National Park Science

A Century of Research in South Africa

South Africa is renowned for its wildlife and environmental conservation in iconic national parks such as the Kruger, one of the world's first formal protected areas. However, this is the first book to thoroughly analyse and explain the interesting and changing scientific research that has been accomplished in South Africa's national parks during the twentieth century. Providing a fascinating and thorough historical narrative based on an extensive range of sources, this text details the evolution of traditional natural history pursuits to modern conservation science in South Africa, covering all research areas of conservation biology and all the national parks around the country. It reveals the interaction between the international context, government, learning institutions and the public that has shaped the present conservation arena. A complex story that will interest and inform not only those involved in conservation science of South Africa, but worldwide.

JANE CARRUTHERS is Professor Emeritus in the Department of History at the University of South Africa (UNISA), Pretoria, and a Research Associate at the Centre for Invasion Biology, Stellenbosch University. A pioneer of environmental history in South Africa, her book, *The Kruger National Park: A Social and Political History* (1995) has become a standard reference work. She has published widely on the history of conservation and science as well as on land reform in both South Africa and Australia. She has been the recipient of numerous academic prizes, including runner-up lifetime achiever for the South African National Science and Technology Forum (2015), the only historian to have received this award. She is a Fellow of the Royal Society of South Africa, Member of the Academy of Science of South Africa, Fellow of Clare Hall, Cambridge and Honorary Fellow of the Rachel Carson Center for Environment and Society in Munich. She is past Chair of the Academic Advisory Board of the Rachel Carson Center, past President of the International Consortium of Environmental History Organizations and past President of the Southern African Historical Society. She has authored six books, co-authored a further one, contributed chapters to 29 edited books and published 58 journal articles.

ECOLOGY, BIODIVERSITY AND CONSERVATION

The world's biological diversity faces unprecedented threats. The urgent challenge facing the concerned biologist is to understand ecological processes well enough to maintain their functioning in the face of the pressures resulting from human population growth. Those concerned with the conservation of biodiversity and with restoration also need to be acquainted with the political, social, historical, economic and legal frameworks within which ecological and conservation practice must be developed. The new Ecology, Biodiversity and Conservation series will present balanced, comprehensive, up-to-date, and critical reviews of selected topics within the sciences of ecology and conservation biology, both botanical and zoological, and both 'pure' and 'applied'. It is aimed at advanced final-year undergraduates, graduate students, researchers, and university teachers, as well as ecologists and conservationists in industry, government and the voluntary sectors. The series encompasses a wide range of approaches and scales (spatial, temporal, and taxonomic), including quantitative, theoretical, population, community, ecosystem, landscape, historical, experimental, behavioural and evolutionary studies. The emphasis is on science related to the real world of plants and animals rather than on purely theoretical abstractions and mathematical models. Books in this series will, wherever possible, consider issues from a broad perspective. Some books will challenge existing paradigms and present new ecological concepts, empirical or theoretical models, and testable hypotheses. Other books will explore new approaches and present syntheses on topics of ecological importance.

Ecology and Control of Introduced Plants
Judith H. Myers and Dawn Bazely

Invertebrate Conservation and Agricultural Ecosystems
T. R. New

Risks and Decisions for Conservation and Environmental Management
Mark Burgman

Ecology of Populations
Esa Ranta, Per Lundberg, and Veijo Kaitala

National Park Science

A Century of Research in South Africa

JANE CARRUTHERS

University of South Africa, Pretoria, South Africa

CAMBRIDGE
UNIVERSITY PRESS

CAMBRIDGE
UNIVERSITY PRESS

University Printing House, Cambridge CB2 8BS, United Kingdom

One Liberty Plaza, 20th Floor, New York, NY 10006, USA

477 Williamstown Road, Port Melbourne, VIC 3207, Australia

4843/24, 2nd Floor, Ansari Road, Daryaganj, Delhi – 110002, India

79 Anson Road, #06-04/06, Singapore 079906

Cambridge University Press is part of the University of Cambridge.

It furthers the University's mission by disseminating knowledge in the pursuit of education, learning and research at the highest international levels of excellence.

www.cambridge.org
Information on this title: www.cambridge.org/9781107191440
DOI: 10.1017/9781108123471

First published 2017

Printed in the United Kingdom by TJ International Ltd., Padstow, Cornwall

A catalogue record for this publication is available from the British Library

Library of Congress Cataloging-in-Publication Data
Names: Carruthers, Jane, author.
Title: National Park Science: A Century of Research in South Africa / Jane Carruthers.
Other titles: Ecology, biodiversity, and conservation.
Description: | Series: Ecology, biodiversity and conservation | Includes
bibliographical references and index.
Identifiers: LCCN 2017006681 | ISBN 9781107191440 (hardback : alk. paper)
Subjects: LCSH: Natural resources conservation areas—South Africa. |
National parks and reserves—South Africa. | Conservation of natural
resources—South Africa. | Ecology—Research—South Africa.
Classification: LCC QH77.S62 C37 2017 | DDC 333.720968—dc23 LC record
available at https://lccn.loc.gov/2017006681

ISBN 978-1-107-19144-0 Hardback
ISBN 978-1-316-64202-3 Paperback

Contents

Colour plates to appear between pp. 246 and 247

Preface

In the short voyage of a lifetime, we can see the eddies and ripples upon the surface, but not the under-currents changing the main channel of the stream. History alone can determine the deep seated causes which have been at work to bring them about.

Thomas Mellon and his Times, p. 338.
Quoted in David Cannadine, Mellon: An American Life
(London: Allen Lane / Penguin, 2006, p. 583)

The twentieth century has been named 'The Age of Ecology' by German environmental historian Joachim Radkau and 'The Ecological Century' by British biologist and conservationist E.B. Worthington.[1] They identify two defining features. The first is that the domination by humanity of the planet has been seismic and irreversible. Nobel Prize-winning chemist Paul Crutzen has even likened our era to a geological epoch by labelling it the Anthropocene.[2] The second is the high profile the 'environment' has achieved over the past 100 years. Terms unknown to earlier generations – biodiversity, ecology, environmentalism, sustainability, ecosystem services – are today in common use.[3] Moreover, the 'environment' is an object of international attention with a plethora of global organisations monitoring what was once called 'nature' and debating how best to care for it.

[1]E.B. Worthington, *The Ecological Century: A Personal Appraisal* (Oxford: Clarendon Press, 1983), vii; J. Radkau, *The Age of Ecology* (Cambridge: Polity, 2014).
[2]P.J. Crutzen and E.F. Stoermer, 'The "Anthropocene"', *IGBP (International Geosphere–Biosphere Programme) Newsletter* 41 (2000): 17–18.
[3]See L. Robin, S. Sörlin and P. Warde, eds, *The Future of Nature: Documents of Global Change* (New Haven, CT: Yale University Press, 2013).

About This Book

This book seeks to explain, in broad political and scientific context, the changing philosophies and mutations in areas of prominence in the research agenda of South Africa's national parks during this ecological century. I hope that the undercurrents as well as the surface eddies and ripples that Thomas Mellon identified as vital to understanding the past are shown to be inextricably intertwined and that, through careful examination through a variety of sources, a valid historical explanation of this complex trajectory is revealed.

The arrangement of this book is both chronological and thematic in dealing with the twentieth century. It is divided into three periods – 1900–1960, 1960s–1990s and 1990 to *c*.2010 – each with its own particular characteristics regarding conservation science and research agendas. I discuss these periods in the three parts of the book and have entitled them in accordance with what I argue are the dominating philosophies of conservation science during those decades. I begin with 'Protecting, preserving and propagating', which were the main elements of nature conservation until after the Second World War, and this is followed by 'Measuring, monitoring and manipulating', principles that dominated professional work in South Africa's national parks from the 1960s until the 1990s. The final part, 'Integration, innovation and internationalisation', explains how conservation science in South Africa has altered in the very recent past and, indeed, remains the dominating paradigm today. This periodisation also generally coincides with distinctive political dispensations in South Africa, and indeed, in the international sphere, the objective being to explain the context in which conservation science took place. Each of the three parts begins with an overview chapter that concludes with a list of key dates, and this is followed by three chapters that provide more detail of the scientific research undertaken in the period in question.

This division into three broad periods should not be understood as presenting three absolutely sequential paradigms within nature conservation in South Africa or that there is an absolutely clear or total break between them. I use them as a device to introduce the new ideas that came into existence in nature research and management and to highlight the dominant and influential personalities and leaders who advocated them. As is almost always the case, older ideas are perpetuated – sometimes in new guises and suited to altered conditions, and may often run in parallel with fresh thinking. Moreover, depending on the research topics under discussion, ideas may integrate and merge in unusual ways that relate more to one branch of science than another.

The content of the book is extremely wide-ranging, but the focus is on that form of protected area dubbed 'national park' in formal legislation, and the role and development of the natural sciences in relation to them. In discussions about the environment, national parks are frequently singled out as welcome spaces protected from change and human rapacity. Because various entities – national, provincial, municipal, private and corporate – own and/or manage South Africa's protected areas, a brief description of them is warranted. The centrepiece is the knowledge generated in national parks managed by a parastatal body currently named South African National Parks (SANParks). In 2016, there are 19 of them, established between 1926 and 2009, and situated in seven of the country's nine provinces. The jewel in the crown is the Kruger National Park (KNP), a very large area along the eastern boundary of South Africa. Because it is older and boasts a rich, intricate and fascinating savannah ecosystem, as well as well-established scientific and administrative structures, Kruger, as will be shown, has attracted the greatest share of research resources and most of the research literature has been devoted to it. However, valuable research has been undertaken in other national parks, and also by outside institutions whose work has impacted on national parks. These too will be discussed in the chapters that follow.

What Is a National Park?

Despite the ease with which the phrase 'national park' trips off the tongue, what exactly such a place is remains a topic of debate.[4] Generally, national parks are creatures of the twentieth century, although a few

---

[4]See, for example, R.F. Nash, 'The confusing birth of national parks', *The Michigan Quarterly Review* 16 (1977): 216–226; R.F. Nash, 'The American invention of national parks', *American Quarterly* 22 (1970): 726–735; W.C. Everhart, *The National Park Service*, 2nd edn (Boulder, CO: Westview Press, 1983); W. Frost and C.M. Hall, 'American invention to international concept', in *Tourism and National Parks: International Perspectives on Development, Histories and Change*, eds W. Frost and C.M. Hall (Abingdon: Routledge, 2009), 30–44; C.M. Hall and W. Frost, 'Introduction: The making of the national parks concept', in *Tourism and National Parks: International Perspectives on Development, Histories and Change*, eds W. Frost and C.M. Hall (Abingdon: Routledge, 2009), 3–15; C.M. Hall and W. Frost, 'The future of the national park concept', in *Tourism and National Parks: International Perspectives on Development, Histories and Change*, eds W. Frost and C.M. Hall (Abingdon: Routledge, 2009), 301–310; A. MacEwan and M. MacEwan, *National Parks: Conservation or Cosmetics?* (London: George Allen and Unwin, 1982).

were established as the nineteenth century wore on.[5] Probably the best-known early park is Yellowstone in the United States, instituted by the federal government on 1 March 1872.[6] Yet Yellowstone was not referred to in the initial legislation as a national park but as a 'public park or pleasuring ground'.[7] The first named national park is the Royal National Park in Sydney, established by the government of New South Wales in March 1879.[8]

The term 'national park' existed for almost a century before an attempt was made to define this form of land use. This occurred in 1969, thanks to the International Union for Conservation of Nature (IUCN), which has designated various categories of protected area from time to time. Its definition of national park has always been fuzzy, to avoid disqualifying or alienating contenders or embarrassing any national state. It has also changed with the years. The initial formulation was a sequel to the first World Parks Congress, held in Seattle in 1962, but underwent revision in 1994 and again in 2008.[9] According to the latest definition, a national park is a 'protected area', and this in turn is 'a clearly defined geographical space, recognised, dedicated and managed, through legal or other

---

[5] They include New South Wales (Royal) National Park 1879, Ku-ring-gai Chase 1891, South Australia, Belair 1891, New Zealand, Tongariro 1884 and Canada, Rocky Mountains (later Banff) 1885.

[6] F. Wagner, *Yellowstone's Destabilised Ecosystem* (Oxford: Oxford University Press, 2006); A. Chase, *Playing God in Yellowstone: The Destruction of America's First National Park* (San Diego, CA: Harcourt Brace, 1987); C.J. Magoc, *Yellowstone: The Creation and Selling of an American Landscape* (Albuquerque, NM: University of New Mexico Press, 1999); J.A. Pritchard, *Preserving Yellowstone's Natural Conditions: Science and the Perception of Nature* (Lincoln, NE: University of Nebraska Press, 1999); J.L. Meyer, *The Spirit of Yellowstone: The Cultural Evolution of a National Park* (Lanham, MD: Rowman and Littlefield, 1996).

[7] In 1899, Mount Rainier National Park was the first protected area in the USA to be called a national park.

[8] L. Robin, 'Being first: Why the Americans needed it, and why Royal National Park didn't stand in their way', *Australian Zoologist* 36, no. 3 (2013): 321–331; M. Harper and R. White, 'How national were the first national parks?', in *Civilizing Nature: National Parks in Global and Historical Perspective*, eds B. Gissibl, S. Höhler and P. Kupper (New York, NY: Berghahn Books, 2012), 50–67.

[9] N. Dudley, ed., *Guidelines for Applying Protected Area Management Categories* (Gland: IUCN, 2008); S. Stolton, P. Shadie and N. Dudley, *IUCN WCPA Best Practice Guidance on Recognising Protected Areas and Assigning Management Categories and Governance Types*, Best Practice Protected Area Guidelines Series No. 21 (Gland: IUCN, 2013); N. Dudley and S. Stolton, eds, *Defining Protected Areas: An International Conference in Almeria, Spain* (Gland: IUCN, 2008); IUCN, *Guide to the WPC Recommendations Procedures Vth World Parks Congress* (Gland: IUCN, 2003), 50–51.

effective means, to achieve the long term conservation of nature with associated ecosystem services and cultural values'. Category II (of six),[10] a National Park, was also amended to read: 'Large natural or near-natural area set aside to protect large-scale ecological processes, along with the complement of species and ecosystems characteristic of the area, which also provide a foundation for environmental and cultural compatible spiritual, scientific, educational, recreational, and visitor opportunities'.[11] These categories were developed as a 'common language' to assist reporting and common communication. However, since 1994 this aim has been distorted. With more than 100 000 protected areas globally, and the increased human pressure upon them, the categories have been utilised in ways that were not originally intended, and 'What began as a simple classification exercise has assumed far greater political importance'.[12]

South Africa is not alone in having a number of national parks – like Bontebok, Mountain Zebra and Addo Elephant – that do not conform to this definition and which could more aptly be categorised as Habitat/ Species Management Areas. This has sometimes been suggested, but legal and political complications, as well as bureaucratic resistance to being relieved of property and power, have proven insurmountable. The definition of national park does not insist that a national government, rather than any other administrative entity (including the private sector), own or manage a national park.[13] While the United Nations Educational, Scientific and Cultural Organisation's (UNESCO) World Heritage Sites, Ramsar Wetlands and Biosphere Reserves have specified criteria, regulatory mechanisms and management standards, no analogous regulatory regime exists for national parks.[14]

Thus, national parks as a concept are amenable to wide interpretation and are almost endlessly flexible. Perhaps, however, it is this very

[10]Others currently are: Ia Strict nature reserve; Ib wilderness area; II national park; III natural monument or feature; IV habitat/species management area; V protected landscape or seascape; VI protected areas with sustainable use of natural resources.

[11]N. Dudley, 'Why is biodiversity conservation important in protected landscapes?', *The George Wright Forum* 28, no. 2 (2009): 31–38.

[12]K. Bishop, N. Dudley, A. Phillips and S. Stolton, *Speaking a Common Language: The Uses and Performance of the IUCN System of Management Categories for Protected Areas* (Cardiff: Cardiff University, IUCN and UNEP, 2004).

[13]Bishop, Dudley, Phillips and Stolton, *Speaking a Common Language*, 4; A. Phillips, 'Turning ideas on their head: A new paradigm for protected areas', *The George Wright Forum* 20, no. 2 (2003): 8–32.

[14]Dudley, 'Why is biodiversity conservation important', 33.

adaptability and imprecision that has ensured the longevity and popularity of national parks and enabled them to serve a variety of purposes, and to mutate according to context and period. Some national parks lie in urban areas, others in rural. Some were established by national governments, others by provinces or regions. Some were the brainchildren of despots, others of local communities. Large areas, small areas, land or sea, rich or poor biodiversity, as well as varying structures of governance – all form part of the global national park community.[15]

As explained by Bishop, Dudley, Phillips and Stolton, more important than 'national parks' is the over-arching category of 'protected areas', no matter by what name they are referred to or by whom they are governed or managed. These authors regard protected areas as being 'at the very heart of national and regional conservation strategies; their existence and continued success are vital to the achievement of global commitments to biodiversity conservation. But protected areas are far more than just places set aside for wild plants and animals. They also provide environmental services, such as soil protection and drinking water supplies, and secure homes for vulnerable human communities including many indigenous peoples. They protect places of cultural and spiritual significance, supply economic benefits, for instance through tourism, and give us all space for recreation and renewal.'[16]

Although there are rich chronicles of national parks in many countries, even analyses of aspects of their histories, there are few comparative studies.[17] Moreover, little detail has been unearthed about the real influence of US national parks on parks elsewhere, although brief allusion to this is often made. Sometimes this is misleading and overstates international indebtedness to the USA. For example, Stankey, Martin and Nash aver that the KNP 'came into being largely because its head ranger demonstrated how the American national park idea applied to the African situation'.[18] This is an oversimplification unsupported by evi-

---

[15] A. MacEachern, 'Writing the history of Canadian parks: Past, present and future', History Publications, Paper 1. http://ir.lib.uwo.ca/historypub/1 (Accessed 20 July 2016).

[16] Bishop, Dudley, Phillips and Stolton, *Speaking a Common Language*, 1.

[17] A comparative study can be found in W. Beinart and P. Coates, *Environment and History: The Taming of Nature in the U.S.A. and South Africa* (London: Routledge, 1995). Recent books that summarise the general literature include K.R. Jones and J. Wills, *The Invention of the Park: Recreational Landscapes from the Garden of Eden to Disney's Magic Kingdom* (Cambridge: Polity, 2005).

[18] G.H. Stankey, V.G. Martin and R.F. Nash, 'International concepts of wilderness preservation and management', in *Wilderness Management*, eds J.C. Hendee, G.H. Stankey and R.C. Lucas (Washington, DC: US Department of Agriculture, Forest Service, 1978), 50.

dence. In fact – as will be described later – the term 'national park' was deemed unsuitable for South African circumstances.

If the definition of 'national park' is problematic, so too are the precise foundational moments. Everhart has described the investigation of their origin in the USA as 'like nailing jelly to the wall',[19] a remark certainly applicable to the South African situation. There is no formal record of the use of the terminology 'national park' in South Africa until the early twentieth century, although by then there were numerous public parks in the country, including botanical gardens, urban parks and game reserves. The first protected area and national park in South Africa consistent with the modern IUCN definition of both was situated in the Drakensberg, a mountain landscape that straddles KwaZulu-Natal, the Free State and the small country of Lesotho. The Natal National Park (after 1947, the Royal Natal National Park) was established in the then British colony of Natal in 1906 and recognised by parliament as late as 1926. Although this park was never brought within the SANParks stable, today almost the entire Drakensberg range is a World Heritage Site and a Ramsar Wetland. It is also becoming the Maloti-Drakensberg Transfrontier Conservation Area. There are elements of the original park that compare well with Yellowstone. It is a relatively large area, scenically and geologically splendid, relatively far from (but accessible to) urban centres and suitable for hiking, mountaineering and fishing. As one later commentator observed, 'India has the Himalayas, North America the Rockies . . . southern Africa's Drakensberg is as notable as any.'[20]

South African society is currently ambivalent about national parks. When the country hosted the Fifth World Parks Congress – the first in Africa – in Durban in 2003, SANParks published a lavish book entitled *South African National Parks: A Celebration*.[21] In the preface, Hector Magome, then director of conservation services, asked: 'Why celebrate a controversy?'[22] In his introduction, Nelson Mandela wrote that 'many of our protected areas have their origins in the colonial past and there

---

[19]W.C. Everhart, *The National Park Service* (Boulder, CO: Westview Press, 1983), 5.

[20]C.S. Stokes, *Sanctuary* (Cape Town: Maskew Miller, 1953), 307, 309. See J. Carruthers, 'The Royal Natal National Park, Kwazulu-Natal: Mountaineering, tourism and nature conservation in South Africa's first national park c.1896 to c.1947', *Environment and History* 19, no. 4 (2013): 459–485.

[21]A. Hall-Martin and J. Carruthers, eds, *South African National Parks: A Celebration* (Johannesburg: Horst Klemm, 2003).

[22]H. Magome, 'Preface', in *South African National Parks: A Celebration*, eds A. Hall-Martin and J. Carruthers (Johannesburg: Horst Klemm, 2003), viii.

is a legacy of alienation from the local people who were excluded from enjoying them or benefiting from them in any way'.[23] Since 1994 and the advent of full democracy in South Africa, national parks have had to reposition themselves by exploring aspects of modern national parks that resonate with a nation which is overwhelmingly black, poor and young, and in which job creation is the paramount national goal. Consequently, while national parks remain playgrounds for whites, what ensures their survival is that they are deemed creators of wealth. There is, however, another key role for national parks: their contribution to scientific knowledge and understanding.

What is Science in a National Park?

In my analysis the emphasis is on the changing shapes of the natural sciences in the twentieth century. They are referred to variously during the period as 'natural history', 'conservation biology', 'conservation science' and 'scientific management' as different nuances around a cluster of similar research objectives. Other branches of knowledge, such as the social sciences and humanities, relevant to national parks and the localities in which they are situated have had a lesser impact on management and conservation, but are examined where appropriate. This book explores two ways of thinking about science in South Africa's national parks: how has science contributed to the development of national parks, and how have national parks served the development of science? Moreover, applied science can often be distinguished from fundamental, hypothesis-driven science.[24] Defining 'science' is even more complex than defining a national park. The disciplines regarded as 'scientific' have changed over time. The term 'scientist' in English was coined by Cambridge polymath and Royal Society Fellow William Whewell in 1833, while the modern concept of science as a profession is a product of the late nineteenth century, with the rise of laboratory studies and the emergence of discrete

[23]N. Mandela, 'Message from Nelson Mandela', in *South African National Parks: A Celebration*, eds A. Hall-Martin and J. Carruthers (Johannesburg: Horst Klemm, 2003), vi.

[24]I would like to thank Roy Siegfried for his advice in connection with defining 'science' and 'scientific research'. See also F. Götmark, K. Kirby and M.B. Usher, 'Strict reserves, IUCN classification, and the use of reserves for scientific research: A comment on Schultze *et al.* (2014)', *Biodiversity Conservation* 24 (2015): 3621–3625, 3622. doi: 10.1007/s10531-015-1011-8.

disciplines within universities and museums. One of the major sciences, or group of sciences, this book deals with – conservation biology – is young, having been named only in the early 1980s.

In the chapters that follow, much of the focus is on conservation biology and the other sciences identified with it, such as biology, botany, zoology, ecology, environmental science, population ecology, landscape restoration and resource management. However, conservation biology is also a human science, in that conservation is a human value pursued nowadays for human benefit of various kinds. Some natural scientists would still agree, however, with Bird's now discredited proposition that '. . . scientific knowledge is something that exists outside [society]'.[25] Thomas Kuhn, by contrast, persuasively argued that any science is merely a *relative* truth about nature, created out of social experience, cultural values and political and economic structures.[26] For example, 'ecology' is certainly a discipline, but to many people it suggests something more, an ethical perspective and even a political movement.[27]

Many years ago, Everett Mendelsohn editorialised in the *Journal of the History of Biology* that 'biology, in particular, must be studied in terms of its relationship with the other sciences, and with the intellectual currents of its day. It may be examined as well for its interaction with the institutions of the society which spawns it.'[28] To this end, the history of biology must be locally grounded.[29] This book seeks to explain how, with reference to South Africa's national parks, nineteenth-century natural history was transformed into a suite of fully fledged modern field sciences. These sciences are themselves complex, because unlike many others, they are specifically goal-directed and thus not strictly 'objective' or 'neutral'. Indeed, Michael Soulé, one of the founders of conservation biology in the 1980s, explicitly refers to it as 'mission-driven'[30] or even

[25]E.A.R. Bird, 'The social construction of nature: Theoretical approaches to the history of environmental problems', *Environmental Review* 11 (1987): 255.

[26]T.S. Kuhn, *The Structure of Scientific Revolutions*, 2nd edn (Chicago, IL: University of Chicago Press, 1970).

[27]S. Bocking, 'Ecosystems, ecologists, and the atom: Environmental research at Oak Ridge National Laboratory', *Journal of the History of Biology* 28, no. 1 (1995): 1.

[28]E. Mendelsohn, 'Editorial foreword', *Journal of the History of Biology* 1, no. 1 (1968): 1–2.

[29]N. Jardine, J.A. Secord and E. Spary, *Cultures of Natural History* (Cambridge: Cambridge University Press, 1996), 7.

[30]C. Meine, M. Soulé and R.F. Noss, '"A mission-driven discipline": The growth of conservation biology', *Conservation Biology* 20, no. 3 (2006): 631–651.

'crisis-driven',[31] a description not readily applicable to, say, mathematics and physics, or even geography.

Together with its value-driven characters, environmental science in national parks differs in that it is, by its very nature, locality based. Thus, the object of scientific inquiry conducted in marine national parks differs from that in savannahs. For this reason, any 'universal truth' may be hard to discern.[32] Nonetheless, the existence of a national park objectifies this landscape, provides distance; indeed, declares it as a study site.[33]

The answers to the questions 'Why do we protect what we do?' and 'What is the purpose of that protection?' are fluid. The quest for knowledge is moulded by social values, public policy and politics. These, rather than linear notions of 'progress', are more helpful in understanding transformations in scientific research. Ideas change, as do priorities. Reminding ourselves that knowledge is contextual and ever-changing is useful, as are reminders that people have little choice but to act within their current circumstances. Praise and blame are therefore not especially illuminating. The past needs to be integrated into the present, with an awareness that no matter how secure the present seems, something new will emerge – that 'black swan'[34] – to overturn accepted thinking and perhaps force a return to basic principles.

From the current vantage point of biodiversity conservation, it needs to be acknowledged that before the 1960s, with one notable exception, South Africa's early game reserves and national parks were not conceived with any scientific purpose in view, but were established on an ad-hoc basis as political context and locality permitted or necessitated. The exception was the Dongola Wild Life Sanctuary, established in the Limpopo River valley in 1947 with a specific research objective. It did not long survive the advent of the new Afrikaner nationalist government in 1948, which in short order abolished it, with the land reverting to agriculture. It was not until the 1960s that scientific priorities and the

[31]M.E. Soulé, 'What is conservation biology?', *BioScience* 35 (1985): 727–734.

[32]L. Robin, 'Resilience in the Anthropocene: A biography', in *Rethinking Invasion Ecologies from the Environmental Humanities*, eds J. Frawley and I. McCalman (London: Routledge, 2014), 45–63.

[33]D.J. Frank, A. Hironaka and E. Schofer, 'The nation-state and the natural environment over the twentieth century', *American Sociological Review* 65 (2000): 96–116.

[34]N.N. Taleb, *The Black Swan: The Impact of the Highly Improbable* (New York, NY: Random House, 2007).

desire to establish a suite of protected areas representative of all biomes came to influence national environmental policy.[35]

In addressing the evolution of nature conservation and its associated sciences as a biological discipline in South Africa in the twentieth and early twenty-first centuries, it is salutary to consider three reference books published by formal scientific associations in 1905, 1949 and 1977, respectively. In the first, *Science in South Africa: A Handbook and Review, Prepared under the Auspices of the South African Governments and the South African Association for the Advancement of Science*, compiled by the Reverend W. Flint, librarian of parliament, and Dr J.D.F. Gilchrist, a marine specialist and government biologist of the Cape colony, and produced for the visit to South Africa by the British Association for the Advancement of Science, nature protection of any kind rated not a single mention.[36] Forty years later, in 1949, *Science in South Africa* was published by the Council for Scientific and Industrial Research (CSIR) for the meeting of the African Regional Scientific Conference that year. In it, one page in the chapter on 'Animal Science' discusses the possibilities of scientific research in South Africa's game reserves and the statement is made that 'apart from the study of animals as potential carriers of disease . . . many important problems are practically virgin fields for investigation in our National Parks and Reserves'.[37] By 1977, in *A History of Scientific Endeavour in South Africa*, edited by A.C. Brown and published by the Royal Society of South Africa, an entire chapter was devoted to 'The history and status of nature conservation in South Africa'. The author was Douglas Hey, a freshwater ichthyologist who had been director of nature conservation in

---

[35]See, for example, W.R. Siegfried and C.A. Brown, 'The distribution and protection of mammals endemic to southern Africa', *South African Journal of Wildlife Research* 22, no. 1 (1992): 11–16; also Hall-Martin and Carruthers, *South African National Parks*.

[36]W. Flint and J.D.F. Gilchrist, eds, *Science in South Africa: A Handbook and Review* (Cape Town: Maskew Miller, 1905); see also S. Dubow, 'A commonwealth of science: The British Association in South Africa, 1905 and 1929', in *Science and Society in Southern Africa*, ed. S. Dubow (Manchester: Manchester University Press, 2000), 66–99; H. Lang, 'Game reserves and wild life protection', in *South Africa and Science: A Handbook Prepared under the Auspices of the South African Association for the Advancement of Science for the Meeting of the British Association in Capetown and Johannesburg, South Africa, 1929*, eds H.J. Crocker and J. McCrae (Johannesburg: South African Association for the Advancement of Science, 1929), 241–250.

[37]Council for Scientific and Industrial Research, *Science in Africa* (Pretoria: CSIR, 1949), 111–113. It is likely that this section of the book was written by R. Bigalke, Director of the National Zoological Gardens.

the Cape province since 1952. Reading this chapter today, one is struck by Hey's proselytising tone.[38] Rather than objectively dissecting the development of scientific thinking on nature protection, Hey is at pains 'to stress the progressive role of certain ideals that are important in the present'.[39] Consequently, he does not uncover 'the historical integrity of that science in its own time',[40] but judges it from his own subjective perspective.[41] Longmore's observation that 'science and scientists, despite the cloak of objectivity, are as much beneficiary and victim of prevailing cultural expressions as everyone else' springs to mind here.[42] A comparison of these three books underscores the course over seven decades of the protection and management of South Africa's natural environment – as an articulated, formally organised science – from a position of negligible national importance to scientific acceptance on par with marine biology, veterinary research, botany or geology.

The current study is thus informed by the growing academic interest in the cultural history of the natural sciences. Conservation biology is maturing into a mainstream applied science[43] and investigating how it has evolved in different parts of the world can shed light on nationalism and identity as well as contribute to the history of science. It has a high profile in South Africa, a country well respected for the success of some of its protected areas. In this respect, South Africa can be regarded as exceptional in African terms, being relatively small, immensely biodiverse and straddling both developed and developing worlds. Moreover, domestic capacity by way of personnel and resources is considerable, obviating much of the need for international funding and external expertise evident in many other African countries. Also, unlike most of the rest of

[38]D. Hey, 'The history and status of nature conservation in South Africa', in *A History of Scientific Endeavour in South Africa*, ed. A.C. Brown (Cape Town: Royal Society of South Africa, 1977), 132–163.
[39]P. Bowler, *The Fontana History of the Environmental Sciences* (London: Fontana, 1992), 23.
[40]Jardine, Secord and Spary, *Cultures of Natural History*, 6–7.
[41]J. Sheail, *Seventy-five Years in Ecology: The British Ecological Society* (Oxford: Oxford University Press, 1987), 1.
[42]R. Longmore, ed., *Biodiversity: Broadening the Debate 3* (Canberra: Australian Nature Conservation Agency, 1999), 28. See also P.L. Farber, *Finding Order in Nature: The Naturalist Tradition from Linnaeus to E.O. Wilson* (Baltimore, MD: Johns Hopkins University Press, 2000); L. Barber, *The Heyday of Natural History, 1820–1870* (London: Jonathan Cape, 1980); B. Lightman, ed., *Victorian Science in Context* (Chicago, IL: University of Chicago Press, 1997).
[43]See A.S. Pullin, *Conservation Biology* (Cambridge: Cambridge University Press, 2002).

Africa, the mining, commercial and industrial sectors are strong in South Africa and the black population has been proletarianised and integrated into the cash economy for more than a century. Against this background, the history of game reserves, national parks and wildlife management in South Africa has played out very differently from other regions in Africa, where the values of the colonial powers have had a greater role in shaping game reserves.[44] Yet it is also true that many of the fundamental reasons for conserving nature have changed over time in South Africa, as elsewhere. As Campbell has observed, we need to 'document our relationship to nature, not just as we wish it could be, but as it has been', taking account of changing philosophies and practices in historical context and 'measuring [nature's] response to social and political circumstances'.[45]

No matter the period and context, however, there is a strong case for claiming that 'national parks remain the best place to share the knowledge that will allow us to sustain biodiversity on this planet'.[46] Anthony Sinclair, the doyen scientist and researcher of the Serengeti, strongly defends the existence of protected areas for their value to baseline studies. Certainly, he argues, they are not enough, but for various reasons they are all we have.[47]

My key research questions have been:

- To what extent were changes in scientific research driven by external or internal circumstances, including the political environment?
- Who have been the 'scientists' in SANParks over the course of its history, what was their range of expertise and their scientific contribution?
- What partnerships and collaborations have been generated over the years?
- How have the scientific outputs of national park research been communicated?
- To what extent has SANParks been influenced by scientific developments in the broader national and international community?

---

[44]See, for example, J.M. MacKenzie, ed., *Imperialism and the Natural World* (Manchester: Manchester University Press, 1990); J.M. MacKenzie, *The Empire of Nature: Hunting, Conservation and British Imperialism* (Manchester: Manchester University Press, 1988).

[45]C.E. Campbell, 'Governing a kingdom: Parks Canada, 1911–2011', in *A Century of Parks Canada, 1911–2011*, ed. C.E. Campbell (Calgary: University of Calgary Press, 2011), 2.

[46]W.C. Tweed, 'An idea in trouble: Thoughts about the future of traditional national parks in the United States', *The George Wright Forum* 27, no. 1 (2010): 6–13.

[47]Anthony Sinclair. Interview with the author. Vancouver, 11 March 2014. See also G.S. Cumming, 'The relevance and resilience of protected areas in the Anthropocene', *Anthropocene* (2016), http://dx.doi.org/10.1016/j.ancene.2016.03.003.

This book argues that scientific research has changed national parks over the past century everywhere in the world and explains how this came about in South Africa. As Patrick Kupper has noted in his fascinating book on the Swiss national park:

> . . . the inclusion of science confronted national parks not only with a new set of rationales but also with new actors and interests. University trained scientists entered national parks as researchers, experts, advisors and managers. Scientific institutions became engaged as research partners and as external reviewers of park performance . . . national parks in most parts of the world had to respond to increasing public and political pressure to become science-based, a pressure that since the 1960s was well orchestrated by internationally organised scientists and conservationists . . . scientific approaches changed the way national parks were managed and conceptualised . . . On the one hand, national parks were used as 'nature's laboratories' as research sites for the scientific study of natural processes . . . On the other hand, scientific research was directed to the needs of park management. Scientific knowledge and authority was used to inform as well as legitimate practices of park management and scientific results could not only trigger profound changes in management . . . The attitudes towards and management of predators and large mammals, of vermin and plagues, of fire and exotic species all changed considerably under the influence of scientific investigations. This was not a linear process . . . but an often extremely complicated process of gaining (and sometimes also losing) different kinds of knowledge, of changing natural and social environments, and of mitigating old and new practices.[48]

The historiography of nature conservation as a science in South Africa is scant and the subject has hardly been touched upon by professional historians, who have not, until recently, shown much interest in the history

---

[48]P. Kupper, 'Nature's laboratories? Exploring the intersection of science and national parks', in *National Parks Beyond the Nation*, eds M. Fiege, A. Howkins and J. Orsi (Norman, OK: University of Oklahoma Press, 2016), 9; P. Kupper, *Creating Wilderness: A Transnational History of the Swiss National Park* (Oxford: Berghahn, 2014); P. Kupper, 'Translating Yellowstone: Early European national parks, Weltmaturschutz and the Swiss model', in *Civilizing Nature: National Parks in Global and Historical Perspective*, eds B. Gissibl, S. Höhler and P. Kupper (New York, NY: Berghahn, 2012), 123–139.

of science at all. Thus, such history has generally been left to scientific practitioners themselves, who have tended to describe the pasts of their own disciplines without historical or political context, and often without critical interrogation. Frequently, this kind of practitioner history tends to be antiquarian, anecdotal, uncritical and lacking in both a clear research premise and an extensive literature survey. It is simply not the case that familiarity with the science always equals understanding of its history. This is not, however, to dismiss out of hand the descriptive records that practising conservation scientists have produced – they can be useful primary sources. Just as it is almost a cliché to describe science as the endeavour to answer, at the most basic level, questions about 'what?', then 'how?' and then to move on to 'why?', the same is broadly true of historical investigation. Yet there are important differences in methodology and training between the natural sciences and the humanities. Australian historian of science, Libby Robin, has expressed this well:

> Donald Worster observed that one of the critical differences between science and history is the assumption in science that the present subsumes and includes all pasts. The date of the paper is 'an index to truth' for a scientist – 'the more recent the date, the more truthful the paper'.[49] Young scientists are trained to feel that there is no point to read anything except the latest paper, as that is . . . the likeliest basis for the future discoveries. Reading is urgent as science marches forward briskly. A historian of science, by contrast, needs to spend time reading all the other papers in order to unpack the intellectual journey, to look at the evolution of the ideas and the sequence of practices, and consider their politics and social context. The historian must 'waste time' considering the possibility of intellectual journeys not taken. Environmental history adds the dimension of watchfulness about place: how local ecologies and the land itself can shape the journey and its politics . . . There is another role for history. The ideas of conservation biology have a history of constructing different understandings of biodiversity, and of the sustainability science that strives to preserve it.[50]

[49]D. Worster, 'The two cultures revisited: Environmental history and the environmental sciences', *Environment and History* 2, no.1 (1996): 3–14, quotation p. 11.
[50]L. Robin, 'New science for sustainability in an ancient land', in *Nature's End: History and the Environment*, eds S. Sörlin and P. Warde (Houndmills: Palgrave Macmillan, 2009), 188–211, quotation pp. 205–206.

Thus far, forays by trained historians into conservation science have been useful, but the literature is patchy, and indeed it is extremely thin as regards South Africa. Moreover, much of this research has appeared in academic journals with a narrow specialist readership. Thus in the absence of an established historiography, this book is an initial attempt to chart the shifts in perspective in conservation biology. The century under discussion has been broadly characterised in three chronological parts relating to what I have called the periods of 'protect, preserve and propagate' (1900–1960), that of 'measure, monitor and manipulate' (1960s–1990s) and, most recently, of 'integrate, innovate and internationalise' (1990s to present). It also points to the need for natural sciences to be reintegrated into cultural concerns about nature instead of being isolated from society at large. A key aim of the book has been to provide context for change, and to offer scientists, non-government organisations and policy-makers a critical perspective on their work. Moreover, through analysis of environmental sciences in places that are expressly 'national', the book seeks to shed light on the creation of wider environmental values.

Environmental History

The sub-field of history germane to this book is known as environmental history, and within this genre, it may also be described as the history of science. In 1972, Roderick Nash gave environmental history its name, its justification and its first teaching syllabus. Since then the field has burgeoned, attracting thousands of scholars and spawning very many journals, books and academic organisations. In its early phases, environmental history was infused with a sense of excitement, innovation and relevance. As was the case with conservation biology, much of that enthusiasm and zeal was directly related to the eco-politics of the second half of the twentieth century. When, in the late 1960s, Lynn White and John Passmore argued that Judeo-Christianity was an ecosystem-unfriendly and nature-destroying belief system,[51] when Rachel Carson drew attention to the environmental damage done to promote short-term human interest and inappropriate notions of 'progress',[52] when wild places and wild animal populations seemed under threat, and when popular ecol-

---

[51]L. White, 'The historical roots of our ecologic crisis', *Science* 155, no. 3767 (1967): 1203–1207; J. Passmore, *Man's Responsibility for Nature: Ecological Problems and Western Traditions* (London: Duckworth, 1974).
[52]R. Carson, *Silent Spring* (New York, NY: Houghton Mifflin, 1962).

ogy vitalised public thinking, history responded enthusiastically. Within a Western paradigm, 'nature', the 'environment' and 'environmentalism' quickly became powerful tropes and environmental history helped to give them an overtly intellectual character. In a relatively short time, environmental history became a vibrant field of study in the United States and historians in other parts of the world began to take note. Professionals in the more established areas of history were encouraged to accept this newcomer as a valid long-term historical pursuit. Much was claimed for this new field, and by 1990 the importance of the environment in shaping culture was considered so fundamental that Donald Worster argued for environmental history's acceptance as central to the discipline as a whole, because it focused on the very intersection between the natural and the cultural.[53]

South African environmental history has bumped up against what C.P. Snow famously called the 'two cultures' in 1959.[54] Historical analysis of science will be found in historical journals, scientific research in science journals. Each has avid readers, but attempts to straddle the two generally offend one constituency or the other, as they cling to their reassuring markers. Scholarly history is not a mere compilation of facts and dates, of anecdotes or reminiscences, although this sometimes appears to historians to be the way scientists regard the discipline, and even use the word 'history' in scientific work. By contrast, scientists are impatient with historical context and lengthy analytical narrative. Yet, as Worster has explained, the task of the environmental historian is to open 'a door in the wall that separates nature from culture, science from history, matter from mind . . . we are arriving . . . not at some point where all academic boundaries and distinctions disappear . . . but . . . where those boundaries are more permeable'.[55] While the natural sciences are engaged and 'useful', the humanities seek to nurture self-awareness, reflectiveness and critical disinterest.[56] As Badsey has wryly observed, history is not an eternal soap opera, it is a thrilling detective story. Historical research requires

---

[53]Worster, 'The two cultures revisited', 3–14.

[54]C.P. Snow, *The Two Cultures and the Scientific Revolution* (Cambridge: Cambridge University Press, 1993).

[55]Worster, 'The two cultures revisited', 4, 13.

[56]P. Vale, 'A sputnik moment? The natural sciences and humanities: An interview with Edward L. Ayers', *South African Journal of Science* 105 (2009): 247–248; S.J. Gould, *The Hedgehog, the Fox, and the Magister's Pox: Mending the Gap Between Science and the Humanities* (New York, NY: Harmony Books, 2003); K. Cuddington and B.E. Beisner, eds, *Ecological Paradigms Lost: Routes of Theory Change* (Burlington, MA: Elsevier, 2005).

the same standards of evidence and analysis as the most taxing physical sciences and it from these findings that historical narratives are composed. However, this also means that even the best historians are experts in only one or two fields, just as scientists are. For the same reason, he says, historians are often spoilsports, modifying or destroying what everyone else believes is true rather than repeating the old platitudes,[57] and this unsettling of generally held views is not always welcomed by experts in other fields.[58]

Sources

This is a work of history, not a scientific treatise. It is written by an historian with a keen interest in the history of South African biological sciences and who is knowledgeable about the history of wildlife and nature conservation and the politics of protection in the region. It has been inspired by histories of science in national parks in other parts of the world, and has benefited immensely from the record contained in scientific journals, management plans and annual reports, and archival sources in national parks and other research institutes in South Africa and elsewhere. I have also been greatly assisted by numerous interviewees, helpful correspondents and critical peers.

[57]S. Badsey, 'A muddy version of the Great War', *History Today* 65, no. 5 (2015): 46–48.
[58]See also M.A. Dennis, 'Historiography of science: An American perspective', in *Science in the Twentieth Century*, eds J. Krige and D. Pestre (Amsterdam: Harwood, 1997), 1–26.

Acknowledgements

This book has been long in the making and over the past few years in which I have been fully engaged in writing it, many people have been extremely generous with their time, expertise and enthusiasm, and it is a pleasure, at last, to be able to thank them all.

The first is William Robertson IV. As head of the Andrew W. Mellon Foundation's programme 'Conservation and the Environment' and the initiator of 'Research Bridges to South Africa', a sub-programme within it, Bill approached me in March 2011 with an invitation to submit a proposal to the Foundation for a publication that would record the history of scientific endeavour in South Africa's national parks. At that time, the Foundation was supporting innovative research in the Kruger National Park and, knowing of my long interest in environmental history and the history of science, he believed that I would be an appropriate person to engage with the topic. Throughout the writing process, Bill was an attentive and extremely helpful mentor and I am deeply grateful to him and the Foundation for giving me a project which has been so enjoyable, so stimulating and so collegial. I very much hope that he and the Foundation will be satisfied with the result.

Although I am solely responsible for the research and writing of this book (and thus for the opinions, interpretations and any remaining errors within it), in many respects this has been a cooperative venture. Assistance has come from organisations – in particular the Andrew W. Mellon Foundation, South African National Parks and the University of South Africa – and from colleagues in many and varied disciplines located all over the world, by way of conversations, interviews and comments on matters of content and emphasis as well as for illustrative material. I have been fortunate to interact with knowledgeable archivists and librarians who are vital to the success of any research-based work. I have benefited from privileged access to scholarly spaces that nurture writers and researchers and from the interventions of Peter Colenbrander, an extraordinarily talented editor, and Marina Pearson, the indexer of some of my previous books. Moreover, the courtesy, efficiency, professionalism and partnership of those in the Ecology, Biodiversity and Conservation series of Cambridge University Press has been outstanding. Family members and friends have taken an interest in my endeavours and provided hospitality and asked kindly after progress. Together with my husband Vincent's constant support, assistance, patience and love, I have been extremely fortunate in every aspect of this work.

The pivotal organisation to acknowledge is the Andrew W. Mellon Foundation based in New York. I twice visited the Foundation and corresponded with many of the staff. Together with Bill Robertson, I would like to acknowledge the then President, Don M. Randel, and Trustees Hanna Gray, Mary Patterson McPherson, Walter Taylor Reveley III and Anne Tatlock with whom I had productive discussions when they visited South Africa in 2012. Stuart Saunders, the Foundation's advocate in South Africa was enthusiastic from the start. In the New York office, Vanessa Cogan, the Database and Records Manager, together with administrators Doreen Tinajaro, Sydney Gilbert and Alex Alberti (more recently and extremely helpfully) guided me through the grant reporting procedures, while librarian Susanne Pichler assisted me with documentation to aid my research.

Also absolutely vital to the project has been South African National Parks, because this book is about the research done by this organisation over the entire course of its history. SANParks has been most generous in every respect, welcoming me to many national parks, opening its archives freely, allowing me to spend time interviewing and meeting staff and, importantly, having confidence in the final product without influencing it in any way. I have been associated with SANParks, and its predecessor the National Parks Board, since the early 1970s when my husband was part of a small team researching amphibians in various national parks and when, some years later, I wrote my doctoral thesis on the social and political history of the Kruger National Park. I would like to acknowledge here my gratitude for the wealth of knowledge I gained at that time from the late U. de V. (Tol) Pienaar, Salomon Joubert, the late Anthony Hall-Martin, Harold Braack and his then wife, the late Toni Braack, M.G.L. (Gus) Mills, L.E.O. (Leo) Braack and Valerius (Vossie) de Vos. Together with G.A. (Robbie) Robinson, who has remained a valued friend and advisor, they laid the foundations on which this book rests.

Another underpinning from past decades is the research I did in the archives of the Stevenson-Hamilton family at Fairholm, Lanarkshire, Scotland, and at their home at White River in Mpumalanga. Jamie and

Jennifer Stevenson-Hamilton generously hosted me for weeks on end as I consulted the voluminous correspondence of Jamie's father, James, the first warden of what became the Kruger National Park, and arguably the first South African modern conservation scientist and wildlife manager. It is a pleasure to thank them again for allowing me to discover the mind and career of the intelligent, important and influential James Stevenson-Hamilton (1867–1957), and encouraging me to write his biography. This was published as *Wildlife and Warfare: The Life of James Stevenson-Hamilton* (Pietermaritzburg: University of Natal Press, 2001).

This book was launched with a lively workshop at SANParks head office in January 2012 when Wendy Annecke, Harry Biggs, Howard Hendricks, Melodie McGeoch, Hector Magome, Danie Pienaar and Rod Randall helped me to refine the relevant research questions and steered me in appropriate directions. Since then, many other SANParks personnel have been of considerable assistance. Among them are the current Chief Executive, Fundisile Mketeni, as well as his predecessor, David Mabunda. I have learnt a great deal from Wendy Annecke, Harry Biggs, Inês Ferreira, Llewellyn Foxcroft, Stefanie Freitag-Ronaldson, Rina Grant, Howard Hendricks, Michael Knight, Melodie McGeoch (now at Monash University in Melbourne), Peter Novellie, Danie Pienaar, Glen Phillips, Dirk Roux, Nicola van Wilgen and Freek Venter. I have also been welcomed at the annual Savannah Science Network Meetings in Skukuza where innovative research is disseminated and shared so generously. Guin Zambatis has been my ally in Skukuza where she maintains a treasure trove of records and information about science in the Kruger National Park. Also there is Itumeleng Khadambi, the head of Information and Records Management, who gave me access to the archival files. I very much hope that SANParks will find this book illuminating and useful and I thank everyone in the organisation for their willingness to assist me in every possible way.

The third organisation to which I owe a large debt is the University of South Africa, where I was employed in the Department of History for more than 30 years. For assistance with this particular project I am indebted to Mamokgethi Phakeng who, when she was Vice-Principal Research and Innovation, supported it and dealt with its management, together with her staff, Lessing Labuschagne and Maishe (Harry) Bopape. In addition, I could not have done without the efficient help of Salomé Schutte in the Finance Department. Unisa's library is incomparable – and so too, are its librarians and archivists. For many decades of the most courteous assistance, I thank Mary-Lynn Suttie, Hleziphi Napaai, Marie Coetzee and Annette le Roux.

In 2015 I was very fortunate to have been awarded a Fellowship at the Stellenbosch Institute for Advanced Studies (STIAS), the Wallenberg Research Centre at Stellenbosch University, during which time I was able to make significant progress with this book. Uninterrupted weeks in the most academically beneficial – and beautiful – environment is a rare privilege, as is the opportunity to interact with an interdisciplinary fellowship of international scholars. I thank all at STIAS for the months of reflection and writing that they afforded me: Hendrik Geyer, Maria Mouton and all the staff.

The other beautiful and nurturing scholarly environment which I have been privileged to enjoy is The Brenthurst Library in Johannesburg. From the mid-1980s I have been welcomed as author, researcher and friend. It is there that I have been cosseted almost every day at a comfortable desk, surrounded by treasures of Africana, and permitted peace in which to research and to write. I would like to thank the Director, Sally MacRoberts, and Inarié de Vaal, Jennifer Kimble and Fylyppa Meyer and the Oppenheimer family for generously allowing me to do so.

Beyond the scientists and managers in SANParks I have relied particularly on the expertise and help of Roy Siegfried, Brian Huntley and Norman Owen-Smith. These three exceptional scientists have been unstinting in their patience from the outset with an historian and her frequent barrages of questions, they have encouraged or corrected my general arguments, pointed out omissions and read and commented on the entire text. Needless to say, however, they are not responsible for the final product or any of its flaws, but it would have been far the poorer without their close interest. I offer them my profound thanks. Other outstanding scholars who have also have been enormously generous with their time and information – and to whom I am most grateful – are Jeremy Anderson, William Bond, Charles Breen, William Beinart, Bruce Brockett, Brian Child, Graham Child, Tim Clynick, Morné du Plessis, Johan du Toit, Saul Dubow, Tom Griffiths, Greg Kiker, Fred Kruger, John Hanks, Eugene Moll, Archie Mossman, Sue Mossman, Banie Penzhorn, Guy Preston, Libby Robin, Kevin Rogers, Bob Scholes, Mary Scholes, Alexis Schwarzenbach, Tony Sinclair, Anthony Starfield, Rudi van Aarde, Brian van Wilgen, Brian Walker and Marinus Werger.

Every seminar and conference that I have attended has been a learning experience, and it is difficult to identify exactly the occasion on which an idea or argument in this book was triggered. I would, however, like to pay tribute to and acknowledge generous colleagues in the Rachel Carson Centre of Environment and Society (Munich), Clare

Hall (Cambridge University), the American Society of Environmental History, the European Society of Environmental History, the Australian National University, the University of Western Australia, the University of Cape Town, the University of the Witwatersrand, the Royal Society of South Africa, and the International Consortium of Environmental History Organisations, who have shaped or otherwise contributed to my ideas over many years.

In December 2015 Norman Owen-Smith put me in touch with Michael Usher, the general editor of the Cambridge University Press series Ecology, Biodiversity and Conservation, as the book Norman had edited with Joris Cromsigt and Sally Archibald was in the pipeline with CUP. Knowing that it would interest me, I was permitted to see the manuscript. This was a very great favour, for not only did I have the benefit of seeing this important book in time to include its wisdom in my own, but I was introduced to the team of the series and thus embarked on the most pleasant publishing experience of a lifetime. For I have been extremely fortunate to have been welcomed into this stable and to have had the professional attention of Michael Usher (the book's final title is his suggestion), Dominic Lewis, Timothy Hyland, Jade Scard and Sara Brunton. They have all gone out of their way to make an historian feel comfortable in a science book series, allowed me latitude regarding style and organisation and encouraged me to include illustrations and images.

For those images and permissions, I appreciate assistance from SANParks (Itumeleng Khadambi, Lazarus Makitla, Reynold Thakuli and Marinda van Graan), Horst Klemm, Vincent Carruthers, Andrew Deacon, Nelson Mandela Metropolitan University (Graham Kerley, Margot Collett and Sharon Wilson), The Brenthurst Library (Sally MacRoberts and Inarié de Vaal), Llewellyn Foxcroft, Kevin Gill, Brian Huntley, Cynthia Kemp, Chantal Knoetze, Carol Knoll, Ria Olivier, Mountain Club of South Africa (Jenny Paterson), Dirk Roux, Joep Stevens, University of Pretoria (Sian Tiley-Nel), Brian van Wilgen and Nicola van Wilgen.

Abbreviations and Acronyms

AENP	Addo Elephant National Park
ANC	African National Congress
AWARD	Association for Water and Rural Development
BAAS	British Association for the Advancement of Science
BRI	Botanical Research Institute
CAO	Carnegie Airborne Observatory
CBD	Convention on Biological Diversity
CCTA	Commission for Technical Co-operation in Africa South of the Sahara
CEC	Commission for Education and Communication, IUCN
CEESP	Commission for Environmental, Economic and Social Policy, IUCN
CEM	Ecology Commission, later named Ecosystem Management, IUCN
CIB	Centre for Invasion Biology, University of Stellenbosch
CITES	Convention on International Trade in Endangered Species of Wild Fauna and Flora
CNPPA	Commission for National Parks and Protected Areas, IUCN
CODESA	Convention for a Democratic South Africa
CRC	Cape Research Centre
CSIR	Council for Scientific and Industrial Research, South Africa
CSP	Cooperative Scientific Programmes, CSIR
CT	Commission of Terrestrial Ecosystems within the IBP United Nations Environment Programme
ESA	Ecological Society of America
FAO	Food and Agriculture Organisation of the United Nations
FFEM	Fondes Francais pour l'Environnement

FRD	Foundation for Research and Development
GEAR	Growth, Employment, and Redistribution
GEF	Global Environmental Fund, World Bank
GRNP	Garden Route National Park
IBP	International Biological Programme
ICOMOS	International Council on Monuments and Sites
ICSU	International Council of Scientific Unions, currently International Council for Science
IFAW	International Fund for Animal Welfare
IUBS	International Union of the Biological Sciences
IUCN	International Union for the Conservation of Nature and Natural Resources, formerly IUPN
IUPN	International Union for the Protection of Nature, later IUCN
JFNC	Johannesburg Field Naturalists' Club
KGNP	Kalahari Gemsbok National Park
KNP	Kruger National Park
KNPRRP	Kruger National Park Rivers Research Programme
LiDAR	Light Detection and Ranging
LTER	Long-Term Ecological Research
MAB	Man and the Biosphere Programme, UNESCO
MRI	Mammal Research Institute, University of Pretoria
NACOR	National Committee for Nature Conservation CSIR
NGO	Non-Governmental Organisation
NIWR	National Institute for Water Research
NMMU	Nelson Mandela Metropolitan University, formerly University of Port Elizabeth
NNP	Natal National Park
NPB	National Parks Board of Trustees
NPER	National Programme for Ecosystem Research, CSIR
NPES	National Programme for the Environmental Sciences, CSIR
NPI	National Productivity Institute
NPS	National Parks Service, USA
NRF	National Research Foundation
NSPU	National Scientific Programmes Unit, CSIR
OAU	Organisation of African Unity
OTS	Organisation of Tropical Studies
PAC	Pan Africanist Congress

PFIAO	Percy Fitzpatrick Institute of African Ornithology, University of Cape Town
RDP	Reconstruction and Development Programme
RRP	Rivers Research Programme
SAAAS	South African Association for the Advancement of Science
SAB	South African Central Government Archives, Pretoria.
SACP	South African Communist Party
SAEON	South African Environmental Observation Network
SAHRA	South African Heritage Resource Agency
SAM	Strategic adaptive management
SANBI	South African National Biodiversity Institute
SANF	Southern African Nature Foundation
SANParks	South African National Parks
SAOU	South African Ornithological Union
SARCCUS	Southern African Regional Commission for the Conservation and Utilisation of the Soil
SCOPE	Scientific Committee on Problems of the Environment
SoK	State of Knowledge
SPFE	Society for the Preservation of the Fauna of the Empire
SPWFE	Society for the Preservation of the Wild Fauna of the Empire. After the First World War renamed the Society for the Preservation of the Fauna of the Empire and after 1950 the Fauna Preservation Society
SRI	Shared Rivers Initiative
SSC	Survival Service Commission, IUCN, later named Species Survival Commission
STIAS	Stellenbosch Institute for Advanced Study
TCNP	Tsitsikamma Coastal National Park
TFCA	Transfrontier Conservation Area
TGPA	Transvaal Game Protection Association
TMNP	Table Mountain National Park
TPC	Threshold of Potential Concern
UCT	University of Cape Town
UK	United Kingdom
UN	United Nations Organisation
UNEP	United Nations Environment Programme
UNESCO	United Nations Educational, Scientific and Cultural Organisation

USA	United States of America
USSR	Union of Soviet Socialist Republics
VOC	Dutch East India Company, Verenigde Oostindische Compagnie
WCED	World Commission on Environment and Development
WCEL	World Commission on Environmental Law, IUCN
WCPA	World Commission on Protected Areas, IUCN, formerly CNPPA
WESSA	Wildlife and Environment Society of Southern Africa, formerly Wild Life Society of Southern Africa
Wits	University of the Witwatersrand, Johannesburg
WSSD	World Summit on Sustainable Development
WWF	Worldwide Fund for Nature, formerly the World Wildlife Fund
WWF-SA	South African Worldwide Fund for Nature

Illustrations

Part I · *Protecting, Preserving and Propagating, 1900 to 1960*

1 · *Overview*

South Africa's protected area estate – whether botanical reserves, forest reserves, game reserves or national parks – did not come into being according to any predetermined plan, but sporadically and even idiosyncratically, depending on changing political, economic, social, institutional and educational contexts. Nonetheless, by the 1960s South Africa's protected estate had taken on many of its modern characteristics. The country's nature custodians had succeeded in saving several species from extinction and in propagating large numbers of formerly diminished populations of plants and animals.

In Part I, comprising four chapters (including this overview) and spanning 60 years, the development and growth of the protectionist ethos and policy are explained in their historical setting and broader national context. In 1900, there was no model of, or for, a national park or national park system and the very concept lacked coherent or established terminology. Certainly there were 'national parks' in the United States as well as in Canada, New Zealand and the Australian colonies. There were also many game reserves – places in which certain animal species were protected – around the world, many of them in Africa. A major step in the theoretical and practical development of national parks worldwide was the conversion of game reserves, from which the public was banned to allow for sport-hunting or the increase of various species, into national parks that might be visited by many thousands of recreational tourists.

The chapters that follow are in chronological order with divisions that broadly reflect key milestones, if not watersheds. The year 1910 marked the establishment of the Union of South Africa and the 1930s heralded a decade in which a number of national parks were established and also the glimmerings of an ecological perspective in science. The fourth chapter discusses the acceleration of biological investigation in protected areas, particularly the Kruger National Park (KNP) but also the few other national parks under the aegis of the National Parks Board of Trustees (NPB) by that time. This section ends in 1960, when, it is argued, there was a distinct change in the scientific function of national parks and the type of science and research their managers believed was achievable. This transformation was part of a worldwide trend at the time, and which had a direct impact on South Africa.

A consistent thread runs through the period 1910–1960: how to protect and preserve desirable wild animal species on one hand, and how to propagate them on the other. Over this half-century these policies proved extremely successful, to the extent that thereafter new scientific challenges arose regarding population over-abundance (at least for some species). Moreover, in these years a strong desire for recreational wildlife viewing took hold among a substantial portion of South Africa's white public, as well, of course, as visitor enjoyment of national parks elsewhere in the world. Popular literature and wildlife movies, even television (books were no longer the main form of knowledge diffusion) disseminated knowledge about wildlife to the public, while professional biologists had come to believe that the careful study of nature in national parks and its management were worthy of serious research attention. Indeed, a new profession emerged. Many 'game rangers', forerunners of conservation biologists, were extremely observant and zoologists were taking a keen interest in what could be learnt in the field. Botanists had developed an interest in wild places even earlier: their tradition of ecological study had deeper roots, while their interest in vegetation in 'natural' places had grown up over centuries. In addition, between 1900 and 1960 the international community had formally coalesced around nature conservation and a number of institutions with worldwide reach had come into being.

The South African Context

By 1900, the once-abundant wildlife herds of the southern African interior had been decimated by firearms in the hands of those whose motives variously related to recreation, income and subsistence. At least two large mammal species had become extinct (the blaauwbok or blue antelope *Hippotragus laucophaeus* and the quagga *Equus quagga quagga*),[1] while others, such as elephant, faced local extinction. The slaughter had taken place despite early legislative attempts in the Cape and Natal colonies and in the republics of the Transvaal and Orange Free State to curtail

[1] R.I. Pocock, 'The quagga', *Journal of the Society for the Preservation of the Fauna of the Empire* 2 (1922): 26–37.

it, or at least to reduce it to sustainable levels so that wildlife populations might recover their numbers. Almost every decade, increasingly stringent hunting regulations were passed in the colonial legislative assemblies and in the republics' *volksrade* (parliaments) to limit hunting seasons, totally ban the killing of certain species, appoint 'gamekeepers', further restrict the rights and bag-limits of landowners to the large mammals on their properties, and very often to prohibit all hunting by black Africans, often blamed for the scale of the slaughter. The prevailing ethic towards the land and its biota was that of a frontier society in the process of being transformed into a land of settlement, with the landscape tamed and brought under cultivation, and into a modern industrial economy.[2]

These laws had little or no effect, and it was clearly proving impossible to curtail hunting within responsible limits. Not only was it difficult in the extreme to arrest and prosecute offenders, but in terms of the region's legal system, wildlife was *res nullius*, an object that cannot be owned. Animals did not belong to the state, nor were they the property of the person on whose land they could be found. Only when dead or captured could a wild animal be a 'possession'.[3] This status, rather like the concept of 'the commons', encouraged the idea that because wild animals belonged to no one, killing them, even in defiance of legislation, was not a 'real' crime. And even when it was admitted to be one, it was by no means comparable with the theft of property or similar serious offences. This legal context encouraged the state and private landowners to resort to the age-old device of game reserves or game sanctuaries, by erecting fences to enclose animals and prevent access by trespassers and potential hunters, who were now effectively recast as poachers. Thus, by 1900 both legislative 'conservation' imperatives and increasingly inaccessible 'preservationist' game reserves existed in southern Africa.

Although 'preservation' and 'conservation' are often used interchangeably and loosely, they do express different values, and there was vigorous debate about both philosophies during this period. Conservation can be

---

[2] J. Carruthers, *Game Protection in the Transvaal 1846 to 1926* (Pretoria: Archives Yearbook for South African History, 1995), 102–103.

[3] The basic law is Roman, mediated, for South Africa, through Roman–Dutch law. All wild animals are, while in the wild, *res nullius*, i.e. unowned. But they can be captured, alive or dead, and a person who captures a wild animal becomes the animal's owner, through a process of acquisition of ownership known as occupatio. Such an animal in captivity is the sole property of the captor, or of anyone who subsequently acquires it from the captor. Thus animals can be freely traded. I am grateful to Kenneth Reid of the University of Edinburgh for clarification on this matter.

viewed as the management and utilisation of any resource in such a way as to ensure its perpetuation – 'wise use', or what today would be called managing for sustainability. This idea was of long standing and in the modern era was strongly associated with forestry in the United States, particularly through the influential philosophy of Chief Forester Gifford Pinchot. Preservation, by contrast, is the prevention of all active interference in managing the resource – an attempt to halt change and prevent any use. The word 'protection' encompasses both these values. In the Cape colony, for example, many forests on the southern coastline were conserved, whereas in game reserves of the interior, certain animals were preserved. Not all wild animals within and beyond game reserves were equally worthy of conservation or preservation. Vermin killing was not only acceptable, it was encouraged and rewarded through the payment of bounties by the state. Many 'vermin clubs' in southern Africa were founded to deplete or extinguish species such as lion, cheetah, leopard and many large avian raptors that predated upon humans or on other species useful to humans. These aroused strong hostility, as did those thought to be ugly – such as hyena and crocodile – or to have 'evil habits' – such as wild dog.[4]

The scientific discipline that was applied to the study of any biota outside a laboratory and in the field came to be known as natural history, the terrain of 'naturalists'. Today these terms have taken on the derogatory connotation of an amateurish interest in nature. However, from the 1600s onwards, many thousands of plant and animal specimens – alive and dead – found their way into the botanical gardens, zoological gardens and menageries of Europe thanks to the work of naturalists. As well as 'living museums', formal museum collections burgeoned with dead examples of wildlife from southern Africa. And within the country, as will be shown, botanical and wildlife reserves played a key part in protection and knowledge generation, but also – and most importantly in the first half of the twentieth century – in propagating those species that had been hunted to near-extinction or that had been decimated by the outbreak of rinderpest, a virulent epizootic disease, in 1896.

In 1900 there was no country called South Africa – the name applied to a large region, not a single polity. The South African War, a bruising conflict between Britain and its two southern African colonies and the two Boer republics, had begun in 1899, engulfed the whole subcontinent and ended in a British victory in 1902 after great hardship on all sides. Warfare devastated the countryside, destroyed infrastructure and

[4]Carruthers, *Game Protection in the Transvaal*, 102.

agriculture and left in its wake hatreds which linger to this day, born of Boer suffering and the British system of concentration camps. After this watershed upheaval and a short interlude of direct imperial and colonial rule, in 1910 the Union of South Africa was created through the unification of the original two British colonies and the two former republics and a state was created that was controlled by white settlers to the almost total exclusion of other peoples. This dominant group was not homogeneous, but was roughly divided between 'Boers', the descendants of earlier and predominantly Dutch immigrants, and those of British extraction.

The creation of the Union was not easy and the ending of colonial rule created novel conditions in the region that had long-term consequences for all aspects of politics, economics and society. While each of the four provinces maintained their own traditions and characteristics, the emergence of a modernising economy and a strong white-minority political state brought about large-scale transformations that had a significant impact.

Game Reserves and National Parks

Game reserves stretch back to the medieval era in the West, but the notion that prominent rulers, princes and kings could set up private hunting reserves was well established in many parts of the world, including Africa. The first game reserves, private and state, in southern Africa were established to keep the public away from these areas so that certain creatures could multiply and live undisturbed within them, or be only hunted by owners of the land. The Old French and Middle English word *parc* or park also derives from the idea of an enclosure for hunting. This was generally a private space, but the opening of London's royal parks to the public in the nineteenth century brought about a new era. In 1842, Victoria Park in London became public, as did Birkenhead Park in Liverpool in the late 1840s, and these inspired Frederick Olmsted's New York Central Park in 1861. In time, however, the phrase 'national park' came to imply, although not through any formal definition, a publicly available space far removed from urban centres.

While, as we will see, the Natal National Park (NNP) was South Africa's first,[5] the passing of the National Parks Act 56 in 1926 established

---

[5] J. Carruthers, 'The Royal Natal National Park, Kwazulu-Natal: Mountaineering, tourism and nature conservation in South Africa's first national park c.1896 to c.1947', *Environment and History* 19 (2013): 459–485.

the KNP as the first protected area under the control of the new NPB. Each of the subsequent national parks established under the board's aegis was the subject of special legislation and all fell under the administrative oversight of this parastatal body. In the 1930s, three small species-specific parks were established in the Cape province (and were more akin to game nurseries and zoos than national parks) – Bontebok National Park (1931), Addo Elephant National Park (1931) and Mountain Zebra National Park (1937). A very large area for the protection of gemsbok (oryx, *Oryx gazella*) was established in the Northern Cape, the Kalahari Gemsbok National Park (1931), while yet another national park, the Dongola Wild Life Sanctuary, was established in 1947, although it was deproclaimed in 1949 for political reasons.

While game reserves were intended to exclude the public, a national park had the express purpose of public access. Not surprisingly, early facilities were rudimentary.[6] Apart from paid staff, no one lived in national parks. Such staff had a dual, and sometimes competing, role of welcoming recreational visitors and of studying the biota within the park. Tourists came to see the 'medley of scientific and natural wonder, novelty and entertainment, grand scenes and spectacle',[7] and scientists were tasked with ensuring that these survived unchanged into the future.

Eventually, protection and propagation proved so successful within the KNP that by the end of the period under discussion, state-sanctioned hunting (culling) was being considered to reduce the number of many previously scarce species. The category of 'vermin' had ceased to exist in protected areas, and animals formerly considered expendable and loathsome had, quite unexpectedly, become visitor favourites. Hunter attitudes had almost completely disappeared in these wild surroundings. Moreover, within the span of 60 years, from its origins in the tradition of gamekeeper and game warden, wildlife management had become a respected profession. The institutionalisation of the knowledge generated about this biota is one of the major themes in the chapters that follow, including the impact of museums, educational bodies, publications and legislation.

---

[6] J. Carruthers, '"Full of rubberneck waggons and tourists": The development of tourism in South Africa's national parks and protected areas', in *Tourism and National Parks: International Perspectives on Development, History and Change*, eds W. Frost and C.M. Hall (London: Routledge, 2009), 211–224.

[7] K.R. Jones and J. Wills, *The Invention of the Park: Recreational Landscapes from the Garden of Eden to Disney's Magic Kingdom* (Cambridge: Polity, 2005), 169.

International Institutionalisation

A further and critical change in this period was that by the 1960s national parks were extremely popular in many parts of the world. Indeed, the international community had become involved by establishing formal structures of nature conservation and national parks, along with several key international institutions, and had entered into a number of international conventions.

Part I opens with the London Convention of 1900 and explains how by the 1960s strong international institutions had come into being that guided and assisted many aspects of nature conservation, including national parks. Early international focus grew out of European imperial interest in the resources of the colonial world and the fascination with large mammal fauna, in particular, and their perpetuation. The role of biology was not dealt with by the Convention, nor highlighted within it. Indeed, protectionism itself was regarded as the appropriate approach to management, and observation and natural history the best means for generating knowledge.

Conservation Science and New Professions

Conservation science arose from the intersection of the long traditions of studying nature and developments specific to the twentieth century. Speculation about, and the study of, the workings of nature have intrigued humans since the beginning of time. However, the delineation of this study has altered over the years, and in English the term 'natural history' was employed as the catch-all phrase for the study of non-human life on earth. Natural history was extremely varied both in relation to the areas of study and the interpretation of the natural world.[8] At the start of the twentieth century, 'biology' had entered the lexicon and crept into educational curricula via zoology and botany, although many years elapsed before the Bachelor of Science degree was instituted.

Thus biology, which now dominates conservation science, is a new discipline.[9] In 1862, the word was first published by George Henry Lewes, partner and later husband of the novelist George Eliot. In his *Studies of Animal Life*, Lewes believed that 'the needful term biology (from bios, life

---

[8] R. Sagarin and A. Pauchard, *Observation and Ecology: Broadening the Scope of Science to Understand a Complex World* (Washington, DC: Island Press, 2012).

[9] E. Myer, *The Growth of Biological Thought* (Cambridge, MA: Harvard University Press, 1982).

and logos, discoveries) is now becoming generally adopted in England, as in Germany. It embraces all the separate sciences of Botany, Zoology, Comparative Anatomy and Physiology.' It did not take long for the word 'biology' to replace 'natural history'.

However, there was a dichotomy between 'field' and 'closet' biology. Field biology was generally the pursuit of amateurs interested in the biographies of animals and the identification of plants and trees in the field. By contrast, closet, or museum, biologists were professionals, who dominated learned societies but often lacked interest in, let alone knowledge of, living animals or plants.[10] As the classification mania spawned by Linnaeus spread, professional and amateur biologists alike were kept endlessly busy and taxonomy, which separated the various orders, families and genera within nature, gave rise to many sub-disciplines of biology.[11] Humanity itself was subjected to biological division and categorisation with the result that museums of the time displayed specimens of people in a manner wholly unacceptable today. There was, however, no particular form of education either for field or closet naturalists and experience was the only measure of their competence. The idea of a 'professional' took time to crystallise, and only in 1924 did all the staff at the South African Museum in Cape Town have university degrees.

So intricate and multi-faceted was biology that by 1952 Ben Dawes listed 26 branches in his *A Hundred Years of Biology*.[12] This excluded conservation biology, which had not then been instituted. The word 'biology' itself indicated a new approach to the study of the living world. It was a branch of physiology and thus marked a divergence from natural history, which mainly concerned itself with classification and description. In the late nineteenth century, physiology became a fundamental science and gave rise to fresh avenues of knowledge through experimentation. This in turn raised the status of biology. In time, further disciplinary separation occurred and distinct professional societies began to proliferate.[13]

Knowledge based on observation was not supplanted by the emergence of laboratory biology. On the contrary, it was characterised

[10]L. Barber, *The Heyday of Natural History, 1820–1870* (London: Jonathan Cape, 1980), 28–29, 40.

[11]L. Merrill, *The Romance of Victorian Natural History* (New York, NY: Oxford University Press, 1989), 66.

[12]B. Dawes, *A Hundred Years of Biology* (London: Duckworth, 1952), 10.

[13]P.L. Farber, 'Discussion paper: The transformation of natural history in the nineteenth century', *Journal of the History of Biology* 15, no. 1 (1982): 145–152.

as cutting-edge 'science' in the conservation of wild animals in game reserves and national parks. It was also often linked with zoological gardens, smaller institutions to be sure, but also concerned with learning about and caring for living creatures. Zookeepers and museologists such as William T. Hornaday, zoologist, taxidermist and first director of the New York Zoological Park (the Bronx Zoo), were leaders in this branch of knowledge, linking it to wildlife protection.[14] In South Africa also museums and zoos played a role in the development of the discipline of conservation. The likes of Jan W.B. Gunning, Alwin Haagner, Austin Roberts and Rudolph Bigalke, all of them employed by what was to become the Transvaal Museum and National Zoological Gardens in Pretoria, and Ernest Warren at the Natal Museum in Pietermaritzburg, were key figures in the development of protectionist thinking and knowledge. As the awareness grew that the extinction of many species was a real possibility, so the prevention of this eventuality itself became a science.[15]

Other relevant sciences also began to make their mark in the late nineteenth century. For instance, in 1893, the BAAS was told that ecology (oecology) was one of the three great divisions within biology – together with physiology and morphology – and the one closest to a 'philosophy of living nature'. In the same year at the International Botanical Congress, the English spelling of 'ecology' (as a branch of biology, not an independent discipline) was adopted.[16] Only after the Second World War did students of ecology emerge in the public domain as an organised, self-aware community of scientists.[17] As for zoology, before the twentieth century it consisted mainly of comparative anatomy or morphology, and only slowly did ethology, a revival of the science of animal behaviour, make an impact.[18] Around 1900, biogeography also emerged as a tool for dealing with distributional patterns, which had hitherto been a descriptive

[14] W.T. Hornaday, *Wild Life Conservation in Theory and Practice* (New Haven, CT: Yale University Press, 1914); S. Bechtel, *Mr Hornaday's War: How a Peculiar Victorian Zookeeper Waged a Lonely Crusade for Wildlife that Changed the World* (Boston: Beacon Press, 2012); C. Yanni, *Nature's Museums: Victorian Science and the Architecture of Display* (London: Athlone Press, 1999), 1–2, 149–150.

[15] Merrill, *Romance of Victorian Natural History*, vii–ix, 6.

[16] P.J. Bowler, *The Fontana History of the Environmental Sciences* (London: Fontana, 1992), 362–366.

[17] T. Dunlap, *Saving America's Wildlife: Ecology and the American Mind, 1850-1990* (Princeton, NJ: Princeton University Press, 1988).

[18] R. Harré, ed., *Scientific Thought 1900–1960: A Selective Survey* (Oxford: Clarendon Press, 1969), 238–239.

project closely related to taxonomy.[19] The earlier approach resulted in anomalies and quirks among those seeking to conserve individual species. Frederick Selous, for example, the well-known hunter-naturalist, did not mourn the extinction of the blue antelope and quagga because they were almost identical to the roan antelope *Hippotragus equinus* and plains zebra *Equus quagga*.[20]

In considering the South African situation, the historian George Basalla's typology of how science develops in the colonial context has some merit. Basalla postulated that colonial science is initially based on the institutions and traditions of a nation with an established scientific culture – in the case of South Africa, this would be Britain. He argued that the conquest and settlement of 'new' lands opened up new fields of science, but that practitioners continued to seek membership in and honours from European scientific societies. Only much later would an independent and local tradition begin to mature.[21] However, to do so, education, financial and institutional support, particularly from government, had to coalesce with ongoing personal networks among individual scientists.

What the above exposition reminds us is that we need to consider the integrity of any science in its own time in order to avoid the sin of presentism or of imposing current categories, interests and values on a world that had no conception of the needs of our own time.[22] We also need to make the effort to remind ourselves of an historical context in which studying of many biota in their natural surroundings was extraordinarily difficult in terms of distance, the absence of technology and the prevalence of endemic diseases.[23]

---

[19]J.B. Hagen, 'Ecologists and taxonomists: Divergent traditions in twentieth-century plant geography', *Journal of the History of Biology* 19, no. 2 (1986): 197; Merrill, *The Romance of Victorian Natural History*, 56.

[20]F.C. Selous, *African Nature Notes and Reminiscences* (1st edn, London: Macmillan, 1908; 2nd edn, Salisbury: Pioneer Head, 1969), 130–131; J. Carruthers, 'Frederick Courteney Selous: Letters to Henry Anderson Bryden, 1889–1914', *The Brenthurst Archives* 2, no. 2 (1995): 9–35.

[21]G. Basalla, 'The spread of western science', *Science* 156 (1967): 611–622.

[22]N. Jardine, J.A. Secord and E. Spary, eds, *Cultures of Natural History* (Cambridge: Cambridge University Press, 1996), 7–8, 152–154.

[23]J. Carruthers, 'Conservation and wildlife management in South African national parks 1930s–1960s', *Journal of the History of Biology* 41, no. 2 (2008): 202–236; J. Carruthers, 'Influences on wildlife management and conservation biology in South Africa c.1900 to c.1940', *South African Historical Journal* 58, no. 1 (2007): 65–90.

How expertise develops is a critically important aspect of any branch of knowledge, and indeed, even today there is contention over what constitutes an 'expert'. In 1900 there was no profession, or professional qualification, appropriate to the post of 'game warden' in a game reserve or, later, a national park. Appointments were made by governments and such expertise as there was came from the paramilitary policing of a closed area. Not accidentally, the first managers of Yellowstone were drawn from the US army. In colonial Africa, the skills expected of land managers were the same as those required of colonial District Officers – sound administration, knowledge of the local language and people, being strict but fair, diligent attention to detail and a strong work ethic. There was no question of being an 'expert' with appropriate formal qualifications for working with wildlife in remote parts of the world. Game wardens certainly made use of their own personal networks and connections, which would have been different, for example, in German, French or British colonies. Invariably, some individuals were more enthusiastic, hard-working and intelligent than others. Needless to say, the inside, on-the-ground knowledge of the 'man on the spot' and his managerial and administrative competence were rated as more important than his zoological or botanical knowledge.

In South Africa, the profession of wildlife, game or national park warden developed over time. It took many years for the requisite personal and professional qualifications to become honed and institutionalised and, with hindsight, it is clear that South Africa was fortunate in the character and work of some of its early game conservators. However, they often locked horns with a well-established veterinary profession intent on protecting an agricultural economy and who regarded themselves as the experts. As South Africa's agricultural and pastoral economy modernised in the twentieth century, veterinary scientists saw themselves as the protectors of the nation's domestic livestock, which they considered as being threatened by diseases among wild animals. These scientists were also close to, and had the ear of, the politicians. They became powerful in the civil service early in the twentieth century and often resented, or overrode, the management philosophy of the wardens and game rangers in South Africa's national parks. South Africa's NPB, established in 1926, lay outside the public service and was thus distinct from the powerful Department of Agriculture, staffed by botanists and veterinarians. The NPB had much less power than a government department and was often at the mercy of inappropriately informed or ignorant Board members. Because it lay outside recognised government service, NPB staffing and promotion issues proved a challenge. There were, however, advantages to this arrangement, including operational flexibility and retention within the institution of the moneys accruing to it. On the other hand, there was no guarantee that the government grant to the NPB would increase regularly. As a parastatal, the NPB was unlike such bodies as the US National Parks Service (NPS), which had an established organisational structure and over whose leadership strict control was exercised.

The following is a list of dates relevant to research into conservation, and the emergence of the science of conservation, in South Africa's national parks, 1800–1960:

1833	'Scientist' was coined by William Whewell in English, thus initiating the concept of 'science' as a profession.
1862	'Biology', described by G.H. Lewes as embracing 'botany, zoology, comparative anatomy and physiology', came into general use.
1866	'Ecology' was first used by Ernst Haeckel, although its precise meaning was unclear and various interpretations have been suggested.
1872	Yellowstone established as a public park in the USA.
1879	Royal National Park, Sydney, established by the government of New South Wales. This is the first explicitly named 'national park'.
1883	The last quagga *Equus quagga quagga*, a female, died in Natura Artis Magistra zoo in Amsterdam.
1884	Tongariro established, the first New Zealand national park.
1885	Rocky Mountains (later called Banff) established, the first Canadian national park.
1886	The Western Districts Game Protection Association founded in the Cape colony.
1889	Pongola Game Reserve, the first in the Transvaal republic, formalised in 1894.
1891	Belair, first national park to be established in the colony of South Australia.
1894	Hunting prohibited in Yellowstone Park (apart from vermin).
1895	St Lucia, Imfolozi Junction, Hluhluwe Valley, Mdlelshe and Mkuzi/Pongola (Reserve No. 5) game reserves established by the British colonial authorities in

	Zululand by Ordinance 12. They were taken over by Natal after Zululand was merged with it in December 1897.
1895	Sabi Game Reserve was established between the Sabie and Crocodile Rivers by the volksraad of the Transvaal republic.
1896	Rinderpest destroyed most of the domestic stock and a great deal of wildlife in southern Africa.
1897	Game sanctuaries established in British East Africa (Kenya).
1898	Springbok Flats and Pretoria townlands and Groenkloof established as game reserves by the volksraad of the Transvaal republic.
1899	Mount Rainier National Park established in the state of Washington, the first legislated 'national park' in the USA.
1899–1902	South African (Anglo-Boer) War.
1900	Convention for the Preservation of Wild Animals, Birds, and Fish in Africa, an initiative of Hermann von Wissman, signed in London (London Convention), initiating the practice whereby one country encourages nature protection in others. Never ratified, it was abandoned in 1914.
1900	Game reserves established in British East Africa (Kenya), Uganda, Nyasa and German East Africa.
1901	William M. Walker, Barberton prospector, appointed warden of Sabi Game Reserve, but dismissed in January 1902 after three months' service.
1902	Transvaal Game Protection Association founded, a resuscitation of the South African Republic Game Protection Association established in 1892.
1902	Transvaal colonial government formally re-proclaimed the game reserves of Sabi (1902), Pretoria/Groenkloof (1902–1903) and responsibility for their administration was given to the Native Affairs Department until 1907, when reserves were transferred to the Colonial Secretary's Department.
1902	James Stevenson-Hamilton employed as warden of Sabi Game Reserve (July 1902) by Native Commissioner Sir Godfrey Lagden.

1903	Society for the Preservation of the Wild Fauna of the Empire founded by E.N. Buxton as a public response to the London Convention.
1904	The *Journal of the Society for the Preservation of the Wild Fauna of the Empire* (after 1921 called the *Journal of the Society for the Preservation of the Fauna of the Empire*, and after 1950, *Oryx*) began publication. The first, and for many decades the only, scientific journal devoted to wildlife study, management and conservation in the British world.
1903	The first of James Stevenson-Hamilton's many publications on wildlife protection and study: 'Game preservation in the eastern Transvaal', *The Field*, 14 March 1903.
1903	Giant's Castle Game Reserve, Drakensberg, established by the Natal Legislative Assembly.
1903	Singwitsi Game Reserve, Transvaal colony, established at the suggestion of L.H. Ledeboer to the native commissioner in Pietersburg. The warden, A.A. Fraser, responsible to Stevenson-Hamilton, was relocated from Pongola Game Reserve.
1903	Bushmanland Game Reserve (sometimes referred to as the Namaqualand Game Reserve) established in the Cape colony.
1905	Stevenson-Hamilton brought wildlife protection into South Africa's formal scientific structures with his publication, 'Game preservation in the Transvaal', in South African Association for the Advancement of Science, comp., *Addresses and Papers Read at the Joint meeting of the British and South African Associations for the Advancement of Science held in South Africa, 1905* (Johannesburg: South African Association for the Advancement of Science, 1905), 350–368.
1906	Swiss Association of the Natural Sciences formed a committee on conservation under Basel naturalist Paul Sarasin.
1907	St Lucia and Umbombo-Mkhuze Game Reserves de-proclaimed by the Natal colonial government.
1908	First Conservation Conference in the US convened by President Theodore Roosevelt and chief of the forest

service, Gifford Pinchot. Terminology and philosophies of 'conservation' (favoured by Pinchot) versus 'preservation' (favoured by national park advocate John Muir) were debated.

1908   Four state farms in Natal Drakensberg were 'reserved for the purpose of forming a national park'. They were taken over by the central government in 1916.

1908   Gordonia Game Reserve, in the Kuruman District of the Cape colony, established comprising 23 900 km^2. The growing availability of water for agriculture and stock-raising resulted in its regular diminution. In 1924, 8805 km^2 remained.

1909   Sweden proclaimed its first two national parks, Abisko and Ängsö. By 1910 there were nine national parks in Sweden.

1909   Rustenburg Game Reserve established by Transvaal Colonial Secretary, Jan Smuts.

1909   North American Conservation Conference convened. The first regional conservation conference, it included the US, Canada and Mexico.

1910   Union of South Africa established from former colonies of the Cape, Natal, Orange River and the Transvaal.

1911   Frederick Vaughan Kirby appointed game conservator in the province of Natal.

1912   *Animal Life in Africa* (London: Heinemann), James Stevenson-Hamilton's highly acclaimed book, published.

1912   Geological Survey of South Africa established.

1912   Mkhuze Game Reserve established by the Natal province for protecting rhinoceros.

1913   First International Conference for the Protection of Nature hosted in Basel by the Swiss government, convened by Paul Sarasin, leader of the Swiss conservation movement. There were delegates from 16 countries. The USA did not attend.

1913   'An oecological survey of the midlands of Natal with special reference to the Pietermaritzburg district', *Annals of the Natal Museum* 2, no. 4 (1913): 485–545 and 'The plant ecology of the Drakensberg range', *Annals of the Natal Museum* 3, no. 3 (1913): 511–566, two papers published by John W. Bews, the earliest South African literature employing the word 'ecology'.

1913   Publication of *Guide to the Study of Animal Ecology* (New York, NY: Macmillan) by Charles Adams.

1913   First appearance of the *Journal of Ecology*, edited by Arthur Tansley, under the auspices of the Central Committee for the Survey and Study of British Vegetation.

1913   Kirstenbosch National Botanical Garden founded in Cape Town.

1914   First World War began (August).

1914   Rustenburg Game Reserve de-proclaimed by Transvaal provincial government.

1914   Swiss National Park inaugurated 1 August.

1915   Ecological Society of America established, with Victor Shelford as president.

1916   Publication of *Plant Succession: An Analysis of the Development of Vegetation* (Washington, DC: Carnegie Institution) by Frederic E. Clements.

1916   United States National Parks Service established.

1916   National Zoological Gardens under Alwin K. Haagner established in the Department of National Education.

1916   South African Biological Society founded.

1916   Natal National Park established.

1918   First World War ended (November).

1918   Botanical Survey Advisory Committee established in the national Division of Botany, part of the Department of Agriculture.

1918   Report of the Commission of Enquiry in the Transvaal into the game reserves of the Eastern Transvaal, paved the way for the Kruger National Park (commission established in 1916).

1919   Imfolozi Game Reserve de-proclaimed by Natal province (re-proclaimed 1930).

1919   Bushmanland Game Reserve (Namaqualand Game Reserve) de-proclaimed by Cape provincial administration.

1921   First National Park conference in the US held in Washington, DC.

1921   Pongola Game Reserve abolished by the Transvaal provincial administration.

1922	Dongola Botanical Reserve established by Department of Agriculture.
1923	An international nature protection conference held in Paris.
1924	Ndumo Game Reserve established by Natal province.
1925	Albert National Park established in the Belgian Congo. Enlarged in 1929, it was both a sanctuary and a research station run by trained biologists.
1926–29	James Stevenson-Hamilton became secretary of the renowned Zoological Society of London.
1926	National Parks Act 56 of 1926 passed in South Africa.
1926	Wild Life Society of South Africa amalgamated various game protection and similar associations in South Africa, but a strong united organisation did not emerge for many years.
1926	H.R. Carey, Harvard Museum of Comparative Zoology, added his voice to calls for a permanent international body for nature protection, and suggested that this be established by the League of Nations. ('Saving the animal life of Africa; A new method and a last chance', *Journal of Mammalogy* 7, no. 2 (1926): 73–75.)
1928	Pieter van Tienhoven of the Netherlands, together with other Dutch and Belgian conservationists, founded the International Office for the Protection of Nature.
1929	South African Academy of Science again published on wildlife protection. See Herbert Lang, American Museum of Natural History, 'Game reserves and wild life protection', in H.J. Crocker and J. McCrae, eds, *South Africa and Science: A Handbook Prepared under the Auspices of the South African Association for the Advancement of Science for the Meeting of the British Association in Capetown [sic] and Johannesburg, South Africa, 1929* (Johannesburg: South African Association for the Advancement of Science, 241–250).
1929	Publication of J. Stevenson-Hamilton's *The Low-Veld: Its Wild Life and its People* (London: Cassell).
1929	American Committee for International Wild Life Protection founded.
1931	Addo Elephant National Park, Cape province, established.

1931	International Congress for the Protection of Nature convened in Paris by P.G. van Tienhoven. South Africa was represented by diplomats Charles te Water (High Commissioner, London) and Arthur Hill. The Convention followed in 1933.
1931	Bontebok National Park in Bredasdorp, Cape province, established to preserve the small herd of rare bontebok *Damaliscus pygargus dorcas*.
1931	The International Council of Scientific Unions (ICSU, currently the International Council for Science) was formed for the promotion of activity in different branches of science and applied science for the benefit of humanity.
1931	Kalahari Gemsbok National Park, Cape province, established.
1932	Bureau of Animal Ecology at Oxford established by Charles Elton.
1932	Mapungubwe's archaeological treasures discovered by local farmers. As a consequence, the land was purchased by government for curation and study by the University of Pretoria, numerous scientific publications followed and the South African Archaeological Survey was established.
1932	The *Journal of Animal Ecology* first appeared. Of 250 members of the society, four were South African. All were botanists: R.S. Adamson (University of Cape Town), J.W. Bews (University of Natal), F.S. Laughton (Assistant Forest Officer, Concordia, Knysna) and J.F.V. Phillips (University of the Witwatersrand).
1932 and 1933	George M. Wright published, at his own expense, two reports on fauna in the national parks of the USA: *Preliminary Survey of Faunal Relations in National Parks* (1932) and *Wildlife Management in the National Parks* (1933).
1933	The Convention Relative to the Preservation of Fauna and Flora in the Natural State (London Convention) signed.
1933	*Game Management* (New York, NY: Scribner's) published by Aldo Leopold.

1934	Momentum grew for a South African Biological and/or Zoological Survey such as existed in the US. The main protagonists were Austin Roberts and Rudolph Bigalke.
1935	Julian Huxley became secretary of the Zoological Society of London (until 1943).
1935	Introduction of the term 'ecosystem' in A.G. Tansley, 'The use and abuse of vegetational concepts and terms', *Ecology* 16 (1935): 284–307.
1937	Mountain Zebra National Park, Cape province, established.
1937	*South African Eden* (London: Cassell), James Stevenson-Hamilton's memoir published.
1939	R. Bigalke, director of the National Zoological Gardens in Pretoria, campaigned for formal biology to be incorporated into the management of South Africa's national parks and published *A Guide to Some Common Animals of the Krüger National Park* (Pretoria: Van Schaik).
1940	Inter-American Convention on Nature Protection and Wildlife Preservation, signed by the United States and 16 Latin American nations.
1942	National Parks Board of Trustees refused to take over Dongola Botanical Reserve and accept it as a formal national park.
1945	Council for Scientific and Industrial Research (CSIR) founded in Pretoria.
1946	Natal Society for the Preservation of Wild Life and Natural Resorts established.
1946	J.A.B. Sandenbergh succeeded Stevenson-Hamilton as warden of the KNP (until 1953).
1947	J. Stevenson-Hamilton published *Wild Life in South Africa* (London: Cassell).
1947	International Union for the Protection of Nature (IUPN) founded at Brunnen under the auspices of UNESCO, with director-general Julian Huxley. After 1956 it was renamed the International Union for the Conservation of Nature and Natural Resources (IUCN).

1947	Natal National Park (NNP) becomes the Royal Natal National Park (under provincial administration) after visit by the Royal Family to South Africa.
1947	Dongola Wild Life Sanctuary Act 6 of 1947.
1947	The Natal Parks, Game and Fish Preservation Board established.
1947	Transvaal Division of Nature Conservation established.
1949	Dongola Wild Life Sanctuary Repeal Act 29 of 1949.
1949	The Nature Conservancy established in Britain.
1950	South African Regional Committee for the Conservation and Utilisation of the Soil (SARCCUS) established.
1951	Victor Cahalane, chief biologist of the US National Parks Service, visited South Africa at the invitation of A.E. Trollip, member of the National Parks Board of Trustees.
1951	*Trees and Shrubs of the Kruger National Park*, Botanical Survey Memoir No. 26 (Pretoria: Department of Agriculture Division of Botany and Plant Pathology) by L.E. Codd.
1951	Biology Section in the Kruger National Park established with T.G. Nel, education biologist formerly with National Zoological Gardens, at its head.
1952	'Hoek Commission of Enquiry into the Management of Various National Parks under the Administration of the National Parks Board', chairman P.W. Hoek. The report of this commission uncovered many instances of negligence, fraud and dereliction of duty and it resulted in substantial changes to the board's mandate and administration.
1952	Cape Department of Nature Conservation established.
1953	Rocco Knobel appointed first full-time director of South Africa's national parks.
1953	In Bukavu, Belgian Congo, a conference was convened by the IUPN to review the 1933 London Convention. *The Preparatory Document for the International Conference for the Protection of the Fauna and Flora of Africa* listed and described many hundreds of game reserves and national parks in Africa. For South Africa, five national parks (as defined in Article 2 of the 1933 Convention)

administered by the NPB and six by the province of Natal – a total of 11 – were listed. In addition ten game reserves in the Transvaal, five in Natal, ten in Zululand, three in the Orange Free State and six in the Cape were mentioned. Regarding the Cape, however, the comment was made that there were many thousands of morgen of conserved state land in that province.

1953 Louis B. Steyn appointed warden of the Kruger National Park (until 1961).

1953 Natal Parks, Game and Fish Preservation Board appointed its first research officer.

1953 *Fundamentals of Ecology* (Philadelphia, PA: W.B. Saunders) published by Eugene Odum, the first English-language textbook on systems ecology.

1955 Steering Committee for Scientific Research established, with chairman H.O. Mönnig, and members, R. Knobel, R. Ortlepp, R. Bigalke and A.P. Goossens.

1958 The IUCN meeting in Athens launched the International Commission on National Parks with an

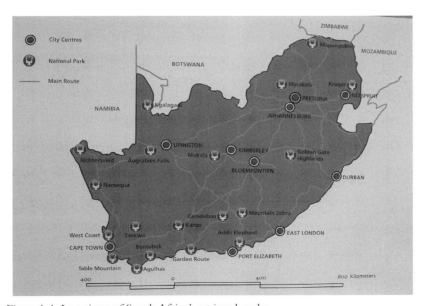

Figure 1.1. Locations of South Africa's national parks.
Courtesy of SANParks.

undertaking to list all existing national parks in the world and to have the first compilation complete for the First World Parks Congress planned for 1962 in Seattle.

1958   *Koedoe*, the research journal of the NPB, first published.

1958   Table Mountain proclaimed a national monument, managed by the Table Mountain Preservation Board.

1959   Bontebok National Park moved from Bredasdorp to Swellendam.

1959   Percy Fitzpatrick Institute of African Ornithology founded at the University of Cape Town (incorporated into the Department of Zoology in 1973).

1959   Zoological Society of Southern Africa established.

2 · Origins of Conservation Science until 1910

During the period up to 1910, Western scientific knowledge had been acquired as travellers, explorers and settlers became familiar with the biology of southern Africa. After that date, however, scientific inquiry and institutions began to take on more modern forms. This evolution relates both to the political history of the country and the kind of society that was evolving. The year 1910 was, as we have seen, a political watershed because it was then that South Africa emerged from its colonial past as a united polity following the acceptance by the Transvaal, Natal, the Cape and the Orange River Colony of the compromise constitution negotiated at the Durban Convention. One can date a national scientific endeavour to that year.

However, educated interest in the natural history of southern Africa, both its fauna and flora, dated back to the 1600s and the beginnings of European occupation of the region by the Dutch East India Company (Verenigde Oostindische Compagnie, VOC). Numerous European visitors marvelled at the variety and beauty of what the Cape offered and left rich records in words, illustrations and preserved specimens.[1] Throughout the VOC era (1652–1795), the short-lived Batavian Republic (1802–1806) and the British colonial era (1795–1802 and again 1806–1910),

[1] P. Kolb, *Naaukeurige en Uitvoerige Beschryving van de Kaap de Goede Hoop* (Amsterdam: Balthazar Lakeman, 1727); F. le Vaillant, *Francois le Vaillant: Traveller in South Africa*. 2 vols (Cape Town: Library of Parliament, 1973); H. Lichtenstein, *Travels in Southern Africa*. 2 vols (Cape Town: Van Riebeeck Society, 1928, 1930); O.F. Mentzel, *A Geographical and Topographical Description of the Cape of Good Hope*. 2 vols (Cape Town: Van Riebeeck Society, 1921, 1944); A. Sparrman, *Voyage to the Cape of Good Hope etc.* 2 vols (London: Robinson, 1786); J. Barrow, *Travels into the Interior of Southern Africa* (London: T. Cadell and W. Davis, 1806); W.J. Burchell, *Travels in the Interior of Southern Africa*. 2 vols (London: Longman, Hurst, 1822, 1824); V.S. Forbes and J. Rourke, *Paterson's Cape Travels, 1777 to 1779* (Johannesburg: The Brenthurst Press, 1980); P.E. Raper and M. Boucher, eds, *Robert Jacob Gordon: Cape Travels, 1777 to 1786*. 2 vols (Johannesburg: The Brenthurst Press, 1988).

wealthy patrons dispatched energetic collectors to the Cape, many of whom sought plants with economic or horticultural potential in Europe.[2] Linnaeus' taxonomic standardisation of 1735 further stimulated the mania for collecting and naming creatures and plants, and private, royal and state accumulations in Europe burgeoned.

Naturally, there was a wealth of African indigenous knowledge about the plant and animal life of the region that dated back many centuries, and the expansion of a settler community into the interior meant that local knowledge increased of necessity. Travellers and settlers, particularly the highly mobile pastoralists, the *trekboers*, learnt from local people about plants that were useful for domestic requirements, such as herbal remedies for humans and domestic stock. Little, if any, of this kind of expertise, however, was formally recorded or found its way into the museums and herbaria of Europe, although some of it was incorporated by later Boer settlers as part of their medical culture and folklore.[3] No institutionalised science developed locally before the 1820s. The zoological knowledge amassed in southern Africa was exported to metropolitan Europe in the form of dried specimens, skins, horns and also by way of wonderful illustrations, and a few live animals were dispatched to menageries and zoological gardens in Europe.[4]

Naming and organising to facilitate collecting and recording were the order of the day.[5] There is a pantheon of collectors, particularly in the Cape Peninsula and its environs, and increasingly proto-scientists travelled deeper into the interior. Complex arrangements for collection, preservation and transportation developed, generally relying on the assistance of local people. Specimens were exported to Europe, but no formal study of natural history grew up in southern Africa itself. However, the region gained a strong reputation in Europe, and the publicity encouraged ever more biologically inclined visitors to come to the region.

[2]See L. Schiebinger and C. Swan, eds, *Colonial Botany: Science, Commerce, and Politics in the Early Modern World* (Philadelphia, PA: University of Pennsylvania Press, 2005).
[3]W. Beinart, *The Rise of Conservation in South Africa: Settlers, Livestock, and the Environment, 1770–1950* (Oxford: Oxford University Press, 2003); W. Beinart and J. McGregor, eds, *Social History and African Environments* (London: James Currey, 2003).
[4]See, for example, G. Mitchell, 'The origins of the scientific study and classification of giraffes: History of science', *Transactions of the Royal Society of South Africa* 64, no. 1 (2009): 1–13.
[5]N. Jardine, J.A. Secord and E. Spary, eds, *Cultures of Natural History* (Cambridge: Cambridge University Press, 1996); L. Merrill, *The Romance of Victorian Natural History* (New York, NY: Oxford University Press, 1989).

By the end of the nineteenth century, Western taxonomy had assumed enormous importance and many of the finest minds in Europe were dedicated to its intricacies. By then, there were fairly strong institutions of learning and study within what was to become South Africa. The institutionalisation of scientific endeavour there began to be consolidated in the nineteenth century, not unexpectedly, in the Cape colony. At that time, after British control over the Cape had been finally formalised after 1814, there was considerable pressure from the local intelligentsia, particularly in metropolitan Cape Town, to establish learned institutions that would amass accurate knowledge, encourage learning and assist in the colony's economic development.[6] In 1814, the Cape was still predominantly Dutch in character and there was no school, no bookshop and no newspaper.[7] Before its bankruptcy in 1795, the VOC had administered the Cape with a view to maximum extraction and minimum investment. Consequently, no attention was given to the 'civilised' accoutrements of permanent colonisation, not even roads and banking institutions, let alone museums and educational facilities.

This situation began to change in the 1820s with the immigration of a significant number of British settlers, some of whom had belonged to the learned societies that had become popular in Britain and were familiar with the institutionalisation of science.[8] In 1824, one of them, John Fairbairn, established the South African Literary Society, the first 'scientific' society on the subcontinent.[9] There followed over the next few years the South African Literary and Philosophical Society and the South African Institution. The mission of the latter was 'to promote general information and encourage Researches into the Natural History and Resources of Southern Africa'. It also produced a research publication, the *South African Quarterly Journal*, which first appeared in 1830 and

[6]J. Carruthers, 'Scientists in society: A history of the Royal Society of South Africa', *Transactions of the Royal Society of South Africa* 63, no. 1 (2008): 1–30; S. Dubow, *A Commonwealth of Knowledge: Science, Sensibility, and White South Africa, 1820–2000* (Oxford: Oxford University Press, 2006); L.D. Bregman, '"Snug little coteries": A history of scientific societies in early nineteenth century Cape Town, 1824–1835' (PhD diss., University College London, 2003). See also C. Russell, *Science and Social Change 1700–1900* (London: Macmillan, 1983).
[7]Dubow, *Commonwealth of Knowledge*, 18.
[8]Bregman, '"Snug little coteries"'.
[9]H.C. Botha, *John Fairbairn in South Africa* (Cape Town: Historical Publication Society, 1984).

sporadically thereafter until 1837.[10] By the early 1830s, Cape Town could boast a library, a museum, botanical gardens and an astronomical observatory, even a proto-university – the South African College – although not all of them were equally thriving. It is salutary to recall that the British Association for the Advancement of Science (BAAS) had been founded only in 1831. As Russell notes, this proliferation of scientific associations and institutions among the growing middle class in Britain and its colonies was fuelled by complex factors, including less-expensive publications, better communication and the desire to achieve upward mobility and political power through learning.[11]

Although the Cape appeared to be well served by institutions promoting the acquisition and dissemination of knowledge, the pool of expertise was extremely small. Even so, the Cape middle class included a number of men who were keen to make their intellectual mark on colonial affairs. Possibly the most notable of these early pioneers was Andrew Smith, an ambitious army surgeon and energetic polymath. A friend of Charles Darwin,[12] Smith was involved in four of the 11 scientific societies that existed in Cape Town between 1824 and 1833.[13] He was a leading promoter of natural history during his sojourn at the Cape, and led two important fact-finding expeditions into the interior. One was to Natal in 1832, and during the other, from 1834 to 1836, he journeyed well beyond the Orange River into what later became the Transvaal. Finance for this second expedition was raised within the Cape colony through the Cape of Good Hope Association for Exploring Central Africa.[14]

Smith's excursions were multidisciplinary and scientifically diverse. He was tasked with recording geology, botany, zoology, anthropology and, in addition, with keeping a sharp eye on the leadership structures and military power of local African communities. He was also instructed to note the increasing number of traders, missionaries and frontier settlers who were moving beyond the bounds of British control. The frontier to the

[10]Bregman, "'Snug little coteries'", 181; Dubow, *Commonwealth of Knowledge*, 40–41.

[11]Russell, *Science and Social Change*, 175–192. In 1868 there were 3520 members of the leading nine mathematical and physical societies and 17 924 members of the leading 13 biological and natural history societies, see p. 222.

[12]Dubow, *Commonwealth of Knowledge*, 39.

[13]Bregman, "'Snug little coteries'", 20–21.

[14]P.R. Kirby, ed., *Andrew Smith and Natal: Documents Relating to the Early History of That Province* (Cape Town: The Van Riebeeck Society, 1955); W.F. Lye, ed., *Andrew Smith's Journal of his Expedition into the Interior of South Africa, 1834–1836* (Cape Town: Balkema, 1975).

GALAGO MOHOLI.
(Mammals Plate 8)

78

Figure 2.1. Galago moholi, named for science by Andrew Smith in 1836.
From A. Smith, *Illustrations of the Zoology of South Africa. Volume 1, Mammals*, p. 78.
Facsimile edition Johannesburg: Winchester Press, 1977.

north of the Cape colony was expanding rapidly for many reasons, not the least of these being the abundance of wildlife in the interior, which sustained commerce and settlement.

His contribution is important not only because of the range and scope of the knowledge he and his party accumulated, but also because, for the first time, the decision was made to house the collected specimens in a South African repository rather than to dispatch them to Europe. Even the type specimens were retained in the South African Museum that Smith had founded in Cape Town in 1825.[15] Indeed, his collections got the museum off to an auspicious start (he became honorary superintendent), but there was no special building for the purpose and no dedicated museum staff. When Smith left the Cape in 1837, the collections fell into

[15]Lye, *Andrew Smith's Journal*; R.F. Kennedy, introduction to *Illustrations of the Zoology of South Africa*, 3 vols, by A. Smith (Johannesburg: Winchester, 1977).

disarray. Although Smith's work and material did not find a publisher at the time (his illustrations, however, were published in parts between 1838 and 1849), the process of localising knowledge obtained and making it available within the colony had begun.[16] It was to develop further during the late nineteenth and early twentieth centuries with the establishment of a number of teaching colleges, museums, learned societies and specialised interest groups.

The public in Britain was highly literate, and scientific and other intellectual pursuits were regarded as integral to an educated society. The accolade 'gifted amateur' was more valuable than any professional qualification of the time – indeed, the very terms 'professional' and 'scientist' had not taken on their current meanings.[17] In the English-speaking world, specialisation and professionalism developed first in physics and chemistry, which had their own particular languages that the lay public could not easily fathom. Natural history held its own for far longer as a field to which any observant person might make a valuable contribution. Natural history societies in Britain peaked in the 1870s and 1880s and were replicated in the colonies.[18] Professions were, however, developing in certain specialisations and jobs were being created in museums and in zoological and botanical gardens. South Africa was part of this process.

Between 1857 and 1877, the mantle of intellectual activity in Cape Town passed from the learned societies to *The Cape Monthly Magazine*. This was issued in three series between 1857 and 1881. The publication dealt with a wide variety of topics, generally – but not invariably – related to colonial themes. Agricultural subjects were covered, as were botany, zoology, geology, literature, travel, African history, linguistics and ethnography, Cape history, education and colonial development. The activities of the Horticultural Society, the Albany Natural History Society and the South African Museum and Library were featured regularly. In March 1860, the *Magazine* included an article on 'The study of science'. While it lauded the attainment of 'truth' as the highest human endeavour, it lamented the neglect of beauty by many scientists in their 'attention merely to the real – that is, to fact'. Nonetheless, scientists were praised as those 'men whose patient labour and deep research are

---

[16] R. Summers, *A History of the South African Museum, 1825–1975* (Cape Town: Central News Agency, 1975).

[17] Russell, *Science and Social Change*, chapter 11.

[18] P.D. Lowe, 'Amateurs and professionals: The institutional emergence of British plant ecology', *Journal of the Society of Bibliography of Natural History* 7, no. 4 (1976): 517–535.

the wonder of mankind. Confining themselves to the accumulation of details, – allowing no deduction until the truth is self-evident, – they reject all assistance from imagination regarding speculation as vain . . . Such are the men, who treating of such dry subjects as botany, anatomy, &c, content themselves with the dry narration of facts.'[19] This article signalled a growing divide in the readership of the *Magazine* between those of literary or artistic inclination and those who preferred the 'dry narration of facts'.

To cater to the latter, in 1877 the South African Philosophical Society was founded on the premise 'that it is desirable to form a Society for Promoting Scientific Inquiry and Original Research in South Africa and Recording its Results'. Shortly afterwards, regular issues of the *Transactions of the South African Philosophical Society* began to appear.[20] A notable early contribution to the *Transactions* was what might now be considered an ecological paper, 'On the peculiar colours of animals in relation to habits of life', by Mary Barber, a corresponding member in Kimberley (and the only woman in the society). In it, she expressed her admiration of Darwin, who put 'us on the right track' and enabled us 'to spell out the book of nature with Mr Darwin's alphabet in our hands'.[21] All scientific disciplines were represented in the society, among them astronomy, archaeology, botany, meteorology and climatology, mineralogy and petrology, physics and engineering, geology and palaeontology, irrigation, mathematics, oceanography, physiology and zoology. There can be no doubt that the growing maturity of South African scientific inquiry owed much to the existence and efforts of the South African Philosophical Society.

In addition to the 'scientific' articles published in these two journals or debated in the learned societies after the mid-nineteenth century, international travellers and collectors published 'travel accounts' about southern Africa. Some of these were entertaining and illuminating and enjoyed a large readership. Sport-hunting exploits were particularly popular and names such as William Cornwallis Harris, Gordon Roualeyn Cumming, H.A. Bryden and Frederick Selous entered the canon of

---

[19] *The Cape Monthly Magazine* 7 (1868): 129–131.
[20] 'Minutes of the South African Philosophical Society, 22 June 1877', archives of the Royal Society, Cape Town.
[21] See W. Beinart, 'Men, science, travel and nature in the eighteenth and nineteenth-century Cape', *Journal of Southern African Studies* 24, no. 4 (1998): 775–799.

'hunting literature'.[22] Their work was perhaps the closest in that era to anything like science, even if the authors – at least before they mellowed with age and experience and became 'penitent butchers'– revelled in killing far more than in aesthetic appreciation or species protection. Although these men were undeniably prolific killers of wildlife, and loathed 'vermin' (as all hunters did at the time), many killed for the benefit of what they believed to be scientific knowledge. They understood that their specimens and their careful descriptions added to the sum of knowledge about wildlife biology, even if the latter were often packaged as tales of derring-do.

As the nineteenth century drew to a close, concern about the decline in wild animal numbers in southern Africa was more frequently expressed. Tales, at times reflecting an attitude of 'possession', at least among British imperialists, were told that lamented the extinction of the blaauwbok or blue antelope *Hippotragus laucophaeus* and quagga *Equus quagga quagga*, and books extolling the wise use and protection of large mammal species began to be published in the popular press.[23]

The aim of many of these authors was both to entertain and to impart knowledge gained in the field. As van der Windt has argued, between 1895 and 1905 'amateur naturalists developed and combined new ideas about nature, its study, its appreciation and its protection' and 'gave shape [to] the conservation movement, including its core message, its

[22]W.C. Harris, *Portraits of the Game and Wild Animals of Southern Africa* (London: n.p., 1840); R.G. Cumming, *A Hunter's Life in South Africa* (Johannesburg: Galago, n.d.); W.C. Harris, *The Wild Sports of Southern Africa* (London: Henry Bohm, 1852); J. Carruthers, 'Frederick Courteney Selous: Letters to Henry Anderson Bryden, 1889–1914', *The Brenthurst Archives* 2, no. 2 (1995): 9–35; H.A. Bryden, ed., *Great and Small Game of Africa* (London: Rowland Ward, 1899); H.A. Bryden, *Gun and Camera in Southern Africa* (London: Edward Stanford, 1893); H.A. Bryden, *Kloof and Karroo: Sport, Legend and Natural History in Cape Colony* (London: Longmans Green, 1889); H.A. Bryden, *Nature and Sport in South Africa* (London: Chapman and Hall, 1897); F.C. Selous, *African Nature Notes and Reminiscences* (London: Macmillan, 1908; 2nd edn, Salisbury: Pioneer Head, 1969); F.C. Selous, *A Hunter's Wanderings in Africa* (London: Richard Bentley, 1881; 2nd edn, Bulawayo: Books of Zimbabwe, 1981); J. Carruthers, *Game Protection in the Transvaal 1846 to 1926* (Pretoria: Archives Yearbook for South African History, 1995), chapter 2.
[23]See, for example, the work of H.A. Bryden in particular, but also J.M. MacKenzie, ed., *Imperialism and the Natural World* (Manchester: Manchester University Press, 1990); J.M. MacKenzie, *The Empire of Nature: Hunting, Conservation and British Imperialism* (Manchester: Manchester University Press, 1988).

Figure 2.2. Quagga stallion, mare and foal displayed in the Natural History Museum, Mainz. Skins acquired in the 1840s.
Photograph by Elke Ackermann.

organisation and its propaganda'.[24] In southern Africa, so rich in wild fauna, the books of sport-hunters facilitated the spread of these ideas.

The influence and wide readership achieved by hunter–naturalists arose from the fact that they were the primary sources about far-flung parts of the world that ordinary people of the time could never hope to visit. They were the 'men on the spot' who had encountered wild animals at first hand and seen them in their natural habitats. Indeed, the high value afforded personal observation and experience continues into the present and underpins the authority of many a modern wildlife biologist.

Since the 1600s, the centre of intellectual life in southern Africa had been the Cape, Cape Town in particular.[25] However, after the South African War (1899–1902), the scientific centre of gravity in the region began to shift significantly. Between 1903 and 1910 the Transvaal began to assert itself in the fields of astronomy, medicine, ornithology, engineering

[24]H.J. van der Windt, 'Biologists bridging science and the conservation movement: The rise of nature conservation and nature management in the Netherlands, 1850–1950', *Environment and History* 18, no. 2 (2012): 209–236.
[25]Carruthers, 'Scientists in society', 1–30; Dubow, *Commonwealth of Knowledge*, 18–19.

and higher education.[26] After the war, eminent English-speaking experts in various fields were attracted to the region, full as it was of the promise of future growth, prosperity (and thus research and other funding), careers and the enhancement of reputations. Moreover, political, aesthetic and cultural nationalism applicable to the whole country came into play at the dawn of the twentieth century. The location and stature of 'national' iconic institutions – national museum, national botanical garden, national university – were matters of discussion and debate. These ideas gained further currency with the establishment of the South African Association for the Advancement of Science (SAAAS) on the occasion of the first visit to the subcontinent of the BAAS, as well as the Royal Society of South Africa.[27]

Natural History, Science and New State Structures

By 1910, some of the contours of scientific institutionalisation and key areas of focus were apparent in South Africa. Many of these trends were important in shaping the trajectory of scientific study in South Africa's future protected areas. As southern Africa fell firmly within the British sphere of influence, it is not surprising that the organisational arrangements and fields of interest replicated those in Britain.[28] A British-style civil service was established in the Transvaal after 1902 and the people involved in the new government in the northern parts of the country worked with energy and enthusiasm, despite post-war economic depression. Perhaps inevitably, new institutions there began to rival and challenge the more established bodies in the Cape.

Museums were the most important state structures dedicated to scientific endeavour. As well-established repositories of scientific knowledge, museums helped shape disciplines and scholarly priorities, and their role in the evolving new science in protected areas deserves consideration.[29] At the beginning of the twentieth century the region's leading museum was undoubtedly the South African Museum in Cape Town, which had moved into an impressive new building in 1895. It was organised along

[26]Dubow, *Commonwealth of Knowledge*, 66–99, 185–186.

[27]Carruthers, 'Scientists in society', 1–30; Dubow, *Commonwealth of Knowledge*.

[28]R. MacLeod, ed., *Nature and Empire: Science and the Colonial Enterprise* (Chicago, IL: University of Chicago Press, 2001).

[29]See J.M. MacKenzie, *Museums and Empire: Natural History, Human Cultures and Colonial Identities* (Manchester: Manchester University Press, 2009).

the lines of the Natural History Museum in London, with which it had close links, with specialist keepers in charge of the various collections. The South African Museum attracted several eminent biologists, some amateur and some professionally trained in Britain. Many of them later enjoyed successful careers in the British Empire.[30] Particularly notable directors in the late 1800s and early 1900s were the ornithologists Edgar Layard and William L. Sclater and the entomologists Roland Trimen and Louis Péringuey, the latter also being an authority on San rock art. Only Sclater, educated at Winchester and Keble College, Oxford, could boast a university education in natural science. He was also responsible for the publication of the *Annals of the South African Museum.*

Other museums in South Africa were linked to the country's emerging universities. At the time, these were still university colleges operating under the aegis of the University of the Cape of Good Hope, established in 1873 as an examination body modelled on the University of London and renamed the University of South Africa in 1916. It spawned most of South Africa's modern universities. For example, Grahamstown's Albany Museum was founded in 1855 by a local 'intellectual' society and until 1902 was run by the town clerk. Thereafter its director was Selmar Schonland, who had a PhD in botany from the University of Kiel, and who became the first chair of botany at Rhodes University College when it was founded in 1904. Similarly, in 1904 the Natal Government Museum was established in Pietermaritzburg, the fruit of the efforts begun by the Natal Society as far back as 1879. The first director, Ernest Warren, was a zoologist whose speciality was skeletal biometrics. By 1910, the Natal Museum was referring to itself as the 'university museum' and Warren was appointed the first professor of zoology at Natal University College.[31] Unlike most other museum directors, he went on to directly influence wildlife conservation science, particularly in Natal.

By 1877, both Durban (Natal) and Bloemfontein (Orange Free State) had museums and the Natural History Society of King William's Town had inaugurated the Kaffrarian Museum in 1884. In the Transvaal Republic, the *Staats* Museum in Pretoria was founded somewhat later, in

[30] P.R. Kirby, 'Andrew Smith: Founder of the South African Museum', *Annals of the South African Museum* 36 (1942–1948): 1–27; Summers, *History of South African Museum.*

[31] S.F. Bush, 'Ernest Warren, DSc, Director, Natal Museum, 1903–1935', *Annals of the Natal Museum* 10, no. 1 (1941): 1–14; S. Brooks, 'Encounters with the colonial: Dr Ernest Warren, science, and new representations of nature at the Natal Museum (1903–1913)', *Southern African Humanities* 17 (2005): 1–31.

1892, lending an air of 'civilised society' to the Boer state. Its first director was Jan W.B. Gunning, a Dutch-born medical practitioner and one of President Kruger's coterie of imported Netherlander officials. What distinguished the *Staats* Museum – apart from its staff's lack of formal training and the absence of university liaison – was that it housed a zoological garden where live animals were displayed.[32]

As with museum scientists elsewhere at the time, South Africa's were more interested in deceased animals than living, and were mostly engaged in systematics or taxonomy.[33] From their dead specimens they compiled comprehensive lists of related taxa in an endeavour to tame nature into a precise and well-ordered hierarchy. In consequence, animal behaviour, habitat and interspecies relationships were neglected, because they did not contribute to the uncovering of organising morphological principles. Research by museum staff was published in museum annals, several of which appeared in the early twentieth century. The South African Museum's journal began in 1898. Significantly, conservation issues or even ecology were first mentioned in its pages only in the mid-1960s. This is hardly surprising, for the specific brief of these annals was publication of 'the results of the original work of the staff', who for many decades engaged in no fieldwork.[34] *The Annals of the Transvaal Museum* began in 1908. In this case, too, most papers focused on taxonomy. One exception, from 1922, was a 'Review of the nomenclature of South African birds', written by the outspoken maverick (and formally untrained) ornithologist and mammalogist Austin Roberts, who boldly declared that cataloguing names 'is the elementary need of science, but not its final objective'.[35]

---

[32]J.W.B. Gunning, 'A short history of the Transvaal Museum', *Annals of the Transvaal Museum* 1 (1903): 1–13; R. Bigalke, *The National Zoological Gardens of South Africa* (Pretoria: Central News Agency, 1954), 3–4, 9–10; S. Dubow, 'A commonwealth of science: The British Association in South Africa, 1905 and 1929', in *Science and Society in Southern Africa*, ed. S. Dubow (Manchester: Manchester University Press, 2000), 75.

[33]See C. Yanni, *Nature's Museums: Victorian Science and the Architecture of Display* (London: Athlone Press, 1999); S. Sheets-Pyenson, 'How to "grow" a natural history museum: The building of colonial collections, 1850–1900', *Archives of Natural History* 15, no. 2 (1988):121–147; P. Davis, *Museums and the Natural Environment: The Role of Natural History Museums in Biological Conservation* (London: Leicester University Press, 1996); J.M. Gore, 'A lack of nation: The evolution of history in South African Museums, c.1825–1945', *South African Historical Journal* 51 (2004): 24–46.

[34]*Annals of the South African Museum* 1 (1898).

[35]*Annals of the Transvaal Museum* 8 (1922): 192.

While South African museums prioritised professional taxonomy, some staff members also wrote for a lay audience and these publications encouraged what today would be called an environmental and nature conservation perspective. Perhaps because the Transvaal Museum showcased both living and dead animals (with the living more popular among the public), a museum staff member wrote one of the earliest 'ecology' books in South Africa in 1908. This was *Sketches of South African Bird Life* by Alwin Haagner, an amateur ornithologist in the employ of the museum, who later became its director. *Sketches* presented illustrated chapters (with photographs in the field) that explained bird biology and behaviour in specific southern African environments and encouraged readers to go birding and to appreciate birds, their habitat, distribution and conservation.[36]

After the end of the South African War in 1902, science was put on a firmer organisational footing with scientists being employed as public servants in the various colonies, as had been the case in the Cape colony. The 1905 visit by the BAAS spurred further interest and provided the opportunity to put local science on show. A book, *Science in South Africa: A Handbook and Review*, edited by the Reverend William Flint (the Cape's librarian of parliament) and John D.F. Gilchrist (the government biologist and a leading member of the South African Philosophical Society), appeared in time for that visit. In his introduction, Leonard Gill (geologist-cum-ornithologist and South African Museum director after 1924) observed that 'with the recent importation of men of trained scientific capacity, as Professors in our colleges, or Government experts, and now with a few sons of the soil who have been trained by them, there is evidence of a marked increase in true scientific work, and a hopeful prospect of more'.[37]

Before 1918, there were no fully fledged universities in South Africa. Indeed, the whole matter of establishing them proved to be one of the most fraught and politically entangled that the colonies in South Africa had had to grapple with after 1902. There was no consistency among the university colleges attached to the University of the Cape of Good Hope. Physics was the first science taught for examination at the

[36] A. Haagner and R.H. Ivy, *Sketches of South African Bird Life* (London: R.H. Porter, 1908). See also J. Carruthers, '"Our beautiful and useful allies": Aspects of ornithology in twentieth-century South Africa', *Historia* 49, no. 1 (2004): 89–109.

[37] W. Flint and J.D.F. Gilchrist, eds, *Science in South Africa: A Handbook and Review* (Cape Town: Maskew Miller, 1905), ix–x.

South African College (Cape Town) in 1873. In 1899 pressure mounted to appoint a biology professor, but proved initially unsuccessful. Four years later, however, professors of zoology and botany were recruited: Arthur Dendy to zoology (his expertise was the fauna of New Zealand) and Harold Pearson to botany. All these colleges were also extremely small. For example, in 1910, the college in Pietermaritzburg had 57 students, almost half of whom were studying law. Grey University College in Bloemfontein had 73 students, the Transvaal University College in Pretoria 93 and Rhodes University College in Grahamstown 153. The School of Mines in Johannesburg – the precursor to the University of the Witwatersrand (Wits) – had 113 students, almost all of whom were working towards mining, engineering and legal qualifications.[38]

In a country poised for modern economic development and seeking agricultural prosperity, as South Africa was at the time, veterinary science was a priority. It, too, was to influence conservation biology, and indeed still does. For decades, understanding, preventing, mitigating and/or eradicating livestock diseases has been high on the scientific agenda. The outbreak of the rinderpest in 1896 had demonstrated the tragedy of a highly contagious disease: most of the domestic livestock of southern Africa had been destroyed by it, plunging the region into poverty and, indeed, in some cases starvation. Arnold (later Sir Arnold) Theiler, the Transvaal's director of veterinary services, had first joined the republic's civil service in 1891, and went on to carve out an illustrious career for himself. He head-hunted extremely competent staff, mostly from Germany and Switzerland. Of particular importance to conservation biology, Theiler and his department were in the forefront of exterminating wild animals believed to harbour diseases fatal to domestic herds, particularly rinderpest, nagana, foot-and-mouth and 's*notsiekte*'.[39]

---

[38]M. Boucher, *Spes in Arduis: A History of the University of South Africa* (Pretoria: University of South Africa, 1973), 94–111; B.K. Murray, *Wits: The Early Years* (Johannesburg: Witwatersrand University Press, 1982); H. Phillips, *The University of Cape Town 1918–1948: The Formative Years* (Cape Town: UCT Press, 1993); R.F. Currey, *Rhodes University, 1904–1970: A Chronicle* (Grahamstown: Rhodes University, 1970).

[39]B.C. Jansen, 'The growth of veterinary research in South Africa', in *A History of Scientific Endeavour in South Africa*, ed. A.C. Brown (Cape Town: Royal Society of South Africa, 1977), 64–191; T. Gutsche, *There was a Man: The Life and Times of Sir Arnold Theiler KCMG of Onderstepoort* (Cape Town: Timmins, 1979); K. Brown and D. Gilfoyle, eds, *Healing the Herds: Disease, Livestock Economies, and the Globalization of Veterinary Medicine* (Athens, OH: Ohio University Press, 2010); W. Beinart and K. Brown, *African Local*

As regards botany, the Cape had a long history. Reference has already been made to the early explorers, travellers and visiting plant collectors. Beyond that, the Cape was granted its first parliament in 1853 and five years later appointed an official botanist, Ludwig Pappe (1803–1862), a German-trained medical doctor with knowledge of and interest in systematic botany, forestry, agriculture and plant diseases. Pappe was an advisor to the United States and Madras governments and corresponded regularly with Sir William Hooker of the Royal Botanic Gardens at Kew. A strong connection with Kew was one of the defining features of the science associated with British imperialism.

Avid collectors and botanists were active not only in and around Cape Town, but also in other districts of the colony. Botanical gardens were established in Grahamstown, Graaff Reinet, Queenstown and King William's Town.[40] In Natal, the Durban Botanic Garden (first established in 1848 when the colony of Natal separated from the Cape) was revitalised by John Medley Wood (1827–1915) and Pietermaritzburg's botanical garden was founded in 1874. These gardens flourished or languished depending on the money available for expansion, maintenance and employing trained staff.

Although all the prominent botanists of the era were interested in southern African indigenous plants, and the colonial botanical gardens and municipal and other public parks displayed a variety of them, the main emphasis until the twentieth century was either economic botany and the 'uses' of plants – indigenous and imported – or on collection and taxonomic determination. The numerous imperial and colonial botanical gardens worked as a vast global network of botanical knowledge and exchange, with Kew as the hub and the institution these gardens served. Before 1900, the independent Transvaal and the Orange Free State were not affiliated with Kew or other European botanical institutions, and thus there was little incentive in those republics to participate formally in the international or scientific botanical world. Although a botanical garden had been suggested in the Transvaal in 1874, and received a boost during the British annexation of 1877–1881, with prisoners providing

Knowledge and Livestock Health: Diseases and Treatments in South Africa (Johannesburg: Wits University Press, 2013).

[40]D.P. McCracken and E.M. McCracken, *The Way to Kirstenbosch* (Cape Town: National Botanical Gardens, 1988); D.P. McCracken and P.A. McCracken, *Natal: The Garden Colony* (Sandton: Frandsen, 1990).

the labour, thereafter the infant institution deteriorated to the point of unrecognisability.

Along with the growth of botanical knowledge and establishment of botanical gardens in southern Africa went the development of herbaria. These arose at first from private plant collections amassed by people such as Pappe or Medley Wood, and other collections were housed in institutions such as the South African Museum and Transvaal Museum.

Public Participation: Citizen Science and Field Naturalists

Scientific wildlife management did not develop out of the museums, and nor was it spawned by the amateur naturalists who abounded in southern Africa before 1910. However, as is the case today, voluntary societies existed and flourished thanks to the curiosity of members and the enthusiasm of the leadership. Certainly, even in that era 'experts' might provide direction, but the interface between formally trained and untrained knowledgeable people was much more porous then than now.

Field naturalists' clubs were a long-established tradition in Britain and had a defining influence on British and colonial intellectual life by enabling amateurs to contribute to natural history and popular biology. The field naturalist movement harked back to the cult of nature associated with Romanticism. Amateurs could participate fully in the enterprise, which, unlike mathematics or physics, required no specialist vocabulary or equipment. Although such clubs had a great impact elsewhere, this was less true of South Africa.[41]

A second significant category of societies founded in the second half of the nineteenth century were the natural history societies. These too derived from British tradition. Such societies sprang up in Port Elizabeth, East London, Grahamstown (Albany), Durban and King William's Town, among other places.[42] However, as with the field naturalist clubs, they were never as strong or popular in South Africa as elsewhere, for instance Australia, whose English-speaking settler population was more homogeneous and offered a greater pool of potential members.[43]

---

[41]See T. Griffiths, *Hunters and Collectors: The Antiquarian Imagination in Australia* (Cambridge: Cambridge University Press, 1996); Russell, *Science and Social Change*, 181–192.

[42]C. Plug, 'Early scientific and professional societies in the Transvaal: Barberton 1889–1889', *South African Journal of Cultural History* 4, no. 3 (1990): 190–199.

[43]Griffiths, *Hunters and Collectors*.

Even so, South Africa had a fair number of clubs of both types. In 1897 the Johannesburg Field Naturalists' Club (JFNC) was founded, and there was a similar organisation in King Williams Town in 1884. By 1905, East London had a Natural History and Scientific Society[44] while Pretoria inaugurated its own Field Naturalists' Club in 1909.[45] The aim of these societies – as expressed by the JFNC – was to combine agreeable communal activities with learning: to hold regular meetings at which all branches of natural history were discussed; to arrange annual and weekend excursions; to host an annual 'Conversazione'; and to publish work of interest. The JFNC expressed a loyalty and dedication to local scientific endeavour, declaring that because of the 'unlimited field of research . . . in a country where comparatively little has been done . . . no more specimens need . . . be sent out of the country for identification and the naturalists of the Transvaal ought to commence to work out their own fauna'.[46] The club lobbied for biological study to become a national priority, advocated the establishment of a museum in Johannesburg and protested strongly when in 1905 the government abolished Professor Henry Lyster Jameson's post as professor of biology at the Technical Institute in Johannesburg, which he had held for three years, for want of student interest.[47]

While some members of these societies were employed at museums and institutions of higher learning, the Transvaal Biological Society, founded in December 1907, had as its nucleus natural scientists attached to government scientific institutions. These included Arnold Theiler, J.W.B. Gunning (director of the Transvaal Museum) and government botanists Illtyd Buller Pole Evans and Joseph Burtt-Davy. However, the initiative was not a great success. Rebranding itself as the South African Biological Society, it soon reverted to its original name, although the comment was

[44]Mentioned in the *Journal of the South African Ornithologists' Union* 1, no. 2 (1905): 64.

[45]A. Graham Cook to Hon. Sec. Pretoria Field Naturalists' Club, 10 July 1909, Correspondence files, Johannesburg Field Naturalists' Club and Johannesburg Field Naturalists' Club Minute Book 12 February 1908, papers of the Johannesburg Field Naturalists' Club, Manuscript Collection A58, University of the Witwatersrand, Johannesburg.

[46]Gunning to Cohen, 22 April 1902, Correspondence files, Johannesburg Field Naturalists' Club, papers of the Johannesburg Field Naturalists' Club, Manuscript Collection A58, University of the Witwatersrand, Johannesburg.

[47]A. Graham Cook to J.C. Smuts, Colonial Secretary, 3 February 1908, Correspondence files, Johannesburg Field Naturalists' Club, papers of the Johannesburg Field Naturalists' Club, Manuscript Collection A58, University of the Witwatersrand, Johannesburg.

made in the 1930s that it ought really to be called the 'Pretoria Biological Society'.[48] While its journal published highly specialised and technical scientific articles, the society was neither a conservation pressure group nor a bridge between game reserves and scientific endeavour. It did, however, host Dr Carl Schröter, renowned botanist and co-founder of the Swiss National Park. In his lecture to the Society on 20 November 1927, a meeting chaired by president Pole Evans, with a welcome to Schröter from the Secretary for Agriculture, the speaker emphasised the scientific interest in glacial landscapes in the Swiss Alps, the protection of vegetation as well as animal life and the strong legislative framework in which nature conservation operated in Switzerland.[49] In contrast, the complete absence in South Africa of links between nature conservation and science at this time can be seen in the non-participation by game wardens and rangers in the activities of the urban-based naturalists' societies, not to mention the Transvaal/South African Biological Society.

Acclimatisation societies were another amateur institution that took hold in South Africa in the early 1900s. The Transvaal boasted a government-supported Trout Acclimatisation Society, whose equivalent in the Cape colony was also extremely active.[50] Their purpose was to improve on nature by augmenting the 'natural' fauna and flora with introduced plants and animals that might be useful for sport or food, or for ornamental or sentimental reasons. Thanks to the activities of such societies and the hatcheries they created in many parts of the country, trout is probably the best established deliberately introduced species in South Africa.

Evidence of synergies between public participation and the state museum service is clearly apparent in the history of the South African Ornithological Union (SAOU). Museums were agents in determining how biology became embedded in South African society, and the

---

[48]A.J.T. Janse, 'A short history of the South African Biological Society', *South African Biological Society Pamphlet* 10 (1939): 49–58.

[49]C. Schröter, 'Protection of wild life in Switzerland and the Swiss National Park', *South African Journal of Natural History* 6, no. 2 (1927): 83–88. See also P. Kupper, *Creating Wilderness: A Transnational History of the Swiss National Park* (New York, NY: Berghahn, 2014).

[50]Carruthers, *Game Protection in the Transvaal*, 112; C. Lever, *They Dined on Eland: The Story of Acclimatisation Societies* (London: Quiller Press, 1992); D. Hey, *A Nature Conservationist Looks Back* (Jonkershoek: Cape Nature Conservation, 1995); D. Hey, 'The history and status of nature conservation in South Africa', in *A History of Scientific Endeavour in South Africa*, ed. A.C. Brown (Cape Town: Royal Society of South Africa, 1977), 142–143.

development of ornithology provides an example of this role in terms of the emergence of a field – or ecological – science. The distinction between 'closet' or 'cabinet' collectors who made no observations from nature and 'field' naturalists was more blurred in the case of ornithology, because museum scientists were dependent on collectors in the field for research material. After the South African War had ended, the new British administrators prioritised the upgrading of the old republican *Staats* Museum in Pretoria.[51] Its extensive collections rivalled those of the older and more professional South African Museum in Cape Town.[52] Even more importantly, there was a collection of living specimens in aviaries in the attached zoological gardens.[53]

The SAOU evolved from the interest in birds and birding expressed, for example, through membership of the JFNC. However, the JFNC was not without its challenges. A society for generalists, its broad focus encouraged wide membership, but also factionalism, and almost from the outset there were problems. For example, for some years the club was dominated by butterfly collectors and there was very little botany. By 1904, the club was flourishing, and there were enough birders to encourage Haagner (a JFNC member and frequent speaker at its meetings) to form the breakaway ornithologists' union.[54] The SAOU went on to produce an authoritative journal, *The Ostrich: A Journal of South African Ornithology*, whose object was 'to promote and foster the study of a branch of science which . . . combines pleasure and physical and mental exercise with practical and scientific utility'.[55] However, although SAOU's start was auspicious, the enthusiasm petered out quickly, despite the fact that

[51]Dubow, 'A commonwealth of science', 75.

[52]A.K. Haagner, 'A short account of the study of ornithology in general and of South Africa in particular', *South African Ornithologists' Union, Popular Bulletin* no. 2 (Pretoria, February 1909), 10.

[53]*The Emu* 2, no. 1 (1902): 117.

[54]Haagner to Johannesburg Field Naturalists Club, 19 March 1904, Correspondence files, Johannesburg Field Naturalists' Club and Johannesburg Field Naturalists' Club Minute Book 12 February 1908, papers of the Johannesburg Field Naturalists' Club, Manuscript Collection A58, University of the Witwatersrand, Johannesburg.

[55]Somewhat surprisingly, a large number of members took exception to this title and it was altered to *The Journal of the South African Ornithologists' Union*. See 1, no. 1 (1905): vi; *Journal of the South African Ornithologists' Union* 2, no. 1 (1906): 45. The outbreak of war in 1914 spelled the end of the SAOU although it did not disappear entirely, but was subsumed within the South African Biological Society and ornithological papers appeared from 1923 onwards in the *South African Journal of Natural History*.

the organisation was pan-South African and that the museum community was well represented in it.

International Diplomacy and Wildlife Protection

By the early 1900s, protecting 'vanishing' species had become an international concern. Within the British Empire, of which South Africa was part, there were many expressions of how best to preserve such creatures. For the first time, states began to accept responsibility for protecting specific landscapes in order to preserve monumental scenery or rare animals.[56] Such initiatives became evident in the USA, Canada, Australia, New Zealand and British East Africa, as well as other colonies in Africa, such as the Sudan. As we have seen, the term 'game reserve' originally involved nobles and other prominent landowners setting aside parts of their holdings to prevent hunting (poaching) of desirable 'game' (sport) species without permission.[57] In keeping with this tradition, areas in Africa (and elsewhere in the empire) set aside to protect wild animal species, specifically hunter's quarry – not carnivora or vermin – were called 'game reserves'.

As regards 'national parks', the Royal National Park in Sydney established in 1879 was the first protected area to be so called. However, it essentially resembled the public parks of urban London. It was the USA that was later to claim the extensive, rural, visitor-friendly national park as its specific, and original, contribution to the modern world.[58] In 1872, in order to preserve Yellowstone from unbridled commercial and

---

[56]D.J. Frank, A. Hironaka and E. Schofer, 'The nation-state and the natural environment over the twentieth century', *American Sociological Review* 65 (2000): 96–116.

[57]M. Cioc, in *The Game of Conservation: International Treaties to Protect the World's Migratory Animals* (Athens, OH: Ohio University Press, 2009), 5, suggests that 'game' derives etymologically from the Old High German *gaman* meaning 'amusement'.

[58]C.J. Magoc, *Yellowstone: The Creation and Selling of an American Landscape* (Albuquerque, NM: University of New Mexico Press, 1999); J.A. Pritchard, *Preserving Yellowstone's Natural Conditions: Science and the Perception of Nature* (Lincoln, NE: University of Nebraska Press, 1999); J.A. Pritchard, 'Charles C. Adams and early ecological rationales for Yellowstone National Park', reprinted in *People and Place: The Human Experience in Greater Yellowstone*. Proceedings of the 4th Biennial Scientific Conference on the Greater Yellowstone Ecosystem (Yellowstone Center for Resources, 2004); F. Wagner, *Yellowstone's Destabilised Ecosystem* (Oxford: Oxford University Press, 2006); B. Gissibl, S. Höhler and P. Kupper, eds, *Civilizing Nature: National Parks in Global and Historical Perspective* (New York, NY: Berghahn, 2012); R.F. Nash, *Wilderness and the American Mind* (New Haven, CT: Yale University Press, 2001); R.F. Nash, 'The American invention of national parks', *American Quarterly* 22 (1970): 970; R.F. Nash, 'The confusing birth of national parks', *The Michigan Quarterly Review* 16 (1977): 216–226; A. Runte, *National*

capitalist development by the state of Wyoming, Washington established a federal 'public park' over the area (which overlaps slightly with Montana and Idaho). Other national parks and key protected areas of this era included Yosemite (California) and Mount Rainier (Washington) in the USA, and Tongariro (New Zealand), Belair (South Australia) and Rocky Mountains (Banff) in Canada. Many game reserves were proclaimed in British East Africa as well as German East Africa and the Anglo-Egyptian Sudan. In 1909, Europe joined the trend when Sweden and Switzerland designated their first national parks.[59]

This frenzy of activity was mirrored in southern Africa. As already noted, British authorities in Zululand founded reserves in St Lucia, Imfolozi Junction, Hluhluwe Valley, Mdlelshe and Mkuzi/Pongola in 1895, and these were taken over by the colony of Natal following the incorporation of Zululand by Natal Act 37 of 1897. The South African Republic (Transvaal) had proclaimed the Pongola Game Reserve (1894), the Sabi Reserve (1895) and the Springbok Flats and Pretoria town-lands and Groenkloof (1898). After the South African War, the Pongola, the Sabi, Pretoria townlands and Groenkloof were re-proclaimed, and the Singwitsi Game Reserve (1903) and the Rustenburg Game Reserve (1909) were founded. Natal established Giant's Castle Game Reserve (1903) and the Natal National Park (1908), while the Cape established the Gordonia Game Reserve (1908).

This widespread thrust to establish protected areas was given further impetus as the wider international community coalesced around issues of nature protection or nature conservation (the terminology varied). In 1908, at a governors' conference on conservation convened by Theodore Roosevelt at the White House, a heated debate raged between the 'pres-ervation' and 'conservation' schools of thought. The former was regarded as the conservative approach to natural resource management, and was advocated by those espousing a quasi-religious, romantic and transcenden-talist approach to the natural world and concerned about the diminishing wilderness in the USA. Conservation, by contrast, was the rallying cry of the progressive lobby. To them, this meant consumption by humans, but within sustainable limits. The protagonists in what became a major politi-cal struggle in the USA were, respectively, John Muir of the national park movement (and founder of the Sierra Club in 1892) and Gifford Pinchot,

---

Parks: The American Experience (Lincoln, NE and London: University of Nebraska Press, 1997).
[59]Kupper, *Creating Wilderness.*

chief of the forestry department.[60] The debate was not about the relative scientific merit of either approach, but the relative public good.

The American president's siding with the conservationists should come as no surprise, given his well-publicised, profligate East African big game hunts, which he had so relished.[61] However, he was wise (or politic) enough to recognise a distinction between national parks (conservation) and 'national wildlife refuges' (preservation), and in 1903 he established the first of the latter at Pelican Island in Florida.[62] Although hunting was permitted in US national parks and predators were destroyed, they were designated national scenic areas for public pleasure and recreation and offered no sporting opportunities comparable to Africa's.

The first international convention relevant to Africa was the London Convention of 1900.[63] Interestingly, the conference that drafted the Convention was not initiated by Britain but by Hermann von Wissman, governor of German East Africa (in 1895). Britain, however, accepted the initiative enthusiastically and soon took charge. Along with many other colonies, the Cape and Natal were invited to send representatives but decided that little would be gained by doing so. Joseph Chamberlain, then colonial secretary, saw no merit in inviting the Transvaal and Orange Free State, then in the throes of the South African War. After considerable discussion, *The Convention for the Preservation of Wild Animals, Birds, and Fish of Africa* was signed on 19 May 1900. Its complicated regulations were impracticable in the African situation, negotiations dragged on for over a decade and it was never ratified. The Convention included no strictly zoological or natural history information, but did strongly advocate the establishment of game reserves along with the destruction of vermin. Despite being ineffectual, the Convention stands as a monument to good intentions and as a forerunner to more effective international instruments in later years.

Public Participation: Game Protection Societies

In this early period, hunter-sportsmen rather than scientists were the main lobbyists for wildlife protection and the study of natural fauna in the wild. They framed their case on the grounds of morality, arguing

---

[60]Carruthers, *Game Protection in the Transvaal*, 95.

[61]T. Roosevelt, *African Game Trails: An Account of the African Wanderings of an American Hunter-naturalist* (New York, NY: Charles Scribner's Sons, 1910).

[62]Cioc, *Game of Conservation*, 83.

[63]Carruthers, *Game Protection*, 95–97; Cioc, *Game of Conservation*, 34–47.

(at times sentimentally and emotionally) that wildlife, or at least certain species, in a natural environment possessed aesthetic beauty, and that causing their extinction was unethical. The major imperial wildlife advocacy organisation was the Society for the Preservation of the Wild Fauna of the Empire (SPWFE) (after the First World War the Society for the Preservation of the Fauna of the Empire, SPFE, and after 1950 the Fauna Preservation Society), founded in 1903 by Edward North Buxton, grandson of the anti-slavery campaigner Thomas Fowell Buxton, and thus no stranger to controversial causes. E.N. Buxton had travelled widely in Africa and authored a book on his experiences in 1912.[64] The society aimed to influence public (and government) opinion in favour of protecting wild animals in Africa and the empire, and to encourage imperial and colonial governments to adopt game-saving programmes as both a serious responsibility and form of moral upliftment.[65] To this end, the SPWFE was to generate what it called 'propaganda' to curtail or prevent hunting that was profligate, cruel or for purely commercial gain.[66] MacKenzie refers to the society as a 'winning combination of aristocrats, hunter-naturalists and officials . . . a pseudo-scientific body which set out to make many of its objectives hard to argue with', and has emphasised its influence in the highest political circles in Britain. Even in its early years, membership was high (around 150) and included professional zoologists such as Michael Oldfield Thomas of the British Museum.[67]

In South Africa, local game protection societies existed that were dedicated to protecting the sport-hunting interests of their members. By 1900, there existed game protection associations in the Transvaal, Natal, Orange River Colony and the western districts (the last founded in Cape Town in 1886). Unlike the membership of the SPWFE, the Transvaal Game Protection Association (TGPA) mainly consisted of settler landowners. It had close ties to the Transvaal Landowners Association and often acted as its mouthpiece. Extremely parochial and vexatious, the TGPA alienated the Transvaal colonial authorities. Its various branches

---

[64]E.N. Buxton, *Two African Trips: With Notes and Suggestions on Big Game Preservation in Africa* (London: Edward Stanford, 1902); D.K. Prendergast and W.M. Adams, 'Colonial wildlife conservation and the origins of the Society for the Preservation of the Wild Fauna of the Empire (1903–1914)', *Oryx* 37, no. 2 (2003): 251–260.

[65]Carruthers, *Game Protection in the Transvaal*, 96–97.

[66]R. Fitter and P. Scott, *The Penitent Butchers: The Fauna Preservation Society, 1903–1978* (London: Collins/Fauna Preservation Society, 1978).

[67]MacKenzie, *Empire of Nature*, 212.

Figure 2.3. Natural history museum in the Surrey home of renowned hunter-collector Frederick Courteney Selous.
From L. Weinthal, 'African trophies', in L. Weinthal, *The Story of the Cape to Cairo Railway and River Route, from 1887 to 1922,* 5 vols. Vol. 3, Plate 7.

constantly quarrelled among themselves, forming fresh breakaway groups, and even disbanding for a year or two at a time. Consequently, government was never able to negotiate with a cohesive body. The Transvaal gained responsible government in 1907 and the fact that TGPA members were almost entirely English-speaking and urban did not endear them to the incoming Boer-led Het Volk government. The selfishness of TGPA members, their targeting of Africans and African hunting dogs, their intense class hatred of Afrikaner biltong and market hunters, their demands for special rights and privileges not enjoyed by other Transvaal citizens discredited such people even in the eyes of the game reserve authorities of the time. Indeed, their principal project in relation to game reserves was lobbying for them to be opened to 'sportsmen'. The fact that TGPA demanded open hunting seasons that aligned better with Christmas holidays than antelope breeding patterns also did not help their cause. Even the Trout Acclimatisation Society in the Transvaal enjoyed more government support and received a small government grant.[68]

Early attempts to merge the various game protection associations in South Africa failed. In 1904 and 1913, the Western Districts Game Protection Association refused to amalgamate with the TGPA.[69] Perhaps the Cape group felt little affinity with the 'big game' hunters elsewhere in the country, because few large mammals remained in the Cape colony, leaving the association to busy itself with other matters, such as trout-fishing in Cape streams, poisoning clubs and praising Rhodes for introducing pheasants and Indian jungle fowl.[70] Whether the societies in the Orange River Colony or Natal were ever invited to amalgamate is not recorded: certainly no national group was founded at this time.

Game Reserves and Emerging Science

Despite their collection and taxonomic classification of indigenous fauna, South African museums and other scientific institutions were not actively involved in wildlife protection or in providing that endeavour with a scientific rationale. As already noted, the conceptual framework underpinning conservation came from the public, sportsmen in particular.[71] By 1900, once-abundant herds of wildlife in the southern African interior had – for various reasons – been decimated and pressure to halt the killing came from the very sportsmen who had contributed to the slaughter. The 'penitent butcher' phenomenon is well known and well studied. Colonial and republican governments in southern Africa and elsewhere responded to pressure from influential persons by creating game reserves in which wild animals were confined and hunting of certain species was totally prohibited for a time. The animals were guarded

---

[68]Carruthers, *Game Protection in the Transvaal*, 112.

[69]Minutes of the Western Districts Game Protection Association, 4 April 1903, 19 February 1904, 2 March 1905, Wild Life Society of South Africa (now the Wildlife and Environment Society of South Africa) archives, Pietermaritzburg.

[70]Correspondence Western Districts Game Protection Association, 11 September 1902, 10 March 1903, Wild Life Society of South Africa (now the Wildlife and Environment Society of South Africa) archives, Pietermaritzburg.

[71]J.G. Reiger, *American Sportsmen and the Origins of Conservation* (Corvallis, OR: Oregon State University Press, 2001).

by a 'game warden' and his staff ('game rangers') and there was no public access without authorisation.[72]

By 1910, a number of game reserves had been established in southern Africa, but no coherent scientific policy underpinned their creation. In administrative terms, they were a colonial, and later a provincial, competency. In South Africa, game reserves were not part of the educational structures, affiliated to museums, or placed within state departments responsible for agriculture or land affairs. The reserves were unstable entities, declared by ad-hoc proclamation in the provincial gazette. They were a low priority within the organs of state, there were no precedents for their administration, there were no agreed objectives, and there were no defined structures within the civil service to administer them.

Unrecognised at the time, game reserves were also based on what was to become an outmoded philosophy of wildlife protection. Game reserves were not established as places for the study of natural history. The aim elaborated in the 1900 London Convention was to encourage the increase in populations of desirable species under controlled conditions of predator or 'vermin' eradication. Poaching was to be prevented, with the possible future aim of allowing fee-paying sport-hunters to crop the excess. Scientific politics and professional values placed a premium on specialised laboratory sciences or sciences that assisted economic growth, and these had no place in the game reserves of the time. Museums were repositories for dead specimens and it was simply not the job of museum keepers to spend long periods in unhealthy and isolated game reserves observing their collections in life. The fact that museum and other trained biologists distanced themselves from the administration of game reserves meant that protected areas were considered as being outside the bounds of any 'science' and as being quite irrelevant to serious academic study.

This divide was further entrenched by the types of men employed by government to manage game reserves – none of whom were scientists or even naturalists. In 1902, when the post of warden of the Transvaal game reserves was to be filled, a number of people applied. One was the university-trained Gerald E.H. Barrett-Hamilton, later of the Natural History Museum, well-known in the field of marine mammal biology (with a special interest in island species) and a prolific author and scientific

---

[72]For a full history of the Transvaal game reserves, see Carruthers, *Game Protection in the Transvaal* and J. Carruthers, *The Kruger National Park: A Social and Political History* (Pietermaritzburg: University of Natal Press, 1995).

traveller who had actually visited South Africa.[73] Without hesitation, Sir Godfrey Lagden, the Transvaal colony's secretary for native affairs under whose aegis game reserves were placed, turned him down.[74] A sportsman himself, Lagden preferred a 'man of action' to a scientific zoologist, and appointed James Stevenson-Hamilton, a Scottish landowner, cavalry officer and sport-hunter. To the colonial government, Stevenson-Hamilton's military experience and administrative ability better qualified him for the post than any marine scholarship.[75] His management task was to *protect* wildlife and ensure the propagation of certain species, not *study* them.[76]

In addition, there was a distinct hierarchy. Stevenson-Hamilton himself was an educated and well-read man with good connections in British upper-class circles, but the game rangers he employed to help him run Sabi and Singwitsi Game Reserves in the eastern Transvaal were, in his words, 'flotsam and jetsam . . . I suppose they think it will be an easy life with not much to do except drink'.[77] They were certainly not scientists. The first South African-born warden was apparently P.J. Rickert (also spelt Riekert) of the Rustenburg Game Reserve, a large area in the western

[73]By 1901 Barrett-Hamilton (who died in 1914) had published the following zoological researches among others: 'Bottle-nosed whale in Wexford and Wicklow', *Zoologist* 3, no. 14 (1890):72; 'Sperm whale Mayo', *Zoologist* 3, no. 14 (1890): 72; 'The white-sided dolphin in Ireland', *Zoologist* 3, no. 14 (1890): 384; 'Sibbalds's Rorqual on the Irish Coast', *Zoologist* 3, no. 15 (1891): 306–308; 'Lesser Rorqual on the coast of Cork', *Irish Naturalist* 8 (1899): 27; 'Probable occurrence of Lesser Rorqual on the coast of Co. Wexford', *Irish Naturalist* 10 (1901): 74; 'On the species of the genus *Mus* inhabiting St. Kilda', *Proceedings of the Zoological Society London* (1899): 77–88; 'On geographical and individual variation in *Mus sylvaticus* and its allies', *Proceedings of the Zoological Society London* (1900): 387–428. He discovered a number of small mammals, travelled extensively throughout the world and was later to be involved in the publication of the multi-volume *A History of British Mammals* (London: Gurney and Jackson, 1910–1921), illustrated by the famous zoological artist Edward Wilson, and co-authored with Martin A.C. Hingston, another talented scientist, who was later to be implicated in the Piltdown forgery and its aftermath.

[74]Carruthers, *Game Protection in the Transvaal*, 125.

[75]See J. Carruthers, *Wildlife and Warfare: The Life of James Stevenson-Hamilton* (Pietermaritzburg: University of Natal Press, 2001).

[76]On the scientific rationale of trophy collecting in South Africa, see J. Carruthers, 'Changing perspectives on wildlife in southern Africa, *c.*1840–*c.*1914', *Society and Animals: Journal of Human–Animal Studies* 13, no. 3 (2005): 183–199 and see also MacKenzie, *Empire of Nature* and MacKenzie, *Imperialism and the Natural World* for the emphasis on the sport-hunting origins of national parks and wildlife protection and the absence of an appropriate scientific discipline that might apply to nature protection.

[77]Carruthers, *Game Protection in the Transvaal*, 131.

Transvaal set aside by Colonial Secretary Jan Smuts. Lacking scientific or administrative experience, his appointment in 1909 seems to have been a political reward, perhaps for services rendered during the South African War. Rickert was incompetent and neglected his duties. Unable to bring orderly administration to the reserve or to prevent poaching, he persecuted the local Tswana communities and was involved in gun-running activities before the rebellion of 1914 (for which he was later imprisoned). Not surprisingly, this heralded the end of the Rustenburg Game Reserve and it was abolished in November 1914.[78] But no matter who the particular incumbent or what the qualities he brought to the job, a game warden was a junior appointment in the civil service and divorced from the scientific bureaucracy.

Yet unusually for a man in his position, Stevenson-Hamilton began to make a considerable mark on game protection and ensured that his reserves – Sabi and Singwitsi – achieved a high profile in scientific and game protectionist circles. In 1905, a commemorative publication recorded the joint meetings between the visiting BAAS and its recently founded South African counterpart. It included an article about the Sabi Game Reserve written by Stevenson-Hamilton. This, the first scientific publication relating to game preservation in South Africa, provided a template that was imitated by many and lasted well into later decades. Stevenson-Hamilton, who had been game warden for just over two years, began by describing the locality, the climate, vegetation, geography, soil and geology of the reserve, as well as the effects of fire, malaria and horse-sickness and some of the human history of the region. Lamenting the extermination of the large herds of antelope, he described some of them in detail, species by species. He explained how the proclamation of the reserve came about and the employment of the first warden, William M. Walker, a prospector from Barberton. He also mentioned the Pongola Game Reserve, which fell within his remit, as did the Singwitsi Game Reserve.

It is clear from Stevenson-Hamilton's article that in the early 1900s the science of wildlife protection in South Africa was indeed *protective*, involving the establishment of administrative order, on business-like lines, and prevention of poaching. By 1905, Stevenson-Hamilton had already divided his reserve into five administrative and management districts, each with a European ranger in charge of a dozen or more African staff. Pairs of African rangers were picketed in strategic positions. In his article,

[78]Carruthers, *Game Protection in the Transvaal*, 152–155.

he knowledgeably described the life cycles of game species – generally antelope – in some detail, together with fish and birds. All staff was required to destroy vermin, even though Stevenson-Hamilton acknowledged that, in nature, they played a role by preying on weak and sick animals and removing them from the system. However, because they also targeted healthy and valuable 'game species', they had to be killed to restore a 'balance of nature', regarded as having been upset by profligate hunting. Stevenson-Hamilton referred to press criticism of game reserves for 'harbouring' carnivora detrimental to farmers outside the reserves. He believed these lion-haters had 'vivid imaginations' and were generally ignorant. It was clear that population dynamics and population ecology (to use modern terminology) already greatly interested Stevenson-Hamilton, and that his strong belief – which never wavered over the course of his long life – in the 'balance of nature' and in not tampering with its workings was already in place.[79]

Stevenson-Hamilton also began to contribute regularly to the *Journal of the Society for the Preservation of the Wild Fauna of the Empire*. Indeed, Prendergast and Adams believe that 'none contributed more to the Society's sense of direction (and its journal) concerning the management and preservation of wildlife than the prolific writer and advisor, Colonel H. [*sic*] Stevenson-Hamilton'.[80] In 1907, Stevenson-Hamilton again defended game reserves against charges that they encouraged lion breeding. He even defended the wild dog, stating that they were rare and thus worthy of protection. Moreover, he firmly held, in the face of claims by the veterinary fraternity, that there was no conclusive proof of a link between rinderpest, tsetse fly and wild animals.[81] In 1909, Stevenson-Hamilton contributed to the *Journal of the South African Ornithologists' Union*, presenting his observations on migratory birds at Komatipoort, and in 1911 contributed to the *Bulletin of Entomological Research*.[82]

---

[79]J. Stevenson-Hamilton, 'Game preservation in the Transvaal', in *Addresses and Papers Read at the Joint Meeting of the British and South African Associations for the Advancement of Science held in South Africa, 1905*, comp. South African Association for the Advancement of Science (Johannesburg: South African Association for the Advancement of Science, 1905), 350–368. See also https://ia802702.us.archive.org/31/items/reportofbritisha06scie/reportofbritisha06scie_bw.pdf (accessed 24 December 2014).

[80]Prendergast and Adams, 'Colonial wildlife conservation', 255.

[81]J. Stevenson-Hamilton, 'Opposition to game reserves', *Journal of the Society for the Preservation of the Wild Fauna of the Empire* 3 (1907), 53–59.

[82]J. Stevenson-Hamilton, 'Observations on migratory birds at Komatipoort', *Journal of the South African Ornithologists' Union* 5, no. 19 (1909): 19–22; J. Stevenson-Hamilton,

Stevenson-Hamilton addressed not only the scientific community, however. He also targeted agriculturalists and sportsmen by writing a number of educational articles about the game reserve in the *Transvaal Agricultural Journal, The Field* and *Blackwood's Magazine*.[83] His 1908 article in the *Transvaal Agricultural Journal* included a graph about birth ratios among impala, showing the effect on populations when females were few. He even argued that these experimental data could be replicated for a number of other species. These were the first hard data collected in a South African game reserve.[84] For Stevenson-Hamilton, his game reserve was science in place, and within a few years he knew its ecology intimately.[85]

Stevenson-Hamilton's responsibility for the Pongola Game Reserve has already been mentioned. This was a small reserve, proclaimed in 1894 by the Transvaal *volksraad* in a politically sensitive area straddling Swaziland, Zululand and the Transvaal Republic. Prior to the South African War, it had been overseen by warden Herman Frederik van Oordt, whose annual reports as a civil servant read far more like those of an intelligence agent than of a game warden. When he was given responsibility for the Pongola Game Reserve in 1902, Stevenson-Hamilton placed Affleck Alexander Fraser – a man with military experience in India and during the South African War – in charge. However, Stevenson-Hamilton became very disappointed in Fraser because he took little trouble to learn any natural history and remained a 'gamekeeper', nothing more. Once Stevenson-Hamilton became aware of the limitations of Pongola as a reserve, he moved Fraser to Singwitsi. Pongola was essentially abandoned because, in Stevenson-Hamilton's opinion, it could only be used as a 'game nursery' in which animals could be bred and tamed and possibly supplied to

---

'The relation between game and tsetse-flies', *Bulletin of Entomological Research* 2 (1911): 113–118.

[83]J. Stevenson-Hamilton, 'Aantekeningen omtrent de wild reserve aan de Sabi', *Het Transvaalsche Landbouw Journaal* 4 (1907–1908): 636–650; J. Stevenson-Hamilton, 'Preservation of female game', *Transvaal Agricultural Journal* 6, no. 23 (1908): 496–497; J. Stevenson-Hamilton, 'Notes on the Sabi Game Reserve', *Transvaal Agricultural Journal* 5, no. 19 (1907): 603–617; J. Stevenson-Hamilton, 'Game preservation in the eastern Transvaal', *The Field*, 14 March 1903. See also A. Sharpe, 'Observations on the game reserves in British Central Africa', *Journal of the Society for the Preservation of the Wild Fauna of the Empire* 3 (1907): 50–52.

[84]Stevenson-Hamilton, 'Preservation of female game', 496–497.

[85]H.A. Bryden, 'The extermination of great game in South Africa', *Fortnightly Review* (October 1894): 538–551.

zoos and farmers. It limped on as a protected area until it was abolished in 1921.[86]

An observant naturalist, Stevenson-Hamilton was also enthusiastic and hard-working. From his many publications it is clear that he soon became familiar with gestation periods, the social structures of various species, together with their tracks and droppings. His science came from close and regular observation and from his wide reading and prolific correspondence.[87] As well as disseminating knowledge, Stevenson-Hamilton promoted an ethic of nature. Believing that it was whites, not Africans, who were mainly responsible for wildlife destruction, he argued for a change of attitude so that the flouting of hunting laws, instead of being a matter of boastful pride, would be one of disgrace and 'studious concealment and remorse'. He argued that in the USA 'the public conscience awoke' only after Yellowstone and Yosemite were guarded by the US cavalry in order to stop despoliation of the geology and wildlife.[88]

Given his frequent contributions to the *Journal of the Society for the Preservation of the Wild Fauna of the Empire*, there can be no question that Stevenson-Hamilton considered the society to be the official and formal forum for expressing his wildlife management philosophy and strategy.[89] The point might also be made that he was obliged to look outside South Africa for professional validation.[90] During his regular periods of long leave in Britain, the socially and politically well-connected Stevenson-Hamilton was courted by his scientific contemporaries. Lord Rothschild personally took him around the museum at Tring, he was entertained by Selous and was fêted at the annual dinner of the SPWFE, attended by Selous, E.N. Buxton, Sir Alfred Pease, H.A. Bryden, Robert Baden-Powell, Lord Lugard and other luminaries.

---

[86]E.J. Carruthers, 'The Pongola Game Reserve: An eco-political study', *Koedoe* 28 (1995): 1–16.

[87]*Annual Report of the Transvaal Museum, 1905 to 1906*, 9; *Annual Report of the Transvaal Museum, 1907 to 1908*, 3.

[88]J. Stevenson-Hamilton, 'Notes on the Sabi Game Reserve', 603–617; Stevenson-Hamilton, 'Aantekeningen omtrent de wild reserve aan de Sabi', 636–650; Stevenson-Hamilton, 'Preservation of female game', 496–497.

[89]For example, J. Stevenson-Hamilton, 'The management of a national park in Africa', *Journal of the Society for the Preservation of the Fauna of the Empire* 10 (1930): 13–20.

[90]See Carruthers, *Wildlife and Warfare*.

Stevenson-Hamilton also had close ties with the renowned Zoological Society of London, founded in 1826.[91] Indeed, for a time in the mid-1920s he was employed as its secretary. In 1910, he accepted a commission from Dr (later Sir) Peter Chalmers Mitchell FRS DSc, the society's powerful secretary from 1903 to 1935 and creator of Whipsnade Zoo, to amass a collection of South African wild animals to present to King George V on his accession. This involved considerable personal travel throughout southern Africa as well as extremely complicated transport logistics for the animals. The collection was safely delivered in London, handed over to the London Zoo, and Stevenson-Hamilton was awarded the society's silver medal in 1912 as a reward. First presented in 1847, it is 'awarded to a Fellow of the Society or any other person for contributions to the understanding and appreciation of zoology, including such activities as public education in natural history, and wildlife conservation'.[92]

Conservation science and zoology associated with South Africa's protected areas – at least in the Transvaal – was thus well recognised in reputable international scientific circles even before the Union of South Africa was established in 1910. These disciplines were to grow in ensuing decades, with Stevenson-Hamilton at the forefront.

[91]In later decades, another South African scientist, Solomon (Solly) Zuckerman (later Lord Zuckerman) was closely involved with the ZSL. See *From Apes to Warlords 1904–1946: An Autobiography* (London: Hamish Hamilton, 1978) and Professor Lord Zuckerman, ed., 'The Zoological Society of London, 1826–1976', in *Symposia of the Zoological Society of London, No. 40* (London: Academic Press for the ZSL, 1976).

[92]P. Chalmers Mitchell, *Centenary History of the Zoological Society of London* (London: Zoological Society of London, 1929), 153–154; Carruthers, *Wildlife and Warfare*, 113–115.

3 · *Consolidating Conservation 1910 to 1930*

There was little change in wildlife protection philosophy and science after the establishment of the Union of South Africa in 1910, but the idea of a national park – indeed all issues 'national' – gained greater urgency with the amalgamation of the four colonies. The process of unification, while relatively quick, was fraught, and only by carrying over aspects of the colonies' administration into the union (for example, education and health) was success achieved. The greatest, and most divisive, issue was, of course, the future of the African majority, and here, despite protests by black South Africans and their champions, an unsatisfactory compromise was reached: 'native affairs' would remain for the time being as it had been in the four colonies and be decided at a later date. This meant the Cape colony's restricted franchise for black and coloured people would remain, but not be extended.

Among the powers the South Africa Act of 1909 devolved on to the four new provincial councils was 'fish and game preservation' (85 (x)). Consequently, game reserves created by the colonies passed under provincial control, as did matters relating to hunting and fishing licences, open and closed hunting seasons, vermin eradication and similar issues. Provincial legislation is easier to change than national laws. For example, game reserves might be abolished by a proclamation of the Administrator, just as hunting regulations could be. National legislation, by contrast, can be altered only by a majority vote in formal House of Assembly and Senate sessions.

Natal National Park

Nonetheless, it is a fact generally unnoticed that when the union came into being in 1910 a formally named 'national park' already existed in the colony of Natal. The Natal National Park (NNP), as it was then called, although sometimes referred to as the Mont-aux-Sources National Park, is situated in the northern Drakensberg, a magnificent mountain range that is the region's most important watershed, straddling the boundaries of the present provinces of KwaZulu-Natal and Free State and the small country of Lesotho. It was established in 1908, becoming the Royal Natal National Park much later, in 1947, following a visit by the British royal family. Today, almost the entire mountain range is part of the uKhahlamba-Drakensberg World Heritage Site, so designated in 2000 on account of its 'mixed' natural and cultural heritage.[1]

The NNP is important to the history of science in South Africa's national parks because it gave rise to the first formal treatise on plant ecology by a university-trained scientist in a national protected area, and it provides a point to illuminate how South Africa's national park philosophy – and its science – eventually came to be almost entirely focused on fauna.[2] This chimed well with an idealised vision of 'primitive Africa' as well as the concerns about marginalised scenic beauty and outdoor recreational pursuits that characterise so many national parks elsewhere in the world.[3]

The idea of a national park in Natal was first mooted in 1896, and found an energetic champion in Maurice Evans, Natal politician, naturalist

---

[1]The total area of 16 000 km² has geological interest and magnificent scenery as well as abundant and high-quality San rock art. It is also a Ramsar Wetland (site 886) and as from 2001 it is in the process of becoming the Maloti-Drakensberg Transfrontier Conservation and Development Area. See T. Sandwith, 'Overcoming barriers: Conservation and development in the Maloti-Drakensberg mountains of southern Africa', *Journal of Sustainable Forestry* 17 (2003): 149–170; J. Hanks, 'Transfrontier Conservation Areas (TFCAs) in southern Africa: Their role in conserving biodiversity, socioeconomic development and promoting a culture of peace', in *Transboundary Protected Areas: The Viability of Regional Conservation Strategies*, eds U.M. Goodale, M.J. Stern, C. Margoluis, A.G. Lanfer and M. Fladeland (New York, NY: Food Products Press, 2003, 127–148); G. Stewart, 'The Maloti-Drakensberg Mountains: Conservation challenges in a region of international significance', *The Journal of the Mountain Club of South Africa* 103 (2000): 146–159; B. Büscher, 'Payments for ecosystem services as neoliberal conservation: (Reinterpreting) evidence from the Maloti-Drakensberg, South Africa', *Conservation and Society* 10, no. 1 (2012): 29–41; and J. Wittmayer and B. Büscher, 'Conserving conflict? Transfrontier conservation, development discourse and conflict between South Africa and Lesotho', *Human Ecology* 38, no. 6 (2010): 763–773.

[2]J.W. Bews, 'The plant ecology of the Drakensberg Range', *Annals of the Natal Museum* 3, no. 3 (1913): 511–566.

[3]J. Carruthers, *The Kruger National Park: A Social and Political History* (Pietermaritzburg: Natal University Press, 1995). See also W. Beinart and P. Coates, *Environment and History: The Taming of Nature in the USA and South Africa* (London: Routledge, 1995); J.M. MacKenzie, *The Empire of Nature: Hunting, Conservation and British Imperialism* (Manchester: Manchester University Press, 1988); and J.M. MacKenzie, ed., *Imperialism and the Natural World* (Manchester: Manchester University Press, 1990).

Figure 3.1. Natal National Park: Mont-aux-Sources and Sentinel Peak. From *The Mountain Club Annual*, no. 14, 1911, opp. p. 84.

and writer. Evans also advocated the establishment of the Giant's Castle Game Reserve further south in the Drakensberg. This came into being in 1903 and was specifically intended to protect the declining herds of eland *Taurotragus oryx* on colonial land in the area. A 'conservator' was appointed and public access and hunting was prohibited.[4] The rationale for protecting this area had much in common with the Sabi and Singwitsi Reserves in the Transvaal and the game reserves of Zululand. By contrast, the NNP had its origins in the tourist industry and in 1908 it was formally proclaimed a 'National Park'[5] for holidaymakers to the mountains and placed under the authority of Natal's Minister for Agriculture and

[4]J. Carruthers, 'The Royal Natal National Park, Kwazulu-Natal: Mountaineering, tourism and nature conservation in South Africa's first national park *c.*1896 to *c.*1947', *Environment and History* 19, no. 4 (2013): 459–485. The boundaries were formalised in 1907. Sydney Barnes was appointed the first conservator (1903–1906), followed by Roden Symons (1906–1915) and Philip Barnes (1915–1949), see C. Wheeler, 'The Barrier of Spears: A survey of the Natal Drakensberg', *The Journal of the Mountain Club of South Africa* 72 (1969): 3–8; C.S. Stokes, *Sanctuary* (Cape Town: Maskew Miller, 1953), 235.
[5]As Natal was one of the four separate British colonies that were united in 1910 the national park was established by the highest legislative authority at the time.

Lands.[6] It was relatively small – comprising only five farms belonging to the Natal government – but was identified in the deeds office as a national park and thus distinguished from a game reserve.[7]

Although South Africa's 1910 constitution gave provinces the responsibility for 'game and fish preservation', a national park was clearly regarded as different: it was a form of land use whose purpose was something other than fauna protection.[8] In 1916, the central government took over the land comprising the NNP from the provincial authorities and the Union's executive council affirmed that it be retained as a national park and recreational area for the people of South Africa for all time.[9] In the following years, more state property was added (including part of an African reserve).[10] The express object of this park was that it be a 'national recreation ground . . . preserved as far as possible in its present natural condition with a view to conserving for future scientists and others the fauna and flora as they at present exist, and that records (including meteorological ones) should if possible be obtained and preserved'.[11] Clearly, scientific study, combined with tourism, was to be a priority of the NNP. Certainly, the area proved popular with mountaineers and hikers, who could visit either from the Orange Free State side of the range or from Natal. Tourist facilities were constructed, access improved and many were the adventures there that mountaineers recorded in almost every issue of *The Annual of the Mountain Club of South Africa*.[12] The NNP was a mountainous landscape and in its geological and historical characteristics

[6]Wheeler, 'Barrier of Spears', 4–5.

[7]Carruthers, 'Royal Natal National Park', 459–485. Mont-aux-Sources was named thus by early French missionaries because of the many headwaters of rivers that rise on the Drakensberg summit plateau.

[8]Section 85 of the South Africa Act 1909, 85(x).

[9]Wheeler, 'Barrier of Spears', 4.

[10]Carruthers, 'Royal Natal National Park', 465; S.H. Haughton, 'The Natal National Park', *The Annual of the Mountain Club of South Africa* 22 (1919): 31–33.

[11]Carruthers, 'Royal Natal National Park', 465.

[12]See Carruthers, 'Royal Natal National Park', 459–485. For example, A.D. Kelly, 'Mont aux Sources: First ascent of the Outer Tower', *The Mountain Club Annual* 18 (1915): 40–45. Most visitors came from Cape Town – the stronghold of the Mountain Club of South Africa founded in 1891 – although there are records of groups arriving from Johannesburg and Pietermaritzburg. Mrs Allderman, 'A trip to the Mont aux Sources', *The Annual of the Mountain Club of South Africa* 24 (1921): 36–43; W.J. Wybergh, 'An attempt on Cathkin Peak', *The Mountain Club Annual* 15 (1912): 59.

it was far closer to the 'Yellowstone model' than any game reserve could ever be.[13]

Another difference between this national park and the game reserves was that there was awareness that it was not 'empty land'. The local African population was substantial and economically active and many of the paths that criss-crossed the mountains in the vicinity of the park were long-standing trade routes. A visitor from Cape Town observed that while 'civilisation seems far removed from these mighty fastnesses', the remoteness was less absolute than in the mountains of the Western Cape owing to the 'maze of the footpaths, cattle-tracks, game-courses and African villages with their cultivated fields and colourfully dressed workers'.[14] While Africans in game reserves were generally denigrated and their presence resented, except for their manual labour, what appears from the mountaineers' records is considerable respect for their African companions. Indeed, many of them were absolutely reliant on the skills of Africans as mountain-guides, horsemen, wagon drivers, cooks and camp assistants in what was referred to as 'the Switzerland of South Africa'.[15] In common with the early national parks of the USA, Canada and New Zealand, visitors were attracted by 'an "atmosphere" for the photographer or the artist, and a paradise for any lover of wide, open spaces'.[16] In 1926, after visiting some of the national parks in North America, the Natal Provincial Secretary expressed the view that when 'compared with the Canadian Rockies, the Drakensberg Range holds the palm'.[17] He also extolled the views of US transcendentalist and nature-lover John Muir that people should 'climb the mountains and get their good tidings. Nature's peace will flow into you as sunshine flows into trees.' A case was being made, with direct reference to the US national parks, that the Drakensberg's 'panoramas gigantic and grand' were as worthy of the name 'national park' as anything that the USA could offer.[18]

---

[13]See K. Jones, 'Unpacking Yellowstone: The American national park in global perspective', in *Civilizing Nature: National Parks in Global and Historical Perspective*, eds B. Gissibl, S. Höhler and P. Kupper (New York, NY: Berghahn, 2012), 31–49.

[14]E.S. Field, 'With the Natal Club: Some impressions of the Drakensbergen', *The Journal of the Mountain Club of South Africa* 38 (1935): 70–71; T.P. Stokoe, 'Mounts and mountaineers', *The Annual of the Mountain Club of South Africa* 31 (1928): 35–42.

[15]Allderman, 'A trip to the Mont aux Sources', 36–43.

[16]Field, 'With the Natal Club', 70–71.

[17]Carruthers, 'Royal Natal National Park', 475.

[18]Stokes, *Sanctuary*, 307, 309.

The history of the NNP raises a number of issues about the transfer of early national park philosophy and management ideas between South Africa and other parts of the world. Elements of the NNP compare favourably with Yellowstone, generally regarded as the first, and exemplary, US national park. The NNP is fairly large, scenically and geologically magnificent with high peaks, waterfalls and streams, relatively far from (but accessible to) urban centres and ideal for recreational hiking, mountaineering, walking and fishing. It contains interesting plants and once-rare wildlife such as eland, but no dangerous mammals such as elephant or lion. The historiography of national parks began with the books of Roderick Nash and Alfred Runte, who argued that American leadership was critical to their international success.[19] Although it is now appreciated that the US model was not diffused globally, there was a broad transnational circulation of growing conservation and outdoor recreation ideas in the early twentieth century, which also affected South Africa.[20] It might be argued that the NNP was, and remains, more 'North American' than any other protected area in South Africa by virtue of its monumental landscape and physical recreational opportunities. Its formal declaration clearly stated that 'The object which the promoters of the Park have in view is the preservation and maintenance for ever of the area as a public park and pleasure ground for the benefit, advantage, and enjoyment of the people of the Union of South Africa.'[21] These were exactly the sentiments upon which the US national parks system was predicated.

Protected areas are significant markers of various forms of nationalism, and encapsulate environmental values and their change over time.[22] The NNP provides an interesting case in point and deserves to be better known for both sets of reasons. The fact that the NNP was South Africa's first national park, established a decade before the Kruger National Park (KNP), is hardly ever mentioned and it is worth determining why

---

[19] R.F. Nash, *Wilderness and the American Mind* (New Haven, CT: Yale University Press, 1983); A. Runte, *National Parks: The American Experience* (Lincoln, NE and London: University of Nebraska Press, 1997).

[20] I. Tyrrell, 'America's national parks: The transnational creation of national space in the Progressive Era', *Journal of American Studies* 46, no. 1 (2012): 1–21; see also A. Howkins, J. Orsi and M. Fiege, eds, *National Parks Beyond the Nation* (Norman, OK: University of Oklahoma Press, 2016).

[21] *The Annual of the Natal Mountain Club* 1 (1920).

[22] R. White, 'The nationalization of nature', *Journal of American History* 86, no. 3 (1999): 976–986.

this primacy has been disregarded.[23] One reason might be because the NNP does not fall under the authority of the organisation currently (since 1994) called South African National Parks (SANParks), formerly (1926–1994) the National Parks Board of Trustees (NPB), which recognises the KNP as 'the first'. Strictly speaking, the KNP was 'the first in the stable of the NPB', rather than 'the first' in South Africa. When the KNP was established in 1926, along with the NPB, the existence of the NNP, as noted above, was already recognised by the Union parliament. During the debate on founding the KNP, House of Assembly member Herbert Papenfus declared: 'So far as I have been able to discover, only one national park has been created by Act of Parliament in South Africa, and that is in Natal. That park is noted for its magnificent scenic grandeur, but it has no faunal wealth worth mentioning.'[24] Parliament, however, took no decision about whether to include the NNP in the NPB stable, or to exclude it.

The Idea of a 'National Park' in South Africa Pre-1930

If the term 'national park' still eludes precise definition in the twenty-first century, it was even more loosely used in the 1920s. In South Africa, it was applied to several types of government-owned nature conservation and outdoor recreation institutions. The question thus arises of how South Africans articulated their philosophies of a 'South African national park', and this has had a direct impact on the kind of scientific knowledge, if any, that these areas might be expected to produce. As noted, the NNP bore many resemblances to a national park in the US in terms of landscape, access and recreational facilities. The KNP, by contrast, was located in very remote savannah country, of which it was said in 1933, 'without the animal life these vast tracts of flat, monotonous country would mean little or nothing to the South African nation'.[25] In the 1920s, it was indeed the animals that came to dominate South Africa's

[23]See www.drakensberg-tourism.com/royal-natal-national-park.html where the statement is made that the 'Royal Natal National Park was proclaimed in 1916, and contains some of the most spectacular scenery in Africa' (accessed 1 March 2012). There is no mention of priority.

[24]*Union of South Africa, House of Assembly Debates, 1926, Vol. 7, 3rd session, 5th Parliament, 22 January to 8 June 1926*, 31 May 1926, col. 4366-4380 and col.4372. Papenfus was later chairman of the NPB and was much involved in the Wild Life Society of South Africa.

[25]A.D. Thomas and W.O. Neitz, 'The importance of disease in wild animals', *South African Journal of Science* 30 (1933): 419–425.

national park philosophy. This may have been because the existence of wildlife evoked a popular, romantic and sentimental veneration of the Highveld past and a hunting frontier in a way that recreational pleasure and natural history in a mountain-scape did not.[26]

Over the years, SANParks and its precursor have attempted to reserve the name 'national park' for only those areas under its management. This is based on the view that SANParks is the only 'national' authority, while other 'national parks', including the NNP and the more recent Pilanesberg National Park (explored in a later chapter), are merely 'provincial parks', because they are managed by provincial authorities, the implication being that they are of less importance in the state hierarchy. Given KwaZulu-Natal's head start in having a 'national park', it is ironic that the province currently has no protected areas administered by SANParks, although the province is home to numerous significant game reserves in Zululand, the iSimangaliso Wetland Park at St Lucia (a World Heritage Site), as well as in the Drakensberg. As a province, Natal has had a rather ambiguous historical relationship with the rest of the country. Strongly English-speaking, pro-British and pro-imperial during the twentieth century, it resented pro-Afrikaner policies and any weakening of ties with Britain. Only reluctantly did it join the Union in 1910 and the Natal Provincial Council was often dominated by an opposition political party in the years that followed. Indeed, it sometimes demonstrated a strong – but invariably unsuccessful – inclination to sever ties with the rest of the country.[27]

Brooks has written extensively on the development of game reserves in Natal, particularly those in Zululand, from the perspective of 'nature tourism' in the province.[28] However, she makes no mention of the NNP: it is as if it did not exist, despite its being called a 'National Park' and its establishment on state land by executive council decision. Her work therefore supports the argument – at least for the northern and inland provinces of South Africa – that it is 'wild Africa' and 'African wildlife', together with a kind of timeless quality and absence of people, that

[26]See J. Carruthers, *Game Protection in the Transvaal, 1846 to 1926* (Pretoria: Archives Yearbook for South African History, 1995).

[27]See P.S. Thompson, *Natalians First: Separatism in South Africa 1909–1961* (Johannesburg: Southern Books, 1990); P.S. Thompson, *The British Civic Culture of Natal South Africa 1902–1961* (Howick: Brevitas, 1999).

[28]S. Brooks, 'Images of "Wild Africa": Nature tourism and the (re)creation of Hluhluwe game reserve, 1930–1945', *Journal of Historical Geography* 31, no. 2 (2005): 220–240.

objectify 'African nature' and national parks, not Alpine scenery, African cultural heritage and outdoor recreational pursuits. Alternatively, her omission perhaps reflects the fact that the imperative to 'save game' was simply the stronger political ideology.

Provincial rivalries may also have played a role in the definition of national park. In the 1920s, there may have been some division of opinion about what constituted such a park as between the public in the Cape and that in the interior, although firm supporting evidence is lacking. For example, in 1929 Cape Town activist Alfred H. Perry wrote in his *National and Other Parks* that these parks were a 'modern' form of land use, the 'home of healthy and delightful open-air recreation' in which 'camping sites, mountains for the climber, streams and pools for the swimmer and angler, peace and solitude for the weary, interest for the lover of nature and joy for the artist' were provided – as was the case in the NNP. Perry also counted Kirstenbosch Botanical Garden along with the adjoining Upper Kirstenbosch Nature Reserve in Cape Town among the national parks and his suggested new parks were in the mountains and forests of the Cape – the Hex River Mountains, the Cederberg and Tsitsikamma.[29]

Perry's book contained a foreword by Robert Harold Compton (1886–1979), a Cambridge-trained taxonomist who was then director of Kirstenbosch Botanical Garden and professor of botany at the University of Cape Town (UCT) (1919–1953). As early as 1909, Harry Bolus, together with other prominent professional Cape botanists, had championed the declaration of Table Mountain as a national park, drawing parallels with Yellowstone in the USA or the National Trust in England.[30] Despite the mountain's iconic and historical status – let alone its distinctive flora – the plea fell on deaf political ears. Twenty years later, Compton was awarded a Carnegie Corporation grant to visit the USA for three months 'to study the system of National Parks and National Monuments established there'. His detailed 1934 report, while not actually disparaging game reserves as national parks, argued that these were but one form of national park, not the norm. The neglect of vegetation and scenic or landscape protection

---

[29] A.H.T. Perry, *National and Other Parks* (n.p.: n.p. [1929]), 12–14.
[30] Cited in S. Dubow, *A Commonwealth of Knowledge: Science, Sensibility, and White South Africa, 1820–2000* (Oxford: Oxford University Press, 2006), 183; see also S. Dubow, 'A commonwealth of science: The British Association in South Africa, 1905 and 1929', in *Science and Society in Southern Africa*, ed. S. Dubow (Manchester: Manchester University Press, 2000), 66–99.

were, Compton considered, a 'national disgrace'.[31] However, Compton's call for floristic or scenic national parks went unheeded by government. Only with the establishment of the Cape Floral Region Protected Areas as a World Heritage Site in 2004, comprising eight protected areas covering 553 000 ha and managed jointly by SANParks and the nature conservation authorities of the Western Cape and Eastern Cape provinces, have these mountain lands been added to South Africa's protected area estate.

Thus, national parks in South Africa had an apparently bifurcated trajectory, and from the 1920s onwards game reserve-type national parks came to dominate to the exclusion of those based on landscape, botanical and archaeological values. Generally speaking, this bias has been mirrored in the emerging conservation biology, which, until recently, was overwhelmingly focused on fauna.

Yet, as already mentioned, it was the atypical NNP that was the site of the first protected area science produced in the country, and this was in accordance with its formal scientific mandate. In 1910, John Bews (1884–1938), an Orkney-born graduate of the University of Edinburgh, was appointed professor of botany at Natal University College in Pietermaritzburg. No sooner had he arrived in South Africa than he was out in the veld studying Natal vegetation, on which he published prolifically. In 1913, for example, he produced 'An oecological survey of the midlands of Natal' and in 1917, 'The plant ecology of the Drakensberg Range', both of which appeared in the *Annals of the Natal Museum*; and in 1920 'The Mont-aux-Sources National Park: Notes on its vegetation' appeared in the *Journal of the Botanical Society of South Africa*.[32] As several of these titles indicate, he was an early plant ecologist and subscribed to ideas about synthesis and the need to 'view the subject as a whole' from an ecological perspective. 'Ecology' was a new field, still fluid in its philosophy

[31]R.H. Compton, *The National Parks of the United States of America* (Pretoria:The Carnegie Corporation Visitors' Grants Committee, 1934).

[32]J.W. Bews, *Plant Forms and their Evolution in South Africa* (London, Longmans: 1925); J.W. Bews, *The Grasses and Grasslands of South Africa* (Pietermaritzburg: P. Davis, 1918); J.W. Bews, 'The plant ecology of the Drakensberg range', *Annals of the Natal Museum* 3, no. 3 (1917): 511–566; J.W. Bews, 'The plant ecology of the coast belt of Natal', *Annals of the Natal Museum* 4 (1920): 367–470; J.W. Bews, 'An oecological survey of the Midlands of Natal with special reference to the Pietermaritzburg district', *Annals of the Natal Museum* 2, no. 4 (1913): 485–545; J.W. Bews, 'The vegetation of Natal', *Annals of the Natal Museum* 2, no. 3 (1912): 253–331; J.W. Bews, 'The Mont-aux-Sources National Park: Notes on its vegetation', *Journal of the Botanical Society of South Africa* 4 (1920): 11–13.

and even its study objectives, and at the cutting edge of new biological thinking,[33] but as part of the British imperial scientific network (including two years at the University of Durham between 1925 and 1927), Bews was well acquainted with the latest ideas in his discipline.

Given their common interest in holism, Bews and South African Prime Minister Jan Smuts were soon mutual admirers. In 1930, Bews went on to become principal of the Natal University College and melded the Durban and Pietermaritzburg campuses into a single institution along holistic ecological lines, using St Andrews University in Scotland (of which Smuts was elected rector in 1931) as his model.[34]

Academic Botany and Zoology

Bews also had the distinction of publishing 'An account of the chief types of vegetation in South Africa, with notes on the plant succession' in one of the earliest issues of the prestigious *Journal of Ecology*.[35] This periodical had been established by the British Ecological Society, one of whose core founders in 1913 had been Robert Adamson (1885–1965), who, from 1923 to 1950, held the Harry Bolus chair of botany at UCT and had also spent time in Australia.[36] The *Journal*, started in 1913, was edited by the renowned Cambridge don Arthur Tansley who, in addition to being the British Empire's leading plant ecologist and promoter of genetic, plant physiological, biochemical and ecological studies as against the more conservative morphological school of botany, was also an active member of the Society for the Promotion of Nature Reserves.[37] The link between plant ecology and nature protection was therefore strong from the outset. The British Ecological Society had grown out of Tansley's Vegetation Committee, founded in 1904. Ecology, while certainly a science, was also a philosophy and an ideology, Darwinian in its slant and based on

[33]A. Bramwell, *Ecology in the 20th Century: A History* (New Haven, CT and London: Yale University Press, 1989), 49.

[34]P. Anker, *Imperial Ecology; Environmental Order in the British Empire, 1895–1945* (Cambridge, MA: Cambridge University Press, 2001), 160–162; see also W. Bizley, 'John William Bews: A commemorative note', *Natalia* 14 (1984): 17–21.

[35]J.W. Bews, 'An account of the chief types of vegetation in South Africa, with notes on the plant succession', *Journal of Ecology* 4 (1916): 129–159; Anker, *Imperial Ecology*, 20–21.

[36]J. Sheail, *Seventy-five Years in Ecology: The British Ecological Society* (Oxford: Blackwell, 1987), 11–12, 25–37.

[37]Bews, 'An account of the chief types of vegetation in South Africa', 29–159; Anker, *Imperial Ecology*, 20–21.

ideas of change over time.[38] Another South African ecological connection was through Charles Moss (1870–1930), a brusque and extremely hard-working Yorkshireman, whose appointment to the newly created post of professor of botany at the School of Mines in Johannesburg in 1917 (after 1922, the University of the Witwatersrand, commonly referred to as 'Wits') was regarded as a great loss to British ecology. After his sudden death in 1930, Moss was succeeded by John Phillips (1899–1988), who through his association with Frederick Clements had closer ties with the US strain of ecology than with the British school.

Yet despite these appointments at institutions of higher learning in South Africa, the natural sciences did not enjoy a high profile in the country. In his presidential address on rural education in 1914 to Section C (bacteriology, botany, zoology, agriculture, forestry, physiology, hygiene and sanitary science) of the South African Association for the Advancement of Science (SAAAS), George Potts (1877–1948), who had a PhD in botany from the University of Halle and had been appointed the first professor of natural science (later changed to professor of botany), at Grey University College, Bloemfontein, had this to say: 'Now to anyone acquainted with University Education, B.A. denotes a man of literature and education, a man of culture, but by contrast, when a B.Sc. is given by the same University it implies a barbaric Goth, a technical expert, a mere specialist, more or less respectable, but not admissible into the cultured caste.' This, he added, was detrimental to the status of the natural sciences, but he agreed with the comment of the eminent imperial educationalist Richard Jebb to the SAAAS in 1905 that the study of the natural sciences could in future denote an 'intellectual culture of the highest order'. Because of their vitally important utility to a modernising society, Potts argued, botany and zoology should be given priority over chemistry and similar disciplines and be accorded equality with the humanities.[39]

When UCT was established in 1918 there was no BSc degree. A BA candidate could major in science with a maximum of seven out of nine

---

[38]L. Robin, 'Ecology: A science of empire?', in *Ecology and Empire: Comparative History of Settler Societies*, eds T. Griffiths and L. Robin (Edinburgh: Keele University Press, 1997), 63; P.G. Ayres, *Shaping Ecology: The Life of Arthur Tansley* (Hoboken, NJ: Wiley Blackwell, 2012).

[39]G. Potts, 'Rural education', *Report of the Twelfth Annual Meeting of the South African Association for the Advancement of Science, Kimberley, 1914* (Cape Town: The Association, 1915), 57–76.

subjects in the sciences, while the other two had to be from the arts. When a BSc in pure science was first introduced in 1922, the seven science subjects became compulsory. This did not yield a flood of students: during the 1920s, only 3% of the student body enrolled for this degree, not least because the South African economy of the day 'needed relatively few highly specialised Science graduates'. However, the teaching staff in the science faculty was large because many subjects – including botany, geology and chemistry – were required for the popular degrees in engineering and medicine.[40] The situation at Wits was similar: far fewer students were enrolled in science than in arts, and of those who were, most were also enrolled for engineering and medicine.[41]

Adamson at UCT, Bews at Natal and Moss at Wits were inspiring teachers and were themselves innovative ecological researchers. Together with other British-educated botanists such as Robert Harold Compton of Kirstenbosch and UCT, and the feisty Welshman Illtyd Buller Pole Evans (1879–1968), who was 'fanatically keen on the preservation of the natural resources of South Africa'[42] and head of the Division of Botany and Plant Pathology in the national Department of Agriculture, they were in the international vanguard of their discipline and extremely important figures in ensuring that botany became one of the most significant sciences in South Africa. Not only was academic botany strong and growing, but there was a readership for the local journals in which research might be published. In the course of just a few years, these publications included the *Annals of the Bolus Herbarium* (1914–1928), the *South African Journal of Botany* (1935–1984), *The Flowering Plants of South Africa* and *Bothalia* (both from 1921). Pole Evans took the lead in establishing the Botanical Survey of South Africa in 1918. It was initially intended to include zoology, a plan that fell through in the absence of a champion for that discipline. The Botanical Survey's advisory committee included South Africa's most prominent botanists, plus a veterinarian and a forester.[43]

[40]H. Phillips, *The University of Cape Town 1918–1948: The Formative Years* (Cape Town: UCT Press, 1993), 45–46.

[41]B.K. Murray, *Wits: The Early Years. A History of the University of the Witwatersrand, Johannesburg, and its Precursors, 1896–1939* (Johannesburg: Witwatersrand University Press, 1982), 150–151.

[42]H. Bloch, 'The case for proclaiming the Dongola Wild Life Sanctuary, 1946', pamphlet collection SQ 590.72 (6825), Johannesburg Public Library.

[43]Pole Evans was its Chairman. Other (honorary) members included Rudolph Marloth and Louisa Bolus (Western and Northern Cape), Selmar Schonland (Professor of Botany, Rhodes University College, Grahamstown, Eastern Cape), John Bews (Professor of

The Botanical Survey had been established without the Secretary for Agriculture's approval and money to begin the survey came courtesy of the 'generosity' of the Department of Mines and Industries, whose secretary, Herbert Warrington-Smyth, was on good terms with Pole Evans. Warrington-Smyth's department was associated with an industrial and scientific advisory committee (based in Johannesburg), which included a botanical sub-committee, whose members Pole Evans did not hold in high regard. Consequently, he made great efforts to ensure this committee did not assume responsibility for the Botanical Survey or provide it with direction and personnel. Indeed, he felt that this committee only intended to insult him and his staff and denigrate the 'most valuable and up-to-date ecological treatises that have yet appeared on South African vegetation' by John Bews in Natal. He was adamant that he would control the survey and its outcome.

Zoology, the other academic discipline that might have made an early contribution to nature and wildlife conservation in South Africa, was less well served in the period from 1910 to 1930. Until he left for McGill in Montreal in 1932, the head of zoology at Wits was Harold Fantham (1876–1937), graduate of Cambridge and London, eminent author of over a hundred research memoirs on parasitology and eugenics, vice-president of the Royal Society of South Africa, president of the SAAAS (1927), fellow of the Zoological Society of London, and recipient of many more honours. Fantham was also an extremely difficult man, 'something of a paranoic', who alienated many of his staff. In fact, it was Fantham who fired the young G. Evelyn Hutchinson (1903–1991) from the department, thus possibly thwarting the development of limnological ecology in South Africa. Hutchinson went on to Yale, where he was in the vanguard of ensuring that systems ecology became one of the most important fields of study in the twentieth century.[44]

UCT's zoology department had been extremely lacklustre under J.D.F. Gilchrist (1866–1926), professor since 1905 at the South African College

Botany, Natal University College, Pietermaritzburg) and George Potts (Professor of Botany, Grey College, Bloemfontein), together with Sir Arnold Theiler (Director of Veterinary Services and plant collector and a close friend of Pole Evans), and Charles Legat (Chief Conservator of Forests). See J. Carruthers, 'Trouble in the garden: South African botanical politics ca.1870–1950', *South African Journal of Botany* 77, no. 2 (2011): 258–267.

[44]Murray, *Wits: The Early Years*, 156–158; J. Carruthers, 'G. Evelyn Hutchinson in South Africa, 1926 to 1928: "An immense part in my intellectual development"', *Transactions of the Royal Society of South Africa* 66, no. 2 (2011): 87–104.

and at UCT until the year of his death. He was in a 'little world of
his own' and 'preoccupied with his pioneering marine biological survey' begun in 1896. Cecil von Bonde, also a marine biologist, had been
Gilchrist's student and considered himself his successor. As the two teachers in the department, Gilchrist and von Bonde 'deviated little from that
pursued in the more staid British departments of the time: a group-by-
group catalogue of the animal kingdom, with a strong emphasis on morphology and classification and plentiful use of wax models and preserved
specimens', which they regarded as more than adequate for the majority
of medical students who were merely doing a half course in zoology.[45]
To von Bonde's great disappointment, Gilchrist was replaced by Lancelot
T. Hogben (1895–1975), a 'tempestuous personality and advanced socialist', a brilliant Cambridge zoology graduate specialising in experimental
biology, one of the founders of the *Journal of Experimental Biology*, and
from 1936 a Fellow of the Royal Society. Hogben, appalled at the low
standard of teaching and research at UCT, set about injecting enthusiasm
and an appetite for controversy into the department. Before long he had
transformed Gilchrist's old-fashioned department into 'a powerhouse
of experimental zoology' and student numbers increased dramatically.
Suspended from his duties at Wits before his formal dismissal, Hutchinson
went to Cape Town where he was inspired by Hogben, who had quickly
appreciated the biological paradise around Cape Town. Hogben drew
Hutchinson's attention to the vleis (lakes and ponds) on the Cape
Peninsula as study sites and the young scientist visited numbers of them,
including Zeekoevlei, Rondevlei and Princessvlei, thus beginning his
career as a limnological ecologist.[46]

---

[45]Phillips, *University of Cape Town 1918–1948*, 56–57.

[46]Hogben's own interests in the lakes and pans around Cape Town resulted in a major
   scientific discovery: that female frogs of the genus *Xenopus* were useful for determining
   pregnancy in human females. Part of his allure for students may have been his extreme
   left-wing Marxist political views and his original, unconventional thinking on a wide
   range of issues. Hogben and his first wife, the statistician Enid Charles, collaborated on a
   number of scientific publications, but additionally, were known to be very sympathetic
   to Africans. One reason for Hogben's leaving South Africa was the couple's abhorrence
   of the growing segregationist and apartheid policies of the late 1920s and early 1930s
   and Hogben was an outspoken opponent of Jan Smuts. Hogben and his students acquit-
   ted themselves well during the 1929 visit to South Africa of the British Association
   of the Advancement of Science, and his growing reputation in Britain – equal to that
   of J.B.S. Haldane, or Julian Huxley – earned him the first Chair of Social Biology at
   the London School of Economics in 1930, where he campaigned against eugenics.

As for Victoria College (later the University of Stellenbosch), Robert Broom (1866–1951), a Scottish-trained medical doctor, who also – in 1905 – obtained a DSc from the University of Glasgow, was the professor of zoology and geology from 1903 to 1910. Broom's all-consuming passion was palaeontology and he was an acknowledged expert on the fossils of the Karoo. Broom promoted evolution and for that reason he was obliged to leave the conservative college.[47] He was succeeded as professor of zoology, geology and mineralogy by the Australian, Ernest Goddard (1883–1948), the recipient of the first doctorate in zoology from the University of Sydney in 1906. The post was altered to professor of zoology alone after Victoria College became a full university in 1918. Goddard's field of research was earthworms and leeches and he also encouraged Antarctic research before leaving South Africa in 1922 to become professor of biology at the University of Queensland.

Perpetually strapped for cash, Rhodes University College fared no better. In 1904 James E. Duerden (1865–1937), an expert on corals, was appointed chair of zoology, his salary being paid initially by the Albany Museum. Upon his retirement 27 years later, the post was abolished for want of funding. Duerden too concentrated on animal anatomy and taxonomy, not the living creature. Apparently, however, he became a specialist in reptiles as well as in ostrich farming and also offered an applied biology course. He was keen to incorporate agriculture into the curriculum, but this did not eventuate. For a time, the department offered a course in 'biology' in conjunction with Selmar Schonland (1860–1940), head of the botany department and curator of the Albany Museum, but it was soon discontinued.[48] However, none of this zoology resembled conservation biology and no school of animal ecology arose in South Africa's universities in this period.

After holding this position for a number of years, he moved on to universities at Aberdeen and Birmingham, the War Office during the war, and finally the University of Guyana, before retiring to Wales. Believing that the responsibility of science was to educate and improve society, as well as scholarly papers he wrote best-selling books, including *Mathematics for the Million* (1936) and *Science for the Citizen* (1938). In addition, he invented Interglossa, a language that is rather like Esperanto.

[47] He went on to work at the Transvaal Museum as a palaeontologist, and made his name by discovering and naming 'Mrs Ples', a young adult Australopithicine from Sterkfontein Caves near Johannesburg in 1947.

[48] A.N. Hodgson and A.J.F.K. Craig, 'A century of Zoology and Entomology at Rhodes University, 1905 to 2005', *Transactions of the Royal Society of South Africa* 60, no. 1 (2005): 1–18.

Early Botanical and Animal Ecology

Historians have begun to analyse South Africa's specific contribution to ecological botany. Like economic ornithology, African plant ecology (and, indeed plant ecology generally in England, most British colonies and the USA) was predicated on its possible benefits for agricultural science: the discipline did not arise specifically out of a concern to protect nature. Nonetheless, the ecological botanists at South African universities and in the civil service knew that their colleagues in Britain worked closely with the Society for the Promotion of Nature Reserves, founded by Charles Rothschild in 1912, to ensure that suitable study areas existed in which 'communities' of plants were available for ecological research. This is certainly what Bews intended with his work in the NNP and its surroundings. As will be seen later, Pole Evans established a botanical reserve in the northern Transvaal for the very purpose of scientific botanical study and conservation.

The philosophy of plant ecology was articulated by Arthur Tansley as early as 1914. He viewed ecology as central to botany because it was the 'study of plants for their own sakes as living beings in their natural surroundings, of their vital relations to these surroundings and to one another, of their social life as well as their individual life . . . [it was not a special branch of botany but] a way of regarding plant life'.[49] Ecology was an exciting new field, and its strong theoretical leanings (especially regarding the nature of a 'community') prompted fierce debate and even warring schools of thought. The theoretical, even philosophical,[50] controversy that split the early plant ecologists concerned the nature of the mature plant community.

This division impacted on thinking in South Africa. John Phillips, using his own ideas, but also influenced by Smuts' ideas of 'holism', took issue with Arthur Tansley. The latter was particular offended by Phillips' article 'The biotic community' that appeared in the *Journal of Ecology* in 1931.[51] To Tansley, Phillips' views 'represented a closed system of religious or philosophical dogma'. In response, Tansley developed the notion of an 'ecosystem', but he did not entirely jettison the philosophies of

---

[49] A.G. Tansley, 'Presidential Address', *Journal of Ecology* 2, no. 3 (1914): 194–203, 195.
[50] E.C. Lindeman, 'Ecology: An instrument for the integration of science and philosophy', *Ecological Monographs* 10, no. 3 (1940): 367–372.
[51] J.F.V. Phillips, 'The biotic community', *Journal of Ecology* 19, no. 1 (1931): 1–24.

'equilibrium' and 'climax'.[52] However, Clements, the American theorist who greatly influenced Phillips, strongly favoured a climax state that would provide environmental stability. There was a life cycle of birth, growth and development with the environment as a stage on which the biota enacted the drama. Tansley's amalgamation, therefore, of biota and environment *as a system* was a conceptual advance 'and opened the door for the wider use of energy theory and matter cycling in ecology'.[53]

South Africa's plant ecologists such as Phillips, Bews and Pole Evans were internationally renowned and their work was fundamental to changing the botanical paradigms of the twentieth century and to reorienting botany out of the laboratory and back into the field. They were intellectually adventurous and formed part of the vanguard of the new paradigm that was later to become fully fledged ecology.[54]

Animal ecology, or ethology, as William Wheeler (1865–1937), first vice-president of the Ecological Society of America (founded in 1915), called it, was far slower to develop. As Bramwell has explained, 'ecology' and 'ethology' were used interchangeably for many years, and only later was the one applied specifically to plant sciences and the other to their animal equivalents.[55] As we have seen, academic zoology in South Africa between 1910 and 1930 was extremely narrow. There was no zoological community keen to utilise ecological knowledge and there were no journals with relatively large readerships, as there were for the numerous botanical publications. Settler societies, like South Africa and Australia, required botanical knowledge to promote agricultural modernisation, to expand the production capacity of healthy grassland, to develop new grasses palatable to domestic stock. Consequently, these countries embarked on vegetation surveys to determine the locations that might support livestock or certain crops. This is the reason the South African Department of Agriculture had a strong Division of Botany, led by the indefatigable Pole Evans. Knowledge was something to be used and, in the early twentieth century, there was no answer as to the possible

[52]F.B. Golley, *A History of the Ecosystem Concept in Ecology: More than a Sum of the Parts* (New York, NY and London: Yale University Press, 1993), 11–16.

[53]Golley, *History of the Ecosystem Concept in Ecology*, 22–24.

[54]S.E. Kingsland, *Modeling Nature: Episodes in the History of Population Ecology* (Chicago, IL: University of Chicago Press, 1985), 178; J.B. Hagen, 'Ecologists and taxonomists: Divergent traditions in twentieth-century plant geography', *Journal of the History of Biology* 19, no. 2 (1986): 197–214; J.B. Hagen, *An Entangled Bank: The Origins of Ecosystem Ecology* (New Brunswick, NJ: Rutgers University Press, 1992), 72–75.

[55]Bramwell, *Ecology in the 20th Century*, 41.

practicability of natural history observations in game reserves. In such places, the only science was management and administration – values of protection, preservation and propagation – to enable 'game' herds to increase. Scientific knowledge was basic, resting on personal observation. And game reserves were closed to public access because no better or more productive use could be devised for the lands owing to their remoteness, endemic diseases and harsh climates.

Between 1902 and 1905 Wheeler published several papers suggesting that zoologists were in great need of a satisfactory term for animal behaviour. Late nineteenth-century naturalists were vague about instinct, often referring to it as 'reflex', but at least this did indicate an interest in the 'whole animal'.[56] In 1924 the Society for the Preservation of the Fauna of the Empire (SPFE) referred to this new science as 'bionomics', a term which in 1910 could be either a 'learned word for "natural history"', 'life history' or the 'lore of the farmer, gardener, sportsman, fancier, and field naturalist'.[57] But whatever it was called, animal ecology was revolutionary in insisting on meticulous observation in natural habitats. It was, in many respects, a return to old-fashioned natural history.[58] Charles Elton, the pioneering animal ecologist at Oxford, in fact called it 'scientific natural history'.[59] Moreover, at the first conference of US national parks in 1921, the education personnel involved were called 'naturalists' and in 1923 the 'chief naturalist' was Ansel F. Hall, a forestry graduate who headed the new Educational Division at Berkeley.[60]

Ecology at the time was as slippery and varied a concept as natural history, and despite thousands of publications in the field and its many specialisations, perhaps remains so even today.[61] When it became

[56]R.P. McIntosh, *The Background of Ecology: Concept and Theory* (Cambridge: Cambridge University Press, 1987), 9; K. Immelman, *Introduction to Ethology* (New York, NY: Plenum Press, 1980), 1–2; P. Crowcroft, *Elton's Ecologists: A History of the Bureau of Animal Population* (Chicago, IL: University of Chicago Press, 1991), xii; P.H. Klopfer and J.P. Hailman, *An Introduction to Animal Behavior: Ethology's First Century* (Englewood Cliffs, NJ: Prentice-Hall, 1967).

[57]*Journal of the Society for the Preservation of the Fauna of the Empire* 4 (1924): 27.

[58]Crowcroft, *Elton's Ecologists*, xv; W.H. Thorpe, *The Origins and Rise of Ethology: The Science of the Natural Behaviour of Animals* (London: Heinemann, 1979), 165.

[59]C. Elton, *Animal Ecology* (London: Sidgwick & Jackson, 1927), 1.

[60]P. Kupper, 'Science and the national parks: A transatlantic perspective on the interwar years', *Environmental History* 14, no. 1 (2009): 58–81.

[61]T.R. Dunlap, *Saving America's Wildlife: Ecology and the American Mind, 1850–1990* (Princeton, NJ: Princeton University Press, 1991), 46.

prominent in the 1920s and 1930s, it was sufficiently broad to include plants, wild creatures and humans. E. Barton Worthington (1905–2001), one of the most influential ecologists of the twentieth century, particularly in Africa, called it a 'scientific cloak for what had long been known as natural history', and regarded it as a method of thought as well as a practical science.[62] Victor Shelford (1877–1968), first president of the Ecological Society of America in 1915 (its journal, *Ecology*, began in 1920), referred to it as 'a set of ideas in search of an organizing principle'.[63] In his 1933 book *Exploring the Animal World*, Elton aimed to 'introduce the public to the new field of ecology by suggesting how they could look scientifically at nature in the course of doing very systematically things the British are famous for doing more casually in the guise of natural history'.[64]

Charles Adams, like Shelford, a student of Henry Cowles at the University of Chicago, was the first to come out with a book expressly entitled animal ecology, namely, his *Guide to the Study of Animal Ecology* published in 1913. Adams was an entomologist, employed in museums and by natural history societies in the USA, but in 1914 he became assistant professor of forest zoology at the New York State College of Forestry before moving on to become director of the New York State Museum.[65] Perhaps more important, and certainly more influential, was *Animal Ecology* by Charles Elton (1900–1991), which appeared in 1927 and greatly influenced Hutchinson among many others.[66] Elton, the English ecologist whose Bureau of Animal Population (established 1932) at Oxford University became world-renowned, referred to his discipline as a 'new mental world of populations, inter-relations, movements and communities . . . to study living nature in the field' that would reject 'easy generalisations about adaptation and the balance of life'.[67] In *Animal Ecology*, Elton conceptualised nature literally as an economy, with energy flowing in terms of supply and demand.[68] He also wrote that 'animals live lives which are socially in many ways comparable with the community

---

[62]E.B. Worthington, *The Ecological Century: A Personal Appraisal* (Oxford: Clarendon Press, 1983), vii–viii.

[63]Dunlap, *Saving America's Wildlife*, 45. See also Crowcroft, *Elton's Ecologists*.

[64]D. Simberloff, 'Charles Elton: Pioneer conservation biologist', *Environment and History* 18 (2012): 183–202.

[65]C.C. Adams, *Guide to the Study of Animal Ecology* (New York, NY: Macmillan, 1913).

[66]Carruthers, 'G. Evelyn Hutchinson in South Africa', 87–104.

[67]Dunlap, *Saving America's Wildlife*, 70–71; see also Crowcroft, *Elton's Ecologists*.

[68]Hagen, *Entangled Bank*, 51.

life of mankind'.[69] He argued that viewing predators and prey as 'enemies' stunted scientific thinking and he advocated the term's replacement with ideas about the optimum density of numbers advantageous to a live animal.[70] Who better to provide information on this than those who worked in the field? Elton admitted he had 'learned a far greater number of interesting and valuable ecological facts about the social organisation of animals from gamekeepers and private naturalists . . . than from trained zoologists'.[71] He referred, for example, to Samuel Cronwright-Schreiner's work on South Africa's famous 'springbok treks'.[72] In 1937, Elton corresponded with KNP warden Stevenson-Hamilton on the possibility of undertaking controlled censuses of animals at fixed points along accessible roads and even of inventing some kind of 'marking bullet' so that animals might be tagged.[73] Various annual reports of the Bureau of Animal Population are to be found among Stevenson-Hamilton's archival papers, indicating a continuing relationship between the two men. Another South African was also involved in this burgeoning discipline. In 1938, the Institute for the Study of Animal Behaviour, part of the Zoological Society of London and headed by Solomon (Solly) Zuckerman, established the *Bulletin of Animal Behaviour*.[74]

In 1932, the *Journal of Animal Ecology* was initiated because of the increasing number of papers on animal subjects being submitted to the *Journal of Ecology*.[75] Its publication coincided with the establishment

[69]D. Spearman, *The Animal Anthology* (London: John Baker, 1966), 136.

[70]A conclusion that Stevenson-Hamilton had also come to by the mid-1920s.

[71]Elton, *Animal Ecology*, 5.

[72]Elton, *Animal Ecology*, 109. On the springbok treks, see C.J. Roche, 'Ornaments of the desert, springbok treks in the Cape Colony, 1774–1908' (MA diss., University of Cape Town, 2004).

[73]Elton to Stevenson-Hamilton, 1 March 1937, Stevenson-Hamilton to Elton, 28 March 1937, in Stevenson-Hamilton family archives, Fairholm, Larkhall, Scotland. See D. Lack, *The Natural Regulation of Animal Numbers* (Oxford: Clarendon Press, 1954), who also deferred to Stevenson-Hamilton's knowledge, see 46, 173–174, 240.

[74]Zuckerman's books, including *The Social Life of Monkeys and Apes* (London: K. Paul, Trench, Trubner and Co., 1932) brought him international renown. He later became a prominent member of Oxford University and eventually chief scientific advisor to the British government. See his autobiography, *From Apes to Warlords, 1904–1946* (London: Hamilton, 1978).

[75]The only South African members of the Society for Animal Ecology, as recorded in the *Journal of Animal Ecology* 1 (1932), were R.A. Adamson (University of Cape Town); J.W. Bews (University of Natal); J.F.V. Phillips (University of the Witwatersrand); and F.S. Laughton, Assistant Forest Officer (Concordia, Knysna).

Figure 3.2. James Stevenson-Hamilton, warden of the Kruger National Park from 1926 to 1946.
Courtesy of SANParks.

of Elton's Bureau for Animal Population and it was edited by Elton and his young assistant A.D. (Doug) Middleton. Birds were the early objects of behavioural investigation because they could be caged and observed under controlled conditions,[76] unlike wild megafauna that were extremely hard to study in the wild.[77] The first article in this journal

---

[76]Edmund Selous, the African hunter's F.C. Selous' equally famous brother, a highly respected ethologist, was writing about bird psychology at this time. See Thorpe, *Origins and Rise of Ethology*, 30; E. Selous, *Evolution of Habit in Birds* (1933), *Realities of Bird Life* (1927). The work of Konrad Lorenz and Nikolaas Tinbergen is well known and they received the Nobel Prize for their endeavours. See R.W. Burkhardt, *Patterns of Behavior: Konrad Lorenz, Nico Tinbergen and the Founding of Ethology* (Chicago, IL: University of Chicago Press, 2005).

[77]Haagner initiated a study of South African wild animals held in captivity in the National Zoological Gardens in Pretoria. See A. Haagner, 'On the variability in the nature or temperament of wild animals in captivity, with special reference to South African species', *South African Journal of Science* 12 (1916): 612–618.

with a South African connection came the following year, in 1933. It was J.M. Winterbottom's 'Bird population studies: A preliminary analysis of the Gold Coast Avifauna', wherein the author elucidated the relative influence of population density and predator–prey relationships in maintaining a 'balance', while conceding that a more general 'balance of nature' does not exist.[78] Of a total of 250 members listed in the journal, only four had links with South Africa, and all of them were plant ecologists – Adamson, Bews, Phillips and F.S. Laughton.

Shelford was adamant that behaviour be 'seen as the primary determinant governing the distribution and development of animal life'.[79] Animal ecology may have got off to a slow start in part because of suspicion towards a discipline that did not lend itself to controlled experiment and for which the observer had to have imagination and empathy in addition to objectivity. 'Where the laboratory biologist eliminates Nature by reducing everything to a controlled environment, the ethologist sees Nature as a reality to be experienced and cherished.'[80] In fact, personal emotion had been part of the vocabulary and values of 'penitent butchers' for decades. 'Instinct' was one of the first animal characteristics to be studied in pursuit of 'more rigorous information about how species function in the wild'.[81] Questions such as 'what did animals think?' or 'how did their minds work?' – issues that had preoccupied sport-hunters – were now being taken seriously by scientists in their quest to understand animal behaviour. Certain members of the SPFE tried to grapple with some of these problems. Stevenson-Hamilton, for example, conducted experiments on the degree of movement and spectrum of colour wild animals could detect. R.W. Hingston wrote on the relationship between animal behaviour and colouration,[82] while Sir Peter Chalmers Mitchell of the Zoological Society of London examined the colour and pattern of

[78]J.M. Winterbottom, 'Bird population studies: A preliminary analysis of the Gold Coast Avifauna', *Journal of Animal Ecology* 2, no. 1 (1933): 82–97. Winterbottom also wrote the first book on southern African animal ecology, J.M. Winterbottom, *An Introduction to Animal Ecology in Southern Africa* (Cape Town: Maskew Miller, 1971). In 1959 he became the first director of the Percy Fitzpatrick Institute of African Ornithology at the University of Cape Town.

[79]G. Mitman, *The State of Nature: Ecology, Community and American Social Thought, 1900–1950* (Chicago, IL: University of Chicago Press, 1992), 3.

[80]P. Bowler, *Fontana History of the Environmental Sciences* (London: Fontana, 1992), 495.

[81]Bowler, *Fontana History*, 486.

[82]R.W.G. Hingston, *The Meaning of Animal Colour and Adornment* (London: Edward Arnold, 1933).

wildlife – 'a very fertile side of zoology in producing theories' he believed.[83] In the 1930s Frank Fraser Darling began to speak of this branch of science as the 'psychology of animals in the wild state', describing it as a branch of knowledge that had hardly been touched.[84]

However, lest it be thought that the ecological perspective evolved out of pure science alone, Dunlap reminds us that the applied science of game management also engendered 'a new view of nature and a new way to study it'.[85] Without doubt it was this kind of study that was emerging in South Africa's game reserves, particularly under Stevenson-Hamilton's direction in the eastern Transvaal. The first formal quantitative game-management population study in the world was conducted on the bobwhite quail (northern bobwhite *Colinus virginianus*) in the state of Georgia (1924–1929). It was undertaken by untrained scientists of the US Bureau of Biological Survey and was based on 'observations and common sense'. Nevertheless, the study itself was innovative and aimed to discover why the birds were declining by using the population in one place as a unit of study.[86] Also in this period (1927–1932), the Murie brothers, Olaus and Adolph, worked in Yellowstone on the population ecology of the coyote *Canis latrans*, just as Stevenson-Hamilton was attempting to do for lions *Panthera leo*.[87]

Working in the remote eastern Transvaal, administering the Sabi and Singwitsi game reserves and some of the private land north of the Sabie River as far as the Olifants River, Stevenson-Hamilton was the first professional game warden in Africa to consider it his responsibility to provide authoritative educational material about the landscape and wild animals within a game reserve to the public and his peers. He thus shunned tales of hunting adventure or near-death experiences, the stock-in-trade of the sport-hunter-naturalist. In the preface to his first book, *Animal Life in Africa* (1912), he expressed a desire to provide 'in condensed form some account of the life economy of the wildlife animals which he finds around him, not only of those popularly known as "game"'.[88] While

---

[83]P. Chalmers Mitchell, *The Childhood of Animals* (London: Heinemann, 1912), 62.

[84]*Journal of the Society for the Preservation of the Wild Fauna of the Empire,* 23 (1934).

[85]T.R. Dunlap, 'Ecology and environmentalism in the Anglo settler societies', in *Ecology and Empire: Comparative History of Settler Societies*, eds T. Griffiths and L. Robin (Edinburgh: Keele University Press, 1997), 76–77.

[86]Dunlap, 'Ecology and environmentalism', 76–78.

[87]Dunlap, 'Ecology and environmentalism', 79–80.

[88]J. Stevenson-Hamilton, *Animal Life in Africa* (London: Heinemann, 1912).

Stevenson-Hamilton's writing at this time was descriptive and lacked an explicit conceptual foundation or innovative understanding of ecosystem theory, he communicated more knowledge and understanding of animal behaviour and habitat use than any earlier writer had done.[89]

As an ecological generalist, fascinated by behaviour and animal psychology, he emphasised how a species functioned while alive. He speculated about population dynamics, the role of colouration and behavioural patterns, thus foreshadowing some modern conservationist attitudes towards wildlife. Stevenson-Hamilton's freshness of attitude and expression appealed to William Hornaday, director of the New York Zoological Park and a leading if controversial US protectionist and scientist of the era. Hornaday had founded the American Bison Society and, with Teddy Roosevelt's support, the first federal game preserve in the USA in 1905, the Wichita National Forest and Game Preserve in Oklahoma. When *Animal Life in Africa* was published (with a foreword by their mutual friend, former US president and African safari-hunter Theodore Roosevelt), Hornaday wrote to Stevenson-Hamilton: 'I have grown weary of tales of slaughter and extermination, and your book of preservation comes like a cold spring bursting forth in a sun-parched desert.'[90] With its novel emphasis on animal behaviour and the connections between wildlife and habitat, *Animal Life in Africa* struck a chord and was enthusiastically reviewed in more than 50 South African and international newspapers and magazines. The *Times Literary Supplement*, no less, praised Stevenson-Hamilton's achievement in creating a new profession and for being at the same time a 'first-class scientific naturalist, an accurate observer and a thoroughly sympathetic animal lover'.[91] Two years later, in 1914, Stevenson-Hamilton ventured into the scientific literature with an article on the colouration of the wild dog *Lycaon pictus*,

---

[89]J. Carruthers, *Wildlife and Warfare: The Life of James Stevenson-Hamilton* (Pietermaritzburg: University of Natal Press, 2001).

[90]Hornaday to Stevenson-Hamilton, 22 August 1912, in Stevenson-Hamilton family archives, Fairholm, Larkhall, Scotland. See also W.T. Hornaday, *Wild Life Conservation in Theory and Practice: Lectures Delivered before the Forest School of Yale University* (New Haven, CT: Yale University Press, 1914); S. Bechtel, *Mr Hornaday's War: How a Peculiar Victorian Zookeeper Waged a Lonely Crusade for Wildlife that Changed the World* (Boston: Beacon Press, 2012); and G. Dehler, *The Most Defiant Devil: William Temple Hornaday and his Controversial Crusade to save American Wildlife* (Charlottesville, VA: University of Virginia Press, 2013).

[91]*Times Literary Supplement*, 2 May 1912. See also Hornaday, *Wild Life Conservation in Theory and Practice*.

published in the *Proceedings of the Zoological Society of London* (currently named the *Journal of Zoology*).[92]

Wildlife and Game Preservation

Stevenson-Hamilton's deliberate use of the phrase 'life economy' in *Animal Life* suggests he was aware, even if inexactly, that there was a developing interest in 'ecology' and 'ethology' as respectable new branches of science and that studies in game reserves might contribute to them. Bramwell refers to a 'holistic biology' that first emerged at the start of the twentieth century, and the warden's writings contain traces of this inclusive line of thinking.[93] Ecology or 'life economy' had little relevance in the then dominant paradigm of formal zoology in South Africa, but the context was about to change. This may have come about because, as Ritvo argues, big game hunting – that 'quintessential activity and symbol of imperialism' – was on the wane.[94] A further South African impetus was that, as we have seen, after 1910 there was growing discussion about 'national parks' along the lines of successful models in the USA, with public access encouraged, as was not the case in game reserves. Upgrading provincial game reserves into national parks was the subject of debate and the values of 'nature' – recreational, aesthetic, and even scientific – were mooted. In January 1913, for example, the Transvaal Game Protection Association (TGPA) publicly asserted that nature should be 'studied', not just 'hunted'.[95] And in 1916, the Transvaal Provincial Council instituted a commission of inquiry to investigate whether to abolish the Transvaal game reserves. Its report concluded that national park status would open up game reserves as 'a training ground for the scientific student, whether in botany, zoology, or other directions' because here 'as nowhere better can the natural surroundings and habits of South African fauna be really studied'.[96]

---

[92]J. Stevenson-Hamilton, 'The coloration of the African hunting dog (*Lycaon pictus*)', *Proceedings of the Zoological Society of London* 27 (1914): 403–405.

[93]Bramwell, *Ecology in the 20th Century*, 39.

[94]H. Ritvo, 'Destroyers and preservers: Big game in the Victorian Empire', *History Today*, January 2002, 34.

[95]Minutes of the Transvaal Game Protection Association, 14 January 1913, Archives of the Wild Life Society of Southern Africa (now Wildlife and Environment Society of Southern Africa), Pietermaritzburg.

[96]Transvaal Province, *Report of the Game Reserves Commission* TP5-18 (Pretoria: Government Printer, 1918).

This line of thinking had been evident in Stevenson-Hamilton when he abandoned the very small Pongola Game Reserve, regarding its optimal future as a 'game nursery' for restocking other areas, an option the Transvaal government supported neither financially nor administratively. The reserve limped on under the charge of local magistrates or a single African guard, and no better use could be found for the malarious area for many years. Eventually, in 1921, the reserve was de-proclaimed and the land earmarked for white settlement, as were other parts of the country in the post-Great War era.[97] The Rustenburg Game Reserve (on the Transvaal boundary with the then Bechuanaland Protectorate between the Groot Marico and Matlabas rivers) fared no better. As we have seen in a previous chapter, it was established in 1909 on the personal initiative of Smuts. After the warden, P.J. Rickert (Riekert) (a friend of Smuts), became embroiled in border politics, poaching and gun-running at the time of the Rebellion of 1914, he was summarily dismissed and the reserve was de-proclaimed in December 1914.[98]

The members of Stevenson-Hamilton's scientific audience were, for reasons outlined above, not university zoologists. However, he received major support at that time from the more practical men who were museum curators and zookeepers, such as his New York admirer Hornaday. Natural history museums were the repositories of many of the trophies and collections of hunters and naturalists, and were keen to add to this store of knowledge. Over the years, Stevenson-Hamilton assisted Alwin Haagner (1880–1962), director of the National Zoological Gardens in Pretoria after it separated from the Transvaal Museum in 1913.[99] Haagner met Hornaday during a visit to New York in 1920 and discovered that they shared an interest in wildlife protection. In 1922, the pair published *The Vanishing Game of South Africa: A Warning and an Appeal*, with the aim not only of education but also of fund-raising. Hornaday contributed chapters on 'The extermination of South Africa's finest game: A warning from friends across the sea' and 'Wild animal extermination, past, present and future', while Haagner wrote 'Vanishing South

[97] E.J. Carruthers, 'The Pongola Game Reserve: An eco-political study', *Koedoe* 28 (1995): 1–16.
[98] Carruthers, *Game Protection in the Transvaal*, 152–154.
[99] For many years there was even a contract between the Sabi and Singwitsi Game Reserves and the Transvaal Museum for the supply of live animals for the zoological gardens in Pretoria. See R. Bigalke, *The National Zoological Gardens of South Africa* (n.p.: Central News Agency, 1954).

African game and its need for protection'. Their main argument for protection was ethical rather than scientific: it was fundamentally 'wrong' for humans to exterminate whole species and populations of wild animals. They gave examples of extinct animals, such as bison *Bison bison*, quagga *Equus quagga quagga* and blaauwbok *Hippotragus leucophaeus*, and warned that the most endangered list of 'vanishing game' at the time included white rhinoceros *Ceratotherium simum*, bontebok *Damaliscus pygargus dorcas*, Cape mountain zebra *Equus zebra zebra*, roan antelope *Hippotragus equinus*, nyala *Tragelaphus angasii*, black rhinoceros *Diceros bicornis*, eland *Tragelaphus oryx*, grey rhebok *Pelea capreolus*, grysbok *Raphicerus melanotis*, southern oribi *Ourebia ourebi*, sable antelope *Hippotragus niger* and kudu *Tragelaphus strepsiceros*.[100]

Notwithstanding his lack of formal biological education, Haagner – who was awarded an honorary doctorate by the University of Pittsburgh in 1922 – was an intelligent man, competent ornithologist and a prolific writer and campaigner for wildlife protection. In 1916, he published two articles in the *South African Journal of Science*, 'Game and bird protection in South Africa: A short comparison with some other countries' and 'On the variability in the nature or temperament of wild animals in captivity, with special reference to South African species'. In 1920 his book, *South African Mammals: A Short Manual for the Use of Field Naturalists, Sportsmen and Travellers*, was published in London and Cape Town.[101]

Another of Stevenson-Hamilton's staunch allies in the museum community was Ernest Warren, director of the Natal Museum in Pietermaritzburg from 1903 to 1935. Warren, who had helped establish the NNP, supported wildlife protection by arguing that national parks and game reserves were places where living representative collections of South African fauna could survive. He asserted that this approach was analogous to the museum collections of dead animals, of which he had

---

[100]W.T. Hornaday and A.K. Haagner, *The Vanishing Game of South Africa: A Warning and an Appeal* (New York, NY and Pretoria: Permanent Wild Life Protection Fund, 1922).

[101]A.K. Haagner, 'Game and bird protection in South Africa: A short comparison with some other countries', *South African Journal of Science* 12, no. 11 (1916): 519–529; A. Haagner, 'On the variability in the nature or temperament of wild animals in captivity, with special reference to South African species', *South African Journal of Science* 12 (1916): 612–618; A. Haagner, 'The conservation of wild life in South Africa', *South African Journal of Industries*, 1925; A. Haagner, *South African Mammals: A Short Manual for the Use of Field Naturalists, Sportsmen and Travellers* (London: Witherby: Cape Town: Maskew Miller, 1920).

particularly fine and well-displayed examples in the well-stocked mammal hall he had developed in 1911.[102]

Stevenson-Hamilton was a meticulous record-keeper, including rainfall and temperature, and his wildlife sightings are supported by observational data. He also kept a detailed daily journal. His regular administrative reports, his correspondence and a large number of photographs – as well as his library of books and papers – can be found in the SANParks archives at Skukuza and in the possession of his descendants in his homes in Scotland and Mpumalanga.[103] His guiding philosophy until the end of his life was 'it is best that a man pick up his biological knowledge direct from the face of nature, unhampered by previous prejudices and preconceived notions'.[104] Among those he interviewed were many Africans who lived in the game reserves in those early days, and in 1929 his regional study of humans and wildlife entitled *The Low-Veld: Its Wild Life and Its People* appeared. It was an unusual book for its time and was based on the notes he had amassed.[105] Unmarried until he was well into his 60s, he had little company for the more than two decades he managed Sabi and Singwitsi Game Reserves. Given the poor communication links with that area of the country, he remained in contact with his many connections by correspondence. He generally spent his long leaves in Britain and in maintaining his networks there.

Stevenson-Hamilton's connection with the SPFE was strong and he contributed regularly to its journal. Clearly this international organisation and its journal provided him with his main professional audience and through both he was able to find validation for himself and his views. The society's *Journal* makes for interesting reading. Every issue advocates game protection and is replete with personal reminiscences and anecdotes, minutiae about hunting regulations, news from game reserves throughout the British Empire, articles on extinct and endangered species and updates on the state of wildlife in many parts of the world, very often based on excerpts from wardens' reports, including those from KNP. Stevenson-Hamilton was a very active member of the

---

[102]S. Brooks, 'Save the Game: Conservationist discourse in early twentieth-century Natal' (paper presented to the South African Economic History Society conference, Pietermaritzburg, July 1992), explains that Warren hoped that national parks would extend and expand in order to protect all the mammal species in the country.

[103]Carruthers, *Wildlife and Warfare*.

[104]Carruthers, *Kruger National Park*, 113.

[105]*The Low-Veld: Its Wild Life and Its People* (London: Cassell, 1929).

Society. His class background allowed him to move easily in a community that has been described as 'high Tory'.[106] Whenever in London, he attended the Society's dinners and lectures, some of which he delivered himself, including, in 1929, a set of lantern slides of the KNP. He knew the Society's leaders well, corresponded and dined with people like Buxton, and visited the homes of famous hunters. He counted among his peers many eminent colonial administrators and sport-hunters such as Alfred Sharpe, F.C.E. Maugham, Robert Coryndon, Chauncey Stigand, F.C. Selous, J.G. Millais and Alfred Pease. He also had a close association with Walter Rothschild and his famous personal museum at Tring, and donated his most interesting finds to the Natural History Museum in London, although he also supported the Transvaal Museum and the South African Museum in Cape Town, where Leonard Gill was a particular friend.

The influence of Stevenson-Hamilton on wildlife protection was transnational. From his solitude in the Lowveld he was in regular communication with British colleagues. When the First World War broke out, Stevenson-Hamilton turned down a military post in South Africa in favour of rejoining his regiment in Britain. His varied war experience included his participation in the Gallipoli campaign in 1915 and his subsequent assignment to the Mediterranean Expeditionary Force's headquarters in Egypt. He disliked this posting so much that he applied for, and was granted, a wartime secondment to the civil administration of southern Sudan.[107] There he remained from 1917 to 1919, visiting again in 1921. This was, for him, an extremely agreeable assignment. In addition to administering a fascinating part of Africa, with its complex community relationships and conflicts, he immersed himself in game protection in what was then part of the Anglo-Egyptian Sudan. In 1919, he published an article about some of the small mammals he encountered in the Bahr-el-Gebel in the *Proceedings of the Zoological Society of London* and an illustrated article in *The Geographical Journal* about the landscape, wildlife and people of the region. However, he also busied himself with game protection in the southern Sudan which, owing to its colonial status, he found to be very different from South Africa. As well as proposing the establishment of several game reserves in the region, at

---

[106]P. Merrington, 'Heritage, pageantry and archivism: Creed systems and tropes of public history in imperial South Africa, *c.*1910', *Kronos: Journal of Cape History* 25 (1998): 129–151.

[107]Carruthers, *Wildlife and Warfare*, chapter 8.

the invitation of the colonial government he spent time in Khartoum in 1921 as the Superintendent, Game Preservation Department, drawing up robust legislation for wildlife protection.[108] Moreover, once the KNP had been founded he was in touch with what was then called 'propaganda' about the national park not only with the SPFE, but also with the Canadian parks publicity, the Naturschutzpark Verein in Germany, the Nederlandsch Commissie voor Internationale Natuurbescherming, the California Academy of Sciences and the National Parks Association of the USA.

Stevenson-Hamilton's world was thus much wider than South Africa. His connections were international and his influence felt throughout game protection circles in the British Empire. He was highly thought of by the SPFE (today called Fauna and Flora International), whose members often approached him for his opinions. In 1940, he was the first to receive the Society's newly created medal. So close were his ties with the Zoological Society of London that he was offered the internationally prestigious post of secretary in the 1920s. Stevenson-Hamilton accepted the offer on an honorary, provisional basis and worked at the Society's offices in London while on long leave from South Africa. Very soon he discovered he intensely disliked claustrophobic confinement in the polluted, crowded, damp and grey London of the time, and working at a desk to arrange lectures and wireless talks and deal with membership and internal political issues. He returned to South Africa and to an outdoor life doing that for which he was best suited – wildlife management.

Founding the Kruger National Park

The transformation of Sabi and Singwitsi Game Reserves, together with the intervening state and private land, into a national park was precipitated by the rapacity of Transvaal farmers, who were lobbying provincial politicians to abolish the reserves and release the land for grazing. With the modernisation of the South African economy after 1910 and improvements in transport and disease control, voters were increasingly reluctant to assume financial responsibility for wildlife reserves that disallowed public access and that effectively prevented the economic development of some 19 000 km^2 of the Transvaal.

---

[108]J. Carruthers, 'Lessons from South Africa: War and wildlife protection in the southern Sudan, 1917–1921', *Environment and History* 3, no. 3 (1997): 299–322.

From the time that Het Volk won the Transvaal colony's elections in 1907, thereby signifying the resurgence of the political power of Afrikaner settler farmers and the waning of British colonial support for game protection, Stevenson-Hamilton, along with others, began to fear that the day of the game reserve was numbered. They started to campaign fairly vigorously for turning these reserves into a national park by removing them from provincial control and placing them under the central government. The term 'national park' thus began to gain wider currency. By about 1914, the large herds of game that had been almost exterminated by the late nineteenth century had rebounded in the reserves and there was a growing sense that the public would probably welcome the chance to view and appreciate wildlife in its natural setting. More leisure time and the expansion of rail and road systems – plus some economic development in the Lowveld in the form of fruit and sugar farming – had made such a transformation feasible. Various politicians, particularly Smuts, appeared to favour a national park, but opposition by the departments of Lands, Native Affairs and Mining, together with the challenges of expropriating the private land (mostly owned by mining companies) administered by Stevenson-Hamilton delayed the transformation for many years. Thus, the path to the assumption of national government control was long and tortuous, and was made more so when Smuts' South African Party ministry fell to a coalition of Hertzog's National Party and Creswell's Labour Party in 1924.

The formal steps in converting the game reserves into a national park began in 1916 with the appointment of a fact-finding commission by the Transvaal government to investigate and report back on the matter of abolition. Thus, while the First World War raged and Stevenson-Hamilton was absent on war service, seven Transvaal Provincial Council members met in the Sabi Game Reserve – time prevented their venturing further afield. So impressed was the group with the experience of viewing the scenery and fauna at first hand, that it recommended transformation from the 'uselessness of having these superb reserves merely for the preservation of the fauna' into 'a great national park where the natural and prehistoric conditions of our country can be preserved for all time'. The commissioners' report identified what they considered to be the four main attributes of a South African national park. First, that it comprise only land belonging to the state (not private land); second, that its permanence be safeguarded by act of parliament; third, that it provide recreational visitors with a glimpse of what the South African landscape was like before the 'advance of civilisation'; and fourth, that it should be a training ground for scientific research generally and biological studies in particular.[109] In the event, only the first three suggestions were taken forward: scientific training and research were not mentioned in the legislation or discussed in parliament. Rather, the latter discussions emphasised the economic development of the Lowveld through local and international tourism.

In 1926, parliament in Cape Town unanimously passed the National Parks Act 56 of 1926, despite difficulties with the word 'park', which has no appropriate Afrikaans equivalent, and reservations among wildlife lovers (Stevenson-Hamilton included) about the applicability of the designation 'national park' to the KNP, even though they recognised its value as a promotional tool. For many, it connoted recreation and pleasure grounds designed for people, rather than 'sanctuaries' in which natural processes could continue free from human interference. In any event, the Act passed and made provision for other national parks to be created by separate legislation. It also inaugurated a centralised management parastatal under a board of trustees. The law did not define national park, but merely delineated the management objectives the 'nation' wished to pursue in such parks. In 1926 these were 'the propagation, protection and preservation therein of wild animal life, wild vegetation and objects of geological, historical or other scientific interest for the benefit, advantage and enjoyment of the inhabitants of the Union' (Section 1). Only in 1962 was the wording amended to include the mandate to 'study' and by 1976 so abundant had many species become that 'propagation' was omitted.

The KNP remains the country's premier national park and enjoys an unequalled international reputation. No other South African park has yet emerged to rival it in terms of visitor numbers or of scientific research. However, it did not long remain the sole national park. The statutory injunction to propagate, protect and preserve certain rare wild animal species inspired the creation during the 1930s of small national parks for this specific purpose.

As the plans to convert the Transvaal's game reserves into a national park neared finality, Haagner, the director of the National Zoological Gardens, described the 'scientific' purpose of national parks as the prevention of species extinction.[110] Perhaps this comment was an attempt to conciliate the state veterinary scientists, whose opposition to national parks was fierce. While ecological botanists could see merit in natural

[109]Transvaal Province, *Report of the Game Reserves Commission*, TP5-18 (Pretoria: Government Printer, 1918).

[110]Haagner, 'The conservation of wild life', 763–765.

areas as study sites, and while university zoologists were aloof from the study of wild animals *in situ*, the veterinarians were deeply involved and totally antagonistic to anything that might compromise the health of domestic stock and thus threaten the country's economy. Scientists in the Department of Agriculture's veterinary division believed that diseases common to wildlife and livestock were spread by free-ranging wildlife. Thus the retention of any large area of undisturbed nature that harboured wildlife and its diseases was to be resisted.[111] In short, conservation of indigenous megafauna and agricultural prosperity were thought to be inimical and it was this conflict that most deeply directed the way in which science in South Africa's national parks first developed.

In this struggle, the vets had 'science' on their side. Just as the Division of Botany had a strong champion in Pole Evans, its veterinary counterpart was led by the extremely talented Swiss-trained Arnold (later Sir Arnold) Theiler, who had joined the Transvaal civil service before the South African War. When the Veterinary Services of the Union of South Africa came into being, Theiler was appointed the first director and he came with a formidable reputation for veterinary research that had either beaten or might beat the many stock diseases endemic in South Africa. Because of the country's peculiar veterinary challenges, Theiler promoted the local training of veterinarians, a function his centre at Onderstepoort fulfilled from 1908. After 1919, Transvaal University College in Pretoria established a faculty of veterinary science, headed by Theiler, and from 1927 veterinary research and veterinary field services were combined into a very powerful arm of government.[112] In her work, Karen Brown has emphasised the high international profile that South African veterinary science enjoyed and its critical role in the development of South Africa's livestock economy, which was eclipsed only by mining in terms of exports, and was vital to meeting the country's internal meat and dairy requirements.[113]

Only one veterinarian in state service was bold enough to come out in print in favour of game preservation during a period of rampant killing because of 'the menace' of tsetse fly and nagana (trypanosomiasis) in Zululand. This was Herbert H. Curson. Born and educated in Natal at a public school, unusually for South African state veterinarians at the time

[111]Carruthers, *Game Protection in the Transvaal, passim*.

[112]T. Gutsche, *There was a Man: The Life and Times of Sir Arnold Theiler KGMG of Onderstepoort* (Cape Town: Timmins, 1979).

[113]K. Brown, 'Tropical medicine and animal diseases: Onderstepoort and the development of veterinary science in South Africa 1908–1950', *Journal of Southern African Studies* 31, no. 3 (2005): 513–529.

he had been educated at the Royal College of Veterinary Surgeons in London as well as in Germany.[114] Curson's co-author of 'Preservation of game in South Africa', which appeared in the *South African Journal of Science* in 1924, was J.M. Hugo, employed in the provincial Administrator's office in Cape Town. They acknowledged the intrinsic worth of protecting wildlife, despite the threat to farmers of diseases and the trampling of crops.[115]

Notwithstanding its influence on government, its funding and the respect it enjoyed, for a number of reasons the veterinary community had insufficient political clout to block the national park initiative altogether. Events of the 1920s highlight how the conflicts of interest between game protectionists and those interested in natural history and those who were trained 'scientists' played out in practice. Zululand's game reserves were situated in an area of endemic nagana (bovine trypanosomiasis), and white settlers and veterinary scientists at the time believed that the disease was harboured and spread by wild animals. The result was the wholesale slaughter of such animals in the region as a precautionary measure.[116] In just two years (1929–1931), at the very time when South Africans were congratulating themselves on their new national park in the Transvaal and considerable numbers of visitors were flocking there to enjoy themselves and admire the wild animals, more than 35 000 such creatures (particularly wildebeest *Connochaetes taurinus*) were destroyed in Natal at a cost to the taxpayer of £25 000, a not inconsiderable sum in those days, far exceeding government financial support for its national park. Warren, the Natal Museum director, feared that the wildlife in the province would never recover from the onslaught – which Dr P.R. Viljoen, acting director of the

---

[114]In 1936, Curson was transferred from the Department of Agriculture to the Department of Native Affairs as deputy-director of Native Agriculture.

[115]H.H. Curson and J.M. Hugo, 'Preservation of game in South Africa', *South African Journal of Science* 21 (1924): 400–424.

[116]See J. Vincent, 'The history of Umfolozi Game Reserve, Zululand, as it relates to management', *Lammergeyer* 11 (1970): 7–49; A.E. Cubbin, 'An outline of game legislation in Natal, 1866–1912 (i.e. until the promulgation of the Mkhuze Game Reserve)', *Journal of Natal and Zulu History* 14 (1992): 37–47; B.H. Dicke, 'The tsetse fly's influence on South African history', *South African Journal of Science* 29 (1932): 792–796; C. Fuller, *Tsetse in the Transvaal and Surrounding Territories: An Historical Overview.* Entomological Memoir No. 1 (Pretoria: Division of Entomology, Department of Agriculture, 1923); K. Brown, 'From Ubombo to Mkhuzi: Disease, ecology and the control of bovine trypanosomosis (Nagana) in KwaZulu-Natal', paper presented at Livestock and Disease Conference, Oxford, June 2005; K. Brown, 'Tropical medicine and animal diseases: Onderstepoort and the development of veterinary science in South Africa 1908–1950', *Journal of Southern African Studies* 31(2005): 513–529.

Division of Veterinary Services, described approvingly as 'complete extermination'.[117] Warren also feared the then rare square-lipped (white) rhinoceros *Ceratotherium simum* might well become extinct in the process.[118]
His own belief was that the nagana scare was just a smokescreen for whites
to hunt legally,[119] and he attempted to save the Natal game reserves by
advocating that they become national parks.[120] This slaughter was of great
concern to the SPFE, who met with the South African high commissioner in London, but to no avail, given the Colonial Office's disinclina-
tion to become involved. Apparently, General Jan C.G. Kemp, a staunch
Afrikaner nationalist and minister of agriculture under J.B.M. Hertzog after
1924, had decided that the 'game must go' and, in the name of the central
government, had overruled the Natal Provincial Council on the matter.[121]

South Africa's wildlife populations were not the only ones in the subcontinent to be threatened with extinction by veterinarians: indeed, this
was general practice. As Graham Child relates, in Rhodesia – as in Natal –
tsetse fly (which had not recurred in the eastern Transvaal Lowveld after
the rinderpest epizootic of 1896) represented the scientific interface
between wildlife and national scientists because no veterinarian of the
time believed domestic and wild animals could coexist. When the votes
of settler farmers aligned with the scientific pursuits of the veterinarians,
the continued existence of free-ranging wildlife under any circumstances
seemed extremely tenuous.[122]

[117]R. Bigalke and J. Skinner, 'The Zoological Survey: An historical perspective',
Transactions of the Royal Society of South Africa, 57 (2002): 38.

[118]For details of Warren's role in game conservation in Natal, see S. Brooks, 'Save the
Game: Conservationist discourse in early twentieth-century Natal', paper presented to
the South African Economic History Society conference, Pietermaritzburg, July 1992.

[119]Brooks, 'Save the Game', 9.

[120]Stevenson-Hamilton to Wilson, Secretary Wild Life Society, 29 May 1929 in Stevenson-
Hamilton family archives, Fairholm, Larkhall, Scotland.

[121]1925 part 5. *Journal of the Society for the Preservation of the Fauna of the Empire.* Discussion
on Zululand report by Austen. Kemp was Minister of Agriculture from 1924 to 1934.
An extremely conservative man who had fought in the Anglo-Boer War and who
had taken part in the 1914 Rebellion, Kemp was devoted to the ideal of an Afrikaner
republic, he had voted against enfranchising women and had advocated South Africa's
neutrality during the Second World War.

[122]See G. Child, 'Growth of modern nature conservation in South Africa', in *Parks in
Transition: Biodiversity, Rural Development and the Bottom Line*, ed. B. Child (London:
Earthscan, 2004), 7–27.

For obvious reasons – and often with good cause, as with the botched handling of the foot-and-mouth outbreak in the 1930s[123] – Stevenson-Hamilton distrusted the veterinary fraternity profoundly. He saw them and their science – communicated through a number of reputable professional journals – as a direct threat to the survival of wildlife in the Transvaal game reserves. Zoologists and/or biologists were one thing in his view, veterinarians quite another.[124]

National Parks Board Organisation

The way in which the national park fitted into the South African institutional structure was critical to its growth and development in the years to come. Locally and internationally, there was as yet no generally accepted template for this task. While the KNP's foundation might be hailed as a small victory for the wildlife preservationists, the government had not provided it with a strong administrative or organisational structure. Unlike the Canadian and US national parks, which had organisational integrity and clear lines of promotion within the Department of the Interior in 1911 and 1916, respectively,[125] with salary scales and other characteristics embedded in the civil service, the South African government preferred to establish a Board of Trustees (as it had done with the Kirstenbosch Botanical Garden in Cape Town) to oversee the national park within the overall remit of the Minister of the Department of Lands. The advantage of this parastatal model was that the board could raise its own funding and keep the profits within the organisation without placing additional strains on the public purse or requiring the diversion of funds from elsewhere, although grants could be, and were, made by the treasury from time to time. One disadvantage was that the position of trustee was seen as a political

---

[123]See J. Stevenson-Hamilton, *South African Eden: The Kruger National Park* (Cape Town: Struik, 1995), 286–290, 302–303.

[124]Brown, 'Tropical medicine and animal diseases', 513–529. See also J.F.V. Phillips, 'The application of ecological research methods to the tsetse (*Glossina* spp.) problem in Tanganyika Territory: A preliminary account', *Ecology* 11, no. 4 (1930): 713–733; C.H.T. Townsend, 'The tsetse problem', *South African Journal of Natural History* 4, no. 1 (1923): 36–45; B.C. Jansen, 'The growth of veterinary research in South Africa', in *A History of Scientific Endeavour in South Africa*, ed. A.C. Brown (Cape Town: Royal Society of South Africa, 1977), 185–187.

[125]C.E. Campbell, 'Governing a kingdom: Parks Canada, 1911–2011', in *A Century of Parks Canada, 1911–2011*, ed. C.E. Campbell (Calgary: University of Calgary Press, 2011), 2, 4. By 1926 Canada had 15 national parks.

Figure 3.3. The National Parks Board of Trustees, 1926.
From R.J. Labuschagne, comp., *60 Years Kruger Park* (1958), p. 41. Courtesy of SANParks.

sinecure, to the detriment of the emergence of a professional or trained leadership. The first board comprised ten members, of whom only Alwin Haagner could claim 'scientific' biological or zoological competence.[126]

Over the years, board members did not attend meetings, made uninformed suggestions for wildlife importations and species extermination and did not even devise an organogram for the nascent structure they oversaw. Moreover, policy was often erratic, lines of organisational responsibility were unclear and administration was haphazard. This later led to difficulties and politicised the national parks. A third weakness was that national parks were separated from the powerful divisions of botany and veterinary science in the Department of Agriculture, making cooperation difficult, discouraging scientific collaboration and information-sharing and even encouraging animosity and distrust, particularly, as we have seen, with the veterinarians.[127]

[126]The others were W.J.C. Brebner, D. Reitz, A. Bailey, R.A. Hockly, W.A. Campbell, G.S. Preller, A.E. Charter, O. Pirow and H.B. Papenfus.
[127]See Carruthers, *Kruger National Park.*

The absence of scientific direction from above – there was no Biological Survey such as existed in the USA – meant that Stevenson-Hamilton had little formal support. During the 1920s, however, two important articles about wildlife protection appeared in the scientific literature. One, in 1929, was by Herbert Lang (1879–1957), a German taxidermist, first employed at the natural history museum at the University of Zurich and later, after emigrating to the USA in 1903, a curator at the American Museum of Natural History and an active member of the American Society of Mammalogists founded in 1919.[128] He visited parts of Africa on numerous occasions in charge of collecting expeditions for the museum and made a name for himself (with Carl Akeley, also a taxidermist) in connection with the establishment of the Albert National Park in 1925 in the Belgian Congo. In the mid-1920s, he apparently settled in South Africa and worked in the Transvaal Museum.[129] In keeping with natural history museums' interest in wildlife preservation, Lang was invited to contribute a chapter on 'Game reserves and wild life protection' to the volume produced by the SAAAS for its joint meeting in South Africa in 1929 with its British counterpart. He was also a co-author with Austin Roberts and Georges van Son (both of the Transvaal Museum) and Frederick FitzSimons (Port Elizabeth Museum), of the mammals chapter in the same book.[130]

International Developments

This local history was taking place against the backdrop of important international developments regarding national park administration and organisation. These had no effect on the trajectory of nature and wildlife protection within South Africa between 1910 and 1930, but they were to become extremely important after the Second World War. Kupper has argued that in the interwar years the twin issues of natural beauty and nature-as-science intersected with the vision of the League of Nations. An international committee was established and the national park idea began its global diffusion, despite differences in strategy and intention

[128]*Journal of Mammalogy* 7, no. 2 (1926): 72.
[129]U. de V. Pienaar, *A Cameo from the Past* (Pretoria: Protea Book House, 2012), 699.
[130]In H.J. Crocker and J. McCrae, eds, *South Africa and Science: A Handbook Prepared under the Auspices of the South African Association for the Advancement of Science for the Meeting of the British Association in Capetown [sic] and Johannesburg, South Africa, 1929* (Johannesburg: South African Association for the Advancement of Science, 1929), 241–250.

Figure 3.4. Vermin culling: lion skulls, 1924.
Courtesy of SANParks.

between the USA and Europe. The notion of national parks as a 'group' or 'community' – an international movement – now took root.

So too did the idea that national parks could be educational, and an educational department was founded within the National Parks Service in the USA. However, educational outreach was not the same as 'science' or scientific or zoological research, and the only 'science' undertaken in US national parks was the regular extermination of vermin and predator species.[131] Even the Audubon Society was determined to destroy all hawks because they preyed on more 'attractive' songbirds. The only protests to save 'varmints' came from a handful of academic zoologists – Charles Adams was one – who took issue with the Biological Survey on this matter on the grounds that the slaughter was unnecessary, rather than for environmental reasons. As Dunlap explains, animals in the USA continued to be divided into 'good' and 'bad' species,[132] and this at a time (1920) when Stevenson-Hamilton was writing in his journal at Skukuza after years of predator control in Sabi and Singwitsi, 'now I think the nearer to nature the better in a reserve, so when I see a lioness with her children, I feel like saying "good luck to you"'.[133]

[131]Kupper, 'Science and the national parks', 58–81.
[132]T.R. Dunlap, 'Wildlife, science and the national parks, 1920–1940', *Pacific Historical Review* 59, no. 2 (1990): 187–202.
[133]Carruthers, *Game Protection in the Transvaal*, 176.

4 · An Emerging Science 1930 to 1960

While the establishment of the Kruger National Park (KNP) was greeted with general public favour and the Board of Trustees began to meet, no botanists, veterinarians or zoologists were involved in determining how best the mandate for 'propagation, protection and preservation' might align with the 'benefit, advantage and enjoyment' that was promised the citizens of the Union. Responsibility for this major omission lay with government. No provision existed in the Act for any management structure or for any expert or scientific representation on the board. None of the board members appointed had any professional qualification for their positions. This meant that in the newly established KNP, Stevenson-Hamilton was generally free to pursue his one-person wildlife management strategies with the help of his small team of white rangers and black staff. Two developments, however, drastically changed his responsibilities.

One was the advent of tourism, which created a tension between the very different mandates of simultaneously providing a game sanctuary and a recreational facility in the same space. Stevenson-Hamilton thought of himself professionally as a game warden. The national park publicist and artist Stratford Caldecott wrote privately to Stevenson-Hamilton shortly after the KNP was established in 1926: 'I understand . . . you have no stomach to see the place full of rubberneck waggons and tourists, but it was vulgarization or abolition, I suppose, and it was at that price only that the animals could be saved.'[1] However, P.G.W. (Piet) Grobler, Minister of Lands from 1924 to 1933 and thus the minister with overall responsibility for national parks, thought quite differently. In persuading parliament to adopt the National Parks Act, Grobler argued that it would be 'a first-class holiday resort',[2] visited by locals and an envisaged 10 000 American visitors annually, who would bring in more than £1 million, 'a sum that

---

[1] J. Carruthers, *The Kruger National Park: A Social and Political History* (Pietermaritzburg: University of Natal Press, 1995), 64.
[2] Union of South Africa, *Debates of the House of Assembly*, 31 May 1926, col. 4371.

should appeal to all South Africans'.[3] As the government grant for the National Parks Board (NPB) was not large, Grobler also hoped the new KNP would not be a financial burden on the state.

The income from tourists was also necessary in order to serve their needs. At that time there was no visitor accommodation in the park, no entry gates, no administrative process, no road or other tourist infra-structure and initially no additional staff to take care of these matters. The access roads from major towns such as Johannesburg, Pretoria or Pietersburg were themselves rudimentary and, in any event, few South Africans owned motor vehicles.[4] Owing to disease (particularly malaria) and the summer heat – let alone staff constraints – the park could not be kept open throughout the year. Parts of the southern portion around what became known as 'Skukuza', Stevenson-Hamilton's African nickname (formerly Sabi Bridge), and Pretoriuskop were opened from 15 May to 14 November, although Pretoriuskop was later opened for day visitors throughout the year. However, much of the former private land to the north together with the old Singwitsi Game Reserve remained closed to tourists for many years.

The warden and his rangers were hard-pressed to cope with this new challenge, which diverted them from their regular duties. The workforce was not large, consisting only of prison labour (mostly Mozambicans who illegally entered South Africa to work on the mines and who served out their two-week sentences incarcerated in moveable lockups and working on the KNP roads) and Africans who had lived for many years within what was now the KNP and who, as tenants on state land, paid rent in labour and in money.[5] Moreover, the park had to be promoted to visitors. Major advertising campaigns were undertaken by South African Railways, which began the 'Round in Nine', a nine-day railway tour around the country that included the KNP, using the recently completed Selati line. This venture proved very popular, particularly in providing exciting visitor experiences (the train stopped overnight in the park) and lion viewings.[6]

[3] J. Carruthers, *Game Protection in the Transvaal 1846 to 1926* (Pretoria: Archives Yearbook for South African History, 1995), 170–175.

[4] E. Prance, *Three Weeks in Wonderland: The Kruger National Park* (Cape Town: Juta, n.d.).

[5] J. Carruthers, '"Police boys and poachers": Africans, wildlife protection and national parks, the Transvaal 1902 to 1950', *Koedoe* 36 (1993): 11–22.

[6] J. Carruthers, '"Full of rubberneck waggons and tourists": The development of tourism in South Africa's national parks', in *Tourism and National Parks: International Perspectives on Development, Histories and Change*, eds W. Frost and C.M. Hall (London: Routledge, 2009), 238–256.

The other change affecting Stevenson-Hamilton was the overall management structure. Previously largely independent of the Transvaal provincial authorities, he now had to report to a new level of central management. The board was the body that employed staff and was legally responsible for 'the control and management of the parks', a mandate that came without further detail.[7] 'Control and management' was henceforward dictated from above by a group appointed by the Minister of Lands. For the rest of his career, which lasted until 1946, Stevenson-Hamilton experienced many difficulties with these people – personal, political and scientific. Given that the majority of board members were politicians loyal to the National Party coalition government (Hertzog's National Party had come to power with the assistance of F.H.P. Creswell's South African Labour Party in 1924 – the so-called 'Pact' government), the KNP warden had little respect for their opinions or their advice on wildlife management. Generally, he regarded them as ignorant and ill-informed. For example, as late as 1936 board member Joseph Ludorf – later to be chairman – proposed that springbok *Antidorcas marsupialis* and blesbok *Damaliscus pygargus phillipsi*, both species with a southern distribution, be introduced into the KNP.[8] The warden also considered them to be unnecessarily interfering in matters he considered to be his responsibility at the expense of providing direction on future vision and principle.[9] In their defence, there was, of course, no precedent for this kind of management and no civil service rules to follow. There were ten board members: the provincial Administrators (or their designates); one representative of the newly established Wild Life Protection Society (a consortium of the older game protection societies); and the remainder ministerial appointees. The secretary was to be a civil servant from the Department of Lands.

Despite the depth of scientific knowledge and research management within the government Departments of Agriculture and Forestry and the growing stature of South Africa's universities, the board did not provide any scientific or professional support for the KNP and its warden. Consequently, there was no one to whom Stevenson-Hamilton could relate professionally, or with whom he could knowledgeably discuss his 'science'. The appointment to the first board of Alwin Haagner, director

---

[7] Act 56 of 1926 paragraph 1; paragraph 5.
[8] U. de V. Pienaar, *A Cameo from the Past* (Pretoria: Protea Boekhuis, 2012), 698.
[9] See J. Carruthers, *Wildlife and Warfare: The Life of James Stevenson-Hamilton* (Pietermaritzburg: University of Natal Press, 1995), *passim*.

of the Transvaal Museum, seemed promising, but in 1926 Haagner suddenly resigned from the museum under a cloud and left South Africa. Further uncertainty related to what kind of knowledge the game reserve was expected to produce in those years – if any. Certainly 'pure science' was unnecessary, and international best practice and leadership in the applied science of 'game protection/preservation' or 'wild life protection/preservation' was to be found in the Society for the Preservation of the Fauna of the Empire (SPFE). Without other professional outlets, Stevenson-Hamilton continued to publish prolifically in its *Journal*. This was a professionally produced periodical, serious in tone, and every issue included news from other protected areas (Australia, Canada, India, etc.), observations and ideas and experimental views about a developing science that was closer to mammalogy than to zoology per se. The *Journal* kept the members of the international community in touch with each other and was a forum for sharing ideas and experiences. In addition, several game protectionists in the English-speaking world published in the *Journal of Mammalogy*, which began publication in 1919 under the auspices of the American Society of Mammalogists. Like the *Journal for the Preservation of the Wild Fauna of the Empire*, it included material on animal behaviour as well as other aspects of mammalian interest.

Promotional and educational material was also important – as it remains today – and Stevenson-Hamilton also wrote for this genre. His was an extraordinarily busy pen. Involved in all aspects of the park's business, in his official reports and private papers he reveals how much he was preoccupied with tourism and in responding to the increasing administrative demands by the board. The latter had no permanent offices during this period and funding was always tight. Additional staff or new divisions within the KNP were unthinkable, and the low calibre and salaries of most of the staff – whites and African – is an indication of how tight-fisted government was, especially during the long years of the Depression. So dire were the Depression's consequences for South Africa that the ruling and opposition parties were forced into a 'Fusion' government in order to handle the situation, with most of Hertzog's National Party and Smuts' South African Party merging to form the United Party in 1934, but with Hertzog remaining prime minister.

The NPB met quarterly. Except when the meeting was held in a national park once a year, few board members regularly attended or even took an active interest in the board's business. Meetings soon degenerated into talk-shops during which members aired their beliefs, prejudices and rural reminiscences. Moreover, board members were often busy in their chosen occupations and board membership was not a priority for them. The first chairman, W.J.C. (Jack) Brebner (1866–1945), may serve as an example. Born and raised in the Orange Free State, Brebner studied law and accountancy at Grey College in Bloemfontein, afterwards joining the civil service and rising through the ranks. During the South African War, he had become very friendly with Hertzog, prime minister when the NPB was founded. Brebner was interested in a political career and became a member of the Orange River Colony's Legislative Council in 1907. He joined Hertzog's National Party when it was established (indeed, helped draft its constitution) and soon afterwards became leader of the Nationalist Party in the senate, the upper chamber in parliament. When Hertzog favoured South African neutrality in the Second World War, Brebner joined Hertzog's breakaway group. In his biography there is no evidence of knowledge of wild animals or even a particular interest in them.[10] As with the majority of the board, his was a political appointment and involved very little responsibility.

Each new national park was to be brought into being by a separate act of parliament. There was no provision for joint management or even for the sharing of knowledge among these parks. In the 1930s, a number of new national parks were established. This was not done in accordance with a predetermined plan, or with landscapes or ecological importance in mind. Rather, it was in terms of the injunction 'to propagate, protect and preserve' wildlife wherever it seemed threatened in the country – and provided it would not prove too costly to do so.

New National Parks in the 1930s

South Africa's National Parks Act of 1926 did not define what a national park should be in terms of optimal size, governance or recreational access, or even explicit conservation objectives. Three very small national parks were proclaimed in the Cape in the 1930s. In terms of current criteria (i.e. protecting the ecological integrity of one or more ecosystems) they would not be worthy of national park status. Each focused on just one small relict population of a rare species. Elephants *Loxodonta africana* were the motivation for the Addo Elephant National Park in July 1931, then comprising 7735 ha. The area had witnessed a long period of government-sanctioned

[10]Human Sciences Research Council, *Dictionary of South African Biography*, vol. 3 (Pretoria: HSRC, 1977), 100–102.

elephant persecution. The extremely dense, succulent karoo vegetation of the Sundays River valley in the Eastern Cape had become the last habitat of the largest southern African herd of about 150 elephants. When a citrus irrigation scheme began in the area in the early 1920s, elephants raided the crops and destroyed water supplies. In a move reminiscent of contemporaneous events in Zululand, to protect the farmers the government stepped in and employed (at considerable expense) Major P.J. Pretorius, a professional elephant hunter, war hero and adventurer, to kill as many of the marauders as he could, all of them if possible. Despite strong protests from the directors of the Port Elizabeth Museum and the Transvaal Museum and others, within a year Pretorius had wiped out all but 16 elephants. Stevenson-Hamilton was naturally perturbed by this and brought it to the attention of the game protection community in 1922 in the *Journal of the Society for the Preservation of the Fauna of the Empire*.[11] However, in a bizarre change of heart, Pretorius began to lobby to conserve the few animals he had been unable to kill. Persuaded that this was a good idea, in 1925 the Cape provincial authorities proclaimed a game reserve, putting J.J. Millard in charge, a man whom Stevenson-Hamilton dismissed as a 'poor white nationalist who had seen an elephant once in four years'.[12] However, as the elephants lived outside the reserve (there was no water for them within it), the proclamation had no effect. Uncertain about how to proceed, the province handed the reserve over to the central government and the NPB accepted it as an addition to its portfolio. A former KNP ranger, S.H. (Harold) Trollope, was appointed warden. He had been a big game hunter before being employed in the Malelane section of Sabi Game Reserve in 1925. He had no need of formal training in any natural science in Addo because his task and that of his successor Graham Armstrong involved no research but rather the implementation of innovative trapping, luring, feeding and fencing techniques to confine the animals within the park.[13]

---

[11]J. Stevenson-Hamilton, 'Empire fauna in 1922', *Journal of the Society for the Preservation of the Fauna of the Empire* 2 (1922): 38–43.

[12]Stevenson-Hamilton to Wilson, Secretary Wild Life Society, 29 May 1929, in Stevenson-Hamilton family archives, Fairholm, Larkhall, Scotland.

[13]M.T. Hoffman, 'Major P.J. Pretorius and the decimation of the Addo elephant herd in 1919-1920: Important reassessments', *Koedoe* 36, no. 2 (1993): 23–44; A. Haagner, *South African Mammals: A Short Manual for the Use of Field Naturalists, Sportsmen and Travellers* (London: Witherby, 1920), xviii–ix, warned against the wholesale extermination of wildlife in Addo and Zululand because the 'facts' were so uncertain; P.J. Pretorius, *Jungle Man: The Autobiography of Major P.J. Pretorius C.M.G. D.S.O. and Bar* (Sydney and London: Australasian Publishing Co., 1948).

Figure 4.1. The fence constructed by Graham Armstrong to restrain the elephants in Addo Elephant National Park within the park boundary.
From R.J. Labuschagne, *The Kruger Park and Other National Parks* (n.d.), p. 137. Courtesy of SANParks.

While the decline of the Addo elephants had been deliberately brought after government bowed to pressure from commercial agriculture, the other two small national parks were established to protect rare and locally endemic subspecies whose habitat had contracted through agricultural development and whose plight concerned local landowners. In 1929, M.J. van Breda, a farmer in the Bredasdorp district of the Cape, alerted government to the rapidly diminishing population of bontebok *Damaliscus pygargus*. Moving fairly quickly, the state purchased 722 ha of the farm 'Bushy Park', known as 'Quarrie Bos', some 27 km south of Bredasdorp. On 3 July 1931 this became the Bontebok National Park and 22 bontebok were relocated there. Fencing began the same year. Jan Jantjes, a coloured man referred to as a 'nature conservator', was appointed as overseer and he was assisted in his duties by the magistrate of Bredasdorp. Despite the absence of zoological oversight or research, the bontebok thrived: in 1939 there were 123 animals, along with other small antelope and many birds. However, by 1940 the little park was regarded as overstocked and a number of animals were captured and distributed to neighbouring farmers and to the National Zoological Gardens in Pretoria.[14] Because of protection and breeding success, the land in the original national park began to deteriorate and became infested with unpalatable renosterbos *Elytropappus rhinocerotis*. NPB members W.A. Campbell (a wealthy Natal sugar-baron who owned property bordering on the KNP)[15] and Brigadier-General C.H. Blaine (then Secretary for Defence) were concerned by this, and suggested that the renosterbos be eradicated and replaced with grass species.

This was accomplished in 1954, but the park did not attract visitors, was proving expensive, and the numbers of bontebok began to decline sharply: between 1945 and 1958 the population almost halved, from 200 animals to only 104. In 1953, biologist T.G. Nel and assistant biologist A.M. Brynard from the KNP visited Bontebok and, together with private veterinarian T. Smuts, concluded that the diet was deficient in certain minerals and trace elements and that the animals were infested with parasites. Numbers were again declining, and the board began to seek additional land. Some animals were immediately moved to 'De Mond', land belonging to the Department of Defence and the Department of Forestry. Matters only worsened. The NPB had no immediate solution and throughout the 1950s the issue was kept alive through questions in parliament. But then a new location, already quite well stocked with other small antelope, was identified in Swellendam, a town not far from Bredasdorp, and was purchased by the state with the help of voluntary donations. Although this upset the Bredasdorp worthies, who took some pride in their national park, the NPB was adamant. Capture and relocation had by then become the major issue

[14]One of the recipients of these translocated animals was F.W.M. Bowker, who owned a farm near Grahamstown. Of his original seven translocations, five survived and by 1947 he had 51 and by December 1953 he had 120. The situation on other farms was similar and many more bontebok were donated to farmers and to the Cape of Good Hope Nature Reserve.

[15]Campbell purchased MalaMala, Eyrefield and Marthly, and subsequently acquired several other adjacent farms. During the early 1930s almost all the farms in the 'Toulon Block' (Sabi Sand), as well as several others in the neighbourhood, were purchased by private individuals.

Figure 4.2. The first site of the Bontebok National Park in 1931 was not a success and the park and the bontebok herd were moved to Swellendam and the new park opened in 1962.
From R.J. Labuschagne, *The Kruger Park and Other National Parks* (n.d.), p. 148. Courtesy of SANParks.

and many were the experiments undertaken to perfect the transporting of the remaining bontebok to their new home. The new national park was officially opened on 10 October 1962, when there were 84 surviving bontebok, and throughout the decade more land was added.[16]

[16]A.P.J. van Rensburg, 'Die geskiedenis van die Nasionale Bontebokpark, Swellendam', *Koedoe* 18 (1975): 165–190; N.J. van der Merwe, 'Die Bontbok', *Koedoe* 11 (1968): 161–168; P.J. Barnard and K. van der Walt, 'Translocation of the bontebok (*Damaliscus*

The Cape mountain zebra *Equus zebra zebra* was also provided with its own national park in the 1930s in a move suggested by the growing international conservation lobby interested in endangered species worldwide. For some years, the South African government resisted this pressure because, given the Depression, it lacked the funds. Eventually, in 1937 a national park for the species was established near Cradock in the Eastern Cape, where the small scattered relict populations were brought together.[17] A nature conservator and four black rangers were appointed, but the NPB seems to have done nothing more. In the 1940s, Ainslie, the senior official at Mountain Zebra National Park, was also officially a full-time farmer who ran his livestock in the zebra camps, chopped down trees in order to sell the wood and cleared state land for his own maize fields. It was concerned local farmers on the Fish River Soil Conservation Committee who brought the soil erosion and decline in the condition and number of zebra in the park to the attention of the board, not the conservator.[18] The international community may have been aware of the deteriorating circumstances in this park by 1950, when, at the second session of the International Union for the Protection of Nature (IUPN, later International Union for the Conservation of Nature and Natural Resources, IUCN) general assembly in Brussels, there was a formal vote congratulating a Mr M.J.K. Lombard of Cradock for his 'generous gift' of land, which had improved the survival prospects of the mountain zebra.[19]

The fourth South African national park established during the 1930s was very much larger than the others, but it too was founded to protect a

pygargus) from Bredasdorp to Swellendam', *Koedoe* 4 (1961), 105; R. Bigalke, 'The bontebok (*Damaliscus pygargus* (Pallas), with special reference to its history and preservation', *Fauna and Flora* 6 (1955): 95–115.

[17] E. Hone *et al.*, *African Game Protection: An Outline of the Existing Game Reserves and National Parks of Africa with Notes on Certain Species of Big Game Nearing Extinction, or Needing Additional Protection*. Special publication of the American Committee for International Wild Life Protection 1, no. 3 (1933): 26–27; R.C. Bigalke, 'Early history of the Cape Mountain Zebra (*Equus zebra zebra*, Linn.)', *African Wildlife* 6, no. 2 (1952): 143–153.

[18] P.W. Hoek, 'Verslag oor' n ondersoek van die bestuur van die verskeie nasionale parke en die nasionale parkeraad se administrasie', unpublished report, 1952, 50–52.

[19] J.C. Phillips, *African Game Protection: An Outline of the Existing Game Reserves and National Parks of Africa with Notes on Certain Species of Big Game nearing Extinction or Needing Additional Protection*. Special Publication of the American Committee for International Wild Life Protection 1, no. 3 (1933). In the sections on the declining Mountain Zebra, noting that the South African government was unwilling at present to save this species owing to the country's poor financial position, it recommended that it did so.

Figure 4.3. Gemsbok in Nossob River in Kalahari Gemsbok National Park.
From R.J. Labuschagne, *The Kruger Park and Other National Parks* (n.d.), p. 166. Courtesy of SANParks.

single vulnerable species, the gemsbok or oryx *Oryx gazella*. In 1931, the Kalahari Gemsbok National Park (KGNP) was established on 1.5 million ha in the Northern Cape bordering on what was then the Bechuanaland Protectorate and South West Africa, a mandate territory under South African control since the end of the First World War.[20] This remote and arid national park, comprising parts of the old Cape provincial Gordonia Game Reserve and private farmland, was to be a sanctuary for South Africa's dwindling numbers of oryx.[21] It was also the 'explicit wish' of the Minister of Lands 'that the park should act as refuge for the Bushmen [San] to save them from extinction'.[22] Despite its enormous size and ecological importance, it was managed by an untrained local farmer with the assistance of four African staff.[23]

[20]In 1938, the Bechuanaland government responded by establishing a large game reserve about 40 km wide on its side of the boundary line, see C. Spinage, *History and Evolution of the Fauna Conservation Laws of Botswana* (Gaborone: Botswana Society, 1991), Part II, 'History and evolution of the protected area system'.
[21]Union of South Africa, *Debates of the House of Assembly*, 5 May 1931. See also J. Pringle, *The Conservationists and the Killers* (Cape Town: Bulpin, 1982), 69–74.
[22]P. van Wyk and E.A.N. Le Riche, 'The Kalahari Gemsbok National Park, 1931–1981', in 'Proceedings of a Symposium on the Kalahari Ecosystem', eds G. de Graaff and D. Janse van Rensburg, supplement, *Koedoe* (1984): 24–25.
[23]Van Wyk and Le Riche, 'Kalahari Gemsbok National Park', 21–32.

Because of its interesting desert ecology and the fact that the land was unattractive to farmers, a national park in the Northern Cape had been mooted in 1913, but war intervened.[24] At that time, the area, on the border with German South West Africa, was of strategic importance. Boreholes were sunk along the Nossob and the Auob rivers to water horses and camels (some of which had come from Australia) for military and police patrols. After the war, the west bank of the Nossob was divided into extremely large farms, but whites proved unwilling to farm in such a hostile environment and so the area was set aside for 'coloureds' instead.[25] The political dispensation of the time dictated that the San could not live among 'coloureds' and would require their own 'reserve' if they did not live within the national park. The solution was to move the coloured people further south and to establish in 1941 a separate San reserve of some 12 000 ha. Thus, San families or groups within the national park deemed 'non-compliant' were evicted to this reserve.[26] For park warden Johannes Le Riche and his brother Joseph, non-compliance included not being 'traditional', having 'mixed' rather than 'pure Bushman blood', and generally acting in a 'modern' way.[27]

Only in the late 1950s did tourists begin to visit KGNP after accommodation was constructed, roads were improved, water was provided for wildlife and a publicity campaign was mounted. In this, the San were to play a part and serve as a tourist attraction, but those who remained within the park were regarded as 'uncooperative' and their increasing demands were resented.[28] So the San had to be evicted because they were not idealised specimens of their 'traditional' society.[29]

Dongola Wild Life Sanctuary

As we have seen, South Africa's national parks of the 1930s were all species-specific and set aside for the propagation, protection and preservation of endangered species. As the sources show, there was no scientific mandate for how this was to be done, apart from confining the animals on

---

[24]W. Macdonald, *The Conquest of the Desert* (London: T. Werner Laurie, 1913).

[25]A.J. Clement, *The Kalahari and its Lost City* (Cape Town: Longmans, 1967), 53.

[26]L.G. Green, *Where Men Still Dream* (Cape Town: Timmins, 1945), 166.

[27]Van Wyk and Le Riche, 'Kalahari Gemsbok National Park', 21–32.

[28]H. Kloppers, *Gee My'n Man* (Johannesburg: Afrikaanse Pers, 1970), 188–190.

[29]Van Wyk and Le Riche, 'The Kalahari Gemsbok National Park', 21–32; J. Carruthers, 'Past and future landscape ideology: The Kalahari Gemsbok National Park', in *Social History and African Environments*, eds W. Beinart and J. McGregor (Oxford: James Currey, 2003), 255–266.

state land and employing a conservator to watch over them. There is no record of involvement in this project by veterinarians or biologists in zoological gardens, even in relation to propagation or diet – matters on which they had some expertise. Nor was there ever any clear distinction between protecting and propagating.

By contrast, the short-lived Dongola Wild Life Sanctuary in the Limpopo valley was South Africa's first ecological park, founded specifically for its value to science. Its failure is particularly instructive.[30] Under the growing influence of the ideas about ecology, in the 1930s Dongola began to take shape. Pole Evans, head of the Botanical Survey within the Division of Botany in the Department of Agriculture, initiated a protected area intended as an ecological showcase for research. He had support from some biologists, botanists and Herbert Curson, the unusual veterinarian who had supported national parks in the 1920s.[31] It was Curson, along with Pole Evans, who believed Dongola would be an ideal research centre for South African biological studies.[32] However, establishing a national park for 'science' proved to be extremely unpopular in the political and social environment of the day. The park's chequered history bears repeating, particularly because of the light it sheds on the NPB's attitudes to professional scientific endeavour.

The area that became the Dongola Wild Life Sanctuary was only slightly less remote than the KGNP. The landscape is arid and bleak, broken only by granite inselbergs that rise out of a stony landscape dotted with sparse and tufted grass. The climate is hot and harsh, and malaria, foot-and-mouth, horse-sickness and nagana were endemic in the early years of the twentieth century. This tropical 'Mopani veld', part of the great African savannahs, is found in many parts of northern South Africa. It was for this reason that Pole Evans had selected it in 1922 for one of the Botanical Survey's experimental research stations. These grew out of Pole Evans' preliminary botanical classification of 1917 and he had high hopes

[30]Further detail about the Dongola Wild Life Sanctuary can be found in J. Carruthers, 'The Dongola Wild Life Sanctuary: "Psychological blunder, economic folly and political monstrosity" or "More valuable than rubies and gold"?', *Kleio* 24 (1992): 82–100 and J. Carruthers, 'Mapungubwe: An historical and contemporary analysis of a World Heritage Cultural Landscape', *Koedoe* 41 (2006): 114.

[31]He had been moved into the Department of Native Affairs in 1936 with responsibility for African agriculture.

[32]Curson had long been interested in the topic of wildlife protection, see H.H. Curson and J.M. Hugo, 'Preservation of game in South Africa', *South African Journal of Science* 21 (1924): 400–424.

of them. They would not only enable survey and systematic work, but also identification of medicinal and economically valuable species and plant pests and the recording of abiotic factors affecting vegetation and general plant distribution. In short, in these stations ecological processes could be monitored.

To this end, in 1918, the government 'at the request of General Smuts set aside a block of nine farms in this area where the wild life and natural vegetation could be preserved'.[33] In the 1920s, it acquired the name Dongola Botanical Reserve, after a volcano-shaped mountain on the farm 'Goeree'. The reserve fell under Pole Evans' responsibility and, personally interested in its development, he visited regularly, sometimes for long periods. In the course of the next few years, the Dongola Botanical Reserve achieved some of its objectives. For example, experiments under Pole Evans' direction led to the development of Limpopo grass *Echinochloa pyramidalis*, which was excellent for hay and for stabilising loose sand. In addition, the keeping of regular scientific records added considerably to the scanty knowledge of the climate and vegetation of the area.

Pole Evans had always enjoyed strong support from his friend Jan Smuts, who became prime minister after Louis Botha's death in 1919. When Smuts was in opposition after 1924, Pole Evans courted National Party politicians by inviting them to visit the reserve. He was greatly encouraged by their enthusiasm and also, no doubt, by the government's penchant for establishing national parks in the 1930s, but nothing further eventuated. When Smuts was returned to government after the collapse of the Fusion government at the time of the outbreak of the Second World War, Pole Evans seized the moment. A number of other considerations may have influenced the evolution of Pole Evans' long-term plans for Dongola. Drought and general economic depression increased the impoverishment of the northern Transvaal and land values remained low. Moreover, Pole Evans was beginning to expound the philosophy of soil conservation and advocated restoration ecology in order to return much of the surrounding degraded veld to its previous biodiversity. This could be achieved by buying up some of the neighbouring farms and applying appropriate veld management. Pole Evans won the favour of Andrew

[33]Its object was to study and to map the vegetation and to assess its agricultural and pastoral value using experimental methods of evaluation: the farms were Goeree 728, Sharlee 729, Rosslynlee 730, Giesdendam 731, Dunsappie 732, Bruntsfield 733, Moerdyk 736, Vernon 737 and Shelton Hall 738.

Conroy, Minister of Lands and Irrigation (1939–48),[34] whose department took over the Dongola farms from the Department of Agriculture. Fearless, outspoken and unpopular in many circles, Conroy took up the cause of converting Dongola from a 'botanical reserve for scientific research' into a 'national park' (possibly to be named after Jan Smuts)[35] with immense passion. The original intention in 1944 was to proclaim 240 000 ha, stretching from 5 km west of Beit Bridge, along the southern banks of the Limpopo to its confluence with the Macloutsie River – an area some 100 km long and 36 km wide at its widest point. The cost of acquiring the land from private owners together with other expenses was estimated at £25 000.

In terms of scientific importance and research in South Africa's protected areas, Dongola has particular significance. The region possesses one of South Africa's greatest archaeological treasures. Large quantities of Stone Age implements have been found and rock art is abundant. Of particular significance is the Iron Age site at Mapungubwe on the farm Greefswald, at the junction of the Limpopo and Shashe rivers. The hill-top structures of Mapungubwe have had a long and significant history and the site became South Africa's first World Heritage Cultural Landscape in 2003.[36] The treasures of Mapungubwe and its environs were discovered by a group of amateur fortune hunters in 1932. Among them was J.C.O. van Graan, a graduate of the University of Pretoria, who reported the find to his *alma mater*. The university moved quickly

---

[34]Board members in 1939 were: Justice N.J. de Wet (Chairman), J.F. Ludorf (Vice-Chairman), members W.A. Campbell, Hon. J.H. Conradie, Brigadier-General F.R.G. Hoare, R.A. Hockly M.P., G.S. Preller, W.H. Rood and D.F. Gilfillan.

[35]The proposal was remarkably similar to the current initiative for the Transfrontier Conservation Area. In 1942 and 1943, with the approval of General Smuts, Prime Minister of South Africa and of Sir Godfrey Huggins, Prime Minister of Southern Rhodesia, three prominent Rhodesians visited Dongola at South African expense to see 'what was being done there towards Wild Life Protection' and with a view to establishing a protected area on their side of the border. The visitors were Sir Robert MacIlwaine, Chairman of the Natural Resources Department of Southern Rhodesia, A.W. Redfern, Member of the Legislative Assembly of Southern Rhodesia and Flight-Lieutenant Pain, Managing Director of the Rhodesian Corporation, which owned a large block of land on the Rhodesian side of the Limpopo River, opposite the Dongola Reserve. The Bechuanaland Protectorate was also approached so that certain farms bordering the Limpopo on the Protectorate side of the Reserve, owned by the Chartered Company might also be included. Had this scheme come to fruition, the first formal international, transboundary conservation area in Africa would have been established.

[36]UNESCO http://whc.unesco.org/en/list/1007 (accessed 10 December 2015).

Figure 4.4. The golden rhinoceros, a treasure of Mapungubwe National Park, housed in the Mapungubwe Collection, University of Pretoria.
Courtesy of the University of Pretoria Museums: Department of UP Arts.

to secure excavation rights and ownership of the site. It was carefully excavated and the findings published a few years later in two enormous volumes by that university's history professor, Leo Fouché, and detailed in the *South African Journal of Science* in 1933.

Further excavations at Mapungubwe were, however, abandoned, in part because of the financial constraints of the Depression and the outbreak of war in 1939, and in part because the University of Pretoria was becoming more narrowly Afrikaner nationalist in its orientation, as a result of which the English-speaking non-political academics in its ranks, such as Fouché, were vilified and precolonial archaeology was downplayed, disputed and ignored. Because of this, Greefswald was placed under the control of Pole Evans in the early 1940s. Archaeology was one of Smuts' scientific interests: he thought it 'a great field awaiting investigation in South Africa', a view not shared by his political opponents. In 1933 Smuts had visited Mapungubwe and, much impressed, had even consulted with a number of prominent archaeologists to establish a Bureau of Archaeology. This was done in 1935; later, it became the Archaeological Survey.

Conroy had approached the NPB to assume responsibility for the Dongola project and he was surprised when the board rejected the scheme out of hand. Unimpressed by the growing potential of the ecological research that might be undertaken in national parks, they argued that the park was unnecessary. Moreover, it would be unattractive to visitors because it had fewer wild animals than KNP and in any case no money was available for another national park. There was also a strong political element: most board members were Hertzog supporters and unwilling to be involved in any scheme initiated by the hated United Party. Vice-Chairman Ludorf, one of the most enthusiastic Afrikaner nationalists on the board, was particularly adamant. It may also have been the case that establishing this national park would have put the spotlight on Mapungubwe and perhaps weakened the myth of the 'empty land' into which whites had allegedly ventured the century before. Certainly, after 1948 the government of D.F. Malan had no interest in archaeology. On coming to power, it revoked Smuts' invitation to hold the second pan-African archaeological congress in South Africa. As Shepherd observes: 'In crucial respects the discipline, which tended to be Anglophile and keyed into the transnational network of the British Empire, found itself at odds with the parochialism of Afrikaner Nationalist politics.'[37]

At the time Conroy's proposal was made, the Wild Life Protection Society's representative on the NPB was J.H. Orpen (1879–1954). He took a principled view, stating that it was the board's duty to expand the protected area estate, and at least board members should visit the area before reaching a conclusion. Conroy tried to placate the board, eventually meeting with Ludorf and offering to fully finance Dongola for five years. Conroy stressed that Dongola was to be a new kind of conservation area. It was not intended to directly compete with the KNP and was to be closed to the public (at least initially) and be available for serious scientific studies and as a 'witness area', i.e. a place where human interference was minimal so that it could serve as a benchmark. However, the idea of a science park in South Africa provoked abhorrence rather than support. A further argument that weighed with the board – and a powerful one – was that white, predominantly Afrikaner, settler farmers – and thus the electorate – rather than disenfranchised black Africans would have their land expropriated for the Dongola National Park.

Despite this hostility, Conroy pressed on with his negotiations. Because private farms would be expropriated for the proposed national protected area, the Dongola Bill was a 'hybrid bill' and a select committee had to be appointed to consider the matter before it could be passed into law.[38] This committee heard objections over a two-year period, posed more than 16 000 questions and finally, in 1945, produced a two-volume

---

[37]N. Shepherd, 'The politics of archaeology in Africa', *Annual Review of Anthropology* 31 (2002): 189–209.

[38]The seven Members of Parliament on this committee were David Jackson, MP Ermelo, United Party; George Henny, MP Swartruggens, United Party; J.G. Carinus, MP Hottentots Holland, United Party; H.J. Cilliers, MP Mayfair, Labour Party; H.O. Eksteen, MP Middelburg, United Party; J.F. Potgieter, MP Brits, Herenigde Nasionale or Volksparty; G.P. Steyn, MP Willowmore, Herenigde Nasionale or Volksparty.

Report of the Select Committee that ran to 1500 pages. The major theme was whether agricultural land should be removed from productive use for wildlife or botanical conservation and research. Discussion of the agricultural and pastoral potential of the district together with the extent and causes of soil erosion and stock disease was intense. Within government itself, the Department of Agriculture opposed the scheme, some officials even actively campaigning against it. Perhaps not surprisingly, the Division of Veterinary Services lodged the 'strongest protest' because stock diseases could spread into South Africa from neighbouring countries if border control was relaxed. The Transvaal Agricultural Union, the South African Agricultural Union and the Zoutpansberg Farmers Union also protested to the committee, claiming that the whole of the Zoutpansberg region would be 'mutilated beyond redemption as a first-class farming district' and recommending that wild animals in the area be killed immediately and turned into biltong for the troops engaged in the war – wildebeest for whites and zebra for Africans. As for troublesome pests such as wild dog and jackal, they would, no doubt, breed in the proposed national park. The Native Commissioner for the area, the Secretary of Mines, and the chairman of Iscor (the state iron and steel corporation) also cautioned against the scheme. Even the nature conservation lobby acting through the Wild Life Protection Society, while supporting the bill generally, acknowledged there were valid grounds for opposition. Indeed, among the opponents of the proposal was the prominent conservationist T.C. Robertson, founder of the Veld Trust. Clearly, any protected area set aside for science alone was extremely unpopular in many quarters.

The debate in parliament was long, acrimonious and extremely personal. Conroy's chief antagonists included General J.C.G. Kemp. It had been Kemp who, as Minister of Lands, was so impressed by the wildlife returning to Dongola when he visited in the late 1920s that he had even suggested the expansion of the botanical reserve. However, he had also sanctioned the mass extermination of wild animals in Zululand in the mid-1920s. He belittled the Dongola project, as did others in his political party, as a sign that the Smuts government cared more for wild animals than for people.[39]

The vote on the Dongola issue was strictly along party lines. The Dongola Wild Life Sanctuary Act 6 of 1947 passed by 35 votes and was

[39]Carruthers, 'Dongola Wild Life Sanctuary', 94.

published in an extraordinary *Government Gazette* on 28 March 1947, with the area much reduced from the original plan (the select committee had recommended reduction from 250 000 ha to 92 000 ha).[40] Thereafter trustees were appointed to a board, money was raised, farms were acquired, and negotiations were begun with neighbouring countries, because the new national park had potential as the first transboundary conservation area in the region. Dongola was poised to fulfil the promise that Conroy, Smuts and Pole Evans (now warden) believed it had.[41] But this was not to be. So politically divisive was Dongola and so intense the hatred it aroused, when the National Party came to power in 1948, funding for Dongola ceased immediately and abolition was debated the following year. Smuts' appeal to the House as a 'botanist and scientist' to reconsider this stance had little effect. The Dongola Wild Life Sanctuary Act was repealed by Act 29 of 1949. Money was repaid to donors, properties returned to their original owners, and the farms that had made up the Dongola Botanical Reserve were allocated for settlement. Given the furore over its foundation, it is surprising that this national park rates no mention in almost all accounts of nature protection in South Africa.[42] Like the Natal National Park, it has faded from public memory, although a very small portion of the Dongola Wild Life Sanctuary is now the Mapungubwe National Park under SANParks control.

Dongola was not the only national park to be turned down in the late 1940s. In January 1948, land at Impenjati on the south coast of Natal was offered as a donation to the board by a wealthy person and the board's

[40] 'Beginning at the north-western corner on the Crocodile or Limpopo River of the farm Samaria 606, Zoutpansberg magisterial district, proceeding thence generally eastwards down the Crocodile or Limpopo River, i.e. along the Transvaal–Bechuanaland boundary and the Transvaal–Rhodesia boundary to the north-eastern corner of the farm Beskow 763 proceeding thence in a south-westerly direction along the boundaries of and including the following farms, viz.: the said Beskow 763, De Klundert 759, Petershof 757, Neanderhohle 758, Rozenthal 735 to the southernmost beacon of the last-mentioned property; thence in a general north-westerly direction along the boundaries of and including the following farms, viz.: Moerdyk 736, Vernon 737, Bruntsfield 733, Hartjesveld 706, Altenburg 626, Kilsyth 622, Hamilton 621, Greefswald 615, and Samaria 606 to the north-western corner of the last-named farm, the place of beginning.'

[41] The trustees were Charles Gordon Saker, H.J. van der Bijl, Bernard Price, Senator John Stuart Franklin and Sir Ernest Oppenheimer.

[42] See, for example, N.J. van der Merwe, 'The position of nature conservation in South Africa', *Koedoe* 5 (1962): 1–122; N.J. van der Merwe, 'The history of game preservation in South Africa', in *Ecological Studies in Southern Africa*, ed. D.H.S. Davis (The Hague: Junk, 1964), 363–370.

recommendation was that it be accepted. The gift was worth around £200 000. There was some procrastination about accepting a seaside resort as a national park but the donor was unwilling to give the land to the province. In the event, the gift was refused, although the board reminded government that its mandate was not merely to protect game, but also to provide recreational facilities to the nation.[43]

The Shape of 'Science'

After his extended long leave in Britain in the mid-1920s, Stevenson-Hamilton feared that under the new regime he – a Smuts and Commonwealth man – would be relieved of his post and replaced by someone more aligned politically with the government. Instead, he was invited by the board to resume his position as KNP warden. He learnt Afrikaans, attended board meetings when invited and continued to write books and articles. He also continued to castigate veterinarians, whom he would apostrophise as 'scientists', for their attempts to interfere with wildlife management. There is no evidence that he was asked to assist in the operational management of any other national park, to use his networks in this regard or even to provide advice. In fact, this treatment of individual national parks as silos, along with the division between 'national' and 'provincial' parks and game reserves, has bedevilled science and management in South Africa's protected areas throughout their history. One consequence has been that, because of the high profile it gained during its early days, KNP has always been the most prominent national park in every way.

No steps were taken by the Department of Lands or the board to include professional scientists of any kind in the national park project. There was a fleeting chance in 1933 when the board considered whether scientific 'liaison' might be instituted through cooperation with certain veterinarians and botanists. Interestingly, no mention was made of ecologists, zoologists or animal behaviourists, or precisely what the scientists would be expected to do. However, nothing came of this initiative; one reason given being that it might lead to a deluge of scientists and scientific institutions wanting to use KNP for their research.[44] The board was not prepared to supply facilities

---

[43]Minutes of a meeting of the NPB, 5 January 1948, SANParks archives, Groenkloof, Pretoria.

[44]S.C.J. Joubert, *The Kruger National Park: A History*. 3 vols (Johannesburg: High Branching, 2012), vol. 1, 42.

for study or experiment. Moreover, people could not be allowed to wander unsupervised within the park no matter how worthy their purpose might be.

Consequently, apart from his professional networks through the Zoological Society of London and the SPFE, Stevenson-Hamilton's knowledge was perforce limited both personally and institutionally. Indeed, his experience of South African animal scientists was mostly unpleasant and ran counter to all he believed a natural environment should be. In his memoir, *South African Eden*, he graphically describes the activities of veterinarians during a foot-and-mouth outbreak in the KNP in the 1930s, on the basis of which they killed not only the livestock of the white rangers but utterly destroyed the livelihoods of the many African families still residing in the park as labour tenants. The state veterinarians by their actions forced many of these people out of the park into the trust lands and to become migrant labourers to urban areas. Stevenson-Hamilton was also highly critical of Siegfried Annecke, whose scientific anti-malarial activities included putting a film of oil on as many KNP waterholes as possible, with dreadful consequences for the wildlife.[45]

Throughout the 1930s and early 1940s, Stevenson-Hamilton continued his preservationist work with enthusiasm and dedication, coping with the growing influx of tourists who, to his surprise, preferred to view 'verminous' carnivores and were increasingly dismissive of the herds of antelope he had spent so many years in nurturing.[46] His frustrations with the board and particularly with H.J. (Hope) van Graan, the secretary in the mid-1930s, are clearly evident in his private journal. Exacerbating these problems was the fact that lines of authority and responsibility were never made clear. Disappointingly, when international conservation organs were being established in the 1930s, he, despite a high professional reputation, was not permitted to attend the overseas meetings for want of money. The South African representative at these gatherings was generally the diplomatic representative who happened to be closest to the meeting venue at the time.[47] Stevenson-Hamilton was very much an imperial and Victorian man and became, as he aged, more set in his ways and less

---

[45]Box K46, file KNP 34, Kruger National Park archives, Skukuza. Although Stevenson-Hamilton decried Annecke's interventions in the KNP, Annecke's work effectively eradicated malaria from the Lowveld.

[46]By 1938 there were 38 014 visitors to Skukuza. The park was closed during the Second World War.

[47]In 1934 the NPB was invited to send a delegate to International Nature Convention in London; the High Commissioner in London attended on the board's behalf.

flexible. Born in 1867, he was nearing 70 by the 1930s. His public profile was high, and he enjoyed a worldwide reputation. In 1935 he received an honorary doctorate from the University of the Witwatersrand and a similar degree from the University of Cape Town ten years later.[48] No other international wildlife warden of his time achieved similar eminence.

Loving the Lowveld and his work, he resisted retirement, despite the increasing burden of tourists, administration, road repairs and construction after every summer rainy season, and the lack of opportunity to travel around the KNP and continue with the environmental observations that he had first started making in 1902. He was also aware that there was no one of comparable stature waiting to replace him. Stevenson-Hamilton hoped to die 'in harness', as he put it, always pleased when his wardenship was extended and he evaded retirement, as was the case during the Second World War when the KNP was closed to visitors. Throughout these years, he maintained his home in Scotland and like so many of his ilk in the dominions, thought of himself as a citizen of the empire, as simultaneously South African and British. Not a great admirer of the USA, he never visited North America. In his personal collection of many hundreds of books and papers on wildlife matters, there is no copy of Aldo Leopold's *Game Management*, which first appeared in 1933. Nonetheless, he would probably have approved of its moral stance, as well as its practical advice. To the end of his life Stevenson-Hamilton believed that observational science, personal knowledge and long familiarity were what generated the science that counted in his emerging profession, not theory or experiment, and certainly not control or manipulation. He had experienced that in Natal, in Addo and in the veterinarians' responses to wild animals and their diseases. In the 1930s and 1940s, he wrote extensively about allowing the KNP to remain a wilderness and never turning into a zoological garden. He also believed, as does conservation biology today, that he was involved in a 'mission'.[49] For him, game protection had a moral purpose; by contrast, the veterinarian's mission, he believed, was materialistic and economic.

There were in South Africa ecologists who played their part in the international development of their discipline, but they had no influence on the government or on the National Party-dominated NPB. In 1939, among the local members of the British Ecological Society were botanists

---

[48]He was made a Vice-President of the SPFE in 1945.

[49]C. Meine, M. Soulé and R.F. Noss, '"A mission-driven discipline": The growth of conservation biology', *Conservation Biology* 20, no. 3 (2006): 631–651.

and foresters R.S. Adamson, F.S. Laughton and J.F.V. Phillips, historian J. Omer-Cooper (Rhodes University), D.H.S. Davis (Department of Public Health, Pretoria), and two zoologists, both from the University of Cape Town, Miss J. Eyre and Professor T.A. Stephenson (Hogben's talented young successor, an ecologically minded marine biologist who appears to have been the first to introduce ecology into a South African university curriculum, earning high praise from Charles Elton for doing so).[50]

Apart from Stevenson-Hamilton and to a lesser extent the museum zoologists Alwin Haagner and Ernest Warren, national park management – or wildlife and protected area management more generally – was without scientific voice in South Africa in the early 1930s. This was to change as the decade progressed and as the idea of what conservation or wildlife science might be took root and found expression by the 1960s. The absence of institutional framework or professional qualification was a major impediment: indeed, no branch of science led directly to study in the wild. If one looks at the 'zoology' or 'biology' degrees of the museum directors, or even some of the first university-trained staff of the Biological Section of the NPB and KNP, they contain, certainly at first glance, no kind of 'outdoor' field science. Botanists were different because, as has been explained, the 'ecological' aspect of botany was well established in South Africa, although ecosystem thinking was not evident and study was predominantly synecological, that is, the study of plant communities.

Moreover, whether national parks were small species-specific reserves or larger parts of ecosystems such as Kruger, Kalahari Gemsbok or Dongola, there was no appropriate government scientific structure to monitor and manage them. In this, South Africa was not alone, for such was also the case in the USA, where the establishment of a Division of Wildlife Studies within the NPS gave rise to fraught relationships. There, between 1929 and 1933, George Wright, a park naturalist at Yosemite with a degree in forestry and vertebrate zoology, personally funded his own survey of national parks, which was published in 1932 and 1933 in a series entitled *Fauna of the National Parks of the United States*. Wright was killed in a motor accident in 1936, and his project died with him, as the NPS was unwilling to continue his work.[51]

[50]H. Phillips, *The University of Cape Town 1918–1948: The Formative Years* (Cape Town: UCT Press, 1993), 352–353.
[51]J. Ise, *Our National Park Policy: A Critical History* (Baltimore, MD: Johns Hopkins University Press, 1961), 593, 595. See also J. Grinnell, 'Natural balance for wildlife in national parks and its maintenance', *Journal of the Society for the Protection of the Fauna of*

Although their rationales may have differed, Stevenson-Hamilton would have agreed with Conrad Wirth, later a director of the US National Parks Service, in distrusting scientific interference and regarding it as outside the national park brief.[52] But then, independent of the national parks service (itself part of the public service), the US bureaucracy had a federal wildlife agency in the Biological Survey, later named the Fish and Wildlife Service.[53] This Survey, which had begun in 1885 as the Division of Economic Ornithology and Mammalogy in the Department of Agriculture, was greatly admired by a number of South Africans, particularly Austin Roberts of the Transvaal Museum and Rudolph Bigalke of the National Zoological Gardens. They contended that South Africa had a Botanical Survey, a Geological Survey and an Archaeological Survey, into which system a Biological or Zoological Survey would fit well.[54] In this argument, Bigalke and Roberts had a precedent in the form of the Biological Survey of Australia, established in 1935 and later to transform itself into the Wildlife Survey Section of the Australian Council for Industrial Research (subsequently the CSIRO). Headed by Francis Ratcliffe, its function was to coordinate the commonwealth-wide conservation of fauna and flora. Bigalke argued that a scientific survey would lead to the more efficient expenditure of resources by the provinces. The survey, he suggested, should become a unit of the Department of

the Empire 24 (1935): 61–66, in which he argued that national parks should be areas of study, to be managed as little as possible and remain as close as possible to natural conditions. R.W. Sellars, *Preserving Nature in the National Parks: A History* (New Haven, CT: Yale University Press, 1997), 96.

[52]Sellars, *Preserving Nature in the National Parks*, 168.

[53]A. Leopold, *Game Management* (New York, NY and London: Charles Scribner's, 1933). Leopold realised (viii) that game management had been an empirical art in Europe for a long time, but he argued that the time had come to adapt that art to biological principles. He stressed that sound biology is 'to avoid artificiality in the manipulation of nature processes for conservation purposes' (396).

[54]Published in Pretoria by the Carnegie Visitors' Grants Committee, 1935. In 1935 the Biological Survey of Australia established a committee to begin a biological survey. War intervened and little was done until the appointment of Francis Ratcliffe as head of the new Wildlife Survey Section of CSIR (later the CSIRO) in 1949 to coordinate commonwealth-wide conservation of fauna and flora in Australia. In the *South African Journal of Science* (November 1934): 396, R. Bigalke pleaded for the inauguration of a biological survey in the Union of South Africa as did C.J. Skead, 'The need for a zoological survey in South Africa', *South African Museums Association Bulletin* 6, no. 4 (1955): 101–103. See also R.D. Bigalke and J.D. Skinner, 'The Zoological Survey: An historical perspective', *Transactions of the Royal Society of South Africa* 57, nos. 1/2 (2002): 35–41.

Agriculture, and focus on solving problems such as the biology and control of predatory animals, noxious rodents and rabies transmitters, and the impact of wild birds on agriculture. He suggested that, in tandem with various museums, a staff of not less than six biologists, trained primarily in zoology but with interests in botany and geology, would suffice.[55]

Perhaps because of the antipathy of the veterinarians – the reason is not clear – no political party in power ever responded positively to these proposals. Feeding this debate – well articulated in the *Journal for the Society for the Preservation of the Fauna of the Empire* and in speeches by British and colonial delegates to the international conferences of the 1930s – was the fact that the term 'national park' itself was problematic. As noted earlier, 'national park' has no easy Afrikaans translation: indeed, the KNP was legislated in 1926 as the *Nasionale Krugerwildtuin* – the Kruger National Game Reserve. Beyond that, the USA did not share this problem with the British world – in Africa particularly. It had never had government-owned 'game reserves', originally intended as wildlife sanctuaries but later converted into national parks. US national parks were recreational areas where people could hike, swim, stay in luxurious hotels and observe immense and beautiful scenery at first hand. Self-evidently, such activities could not be pursued in places abounding with dangerous large mammals.[56]

The Depression of the 1930s, the rise of Afrikaner nationalism and deep divisions over whether South Africa should enter the Second World War had created 'an explosive cocktail of political poisons' in South Africa by the 1940s.[57] In 1948 there was a surprise (and very narrow) victory by D.F. Malan and Smuts was ousted. Back in 1934, a hard-line Afrikaner nationalist group under Malan's leadership had broken away from Hertzog and formed the 'Purified National Party' (*Gesuiwerde Nasionale Party*) and it was this faction that now took power. The following general election (1953) gave Malan an increased majority and the 1950s and 1960s became the era of 'grand apartheid'. By 1961, the longer-term consequences were apparent: a new South African constitution created a republic outside

---

[55]R. Bigalke, 'A Biological Survey for the Union', *South African Journal of Science* 31 (1934): 396–404.

[56]In addition, the US NPS took care of historical monuments – which may have influenced its philosophy – while in South Africa these were separately managed and administered under the Monuments Council.

[57]S. Dubow and A. Jeeves, eds, *South Africa's 1940s: Worlds of Possibilities* (Cape Town: Double Storey, 2005), 2.

the British Commonwealth, the country was excluded from many global institutions on account of its racist policies, and authoritarianism, social engineering and discriminatory legislation permeated all aspects of South African life.

For protected areas, two processes were at work in this period. The first was bringing national parks within the Afrikaner nationalist cultural ambit. This was relatively quick and very successful after 1948, particularly as it coincided with the retirement of Stevenson-Hamilton, with his close ties to Britain and its protectionist network. The myth that national parks were the brainchild of Paul Kruger, president of the Transvaal Republic before the South African War (1899–1902), gained purchase. There was now aggressive preferential employment of government supporters in an expanding civil service so that by the mid-1960s South Africa's national parks were integral to '*volkshuishouding*',[58] a complex word suggesting that they had been assimilated into the ethos of the Afrikaner *volk* [people]. Many international intellectual exchanges between Europe and South Africa that had been taken for granted ended as this new inward-looking perspective – associated with growing isolationism, national self-reliance and dependence on people trained in South Africa – took hold. The absence of foreign stimulation and connections by way of, for example, sabbatical leave abroad or the use of internal not external PhD examiners led to scientific thinking, particularly on the part of Afrikaans-speakers who were reluctant to engage with international colleagues (because of linguistic challenges), that was often derivative and descriptive rather than innovative. This situation was to continue well into the late 1980s.

In addition, there were changes in the nature conservation arena. These were sparked by legislation in 1945 relating to central government finances that obliged the provinces to reformulate their nature conservation structures.[59] Consideration was also given to instituting national coordination of protected areas, but this initiative floundered in the face of strong provincial opposition. In 1945 a provincial consultative committee was appointed to coordinate the activities of all bodies controlling national parks, game reserves and botanical gardens, but it never really got off the ground.[60] Then in January 1949, a Scientific Advisory Council for

[58]Minutes of a meeting of the NPB, 11 March 1968, SANParks archives, Groenkloof, Pretoria. Literally the 'national economy'.

[59]Financial Relations Consolidation and Amendment Act 38 of 1945.

[60]The documents are in Secretary for Home Affairs, BNS files 1/1/477 and 6/5/85, Central Archives Depot, National Archives of South Africa, Pretoria.

National Parks and Nature Reserves was created. One council member, Pretoria's National Zoological Gardens Director Rudolph Bigalke, wrote triumphantly to Herbert Smith, Secretary of the British Correlating Committee for the Protection of Nature in London in January 1949, that a three-year campaign had resulted in the new Minister of Lands and Irrigation, J.G. Strijdom, agreeing to the creation of a Scientific Advisory Council for National Parks and Nature Reserves: 'Remarkable as it may seem, this is the first time in the history of South Africa that a Council of scientists will advise the Union Government on matters pertaining to the country's National Parks and Nature Reserves. I expect great things from this body.'[61] It was an unpaid group with an advisory mandate only, but it was a start.[62]

Disappointingly, no such 'great things' were forthcoming: this advisory group, too, did not last long. Nonetheless, Bigalke went on to play a major role in injecting formal research techniques into the NPB. Born in Kimberley, he had studied first in South Africa before obtaining a PhD in 1926 (topic unrecorded) in Berlin.[63] A keen writer and educationalist familiar with the work of the US National Park Service, he published prolifically on science and nature conservation in the late 1930s.[64]

Stevenson-Hamilton's *laissez-faire* approach of leaving nature to be respected, appreciated and observed came under increasing pressure as

---

[61]Bigalke to Smith, 5 January 1949, Bigalke archives, Pretoria. (Per kind favour of Dr R. Bigalke.)

[62]The zoologists were R. Ortlepp and R. Bigalke, botanist Professor R.H. Compton, forester L.C. Wicht, geologist L.C. King, veterinarian P.J. du Toit and agronomist J.C. Ross.

[63]J.D. Skinner, 'Obituary Dr Rudolph Bigalke FRSSAf', *Transactions of the Royal Society of South Africa* 47, no. 3 (1990): 360–361.

[64]For example, R. Bigalke, 'Science and the conservation of wild life in South Africa', *Journal of the South African Veterinary Medical Association* 21 (1950): 166–172; R. Bigalke, 'Krugerwildtuin buitengewone geleenthede om dierelewe tydsaam te bestudeer', *South African Railways and Harbours Magazine*, August 1949: 559–563; R. Bigalke, 'Roofdiere van die Krugerwildtuin', *Huisgenoot*, 19 January 1940: 25, 61; R. Bigalke, 'Science and nature conservation in Transvaal: A short historical account', *Fauna and Flora* 27 (1976): 13–15; R. Bigalke, 'Our National Parks, past and future', *South African Journal of Science* 40 (1943): 248–253; R. Bigalke, *Animals and Zoos Today* (London: Cassell, 1939); R. Bigalke, *A Guide to Some Common Animals of the Kruger National Park* (Pretoria: Van Schaik, 1939); R. Bigalke, *National Parks and their Functions, with Special Reference to South Africa*. Pamphlet No. 10, South African Biological Society (Pretoria: Biological Society, 1939); R. Bigalke, 'Wild life conservation in the Union of South Africa', *Fauna and Flora* 1 (1950): 5–42; R. Bigalke, 'Suid-Afrika se eerste wildreservaat', *Fauna and Flora* 17 (1966): 13–18.

agricultural and pastoral development hemmed in the KNP, the African population on its borders increased, and the number of tourists grew, requiring the provision of further recreational services. There were also changes in the international nature protection environment. By the late 1940s, calls for 'scientific wildlife conservation' that would take account of the changing socio-political and economic milieus were becoming more vociferous thanks to the work of, for example, Aldo Leopold as well as international cooperative structures. The word 'science' became a mantra. The desired characteristics of wildlife science were spelt out by Bigalke, the most outspoken individual on this subject. He was troubled that South Africans knew so little about the country's indigenous fauna, even though they spent a great deal of time outdoors. Given his familiarity with the US situation, he advocated a strong educational drive by way of guidebooks, a museum and library situated within the KNP, and employment of 'ranger-naturalists' to impart information to visitors (as in the US national parks).[65] More than this, however, he argued that formal academic research should be conducted in national parks, starting with baseline studies on the effects of alien invasive species, distribution surveys and problem animal (such as lion and elephant) management.[66] By 1945, Bigalke was insisting that 'game preservation is the task of the scientist, i.e., the work of the biologist' and that the lack of organised scientific knowledge was leading to human–wildlife conflict and animal diseases. The South African Association for the Advancement of Science (SAAAS) agreed: what was required was the 'continuous study of the distribution, density, habits of each species and their inter-relationships, the progressive disappearance of species from many of their old habitats, etc.... the scientific aspect cannot be sufficiently stressed'. Another commentator put it thus: 'I strongly urge that the future control of our fauna and the business administration of our reserves should undergo a radical change of policy . . . I suggest that the study and control of our fauna in our reserves should be entrusted to a scientifically trained director'.[67] Science was becoming a persistent refrain in a world dominated by science and technology and Professor George Potts' long-ago lament that a scientist was viewed as 'a barbaric Goth, a technical expert, a mere specialist' no longer held true.

[65]For instance Bigalke, *National Parks and their Functions*.
[66]Bigalke, *Animals and Zoos Today*, 7, 23, 125–127, 142, 149.
[67]Transvaal Province, *Report of the Game Commission of Inquiry (TP6-1945)* (Pretoria: Government Printer, 1945), 24.

The NPB, however, took little note of Bigalke's concerns and no scientific director was appointed. Moreover, given their passion for 'scientific management' of national parks, Bigalke and others like him were dismayed when Stevenson-Hamilton was replaced upon his retirement in 1946 by a retired air force officer, Colonel J.B. Sandenbergh.[68] While not actually hand-picked by Stevenson-Hamilton, Sandenbergh was cut from much the same cloth – a military man with sound administrative skills and some interest in wildlife. However, for people like Bigalke, with the rather arrogant and experienced Stevenson-Hamilton out of the way, the board had missed an opportunity to establish a professional scientific division within the national parks to assist the new warden.[69]

Bigalke was himself appointed to the NPB in 1949.[70] He was the first professional scientist on the board and he took his responsibilities seriously. He was adamant that a formal scientific division was required within the national park structures,[71] warning that wildlife conservation 'would fail if divorced from scientific research' and that 'conservation necessitates the deliberate control of wildlife and its environment, where necessary, for the "wise use of man"'.[72] He advocated proper scientific procedure for establishing new national parks, expanding others and for determining ecologically appropriate boundaries.[73] Wildlife or game management was asserting itself in the scientific world, particularly in the USA, where in 1933 Aldo Leopold had promoted it as a proactive discipline, not merely the prevention of destruction.[74] This was a science with potential for game reserve-type national parks and it began a shift away from the principles of 'propagation, protection and preservation' towards a more interventionist philosophy.

Given his tremendous enthusiasm as an NPB member, let alone his expertise, it is surprising to learn that in 1952 Bigalke suddenly resigned

---

[68]A.J.A. Roux to Blaine, 6 November 1946 Stevenson-Hamilton Documents in Trust, Kruger National Park archives, Skukuza; Minutes of a meeting of the NPB, 6/7 November 1946, SANParks archives, Groenkloof, Pretoria.

[69]Sandenbergh to NPB, file K8, 'Carnivora control and factors necessitating such control', 2 August 1949, Kruger National Park archives, Skukuza.

[70]Minutes of a meeting of the NPB, 19 September 1949, SANParks archives, Groenkloof, Pretoria.

[71]See, for example, Minutes of a meeting of the NPB, January 1950; 24 January 1950; 13 November 1950, SANParks archives, Groenkloof, Pretoria.

[72]Bigalke, 'Wild life conservation in the Union of South Africa', 5–42; Bigalke, 'Science and the conservation of wild life', 166–172.

[73]Bigalke, 'Wild life conservation in the Union of South Africa', 5–42.

[74]Leopold, *Game Management*.

from the board.[75] As a scientist, he was extremely disappointed to discover that objectivity did not prevail within the NPB and was dismayed to learn at first hand that the board and its growing administrative structures were rife with political agendas and personal squabbles, some of which involved even his personal friends.

The Hoek Inquiry

As noted, the NPB as constituted in 1926 was not made up of expert advisors or knowledgeable managers.[76] In the 1930s, there was frequent tension between the NPB and Stevenson-Hamilton, originating in the National Parks Act of 1926's failure to define the precise organisational structure and administrative responsibilities of the parties involved. While the KNP was in its infancy, this did not much matter, but when thousands of visitors demanded sophisticated facilities and other national parks were established, some kind of head office and formal bureaucracy was required. Bigalke thought there was much room for improvement and in 1951 he persuaded the board to appoint a commission of inquiry to investigate the organisation and clarify areas of responsibility and overlaps. What he did not expect was the controversy that the (closed) commission unleashed, given the strains that had built up over many years in the national parks organisation.

Chaired by Professor P.W. Hoek, a chartered accountant, the commission sat from February to September 1952.[77] Some of the pent-up anger that spilt out before Hoek can be attributed to post-war sociopolitical transformations in the country, but there can be no doubt South Africa's national parks were in deep trouble.[78] From graphic testimony, Hoek learnt of widespread disorganisation and mismanagement: functions were not defined, accountability was absent, attempts to undermine people were common, personnel were unqualified for their posts,[79] and financial record-keeping was so poor that it encouraged fraud and corruption, particularly in land acquisition. Many employees did no work at all and there were accounts of wildlife smuggling and embarrassing

[75]*Pretoria News*, 22 December 1952.

[76]Stevenson-Hamilton, journal entry 13 November 1942, in Stevenson-Hamilton family archives, Fairholm, Larkhall, Scotland.

[77]Hoek, 'Verslag', 3–4.

[78]Hoek, 'Verslag', 150.

[79]Hoek, 'Verslag', 7.

public drunkenness among senior officials, including the KNP's senior game ranger, Louis B. Steyn.[80]

Equally significant, however, was the evidence about what ought to have been professional wildlife management. So toxic were the internal politics and personal squabbling that the core business of nature protection had been completely lost sight of. No national park was an ecological unit, many were infested with alien plants, and the handful of reports that had been done (soil, fish and trees) were fragmented and incomplete.[81] It appeared that the absence of overall policy together with mismanagement had actually resulted in the near-extinction of species, such as the black rhinoceros *Diceros bicornis*, oribi *Ourebia orebi*, red duiker *Cephalophus natalensis*, mountain zebra *Equus zebra zebra*, boekenhout *Rapanea melanophloeos* and red ivory *Berchemia zeyheri*.[82] Even the newly appointed biologist in the KNP, T.G. Nel, formerly Bigalke's educational officer in the National Zoological Gardens, had become mired in the vicious internal politics. Nel had been given no authority by the board and was constantly undermined by certain antagonistic board members and particularly by the game ranger staff.[83]

Many of the problems relating to professional values were ascribed to the poor relationships and unclear lines of authority among the board, managers, wardens and game rangers. Staff numbers were increasing and proper lines of authority and areas of responsibility and accountability were badly needed. There was a relatively large permanent staff. At head office in Pretoria, there were eight whites and one African; at Addo, one white and eight Africans; at Bontebok, just one African; at KGNP, one white and eight Africans; at Mountain Zebra, one white and one African; and at KNP, 18 whites and about 400 Africans, with about 150 more people of both races serving tourists. Of the 29 permanent white staff in the KNP, three were described as 'scientists and educationalists'.[84] There was no one of this description in the other four national parks, nor was there anyone at head office – or even formally on the board – responsible for scientific or educational liaison.

No game ranger had training in natural history. Worse, many had no inclination to acquire it, actually thwarting attempts to improve their

[80]Hoek, 'Verslag', 21–25.
[81]Hoek, 'Verslag', 25–26.
[82]Hoek, 'Verslag', 12, 26, 34.
[83]Hoek, 'Verslag', 21, 25.
[84]Hoek, 'Verslag', 7.

wildlife skills and refusing to report sightings of fauna or flora.[85] In the KGNP, Le Riche spent far more time tending to his private flock of sheep than attending to his nature conservation duties.[86] Over 14 years of service (approximately 3710 working days), Le Riche could give no account of his activities for 2479 of them.[87] Ainslie, the ranger at Mountain Zebra National Park, totally neglected his duties.[88] With one exception, rangers in all the parks devoted only between 6% and 14% of their time to matters to do with nature, the rest being spent either doing nothing at all, or engaged in 'admin', for which no records could be produced.[89]

The problems that had arisen in South Africa's parks had been avoided in the USA, where the NPS, an arm of government, comprised three separate divisions: 'ranger', 'naturalist' and an educational division, which was, in fact, the 'birthplace and nursery of ecological ideas within the NPS'.[90] Scientists such as Bigalke advocated similar structures for South Africa. It was unfortunate that the chief biologist of the NPS (from 1939), Victor Cahalane, visited South Africa during this period of upheaval between November 1950 to February 1951, because so much more could have been made of his advice had the situation within the NPB been more settled politically and administratively.[91] Cahalane (1901–1993) – the author of *Mammals of North America* (1947), a book very much like Stevenson-Hamilton's *Wild Life of South Africa* of the same date, as well as other publications – was a landscape gardener and forester by training. However, he was also a museum director, a director of the Cranbrook Institute of Science and a deer investigator with the University of Michigan in Lansing. Cahalane's visit was at the invitation of then board chairman A.E. (Alf) Trollip. Trollip served on the NPB from 1945 (when, as a prominent United Party MP, he was appointed by Conroy) to 1950 (when the National Party was back in power).[92] In 1950, Trollip asked the NPS director, Newton Drury, if Cahalane could visit the NPB to establish a 'wildlife management program' in

---

[85]Hoek, 'Verslag', 20, 26.

[86]Hoek, 'Verslag', 32.

[87]Hoek, 'Verslag', 77–79.

[88]Hoek, 'Verslag', 50–52.

[89]Hoek, 'Verslag', 74.

[90]J. Pritchard, *Preserving Yellowstone's Natural Conditions: Science and the Perception of Nature* (Lincoln, NE: University of Nebraska Press, 1999), 48–52.

[91]See Sellars, *Preserving Nature in the National Parks*, 165, 169; Ise, *Our National Park Policy*, 99.

[92]Trollip, the Member of Parliament for Brakpan, who was English-speaking, later changed sides, joining the National Party and becoming a Cabinet Minister.

the national parks. Once outside funding had been obtained from the Carnegie Foundation, Cahalane travelled to South Africa to train 'South Africans in the management of large wildlife species', although there is no record of what kind of training took place.[93]

Bigalke, who particularly admired the NPS' educational branch (which was never replicated in South Africa), was no doubt one of those to welcome the distinguished visitor. Cahalane spent two weeks in the KGNP and also visited the Mountain Zebra and Addo Elephant National Parks. He found all of them magnificent, and in an article in the *Farmer's Weekly* said that nothing had prepared him for the grandeur and wealth of life he had seen. This did not, however, prevent him from voicing many criticisms. These included the woefully inadequate tourist facilities and services, in terms both of quantity and quality, that he had experienced in the KNP. He was alarmed by the prevalence of invasive vegetation in the Cape of Good Hope Nature Reserve, postulating that unless it was controlled, within 40 years the fynbos would be doomed. He was also disappointed in the lack of pride that South Africans took in their national parks, signified by the continuing high level of poaching by biltong-seeking whites and the feeding of wild animals.[94]

Despite its potential importance, Cahalane's visit became a side-show to the main event, the Hoek inquiry. In the event, Hoek's final recommendations were straightforward. An appropriate corporate culture needed to be developed and this required proper management structures with agreed policies, procedures and a healthy public relations outlook.[95] He proposed the establishment of three separate departments: biology, management and park development and tourism. Hoek further recommended that the chair of the board should be a professional biologist and that there should be a formal director of national parks to whom other department heads and all wardens would report directly.[96]

[93]T. Young and L.M. Dilsaver, 'Collecting and diffusing "the world's best thought": International cooperation by the National Park Service', *The George Wright Forum* 28, no. 3 (2011): 269–278; see also V. Cahalane, 'A report to the National Parks Board of Trustees, South Africa 1951', in L66, Foreign Parks and Historic Sites, Africa, 1961–1969, Box 2171, Appendix 3, RG 79 (National Park Service), US National Archives (NARA), College Park, Maryland.
[94]Anon., 'American authority's impressions of Union's game reserves', *Farmer's Weekly* 80 (1951): 58.
[95]Hoek, 'Verslag', 30.
[96]Hoek, 'Verslag', 39–41.

Immediately after the Hoek inquiry (which was handed to the attorney-general but never made public because of fears of libel),[97] NPB secretary van Graan, much disliked and distrusted by Stevenson-Hamilton, was dismissed. The way thus cleared, restructuring of the organisation could begin.[98] The government simply ignored the recommendation that the board chair be a scientist, because no politically reliable scientist was at hand. Instead, Malan's Minister of Lands, J.G. Strijdom, appointed F.H. (Fox) Odendaal, a lawyer who, according to his biography, had no specific interest in wildlife protection.[99] His qualifications for the post were that he was a great friend of Strijdom as well as a political ally and business partner (and was later Administrator of the Transvaal). Odendaal was to remain chairman until 1965. Rocco Knobel, another man with the correct political credentials, was appointed to the new position of director of national parks in April 1953. In 1973, on the twentieth anniversary of his appointment, Knobel (1914–2002) recounted to his fellow board members how he, a social worker and family counsellor for the Dutch Reformed Church in Krugersdorp – a small town close to Johannesburg – applied on a whim for the directorship and, without supplying any references, found himself catapulted into this exalted position on 1 April 1953.[100] Knobel never abandoned his church and counselling background and training, and strongly believed in the national parks' social programme, including their role as moral bastion against 'outside influences'.[101] He began board

[97]*Rand Daily Mail*, 27 October 1952 and 1 November 1952.

[98]D. O'Meara, *Forty Lost Years: The Apartheid State and the Politics of the National Party, 1948–1994* (Johannesburg and Athens, OH: Ravan Ohio University Press, 1996), 43–44; S. Dubow, *A Commonwealth of Knowledge: Science, Sensibility, and White South Africa, 1820–2000* (Oxford: Oxford University Press, 2006), 252. The Broederbond affiliations among board members and NPB employees has yet to be fully researched, a difficult task because of the secrecy involved. E.A.N. le Riche, of the Kalahari Gemsbok National Park, and F.C. Eloff, board member, University of Pretoria, were formally recorded as members in I. Wilkins and H. Strydom, *The Super-Afrikaners: Inside the Afrikaner Broederbond* (Johannesburg: Jonathan Ball, 1978) (Le Riche, A146; Eloff, A36).

[99]Human Sciences Research Council, *Dictionary of South African Biography*, vol. 4 (Pretoria: HSRC, 1981), 417–418.

[100]Born in Kimberley in 1914, Knobel was the son of a missionary and spent part of his childhood in the Bechuanaland Protectorate. He became assistant director of the Johannesburg Municipal Welfare Department (1940–1951), chief professional officer of the Armesorgraad van die Witwatersrand (1951–1953) and first chairman of the Social Worker's Association of South Africa.

[101]Minutes of a meeting of the NPB, 23 June 1967, SANParks archives, Groenkloof, Pretoria.

meetings with what can only be described as a sermon and often asserted that the Creator spoke through nature and that it was the duty of NPB officials to assist Him in this.[102] For example, he opened the August 1966 meeting with reflections on *erkentlikheid* (recognition) and *eerlikheid* (honesty);[103] that of August 1969 on limits to freedom (*vryheid*);[104] and after a senior and greatly trusted official was fired for fraud and theft, Knobel's homily concerned, perhaps predictably, the lesson of Judas, the traitor.[105]

Unsurprisingly, it was not long before the Afrikaans-speaking National Party supporter Knobel and the English-speaking Sandenbergh locked horns. Refusing to resign in response to political pressure, the KNP warden was dismissed in 1954 for financial malpractices allegedly perpetrated by a member of his staff.[106] What was unexpected, given his lack of academic and professional training and the accounts of his bad behaviour and disruptiveness that had surfaced during the Hoek inquiry,[107] was that Senior Game Ranger Louis B. Steyn was appointed warden in his stead. Before his appointment as a ranger by Stevenson-Hamilton in 1929, Steyn – an outspoken and devoted Afrikaner nationalist whom Stevenson-Hamilton later came to distrust and suspect of being cruel to his African staff – had been a teacher and big game hunter in East Africa.[108]

Formal Biology

However, if a scientist had not been appointed to the NPB after Bigalke resigned, or to the directorship of the NPB, or even to the wardenship of the KNP, at least there was now a biologist on the staff of the KNP, in the

[102]Minutes of a meeting of the NPB, 23 June 1967, SANParks archives, Groenkloof, Pretoria.

[103]Minutes of a meeting of the NPB, 11 August 1966, SANParks archives, Groenkloof, Pretoria.

[104]Minutes of a meeting of the NPB, 19 August 1969, SANParks archives, Groenkloof, Pretoria.

[105]Minutes of a meeting of the NPB, 17 February 1970, SANParks archives, Groenkloof, Pretoria.

[106]Minutes of a meeting of the NPB, 1 February 1954, SANParks archives, Groenkloof, Pretoria; U. de V. Pienaar, *Goue Jare: Die Verhaal van die Nasionale Krugerwildtuin 1947–1991* (Stilbaai: The Author, 2010), 631.

[107]Minutes of a meeting of the NPB, 20 October 1952, SANParks archives, Groenkloof, Pretoria. See also Sandenbergh to van Graan, 27 July 1951; Steyn to van Graan, 16 May 1951, Box K2/1/1/, archives of the Kruger National Park, Skukuza.

[108]Stevenson-Hamilton, journal entry, 8 January 1934, in Stevenson-Hamilton family archives, Fairholm, Larkhall, Scotland.

person of T.G. Nel. He had previously been seconded by the Department of Education to Bigalke's National Zoological Gardens as guide-lecturer and was subsequently elevated to conservator in the newly established Transvaal Division of Nature Conservation in 1947.[109] In 1950, when the NPB advertised the post of 'biologist', Nel was successful and he was tasked with establishing the research section. There was, of course, no precedent for a research section within the NPB. To work under Nel's direction, the board employed two botanists, H.P. van der Schijff in 1951 (referred to as an 'ecologist')[110] and A.M. Brynard[111] in 1952, and an information officer, R.J. Labuschagne.[112] The mandate of the two scientists was to initiate and carry out wildlife research in all national parks and that of Labuschagne was to organise an educational service, whose activities would include producing appropriate wildlife literature.

In 1951 Nel submitted his first annual report[113] and in 1952 he stated his research priorities as determining ecological boundaries, pasture and burning, population studies, ecological factors and influences, e.g. tourism. This earned him – not surprisingly – high praise from Bigalke.[114] By 1954, despite unsatisfactory practical work and his difficulties in preventing the game rangers from killing lions and wild dog as freely as they wished,[115] Nel had considerable achievements to record. He had already produced a number of research reports and started surveys of insects, fish,

[109]R. Bigalke, *The National Zoological Gardens of South Africa* (Johannesburg: Central New Agency, 1954), 63–68.

[110]H.P. van der Schijff, 'An ecological study of the flora of the Kruger National Park' (DSc diss., Potchefstroom University, 1957).

[111]Brynard grew up near Calvinia, Cape province, and earned an MSc degree from Potchefstroom University for his study of *Senecio retrorsus*. Stationed at Mountain Zebra National Park, near Cradock, in 1955 he was given leave to begin doctoral studies at Aberdeen University in Scotland. His research was a comparative study of two *Erica* species, *E. tetralix* and *E. cinerea*. This, however, was never completed as the experimental and field data were stolen from his motor vehicle and never recovered.

[112]National Parks Board, *Annual Report 1952*, 1.

[113]*Annual Report of the Biologist, Kruger National Park 1951*, 97.

[114]Bigalke (Secretary to the Scientific Advisory Committee) to NPB Director, 15 February 1954, Bigalke archives, Pretoria. (Per kind favour of Dr R. Bigalke.)

[115]Nel to Warden, 30 November 1953 requesting immediate cessation of carnivora control as being in conflict with the national park ethos, 'The time for a carnivore guilty until proven innocent is over', he wrote. In this instruction, Nel was countermanded by the Director (Knobel), who on 23 February 1954 gave permission to control all predators, including lions and crocodiles and, if necessary, wild dogs. Extract from Board meeting 25 September 1953, box K1/11(I) 1953–1962, Kruger National Park archives, Skukuza.

birds and mammals. Boundary studies had proceeded, plant samples had been collected and pamphlets on trees, fish, birds and reptiles had been published for tourists. L.E.W. Codd, employed by the Division of Botany in the Department of Agriculture, had been persuaded in 1951 to produce a Botanical Survey Memoir, a handy, well-illustrated (including colour plates) book for visitors entitled *Trees and Shrubs of the Kruger National Park*. As far as animal life was concerned, in 1939 Rudolph Bigalke had authored *A Guide to Some Common Animals of the Krüger National Park*, illustrated with photographs, while in 1951, C.T. Astley Maberly, a well-known artist and naturalist, published a book of sketches that showed sexual dimorphism and different ages of various large mammals, called *What Buck is That? A Guide to the Antelope and Other More Notable Animals of the Kruger National Park*.[116] Nel had himself begun a report on the bio-ecology of lion (although this stalled because of difficulties with the uncooperative game rangers) and had started a mammal census.

If Nel began as an educationist, he showed himself adept at expanding his expertise to include international nature conservation. During his tenure at KNP, he was the only African member on the world committee of the IUPN, an arm of UNESCO (United Nations Educational, Scientific and Cultural Organisation), and was invited to participate in gatherings such as the African ornithological conference in Livingstone, Northern Rhodesia, and the Scientific Council for Africa South of the Sahara.

What is remarkable is how much Nel achieved, given the often unsupportive milieu in which he worked. Steyn, the new warden, was extremely hostile to science. His 1951 diary records: 'This questionnaire of Nel's that wants to know everything about a lion from conception to death is a farce and I have treated it as such, except where the questions relate to whether there are too many lions. I do not believe that such a set of questions about any wild animals in Africa can ever be answered by all the scientists in the world together – certainly not by imitation scientists.'[117] Naturally, this attitude proved discouraging to the scientific staff and in January 1955 van der Schijff, who had begun to amass a considerable herbarium in the KNP, resigned, citing dissatisfaction with the organisation in general, the appointment of Steyn as warden in particular, and the lack of support given to scientific reports. He later became a

---

[116]Bigalke, *Guide to Some Common Animals of the Krüger National Park*; C.T. Astley Maberly, *What Buck is that? A Guide to the Antelope and Other More Notable Animals of Kruger National Park* (Bloemfontein: A.C. White, 1951).
[117]Hoek, 'Verslag', 28.

prominent professor of botany at the University of Pretoria. Many South African scientists were concerned by this turn of events and a newspaper reported that several of the most prominent of them had gone to the prime minister to ask that something be done.[118]

The adversarial relationship between the biologists (who reported to the director) and the game rangers (who reported to the warden) came to a head at a national conference on nature conservation held in the KNP in 1955. The solution was to divide the administrative from the nature conservation duties and to place the game rangers in the latter division. A promising scientific development related to the establishment of a state-supported Ecological Institute for the Lowveld. The NPB had at first supported this proposal in 1953, but the government subsequently pulled out of the project and decided not to fund it. A solution was found by creating a steering committee for scientific research in the national parks in cooperation with the Scientific Advisory Council for National Parks and Nature Reserves. At the 1955 conference, this steering committee was set in motion under the chairmanship of the eminent entomologist and veterinarian Professor H.O. Mönnig, and with Knobel, veterinarian R. Ortlepp, Bigalke and Professor A.P. Goosens, head of the department of botany at Potchefstroom University, as members. They agreed that game rangers should have proper job descriptions: their functions should be to protect wildlife from destruction; to control destructive and dangerous animals; to investigate animal–human conflict; to study animal populations; to disseminate information to the public; and to observe characteristics and life cycles of the fauna and flora.[119]

In the same year, 1955, Nel persuaded the board to employ U. de V. (Tol) Pienaar, as assistant biologist. He had a PhD in histology and embryology from the medical school of the University of the Witwatersrand and had since chosen to become a game ranger in the KNP. With his joining the team, the conservation division was at full strength once more.[120] In time, Pienaar became extremely influential, rising to become warden of the Kruger National Park in 1978 and chief director of South Africa's National Parks Board from 1987 until 1991.

---

[118]*Rand Daily Mail*, 13 January 1955.

[119]C.S.L. Schutte, 'Oor die hoofdoel van nasionale parke en die stigting van 'n ekologiese instituut', n.d. 5, KNP K8. See also KNP K1/13, NPB meeting, 22/23 September 1954, item 13, files K1/16, K1/19/1, K1/20, file K1/19/1/. Minutes of the first meeting of the Steering Committee, 10 May 1955; NPB meeting, 23 March 1956, item 25F, annexure L, Kruger National Park archives, Skukuza.

[120]National Parks Board of Trustees, *Annual Reports* 1951, 1952 and 1953.

While there was little in Nel's scientific achievements to quibble with, his tenure was politically precarious because he was not an overt National Party man. Bigalke was keen for him to become head of the NPB's nature conservation division, and in September 1955 he wrote to a fellow steering committee member to gather support for Nel, because he suspected that the NPB (of which he was no longer a member) wanted to get rid of Nel and put in its own politically reliable man, R.J. Labuschagne, the liaison and information official appointed in 1951. Bigalke considered Labuschagne unsuitable to lead the division (he was ultimately proved correct in this assessment), and to head off his appointment suggested that the incumbent should have a doctorate in zoology and preferably also competency in botany, together with experience in nature conservation in South Africa – none of which Labuschagne had.[121] Political intrigue delayed the establishment of the new division for three years and it took effect only in April 1958. By then Bigalke – and Nel – had been outmanoeuvred: Nel had resigned and Labuschagne was appointed chief of the nature conservation division and was later to become the deputy-director of the NPB. Labuschagne, a non-scientist, was thus in control of all the game rangers and responsible for the entire portfolio of conservation, scientific studies and educational work.[122] Bigalke must have been extremely disappointed to have his years of hard work on behalf of formal science in the KNP end so ignominiously and for political reasons, although at least Brynard headed up the research section.

While all this was brewing, Bigalke and Nel corresponded with each other. Their letters do not detail the reasons Nel considered his position to have become untenable, but they suggest he had become the object of political intrigue of the kind that Hoek had uncovered a few years earlier. Bigalke encouraged Nel to involve the other biologists who had resigned to collaborate in approaching the Secretary of Lands, call for a commission of inquiry and put their case forward. However, having witnessed the Hoek Commission and the subsequent promotion of Steyn to the post of warden, Nel had no appetite for such a bruising and uncertain course of action.[123]

Once the structures of the organisation had been settled, Afrikaans became the dominant language and correspondence and other communication in English became a thing of the past. There was, however,

[121]Bigalke to Goossens, 3 September 1955, Bigalke archives, Pretoria. (Per kind favour of Dr R. Bigalke.)
[122]Later to become Assistant Director, he was fired for corruption.
[123]Bigalke to Nel, 13 February 1957, Bigalke archives, Pretoria. (Per kind favour of Dr R. Bigalke.)

a rapprochement between the practical men in the field – the game rangers – and the biologists, who, together were to be responsible for nature conservation management.[124] When Steyn retired as warden in 1961 he was succeeded by Brynard: at last, a trained scientist headed the overall management of the KNP. With the departure of Steyn and the changes in personnel and organisational structure, the institutional politics calmed down enough to allow the ethos of 'scientific management' to grow. Increasingly, the KNP was managed along the then current agricultural principles of productivity, linked to an ecological paradigm of 'stability' and 'climax'. Fencing the western boundary was completed, artificial water points proliferated so that wildlife did not have to search for water, and the park was divided into 'blocks' that were burnt regularly according to a predetermined schedule. Later scientists have observed that management of the Kruger and other national parks was conducted on a commercial agricultural model, with stock management or 'carrying capacity' as a guiding principle, just as Stevenson-Hamilton had feared. Destructive wildfires were curtailed by the block burning system, which, while providing fresh grass and foliage for browsing in different parts of the park in different years, has in the longer term reduced heterogeneity. Artificial water points (a particular penchant of Sandenbergh and the board of his time) were designed to prevent over-grazing in any one area and to ensure an even distribution of animals throughout the range. In fact, this water manipulation has advantaged water-dependent species, and is probably one of the factors in the declining numbers of roan antelope *Hippotragus equinus* and sable antelope *Hippotragus niger* in the KNP. Moreover, the provision of year-round water has affected the delicate arid ecology of the KGNP.[125]

The International Milieu and South Africa's Role

Between 1930 and 1960 there were many important international developments in wildlife protection of which South Africa was, in one way or another, part. Mainly focused on the organisation and structure of

---

[124]National Parks Board, *Annual Report of the Assistant Biologist 1957–1958*, 1.

[125]See N. Owen-Smith, ed., *Management of Large Mammals in African Conservation Areas: Proceedings of a Symposium held in Pretoria, South Africa, 29–30 April 1982* (Pretoria: HAUM, 1983); and H. Biggs and P. Novellie, 'Science for biodiversity management', in *South African National Parks: A Celebration*, eds A. Hall-Martin and J. Carruthers (Johannesburg: Horst Klemm, 2003), 69–71.

national parks and protectionism worldwide, they later came to have a considerable impact on science. The 1930s began with 'an important International Congress for the Protection of Nature' convened in Paris from 1 to 4 July 1931. Fourteen countries were represented, and Lord Onslow's message on behalf of Great Britain was reproduced in the *Journal for the Preservation of the Fauna of the Empire*. No delegate from the British colonies and dominions attended, although there were two representatives from the SPFE, Stevenson-Hamilton's correspondents and friends K. Caldwell and C. W. Hobley. The first of the general resolutions passed was that governments should endeavour to spread the 'importance of the idea of the Protection of Nature from the scientific, economic, and educational point of view'. Second, there was an important presentation in London of the Royal Geographical Society in 1931 on 'Proposed British National Parks for Africa'. As he was in South Africa, Stevenson-Hamilton was unable to attend, but his memorandum on the KNP and its successes in increasing the number of animals and species, the cessation of routine predator control and the growing number of visitors (and thus income) was read during the discussion.[126]

Both the 1931 meetings took the view that a new conference on wildlife protection in Africa was due.[127] This occurred in London in 1933 (31 October to 8 November). Planned as a delayed follow-up to the failed London Convention of 1900, it was attended by an official South African delegate, Charles te Water, the Union's high commissioner in London. Admitting that 'in South Africa there is hardly a young man who doesn't get his gun and go out on the veldt', te Water was pleased to inform the gathering that hunting was prohibited in South African national parks and that all of them were on government-owned land. The meeting lauded South Africa for its game laws, commenting favourably on the KNP, 'whose establishment in 1926 made the Union a standard bearer in the sanctuary field' and approved the recent establishment of the KGNP, Addo and the Bontebok National Park. Onslow, again the British delegate, suggested there might be another important kind of reserve that totally excluded people, even visitors. In this context, Albert Park in the Belgian Congo was commended for being organised 'along

---

[126]R. W. G. Hingston, 'Proposed national parks for Africa', *The Geographical Journal* 97, no. 5 (1931): 401–428.

[127]'International Congress for the Protection of Nature', *Journal of the Society for the Preservation of the Fauna of the Empire* 15 (1931): 43–52.

scientific lines'.[128] The meeting culminated with the signing of a fresh *London Convention for the Protection of the Fauna and Flora of Africa* on 8 November 1933, and marked the first attempt to clarify the terminology of protected areas.[129] Te Water and Sir Arthur Hill, director of the Royal Botanic Gardens, Kew, signed on behalf of the Union of South Africa. The treaty distinguishes between a national park and a 'strict nature reserve', a 'fauna and flora reserve' and a 'reserve with prohibition for hunting and collecting'. While most clauses deal with hunting restrictions and legislation, one (8.4) mentions science, in that plants and animals of 'special scientific interest' are to be protected.[130]

In this decade the USA began to play a part in African protectionist affairs. In 1933, the American Committee for International Wild Life Protection prepared an influential publication entitled *African Game Protection: An Outline of the Existing Game Reserves and National Parks of Africa with Notes on Certain Species of Big Game Nearing Extinction or Needing Additional Protection*. Stevenson-Hamilton's publications were among the references and these, together with the work of Leonard Gill

---

[128]S.S. Hayden, *The International Protection of Wild Life: An Examination of Treaties and Other Agreements for the Preservation of Birds and Mammals* (New York, NY: Columbia University Press, 1942), 22, 55–56.

[129]The 1933 convention defined a national park as an area:

Placed under public control, the boundaries of which shall not be altered or any portion be capable of alienation except by the competent legislative authority;

Set aside for the propagation, protection and preservation of objects of aesthetic, geological, prehistoric, historical, archaeological, or other scientific interest for the benefit, advantage or enjoyment of the general public;

In which the hunting, killing or capturing of fauna and the destruction or collection of flora is prohibited except by or under the direction or control of the park authorities. In accordance with the above provisions, facilities shall, so far as possible, be given to the general public for observing the fauna and flora in national parks.

[130]Details of the Convention are reproduced in *The London Convention for the Protection of African Fauna and Flora*, Special Publication of the American Committee for International Wild Life Protection, No. 6 (Cambridge, MA: American Committee for International Wild Life Protection, 1935). The foreword, by John C. Phillips, emphasised that the USA had no special standing in regard to Africa, but followed African wildlife protection with great interest. Interestingly, a different range of classification was incorporated into the 1942 Pan American Convention on Nature Protection and Wildlife Preservation in the Western Hemisphere where 'wilderness' was an important consideration, namely, national park, national reserve, nature monument and strict wilderness reserve: K. Bishop, N. Dudley, A. Phillips and S. Stolton, *Speaking a Common Language: The Uses and Performance of the IUCN System of Management Categories for Protected Areas* (Cardiff: Cardiff University, IUCN and UNEP, 2004), 44.

(director, South African Museum) and Alwin Haagner (formerly of the National Zoological Gardens), were quoted extensively.[131] At the Second International Conference for the Protection of the Fauna and Flora of Africa held in London from 24 to 27 May 1938, te Water was again the South African representative. He told the meeting that fauna and flora was a 'constantly alive' subject in South Africa thanks to the KNP, but he also criticised the gathering for being too narrow and for excluding men of experience such as Stevenson-Hamilton.[132]

There was also another, separate strand of international protection, which emanated from Europe, particularly the Netherlands and Switzerland, and had more to do with science and with 'natural monuments' (*naturdenkmal*) than with the protection of Africa's large mammals.[133] The leadership of this group was different, although there were links with Buxton and Onslow of the SPFE. Numerous accounts exist of the efforts to this end of the Swiss naturalist and explorer Paul Sarasin and of Pieter van Tienhoven, who had established a Foundation for International Nature Protection in November 1930.[134]

[131]Phillips, *African Game Protection*.

[132]The second International Conference for the Protection of the Fauna and Flora of Africa was held in London from 24 to 27 May 1938; Charles te Water, the South African High Commissioner in London, averred that fauna and flora was a subject constantly alive in South Africa, 'a national pride that has grown up in later years' due to the success of the KNP. He requested that a wider conference be held that included the men with experience, e.g. Stevenson-Hamilton. Cabinet Papers CAB 58/93, International conferences 1933 and 1938, National Archives, Kew, London.

[133]IUPN, *Proceedings of the Third International Conference: Protection of the Fauna and Flora of Africa* (Bukavu: Belgian Congo, 1953).

[134]See B. Gissibl, S. Höhler and P. Kupper, eds, *Civilizing Nature: National Parks in Global and Historical Perspective* (New York, NY: Berghahn, 2012); P. Kupper, 'Science and the national parks: A transatlantic perspective on the interwar years', *Environmental History* 14, no. 1 (2009): 58–81; P. Kupper, *Creating Wilderness: A Transnational History of the Swiss National Park* (Oxford: Berghahn, 2014); H.J. van der Windt, 'Biologists bridging science and the conservation movement: The rise of nature conservation and nature management in the Netherlands, 1850–1950', *Environment and History* 18, no. 2 (2012): 209–236; W.M. Adams, *Against Extinction: The Story of Conservation* (London: Earthscan, 2004); M. Cioc, *The Game of Conservation: International Treaties to Protect the World's Migratory Animals* (Athens, OH : Ohio University Press, 2009); B.J. Lausche, *Weaving a Web of Environmental Law* (Berlin: IUCN Environmental Law Programme, 2008); P. Jepson and R.J. Whittaker, 'Histories of protected areas: Internationalisation of

These three movements – from the British Empire, the USA and Europe – coalesced in 1948 when the IUPN was established at a meeting at Fontainebleau under the auspices of UNESCO, whose director-general was Julian Huxley, the British conservationist, naturalist, national park advocate and evolutionary biologist. Huxley considered UNESCO an appropriate home for nature protection because he believed the 'science' in the title to be cultural and institutional, as well as international. The IUPN held a number of meetings in the 1950s: Brussels 1950, Caracas 1952, Copenhagen 1955, Edinburgh 1956, Athens 1958 and Warsaw 1960. Charles Bernard (chair of the 1947 Brunnen meeting that drafted the IUPN constitution) was president of the IUPN, whose members included 18 governments, seven international organisations and 107 national organisations concerned with nature protection. There was also representation from 33 countries. No African countries were present, nor was there a British imperial representative.[135] Despite a shortage of funding (UNESCO ended its financial support in 1954), the IUPN grew quickly, and 35 new members were admitted in 1950, including South Africa, represented by C.H. Taljaard, secretary of the South African legation in Brussels. New members mentioned on this occasion included the NPB and the South African Wild Life Protection Society, which had been recruited by Jean-Paul Harroy, the IUPN general secretary, during a visit to South Africa. It was Harroy who acknowledged that nature protection could no longer be an emotional and moral issue. Instead, he argued, in a world filled with economic foreboding after the Second World War, the protection of nature needed a utilitarian perspective. If nature and the economy were to be linked, he continued, the scientific study of natural communities was required 'and ecology appeared to be the appropriate science'.[136]

At the Caracas meeting in 1952, the Natal Parks, Game and Fish Preservation Board joined the organisation and KNP biologist T.G. Nel was elected to the Commission on Education, the only operational

---

conservationist values and their adoption in the Netherlands Indies (Indonesia)', *Environment and History* 8 (2002): 129–172; M.W. Holdgate, *The Green Web: A Union for World Conservation* (London: Earthscan, 1999).

[135]In 1948 the International Union for the Protection of Nature was founded and it held its first formal gathering in 1950 to report on *The Position of Nature Protection Throughout the World in 1950* during which South Africa was only very briefly mentioned.

[136]D. Bergandi, ed., *The Structural Links between Ecology, Evolution and Ethics: The Virtuous Epistemic Circle* (Boston, MA: Boston Studies in the Philosophy and History of Science, 2013), 87.

commission at the time. South Africa was among the highest financial contributors (after the USA, the United Kingdom and Belgium). At this meeting, the threatened species in the xerophile bush near Grahamstown, cycads and cushion bush *Oldenburgia arbuscular* were mentioned as being of concern. In the 1950s, the NPB and other South African organisations consistently attended IUPN meetings and their influence appeared to be growing. Both Knobel of the NPB and Jack Vincent from Natal, for example, attended the Edinburgh meeting and Knobel began to take a leadership role, joining the Survival Service Commission.[137] Not a scientist himself, Knobel proved a professional, competent and inspiring leader. He reported that he had devoted himself to the gatherings dealing with the management of nature reserves. At the request of the NPB, Knobel was actively involved in the international debates on whether the heads of parks organisations and wardens of national parks should be 'biologists'. He reported that the consensus was that although biologists should not be excluded from these management positions, such roles would cut into their research time. Thus, in his report in the *South African Biological Society Pamphlet* 18 of 1956, Knobel quoted international scientific luminaries E.B. Worthington and J.D. Ovington as agreeing that 'there is not much modern scientific knowledge yet available for direct application in conservation' and scientists should therefore be encouraged to remain scientists. 'Research staff must not be burdened with management projects and management staff must be supplied with the most recent and controlled scientific data to enable them to manage the project with due regard to scientific principles involved.' As this was the current management philosophy of the NPB, Knobel came away convinced that South Africa was on the right track, particularly in that protected area research should be applied, and that 'no research need be considered which does not represent a prototype or test able to contribute to some possible management treatment'.[138] In Athens (1958), the presence of both Knobel and Labuschagne was noted, as was that of Douglas Hey of the Cape Department of Nature Conservation. On this occasion, Knobel was elected to the executive board (a four-year term) and also to the Commission on National Parks, while Hey became a member of the

---

[137]R.F. Nash, 'The exporting and importing of nature: Nature-appreciation as a commodity, 1850–1980', *Perspectives in American History* 12 (1979): 519–560.
[138]R. Knobel, 'The IUCN', *South African Biological Society Pamphlet* 18 (Pretoria: Biological Society, 1956): 26–33.

game management committee and Labuschagne of the Survival Service Commission.[139]

South Africa had an important African presence in 1953, when the Third International Conference on the Protection of the Fauna and Flora of Africa was held in Bukavu in the Belgian Congo (24–27 May). The conference began from the premise that since the 1930s research perspectives had changed from conservation management as a 'negative form of protection' to a discipline based on knowledge. Such studies would need 'modern' ecological methods, 'undertaken and developed by groups of specialists working with assurance of permanence and continuity'.[140] The comprehensive questionnaires completed by all the African colonies and countries are instructive about their national parks and strategies for protecting nature in Africa.

South Africa was well placed to continue active participation in this international community, and even to become the African leader. This was not to be. Instead, apartheid policies complicated continued NPB involvement in African affairs, and many meetings, including those related to Africa specifically, took place without South Africa being present. Yet, some South African institutions – including the NPB's representation in the IUCN – were never expelled from these scientific organisations and in time, in the era of grand apartheid, these international nature conservation structures proved very useful as platforms for parading South Africa's achievements in an era when the country was vilified in so many other international forums.

In 1958 the NPB initiated *Koedoe*, a bilingual annual research journal.[141] It may have been the first journal produced by a national park organisation and continues to exist. Like many journals, the quality fluctuated depending on the peer review it underwent as well as its professional editorship. It is not clear who first suggested that the NPB publish its own annual journal to disseminate its views and research, but one can assume that the senior management cohort at the time, especially the biologists – people like Nel, Brynard and van der Schijff – had a big hand in it. No doubt, too, these people felt the absence of opportunity to publish in journals and reports of the kind produced by the Biological Survey of the US NPS and thus decided to inaugurate their own publication. The first issue was impressive, with articles on an early expedition to the Lowveld from

[139]Knobel, 'The IUCN', 6–33.
[140]*Proceedings of the Third International Conference*, 534.
[141]It became a bi-annual publication in 1989.

Mozambique in 1725, a list of mammals around Mountain Zebra National Park in the Eastern Cape, a mosquito survey and fire research in the KNP, hyena observations and seven articles on the animals of the KGNP. Five articles were in Afrikaans, eight in English; only two were by NPB staff – Brynard (on conditions in the KGNP) and van der Schijff (fire research in the KNP). Naturally, as an in-house journal, the interest, importance or topicality of an article has often exceeded the quality of the research it communicates. However, that does not detract from its utility as a record and as a platform for disseminating or stimulating research.

It is useful to end this chapter by referring to N.J. van der Merwe's article in the 1962 issue entitled 'The position of nature conservation in South Africa'. Van der Merwe was then the NPB's liaison officer. He took the view that South African history began with white settlement in 1652 and, not surprisingly, his is an Afrikaner nationalist perspective on the history of nature conservation in the country. Neither the Natal National Park nor Dongola is mentioned. Useful summaries are provided of the current status of the NPB, its members, its staff and its responsibilities in all the national parks. From the sketchy personnel complement Stevenson-Hamilton had at his disposal in the KNP in 1926, by 1962 the various divisions accounted for more than 300 permanent staff responsible for tourism, engineering and nature conservation and some 700 temporary African labourers, mostly in the KNP. Van der Merwe identified many scientific partners, mostly government departments, but also including five universities (Pretoria, Potchefstroom, Witwatersrand, Rhodes and Natal) and one museum (Transvaal). He noted that *Koedoe* was already proving useful for exchange purposes and that the library in Skukuza had received 92 scientific journals, 28 semi-scientific journals and 27 annual reports. From its modest beginnings in 1926, the NPB was growing into a large and formidable organisation whose influence would be increasingly felt in the decades to come.

Part II · *Measuring, Monitoring and Manipulating, 1960s to 1990s*

5 · *Overview*

By the early 1960s, in comparison with later years, the scientific value of protected areas had not been unlocked and the management of national parks was largely protective, rather than academic or actively managed. This was to change dramatically in the years that followed, not only in South Africa, but also elsewhere. Aspects of protection, preservation and propagation gave way to meticulous measurement and to monitoring and manipulating landscapes and biota. In part this was due to the growing maturity and acceptance of the environmental sciences, but also to new bureaucratic and scientific institutions. Moreover, public enthusiasm for national parks and protected areas burgeoned around the world, aided by social and political environmental activism and greater ease of travel.

The direction of scientific research and management in South Africa's national parks altered in the three decades that followed the reorganisation of the National Parks Board (NPB) in the late 1950s and early 1960s. A number of characteristics distinguished this period and in the overview that follows the major ones will be identified, with further details provided in the subsequent three chapters. Essentially, all the developments in these decades were possible only because the previous preservation and protection of wildlife species and intact landscapes within specified areas had been so successful. This is not to say that elements of the 3Ps did not survive: they did. Certainly there was relentless vigilance against poaching, protective fencing of various parks continued unabated (indeed, in many instances it accelerated on account of increased population density on park boundaries) and even new techniques, such as wildlife translocation, can be construed as within the 'propagation' frame of reference as well as within ideas around 'manipulation'. Nonetheless, in general, with new scientific managers and a politically altered South Africa – let alone a changed world – there are distinct elements of difference that, it can be argued, constitute real change.

In South Africa, the National Party government had come to power in 1948 and, making a relatively clean sweep of the civil service by removing an English-speaking old guard, it gave its support to a fresh cohort of managers and scientists, the majority of whom devoted themselves to matters of technology and studies to enhance national security. Moreover, in the boom years of the 1960s and early 1970s, the South African government expended money on white, and primarily Afrikaans, universities for institutes, units and teaching and research centres that could be regarded as environmental or ecological. These initiatives included nurturing the profession of nature conservation through locally focused zoological, particularly mammalian, studies. Moreover, money was finally available by the National Party government at this time of financial prosperity for establishing and staffing protected areas on a scale previously unheard of.

The predominant political policy between 1960 and 1990 was indubitably apartheid. It entailed an over-arching bureaucratic mind-set of demarcation, order and measurement, whose influence was also apparent in the management of protected areas, indeed all aspects of South African governance. The racist policy that disenfranchised all except South African whites divided people into groups, counted them, placed them in discrete localities based on racial profiles and applied the most stringent urban influx controls that also gave birth to countless committees and institutions to implement it. This approach chimed well with the kinds of measuring, monitoring, describing and also controlling of plants and wild animals that were encouraged in South Africa's national parks. A political philosophy and national demographic policy was not, of course, solely – or even mainly – responsible for the type of science that took place in the country's protected areas, but they provided an enabling environment for accumulating and recording that detail.

By 1960, the Cold War had split the world into two competing and hostile blocs under the leadership of the Union of Soviet Socialist Republics (USSR) and the USA, respectively. Britain and Europe had dwindled in influence and power, especially in Africa, where decolonisation accelerated. This period also saw the maturation of a number of important international organisations that had emerged at the end of the Second World War to police and protect the fragile post-war equilibrium. Leadership in this regard came from the ever-stronger United Nations Organisation (UN) and its subsidiary bodies, including the newly established International Union for the Protection of Nature (IUPN) within UNESCO, which was so critically important to national parks.

This institutional evolution coincided with the emergence of environmentalism as a form of social and civic activism, particularly in the

USA, where the publication of Rachel Carson's *Silent Spring* in 1962 heralded the 'age of environmentalism' and the acceptance of ecology as a platform for action as well as a field of study.[1] Although environmentalism was not as evident in South Africa as elsewhere, because civil society in that country was more preoccupied with the political than the environmental future, it did have an impact on many scholars, academics and civil servants. Previous chapters have examined the role of vegetation studies in spearheading ideas about ecology. In the period under review, zoology – particularly mammalogy or animal studies – not only caught up with botany, but surged ahead. This was fuelled by local tourist interest in the 'Big Five'[2] and also by the rapid technological developments that made tranquillisation, translocation and detailed study of live animals possible. In turn, these innovations were made easier by the fact that South Africa is one of a very few countries in which the sale of indigenous animals is legal. Undoubtedly, too, wildlife husbandry was spurred by growing international concern about feeding an exponentially growing human population: the increased interest in the subject arose in part in anticipation of using indigenous animals for food.

Outside the rather closed scientific research environment within South Africa's national parks, a group of local scientists made an especially important mark on conservation science. This significant initiative came from other important quasi- or partly governmental scientific institutions. These included the Council for Scientific and Industrial Research (CSIR), a nominally non-governmental research institute established by the Smuts government in 1945,[3] and nature conservation bodies such as the Transvaal Division of Nature Conservation, the Natal Parks

---

[1]In his article, 'What does "ecology" mean?', *Tree* 12, no. 4 (1997): 166, Mark Westoby lamented the confusion, as he saw it, between 'the academic's definition of ecology as a branch of disinterested science, and the general public's understanding of ecology as a life philosophy or quasi-religion that connects interpretations of how ecosystems function to moral imperatives and spiritual significance'.

[2]These are the five large mammal species that are most avidly sought by visitors: lion, elephant, black rhinoceros, buffalo and leopard.

[3]Excluded from the ambit of the CSIR was agricultural research – the responsibility of the Department of Agriculture – and research on the human sciences, later catered for by the institution of the Human Sciences Research Council founded in 1969. The CSIR was instituted to focus on industrial applications whether fundamental or applied, and it comprised a strong information service and overseas offices. In time, a number of other focused research institutions were formed from the nucleus of the CSIR, e.g. the National Institute for Water Research.

Game and Fish Preservation Board and, perhaps surprisingly, the natural resource and agricultural agencies of the various apartheid-era African 'homelands' or Bantustans. It was these institutions that, constrained less by the rules and bureaucracy that characterised the NPB, initiated considerable scientific and managerial experimentation, at times eclipsing the NPB in important respects.[4]

South African Context

If developments in environmental sciences in South Africa's national parks and elsewhere over the 30 years of apartheid appear progressive in what follows, it is worth recalling the political context in which they occurred. Important though these developments may have been, they were minor in terms of the overall and tumultuous history of the country.

The period opened with serious revolts by Africans in Durban's Cato Manor and in Pondoland in the Eastern Cape, and with sporadic incidents of sabotage and violence. In a speech to South Africa's parliament on 3 February 1960, British Prime Minister Harold Macmillan warned the country's leaders that fighting against the 'wind of change' in Africa with ever-more repression would lose the country international support and harm it irreparably. His words proved to be prophetic as regards the next 30 years of South African history.

The first of many serious crises erupted just a month after Macmillan's visit, when police killed and wounded many people on 21 March 1960 at Sharpeville, near Vereeniging, in the Transvaal, during a protest by thousands of Africans against 'passes', documents that restricted them to demarcated areas and prevented freedom of movement and free access to employment. Repeatedly, the UN implored South Africa to abandon apartheid. Almost every year, apartheid – acknowledged as a crime against humanity in 1967 – was punished with increasing sanctions and embargoes (at first partial, later total) and expulsion from international

---

[4]J.P.G.M. Cromsigt, S. Archibald and N. Owen-Smith, eds, *Conserving Africa's Mega-Deversity in the Anthropocene: The Hluhluwe-iMfolozi Park Story,* (Cambridge: Cambridge University Press, 2016) and S.R. Johnson, W. Boonzaaier, R. Collinson and R. Davies, 'Changing institutions to respond to challenges: North West Parks, South Africa', in *Evolution and Innovation in Wildlife Conservation: Parks and Game Ranches to Transfrontier Conservation Areas*, eds H. Suich, B. Child and A. Spenceley (London: Earthscan, 2009), 373–391.

institutions and organisations. There was no compromise in South Africa: almost every year, under harsh laws the government banned 'subversive' organisations and their leaders — church leaders included — deported 'undesirable aliens', imprisoned and tortured many without trial and placed hundreds of others under house arrest. South Africa became a pariah state, not only because of its internal politics but also over the execution of its mandate in South West Africa (Namibia).

A referendum among whites in October 1960 narrowly opted to alter the 1909 Union constitution in order to establish a republic totally independent from Britain. Although this was a political victory, very little changed in practical terms. The governor-general was replaced by a state president and all references to 'royal' in documentation and institutions came to an end. While many believed that South Africa could remain within the Commonwealth under this new dispensation, in 1961 South Africa left that body ahead of possible expulsion. Consequently, without formal connection to, or protection from, the Commonwealth and UK, the African National Congress (ANC, founded in 1912 to protest the 1909 constitution) abandoned its previous stance of peaceful negotiation to gain equality and enfranchisement. With the establishment of the militant Umkhonto we Sizwe armed wing of the ANC in 1961 and the growing strength of other local liberation organisations, such as the Pan Africanist Congress and later the Black Consciousness Movement, a struggle akin to civil war began. As resistance escalated into large-scale strikes, sabotage and later widespread civil disobedience, white South Africans responded at every general election — 1961, 1966, 1970, 1974, 1977 and 1981 — by giving increasing backing to the National Party. In 1981, the party won 131 of 165 seats in parliament (proportional representation was only instituted in the post-apartheid era after 1994). Given this support, the government confidently believed it had a mandate from the white electorate to implement its full programme of apartheid, which involved removing every vestige of black participation in the institutions of South Africa and establishing separate polities for the various 'ethnic groups'.[5] Even 'Coloureds', 'Malays' and people of Chinese and Indian descent were forced to live in separate suburbs and locations away from 'white' towns and cities. The African reserves changed name as the institutions and the authorities that governed them metamorphosed

---

[5]For example, in 1971 after 100 years 'Coloured' people were removed from the common voters roll in local authorities in the Cape province.

into 'Bantustans' and 'black/Bantu homelands'. Some of these were given partial autonomy and declared 'self-governing' or even 'independent', as was the case in Transkei, Bophuthatswana, Venda and Ciskei.

In the event, the apartheid system was not sustainable, even with tacit US support for South Africa during the Cold War. Increasing uprisings such as that in Soweto from 1976, the mounting costs of internal and external policing and the financial effects of boycotts and sanctions began to tell on the South African economy by the late 1980s. The regime's long-term ability to maintain the status quo diminished with every passing year.

Even to the government it began to be evident that the current situation could not continue indefinitely. The process of reform began hesitantly with a white referendum in August 1983 that altered the constitution yet again. The senate (upper chamber) was abolished and a 'multi-racial' president's council was appointed in its place to oversee the introduction of a tri-cameral parliament, with separate chambers for whites, 'Coloureds' and 'Indians'. Coming as it did during a period of sabotage, violence, boycotts and attempts to render the country 'ungovernable', and with an extremely low voter turn-out for the 'non-white' chambers, the initiative proved a total failure. Not surprisingly, the UN was only one among many international institutions that dismissed it as window-dressing. By 1986, when South Africa was again mired in a prolonged state of emergency, and with yet another world conference taking place about the country's policies, the cracks were becoming increasingly visible. Clearly, this was a state without long-term prospect of survival, and the situation was being made worse by the escalating and seemingly unstoppable violence between the ANC and Inkatha in Natal.

In an effort to defuse the situation, the government abolished some of the petty apartheid laws. Moreover, businessmen and even government officials began to put out feelers in the rest of Africa to begin a dialogue. The government even offered to release certain political prisoners, provided they abided by certain strict conditions. The ANC, by now recognised by the international community as the sole legitimate voice of the African majority in South Africa and thus even more likely to replace the National Party in any new dispensation, also became more amenable to compromise so as to avoid the utter devastation witnessed in neighbouring countries such as Angola and Mozambique. The ANC, operating within and outside South Africa, was facing leadership tensions. Most importantly, the impending collapse of the USSR and end of the Cold War meant that the ANC would lose much-needed financial and moral support from the Eastern bloc. In 1990, Nelson Mandela was released from prison, the state of emergency was lifted and South West Africa became the independent Namibia. After another whites-only referendum in 1992, which garnered the support of 70% of respondents for a reform process that would lead to a new constitution, the two sides were, at last, ready to negotiate.[6]

It is against this background of a beleaguered, inward-looking and increasingly authoritarian state and countrywide violence that the environmental sciences within and beyond South Africa's national parks must be evaluated. The NPB and the conservation sector were deeply embedded in this political, social and economic matrix and dependent on it for support and opportunity. By the 1960s, the civil service had been largely purged of English-speakers, few of whom remained in positions of political power either. Funding was relatively generous, because generally the state supported institutions such as national parks and game reserves that were recreation destinations for whites. Despite its advanced economy, South Africa had no television until 1976 and the viewing of wildlife documentaries, so important elsewhere, was not a factor.[7]

By the 1960s, there were many national parks in the rest of Africa. Indeed, in 1960, Kwame Nkrumah, Ghana's high-profile leader, even asked NPB director Rocco Knobel for advice on a national park in his country.[8] More generally, international conservation attention was focused on the Africa Special Project. This was finally approved in Cape Town at the 11th session of the UNESCO Scientific Council for Africa South of the Sahara, founded in 1949 and headquartered in Lagos.[9] In the long run, however, South Africa was not part of this initiative. South Africa's relationship with the continent became increasingly hostile and tense. Vilified by the Organisation of African Unity (OAU, founded in May 1963), it

---

[6]For further information on the struggle against apartheid, see, for example, T. Lodge, *Black Politics in South Africa since 1945* (New York, NY: Longman, 1983) and T. Lodge, *Sharpeville: An Apartheid Massacre and its Consequences* (Oxford: Oxford University Press, 2011).

[7]For example, David Attenborough's BBC Natural History Unit's 'Zoo Quest', initially co-starring Julian Huxley, began in 1957. The USA's 'Wild Kingdom' and subsequently the National Geographic series began in the 1960s.

[8]Julian Huxley to Lady Jackson, 6 August 1960, box 30, folder 2, Woodrow Wilson Research Center, Rice University, Houston, Texas. I am grateful to Elke Ackermann for this reference.

[9]Minutes of the Nature Conservancy, Scientific Policy Committee, 18 October 1960, box 114, folder 7, Woodrow Wilson Research Center, Rice University, Houston, Texas. I am grateful to Elke Ackermann for this reference.

was viewed as an enemy by almost all the independent countries of Africa, whose number only grew. Its scientific communications with the rest of the continent through UNESCO also soon came to an end, and nor was it among the 30 African countries that signed the African Convention on the Conservation of Nature and Natural Resources in Algiers in 1968. Whereas under the Smuts government South Africa had enjoyed a strong influence on Lord Hailey's Africa Survey and through the contributions of E.B. Worthington, J.F.V. Phillips and I.B. Pole Evans, for example, its apart-heid policies were now isolating it from the continent, notwithstanding the contribution it could have made to attempts by the world conservation lobby to ensure the survival of wildlife in Africa.[10] With imperial rulers having saved some of the 'vanishing herds', decolonisation brought with it a fear that over-exploitation would again take place. South Africa shared this fear. In parliament in 1961, Paul Sauer, then Minister of Lands, stated that wildlife, 'the greatest asset of Africa', would not survive in post-colonial Africa because 'uncivilised' Africans would simply destroy it. Describing the Serengeti as 'cleared out' and believing the same to be true of Rwanda and Kenya, Sauer foresaw that it would not be long before South Africa, in withstanding the 'wind of change', would be the only African country to have preserved its wildlife 'on a scientific basis' for posterity.[11]

By 1986, the country's political situation was having a significant impact on the NPB and particularly the Kruger National Park (KNP). There was little to celebrate on the 60th anniversary of the National Parks Act and the establishment of the park. Internal political unrest and violence was widespread, despite the state of emergency and strict media censorship. There was a concerted international political campaign against South Africa as well as sanctions. Moreover, inflation was high, and the Rand currency had plummeted in value. As regards the KNP in particular, despite very low rainfall, malaria was rampant, few international tourists came to visit, and streams of people from Mozambique traversed the park, many of them poachers, others arsonists. Incidents of stone-throwing occurred in the park, the army took over border responsibilities from the police and military posts were established in the park for security reasons. All game rangers had to undergo paramilitary training.[12]

---

[10]In later years assistance was given to independent states in Africa that were 'friendly' to South Africa, for example, Malawi and Ivory Coast.

[11]Union of South Africa *Debates of the House of Assembly*, vol. 108, 1 to 26 May 1961, cols. 7291–7315.

[12]National Parks Board of Trustees, *Jaarverslag Nasionale Kruger Wildtuin, 1986–1987*.

Yet despite these travails, broader environmental policy did develop within the apartheid state – as it did elsewhere – that focused on more than protected areas. As part of the process of physical design, critical to dividing the country into racially separated political entities, national natural resource planning assumed greater urgency. With more money in the state coffers in the 1960s, industrial expansion was encouraged through tax and other incentives. Planning control was crucial if industrialisation was to subserve apartheid, but until 1967 the state lacked the legislative wherewithal to plan the landscape at a national level.[13] This power was obtained with the Physical Planning and Utilisation of Resources Act 88, a piece of legislation resisted vehemently by the opposition for being based on apartheid considerations, not on sound economics.[14] But then, in 1975, the Physical Planning Act was amended and renamed the Environmental Planning Act. Further clarification was provided by the Environmental Conservation Act 100 of 1982, which specifically included conservation measures and made provision for a separate Department of Environment Affairs in 1984. In 1989, yet another Environmental Conservation Act was passed. These laws applied environmental thinking to the country as a whole, but the NPB remained within the Department of Lands, and national parks continued to fall under different legislation.

International Institutionalisation

In early January 1961, UN Secretary-General Dag Hammarskjöld visited South Africa. The South African government used the opportunity to defend apartheid and took control of his itinerary. Even so, he was greeted by anti-apartheid protests almost everywhere he went. He was prevented from meeting any African leader who was not a government supporter (such as the banned ANC leader and Nobel Peace Prize laureate Albert Luthuli) and, under close police supervision, only managed to get glimpses of African townships and rural areas. Despite the orchestration, the head of

---

[13]Previous to this date, the Natural Resources Development Act 51 of 1947 regulated planning by consultation only.

[14]For details of legal developments in environmental conservation in South Africa, see D. Barnard, *Environmental Law for All* (Pretoria: Impact Books, 1999); R.F. Fuggle and M.A. Rabie, *Environmental Concerns in South Africa: Technical and Legal Perspectives* (Cape Town: Juta, 1983); A. Rabie, *South African Environmental Legislation* (Pretoria: University of South Africa, 1976); J. Glazewski, *Environmental Law in South Africa* (Durban: Butterworths, 2000).

the UN was not inclined to revise his opinion of apartheid and nor was the organisation he headed until his untimely death in a plane crash later that year. In the years that followed, the boycotts of South Africa increased until, by the 1980s, the country had few friends among the international community and had been expelled from, or had left, many of the international institutions that had been created after the Second World War. It was even suspended from the World Meteorological Organisation in 1975. Some branches of South African science managed to retain their links with older, British-based, scientific bodies, such as the International Union of Forest Research,[15] but the dominant trend at all levels and in all spheres was isolation. Certainly, it would have been disadvantageous for any organisation to have had a South African as a prominent leader.

South Africa was not expelled from UNESCO, the International Union for the Conservation of Nature and Natural Resources' (IUCN) host organisation, but withdrew in 1956,[16] claiming that the organisation's public statements and activities against apartheid constituted unacceptable interference in the country's internal policies.[17] One important consequence was that South Africa was excluded from the World Heritage Convention of 1972, which linked natural and cultural heritage through the ties between the IUCN and the International Council on Monuments and Sites (ICOMOS).[18] Nor did it become a member of UNESCO's Man and the Biosphere Programme (MAB) in the 1970s. This outsider status meant that the range of protected areas available to South Africa was limited. However, a number of South African institutions, including the NPB, were able to remain members of the IUCN, although the country itself, as a state member, was able to join only in 1993. Thus, throughout the years of apartheid, the NPB, together with other official and non-governmental conservation bodies, attended and contributed to meetings of the IUCN (with the exception of those held

---

[15]S. Pooley, *Burning Table Mountain* (Houndmills: Palgrave Macmillan, 2014), 105–106.
[16]It rejoined in 1994.
[17]It was not the only country to leave UNESCO, which was the most controversial of the UN organisations as it often appeared to attack the West, especially the USA. This was the case particularly under Amadou-Mahtar M'Bow, Director-General from 1974 to 1987, who was frequently accused of undermining the goals of UNESCO and politicising its operations, as well as criticised for his administrative and budgetary practices. The USA was absent between 1985 and 1993; the United Kingdom between 1986 and 1997 and Singapore from 1986 to 2007.
[18]South Africa signed the Convention and thus became a member in 1997.

in African or other overtly hostile countries) and also participated in the World Parks Congresses, held at ten-yearly intervals from 1962.

There were, however, UN environmental initiatives in this period that transcended national park affairs and produced the most significant thinking and modern science regarding sustainability, climate change and millennium development goals, and which initiated and consolidated the linkage between environmental health and human development. From these, the NPB stood apart. The most important global environmental initiative of these decades was the 1972 UN Conference on the Human Environment held in Stockholm. South Africa attended (one of 113 delegates) but, ironically, with the Soviet Bloc, voted against the draft resolution expressing satisfaction with the outcome of the meeting. This was politically motivated because the amendments proposed by Tanzania included the phrase that 'crimes committed against mankind by advocates of apartheid, colonial and racialist practices . . . also threaten the human environment'. This was taken by South Africa as interference in its 'internal affairs'.[19] South Africa alienated itself still further by having no presence in the United Nations Environment Programme (UNEP), a UN agency founded in 1972 after the Stockholm conference and headquartered in Nairobi.[20] Among UNEP experts, the idea of the environment expanded to encompass socio-economic welfare and ethical human development, while 'conservation' in the sense of wildlife, national parks and recreation reigned within the IUCN.

South Africa remained a member of some of the international initiatives specifically focused on nature protection under the aegis of the IUCN. This enabled the country to participate in certain international developments and become a signatory to specific legal instruments. These included being a founding member of the Convention on International Trade in Endangered Species of Wild Fauna and Flora (CITES, agreed

---

[19] See L.B. Sohn, 'The Stockholm Declaration on the Human Environment', *Harvard International Law Journal* 14, no. 3 (1973): 423–514 (see 454–455). See also P. Steyn, 'Apartheid South Africa's participation in United Nations-organized international environmental initiatives in the 1970s: A reassessment', *Journal of Contemporary History* 52, no. 2 (2017), doi: 10.1177/0022009416678918. Steyn provides a thorough and fascinating analysis of the South African government's complex responses to involvement in international conservation initiatives, avoiding particularly any that linked environmental management to national politics.

[20] With the ending of apartheid, however, South Africa was reconciled to the organisation and even hosted the Earth Summit of 2002 in Johannesburg.

1973, in force 1975, also referred to as the Washington Convention).[21] It was also an original signatory of the Ramsar Convention (on wetlands of international importance) adopted in Iran in 1971 (ratified in 1975), also an IUCN initiative.

However, South Africa was expelled from the UN's Food and Agriculture Organisation in 1963. The FAO was extremely influential in Africa and, of particular relevance, led an African wildlife conservation and game ranching initiative based on many of the principles of scientific wildlife management.[22] Together with the IUCN, the Commission for Technical Co-operation in Africa South of the Sahara (CCTA) and UNESCO, the FAO convened a pan-African symposium on the conservation of nature and natural resources in modern African states in September 1961. This resulted in the Arusha Manifesto, or Arusha Declaration, and the initiation of international support and advice to African governments through the Africa Special Project led by E.B. Worthington.[23] This initiative culminated in 1968 in the African Convention on the Conservation of Nature and Natural Resources adopted by the OAU in Addis Ababa, which promoted the management of the continent's natural resources, including soil and water, 'in accordance with scientific principles'.[24]

---

[21]The matter of illegal and widespread international animal and plant trade had been raised at an IUCN meeting in Washington in 1963 and had resulted in an international agreement in 1973 that entered into force in 1975.

[22]E.S. Reddy, 'The United Nations and the struggle for liberation in South Africa', in *The Road to Democracy in South Africa: South Africans Telling their Stories*, SADET, vol. 3, part 1 (Pretoria: Unisa Press, 2008), 109.

[23]See E.B. Worthington, *The Ecological Century: A Personal Appraisal* (Oxford: Clarendon Press, 1983), 153. See also E.B. Worthington, *Science in Africa: A Review of Scientific Research Relating to Tropical and Southern Africa* (London: Oxford University Press, 1938); W.M. Adams, *Green Development: Environment and Sustainability in the Third World* (London: Routledge, 1992). President of Tanzania, Mwalimu Julius K. Nyerere's Arusha Manifesto reads as follows: 'The survival of our wildlife is a matter of grave concern to all of us in Africa. These wild creatures amid the wild places they inhabit are not only important as a source of wonder and inspiration but are an integral part of our natural resources and our future livelihood and well-being. In accepting the trusteeship of our wildlife we solemnly declare that we will do everything in our power to make sure that our children's grand-children will be able to enjoy this rich and precious inheritance. The conservation of wildlife and wild places calls for specialist knowledge, trained manpower, and money, and we look to other nations to co-operate with us in this important task – the success or failure of which not only affects the continent of Africa but the rest of the world as well.'

[24]Adams, *Green Development*, 33; also F. Vollmar, 'Conserving one earth: A look at world conservation', in 'Proceedings of a symposium on the state of nature conservation in

In giving this initiative its full support, the IUCN was keen to make a mark in developing countries and to shed its Eurocentric image.[25] South Africa, long criticised by the OAU, was not party to the convention.[26]

However, throughout these difficult years, South Africa was able to retain its membership in the International Council of Scientific Unions (ICSU, now the International Council for Science), established in 1931[27] and the first non-governmental organisation to be formally affiliated with UNESCO (in December 1946).[28] Its membership is wide, embracing scientific academies and nation states. Interdisciplinary in scope, its mission was, and remains, the development of a global scientific community based on an underlying philosophy of the universality of science. Although there is cooperation with other international bodies, including the UN (e.g. the Rio Earth Summit of 1992 and the World Summit on Sustainable Development in Johannesburg in 2002), it is not a UN organ. Important international ICSU initiatives have included the International Geophysical Year (1957–1958) and the International Biological Programme (IBP) (1964–1974). As Worthington has explained, the IBP was of particular importance to the developing world and was to have considerable impact on South Africa's environmental sciences.[29] The NPB, while not a participant in the IBP, did benefit from the science that flowed from it and from the knowledge generated by individual participants.[30] Another significant non-governmental scientific organ that continued to include South Africa was the Scientific Committee on Problems of the Environment (SCOPE), established in 1969 through the ICSU. Taking account of the growing global importance of environmental issues, SCOPE was tasked with identifying and undertaking analyses of those problems caused by, or impacting upon, humans and the environment. Its early priority was

---

southern Africa, Kruger National Park, 1976', eds G. de Graaff and P.T. van der Walt, supplement, *Koedoe* (1977): 10–23; N. Myers, 'National parks in Africa', *Science* 178 (1972): 1255–1263.

[25]Adams, *Green Development*, 31–33.

[26]P.L. Dekeyser, 'Nature in Africa: A lasting reality', *Impact of Science on Society* 12, no. 4 (1962): 255–277.

[27]ICSU began life in 1931 as the merger and extension of the International Association of Academies (1899–1914) and the International Research Council (1919–1931).

[28]V. Enebakk, 'The S in UNESCO: Post-war visions of science and democracy', 3rd Conference on Knowledge and Politics at the University of Bergen, May 2005.

[29]See Worthington, *Ecological Century*, 153.

[30]B.J. Huntley, 'Ten years of cooperative ecological research in South Africa', *South African Journal of Science* 83, no. 2 (1987): 72–79.

promoting East–West dialogue by providing a 'safe meeting ground' for them,[31] and it was indeed to prove so.

Game Reserves and National Parks

Given the close association between the South African government and the national parks as a parastatal entity, the boom years of the 1960s and the attention to white concerns benefited the NPB enormously. The organisation aligned itself fully with government policy on matters of race, to the extent of procrastinating about making an offer to host the second Pan African Ornithological Congress in the KNP in 1969 for fear that some delegates might be 'non-whites'.[32] Not so many years previously (1949) it had only narrowly avoided having the KNP divided into separate 'white' and 'non-white' sections, a plan that originated with the Minister of Lands, J.G. Strijdom.[33] What the NPB did, however, begin to do was to replace skilled African labour with whites in the KNP, while its focus on the mythology of Paul Kruger as the founder and hero of the KNP helped entrench an invented tradition of Afrikaner leadership.[34] In this narrative, Hendrik Verwoerd, the architect of apartheid, was included in the pantheon and credited with having the Augrabies Falls National Park established in 1966 after a 'great struggle'. Many publications about South Africa's national parks in this period could be read as if there were no black Africans in South Africa at all, let alone living in areas adjacent to the national parks. As late as 1988, an article in *Koedoe* on 'Social science research projects in South African national parks' made many references to the effect of national parks on the 'quality of life of everyday people living in the Republic of South Africa', and to 'conservation [as] a human activity performed for the benefit of humanity'. What is striking about such statements is that they simply ignore any African relationship at all with the country or with national parks.[35]

[31]G. Oldham, prep. *A Review of the Scientific Committee on Problems of the Environment (SCOPE)* (ICSU, 2008), Appendix 4, J. Melillo, 31.

[32]Minutes of a meeting of the NPB, 30 November 1964, SANParks archives, Groenkloof, Pretoria. The congress, an initiative of the Percy Fitzpatrick Institute of African Ornithology, established at the University of Cape Town was held in Pretoriuskop in the KNP, but no indigenous Africans attended. Naturally, this limited the 'pan African' nature of the gathering.

[33]J. Carruthers, *The Kruger National Park: A Social and Political History* (Pietermaritzburg, University of Natal Press, 1995), 98.

[34]In later years, the board's ambitious plans for a 'Mount Rushmore style' bust of Paul Kruger in the KNP carved out of granite created a storm of protest.

[35]A.W. Odendal and I.M. Krige, 'Social science research projects in South African National Parks: Introductory notes', *Koedoe* 31 (1988): 105–113.

When Verwoerd, who had been welcomed in the KNP to recuperate from the injuries he received during the first attempt on his life in 1960, was assassinated in 1966, the NPB recorded its gratitude to him personally for its 'good progress' over the past few years. And indeed, there was progress to report in terms of new national parks and of the doubling of the government's grant-in-aid.[36] Figures provided in the NPB minutes of March 1966 indicate that in 1952 the whole NPB budget was R300 000, whereas by 1966 it had risen to R3 million – a not inconsiderable sum.[37] In this supportive political atmosphere, the NPB was able to persuade government to establish several new national parks and an NPB presence in various parts of the country. Between 1960 and 1990 some parks were enlarged (Bontebok and West Coast) and others established (Golden Gate Highlands (1963); Tsitsikamma Coastal and Forest National Park (1964); Augrabies Falls (1966); Karoo (1979); Knysna Lakes (1985); Tankwa Karoo (1986); Vaalbos (1986); and Wilderness National Park (1983), comprising part of the Wilderness National Lake Area).[38] None of them ever rivalled the KNP in terms of public and government interest or of scientific output and management, but they represented, at least, modest protection of a wider variety of biomes.

The financial value of national parks to the country was spelt out in 1970. There was their obvious contribution to tourism and national revenue, but national parks on South Africa's borders, KNP and KGNP, also played an important military and security role in terms of securing those boundaries. This the Board considered to be worth R1.5 million annually and decided to ask the government for this sum, with a 6% increase for inflation each year in addition.[39]

While many official NPB publications from this period ignore black South Africans and convey the impression that only white managers, game rangers and tourists were associated with the national parks, this was most certainly not the case in reality. None of the national parks would have existed or could have been efficiently run without the many, many

---

[36]Minutes of a meeeting of the NPB, 30 November 1964, SANParks archives, Groenkloof, Pretoria.

[37]Minutes of a meeting of the NPB, 22 March 1966, SANParks archives, Groenkloof, Pretoria.

[38]National Parks Board, *Jaarverslag April 1987 tot Maart 1988: Kusgebiede; Jaarverslag Binnelandse Parke 1987–1988*. These annual reports are extremely detailed, often recording sightings of various individual animals but they lack integration and analysis.

[39]Minutes of a meeting of the NPB, 18 September 1970, SANParks archives, Groenkloof, Pretoria.

black labourers on roads and other infrastructural projects or as cleaners, waiters and general servants and assistants. In 1964, for example, a total of 1407 Africans were in the employ of the NPB, 335 in the Division of Nature Conservation alone.[40] The research and scientific section was supported by African staff, but seldom is their contribution acknowledged. Indeed, it is often difficult to discern exactly how Africans assisted with capture and immobilisation, observation, tracking and data collecting, and in constructing makeshift roads that allowed formally trained researchers to conduct their work and to do so in safety, because so little is recorded of what they saw and did. They are shadowy figures in most narratives and there is no written record by any of them of their experiences. One exception is *Lion*, a book by G.L. (Butch) Smuts, who worked in the KNP and who acknowledges his lion capture team as comprising himself, Ian Whyte, Lazarus Mangane and Philemon Chauke.[41] This informal and respectful camaraderie may well have been more common than published narratives indicate. However, until 1994 there was no opportunity for talented black trackers, rangers and technicians to obtain wildlife management or zoological training or to be appointed to any position held by, or reserved for, whites, and thus obtain a commensurate salary. Joubert records the appalling conditions in the separate 'compounds' that accommodated the black workforce in the KNP. Even in the late 1970s, many of them lacked electricity, hot water or cooking shelters, let alone a general dealer or a dining hall. The Commissioner of Bantu Affairs issued a highly critical report that obliged the NPB to upgrade the KNP compounds and to provide recreational facilities and other amenities.[42]

Despite the establishment of many national parks between 1960 and 1990, the NPB had originally set its sights far higher, requesting the inclusion of the Cango Caves at Oudtshoorn (in preference to a marine national park at Tsitsikamma);[43] the Cederberg mountains; Cape Point; an (unspecified) area in Zululand; a mountain park; an indigenous forest park; and a typical 'Highveld' area. In 1967, potential national parks on which the NPB

[40]Minutes of a meeting of the NPB, 22 September 1964, SANParks archives, Groenkloof, Pretoria.

[41]G.L. Smuts, *Lion* (Johannesburg: Macmillan, 1982), 123–124. The book contains a delightful photograph of the whole group toasting their success – with raised cans of 'Lion' brand lager – at capturing the first 1000 lions (opposite p. 170).

[42]S. Joubert, *The Kruger National Park: A History*, vol. 2 (Johannesburg: High Branching, 2012), 14–15.

[43]The Oudtshoorn Town Council remained adamantly opposed to losing control of the Caves, although the NPB took no heed and made the application in any event.

had its sights eye areas on the east and west coasts (Namaqualand and Zululand); Makapansgat and Sudwala caves (Transvaal); mountains in the Cape Fold Belt and the Drakensberg; and areas of archaeological or historical importance, including Mapungubwe and unspecified areas under the control of the Departments of Forestry and Native Affairs.[44]

In these deliberations and in the establishment of new national parks, there was no formally recorded elaboration of what their value to science might be or their usefulness in terms of extending scientific knowledge. Although the NPB may well have been influenced in this period by scientific ideas about island biogeography and the philosophy of protecting a variety of ecological communities in 'reserves', this influence is not evident in the minutes of NPB meetings. What is clear is that the NPB was in an expansionist mode. Not only was it acquiring new properties to manage and keen to have even more of them, it was also emerging as a substantial bureaucracy, replete with impressive headquarters at Groenkloof on land provided by the Pretoria city council.[45] Its personnel, all in standardised uniforms after 1960, were well paid (the director not far behind a secretary in a state department[46]) and had grown in number. It had also grown in self-confidence (some might say arrogance) to the extent that it had begun to press government to centralise all nature conservation in South Africa under its control: as early as 1960 it was discussing the possibility of taking over all protected areas from the provinces.[47]

Systematic data collection and recording took place according to pigeonholes of disciplines or biota and accelerated, together with careful observational study, particularly, but not only, in the KNP. The underlying question of the scientific data, as well as philosophically, was 'what do we have?' Believing that sound management could only occur once

---

[44]Minutes of a meeting of the NPB, 23 June 1967, SANParks archives, Groenkloof, Pretoria.

[45]Minutes and agenda of a meeting of the NPB, 28 November 1963, SANParks archives, Groenkloof, Pretoria. The former offices were located in the Sanlam Building, corner of Andries (now renamed Thabo Sehume) and Pretorius Streets, Pretoria.

[46]Minutes of a meeting of the NPB, 28 November 1963, SANParks archives, Groenkloof, Pretoria. The salaries were director, R7200; deputy director, R5700, biologist and nature conservator in the KNP, R3600 and in KGNP, R3120. For comparison, at that time the heads of service in the South African Broadcasting Commission earned R5088, a secretary (director-general) in a state department, R8100 and a research officer in the CSIR, R2040.

[47]Minutes and agenda of a meeting of the NPB, 4 April 1960, SANParks archives, Groenkloof, Pretoria. This was motivated by the fact that in 1945 chief state veterinarian P.J. Du Toit had suggested this course of action in order to give government direct control over all animals, wild and domestic, because of the threat of disease.

the biota was known and listed, the board placed the emphasis on monitoring and recording. Documentation was carefully maintained, but as Werner Heisenberg famously said in *Physics and Philosophy* (1958), 'What we observe through science is not nature itself, but nature exposed to our method of questioning',[48] a quotation perhaps more applicable to the natural than to the physical sciences.

Until 1962 there was, in fact, no legal mandate for the NPB to study any aspect of nature or history in South Africa's national parks. The legislation governing the parks only made provision for 'the propagation, protection and preservation therein of wild animal life, wild vegetation and objects of geological, historical or other scientific interest for the benefit, advantage and enjoyment of the inhabitants of the Union'.[49] As has been recorded, the '3Ps' had been extremely successfully applied by the late 1950s in parks such as KNP, Bontebok, Mountain Zebra, Addo and KGNP. It took an opposition member in the House of Assembly (the lower house), rather than a politician involved with the NPB, to suggest that scientific study should become a new legal obligation. In 1961, when a few minor issues relating to national park legislation came up for debate, Douglas Mitchell, formerly the Administrator of the Natal province, a prominent opposition party politician and MP for Natal South Coast, expressed concern at the phrase 'for the benefit and enjoyment of visitors'. Expressing his views as the principal architect of the legislation that established the Natal Parks, Game and Fish Preservation Board in 1947, and that Board's deputy chairman, he argued that while visitors were important, 'the protection of . . . wild life can give intense enjoyment to people who do not necessarily even visit our parks, but through reports and papers and the material which is made available, through scientific institutions, immense interest is manifested . . . I cannot over-emphasise the necessity for methodical scientific research in connection with the flora and fauna in our game reserves.' The minister agreed, asked Mitchell to discuss the issue with his department, and the word 'study' found its way into the final legislation.[50]

---

[48]W. Heisenberg, *Physics and Philosophy: The Revolution in Modern Science* (New York, NY: Harper, 1958).

[49]National Parks Act 56 of 1926 (as amended by National Parks Amendment Act 20 of 1935 and National Parks Amendment Act 9 of 1936).

[50]Union of South Africa, *Debates of the House of Assembly*, vol. 108, 1 to 26 May 1961, cols. 7291–7315. The final wording of Section 4 in Act 42 of 1962, enacted to 'consolidate the laws relating to national parks and matters incidental thereto' was 'The object of the

The KNP was the location in which any form of 'study' was undertaken. Although P.J. Barnard was employed as the biologist in charge
of parks other than the KNP, then referred to as the 'Cape Parks', all of
them (except KGNP) were small and unattractive to those interested
in scientific research or to the emergent wildlife management based on
scientific principles. Moreover, basing well-qualified senior staff in these
small parks was not financially viable. Because of its large size, the variety
of its habitats, and the opportunities these afforded people who enjoyed
natural history and wanted to study it, the KNP was the strongest magnet,
eclipsing all the others by far. This is obvious from the NPB minutes, in
which many pages are devoted to research in the KNP, while a paragraph
generally sufficed for the other national parks.

The period 1960 to 1990 thus demonstrates a clear shift from a
custodial 'protect and preserve' model to active measuring and monitoring. Before long, manipulation was added to the mix, and the '3Ms'
became the dominant philosophy of intensive management. Plants and
animals were measured and monitored, rather than, as today, ecological
processes and functions. Consequently, manipulation of wildlife population numbers was a cardinal tenet of the 'management by intervention'
philosophy, also known as 'command-and-control'. This approach was
based on an agricultural model. To ensure that the number of animals
in an area remained in 'equilibrium' with the food supply, much work
was done on population dynamics and herd structures in South Africa's
national parks. Vegetation was monitored from fixed-point photographs
to detect change. By means of concrete tanks and dams, water was
provided to areas where it was absent so that animals would be more
evenly spread and grazing more evenly utilised. In the 1980s, basic
computer modelling to help understand population dynamics and the
consequences of interventions was introduced and aerial census methods,
using fixed-wing aircraft and helicopters, were developed. This, in turn,
led to advances in animal translocation, as certain large mammals (e.g.
rhinoceros) were moved from one protected area to another. As will be
explained, the NPB did not invent translocation methods, but it adopted
them quickly and much to its advantage. Game capture, sedative darting and translocation created problems that were solved by biological
study and by developing and refining equipment, technology and tactics.

---

constitution of a park is the preservation and study therein of wild animal and plant life
and of objects of geological, archaeological, historical, ethnological and other scientific
interest and the benefit and enjoyment of visitors to the park.'

This form of management also led to the most controversial of practices, the culling of 'excess' animals, a direct intervention to maintain what was then thought to be 'the balance of nature', the most desirable ecological state. As the '3Ms' replaced the '3Ps', culling became a refined art with the aid of aerial censuses, drugs and darting techniques and ideas about the optimum regulation of different species. For example, by studying the social structure of elephant herds, it was deemed desirable to kill an entire family group, rather than just a few individuals or adults. Culling was an extremely controversial intervention and remains so, because the deliberate killing of indigenous animals in protected areas has ethical implications and is not only a practical issue.

South Africa, the IUCN and WWF

In 1962, following the introduction of Mission 66, the process of upgrading all US national parks was proceeding well, and with growing civic interest in environmental issues, the USA hosted the First World Conference on National Parks in Seattle. It was at this point that the regulatory and coordinating procedures for national parks began in earnest. The vice-president of the IUCN's Commission on National Parks, Jean-Paul Harroy, a Belgian soil scientist who had worked in the Congo as secretary to the Belgian Institute of Scientific Research in Central Africa and had also been deputy governor-general of Ruanda-Urundi, took on the task of listing the world's national parks with the assistance of a parks planning committee. Thenceforward, national parks became part of an international system, and in 1969 the *United Nations List of National Parks and Equivalent Reserves* was published, and thereafter regularly updated and revised.[51] The explicit linking of national parks with heritage and moral purpose for the future was taken a step further in 1982 at the Third World Parks Congress in Bali, Indonesia, with the theme 'Parks for Development', and in 1992 at the fourth, in Caracas, Venezuela, titled 'Parks for Life'.[52]

---

[51]Vollmar, 'Conserving one earth', 21–23; R.F. Nash, *Wilderness and the American Mind* (New Haven, CT: Yale University Press, 1983), 363–368. The International Commission on National Parks was established in 1960, but soon became known as the Commission on National Parks and Protected areas (CNPPA). Since 1996 it has been the World Commission on Protected Areas (WCPA). K. Bishop, N. Dudley, A. Phillips and S. Stolton, *Speaking a Common Language: The Uses and Performance of the IUCN System of Management Categories for Protected Areas* (Cardiff: Cardiff University, IUCN and UNEP, 2004), 11.

[52]M.V. Moosa and M. Morobe, 'The future', in *South African National Parks: A Celebration*, eds A. Hall-Martin and J. Carruthers (Johannesburg: Horst Klemm, 2003), 247. See also

South Africa, through the NPB, was extremely active in attending and participating in the national park aspect of the IUCN's work, and members of the NPB were important contributors to the various congresses. However, in the regular IUCN meetings they shared the platform with other South African conservation bodies and non-governmental organisations (see Chapter 6).

Discussion of the international organisations in which South Africa played a part would not be complete without mention of the World Wildlife Fund, currently named the Worldwide Fund for Nature (WWF).[53] Arguably more powerful than the IUCN, the WWF was founded in Morges, Switzerland in 1961. The IUCN consisted of governments and other agencies that recognised the importance of 'nature conservation' but were unwilling or unable to commit resources to it. These financial difficulties were the major factor behind the founding of the WWF, for it was to be the funding agency that would operationalise the IUCN. What differentiated WWF from other 'nature conservation' organisations of the time was its membership: it was not made up of civil servants or sentimental nature lovers, but businessmen with highly developed diplomatic skills. They appreciated that without sound governance, advertising, and attention-grabbing campaigns and competent spokespeople, no money would be forthcoming from the public or from corporations to 'Save the World's Wildlife'. This approach was true of both the WWF International board and many of its national organisations. Businessmen, together with appropriate scientists, determined which programmes would yield the best financial results. Among the most prominent of these corporate leaders was the South African tobacco, wine and luxury goods magnate, Anton Rupert.[54]

Also integral to the story of the WWF is Rocco Knobel, the director of the NPB, who was one of the original signatories of the Morges Declaration. Not long afterwards, because of the high international

---

A. Phillips, 'Turning ideas on their head: A new paradigm for protected areas,' *The George Wright Forum* 20, no. 2 (2003): 8–32; M. Hockings, J. Ervin and G. Vincent, 'Assessing the management of protected areas: The work of the World Parks Congress before and after Durban', *Journal of International Wildlife Law and Policy* 7 (2004): 32–42; and G. Wandesforde-Smith, 'The future of wildlife and the World Parks Congress', *Journal of International Wildlife Law and Policy* 7 (2004): 1–7.

[53] The World Wildlife Fund was renamed the World Wide Fund for Nature in 1986, retaining the initials WWF. However, it remains officially the World Wildlife Fund in Canada and the USA.

[54] E. Dommisse, *Anton Rupert: A Biography* (Cape Town: Tafelberg, 2009).

regard in which South Africa's KNP was held, and despite the country's international unpopularity because of apartheid, Rupert was recruited into the WWF family by his friend Prince Bernhard of the Netherlands and Peter Scott, the artist-conservationist, in order to establish a national WWF organisation in South Africa. This initiative had a bumpy beginning. Then Prime Minister Verwoerd 'was so irritated by Bernhard's interference that he actively opposed the establishment of WWF in South Africa' and no progress was possible until after Verwoerd's assassination in 1966.[55] Moreover, concerned at the prospect of a rival organisation, the South African Wild Life Society insisted that, unlike other national WWF organisations, the South African version would not compete for individual membership and in securing funding and donations. The South African Nature Foundation (as it was called) in South Africa was thus allowed to accept only corporate donations and was prohibited from building up a membership base. Initially named the Southern African Wildlife Foundation (1968–1972), and thereafter the Southern African Nature Foundation, it adopted the name WWF-SA only in 1994.

In 1968 Rupert became a trustee of WWF International and remained on the board until 1989. Charles de Haes, a lawyer, economist and Rupert employee, who, although born in Antwerp, grew up in the Eastern Cape, launched the highly successful and prestigious 'The 1001 – A Nature Trust' in 1970. This was a campaign that raised a great deal of money from Prince Bernhard and 1000 anonymous donors in order to finance WWF International's ongoing administrative expenses, and thus allow maximum use to be made of subsequent individual donations for projects rather than overhead and running costs. Of the 1000 large donors, 65 were South African, the fourth highest number after the USA (177), UK (157) and the Netherlands (107). In 1975 de Haes became joint director-general of WWF with Fritz Vollmar, an economist, political scientist and journalist, who had been involved with the Red Cross and who had been the first secretary-general of WWF in 1962. De Haes took responsibility for fund-raising and public relations while Vollmar was responsible for conservation, education and international representation. This never became a harmonious partnership, and the leadership was split. Vollmar resigned in 1977 and de Haes carried on

---

[55] A. Schwarzenbach, *Saving the World's Wildlife: WWF – The First 50 Years* (London: Profile Books, 2011), 120.

as sole director-general until 1993, his imperious style of management increasingly resented.[56]

In August 1974 Bernhard and 20 members of the 1001 Club visited the KNP as part of a group of 50 guests. The NPB was well aware of the importance of this prestigious assembly. Instructions for their visit were detailed, Knobel writing to the staff at Skukuza, 'You know that they are individuals who are used to having their own way . . . We must ensure that everything is 101% as usual [and that] everything that follows on KNP must be an anti-climax.' The party was treated to game drives, a talk about Kalahari lions, a film and a visit to MalaMala, the luxury private reserve along the KNP boundary.[57]

Conservation Science and New Professions

A key moment in defining twentieth-century environmental thought was the 1972 photograph of Earth taken from space by Apollo 17. This image of our planet, so fragile against the dark void of the universe, affected the thinking of millions of earthlings about the natural resources and exquisite treasure that is our home in the galaxy. By the early 1970s, the environmental movement had already begun to carve out a signif-icant place in civil society in many parts of the world. Crucial in this regard was the work of Rachel Carson – whose *Silent Spring* (1962)[58] had galvanised millions of readers – and others who warned of impending disaster if the human ecological footprint increased exponentially and exceeded the sustainability of limited natural resources.[59] Foreshadowed by publications such as William Vogt's *Road to Survival* (1948), and Fairfield Osborn's *Our Plundered Planet* (1948), this 'style of thought within the newly secular realm on the fate of the world' with its doomsday scenario

---

[56]Schwarzenbach, *Saving the World's Wildlife*, 217. The most interesting chapter in the book for South Africans is the story of 'Operation Lock'. In 1994, the Kumleben Commission appointed by President Nelson Mandela explored this awful 'chapter of the history of apartheid South Africa'. See also J. Hanks, *Operation Lock and the War on Rhino Poaching* (Cape Town: Penguin, 2015).

[57]Knobel to director of nature conservation, Skukuza, 4 August 1974, A/21 Wetenskaplike skakelings. KNP archives, Skukuza. Translated from Afrikaans.

[58]R. Carson, *Silent Spring* (New York, NY: Houghton Mifflin, 1962).

[59]For a handy and scholarly reference on many of these ideas, see L. Robin, S. Sörlin and P. Warde, eds, *The Future of Nature: Documents of Global Change* (New Haven, CT: Yale University Press, 2013).

was extremely influential and spread rapidly.[60] Not only did Carson and her fellow-thinkers and followers point to the negative environmental potential of human- and machine-power, but there was also growing concern that the ever-increasing human population would overwhelm the already-dwindling wild places of the earth.[61] Concerns shifted from isolated rare species (although these remained important) to the basic question of life on the planet.[62]

Many factors, events and publications highlighted these environmental concerns for individual nations and the international community. Within the arena of 'the environment', scientific, socio-economic and cultural–philosophical concerns meshed closely. People and 'nature' became linked in a manner not previously seen. Extremely influential in this regard was the first Earth Day held in April 1970, and the publication of *The Limits to Growth* in 1972, the work of the multidisciplinary think-tank, the Club of Rome.[63] There followed the UN Conference on the Human Environment the same year in Stockholm, the institutionalisation of UNEP and the later World Commission on Environment and Development (the Brundtland Commission), whose conclusions were published as *Our Common Future* in 1987.[64] Non-governmental environmental organisations thrived internationally and within South Africa. The sea change in environmental thinking that was taking place was so all-encompassing that the century now became known as *The Ecological Century*[65] or *The Age of Ecology*.[66] Not only was there intense interest in the future of the planet, human life on it and in its workings in practical, measureable terms, but an entirely new school of philosophy opened up as well. Subsequently, environmental philosophy has become a powerful

---

[60]S. Sörlin, 'Commentary', in Robin, Sörlin and Warde, *Future of Nature*, 191–194.

[61]P. Ehrlich, *The Population Bomb* (New York, NY: Ballantine Books, 1968). Paul and Anne Ehrlich were invited to South Africa by Brian Huntley in 1989 and they spent a few days in the KNP.

[62]A-K. Wöbse, 'Framing the heritage of mankind: National parks on the international agenda', in *Civilizing Nature: National Parks in Global and Historical Perspective*, eds B. Gissibl, S. Höhler and P. Kupper (New York, NY: Berghahn, 2012), 148.

[63]D.H. Meadows, D.L. Meadows, J. Randers and W.W. Behrens, *The Limits to Growth: A Report of the Club of Rome's Project on the Predicament of Mankind* (New York, NY: Universe Books, 1972).

[64]World Commission on Environment and Development (WCED), *Our Common Future (The Brundtland Report)* (Oxford: Oxford University Press, 1987).

[65]Worthington, *Ecological Century*.

[66]J. Radkau, *The Age of Ecology* (Cambridge: Polity, 2014).

field of inquiry that comprises many branches, including deep ecology, ecofeminism, animal rights, ethics and religion and many more.[67]

The internationalisation of environmental issues was extremely important in the public sphere and civil society, and political leaders and scientists rethought the matter of what nature and its concomitant values meant to human beings. New sciences came into being, many with roots in older disciplines. Numerous practitioners in the protectionist arena enthusiastically married the moral imperative of 'preserving, protecting and propagating' nature that had been evident from the earlier years of the century, with modernised and more nuanced versions of 'natural history'. The word 'environment' itself became imbued with new meaning and people began to refer to an 'environmentalism' that could be interpreted as scientific, political, social, philosophical or economic.[68] The effect of environmentalism on the version of ecology that began to emerge at this time was to shape conservation thinking.[69]

Another outcome of the environmental revolution was intensified interest in wilderness, and in protected areas such as national parks that might contain landscapes useful for testing ecological ideas and for promoting creative environmental thinking. The national parks in South Africa that appeared to provide such localities were the larger parks, specifically KNP and KGNP, and the provincial game reserves in Zululand. These, administered by the Natal Parks, Game and Fish Preservation Board, were frequently well ahead of the NPB in the quality and reach of conservation research.[70] Although it was the custodian of some of the best of South Africa's 'wilderness', the NPB was reluctant to adopt wilderness protection as a policy. Indeed, the board gave it short shrift when the American environmental historian Roderick Nash, after a visit to the KNP in 1989, presented them with a detailed template for wilderness action.[71] Given the

---

[67]I.D. Barbour, ed., *Earth Might Be Fair: Reflections on Ethics, Religion and Ecology* (Englewood Cliffs, NJ: Prentice-Hall, 1972); M. Bates, *Man in Nature* (Englewood Cliffs, NJ: Prentice-Hall, 1964). See also the useful summary by F. De Roose, 'Editorial Introduction' to the special issue on environmental ethics of *Philosophica* 39, no. 1 (1987): 3–10. The classic on animal ethics is P. Singer, *Animal Liberation* (Wellinborough: Thorsons, 1983).

[68]T. O'Riordan, *Environmentalism* (London: Pion, 1976).

[69]S. Bocking, *Ecologists and Environmental Politics: A History of Contemporary Ecology* (New Haven, CT: Yale University Press, 1997), 1.

[70]Cromsigt, Archibald and Owen-Smith, *Conserving Africa's Mega-Deversity*.

[71]Nash, *Wilderness and the American Mind*. See also Nash to Joubert, 16 May 1989; Joubert to Nash, 30 May 1989, A/4 Besoeke van Wetenskaplike en andere [Visits from scientists and others] 1980–1982, Kruger National Park archives, Skukuza.

size of the KNP and KGNP and fears about attacks by dangerous animals and the adverse publicity that would ensue, the state was extremely reluctant to allow hiking of any kind in national parks. In the KNP, in 1981 its managers did divide the park into various usage sections, excluding large areas from tourist traffic altogether as 'wilderness', while expanding and concentrating visitor facilities in specific locations.[72] However, leadership of wilderness philosophy was captured during this period by the Natal Parks Board and by Ian Player in particular, who founded the Wilderness Leadership School in 1963. Player, warden of the Umfolozi Game Reserve (today the Hluhluwe-iMfolozi Park), was a leader in the international wilderness movement, having established a formal wilderness area in that game reserve in 1958 and convening in South Africa the first World Wilderness Congress in 1977.[73]

In contrast with NPB's caution as regards the wilderness movement – with its associations with aesthetics, individual experience and (often Jungian) psychology – the NPB engaged with many of the disciplines and techniques that were focused on the active management of landscapes and its biota. This included attempting to replicate what was regarded as 'appropriate' populations of vegetation and wild animals. These populations were to be enclosed in protected areas 'intact' for future generations, areas in which humans might find recreation, reflection and an escape from the fast pace of urban life. Wilderness areas could provide respite only for the intrepid few: most people – and certainly visitors to South Africa's national parks – demanded an acceptable level of comfort as well as the certainty of seeing their favourite animals, including the 'Big Five', from the comfort and security of their motor vehicles.

For many years, then, there were no facilities for walking or hiking in South Africa's national parks. However, the wilderness movement did have an effect on the NPB because, finally, in July 1978, the first walking trail – the Wolhuter – was opened in the southern part of the KNP.[74] Even before this, however, a hiking trail, the Otter Trail, had been established some years before in the Tsitsikamma Coastal National Park and its popularity was immediate.

Another proposal regarding sectioning the KNP was made in 1987 by M.G.L. (Gus) Mills, whose support of science in national parks has always been passionate and professional. A carnivore expert acclaimed

[72]Joubert, *Kruger National Park*, vol. 2, 213–216.
[73]I. Player, ed., *Voices of the Wilderness* (Johannesburg: Jonathan Ball, 1978).
[74]National Parks Board, *35th Annual Report for the Year 1978–1979*.

internationally for his outstanding work, he was employed first in 1974 in the KGNP as a researcher and in the KNP from 1977. He submitted a proposal in August 1987 to establish a low-intensity management, high-intensity research area in the KNP so that controlled experiments could be conducted. Concerned that the management regime was not accomplishing what it was intended to, he argued that more research questions needed to be asked and addressed. He suggested that tourists be informed of the projects and encouraged to take an interest.[75] His suggestion was not adopted, but the issue of a specified research locality has been raised time and again since.

From the growing international environmental concerns there emerged new disciplines that aimed at studying aspects of the planet's natural resources. Of particular relevance to national parks were those fields currently referred to as conservation biology. Orienting older scientific terms towards applied sciences, e.g. 'natural history', 'biology', 'zoology' and even 'ecology', the new sciences were an indication that specific and particular training – professionalisation, in fact – was needed in caring for the earth. These sciences are unusual in straddling the 'hard' and the 'soft' in a partnership between scientific output and overtly moral purpose, as well as in straddling theoretical and applied sciences.

Chisholm notes that many people first heard the word 'ecology' in the Reith Lectures given by Frank Fraser Darling in 1969. 'Ecology, it appeared, was the science which could interpret the fragments of evidence that told us something was wrong with the world', providing 'a new morality and a strategy for human survival rolled into one'.[76] As outlined previously, ecology – both plant and animal – had origins in both Britain and the USA. The word 'ecosystem' had earlier been used by British botanist Arthur Tansley in an article in *Ecology* entitled 'The use and abuse of vegetational concepts and terms'. In it, he took issue with the view of Frederick Clements of the USA and his acolyte, South African botanist John Phillips, that succession is organic and develops towards a mono-climax. Tansley offered the idea of the ecosystem with energy flows and nutrient cycles. This was a concept that incorporated

---

[75]M.G.L. Mills, 'A proposal for a low-intensity management, high intensity research area in the KNP' [26 August 1987], F19 Navorsing met betrekking tot ekosisteem bewaring [Research in connection with ecosystem conservation], Kruger National Park archives, Skukuza.

[76]A. Chisholm, *Philosophers of the Earth: Conversations with Ecologists* (London: Sidgwick and Jackson, 1972), x.

both animals and plants at the system level, rather than merely climax vegetation.

Tansley's ideas, and the word he popularised, soon became the order of the day.[77] Ecology, in this interpretation, was a field of study in itself, and not just a branch of zoology or botany. Kingsland refers to ecosystem ecology as 'a thoroughly modern response to the challenges of the post-war period, an effort to convert the "soft" science of ecology into a "hard" science and show that the subject could command intellectual respect'.[78] McIntosh has argued that ecology, at first a fuzzy, obscure field of study, came to be applied to a distinct and respectable science, in the process supplanting the other word with a very similar meaning, bionomics.[79] In practice, however, ecology became a catch-all phrase, as the documents emanating from NPB scientists testify: the word is loosely used in the heading of many reports.

Certainly, ecology became a buzzword in South African biological and landscape studies from the 1970s. From a period, as explained in previous chapters, when botany and, particularly, zoology as taught in South African universities was generally old-fashioned, and when students such as Brian Huntley, in 1966 a recent graduate from the University of Natal, looked forward to a time that 'a progressive school of ecology is established in South Africa with Pietermaritzburg as its centre, for its past history has been strongly flavoured by ecologists',[80] this was to happen in the 1970s. As a place-based science with relevance to a country with a wide variety of biomes, it was soon picked up by a number of local universities, either as an addendum to existing disciplines, or often in the form of a separate institute or centre, or a personal professorial chair. Brian Walker, for example, a leading thinker on ecosystem resilience (1973) and involved in the National Programme for Ecosystem Research (NPER)

---

[77] Regarding Phillips' role, see P. Anker, *Imperial Ecology; Environmental Order in the British Empire, 1895–1945* (Cambridge: Cambridge University Press, 2001).

[78] The ecosystem concept grew out of the early work of G.E. Hutchinson and his students Raymond Lindeman and Tom Odum; see S.E. Kingsland, *The Evolution of American Ecology 1890–2000* (Baltimore, MD: Johns Hopkins University Press, 2005) and F.B. Golley, *A History of the Ecosystem Concept in Ecology: More than a Sum of the Parts* (New Haven, CT and London: Yale University Press, 1993).

[79] R.P. McIntosh, *The Background of Ecology: Concept and Theory* (Cambridge: Cambridge University Press, 1985), 26–27.

[80] B.J. Huntley, *Exploring a Sub-Antarctic Wilderness: A Personal Narrative of the First Biological and Geological Expedition to Marion and Prince Edward Islands 1965/1966* (Stellenbosch: Antarctic Legacy of South Africa), 120.

on terrestrial ecosystems, taught ecology at the University of Rhodesia (1969–1975) before becoming the founding director of resource ecology at the University of the Witwatersrand in 1975. He remained there until 1985, when he left for a career in the Australian CSIRO. John Hanks became founding director of the Institute for Natural Resources at the University of Natal in the mid-1970s, while in 1972 Richard Fuggle took up the Shell Chair of Environmental Studies at the University of Cape Town. Palynologist Eduard van Zinderen Bakker held a similar post in the Institute of Environmental Sciences at the University of the Orange Free State from 1972 until 1976. Resilience, defined in 1973 by Canadian ecologist C.W. (Buzz) Holling[81] and institutionalised in the Resilience Alliance, introduced a crucial new concept. Ultimately, the whole idea of any 'balance of nature' was discredited and it was replaced by non-equilibrium concepts generally.[82] This idea was well understood in South African academia through Walker's networks, but was to take many years before becoming accepted philosophy and management policy in South Africa's national parks.

From the 1960s to the 1990s, the principal field of study undertaken by the NPB remained wildlife management, with vegetation studies important principally because of the need for healthy vegetation to support wild animal life. This is akin to an agricultural model of productivity rather than an understanding of a natural ecosystem. To support the growing field of wildlife biology within national parks, there was a number of specialised institutes and departments that had been established earlier than the more general environmental or ecological bodies mentioned above. These were the Percy Fitzpatrick Institute for African Ornithology at the University of Cape Town (1959)[83] and the Mammal Research Institute at the University of Pretoria in 1966.[84] Stellenbosch University followed suit by appointing Rudolph Bigalke, principal

---

[81]C.S. Holling, 'Resilience and stability of ecological systems', *Annual Review of Ecology and Systematics* 4 (1973): 1–23.

[82]L. Robin, 'Resilience in the Anthropocene: A biography', in *Rethinking Invasion Ecologies from the Environmental Humanities*, eds J. Frawley and I. McCalman (London: Routledge, 2014), 45–63.

[83]An MSc course in conservation biology was instituted at the PFIAO in 1991.

[84]N. Bennett, 'The Mammal Research Institute 1966–2006', *Transactions of the Royal Society of South Africa* 63, no. 1 (2008): 53–60. The University of Pretoria had established a postgraduate degree in wildlife management in 1965. Led by George Petrides, James Teer and Russ Mumford, all North Americans, it was a practical, not a theoretical course.

research officer at the Natal Parks Board and nephew of national zoo director Rudolph Bigalke, as head of its newly established Department of Nature Conservation (funded by the South African Nature Foundation). The department was responsible for the final two years of specialisation in nature conservation within a four-year degree. Huntley records that between 1970 and 1974, 36 diplomas were awarded by southern African universities in wildlife management and research, along with 10 BScs, 37 BSc (Hons), 36 MScs and 3 DScs. At the time, it was felt this large number would flood the limited market in South Africa and the then Rhodesia.[85] Certainly, the early view that there was no 'profession' for people interested in wildlife was changing, and standards were developing such as those 'well established for agriculture, veterinary services, forestry and fisheries'.[86]

Adding to the academic interest was the Zoological Society of Southern Africa, first founded in 1959 (with 151 members). It paid particular attention to wildlife zoology and after 1965 published *Zoologica Africana*, a highly regarded academic journal.[87] A Limnological Society of Southern Africa was founded in 1963[88] and in 1970 the Southern African Wildlife Management Association (which produced the journal *South African Wildlife Research*) came into being. It was, however, the connection with the University of Pretoria that was to serve the NPB best, given its proximity to the KNP and its focus on mammal research, although there were also close ties with the department of botany at that institution. Moreover, Pretoria University was the first academic institution to focus on indigenous live fauna rather than on the more traditional zoological science.[89] The South African Institute of Ecologists, founded in 1981, was for a while very active.[90] Its work was bedevilled and weakened by the

---

[85]B.J. Huntley, 'Ecosystem conservation in southern Africa', in *Biogeography and Ecology of Southern Africa*, vol. 2, ed. M.J.A. Werger (The Hague: Junk, 1978), 1339.

[86]Minutes of the Nature Conservancy, Meeting on Conservation Problems Overseas, 18 October 1960, box 114, folder 7, Woodrow Wilson Research Center, Rice University, Houston, Texas. I am grateful to Elke Ackermann for this reference.

[87]The journal is now entitled *African Zoology* and combines *Zoologica Africana* with the *South African Journal of Zoology*.

[88]Founded with 73 members, by the following year there were 121. In 1984 the name was changed to the Southern African Society of Aquatic Scientists.

[89]Banie Penzhorn. Interview with the author. Pretoria, 19 June 2015.

[90]In 1983, the office bearers were Brian Walker (Chair), Roy Siegfried (Vice-Chair). Other board members were Brian Huntley, Richard Fuggle, John Grindley, Graham Noble and Daan Toerien.

fact that ecology meant 'different things to different people'. In addition, the then very conservative South African Council of Natural Scientists was reluctant to recognise 'ecology' as a discipline, insisting that 'proper' scientists could not engage in multi- or interdisciplinary studies and had to be registered in traditional fields such as botany and zoology.[91]

Some sense of this outpouring of research can be gained from the scientific archives at Skukuza, which are extremely well kept and efficiently run by Guin Zambatis. Currently, she is officially a biotechnician in the Biological Reference Museum and her duties include the curation of the museum and its bottled and dried specimens as well as the herbarium. Her responsibility encompasses a strong-room packed with files of raw data (weekly malaria reports, anthrax field forms, carrion data-sheets, game count sheets, predator returns, cheetah register, etc.), photograph albums of the regularly monitored vegetation plots as well as other material collected over the years. In this treasure trove, there are also many hundreds of publications, journal articles relating to the Kruger Park, and master's and doctoral theses deposited by their authors after graduation. These publications and theses are available on a computer database that runs to a very large number of pages and can be searched using various keywords and organisational techniques. This is an almost complete, and probably unique, record of research initiatives in a national park concerning wildlife research and management issues. While the reference collection refers principally to the KNP, Zambatis currently includes any scientific material relating to a South African national park that she comes across. The range of scientific knowledge that has been amassed in this way – with its journal articles and theses as well as raw data – is extraordinary.[92] In time, one hopes the data will be analysed to identify gaps, overlaps and to distinguish between merely average and outstanding research, and that this material will be integrated with other collections in the country.[93] Most of the doctoral work emanates from South African universities – principally Pretoria (not surprisingly) – but there is a scattering of international PhDs as well. Owing to the perennially unsettled organisational state of research in national parks other than Kruger and to their smaller size and lesser scientific interest, no similar archive exists

[91] *South African Institute of Ecologists: Bulletin* 2, no. 1 (1983); 6, no. 1 (1987).
[92] Many of the annual reports provide information on publications and other outputs. For example, see NPB, *Jaarverslag Navorsing en Inligting 1 April 1986–31 Maart 1987*.
[93] G. Zambatis, Data-sheets, Biological Reference Museum, Skukuza.

for those national parks, although individual parks do have small research collections.

Criticism of the absence of integrative, multidisciplinary and analytical approaches to ecological training and practice in South Africa is not new. In 1977, it was made in a hard-hitting article by Brian Huntley in the *South African Journal of Science* and, it might be argued, many of his conclusions remain valid. Huntley noted how 'wildlife ecology' was often sentimental rather than scientific; how specialist, even esoteric, interests drowned out the self-criticism that was evident internationally; and how descriptive studies of large mammals or classification of plant communities were undertaken more to impress colleagues than to advance the research agenda. Moreover, Huntley averred, the absence of coordination and synthetic research meant that the more significant project of developing new concepts and fresh and imaginative approaches, and of exploring rates and causes of change or the processes involved in those changes, were regarded with suspicion. He also commented on the low level of ecological education in South Africa and argued that the poor salaries paid to biologists accounted for the preference among many talented scientists to study and work abroad.[94]

Like 'ecology', 'biodiversity' was also new to the lexicon after 1960. Chester claims it was first used in 1955 as 'biological diversity', with the contraction into biodiversity rapidly gaining ground thereafter. From its beginnings, it was linked with 'conservation biology' (a field very different from 'biology' in its original meaning of physiology). Thomas Lovejoy is generally credited with popularising the concept in its present meaning in 1980 in his foreword to *Conservation Biology*, a collection of papers edited by Michael Soulé and Bruce Wilcox that emerged out of the first Conservation Biology conference held in 1978 at the University of California, San Diego. Lovejoy spoke of his belief that the 'reduction in the biological diversity of the planet is the most basic issue of our time'. He was referring specifically to species diversity, the focus of the book. However, Norse and McManus[95] use the terms as a new concept for unifying the conservation world. Thus, biodiversity and conservation

[94]B.J. Huntley, 'Terrestrial ecology in South Africa', *South African Journal of Science* 73, no. 1/2 (1977): 366–370.

[95]E.A. Norse and R.E. McManus, *Environmental Quality 1980: The Eleventh Annual Report of the Council on Environmental Quality* (Washington, DC: Council of Environmental Quality, 1980), 31–80.

biology were linked from the outset.[96] Nonetheless, more than 25 years later, the comment can be made that 'species diversity' and 'biological diversity', while widely used, are rarely defined, confusing, vague, and varyingly applied in the literature.[97]

Although it was the major practical 'conservation biology' institution in South Africa, the NPB was not the first to introduce this concept into the country. This happened after Brian Huntley, in his capacity as one of the heads of the NPER programme, invited pioneer conservation biologist Michael Soulé to attend a workshop in Cape Town, just two years after the initial meeting in California. More will be said about this later. Early South African literature provided another spin on the phraseology, in particular Huntley's own edited book called *Biotic Diversity in Southern Africa: Concepts and Conservation* (1989), the result of a conference entitled 'Conserving biotic diversity in southern Africa' at the University of Cape Town the previous year and sponsored by the NPER. Interestingly, not a single scientist author was formally attached to the NPB or any other state or provincial conservation organisation, apart from the Cape (Jonkershoek) and the Sea Fisheries Research Institute.

The following is a list of dates relevant to research into conservation, and the emergence of the science of conservation, in South Africa's national parks, 1960 to 1990.

1960   National Parks Board discussed ambitious plans for future national parks and recorded its intention to take control of protected areas away from the provinces.

1960   Rocco Knobel and R.J. Labuschagne, director and deputy-director of the National Parks Board, respectively, attended the 7th General Assembly of the IUCN in Warsaw, during which the

---

[96]See, for example, C.C. Chester, 'Biodiversity', in *The Palgrave Dictionary of Transnational History*, eds A. Iriye and P.-Y. Saunier (Houndmills: Macmillan, 2009), 83–89. Important literature from this period includes M.E. Soulé and B.A. Wilcox, eds, *Conservation Biology: An Evolutionary-Ecological Perspective* (Sunderland, MA: Sinauer Associates, 1980); M.E. Soulé, 'History of the Society for Conservation Biology: How and why we got here', *Conservation Biology* 1 (1987): 4–5; M.E. Soulé, ed., *Conservation Biology: The Science of Scarcity and Diversity* (Sunderland, MA: Sinauer Associates, 1986); T. Farnham, *Saving Nature's Legacy: The Origins of the Idea of Biological Diversity* (New Haven, CT: Yale University Press, 2007); P. Sarkar, 'Defining "biodiversity"; assessing "biodiversity"', *The Monist* 85, no. 1 (2002): 131–155.
[97]A. Hamilton, 'Species diversity or biodiversity?', *Journal of Environmental Management* 75 (2005): 89–92.

Africa Special Project was launched. After this meeting, Knobel visited the US and many of its national parks.

1960 Red Data books first mooted by the IUCN.

1960s Raymond Dasmann, Thane Riney and Archie Mossman, supported by FAO, began game farming research in Rhodesia.

1960 Technology of capture becomes a significant feature of national park management.

1960s International standardisation for national parks began.

1960s Environmental revolution took hold and political and public influence of ecologists grows.

1961 Foundation of the World Wildlife Fund.

1961 Republic of South Africa established. Left the British Commonwealth.

1962 Conference on nature conservation held at Skukuza and a national Nature Conservation Coordinating Committee established in 1963, with chairman veterinarian H.O. Mönnig.

1962 Change in wording of the National Parks Act includes the duty to 'study'.

1962 'First World Conference on National Parks' held in Seattle. As vice-chair of International Commission on National Parks, J.-P. Harroy was tasked with revising the list of the world's national parks.

1962 Publication of Rachel Carson's *Silent Spring*.

1963 Golden Gate Highlands National Park established.

1963 After criticism from the US National Academy of Sciences, the NPS in the USA established a special advisory committee under A. Starker Leopold to report on science and management to assure preservation of the parks' ecological systems.

1963 Limnological Society of South Africa established.

1964 C.G. Hide and B. de Winter attended the formal launching of the IBP at the 1st General Assembly of IBP in Paris.

1964 Tsitsikama Coastal and Forest National Park proclaimed. (The spelling was later altered on the advice of G.A. Robinson and expert Khoisan linguists to Tsitsikamma.)

1964 *Journal of Applied Ecology* first published.

1964 First Red Data List published by the IUCN: *The Red List of Threatened Plants*.

1964 Culling begins in KNP with 104 hippo culled, while 80 rhinoceros were released into the park.

1965   Formal decision to control numbers and cull animals taken after a symposium attended by other South African nature conservation bodies.

1965   Inauguration of a one-year practically oriented postgraduate course in wildlife management at the University of Pretoria, led by North Americans George Petrides, James Teer and Russ Mumford.

1965   *Zoologica Africana* published.

1966   Augrabies Falls National Park established.

1966   Mammal Research Institute founded in the department of zoology at the University of Pretoria.

1967   Robert MacArthur and Edward O. Wilson published *The Theory of Island Biogeography* (Princeton, NJ: Princeton University Press).

1967   Zoological Society of SA held its symposium on Terrestrial Mammal Ecology in southern Africa.

1968   *Biological Conservation* journal began.

1968   Raymond Dassman published *Environmental Conservation*.

1968   South African Nature Foundation begun by Anton Rupert. Its scientific committee was chaired by Rocco Knobel.

1968   OAU African Convention on the Conservation of Nature and Natural Resources signed in Algiers, 15 September.

1968   KNP Biologist U. de V. Pienaar visited Europe and Israel.

1969   First international definition of national park. (US definition: 1916.)

1969   Tsitsikamma scientist G.A. Robinson published on marine conservation in the national park in *Biological Conservation*.

1969   Scientific Committee on Problems of the Environment (SCOPE) began work.

1970   Eugène Marais Chair in Wildlife Management established at the University of Pretoria.

1970   Launch of the UNESCO Man and the Biosphere Programme, formally established in 1977.

1970   Southern African Wildlife Management Association founded with membership of more than 400, publication of *South African Journal of Wildlife Research* began.

1971   KNP biologist Piet van Wyk visited the US for six weeks.

1971   Ramsar Convention concluded.

1972   World Heritage Convention concluded.

1972   Second World Parks Congress held in Yellowstone National Park, USA.

1972 Degree course in nature conservation established at Stellenbosch University in the Forestry Faculty.

1972 Shell Chair of Environmental Studies established at the University of Cape Town.

1972 Beginning of the South African National Programme for Environmental Sciences (NPES), administered by the National Committee for Environmental Sciences (through CSIR).

1972 United Nations Conference on the Human Environment, Stockholm.

1973 CITES convention concluded.

1973 Ecological Institute established in the department of botany at the University of the Orange Free State.

1973 Foundation of the Endangered Wildlife Trust.

1973 Publication of C.S. Holling's 'Resilience and stability of ecological systems' in the *Annual Review of Ecology and Systematics*.

1974 CSIR began the Cooperative Scientific Programmes, seizing the opportunity afforded by SCOPE (founded in 1969).

1974 Prince Bernhard of the Netherlands and 20 members of the WWF 1001 Club visit South Africa and the KNP.

1978 First International Conference on Conservation Biology held at the University of California.

1979 Articulation by S.J.C. Joubert of the idea that the KNP research programme has as a major objective the study and analysis of the ecosystem.

1979 Karoo National Park established.

1979 Committee for Nature Conservation Research established within the NPES.

1980 World Conservation Strategy.

1980 Publication of M.E. Soulé and B.A. Wilcox, eds, *Conservation Biology: An Evolutionary–Ecological Perspective* (Sunderland, MA: Sinauer Associates).

1980 First definition of 'biological diversity' published.

1980 Michael Soulé visited Cape Town to speak at the International Symposium on the Conservation of Threatened Natural Habitats held at UCT.

1981 South African Institute of Ecologists founded.

1980 Publication of P.A. Jewell and S. Holt, eds, *Problems in Management of Locally Abundant Wild Mammals: A Workshop to Examine the Need for and Alternatives to Culling of Wild Animals, 29 September– 3 October 1980, Cape Cod* (New York, NY: Academic Press, 1981).

1982 United Nations accepted World Charter for Nature.

1982 IUCN Third World Parks Congress in Bali, 'Parks for Development' (The Bali Declaration).

1982 Council for the Environment established with 22 members in terms of the Environmental Conservation Act of 1982 to advise the minister. Idea to take a fresh look at environmental issues in South Africa, develop policy documents that would lead to a 'National Environmental Policy and Strategy'.

1982 South African Council of Natural Scientists formed, president Professor V. Pretorius.

1983 Publication of A.A., Ferrar ed., *Guidelines for the Management of Large Mammals in African Conservation Areas*. South African National Scientific Programmes Report 69 (Pretoria: CSIR, 1983).

1983 Publication of R.F. Fuggle and M.A. Rabie, *Environmental Concerns in South Africa: Technical and Legal Perspectives* (Cape Town: Juta, 1983).

1983 Publication of N. Owen-Smith, ed., *Management of Large Mammals in African Conservation Areas: Proceedings of a Symposium held in Pretoria, South Africa, 29–30 April 1982* (Pretoria: HAUM, 1983).

1983 Wilderness National Park established.

1984 Publication of T. Greyling and B.J. Huntley, *Directory of Southern African Conservation Areas*. South African National Scientific Programmes Report 98 (Pretoria: CSIR, 1984).

1985 Second International Conference on Conservation Biology, University of Michigan, and founding of the Society for Conservation Biology.

1985 Knysna National Lake Area established.

1985 West Coast National Park established.

1986 Tanqua (Tankwa) Karoo National Park established.

1986 Vaalbos National Park established.

1987 Brundtland Report, World Commission on Environment and Development.

1987 Publication of the journal *Conservation Biology* (outcome of Society for Conservation Biology).

1989 Publication of B.J. Huntley, ed. *Biotic Diversity in Southern Africa: Concepts and Conservation* (Cape Town: Oxford University Press, 1989).

6 · Biodiversity, New Sciences

Between 1960 and 1990 the whole issue of protected areas changed in almost every respect. The international community became extremely active in what came to be called 'the environment' and international organisations such as the International Union for the Conservation of Nature and Natural Resources (IUCN), World Wildlife Fund (WWF) and the United Nations Environment Programme (UNEP) energised the international governance of nature protection and sustainable resource use. New disciplines emerged that dramatically changed the ways in which the natural world was studied. These developments had a great impact on South Africa which, as has been explained, was also experiencing sea changes in politics and international relations. The development of conservation science in the country's national parks in various ways, but not always, mirrored these changed diplomatic and scientific circumstances.

International Organisations and Developments

As noted in the previous chapter, after 1960 environmental concerns proliferated dramatically around the world. The IUCN held its triennial general assemblies in locations as diverse as Kenya (1963), Europe (1966, 1977 and 1984), India (1969), Canada (1972), the Democratic Republic of Congo (1975), Russia (1978), New Zealand (1981) and Costa Rica (1988).[1] Business was conducted through working commissions that met regularly and reported to the general assembly. The commissions

---

[1] General assemblies were held as follows: 8th General Assembly, 1963 – Kenya; 9th General Assembly, 1966 – Lucerne, Switzerland; 10th General Assembly, 1969 – New Delhi, India; 11th General Assembly, 1972 – Banff, Canada; 12th General Assembly, 1975 – Kinshasa, Democratic Republic of Congo; 13th (Extraordinary) General Assembly, 1977 – Geneva, Switzerland, 14th General Assembly, 1978 – Ashkhabad, USSR; 15th General Assembly, 1981 – Christchurch, New Zealand; 16th General Assembly, 1984 – Madrid, Spain; 17th General Assembly, 1988 – San José, Costa Rica.

dealt with Education and Communication (CEC); Environmental, Economic and Social Policy (CEESP); Environmental Law (WCEL); Ecology (founded in 1954 and later renamed Ecosystem Management, CEM); Survival Service Commission (later named the Species Survival Commission, SSC); and National Parks and Protected Areas (CNPPA, from 1996 the World Commission on Protected Areas, WCPA).[2] Riding the wave of interest in nature at a time of global economic growth, the IUCN, despite its own precarious finances, was able to benefit from voluntary work done by commission members whose home organisations supported their travel and other expenses.

Despite his lack of training in international diplomacy, nature conservation or biological science, National Parks Board (NPB) Director Rocco Knobel threw himself into IUCN activities with energy and ability, focusing on national parks. Nominated to the CNPPA in 1958, he was one of its first 11 members.[3] Two years later, at the seventh general assembly in Poland, he was elected to the IUCN executive board. By that time there was a growing South African presence. Knobel was accompanied by NPB biologist Andrew Brynard, along with Jack Vincent and Rudolph Bigalke of the Natal Parks Board (nephew of National Zoological Gardens director Rudolph Bigalke), J.G. van der Wath from the Transvaal Division of Nature Conservation and Robert Rand from the Cape Nature Conservation authority. At this meeting the decision was taken to hold the first International Conference on National Parks in 1962 in Seattle.[4]

After the meeting in Poland, Knobel made an extended visit to the USA. During the course of his travels he obtained valuable information about national park administration. Appreciating that US national parks were managed for the twin purposes of landscape protection and

[2]Commission on Education and Communication (formerly Commission on Education, then Education and Training); Commission on Environmental, Economic and Social Policy (formerly Landscape Planning Commission, Commission on Environmental Planning, Commission on Environmental Strategy and Planning, then Commission on Sustainable Development); World Commission on Environmental Law (formerly Legislation Committee, then Commission on Environmental Policy, Law and Administration); Commission on Ecosystem Management (formerly Commission on Ecology); Species Survival Commission (formerly Survival Service Commission); Commission on Protected Areas (formerly Commission on National Parks and Protected Areas). See R. Boardman, *International Organization and the Conservation of Nature* (London: Macmillan, 1981).
[3]Newsletter of the CNPPA no. 44, July/August/September 1988, File A/18 IUCN and IBP, Kruger National Park archives, Skukuza.
[4]In 1960 the 7th General Assembly met in Warsaw and in Cracow.

Figure 6.1. Rocco Knobel, Chief Director of the National Parks Board from 1953 to 1979.
From R.J. Labuschagne, comp. *60 Years Kruger Park* (1958), p. 59. Courtesy of SANParks.

management-directed research, he concluded that more research was taking place in South Africa's national parks than in the USA. Having witnessed the private investment and concession policies of the USA, he was relieved that in South Africa's protected areas such involvement was excluded. On the other hand, he was so impressed by the standard National Parks Service (NPS) uniform that on his return to South Africa he implemented a similar dress code for NPB staff. Knobel also attended the fifth World Forestry Congress in Seattle as an IUCN representative. Viewing the invitation as an honour for South Africa, he particularly benefited from his discussions with representatives of those countries whose national parks were managed by departments of forestry. Called upon to speak to numerous audiences, he experienced no political animosity towards South Africa when he provided the 'true facts' about his country's problems, which he thought were 'fairly small' in comparison with those of the USA.[5]

[5]Minutes of a meeting of the NPB, 24 November 1960, SANParks archives, Groenkloof, Pretoria.

However, those 'fairly small' South African problems prevented Knobel from attending the IUCN's eighth general assembly in Nairobi in 1963.[6] The then president of the IUCN (from 1958 to 1963), Swiss parasitologist Jean George Bauer, communicated his disappointment to the Kenyan government.

It is . . . most regrettable that for extraneous reasons these meetings have been deprived of the presence and experience of several participants among whom is a member of the Executive Board [i.e. Knobel] who over the past six years has given constant and ample proof of his support to conservation on a worldwide scale. The National Parks Board of South Africa represents one of the pioneer organisations that more than any other has opened new roads and introduced new methods that are today the scientific basis for conservation in Africa. In scientific circles any form of discrimination is contrary to the true spirit of international cooperation . . .[7]

Despite his exclusion from the conference, Knobel contributed to a key IUCN publication on Africa that year, Gerald Watterson's *Conservation of Nature and Natural Resources in Modern African States* (1963). Knobel's chapter was entitled 'The economics of tourism in national parks and nature reserves'. In it, he pointed out the benefits that could accrue to Africa from eco-tourism in its protected areas.[8] What South Africa contributed by way of 'science' is, unfortunately, not evident in any IUCN documentation. One may, however, surmise that such contribution derived from the energy of the South African delegation, their experience of efficient national park administration, their systems of data collection and record-keeping and the in-house journal *Koedoe*. Charles Darwin's fundamental precept that 'all observation must be for or against some view if it is to be of any service' was simply ignored.[9]

---

[6]Only one person with a South African connection attended the Nairobi meeting; this was Jack Vincent, who had been first Director of the Natal Parks, Game and Fish Preservation Board (1947–1963), and he did so in his capacity as an employee of the International Council for Bird Preservation in Morges, Switzerland.

[7]IUCN 8th General Assembly, Nairobi, Kenya, 1963.

[8]G.G. Watterson, comp., *Conservation of Nature and Natural Resources in Modern African States*. IUCN Publications, New Series No. 1 (Morges: IUCN, 1963). Watterson was employed by the FAO and seconded to the IUCN.

[9]Expressed in a letter from Darwin to Henry Fawcett in 1861, quoted in S.J. Gould, *Dinosaur in a Haystack: Reflections in Natural History* (London: Jonathan Cape, 1996), 148.

However, opinions on the quality of South Africa's national park science were not uniformly high. A few years later (1972) at the World Parks Congress in Yellowstone (on its centenary), Jean-Paul Harroy informed the gathering that the Swiss led the world in bringing science to national parks and that their closest rival was the USSR, not South Africa.[10] This high opinion of the Swiss was echoed by Harold Coolidge, president of the IUCN from 1966 to 1972,[11] and by Bauer, who, proud of the scientific emphasis of the national parks in Switzerland, declared (without elaboration) that nature conservation 'constitutes a branch of science'.[12]

In the meantime, South Africa continued to be well represented at IUCN meetings. In 1966 in Lucerne, for example, the NPB was represented by board member D.H.C. du Plessis and deputy-director Rudolph J. (Lappies) Labuschagne. The remainder of the South African group comprised John Geddes Page (Natal Parks Board), Douglas Hey (Cape Division of Nature Conservation) and Jack Mackie-Niven (Wild Life Protection Society of South Africa), and his wife, Cecily (née Fitzpatrick), who represented the Percy Fitzpatrick Institute of African Ornithology (PFIAO), a new member. South African attendance at subsequent general assemblies remained good,[13] one exception being the 1978 assembly at Ashkhabad (Ashgabat/Aşgabat), then part of the USSR (now in Turkmenistan). At this meeting the World Conservation Strategy was discussed. The sole South African present was Brian Huntley, a savannah ecologist and representative of the Wild Life Protection Society of South Africa.[14]

By the 1980s a number of South Africans had found positions on IUCN commissions: Brynard (CNPPA), Huntley (SSSC) and Graham Noble (Ecology).[15] Other regular attendees were Geddes Page and Dering

---

[10]P. Kupper, 'Translating Yellowstone: Early European national parks, *Weltnaturschutz* and the Swiss model', in *Civilizing Nature: National Parks in Global and Historical Perspective* eds, B. Gissibl, S. Höhler and P. Kupper, (New York, NY: Berghahn, 2012), 123–139. See also D.R. Weiner, *Models of Nature: Ecology, Conservation and Cultural Revolution in Soviet Russia* (Pittsburgh, PA: University of Pittsburgh Press, 2000).

[11]P. Kupper, *Creating Wilderness: A Transnational History of the Swiss National Park* (New York, NY: Berghahn, 2014), 61–62.

[12]IUCN 9th General Assembly, Lucerne, 1966.

[13]IUCN 11th General Assembly, Banff, 1972. Applications for membership had come from the Division of Nature Conservation of the Provincial Administration of the Orange Free State and from the CSIR.

[14]IUCN 14th General Asembly, Ashkhabad, USSR, 1978.

[15]B.J. Huntley and S. Ellis, 'Conservation status of ecosystems in southern Africa', in *Proceedings of the 21st Working Session of the Commission for National Parks and Protected Areas*, (Gland: IUCN, 1984), 13–22.

Stainbank (Natal Parks Board), Wolfgang Morsbach (Cape Department of Nature and Environmental Conservation) and NPB member A.E.G. Trollip, who had been on the Commission on Environmental Policy, Law and Administration since the early 1970s.[16] By the mid-1980s even more South Africans were involved: 10 in 1984 and 11 in 1988.[17]

The NPB: An International Comparison

In 1963 the NPB asserted that 'science' and 'research' in South Africa's national parks had since 1960 'opened new roads and introduced new methods that are today the scientific basis for conservation in Africa'.[18] In light of this claim, a few brief comparisons are in order to provide perspective.

Recent literature has highlighted the strong scientific focus of the Swiss national parks and Kupper has argued convincingly that Switzerland was the world leader in this regard.[19] South Africa had foregone the opportunity to have a 'scientific' national park when it abolished the Dongola Wild Life Sanctuary in 1949, at the time clearly preferring aspects of the 'Yellowstone model', with its strong emphasis on the recreational visitor experience. For many years, US national parks were predicated upon scenic beauty, and there is no shortage of evidence on the priority the NPS afforded aesthetics and visitor satisfaction over wildlife preservation or management. Tourists flocked to the US national parks in the West once the motor car had become ubiquitous, and only slowly did the wildlife in those parks become objects of scientific study. By contrast, until the mid-1960s all South Africa's national parks under the NPB were wildlife reserves in which the thrill for visitors was the opportunity for wildlife viewing at close range, although through vehicle windows.

---

[16]IUCN 15th General Assembly, Christchurch, New Zealand.
[17]IUCN 16th General Assembly, Madrid, 1984. Attending were Brynard and his wife and Trollip and his wife (NPB); Keith Cooper; Richard Fuggle; John Hanks; Douglas Hey; Brian Huntley; Roy Siegfried; R. Soutter (SANF); and P.S. Swart (SWA). At the IUCN 17th General Assembly in Costa Rica, South Africans who attended were Blythe Loutit (recipient of a Peter Scott Medal) whose husband was head of nature conservation in South West Africa; George Barkhuizen, OFS provincial authorities; Michael Cohen, Department of Environmental Affairs; F.C. Eloff, NPB; Hall-Martin, NPB; Trollip, NPB; Geddes Page, Natal Parks Board; Huntley, CSIR and Botanical Society; Roy Siegfried PFIAO; Soutter, SANF; and P.S. Swart, South West Africa.
[18]IUCN 8th General Assembly, Nairobi, Kenya, 1963.
[19]Kupper, *Creating Wilderness*, 61–62.

During the 1960s almost all countries with national parks began logical, coordinated management and research.[20] As Wright has explained, the environmental movement and the NPS Mission 66 meant that 'for the first time scientists began to recognise the value of national parks as preserving integral parts of the global ecosystem'.[21] After a thorough, in-house evaluation led by Harold Stagner, the administrator of Mission 66, an external impartial review was conducted by the National Academy of Science Research. Many of its recommendations concerned administration, and it 'did not fully endorse the idea that NPS scientists should conduct basic research in parks'. However, because Stagner's review had not given clear guidance on how to deal with public criticism of elk culling in Yellowstone and Rocky Mountain National Parks, Secretary of the Interior Stewart Udall established a special advisory board to do so. Its 1963 report, *Wildlife Management in the National Parks*, usually referred to as the 'Leopold Report' after its chairman, A. Starker Leopold (zoologist son of Aldo Leopold), was comprehensive. It endorsed the need for 'mission-oriented' research rather than 'science for science's sake', although Leopold recognised the inextricable links between the two. 'Mission-oriented' was also how Michael Soulé described the general field of conservation biology some years later, although, as reflected by articles in the journal *Conservation Biology*, he did not exclude fundamental research from its brief.[22] However, in short, the main aim of the protected area authorities was to directly link research to management 'problems', thus creating a culture of purpose-driven, rather than understanding-driven, research.

In 1971, as a consequence of the Leopold Report and of the Robbins Committee (1963) on research in the parks, NPS Director George Hartzog reorganised the administration of science. The authority of the chief scientist was removed and delegated to the director or superintendent of a particular park. Hartzog's strategy had far-reaching consequences for the

[20]The Serengeti Wildlife Research Institute was founded in 1961. See A.R.E. Sinclair, *Serengeti Story: Life and Science in the World's Greatest Wildlife Region* (Oxford: Oxford University Press, 2012).

[21]R.G. Wright, *Wildlife Research and Management in the National Parks* (Urbana and Chicago, IL: University of Illinois Press, 1992), 25–30; J.G. Dennis, 'Building a science program for the national park system', *The George Wright Forum* 4, no. 3 (1985): 11–20. See also E. Carr, *Mission 66: Modernism and the National Park Dilemma* (Amherst, MA: University of Massachusetts Press, 2007).

[22]C. Meine, M. Soulé and R.F. Noss, '"A mission-driven discipline": The growth of conservation biology', *Conservation Biology* 20, no. 3 (2006): 631–651.

NPS, depriving it of unified policy direction, fostering unequal attention to science by making it dependent on the management of an individual park, and breaking down communication among the NPS scientific community.[23] Clearly, the problems associated with the administration of 'science' by a national park organisation were not unique to the South African NPB and the provincial nature conservation bodies. What was different, however, was that whereas NPS had no statutory obligation to develop a science programme, after 1962 the NPB did.

The aim of the World Parks Congress in Seattle in 1962 was to establish an effective understanding of national parks and to encourage the national park movement worldwide. Ten years later, much had been achieved in terms of 'national park' brand recognition. Thus, the second congress in Yellowstone was entitled 'A Heritage for a Better World', a tag-line that made national parks' moral role more explicit.[24] Even by 1962 it was clear that the USA had taken the lead in the national parks movement. Indeed, the year before the NPS had founded its Division of International Affairs (currently called the Office of International Affairs), comprising US experts prepared to travel the world dispensing advice and tips on 'how to do national parks'. It was active in countries as diverse as Jordan, New Zealand and Canada.[25]

South African national park personnel also dispensed advice when given the opportunity. In 1968, U. de V. (Tol) Pienaar, the KNP biologist, visited Israel, and told conservationists there 'that the time is ripe now for an intensification of scientific research, particularly ecological research in the National Parks and Nature Reserves of Israel, in order to provide a sound basis for future management policies' and that 'this only comes after intensive and often painstaking research'.[26] Clearly, these sentiments reflected his beliefs about what his own organisation was achieving, but

---

[23]Wright, *Wildlife Research and Management*, 30.

[24]A. Phillips, 'Turning ideas on their head: A new paradigm for protected areas', *The George Wright Forum* 20, no. 2 (2003): 8–32; M. Hockings, J. Ervin and G. Vincent, 'Assessing the management of protected areas: The work of the World Parks Congress before and after Durban', *Journal of International Wildlife Law and Policy* 7 (2004): 32–42; G. Wandesforde-Smith, 'The future of wildlife and the world parks congress', *Journal of International Wildlife Law and Policy* 7 (2004): 1–7.

[25]T. Young and L.M. Dilsaver, 'Collecting and diffusing "the world's best thought": International cooperation by the National Park Service', *The George Wright Forum* 28, no. 3 (2011): 269–278.

[26]Pienaar to Rosenberg, 12 December 1968, A/21 Wetenskapleke Skakelings [Scientific links], Kruger National Park archives, Skukuza.

he did not elaborate on the kind of research being done, or the principles underpinning it.

South African national parks were also closely connected with the southern African region. South Africa had a mandate over South West Africa, was friendly with Rhodesia, which had unilaterally declared its independence in 1965, and remained on relatively good terms with Botswana. It is useful to compare South Africa very briefly with Rhodesia. There, the Wild Life Conservation Act of 1960 had transformed the Rhodesian Game Department into the Department of Wild Life Conservation, which became more scientifically oriented, a move that, surprisingly, was widely criticised. As a result, in 1970 a parliamentary wildlife commission was appointed with the assistance of KNP biologist Pienaar and George Petrides (Michigan State University, East African ecologist and in 1966 first visiting lecturer in the newly established masters degree programme in wildlife management at the University of Pretoria). The commission recommended a scientific approach to conservation leadership in Rhodesia, and the first director, Graham Child, was appointed in 1971 (he remained until 1986).

Another coordinated regional development was the Southern African Regional Commission for the Conservation and Utilisation of the Soil (SARCCUS), whose remit actually included conservation of all renewable resources. Similar intergovernmental networks of agriculturalists existed in East and West Africa. SARCCUS was reorganised in 1968, when a standing committee for conservation, management, and use of wildlife and nature areas (MUNC) was formed. South African scientists, through their membership of both bodies, had a window into what was happening internationally via neighbouring Zimbabwe, which was better connected internationally in these decades than South Africa.

Environmental Science in South Africa: The CSIR

The NPB and the provincial nature conservation departments were not the only organisations involved in conservation and environmental science in South Africa. Therefore, the contribution of the NPB needs to be evaluated in a national, as well as an international, context. In terms of scientific study and understanding, innovation and importance, the activities of all the state conservation bodies were eclipsed by the Cooperative Scientific Programmes (CSP) conducted by the Council for Scientific and Industrial Research (CSIR) between 1975 and 1988. The CSIR had been established in 1945 to promote the technical and physical sciences and its mandate did not include research into living plants and animals, apart from funding basic research at universities. Although state-funded, the CSIR was not part of the civil service, but governed by legislation and was based on a research model that encouraged collaboration between government and universities in terms of funding and project evaluation. The CSIR was thus well placed to encourage research that straddled disciplines.[27]

C. van der Merwe Brink, president of the CSIR from 1971 to 1980, was an enthusiastic proponent of cooperative research. An ideal opportunity for a holistic approach to studying the South African environment arose for the CSIR in the 1970s. By then, the environmental sciences had gained in prominence as a result of the growth of international environmentalism and the international energy crisis. Structured interdisciplinary cooperation on ecological issues had begun in 1964 when the International Council of Scientific Unions (ICSU), in which South Africa had retained membership, launched the International Biological Programme (IBP) under the overall direction of E.B. Worthington.[28] This was a coordinated programme, modelled on the 1957 International Geophysical Year, to incorporate ecosystem ecology and other environmental issues into the international research arena and to provide substantial funding for them. The IBP fitted well into the overall goals of the IUCN.

Not without its critics at the time and subsequently, the IBP was divided into three over-riding themes, including conservation, in which the 'biome' emerged as the prime focus.[29] The IBP lasted for a decade and the CSIR became the facilitating partner in South Africa. Heading the local IBP committee was Professor C.A. du Toit, a comparative anatomist at Stellenbosch University, who had been a member of the African Scientific Council in 1949 and was a CSIR council member.[30] Two South Africans participated in the first IBP general assembly in Paris in 1964 – C.G. Hide, from the science cooperation division of the CSIR (and later scientific counsellor at the South African embassy in Washington), and Bernard de Winter from the Botanical Research Institute. Moreover, when the first

---

[27] For a history of the CSIR, see D.R. Kingwill, *The CSIR: The First 40 Years* (Pretoria: CSIR, 1990).

[28] E.B. Worthington, ed., *The Evolution of IBP*. International Biological Programme 1 (Cambridge: Cambridge University Press, 1975).

[29] S.E. Kingsland, *The Evolution of American Ecology 1890–2000* (Baltimore, MD: Johns Hopkins University Press, 2005), 221–223.

[30] Kingwill, *CSIR*, 41–73.

IBP Intergovernmental Conference on the Organisation of Research and Training in Africa was held in Lagos later that year, South Africa was again represented by Hide and de Winter, but also by Phillip Tobias, a young and later eminent palaeo-anthropologist from the University of the Witwatersrand. The following year (1965), Rudolph Bigalke, chief research officer of the Natal Parks Board, U. de V. (Tol) Pienaar from KNP and Berend Jansen, director of veterinary research at Onderstepoort, attended the IBP meetings in Aberdeen and Cambridge.[31] In 1971, the CSIR even arranged for the executive committee of the International Union of the Biological Sciences (IUBS) to meet in Cape Town. It appeared that South Africa and the NPB were poised to make a contribution to the international ecological sciences, in which theories such as stability, diversity, resilience and regulation were already being hotly debated.

The archives of the KNP contain many documents about the IBP as well as typescript articles written by the most eminent people involved in it at the time, including Raymond Dasmann, E.B. Worthington and Frank Fraser Darling.[32] It is clear, therefore, that NPB biologists were not only aware of international developments, but also, for a time, played an active part in them. Roelf Attwell, then interim convenor of the important Commission of Terrestrial Ecosystems (CT) within the IBP, wrote to Pienaar in anticipation of the latter's serving on the South African CT committee, and invited him to a meeting in this connection in Pietermaritzburg in December 1965. It is not clear whether Pienaar attended, but he wrote a paper (in Afrikaans) about the role of nature conservation in the IBP. In it, Pienaar maintained that the scientific value of nature conservation lay in the ecological importance of forms of wildlife, about which he believed comparatively little was understood. It was to fill this gap, he argued, that the IBP had begun its worldwide programme for advancing knowledge of biological processes and he described how protected areas would be important in assisting the project. This was so, he stated, because some were natural ecosystems. They were thus targeted for study by the CT committee of the IBP owing to their size and heterogeneity, their potential as outdoor botanical and zoological laboratories, as well as their use as outdoor museums for education and public enjoyment. Although there was no explicit identification of what kind of work in national parks would advance the IBP

[31]See File A/18 IUCN and IBP, Kruger National Park archives, Skukuza.
[32]See File A/18 IUCN and IBP, Kruger National Park archives, Skukuza.

research, Pienaar's paper attracted press interest in July 1967, when the South African Association for the Advancement of Science (SAAAS) was arranging its 65th congress in Pretoria.[33]

In 1971, Pienaar, by then nature conservator (warden) of the KNP, articulated the scientific responsibilities of the KNP. First was data collection and the storage of long-term monitoring data of important factors in the ecosystem. Second was the analysis and interpretation of these processes to provide an understanding of the ecosystem and as necessary background for management policies. Third was a feedback system to monitor the effectiveness and impact of management strategies and other man-induced effects on the ecosystem. Finally, all findings were to be published for critical evaluation by the scientific world at large and as a public source of information to assist in the fuller appreciation and enjoyment of the KNP ecosystem.[34] How this was to be achieved in practice, particularly for the second point, was not spelt out, nor was any definition of 'ecosystem' provided. While the CSIR programmes leant in the direction of inclusiveness, the NPB took a long time to follow suit. Given the lack of baseline information in the KNP and elsewhere, its collection was conducted with gusto by the team in Skukuza. The '3Ps' took a back seat to the '3Ms' of monitoring, measuring and manipulating the discrete elements of the ecosystem. Agee argues that there are two distinct views of ecosystems, one the population community view (the focus of many South African studies in the period under review), and the other concerned with flows of energy and cycles of nutrients through the whole system, which was adopted only much later.[35]

Meanwhile, the IBP had encouraged studies on the structure and functioning of ecosystems, thus introducing 'big science' to environmental research and displacing small-scale or localised descriptive work.[36] The time had come for South Africa to move beyond 'a strong emphasis

[33]News No. 8. U. de V. Pienaar, manuscript: 'Die rol van natuurbewaring in die Internasionale Biologiese Program'; SAAAS to Pienaar, 9 June 1967. File A/18 IUCN and IBP, Kruger National Park archives, Skukuza.

[34]U. de V. Pienaar, 'The Kruger Park Saga 1898–1981', 73–74. Unpublished manuscript, Kruger National Park archives, Skukuza.

[35]J.K. Agee, 'Ecosystem management: An appropriate concept for parks', in *National Parks and Protected Areas: Their Role in Environmental Protection* ed., R.G. Wright (Cambridge, MA: Blackwell Science, 1996), 31–44. See also F.B. Golley, *A History of the Ecosystem Concept in Ecology: More than a Sum of the Parts* (New Haven, CT and London: Yale University Press, 1993).

[36]Kingsland, *Evolution of American Ecology*, 220.

on wildlife management and the description and understanding of individual species' into a new kind of environmental science.[37]

South African natural resource scientists were able to put IBP principles to use when ICSU created the Scientific Committee on Problems of the Environment (SCOPE) in 1969 to identify and analyse emerging environmental issues that were caused by, or impacted upon, humans. With support from the National Committee for Nature Conservation (NACOR), and using the examples created by the IBP and SCOPE, the CSIR established the National Scientific Programmes Unit (NSPU, later CSP, the Cooperative Scientific Programmes) – under the visionary leadership of R. Graham Noble, an aquatic ecologist and the driving force behind cooperative science in South Africa. The management of the CSP reported directly to the CSIR president, who in turn appointed a number of advisory committees 'to identify problems peculiar to South Africa which, because of their magnitude and complexity, required the co-ordinated effort of a number of different organizations in planned research programmes'. The National Programme for the Environmental Sciences (NPES) evolved into the National Programme for Ecosystem Research (NPER) in 1975. The Savannah Ecosystem Project at Nylsvley, initiated in 1974, was one of the first major investments of the CSP, strongly supported by S.S. du Plessis of the Transvaal Division of Nature Conservation, A.J. (Pine) Pienaar of the Department of Agricultural Technical Services, Christopher Cresswell and Brian Walker of the University of the Witwatersrand and J.O. Grunow of the University of Pretoria. The NPB, although invited, did not engage with the project.[38] Within the NPER were four sub-programmes: inland water ecosystems, terrestrial ecosystems, nature conservation research and human needs and, fourthly, resources and the environment. The time, the opportunity, the support and the expertise had converged to energise South African environmental research on a very large scale.

Well funded and located outside individual universities, research institutes or government structures, and capitalising on the contributions of groups of like-minded men from different disciplines (very few women were involved), these innovative research projects galvanised practical and theoretical ecological research in South Africa. The NPER was extremely ably managed by Brian Huntley, an ecologist trained at the University of

---

[37]Anon., *Environmental Research Perspectives in South Africa*. South African National Scientific Programmes Report 66 (Pretoria: CSIR, 1982), 1, 25.
[38]Kingwill, *CSIR*, 41–73.

Natal. Highly influential on the NPER was Brian Walker, also a graduate from the University of Natal and of the University of Saskatchewan, a savannah ecologist and innovative thinker who was even then involved in the promising environmental science of resilience with numerous international colleagues. A number of fynbos ecologists, such as Frederick J. Kruger and Roy Siegfried, contributed important ideas around what has come to be called the Cape Floristic Region. These studies provided the springboard for ecosystems approaches in southern Africa and for 'resilience thinking' more globally.[39]

Between 1975 and 1988, the various groups (22 cooperative ventures) and individuals (208 individual projects) within the CSP produced 151 reports and papers at a cost of R9.2 million.[40] The projects mobilised more than 500 participants from 13 universities, four government and five provincial departments,[41] seven statutory organisations, seven museums and three voluntary organisations, as well as 'several dozen' international scientists.[42] Many projects were completed within the six programmes of inland water ecosystems, terrestrial ecosystems, human needs, marine pollution, the atmosphere and waste management.

The CSP included research on topics as varied as savannah and fynbos ecosystems; pollution and waste; compilation of Red Data books; numerous checklists; freshwater, estuary and marine science; fynbos; fire; Antarctic research; invasion biology; palaeo-ecology; rural needs; construction and building; island ecology; forestry; and the atmosphere. All these initiatives are evidence of an unusual burst of activity in South Africa, with scientists at various levels of expertise working collaboratively and actively, and with financial and other support from the CSIR and other organisations. The upshot was a profound change to the course of South African ecological thinking.

Although South African scientists were generally unwelcome abroad, CSP leaders were free to invite foreign scientists into the country. The initial reluctance of some to accept financial support from the South African government could be overcome, because the costs were explicitly

[39]See L. Robin, 'Resilience in the Anthropocene: A biography', in *Rethinking Invasion Ecologies from the Environmental Humanities*, eds J. Frawley and I. McCalman (London: Routledge, 2014), 45–63.

[40]B.J. Huntley, 'Ten years of cooperative ecological research in South Africa', *South African Journal of Science* 83, no. 2 (1987): 72.

[41]The newly formed Department of Environment Affairs was one.

[42]Huntley, 'Ten years of cooperative ecological research', 72–79.

Figure 6.2. Delegates to an international ecology workshop convened by Brian Huntley at Tsitsikamma National Park in September 1980.
Photograph by Brian Huntley.

covered by the CSIR, an independent research body. Many internationally renowned figures took advantage of the opportunity to visit South Africa and contributed to the 24 workshops organised by Huntley. Among the visitors were major environmental leaders and scientists such as Michael Soulé, Jared Diamond, Peter Raven, Daniel Botkin, Raymond Specht, Imanuel Noy-Meir, Francisco di Castri, Harold Mooney and Paul Ehrlich. Their work was thus brought to South African attention, and the country benefited enormously.[43]

The specific engagement of the NPB with the CSP will be discussed in greater detail in Chapter 8, because NPB staff principally involved themselves in the debates about controlling 'surplus' animals in national parks. It is sufficient to note here that the smallest of the three major sub-programmes within the NPER was Nature Conservation Research, coordinated by A.A. (Tony) Ferrar, the larger two being Inland Water Ecosystems and Terrestrial Ecosystems. Nature Conservation had 25 projects (compared with 56 for Inland Water and 127 for Terrestrial), funding of R982 000 (compared with R2.7 million and R5.5 million,

[43]See Kingwill, *CSIR*, 71–72.

respectively) and 32 papers and one thesis (compared with 95 and 19 and 206 and 35, respectively). Research themes within the Nature Conservation Research programme were threatened species, habitat conservation, invasive biota (the largest with ten projects), management and utilisation and conservation behaviour. There were none on ecosystem research in or for protected areas.[44] Predicting responses to stress and disturbance was a key objective of the more fundamental research within the various terrestrial biomes and freshwater systems of the NPER.

Koedoe 1974 should have been a landmark issue of the journal, because it contained three surveys that might have assisted protected area planning in South Africa. One of them – a register of permanent conservation areas in South and South West Africa – was produced by NACOR. However, they had no effect on government or on NPB planning at the time.[45] A decade later, the CSP also published a full directory of southern African conservation areas. The directory was an inventory of 155 areas that were larger than 1000 ha, giving details of physical characteristics, soils, elevation, dates of establishment and administrative regime.[46] Again, there is no evidence that this information was put to practical use by government or the board.

In 1989, as the CSP was being phased out, independent reviews were solicited. Michael Usher, forester, ecologist and professor of biology at the University of York, evaluated the NPER Nature Conservation Programme. Some details from his evaluation are worth relating because of their relevance to science in national parks. Established in 1980 at the request of official nature conservation agencies through NACOR, the Programme aimed to stimulate and coordinate nature conservation research by funding new projects not adequately covered by government agencies. Usher listed 66 research projects that had been undertaken and showed how these had spawned many articles in the open literature as well as 70 in refereed journals and 65 in popular journals.[47] Most important in his view

---

[44]Huntley, 'Ten years of cooperative ecological research', 72–79.
[45]D. Edwards, 'Survey to determine the adequacy of existing conserved areas in relation to vegetation types: A preliminary report', *Koedoe* 17 (1974): 3–38; W. von Richter, 'Survey of the adequacy of existing conserved areas in relation to wild animal species', *Koedoe* 17 (1974): 39–69; R.G. Noble, 'An evaluation of the conservation status of aquatic biotopes', *Koedoe* 17 (1974): 71–83; Editorial Committee, 'Register of permanent conservation areas in South and South West Africa (August 1973)', *Koedoe* 17 (1974): 85–119.
[46]T. Greyling and B.J. Huntley, eds, *Directory of Southern African Conservation Areas*. South African National Scientific Programmes Report 98 (Pretoria: CSIR, 1984).
[47]Huntley to Joubert, 22 February 1989; Huntley to Colleagues, 23 March 1989, File A/21, 1989, Kruger National Park archives, Skukuza.

were three textbooks that would be a major and long-lasting contribution to South Africa's conservation science: B.J. Huntley, ed., *Biotic Diversity in Southern Africa: Concepts and Conservation*,[48] I.A.W. Macdonald, F.J. Kruger and A.A. Ferrar, eds, *The Ecology and Management of Biological Invasions in Southern Africa*,[49] and N. Owen-Smith, ed., *Management of Large Mammals in African Conservation Areas: Proceedings of a Symposium held in Pretoria, South Africa, 29–30 April 1982*.[50]

Despite earlier interest in the IBP, very few NPB scientists participated in the CSP projects and none led any of them. The two in which a few NPB people did participate were the management of large mammals (1983) and rivers research (1988).[51] Given the KNP's high profile, large staff, long history and good finances and incomparable natural resources and landscapes, it is surprising that the study site chosen for the major savannah ecosystem project within NPER's Terrestrial Ecosystems was a Transvaal provincial nature reserve called Nylsvley. It is difficult to explain why the NPB did not take a lead, and there is nothing to be found in the formal record. Informally it has been suggested that Nylsvley was selected because it was closer and more convenient to the major cities of Pretoria and Johannesburg at a time when there were petrol restrictions; that the NPB was protective of its turf and refused to allow the KNP to be opened up to competition and investigation by outside scientists, particularly for the intrusive research that was required; that it was supremely self-confident and regarded outside interest as 'unwarranted interference'. This is certainly how the government of South Africa reacted to criticism at that time, often reiterating that the rest of the world had nothing to offer South Africa, which had (it was said) world-class technology and sound human relations. An element of personal insecurity may also have played a role because the majority of the senior NPB staff were Afrikaans-speaking and unused to expressing themselves in English or interacting with international, English-speaking scientists. It has also been suggested that Pienaar, who had been promoted to assistant-director of conservation in 1970, director in 1974 and warden of the KNP in 1978, did not consider these projects to be

---

[48](Cape Town: Oxford University Press, 1989).
[49](Cape Town: Oxford University Press, 1987).
[50](Pretoria: HAUM, 1983).
[51]Director's Archive File Index, Nature Conservation and Research updated in 2006. Also NK1 – NK/53, File A/7/1 Algemeen Ekosisteemprojek. Kruger National Park archives, Skukuza.

directly relevant to wildlife management or to the type of conservation science that he believed to be his brief. It is also possible that, given the almost constant organisational upheavals in the NPB from 1970 to 1980, including changes in the responsible ministry and alternating centralisation and decentralisation, the organisation was simply paralysed.[52] In any event, the NPB staff in the KNP and other parks did not take the opportunity to engage actively in an extremely important initiative.

It may also have been that the NPB believed it should be more strongly allied to the IUCN than to ICSU, and thus did not consider the CSP to be germane to it. A hint of this can be found in correspondence in December 1982 between Gerrit de Graaff, assistant head (scientific liaison) of the NPB, and John Hanks at the Institute of Natural Resources at the University of Natal. The matter at hand was the completion of a detailed questionnaire requested by the IUCN. De Graaff's letter expressed keenness to 'enhance our standing with the IUCN', while admitting that the CSIR had coordinated the 'lion's share' of ecological and environmental research. He was silent on the issue of scientific management and best practice for national parks, their contribution to South Africa's ecological knowledge, or even the contribution of its scientists to the literature.[53]

A sense of the NPB's attitude can be gleaned from a brief outburst in a letter of September 1987 from Willem Gertenbach, general manager of nature conservation in the park, to Huntley in September 1987. It can be found in the KNP archives. In it, he stated that funds, rather than going to the CSP, should instead be assigned to helping local management understand the functioning of the KNP ecosystem. Efforts should be focused on local scientists and local concerns, and he was averse to being manipulated (*manipuleer*) by other scientists in the Savannah Ecosystem Project. He thought Nylsvley had bad connotations (which he did not specify), and he took issue with some members of the steering committees, whose personalities clearly clashed with his own.[54] In reply, Huntley – as programme manager of the NPER – reminded Gertenbach that the project was designed to develop predictive understanding, not

---

[52]S.C.J. Joubert, *The Kruger National Park: A History*, vol 2 (Johannesburg: High Branching, 2012), 2–10.

[53]De Graaff to Hanks, 27 December 1983, A/21 Wetenskaplike Skakelings [Scientific links]. Kruger National Park archives, Skukuza.

[54]Gertenbach to Huntley, 16 September 1987, A/21 Wetenskaplike Skakelings [Scientific links]. Kruger National Park archives, Skukuza.

answer specific management-related questions. Huntley asked to be provided with details of the KNP research programme and strategy so that synergy could be generated and overlap (particularly in the use of funds) be avoided. He also fairly sharply reminded Gertenbach that it was not the place of the NPB to interfere in the appointment of CSIR project coordinators.[55] Clearly the relationship was not altogether harmonious.

That same month, September 1987, Salomon Joubert, then warden of KNP, who took an active interest in the CSP, listed the nature conservation achievements of the NPB in an in-house document. The KNP Research and Management Strategy was, he said, exclusively directed towards maintaining pristine ecosystems, and that all research inputs had been designed to analyse and interpret the functions and dynamic aspects of those 'natural' ecosystems. This work included an annual census of 16 large mammal species, relating their distribution and densities to nine environmental parameters. It also involved an extensive programme on vegetation monitoring and photographic images, and he mentioned that the KNP worked with other research institutions, particularly the Department of Water Affairs, on perennial water systems. Moreover, the NPB had maintained an active programme of saving species before they became extinct, including – as part of the manipulation process – translocating white and black rhino and reintroducing Lichtenstein's hartebeest.[56]

What Joubert did not stress was his own contribution in terms of the comprehensive KNP masterplan devised in 1984, which followed on his first plan of 1975.[57] This was an important document and it has been a benchmark for those that followed. Naturally, it is a product of its time, written from the perspective of its author, reflecting his personality and his institutional culture. Joubert began his career in the KNP working part-time as a game ranger when he was a BSc student at the University of Pretoria and he joined the permanent staff in 1964 as a section ranger. After obtaining his MSc in 1967, he was transferred to the research section, completing his PhD on the population ecology of roan antelope in 1976. He became head of that section and in 1987, on the promotion of

[55]Huntley to Gertenbach, 12 October 1987, A/21 Wetenskaplike Skakelings [Scientific links]. Kruger National Park archives, Skukuza.

[56]Joubert to Gertenbach, September 1987, A/21 Wetenskaplike Skakelings [Scientific links]. Kruger National Park archives, Skukuza. See also B.L. Penzhorn, 'An old reference to "hartebeest" in the Transvaal lowveld', *Koedoe* 28 (1985): 69–71.

[57]Joubert's Masterplan of 1975 was an internal document that is mentioned in W.P.D. Gertenbach, 'Landscapes of the Kruger National Park', *Koedoe* 26 (1983): 120.

Pienaar to the position of the NPB's chief director, warden (director) of the KNP. He retired in 1994.

Identifying the prime management objective as being 'to preserve all the intrinsic values of the ecosystem in the KNP and to limit managerial involvement to those aspects where man-induced or other identified unnatural pressures have led to deviations in the ecological structure and natural processes',[58] Joubert's masterplan was a detailed chronology and compilation of facts about the KNP,[59] and contained no explicit scientific strategy. Summarising the philosophy of the KNP as a rather unscientific 'concept of life', Joubert described the national park as follows: 'The KNP is, indeed, a most beautiful lady, worthy of all the love and care, respect and appreciation that we may command: the Cinderella who became a Princess; the Princess who has been crowned as Queen.'[60] This anthropomorphising (and feminisation) of the national park and valorising of the 'concept of life' – rather than the ecosystem, or even biodiversity – resonates with a book published around the same time by theologian W.S. Vorster. This was entitled *Are We Killing God's Earth? Ecology and Theology* and it eschews environmentalism in its civic and political forms. Indeed, it argues against the views of John Passmore and Lynn White and emphasises a convergence between religion and conservation, through repentance, creation and celebration.[61] An extremely able wildlife manager, it is perhaps regrettable that Joubert, so firmly within the bastion that was the NPB, had little interaction with men like Brian Walker or Richard Bell who could have moulded his synthesis and interpretation of information into a less romantic response. Moreover, had more NPB personnel attended workshops and symposia in South Africa that included international luminaries in the conservation science field, the course of NPB science might have been different, innovative and path-breaking before the mid-1990s.

While synthesis and a scientific paradigm are hard to discern in the first masterplan document, it became more explicit in Joubert's 1986 article in *Koedoe*.[62] There, stressing the strictures in the National Parks Act

---

[58]S.C.J. Joubert, 'Masterplan for the management of the Kruger National Park' (1984/5), 3. Unpublished NPB manuscript, Kruger National Park archives, Skukuza.

[59]Joubert, *The Kruger National Park*.

[60]Joubert, 'Masterplan'.

[61]W.S. Vorster, ed., *Are we Killing God's Earth? Ecology and Theology* (Pretoria: University of South Africa, 1987).

[62]S.C.J. Joubert, 'Management and research in relation to ecosystems of the Kruger National Park', *Koedoe* 29 (1986): 157–163.

57 of 1976, Joubert maintained the KNP's commitment to the preservation and perpetuation of ecosystems. However, as expressed in *Koedoe*, the value of these ecosystems did not lie in how they might be understood, but in how these 'living organisms' (vocabulary harking back to J.F.V. Phillips) were useful as recreational facilities for 'modern day technological man', and also counteracted the tendency to deplete natural resources. Management options were to be guided by the 'minimum intervention' principle, although precisely how and when such intervention might be scientifically determined was left unstated. There is little appreciation of a need to understand before intervention took place, or what 'minimum' implied. Joubert's priorities for what he referred to as ecosystem-oriented research lay in monitoring, identifying and mapping all elements of the system – including geology and geomorphology – so that changes could be identified within communities, not within the system itself.

In this period, South African environmental science outside the NPB appears to have been far more sophisticated. The 1982 CSP report by W.R. Siegfried and B.R. Davies on *Conservation of Ecosystems: Theory and Practice* (South African National Scientific Programmes Report 61) will serve as an example. This overview of a workshop held in Tsitsikamma in September 1980 detailed many aspects of ecosystem conservation – goals, obstacles, ecological characteristics, etc. – placing particular emphasis on protected areas as 'islands' and applying theories of island biogeography to them. The participants warned that islands become increasingly impoverished and that integrating protected areas with human activities would be the optimum path. The entire report advocates a philosophical understanding of ecosystems (rather than a tinkering with them) and a strategic approach based on an understanding of ecosystem functioning. The only representative from the NPB at this workshop was G.R. (Robbie) Robinson, a marine biologist who had been warden of the Tsitsikamma Coastal and Forest National Park[63] before being promoted in 1978 to head up what was called 'Southern Parks' – all parks apart from the KNP. And this was despite the vital relevance of the workshop to core NPB business, in particular the understanding of key processes in conserved ecosystems. Report 61 discussed moving away from traditional wildlife management that aimed at managing and minimising change or disturbance towards acceptance of the dynamism of ecosystems.[64] Two years later (1982), the

---

[63]The spelling was originally Tsitsikama but, on advice from specialists in the Khoisan languages, Robinson altered it to Tsitsikamma.

[64](Pretoria: CSIR, 1982).

CSP report on environmental research perspectives identified collabora-tive programmes specifically targeted at increasing research capacity, and stimulating and coordinating them to the benefit of the country.[65] This again suggests that in the 1970s and 1980s opportunities for productive interchange between NPB scientists and their colleagues were lost.

Two of South Africa's most eminent scientists of the 1970s were direct in expressing their opinions about the state of science in the country at the time. One was Chris van der Merwe Brink, the CSIR president. For him, science needed to find general solutions to complex problems – as the CSP had attempted to do. He hailed the programme for bringing together the best available skills where they were most needed and for inaugurating an era of interdisciplinary research. The NPER came in for special acclaim. Brink regarded it as having contributed significantly to a fresh conception of ecosystems. He was concerned at the absence of integrated research and the continued privileging of a single species – an approach favoured by the NPB. For this reason, he singled out the Savannah Ecosystem Project for praise.[66]

The other South African scientist to pronounce on the state of the coun-try's science was eco-physiologist Gideon Louw, internationally acclaimed head of UCT's department of zoology. Louw's research on the physiology of muscle functioning in ungulates was truly ground-breaking and it was eventually applied in overcoming 'overstraining' of animals stressed in cap-ture. Speaking of the biological sciences, he noted in 1978 the revolution-ary change that had taken place since the 1940s. Such sciences had been transformed into a rigorous quantitative study supported by the physical sciences. Describing ecological training and research in South Africa as being 'mediocre', he felt that the CSP had exposed 'our weaknesses in the field of ecology' and hoped that through international contacts and national coordination, matters might improve. Nature conservation, an applied science, had progressed, but he warned that if national parks were to fulfil their function, they would have to work more closely with univer-sity research institutes and minimise 'red tape'.[67]

---

[65] Anon., *Environmental Research Perspectives*; also W.R. Siegfried and B.R. Davies, eds, *Conservation of Ecosystems: Theory and Practice*. South African National Scientific Programmes Report 61 (Pretoria: CSIR, 1982).

[66] C. v.d.M. Brink, 'Trends and challenges for science in South Africa', *Transactions of the Royal Society of South Africa* 43 (1978): 223–239.

[67] G.N. Louw, 'The biological sciences in South Africa: Present state and future trends', *Transactions of the Royal Society of South Africa* 43 (1978): 261–265.

The CSP projects lost momentum when the CSP and the Main Research Support Programme (Research Grants Division) were combined to form the Foundation for Research and Development (FRD), a model akin to the German Forschungsgemeinschaft. The CSIR moved away from the open debate established by the CSP and marginalised 'soft science' research that was published in the 'grey literature', principally in workshop reports. From then on, the FRD (and its successor, the National Research Foundation) focused on, and funded, individual, peer-reviewed research done primarily by university academics,[68] to which, to be sure, many scientists in the CSP had also contributed. Three important consequences flowed from the change from cooperation to support for an elite corps of scholars. One was that it stifled opportunities for incorporating untrained South Africans in funded scientific research, even in assistant positions; another was that conservation administrators unfamiliar with academic journals were not supplied with accessible information; and the third was that blue-sky, primary university-funded research replaced applicable, mission-oriented, multi-organisational projects. The new emphasis brought South Africa into the changing international research landscape with its emphasis on quality work, published mainly in academic journals and adjudicated by peer review.

Conservation Biology

The environmental research being conducted in South Africa, whether of the NPB's monitoring and measuring kind or the CSP's more eco-system-related work, lacked a generally agreed disciplinary name. By the mid-twentieth century, 'natural history' had come to suggest an amateurish, observational interest in the environment, hence its supersession by 'biology', the name adopted for the first scientific research and researchers in the NPB. Biology, however, soon became problematic itself. Many biologists had little in common with each other and biology was increasingly becoming a laboratory science. The emergence of the environmental movement accelerated the search for a named discipline applying specifically to environmental research or to nature conservation practice. 'Ecology' was one of the first to come into prominence with the publication of E.P. and H.T. Odum's 1953 textbook, *Fundamentals of Ecology*. This introduced the concept of an ecosystem to a far wider

[68]Brian Huntley. Interview with the author. Betty's Bay, Western Cape, 1 September 2013.

audience than Tansley had done. It implied flows of nutrients and energy between biotic and abiotic elements in an interconnected system.[69] In South Africa, as elsewhere, botanists, zoologists, animal behaviourists and many others working in protected areas began to refer to themselves as 'ecologists' studying 'ecosystems'. However, an ecosystem is extremely difficult to define, let alone understand and study, and most South African ecologists of that time – particularly in the NPB – might more accurately have been described as bio-geographers, studying populations and communities in particular habitats. There was considerable truth to the 1982 comment that many 'ecologists' ignored the ecosystem.[70]

In unpacking the history of ecology, Kingsland has argued that recognition of an ecological perspective does not necessarily imply there ought to be a separate discipline called ecology. In regarding nature conservation as an applied science, ecology merely became a convenient term for the research side of conservation. What promoted ecology from the junior ranks and transformed its 'subversive' nature was, on one hand, its institutionalisation within the sciences, and on the other its elevation to scientific social responsibility by the thinking of Rachel Carson and the environmental movement in general.[71] In addition to 'ecology', there were other contenders for prime position as *the* science of conservation. *Wildlife Biology* was one – the title of Raymond Dasmann's 1964 book, which, incidentally, praised Stevenson-Hamilton's *Animal Life* and endorsed the warden's views.[72] In 1970, Ehrenfeld came up with *Biological Conservation*[73] while *Conservation Biology* came into its own with the book edited by Michael Soulé and Bruce Wilcox in 1980.[74] In time, the name conservation biology, which incorporated an outcome with a science, eventually became widely accepted in the world.

A clear exposition of the development of conservation biology was published by Curt Meine, Michael Soulé and Reed Noss in 2006.[75] They mention how it brought together scientists from several disciplines – pure

---

[69]The first textbook appeared in 1953: Eugene Odum's *Fundamentals of Ecology.*

[70]Anon., *Environmental Research Perspectives*, 25.

[71]Kingsland, *The Evolution of American Ecology*, *passim*; M. Westoby, 'What does ecology mean?' *TREE* 12, no. 4 (1997): 166.

[72]R.F. Dasmann, *Wildlife Biology* (New York, NY: John Wiley, 1964), 100.

[73]D. Ehrenfeld, *Biological Conservation* (New York, NY: Holt, Rinehart and Winston, 1970).

[74]M.E. Soulé and B.A. Wilcox, eds, *Conservation Biology: An Evolutionary–Ecological Perspective* (Sunderland, MA: Sinauer Associates, 1980).

[75]Meine, Soulé, and Noss, '"A mission-driven discipline"' 631–651.

and applied – to construct 'not so much . . . a new science as a more comprehensive, better-integrated response to problems that were themselves more extensive, more urgent and more complicated than most had realised in 1970'. It was also helpful that those who adopted this label for their work did not have to abandon their other disciplinary homes, for instance, zoology or botany, in pursuing a 'conservation need'. Meine *et al.* note the emergence of the discipline of conservation biology in the first international conferences of 1978 (California) and 1985 (Michigan), the establishment of the Society for Conservation Biology and the publication of the journal *Conservation Biology* in 1987. In the first issue of the journal, Ehrenfeld described it as 'a discipline, a recognisable and coherent body of facts, theories and technologies'. He divided it into three parts: taxonomy and systematics, population biology, and ecology concerned with ecosystem functioning. Management was described as requiring and integrating all three aspects.[76] The term had already arrived in South Africa during its emergent phase in 1980, when one of the CSP's most important workshops included luminaries such as Soulé, Specht and Diamond.

The phrase 'biological diversity', or 'biodiversity', is often taken for granted as the prime goal of conservation biology in protected areas. It was a term that arose in the formal conservation literature in 1980 at the same time as 'conservation biology'. Indeed, it was argued that conservation biology was in the service of biological diversity.[77] Farnham has written extensively about the origins of the term and the concept of biodiversity. He records that in 1986 there was just one reference to biodiversity in the literature, but by 2001 it had increased to 872, and two years later (2003) to 2177. Such references currently number in many thousands. He surmised it had become a mantra because 'it succeeded in expressing a range of values and concerns which previously were scattered disparately through the scientific and conservation communities'. Although originating in microbiology, the word biodiversity migrated into environmentalism through the work of Norse and McManus.[78]

---

[76]D. Ehrenfeld, 'Editorial', *Conservation Biology* 1, no. 1 (1987): 6–7.
[77]Meine, Soulé and Noss, '"A mission-driven discipline"', 631–651.
[78]T. Farnham, *Saving Nature's Legacy: The Origins of the Idea of Biological Diversity* (New Haven, CT: Yale University Press, 2007), 6. Biological diversity surfaced first as a term in the 1960s then applied to microbiology, although N.W. Moore, in an article titled 'Experience with pesticides and the theory of conservation', came closest to its modern usage in 1969.

They argued that both genetic and ecological diversity were fundamental to the functioning of ecological systems. With acceptance of biodiversity as the goal, conservationist concern broadened from unique species to the biota as a whole. Norse believed that 'the concept had real value . . . it looked at conservation differently. It had the potential to bring people together who had not been together before . . . It was an idea whose time had come.'[79]

The first time 'biodiversity' was a keyword in an article published in *Koedoe* was only in 1997, and it was applied to a vegetation study of a small nature reserve in Witbank, not a national park.[80] It then took another two years for 'biodiversity' to appear as a keyword for a contribution relating to a national park – almost 20 years after it had entered the lexicon of conservation biology.[81]

The National Parks Board

In the absence of an agreed definition in the 1950s, the typology of national parks was unclear. In 1962, Cahalane wrote *National Parks: A World Need*. In it, he identified four types of national parks: African wildlife sanctuaries; US scenic parks; cultural landscapes in Britain and Japan; and parks in Switzerland, Congo and French West Africa that were 'extensive outdoor laboratories', not recreational amenities. South Africa was unusual in having a national park, at least in the KNP, that seemed to straddle the categories of outdoor laboratory and wildlife sanctuary.[82]

The IUCN first defined a national park in 1969 at its tenth general assembly in New Delhi. This included the requirement that it be 'large', contain one or more materially unchanged ecosystems of special interest or have components of special interest. Public access, even if under special conditions, was a necessity. In 1971, the definition was revised. This specified a minimum size of 1000 ha, statutory legal protection, an

[79]Farnham, *Saving Nature's Legacy*.
[80]C.M. Smit, G.J. Bredenkamp, N. van Rooyen, A.E. van Wyk and J.M. Combrinck, 'Vegetation of the Witbank Nature Reserve and its importance for conservation of threatened Rocky Highland Grassland', *Koedoe* 40, no. 2 (1997): 85–104.
[81]I.J. Whyte, H.C. Biggs, A. Gaylard and L.E.O. Braack, 'A new policy for the management of the Kruger National Park elephant population', *Koedoe* 42, no. 1 (1999): 111–132.
[82]V.H. Cahalane, ed., *National Parks: A World Need* (New York, NY: American Committee for International Wildlife Protection, 1962).

adequate budget and staff, and the prohibition of any natural resource exploitation, such as mining. As the definition post-dated the establishment of many national parks around the world, the title 'national park' did not always coincide with the definition. There were, however, definitions of other types of protected areas. They included Strict Nature Reserve, Wilderness Area, Habitat/Species Management Area, National Monument and Protected Landscape. Since these first efforts, there have been several changes both to the schedule and to the definitions and they are regularly reviewed in light of changed environmental priorities, international politics and economic conditions.[83]

In 1960, there were five national parks in South Africa: KNP, Addo, Bontebok, KGNP and Mountain Zebra. Given economic prosperity, the explosion of environmental thinking and the attention given to national parks at the first World Parks Congress of 1962, there was a rash of new proclamations: Golden Gate Highlands (1963), Tsitsikamma (1964), Augrabies Falls (1966), Groenkloof (1968, the site of the NPB head office in Pretoria), Karoo (1979), Wilderness (1983), Knysna National Lake Area (1985), West Coast (1985), Zuurberg (1985), Tankwa Karoo (1986) and Vaalbos (1986). In 1966 there was a concerted effort by the SAAAS to resuscitate the Dongola National Park, but despite considerable public support, the initiative ultimately failed.[84]

After the organisational upheavals of the 1950s, the NPB entered a stable phase and developed a corporate image and defined line management functions. Expansion became structurally possible. Some regarded the quest for new national parks to be almost manic. Early in 1962, during the first reading of the National Parks Amendment Bill (to clarify certain

---

[83]See R.F. Dasmann, 'Towards a system for classifying natural regions of the world and their representation by national parks and reserves', *Biological Conservation* 2 (1972): 247–255; R.F. Dasmann, *A System for Defining and Classifying Natural Regions for Purposes of Conservation.* IUCN Occasional Paper No. 7 (Morges: IUCN, 1973), iii–47; IUCN, *United Nations List of National Parks and Equivalent Reserves.* IUCN Publications No. 33 (Morges: IUCN, 1975); IUCN Commission on National Parks and Protected Areas, *United Nations List of National Parks and Equivalent Reserves* (Gland: IUCN, 1980); IUCN Committee on Criteria and Nomenclature Commission on National Parks and Protected Areas, *Categories, Objectives and Criteria for Protected Areas: A Final Report* (Morges: IUCN, 1978); IUCN, *Guidelines for Protected Area Management Categories* (Gland and Cambridge: IUCN, 1994).

[84]J. Carruthers, 'The Dongola Wild Life Sanctuary: "Psychological blunder, economic folly and political monstrosity" or "more valuable than rubies and gold?"' *Kleio* 24 (1992): 82–100.

legal issues), three prospective parks were announced by the Minister of Lands. They included 'a coastal park, a sea park or a beach park (call it what you may) ...' along the Tsitsikamma coast of the Western Cape. This would be a recreational 'angling park', although on-site bait collection would not be allowed. Another was a 'primeval forest' in the same general area, involving the Department of Forestry, while the third was the Augrabies waterfall in the Northern Cape, the highest in the country. The falls apparently needed protection 'from the spoliation which often takes place when a beautiful bit of nature is left at the mercy of the public without . . . supervision'.[85] According to the minister, the NPB was 'amazingly enthusiastic . . . I think they would even declare me a national park if they had the opportunity. I have to deal with their requests . . . with a certain measure of circumspection, and I have to apply the brake every now and then . . .'.[86]

Given the level of development in South Africa and its large population, there was no question of fashioning a national park *ab initio* from extensive vacant lands and interesting ecosystems. Moreover, the 'homelands' for black Africans were not regarded by government as part of white South Africa and were thus beyond the ambit of the NPB. This is not to say that no protected areas came about in those localities. The best known of these is the Pilanesberg National Park (regarded by the Bophuthatswana government as being 'national'). This was extremely innovative in terms of management and design, restoration ecology and research. Indeed, lacking a large, conservative bureaucracy at its helm, it later became a model for community conservation and the empowerment of local people.[87]

Under the enthusiastic leadership of Director Rocco Knobel, the new national parks of the 1960s brought a variety of landscapes under NPB control as well as change to the exclusive focus on wild animals. Control over the Augrabies Falls had been approved in principle by the NPB as early as 1955, but there had been considerable difficulty with

[85]Republic of South Africa, *House of Assembly Debates*, 27 February 1962, cols. 1622–1626.

[86]Republic of South Africa, *House of Assembly Debates*, 27 February 1962, see also 26 May 1961, cols. 7292–7316.

[87]J. Carruthers, 'Designing a wilderness for wildlife: The case of the Pilanesberg National Park, South Africa', in *Designing Wildlife Habitats*, ed. J. Beardsley (Washington, DC: Dumbarton Oaks Research Library and Collection, 2013), 107–130; J. Carruthers, 'Pilanesberg National Park, North West Province, South Africa: Uniting economic development with ecological design – a history, 1960s to 1984', *Koedoe* 53, no. 1 (2011), doi 10.4102.

the land acquisitions.[88] Because the need for marine national parks had been raised in IUCN circles and discussed at the 1962 Word Parks Congress (Recommendation 15), much impressing NPB delegates Knobel and Labuschagne in the process, such a site was also sought by the NPB. However, finding an appropriate part of the coastline was not simple, given the regional politics of the provinces. Cape Point was investigated, as was Tsitsikamma, because state land was available there.[89] Tsitsikamma was declared a national park, as was, eventually in the late 1990s, Cape Point. Perhaps one of the 'brakes' the minister had to apply was in respect of Cango Caves, upon which the NPB, supported by the Historical Monuments Commission and the South African Speleological Association, had set its sights. However, the municipality of Oudtshoorn adamantly refused to relinquish control over the landmark.[90]

Golden Gate Highlands National Park was the first to include mountain landscape and was in a province, the Orange Free State, which had no national parks. The area was fairly remote and when, in 1962, a few families decided to sell their farms, they were purchased by the provincial administration and handed over to the Department of Lands as a national park the following year.[91]

Marine parks joined the growing protected estate. First was Tsitsikamma, then Knysna and then Langebaan (West Coast) National Park in 1985. A marine park also marked a new managerial departure and warden Robbie Robinson became a pioneer in marine conservation in the NPB, in handling difficult landowners and in encouraging a different tourist experience by promoting hiking trails. The success of the Otter Trail led to the later development of trails in the KNP. Having studied in the USA, where modelling fish stocks was well-established

---

[88]Minutes and agenda of a meeting of the NPB, 23 March 1960, SANParks archives, Groenkloof, Pretoria.

[89]Meeting and agenda of a meeting of the NPB, 7 December 1959, SANParks archives, Groenkloof, Pretoria. The matter of a 'Sea Coast Park' had been item 72G on the NPB agenda of 6 December 1956, SANParks archives, Groenkloof, Pretoria. See also G.A. Robinson, 'Marine conservation in the Republic of South Africa with special reference to marine parks and reserves', in 'Proceedings of a symposium on the state of nature conservation in southern Africa, Kruger National Park, 1976', eds G. de Graaff and P.T. van der Walt, supplement, *Koedoe* (1977): 230–242.

[90]Minutes and agenda of a meeting of the NPB, 19 September 1960, SANParks archives, Groenkloof, Pretoria.

[91]A.P.J. van Rensburg, 'Golden Gate: Die geskiedenis van twee plase wat 'n nasionale park geword het', *Koedoe* 11 (1968): 83–138.

Figure 6.3. Former State President C.R. Swart in Golden Gate Highlands National Park.
From R.J. Labuschagne, *The Kruger Park and Other National Parks* (n.d.), p. 141. Courtesy of SANParks.

practice, Robinson was also responsible for initiating the first computer modelling by the NPB.

In 1973, even more national parks were under consideration, the board now attempting to have a national park in every habitat in South Africa. However, there were cultural as well as ecological aspects in play. The rationale for the Karoo National Park, for example, was that according to Knobel the Beaufort West landscape was integral to the history of 'our people' (*volksgeskiedenis*), and to its literature and other art forms, and thus worthy of protection on cultural grounds.[92]

While the NPB was a parastatal with wide powers, those powers devolved from parliament. National parks were thus the ultimate responsibility of

[92]Minutes and agenda of a meeting of the NPB, 22 June 1973, item 35, SANParks archives, Groenkloof, Pretoria. Other karoo landscapes that were also suggested at this time were Baviaanskloof and Graaff-Reinet in the Eastern Cape. See G. de Graaff, G.A. Robinson, P.T. van der Walt, B.R. Bryden and E.A. van der Hoven, *The Karoo National Park, Beaufort West* (Pretoria: National Parks Board, 1979).

government. Every national park required a separate Act and the general legislation applying to national parks also needed regular updating. For example, the Act was changed in 1962 to permit donations, the sale of liquor in national parks, the prohibition on feeding wild animals and even a change in the definition of 'animal', because in terms of the extant legislation killing even an insect was illegal.

As already noted, the kind of science in which national parks should engage was also aired in parliament. In urging that 'study' be added to the purpose of the country's national parks, Douglas Mitchell explained how the Natal Parks Board was using the 'latest technique' of tranquillisation and translocation of wildlife. He also told the House that a full-time 'ecologist' had been employed in the Natal game reserves from the 1950s to investigate the phenomenon of bush encroachment and the promotion of what he called 'methodical scientific research'.[93] Mitchell did not then expand on the research being conducted in his provincial game reserves, but had he done so, the comparison with the poorer studies in the NPB would have been illuminating, because the Natal Parks Board was introducing professional management planning and, with his international links, George Hughes was producing innovative research work on marine turtles.[94]

Moreover, the exact positioning of science within the NPB organisation required a decision. In 1962 the title of the head of a national park was changed from 'Warden' (*Opsiener*) to 'Nature Conservator'. The first KNP head with the new title was 'biologist' Andrew (Dolf) Brynard, who took over from Louis Steyn in 1961. This change brought together the previously separate sections of rangers and biological (research) under a single manager with potential benefits for research. Writing in 1964, Liaison Officer N.J. van der Merwe credited Minister of Lands J.G. Strijdom with exerting pressure on the NPB to establish the research section.[95]

However, the placement of the research function constantly changed in response to the prevailing winds of centralisation or decentralisation. In 1970, non-scientist R.J. Labuschagne became Director: Nature

---

[93]Union of South Africa, *House of Assembly Debates*, 26 May 1961, cols. 7292–7316.

[94]See J.P.G.M. Cromsigt, S. Archibald and N. Owen-Smith, eds, *Conserving Africa's Mega-Diversity in the Anthropocene: The Hluhluwe-iMfolozi Park Story*, (Cambridge: Cambridge University Press, 2016).

[95]N.J. van der Merwe, 'The history of game preservation in South Africa', in *Ecological Studies in South Africa*, ed. D.H.S. Davis (The Hague: Junk, 1964), 368–369.

Conservation, managing two teams headed by assistant directors of research and of wildlife management, who were responsible for all the national parks. Labuschagne's dismissal in March 1970 on charges of serious fraud necessitated another commission of inquiry, led by W.E. Purvis. His was a confidential report, delivered in December. Immediately, reorganisation of NPB's top management team followed, together with tighter budgets and financial controls. There were fears that the board might have been fatally harmed by Labuschagne, but Knobel repeatedly explained that only one Judas was to blame and that there was no fundamental flaw.[96]

Further restructurings took place in 1974, and again in 1978 and 1979. In 1978, KNP was split from 'Southern Parks', with the head of the park made responsible for research, wildlife management and information. In 1979, the research and information department was upgraded and headed by the deputy chief director, while the other part of what had been 'Nature Conservation' became the division of wildlife management.[97] The division was divided again, with Pieter van Wyk as head of department (he moved from Skukuza to Pretoria to take charge of research, photography and scientific liaison),[98] while Valerius (Vossie) de Vos, previously the veterinary ecologist, became assistant head of research and information and was stationed at Skukuza. Organisational changes to the NPB's research arm were paralleled by changes to the general administration of the parks. The coastal areas office came into being in April 1983, when part of the Wilderness Lake Area became the fully fledged Wilderness National Park. The Tsitsikamma National Park was expanded, as was the West Coast National Park, which at the time was considered to have the potential to develop into a meaningful national park. By 1988, the inland parks (as they were termed) comprised Addo, Augrabies, Mountain Zebra, Golden Gate, KGNP, Karoo, Vaalbos, Zuurberg and Tankwa-Karoo with Marakele about to come on-stream.

In 1986 there were 23 senior posts in the research section: 11 were resident in KNP, six were allocated to other national parks and six were

---

[96]Minutes of a meeting of the NPB, 13 March 1970, SANParks archives, Groenkloof, Pretoria.

[97]Joubert, *The Kruger National Park*, vol. 2, 4–9.

[98]Van Wyk, who never obtained a PhD degree, studied at the University of Potchefstroom and was engaged in pasture science research at the Potchefstroom College of Agriculture until he joined the KNP as assistant biologist in 1961. He was promoted to senior biologist in 1969 and chief research officer in 1970.

given more general responsibilities. This was an impressive enterprise, with 159 outside scientists involved in NPB research in that year, most from South African research institutions (the majority from the University of Pretoria) but a few from abroad. Because so many NPB staff researchers were involved, and many of them worked on numerous projects, it is difficult to untangle the influence of the outside researchers. The overwhelming majority of research projects relate to the KNP. The annual research reports are voluminous, but they list projects and provide no syntheses; they are repetitive (some projects lasted many years); and there is no tabular record of ensuing publications or completed degrees.[99] In 1987, 88 articles relating to South Africa's national parks were published in 22 non-South African journals. What is noteworthy is that very few NPB staff members published in them.

By this time, there was an urgent need for an annotated bibliography of research literature on the national parks of South Africa. This was duly compiled by V. de Vos, H. Bryden and P. Retief. Other sorely needed research material included copies of all known scientific literature on the national parks of South Africa, to be kept in well-organised fashion in the Stevenson-Hamilton Library at Skukuza. In April 1988, R.M. (Rod) Randall, from the Karoo National Park, became the chief research officer for coastal areas and moved to George to coordinate research in the coastal parks. The computer age had arrived by this time and in August 1988 a course on using the computer for nature conservation had been arranged in the Pilanesberg National Park in conjunction with the CSIR. It was attended by 50 researchers, including Peter Retief, a quantitative biologist employed by the NPB, who served as one of the course leaders.[100]

In 1988, de Vos, then head of NPB research, could boast that the division now had 50 staff members, including 17 professional research officers. There were 152 registered research projects, some being undertaken in conjunction with other institutions. Of these, 73 were in the KNP, although many were being done by the same person. As before, no other park even came close. There were 17 multi-park projects, but just two in each of Addo, Bontebok, Tankwa Karoo and West Coast, three

---

[99]National Parks Board of Trustees, *Jaarverslag Navorsing en Inligting 1 April 1987–31 Maart 1988.*

[100]National Parks Board of Trustees, *Jaarverslag April 1987 tot Maart 1988: Kusgebiede; Jaarverslag Binnelandse Parke 1987/1988; Department Navorsing en Kommunikasie Jaarverslag 1988/89.*

in Golden Gate and Wilderness Lakes, one in the Zuurberg and five in the Karoo. There were ten in Tsitsikamma, although five were being conducted by the same researcher, and there were 24 in the KGNP, six by the same researcher.[101]

By the 1980s, South African environmental scientists outside the NPB were giving attention to ecosystem management but, as has been explained, they were not focused on solving immediate problems. Indeed, most ecologists had by then begun seriously to question, if not jettison, the idea that there was a 'pristine' ecosystem that could be stabilised through management.[102] Perhaps influenced by the CSP initiatives, as early as 1978 KNP biologist Salomon Joubert had circulated the KNP's research objectives to a wide variety of institutions and scientists for comment. Among the few surviving replies are those from J. (Jan) Bothma, the Eugène Marais Chair of Wildlife Management at the University of Pretoria, and Bob Crass, a fisheries biologist, the first scientist on the staff of the Natal Parks Board (an expert in trout who was employed to manage the riverine fish of the province for the benefit of recreational anglers) and later its principal scientific officer.[103] They are worth recounting. Bothma believed that the scientists in national parks had a right to expect that outside experts, acting in the national interest, would assist in solving problems at little or no cost. However, it was park biologists who set the agenda and decided what problems required resolution, and they did not necessarily have to take the advice given. In this way, national parks personnel became research gatekeepers. In addition to praising the NPB for its maps, vegetation studies and zoogeographical surveys and effective veld burning policy, Crass congratulated Joubert on his openness and hoped it would lead to an exchange of ideas and

[101]National Parks Board of Trustees, *35th Annual Report for the Year 1987–1988*, National Parks Board of Trustees, *Research Division, Report 1987/1988.*

[102]B.J. Huntley, 'Ecosystem conservation in southern Africa', in *Biogeography and Ecology of Southern Africa*, vol. 2, ed. M.J.Werger (The Hague: Junk, 1978), 1333–1384. See also D. Hey, 'The history and status of nature conservation in South Africa', in *A History of Scientific Endeavour in South Africa*, ed.A.C. Brown (Cape Town: Royal Society of South Africa, 1977), 132–163; N.J. van der Merwe, 'The position of nature conservation in South Africa', *Koedoe* 5, 1962, 1–127; van der Merwe, 'The history of game preservation in South Africa', 363–370.

[103]B. Crass, 'Early days with the Natal Parks Board: Some personal reminiscences by a former principal scientific officer', *Natalia* 41 (2011): 82–89, 85; G.R. Hughes and M. Coke, 'Robert Sanderson ["Bob"] Crass (26 June 1921–13 January 2011)', *African Journal of Aquatic Science* 36, no. 1 (2011): iii. doi: 10.2989/16085914.2011.585600.

information among conservation agencies. In the event, provincial rivalries proved too strong for even a body such as NACOR to overcome.[104]

One must conclude that a specific understanding of research prevailed in the NPB. In 1986, Joubert acknowledged that the concept of ecosystem was 'of the utmost importance in modern scientific thought' and that 'the management and research strategies of the KNP are designed to take cognisance of the complex, dynamic nature of ecosystems'.[105] These were remarks with which the scientists of the CSP would agree. However, Joubert had begun with the premise that nature was 'orderly' and that 'in ecosystem research the emphasis falls on monitoring that order'. Many ecologists would have taken issue with that view, as they would with Joubert's opinion that recording events as they occurred, and 'identifying changes and associated responses amongst the various components of the ecosystem is the most important consideration once the individual components have been identified and described'.[106] Some would have countered that understanding ecosystem functioning was the more critical research requirement. Undeterred by any such concerns, in the late 1980s the NPB announced that with the appointment of a quantitative biologist and computer expert 'the modern approach of ecosystem analysis in the Board's research program is fully implemented'.[107]

Analysis of the contents of *Koedoe*, the in-house journal, also provides insight into scientific research in the NPB, although a list is not, of course, an indication of quality. Perusing *Koedoe* is also instructive about the reference material used by the authors of the articles. Generally, the reference lists are thin, demonstrating unfamiliarity with the international literature and the non-utilisation of comparative material from other national parks

---

[104]Navorsing met betrekking tot Ekosisteem Bewaring 1978, box F9, Kruger National Park archives, Skukuza. In 1963, the National Committee for Nature Conservation (NACOR) was originated in the portfolio of Paul Sauer, then Minister of Lands.

[105]Joubert, 'Management and research in relation to ecosystems', 157–163.

[106]Joubert, 'Management and research in relation to ecosystems', 157–163.

[107]NPB, *35th Annual Report for the Year 1987–1988*, 5 and NPB *Research Division, Report 1987/1988.* Some years earlier, Robinson had apparently drafted a proposal to establish a more analytical/quantitative approach to research and recommended the appointment of a quantitative ecologist. The proposal met with the support of the board and the post was created and it was offered to Robinson, provided he moved to Skukuza, which, as a marine biologist, he was extremely reluctant to do. Peter Retief was appointed. See also F. Venter, R. Naiman, H. Biggs and D. Pienaar, 'The evolution of conservation management philosophy: Science, environmental change and social adjustments in Kruger National Park', *Ecosystems* 11 (2008): 173–192.

Figure 6.4. Covers of *Koedoe*, the research journal of SANParks.
Photograph by the author.

and protected areas. In fact, in 1986 the profile of *Koedoe* was so low that it was in danger of losing its official scientific accreditation. It was only spared this ignominy by the appointment of a new editorial board, which included several men of scientific stature.[108]

Koedoe is, nonetheless, an extremely useful record of the activities and scientific priorities deemed worthy of publication.

Between 1958 and 1983, the majority of articles (90) concerned mammalian zoology, while plant physiology garnered only two. There were 63 articles on wildlife conservation and techniques, 34 on mammal ecology and behaviour, 42 on invertebrates, and 8, 10 and 11 on amphibians, reptiles and fish, respectively. As to botany, there were 17 articles on

[108]NPB, *Jaarverslag Navorsing en Inligting 1 April 1986–31 Maart 1987*, 64–65.

ecology and 10 that were regional or geographic and that included other parks (Bontebok, KGNP, Mountain Zebra, Addo and Golden Gate). Fourteen articles dealt with archaeology and history.[109] In total, between 1958 and 2006, 35.3% of the articles related to the KNP.[110]

Some issues of *Koedoe* mark an important moment, or provide a snapshot of the state of science in NPB. One of these is the *Koedoe* supplement of 1977, 'Proceedings of symposium a "the state of nature conservation in southern Africa"', held to commemorate the 50th anniversary of the National Parks Act. The celebratory meeting was a huge affair with about 200 participants from southern Africa, including Swaziland, Rhodesia, Lesotho and Botswana, as well as QwaQwa, 'Vendaland', 'Zululand', Ciskei and other 'self-governing' states in South Africa. It was held in the KNP, with a keynote address by Fritz Vollmar, who represented the WWF and the IUCN, and was chaired by Knobel. The proceedings were wide-ranging, and encompassed wilderness, education, private nature reserves, the status of nature conservation in various states and regions, tourism, marine parks and botanical and zoological gardens. The occasion served as a mirror of the southern African nature conservation fraternity at that time. Apart from Vollmar, there was only one other international delegate, N.J. Shaw from Australia. A few presentations were in Afrikaans; the only woman on the programme was Elizabeth Reilly, who joined her husband Ted in giving an overview of nature conservation in Swaziland.[111] Substantial funding was provided by the Rembrandt Group, United Tobacco, Coca Cola and Total Petroleum.[112]

Of the many contributions, one of the few to deal explicitly with research was Pienaar's 'Research objectives in South African National Parks'.[113] Perhaps the fact that his was just one of 27 presentations reflects the low importance afforded scientific research in the pantheon of nature conservation subjects. Pienaar outlined the purpose of a national park as

[109]See J.C. Rautenbach, comp., 'Second cumulative index to *Koedoe* volumes 26–35/1 (1983–June 1992)', *Koedoe* 35, no. 1 (1992): 131–151; J.C. Rautenbach, comp., 'Third cumulative index for Koedoe: volumes 35/2–44/1', *Koedoe* 44, no. 2 (2001): 85–113.

[110]S. Webb, 'A bibliometric survey of the *Koedoe* journal publications from 1958–2006'. Unpublished report [2006], SANParks archives, Groenkloof, Pretoria.

[111]S.G.J. van Niekerk, 'Word of welcome', in 'Proceedings of a symposium on the state of nature conservation in southern Africa, Kruger National Park, 1976', eds G. de Graaff and P.T. van der Walt, supplement, *Koedoe* (1977): v.

[112]Vollmar, 'Conserving one earth', 10–23.

[113]Another is Joubert, 'Management and research in relation to ecosystems', 157–163.

being to maintain 'an area's ecosystems in as nearly pristine a condition as possible', with only non-consumptive uses being permitted. In this, he took his wording from an article in *Science* in 1971 by Douglas Houston, a research biologist in the NPS. Houston, an advocate of active management to 'maintain or restore the ecosystem', in turn took his wording from the NPS policies of the time.[114] Pienaar went on to observe that 'few, if any, of our South African national parks . . . are completely self-contained natural units'. It was therefore 'obvious' that management was required to maintain these ecosystems to compensate for 'man's altering of natural ecological conditions', particularly tourist impacts. Leaving nature alone was, he believed, an untidy and unscientific approach, while minimum interference based on firm and factual biological data could maintain an ecosystem in a 'pristine condition'. For this reason, the primary research objective should be 'the study of ecosystems and their interrelationships' in order to manage those systems. In pursuing this goal, the recording of activities through detailed factual itemisation was critical.[115] Pienaar was silent on how management and maintaining the ecosystem align, or which would take precedence, and this was the very problem facing many national parks around the world.

In summarising the proceedings, Olaf Martiny, president of the Wild Life Society of Southern Africa, mentioned research only briefly. 'My plea at this symposium would be that scientists especially, see eye to eye, for they are always at each other because one is pinching the other's research, or the one does not agree with the other.'[116]

Scientific Literature

It is useful to conclude by summarising a few of the key publications on conservation biology, or which regarded themselves as 'ecological', that appeared in South Africa during the period 1960–1990 to illustrate how

---

[114]D.B. Houston, 'Ecosystems of national parks', *Science* 172, no. 3984 (1971): 648–651. Houston was one of the biologists who worked on elk management in the 1980s.

[115]U. de V. Pienaar, 'Research objectives in South African National Parks', in 'Proceedings of a symposium on the state of nature conservation in southern Africa, Kruger National Park, 1976', eds G. de Graaff and P.T. van der Walt, supplement, *Koedoe* (1977): 38–48.

[116]O. Martiny, 'Summary of the proceedings of the symposium, The State of Nature Conservation in Southern Africa', in 'Proceedings of a symposium on the state of nature conservation in southern Africa, Kruger National Park, 1976', eds G. de Graaff and P.T. van der Walt, supplement, *Koedoe* (1977): 248–254.

'ecology' and 'conservation biology' were being construed at that time, with particular reference to national parks.

In addition to *Koedoe*, the NPB was associated with, or published, several informative books for visitors on trees, frogs, fish, small mammals and birds, as well as the large and more obvious large mammal species. Pienaar, energetic, competent and professional, strongly encouraged the collection of records, the discovery of new species and, like Stevenson-Hamilton, was interested in all forms of wildlife and meticulous in his work. No book, however, dealt with conservation biology in general or with wildlife management specifically.

An important and long-lasting initiative in South Africa has, however, been the Southern African Wildlife Management Association. Its journal, the *South African Journal of Wildlife Research* (recently renamed the *African Journal of Wildlife Research*), was launched in 1970 and provided a peer-reviewed forum for experts in the field as well as information on topics relevant to professional wildlife management, but not necessarily to national parks.

The first appearance of 'ecological' in the title of a major South African work was *Ecological Studies in South Africa*, two volumes edited by D.H.S. Davis and published in the Netherlands in 1964. In it, 'ecology' or 'ecological' is never defined. Davis, employed by Medical Ecology centre in the state Department of Health and based in Johannesburg, was an expert in the ecology of bubonic plague. In the introduction, Davis explains that the book came about after a visit to South Africa in 1956 by F.S. Bodenheimer, an entomologist at the Hebrew University in Jerusalem who had a passion for insect population ecology.[117] In South Africa, Bodenheimer had met various biologists and had briefly visited the KNP. Impressed with the work done in South Africa, Bodenheimer invited Davis to write a book as a companion volume to one envisaged for Australia. After Bodenheimer's sudden death, other editors came on board and the book took shape. In the absence of a framing philosophy or scheme, it is a wide miscellany of unrelated chapters, ranging from the Pleistocene environment, San hunter-gatherers, forest fauna, an ecological survey of the Berg River, Australian wattles, amphibians, the genetics of two mouse subspecies, gerbil fleas, bilharzia to the classification of flies. There is no explanation of how the authors were selected, and the only hint by Davis of an ecological philosophy in the book is his

---

[117]F.S. Bodenheimer, *Animal and Man in Bible Lands* (Leyden: Brill, 1960).

quotation from Elton, that study is required that 'will maintain a permanent balance in each community'. That, Davis added, 'in a nutshell, is the ecologist's task'.[118]

The last two chapters in Davis' book are relevant to national parks. One, on the history of game preservation, was written by N.J. van der Merwe, the scientific liaison officer of the NPB. It is an abbreviated version of his 1962 article in *Koedoe* and includes no mention of ecological research.[119] The other is by Brynard, the biologist, and deals with veld burning in the KNP. He provides a brief chronology of what was considered to be a precolonial fire regime and a general overview of fire policy. He also provides a narrative description of the effects of fire on various plants and animals and notes with pleasure that vegetation had begun to assume equal importance with animals in KNP management practices. There is no mention of ecology, or the ecosystemic function of fire, although he conceded that more experimentation was being undertaken.[120]

In 1978 the important two-volume publication *Biogeography and Ecology of Southern Africa* appeared. Edited by Marinus Werger, it was also published in the Netherlands.[121] Educated at the University of Utrecht, Werger was attracted to South Africa by its arid plant community and its distinctive ecology (phytosociology). He worked with ecologist Denzil Edwards at the Botanical Research Institute (BRI) in Pretoria. As Werger explained, the ecology section of BRI classified vegetation into 'types' or 'communities' and mapped those communities as 'a sort of natural entity' in the field (or through aerial photography). It was assumed that a specific vegetation type fully correlated with a specific habitat type and that by distinguishing a specific plant community one could 'read' the environmental conditions typically associated with that community. On his return to Holland, Werger was encouraged by Junk Publishers to update Davis and he invited various notable researchers to join the authorial team.[122] Of the 20 chapters (the majority on vegetation), one in

[118]D.H.S. Davis, ed., *Ecological Studies in South Africa* (The Hague: Junk, 1964), 151.

[119]Van der Merwe, 'The position of nature conservation in South Africa', 1–127; van der Merwe, 'The history of game preservation in South Africa', 363–370.

[120]A.M. Brynard, 'The influence of veld burning on the vegetation and game of the Kruger National Park', in *Ecological Studies in Southern Africa*, vol. 2, ed. D.H.S. Davis (The Hague: Junk, 1964), 371–393.

[121](The Hague: Junk, 1978).

[122]Marinus Werger, email message to author, 9 December 2013.

particular – the last – is important as a benchmark for ecosystem thinking in South Africa in the 1970s.

Authored by Brian Huntley, the chapter emphasised the international political attention conservation was enjoying and its development as a science based on research and planning. He outlined the scientific criteria for protected areas that had been summarised by KNP biologist Gerrit de Graaff (1973) and ecologist Ken Tinley (1969), but acknowledged the difficult practicalities of setting land aside for such purposes outlined by Pienaar (1979). The importance of ideas about wildlife capture, game utilisation and wildlife breeding programmes and education were explained, with special attention being given to how the 'balance of nature' had been replaced by ecosystem dynamics and how ideas about stability and resilience had come to the fore. Moreover, he highlighted the importance of rural community participation in the conservation endeavour – to the point of shaping it to protect community welfare – as crucial to its success. On the image of 'old Africa' being perpetuated in many of Africa's national parks, he commented unfavourably. The main thrust of the chapter was, however, ecosystem thinking, which Huntley defined and explained. He listed some of the most important ecosystems and provided data on their conservation status. Drawing attention to the fact that only three of the 190 professional staff in southern African conservation departments were ecological planners, he argued that drastic changes in research and management would be required if endemic diversity was to be maintained.[123]

A decade later, Huntley himself edited a very significant book, *Biotic Diversity in Southern Africa: Concepts and Conservation*. This arose from a conference held in Cape Town in 1988 under the auspices of the NPER. Recognising that the discipline of conservation management had changed since the 1960s, he reflected on how it had become a self-conscious hard science that drew on genetics, parasitology, community ecology and many other disciplines. Theory, too, had become the object of study, providing 'a breath of fresh air that is blowing through the stagnant territory of plant phytosociologists, animal behaviourists and the hunting and fishing fraternity'.[124] Huntley was also correct in identifying the conceptual and practical impact of the conservation of biotic diversity on South Africa's socio-economic landscapes and national and

---

[123]Huntley, 'Ecosystem conservation in southern Africa', 1333–1384.
[124]B.J. Huntley, ed., *Biotic Diversity in Southern Africa: Concepts and Conservation* (Cape Town: Oxford University Press, 1989), xiii–xix, xv.

international policy. The 22 chapters included discussions on the conservation status of the country's terrestrial and aquatic biomes; policy directions; human dependence on biotic diversity; survey, evaluation and monitoring; and the nature of biodiversity itself. It is notable that of the 36 contributing authors, not one was from the NPB. Exactly why the board remained aloof from the major conservation biology developments in the country is not a matter of record. However, it may be that as the prime conservator of the nation's protected areas it felt it could do its work without engaging with wider society or even disciplinary peers.

Another important publication was that edited by A.V. Hall in 1984, *Conservation of Threatened Natural Habitats*, Report No. 92 of the South African National Scientific Programmes. The material was based on an international symposium on conservation of threatened natural habitats at the University of Cape Town in 1980. Organised by Huntley and thanks to his powers of persuasion as well as his distance from the political dispensation of the time (perhaps combined with his being English-speaking), it was attended by the likes of Norman Myers, Michael Soulé, Daniel Botkin and Jared Diamond. The consensus in the symposium report was that horizons needed to extend beyond protected species and include 'the physical and biological features; including humanity that make up the habitats in which organisms live'. The report also suggested that conservation biology be integrated into academic curricula and research programmes.[125] A further key meeting was held at Houwhoek, near Hermanus, in 1984 on 'Paradigms in South African ecology'. At it, too, were important people in South African ecology and international figures such as Jared Diamond, but also Salomon Joubert from the KNP. Regrettably the proceedings of this gathering were never published, despite its importance on future thinking.

The context outlined above is important in analysing the detailed disciplinary studies conducted in South African national parks. It is to those we now turn.

[125]A.V. Hall, ed., *Conservation of Threatened Natural Habitats*. South African National Scientific Programmes Report 92, 1984 (Pretoria: CSIR, 1984), iii–iv.

7 · *Botany and Beyond*

After the internal upheavals of the 1950s, the National Parks Board (NPB) unleashed a great deal of research activity in almost all of South Africa's national parks. Indeed, there was almost a frenzy of measuring and recording the contents of the protected estate. Apart from the research facility started in the Kruger National Park (KNP), in the Kalahari Gemsbok National Park (KGNP) specialist biologists were appointed and formal sorties were made into the furthest localities of many national parks to conduct vegetation and ground surveys. Because this was, at least initially, a period of economic prosperity, the staff complement expanded, buildings for research activities were erected and herbaria and local museum collections were initiated.

A further factor galvanising the predominantly Afrikaans-speaking NPB was a sense of pride in the new republic: the personnel were imbued with a belief that national parks were part of the nation-building project and that their work was of national importance. The shared social and linguistic culture among staff contributed to this belief, but there was also a shared research culture that was different from the Cooperative Scientific Programmes (CSP) of the Council for Scientific and Industrial Research (CSIR). It is the case that at this time Afrikaans educational institutions, including the universities, placed greater emphasis on rote learning than creative thinking, and they encouraged an attitude of respect for educators and national authorities. This was in contrast to the assertive questioning, curiosity and scepticism – and cutting-edge scholarship – that generally characterised staff and students of the politically liberal English-speaking universities. Thus, the KNP research team demonstrated many of the characteristics of this conformist educational philosophy. If a shared culture, national pride and research interaction underpinned this corporate identity, it was given expression through a highly organised, efficient and bureaucratic management system.[1]

[1]Minutes of the Steering Committee for Scientific Research, Skukuza, 2 October 1959, Kruger National Park archives, Skukuza. The members were Mönnig, Goossens, Bigalke, Ortlepp and Knobel and attending as officials were Labuschagne, Brynard and Pienaar.

In perusing the large body of information produced between 1960 and 1990 one can almost sense the excitement the NPB's research activities elicited. These were presided over by an able and enthusiastic leadership. Clearly, the hard-working directorate in Pretoria were held in high regard. Knobel remained as director until 1979, followed by Andrew (Dolf) Brynard until 1986. Brynard's appointment was the much delayed realisation of the recommendation made in 1952 in the Hoek Report that the head of the NPB be a scientist. Irrespective of the quality of the research projects, publications and other scientific activities throughout the national parks, their proliferation can be attributed to his direction and interest. In addition, in the KNP, U. de V. (Tol) Pienaar, originally a histologist but also a polymath of very definite views, provided enormous inspiration, direction and support to his staff and clearly took great interest in their professional activities as well as their personal lives.[2] A strong leader, he was appointed warden of the KNP in 1978. Subsequently, he succeeded Brynard as chief director of the NPB, a position he held until his retirement in 1991.

Along with referring to people by their academic titles, as was customary in the NPB, went the more informal, but also respectful, form of Afrikaans greeting of 'Oom' or 'Tannie' (uncle and aunt) for older people. The atmosphere, particularly in the KNP, was like that of a close-knit family: hospitable to, but wary of, strangers. Pienaar, among others, established a particular NPB culture of research and a delight in gathering accurate factual knowledge. The research activities he directed in the KNP were wide-ranging and well administered. In time, however, a sense of 'we know best' came to permeate the organisation, which became increasingly reluctant to accept new ways of thinking and acting.

Other national parks were less fortunate in their research leadership. They varied widely in location, landscape, size and scientific intention, and required too wide a disciplinary expertise to be managed or researched as a coherent unit. Moreover, they continued to proliferate, far outstripping the NPB's ability to research and manage them appropriately. It was not that expertise was lacking, but rather that the human resources were stretched too thinly. Large salary outlays were one impediment, but so was the fact that there was little of scientific interest in the smaller national parks that required specialised research and warranted targeted outlays. Only the KGNP attracted anything like the research

---

[2]See biographical sketches in U. de V. Pienaar, *Goue Jare: Die Verhaal van die Nasionale Krugerwildtuin 1947–1991* (Stilbaai: The Author, 2010), Appendix C.

devoted to KNP: even so, this was on a much lesser scale because of the remoteness of the area and difficulty of access. The KNP held on to its research and tourist laurels because of its size, diversity, accessibility, healthy wildlife populations, its long history as a British imperial game reserve and national park, and its reputation for being one of the few accessible places in which many animal species of 'wild Africa' might be encountered.

Managing the other national parks proved more challenging. Over the years, the NPB attempted various organisational solutions. Yet NPB leadership of these 'other' parks remained often weak and incoherent. In 1972, Gerrit de Graaff, a rodent specialist, was put in charge of the 'Cape parks' (Addo, Augrabies Falls, Mountain Zebra, KGNP, Tsitsikamma and Golden Gate Highlands, which was actually in the Orange Free State). It is not clear how de Graaff organised research in these parks, but probably with difficulty in terms of finding appropriate and willing personnel. In many years, official reports recorded that no 'scientific research' had been done, as, for example, in 1972 in both Mountain Zebra and Augrabies.[3]

The research team elsewhere in the NPB was young, energetic and dedicated. The organisation was, however, inward-looking and there were few avenues for advancement outside its corporate structure. Over time, it became self-referencing and, in later years, more and more distanced from the concerns of wider South African society, especially black society. Those not involved in the NPB accused it of becoming a 'laager' (fortress) and considered it to be aligned with the laager-mentality of South Africa's government. It was certainly somewhat isolated from mainstream South African biology. In terms of stature and influence, none of the scientists employed by the NPB were prominent contributors to the proceedings of the South African Academy for the Advancement of Science (SAAAS) or the South African Biological Society, both well-established national scientific forums of the time.

In 1960, a work plan for the national parks was articulated. For the KNP, this included a special study of the mopane veld, an area dominated by *Colophospermum mopane*; long-term projects like zoological community studies, vegetation and species studies and research into veld fires. Aspects of drainage, topography and abiotic elements were also put on the research agenda. There was much to do in the KNP and KGNP, and

[3]Minutes of a meeting of the NPB, 1 September 1972, SANParks archives, Groenkloof, Pretoria.

in the 1960s the board was concerned that research in other parks was being largely neglected.[4] In 1962, N.J. van der Merwe, the NPB liaison officer, outlined the NPB's research strategy. Given the scope of the work and the relatively limited in-house staff, the plan envisaged collaboration with the Council for Scientific and Industrial Research (CSIR), the universities of Pretoria, Potchefstroom and the Witwatersrand, as well as the Transvaal Museum and the Departments of Nature Conservation in all four provinces. To attract these partners, van der Merwe emphasised that Skukuza had a 'well equipped research laboratory', while the KGNP had a herbarium and museum at Twee Rivieren as well as the Rembrandt Field Laboratory with accommodation for visiting scientists. Van der Merwe also stressed that NPB staff would be in control of planning surveys and in deciding what research would be done. Respectable publications were highlighted as important outlets, and van der Merwe further noted *Koedoe* as a vehicle for disseminating research on national parks and lauded the scientific and research journal collections maintained in the head office library in Pretoria. In addition, education was earmarked as an important facet of NPB outreach: apart from the liaison officer, there were another six education officers.[5]

However, outside researchers were in practice often seen as more of a burden than a help to the NPB. Only in rare instances were they free to follow their own research interests. For obvious management reasons, or for reasons associated with problems that confronted them, the NPB sought assistance with work that fed directly into its management regime. Part of the frustration for outside researchers with an interest in environmental studies was that there was no other national structure that held large and important areas of land under its control, apart from the Department of Forestry, which was obviously limited in its potential.

The autonomy and influence of the NPB was also boosted by the fact that, unlike Australia with its Wildlife Survey Section of the CSIRO (founded in 1949), there was no other national scheme to give guidance and help, and no involvement by the SAAAS or the Akademie vir Wetenskap and Kuns. It was the NPB that gave direction to the 'national' conservation research endeavour, and even the CSIR's arguably more important CSP could not compete in terms of public profile. Over time,

[4]Minutes of a meeting of the NPB, 4 June 1960, 'Work Programme for the Biological Section 1960/1961', SANParks archives, Groenkloof, Pretoria.
[5]N.J. van der Merwe, 'The position of nature conservation in South Africa', *Koedoe* 5 (1962): 1–127.

the NPB became increasingly proprietorial, a development consolidated by the fencing of the KNP (and other parks) so that they became – in the opinion of some – more like exclusive, privately managed farms, at least in the scientific sense.

Much is made of 'research' in NPB publications and publicity and the word can mean many kinds of organised, even applied, knowledge. As has already been highlighted, it is a contested term. In the 1960s, none of the fields of study currently familiar to conservation scientists was well established. Even now, conservation science is not a tightly integrated discipline. Nonetheless, it is not difficult to discern the underlying philosophy of knowledge-gathering that permeated the NPB between the 1960s and the early 1990s. Research focused exclusively on the discovery of facts, listing biota, and on monitoring and measuring very specific aspects of the natural world. It was managed along highly organised principles, and focused on tabulation rather than hypothesis. Recording was meticulous and data collection obsessive. Much that was scientifically debatable (e.g. the state of the habitat, or population dynamics and over-population) was considered 'obvious'. Thus, when habitat appeared 'degraded', it was 'obviously' not pristine and was in need of active management. By the early 1980s, even within the organisation, the realisation had dawned that 'the intensity of these surveys has . . . apparently surpassed the practical application of the results'.[6]

Vegetation and Botany

By the late 1950s wild animals had increased in number in all of South Africa's national parks. As the following chapter will explain, ideas about over-population had come to the fore and culling began. The spotlight now shifted from the growing mammal populations to the vegetation needed to provide them with appropriate sustenance. Not only was vegetation tabulated, but there was a new focus on the importance of landscape – not necessarily scenic landscapes (although these were important for the tourist industry), but landscapes comprising particular vegetation types. As we have seen, one outcome of this between 1960 and 1990 was the establishment of new national parks specifically to conserve certain vegetation and its landscape value. Together with the small parks of the 1930s – Addo Elephant, Bontebok and Mountain

---

[6]W.P.D. Gertenbach, 'Landscapes of the Kruger National Park', *Koedoe* 26 (1983): 9–121.

Zebra – this suite of landscapes and their accompanying biota offered new research opportunities.

Although national parks were part of a single administrative structure, they were managed as discrete entities. This was almost inevitable given that the vegetation types and landscapes were so very diverse. Particularly in the small national parks focused on propagating the rare species after which they were named – bontebok, mountain zebra and Addo elephant – it was the food and water supply that was the critically important objective. This meant managing the area in accordance with the articulated agricultural principle of 'carrying capacity'. The science of national park management was then in its infancy worldwide and there seemed to be no other useful, well-established model to compete with this agricultural paradigm. An alternative measure, such as energy flows, based on ecological systems theory and simulation, as was suggested by Brian Walker in 1974 and appreciated by the International Biological Programme (IBP) and South Africa's CSP,[7] was not considered by the NPB for many years.[8] Balance remained the desired 'pristine' state – unchanged from what 'nature' intended.[9] Although the vocabulary had changed, the underlying ideology was similar to Stevenson-Hamilton's 'balance of nature', although what he described was a very dynamic 'balance', arguing that good times for game and for predators alternated, thus anticipating later concepts of disequilibrium dynamics.[10]

Tourists were the financial and cultural lifeblood of national parks, and the NPB's management approach was aimed at least as much at them as at the landscape and animals, perhaps even more so. By maintaining stability, managers and scientists sought to ensure that tourists did not encounter unsightly landscapes, except of course, in times of drought. Manipulation and micro-management therefore suited a variety of objectives – philosophical, practical and economic.

The knowledge that was gained along the way was disseminated throughout the organisation through board minutes and other well-established

---

[7]B.H. Walker, 'An appraisal of the systems approach to research on and management of African wildlife ecosystems', *Journal of the Southern African Wildlife Management Association* 4, no. 3 (1974): 129–135.

[8]E.B. Worthington, *The Ecological Century: A Personal Appraisal* (Oxford: Clarendon Press, 1983), 170.

[9]See H.P. van der Schijff, 'Weidingsprobleme en natuurbewaring: Deel II', *African Wildlife* 23, no. 2 (1969): 105–128.

[10]I am grateful to Norman Owen-Smith for clarification on this point.

reporting procedures. There was, however, no exchange between or among parks, and no annual research meeting where managers and scientists could share information. However, projects were communicated in the popular press and the NPB magazine *Custos* (from 1971)[11] and to the more academic audience – including professional staff – through the in-house research journal *Koedoe*, which first appeared in 1958. From the latter and the annual research reports it is clear that an energetic research culture was being nurtured in all national parks, but particularly in the KNP.[12]

Koedoe is an interesting and perhaps rather unusual interdisciplinary journal. Initially an annual publication, after 1989 it appeared twice a year. Over time the content has varied enormously in scope and quality: there have been substantial articles and extensive lists of plants, but also, often, short pieces of a page or two about an unusual sighting or a new record. There is no apparent editorial policy or hierarchy of information, and the absence of peer review is evident in the earlier volumes. The trivial and the important enjoy equal space; associations and conclusions from data are not always articulated; the material seems idiosyncratic; and there is no sense of a posed research question and evidence to answer it. Moreover, the contributions appear in no particular order so it is difficult to sense, even within an issue, what the most significant material might be. Finally, there is a sprinkling of information about conservation areas outside the national parks, without explanation for its inclusion.[13] Although it was bilingual, from the start English-language contributions dominated. Despite these criticisms, it is worth emphasising the novelty and importance of such an interdisciplinary research journal and its pioneering role in providing a platform for national park matters relating to knowledge collection, conservation biology and park management. It was, as far as can be ascertained, the first of its kind and some of the early material is still regularly cited.[14] For the historian recording a long period of locality-based research, it is an incomparably rich resource.

[11] *Custos* began publication in December 1971 and ended in 1998. A special 60th anniversary issue was published in 1986 that summarised for the general public some of the management and scientific research issues in the national parks.

[12] See, for example, 'Annual Report of the Biologist, 1958/1959', *Koedoe* 3 (1960): 1–205.

[13] See B.R. Roberts, 'Ondersoek in die plantegroei van die Willem Pretorius-wildtuin met spesiale verwysing na die veldbenuttiging', *Koedoe* 6 (1963): 137–164.

[14] L. Foxcroft, 'Fifty years of *Koedoe*: Current status and future directions', *Koedoe* 50, no. 1 (2008): 1–2.

The first organised vegetation survey in Kruger appeared in 1951, even before the research section under T.G. Nel had been properly formalised. Leslie Codd, from 1937 an eminent botanist in the Department of Agriculture's Division of Botany (later the Botanical Research Institute – BRI – of which he became director), compiled *Trees and Shrubs of the Kruger National Park*, which was also published in Afrikaans. This important book appeared in the *Memoir* series of the Botanical Survey, strongly supported by National Zoological Gardens Director Rudolph Bigalke and partly subsidised by the NPB. In the foreword by R.A. Dyer, director of the Botanical Survey, the point was made that the book was directed at the scientist and botany student, like the majority of the *Memoirs*, but also at the general public. Tourist interest in the trees and shrubs of the KNP needed to be encouraged to complement the more usual interest in the natural history of large mammals.[15]

Codd's book was only superseded some 20 years later by the monumental two-volume *Trees of the Kruger National Park* (1972 and 1974) by Pieter van Wyk, a staff biologist trained at the University of Potchefstroom.[16] It, too, appeared in both official languages. Ten years later, van Wyk was persuaded to produce a handier *Field Guide to the Trees of the Kruger National Park*.[17] Checklists of plants in Kruger were regularly compiled and, over time, these formed the basis for synecological and landscape studies.[18]

In terms of the distribution of botanical research projects, a fairly typical snapshot is provided by the projects in South Africa's national parks for the year 1987/1988. The KNP topped the list with 75 projects, while the KGNP was second with 29. Of these, however, many had the same principal investigator. In the KGNP, for example, of 29 projects, Michael Knight and his wife were involved in eight. Mountain Zebra was third with 11 projects (of which Peter Novellie had four), and Tsitsikamma 10. Addo Elephant, Wilderness and Golden Gate each had

---

[15]L.E.W. Codd, *Trees and Shrubs of the Kruger National Park*. Department of Agriculture Division of Botany and Plant Pathology. Botanical Survey Memoir No. 26 (Pretoria: Government Printer, 1951).

[16]P. van Wyk, *Trees of the Kruger National Park*. 2 vols (Cape Town: Purnell, 1972 and 1974); P. van Wyk, *Field Guide to the Trees of the Kruger National Park* (Cape Town: Struik, 1984).

[17]F.J. Venter and W.P.D. Gertenbach, 'A cursory view of the climate and vegetation of the Kruger National Park', *Koedoe* 29 (1986): 139–148.

[18]See, for example, H.P. van der Schijff, *A Check List of the Vascular Plants of the Kruger National Park*. Publications of the University of Pretoria, New Series, No. 53 (Pretoria: University of Pretoria, 1969).

Cythna Letty.

PLATE IV.
Fruits of some lowveld trees: (a) *Ochna pulchra*, Lekkerbreek (see page 124);
(b) *Combretum transvaalense*, Russet Bush-willow or Kierieklapper (page 133);
(c) *Terminalia prunioides*, Lowveld Terminalia or Sterkbos (page 134).

Figure 7.1. Fruits of *Ochna pulchra*, *Combretum transvaalense* and *Terminalia prunioides*, painted by Cythna Letty.
From L.E.W. Codd, *Trees and Shrubs of the Kruger National Park* (1951), Plate IV, opp. p. 98.
Courtesy of the South African National Biodiversity Institute.

three projects, West Coast and Bontebok, two. The Zuurberg had one, and 17 multi-park projects were recorded.[19]

As can be seen, the smaller parks were not entirely neglected. By November 1963, plant checklists were being compiled in Golden Gate and invasive plants were being chemically controlled in Addo. Moreover,

[19]NPB, *Research Report 1987/1988.*

because of its importance for bontebok, renosterbos *Elytropappus rhinoc-erotis* was being surveyed in Bontebok National Park.[20] Sometimes, the NPB could rely on outside research assistance in the smaller parks. In 1969, the work on Golden Gate by Brian Roberts of the department of pasture science at the University of the Orange Free State was published. Roberts had investigated grazing and carrying capacity in a predominantly sourveld area subject to harsh winter conditions into which wildlife had been artificially introduced.[21]

Another prominent figure in this context was Banie Penzhorn. After graduating from the University of Pretoria, he was appointed NPB biologist with responsibility for Addo and Mountain Zebra, where he was stationed. Although not a botanist by training, he published a list of the flowering plants in the new Mountain Zebra herbarium in 1970. In 1974, together with Petrus Robbertse and Maria Olivier, both of the department of botany at the University of Port Elizabeth, Penzhorn published a checklist of the flowering plants of Addo and an article outlining the effect on the park's vegetation of the growing number of elephants.[22] For the latter paper, Penzhorn drew on earlier work on the park by Eily Archibald (later Gledhill) published in the *South African Journal of Botany* in 1955. Archibald, who had obtained her PhD in plant population studies from London University, was by 1974 at Rhodes.[23] During the eight years he was employed by the NPB, Penzhorn was extremely active. He also encouraged work by others, for example P.T. van der Walt on the phytosociological aspects of the Mountain Zebra National Park.[24]

---

[20]Minutes of a meeting of the NPB, 28 November 1963, SANParks archives, Groenkloof, Pretoria.

[21]B.R. Roberts, 'The vegetation of the Golden Gate Highlands National Park', *Koedoe* 17 (1974): 15–28.

[22]B.L. Penzhorn, 'Toevoegings tot die blomplantlys van die Bergkwagga Nasionale Park', *Koedoe* 20 (1977): 203–204; B.L. Penzhorn, P.J. Robbertse and M.C. Olivier, 'The influence of the African elephant on the vegetation of the Addo Elephant National Park', *Koedoe* 17 (1974): 137–158; B.L. Penzhorn and M.C. Olivier, 'A systematic check list of flowering plants collected in the Addo Elephant National Park', *Koedoe* 17 (1974): 121–136.

[23]Minutes of a meeting of the NPB, 21 March 1973, SANParks archives, Groenkloof, Pretoria. E.A. Archibald, 'Ecological survey of the Addo Elephant National Park', *South African Journal of Botany* 20 (1955): 147–155.

[24]P.T. van der Walt, 'A phytosociological reconnaissance of the Mountain Zebra National Park', *Koedoe* 23, no. 1 (1980): 1–32; N. van Rooyen, D.J. van Rensburg, G.K. Theron and J. du P. Bothma, 'A check list of flowering plants of the Kalahari Gemsbok National Park', *Koedoe* 31, no. 1 (1988): 115–135; N. van Rooyen, ''n Ekologiese studie van die

Later, he studied wildlife science at Texas A&M University and obtained his doctorate from Pretoria on the ecology and behaviour of the Cape mountain zebra. Subsequently, he left the NPB and taught veterinary science at Onderstepoort.[25]

The KGNP also gave rise to a number of early botanical reports, checklists and data collections. A checklist of the edible plants of the park was compiled by M.I. Keith (CSIR) and A. Renew in 1975 (they were both then stationed at the S.A. Lombard Transvaal provincial nature reserve), while a checklist of the flowering plants, compiled by N. van Rooyen, D.J. van Rensburg, G.K. Theron and J. du P. Bothma (all of Pretoria University), was published in 1988.[26]

Individual plant species in these parks and in KNP also received attention, for example, the chemical investigation of *Senecio* spp. in Kruger that appeared in *Koedoe* in 1964, by H.L. de Waal and P. van Twisk (Pretoria University); a study of the 'sleep-movements' of the leaves of South African *Acacia* species (1972) by P.J. Robbertse; and Elzabe Schoonraad's study of the morphology of *Podocarpus* spp. in the Tsitsikamma National Park in 1973.[27] Nonetheless, much more attention was given to vegetation communities, habitat preferences and plant ecology within the paradigm of climax vegetation studies than to individual species.

This was an exciting time in this branch of ecology, with competing (and complementary) methods of analysis coming to the fore, as well as improved methods of mapping and aerial survey.[28] It was

---

plantgemeenskappe in die Punda Milia-Pafuri gebied van die Nasionale Krugerwildtuin' (MSc diss., University of Pretoria, 1976).

[25]Penzhorn, Robbertse and Olivier, 'The influence of the African elephant'; Penzhorn and Olivier, 'A systematic check list of flowering plants collected in the Addo Elephant National Park'.

[26]M.I. Keith and A. Renew, 'Notes on some edible wild plants found in the Kalahari', *Koedoe* 18, no. 1 (1975): 1–12; van Rooyen, Van Rensburg, Theron and Bothma, 'A checklist of flowering plants of the Kalahari Gemsbok National Park'.

[27]H.L. de Waal and P. van Twisk, 'Die chemiese ondersoek van vier *Senecio* spesies van die Nasionale Krugerwildtuin', *Koedoe* 7 (1964): 40–42; P.J. Robbertse, 'Slaapbewegings by die blare van die Suid-Afrikaanse *Acasia*-spesies', *Koedoe* 15 (1972): 83–89; E. Schoonraad, 'Enkele morfologiese aspekte van die *Podocarpus*-soorte van die Tsitsikama- Bos en -Seekus nasionale parke', *Koedoe* 16 (1973): 59–75.

[28]B.H. Walker, 'An evaluation of eight methods of botanical analysis on grasslands in Rhodesia', *Journal of Applied Ecology* 7 (1970): 403–446; M.D. Panagos, 'A comparative classification of the sourish-mixed bushveld on the farm Roodeplaat (293JR) using quadrat and point methods' (MSc diss., University of Natal, 1995); M.J.A. Werger, 'On concepts and techniques applied in the Zurich–Montpellier method of vegetation

clearly a popular field of study at a number of South African universities, including Potchefstroom and Pretoria. The particularly useful Zurich–Montpellier method of vegetation survey, or the Braun-Blanquet method of studying plant communities (plant sociology), had been introduced into South Africa by Denzil Edwards, of the Botanical Survey section of the BRI. As an indication of the various schools of ecological thought that were being introduced into South African academia, in 1966, while on Marion Island as a student botanical researcher, Huntley commented that Van Zinderen Bakker expected him (Huntley) to use the European Braun-Blanquet methodology that required knowledge of all types of plants in a community. This he found challenging, as his training at the University of Natal had followed the British and US traditions of Tansley and Clements that concentrated on dominant species.[29]

Edwards was very familiar with the major European and North American institutes of ecology and with the philosophical and theoretical elements of plant community studies. Highly regarded as the then head of the BRI's ecology section, Edwards, with the encouragement of Van Zinderen Bakker of the Institute for Environmental Sciences at the University of the Orange Free State, was able to recruit Marinus Werger, a talented graduate of the University of Utrecht, to work in South Africa. As Werger – who, in 1978, edited the first book explicitly on the *Biogeography and Ecology of Southern Africa*[30] – explained, vegetation mapping was then a major thrust of plant ecology in order that vegetation types could become recognisable as natural entities and fully correlated with a specific habitat type. Thus, one might 'read' the environmental conditions that were typically associated with that plant community. Such maps could be combined with other studies to estimate, for instance, the productivity of a site, its carrying capacity, erodibility,

---

survey', *Bothalia* 11 (1974): 309–323; J. Braun-Blanquet, *Plant Sociology; The Study of Plant Communities* (New York, NY and London: McGraw-Hill, 1932); M.E.D. Poore, 'The use of phytosociological methods in ecological investigations: The Braun-Blanquet system', *Journal of Ecology* 43 (1955): 226–244; M.E.D. Poore, 'The use of phytosociological methods in ecological investigations: Practical issues involved in an attempt to apply the Braun-Blanquet system', *Journal of Ecology* 43 (1955): 606–651.

[29] B.J. Huntley, *Exploring a Sub-Antarctic Wilderness: A Personal Narrative of the First Biological and Geological Expedition to Marion and Prince Edward Islands 1965/1966* (Stellenbosch: Antarctic Legacy of South Africa), 158.

[30] M.J.A. Werger, ed., *Biogeography and Ecology of Southern Africa* (The Hague: Junk, 1978).

suitability as arable land, or its status as a fire hazard.[31] This seemed to be an entirely appropriate scientific technique for identifying and studying vegetation in national parks.

At the BRI, Werger was responsible for analysing the vegetation of a large area along the upper Orange River where two major dams were under construction. He aimed to combine the Braun-Blanquet method with new statistical classification procedures developed in the UK. This led Werger and his colleagues to conduct short surveys in protected areas close by and in the 1970s he worked in the KGNP and Addo.[32] The KGNP was a popular site for vegetation studies in this period because of the prevailing international focus on arid area science.[33] Little work had been done in the KGNP since its proclamation in 1931 (it was not open to the public for many years) and the first survey – of the vegetation as well as geology, habitats and other aspects of the park – was conducted by Brynard and published in *Koedoe* in 1958.[34] The following year, Leistner's vegetation survey and a further list of plants were published and, in 1967, he elaborated on the plant ecology.[35] Leistner and Werger published the first phytosociological survey in 1973 and published their assessment of 12 plant communities in KGNP in the journal *Vegetatio*.[36] At the time, a habitat map of this park appeared, compiled by Bothma and de Graaff, who had determined that there were six major habitats.[37] Only much later, in 1989, was a vegetation survey of Tsitsikamma National Park published in *Koedoe* by N. Hanekom, then stationed there as research

---

[31] Marinus Werger, email message to author, 9 December 2013.

[32] M.J.A. Werger and B.J. Coetzee, 'A phytosociological and phytogeographical study of Augrabies Falls National Park, South Africa', *Koedoe* 19 (1977): 11–51; M.J.A. Werger, 'Phytosociology of the Upper Orange River valley, South Africa. A syntaxonomical and synecological study' (PhD diss., University of Nijmegen, 1973).

[33] B. Walker and M. Westoby, 'States and transitions: The trajectory of an idea, 1970–2010', *Israel Journal of Ecology and Evolution* 57 (2011): 17–22.

[34] A.M. Brynard, 'Verslag insake voorlopige ondersoek rakende toestande in die Nasionale Kalahari-Gemsbokpark', *Koedoe* 1 (1958): 162–183.

[35] O.A. Leistner, 'Preliminary list of plants found in the Kalahari Gemsbok National Park', *Koedoe* 2 (1959): 152–172; O.A. Leistner, 'Notes on the vegetation of the Kalahari Gemsbok National Park with special reference to its influence on the distribution of Antelopes', *Koedoe* 2 (1959): 128–151.

[36] O.A. Leistner and M.J.A. Werger, 'Southern Kalahari phytosociology', *Vegetatio* 28 (1973): 353–397.

[37] J. du P. Bothma and G. de Graaff, 'A habitat map of the Kalahari Gemsbok National Park', *Koedoe* 16 (1973): 181–188.

officer, together with A. Southwood, of the Department of Nature and Environmental Conservation, and the forester M. Ferguson.[38]

Koedoe and the NPB annual reports are replete with plant community studies influenced by the Braun-Blanquet school of thinking and its variants.[39] These had commenced with the work of Hermanus (Manie) van der Schijff, the first person to gain a DSc for work done in the KNP. His thesis ''n Ekologiese studie van die flora van die Nasionale Krugerwildtuin' ('An ecological study of the flora of the Kruger National Game Reserve') was accepted by the University of Potchefstroom in 1957.[40] He followed this up with an article in *Koedoe* on the grazing potential and problems of the KNP.[41] Van der Schijff left the NPB in 1956 to join the department of botany at the University of Pretoria, where he later became head of department and dean of science. Involved in South Africa's national scientific organisations, he continued to work, however, in the KNP fairly regularly over many years, as his publications attest.[42]

By the mid–1980s, so much basic recording had been accomplished that F.J. (Freek) Venter, the first soil scientist employed in Kruger, and botanist Willem Gertenbach were able to declare in 1986 that the park contained around 1968 plant species, of which 457 were trees or shrubs, 235 grasses, 27 ferns, 16 wood lianas, 20 aloes and 1213 forbs.[43] This statement was made possible in part by the consolidation of many plant checklists and studies in Gertenbach's major 1983 *Koedoe* publication 'Landscapes of the Kruger National Park'.[44] Gertenbach had obtained his Masters from the University of Potchefstroom in 1978 on the plant communities of

---

[38]N. Hanekom, A. Southwood and M. Ferguson, 'A vegetation survey of the Tsitsikamma Coastal National Park', *Koedoe* 32, no. 1 (1989): 47–66.

[39]A Swiss, Josias Braun-Blanquet was to become deeply involved in the Swiss National Park. See P. Kupper, *Creating Wilderness: A Transnational History of the Swiss National Park* (Oxford: Berghahn, 2014).

[40]H.P. van der Schijff, ''n Ekologiese studie van die flora van die Nasionale Krugerwildtuin' (DSc diss., Potchefstroom University, 1957).

[41]H.P. van der Schijff, 'Weidingsmoontlikeheded en weidingsprobleme in die Nasionale Kurgerwildtuin', *Koedoe* 2 (1959): 110–127. See also H.P. van der Schijff, *A Check List of the Vascular Plants of the Kruger National Park*. Publications of the University of Pretoria, New Series, No. 53 (Pretoria: University of Pretoria, 1969).

[42]H.P. van der Schijff, 'Die ekologie en verwantskap van die Sandveld-flora van die Nasionale Krugerwildtuin', *Koedoe* 7 (1964): 56–76; H.P. van der Schijff, 'The affinities of the flora of the Kruger National Park', *Kirkia* 7 (1969): 109–120.

[43]Venter and Gertenbach, 'A cursory view of the climate and vegetation of the Kruger National Park'.

[44]Gertenbach, 'Landscapes of the Kruger National Park'.

the northern district of the KNP,[45] and the vegetation information at his disposal had been amplified by the PhD material of Ben J. Coetzee on the phytosociology, vegetation structure and landscapes of the central KNP in 1982, and on Coetzee's earlier (1977) work with the CSP on a phytosociological classification of the Nylsvley Nature Reserve.[46] Thus, initial vegetation surveys and checklists were followed by more intensive, refined and complex analyses of plant communities, species composition and vegetation structures. By 1986 these analyses were being correlated with the abiotic environment into 'landscape types', which had become the key planning units.[47]

In the Tsitsikamma National Park, warden Robinson began to make his mark by collecting identification data and soon this national park was well recorded. A number of guidebooks, based on professional identification, were published in an effort to attract people to the park and to inform them of its biota. In terms of vegetation, a popular book by Stanley Seagrief, head of the department of botany at Rhodes University – an institution renowned for its aquatic science and ichthyology – on the seaweeds of the Tsitsikamma Coastal National Park was published in 1967, just a year after the proclamation of the park.[48] That same year, Marjorie Courtenay-Latimer and Gerald Smith, both associated with the East London Museum, were responsible for another identification guide, *The Flowering Plants of the Tsitsikama Forest and Coastal National Park*.[49]

Fire Ecology

As noted earlier, Stevenson-Hamilton had held the view that fires – many of which he had seen run out of control during his long stint as KNP

---

[45]W.P.D. Gertenbach, 'Plantgemeenskappe van die Gabbro-complex in die noordweste van die sentrale distrik van die Nasionale Krugerwildtuin' (MSc diss., Potchefstroom University, 1978).

[46]B.J. Coetzee, 'Phytosociology, vegetation structure and landscapes of the Central District, Kruger National Park' (DSc diss., University of Pretoria, 1983); B.J. Coetzee, F. van der Meulen, S. Zwanziger, P. Gonsalves and P.J. Weisser, *A Phytosociological Classification of the Nylsvley Nature Reserve*. South African National Scientific Programmes Report 20 (Pretoria: CSIR, 1977).

[47]S.C.J. Joubert and J.J. Kloppers, 'Advancing by the decade', *Custos* 15, no. 6 (1986): 16–23.

[48]S.C. Seagrief, *The Seaweeds of the Tsitsikama Coastal National Park/Die Seewiere van die Tsitsikama-Seekus Nasionale Park* (Pretoria: National Parks Board, 1967).

[49]M. Courtenay-Latimer and G.G. Smith, *The Flowering Plants of the Tsitsikama Forest and Coastal National Park* (Pretoria: National Parks Board, 1967); R.M. Tietz and G.A. Robinson, *The Tsitsikama Shore: A Guide to the Marine Invertebrate Fauna of the Tsitsikama Coastal National Park* (Pretoria: National Parks Board, 1974).

warden – replenished the savannah grassland and provided fresh shoots and leaves for browsers and grazers. However, such was the turmoil about the role of fire and its impact on vegetation in intellectual and scientific circles at the time, his successor, Col. J.A.B. Sandenbergh, adhered strictly to the Soil Conservation Act 45 of 1946, whereby veld burning in nature reserves required the permission of the Department of Agriculture. With unanimous board approval, he banned all deliberate fires and required those begun accidentally be extinguished as quickly as possible. However, given the wider uncertainty about fire policy, a decision was taken as early as 1948 that while accidental fire was outlawed, controlled burning might be undertaken, but only in spring and no more often than every five years.

At the time, the debate about fire management raged not only in respect of savannah environments but also of the fynbos of the Western Cape. There was in this era no well-recognised science named 'fire ecology' and there had been no scientific or comparative experiments that shed light on the role, frequency and effects of fire. To all pastoralists it was evident that fire encouraged fresh annual growth and thus nurtured herds of domestic stock. However, to those who cared for the floral wealth of the fynbos, fire seemed to the human eye to be totally destructive of plant life, which took years to recover. However, by the 1950s in the KNP the fuel load had accumulated so much that, in the agricultural-type management perspective of the time, it became clear that regular burning would be advantageous. Apparently, a solution became more urgent after uncontrolled wild fires burnt almost a quarter of the total area of the KNP in 1954.[50] However, there was no organised burning until 1956, and thereafter fire management dominated KNP research, although this was not the case in the other national parks.

Veld burning (as it was called before acquiring the more exalted label of fire ecology) was given attention in the very first issue of *Koedoe* in 1958.[51] In an extended article, van der Schijff explained why regulated burning was necessary. Using J.P.H. Acocks' *Veld Types* of 1953,[52] van der Schijff utilised four veld types for his experiment. Apparently,

[50]R. Biggs, H.C. Biggs, T.T. Dunne, N. Govender and A.L.F. Potgieter, 'Experimental burn plot trial in the Kruger National Park: History, experimental design and suggestions for data analysis', *Koedoe* 46, no. 1 (2003): 1–15.
[51]H.P. van der Schijff, 'Inleidende verslag oor veldbrandnavorsing in die Nasionale Krugerwildtuin', *Koedoe* 1 (1958): 60–94.
[52]J.P.H. Acocks, *Veld Types of South Africa*. Memoirs of the Botanical Survey of South Africa 28, 1953, 1–192.

the Department of Agriculture had offered to help in the early 1950s, but KNP researchers modified the official suggestions and set up regular, controlled burning. This took place at different seasons and frequencies and included fire exclusion plots. Later, a simplified regime of regular triennial spring burning was adopted. Others assisted in the identification of 'burning blocks' and their extent. For example, in 1961 R.L. Davidson, P. Gillard, G. Lecatsas and J. Leigh of the University of the Witwatersrand and based at the Frankenwald Field Research Station that specialised in pasture research published an article on potential ways of calibrating the *Combretum* veld for fire purposes.[53]

Deeply involved in fire research was Brynard, Kruger's chief biologist and after 1961 nature conservator (warden). In 1964 he contributed a chapter on 'The influence of veld burning on the vegetation and game of the Kruger National Park' to *Ecological Studies in Southern Africa*, the book edited by D.H.S. Davis. This classified Kruger into six veld types (following van der Schijff, 1958). After describing each type in detail (and explaining the effect of fire on each of them, species by species, with numerous photographs), Brynard arrived at the nub of his contention: the bushveld as observed is not a climate, topographic nor edaphic climax, but rather a successional 'pyrophilous' climax. He decried the loss of tree and plant species owing to fire, and believed fire to be responsible for desiccation and bush encroachment, as well as being detrimental to animal life. He advocated that burning should, nonetheless, be regular and controlled, and that any experimentation should be flexible.[54]

Some years later, in 1971, when he was deputy-director of the NPB, Brynard attended the Annual Tall Timbers Fire Ecology Conference in Tallahassee, Florida, on the theme of 'Fire in Africa' (co-chaired by John Phillips of the University of Natal). There, he presented a paper on 'Controlled burning in the Kruger National Park – History and development of a veld burning policy'. Illustrated with photographs of wild animals (no trees or fire scenes), it summarised the locality and history of

[53]R.L. Davidson, A.M., Brynard, P. Gillard, G. Lecatsas and J. Leigh, 'Veld burning: (c) Calibration of the belt transect method in *Combretum* woodland in the Kruger National Park', *Koedoe* 4 (1961): 31–44; see also J.H. Leigh, 'Persistence of some varieties of pasture grass and their susceptibility to invasion by other species', *Journal of Ecology* 49, no. 2 (1961): 341–345.

[54]A.M. Brynard, 'The influence of veld burning on the vegetation and game of the Kruger National Park', in *Ecological Studies in Southern Africa*, ed. D.H.S. Davis (The Hague: Junk, 1964): 371–393.

Figure 7.2. The vegetation of a demarcated plot at Mooiplaas as regularly recorded in the KNP from 1958 to 1998.
Photograph by Guin Zambatis.

Kruger, before discussing the hundreds of miles of firebreaks that divided the park into burning blocks (eventually some 456),[55] although by then wetlands, areas with shallow soils and steep slopes had been removed from the burning roster. While Brynard did not expand on the ecological reasons for the KNP's decisions of this kind, it is clear they emanated from climax ideas and an agricultural model.[56]

Pieter van Wyk, chief research officer at KNP, also presented a paper to the conference, 'Veld burning in the Kruger National Park: An interim report of some aspects of research'. He lamented the 'frightening lack of information on the subject' in the 1950s and described how the NPB had been obliged to undertake its own research by de-limiting experimental

[55] W.S.W. Trollope, 'Fire regime of the Kruger National Park for the period 1980–1992', *Koedoe* 36, no. 2 (1993): 45–52, 47.

[56] A.M. Brynard, 'Controlled burning in the Kruger National Park: History and development of a veld burning policy', *Proceedings of the Annual Tall Timbers Fire Ecology Conference, April 22–23, 1971, Tallahassee, Florida. No. 11* (Tallahassee, FL: Tall Timbers Research Station, 1972), 219–231.

244 · **Botany and Beyond**

burning blocks, keeping records of climatic and other conditions at the time of burning (including fire temperatures) and measuring and monitoring the recovery rate of vegetation. 'Uncontrollable factors', he added, had made research difficult, including over-grazing, drought, exceptionally low temperatures and times of the year when burning was ineffective or unsuccessful.[57] The meeting discussed different environmental conditions and practical issues related to appropriate management policy, but it was clear that this was still a topic about which little was known.

The meeting in Tallahassee provided a rare opportunity for fire researchers from many parts of Africa to share their experiences and findings and must have been enlightening for the NPB representatives, who had previously had limited exposure to international ideas about 'eco-pyrology'. Papers were delivered by conservation officials and fire managers from national parks in Tanzania, Kenya, Uganda and Rhodesia as well as Côte d'Ivoire and other parts of West Africa. There were two other South Africans present. One of them was J.D. Scott, a pasture ecologist and pioneer fire ecologist who had worked under Phillips in Tanzania, and who was professor of pasture science and dean of agriculture at the University of Natal from 1948 to 1973. Scott limited his address to veld burning in Natal, where he oversaw the university research farm.

The other South African present was Winston Trollope, a young scientist who had completed his MSc under Scott's supervision and who was later to become eminent in the field of fire ecology. Trollope's MSc had been on the relationship between fire and the spread of undesirable macchia species (*Helichrysum*) in the grassland vegetation of the mountainous localities in the Ciskei region in the Eastern Cape. For him, attendance at Tallahassee was a 'turning point in both my research career and fire ecology in South Africa'. He came to realise that the effects of season and frequency that had dominated research thus far totally neglected the potentially more important effects of the type of fire and its intensity.[58]

It was clear to many people by the mid-1970s that the fire experiments undertaken to date had not been replicating nature as intended, but were having detrimental effects on the vegetation, often homogenising species

---

[57]P. van Wyk, 'Veld burning in the Kruger National Park: An interim report of some aspects of research', *Proceedings of the Annual Tall Timbers Fire Ecology Conference, April 22–23, 1971, Tallahassee, Florida. No. 11* (Tallahassee, FL: Tall Timbers Research Station, 1972), 9–31.

[58]Winston Trollope, EcoRestore. www.ecorestore.co.za/winston-trollope (accessed 22 May 2015).

Figure 7.3. A ranger and a game guard using a gas flame-thrower to start a counter blaze along a firebreak to halt a major conflagration from an approaching bush fire. From R.J. Labuschagne, *The Kruger Park and Other National Parks* (n.d.), p. 113. Courtesy of SANParks.

distribution. Changes to the burning programme were made. In 1980, fire information for Kruger was computerised and Trollope, based at the University of Fort Hare, was invited to use it to consider tree mortality and other issues that had not previously been taken into account. After reviewing the evidence, Trollope concluded that the simple, identical blocks of the 1950s (even with their later modification) had not been successful as an appropriate ecological management tool. And despite regulated burning, the KNP fire regime remained complex and in a state of flux, principally because the source of ignition was so varied and could not be controlled. Fires included 'controlled' burns (47%), ignition by Mozambican refugees (24%), 'other' (namely, tourists, poachers, accidents, etc.) (20%) and lightning (10%). This variety, even if unintended, was positive for biodiversity as well as for habitat diversity and savannah heterogeneity, Trollope concluded in 1993.[59]

Fire management in the smaller national parks was not as significant an issue. In Golden Gate, for example, a small park into which black wildebeest, blesbok, plains zebra, grey rhebuck, mountain reedbuck, oribi

[59]Trollope, 'Fire regime of the Kruger National Park', 52.

and springbok had been reintroduced, the management objective was to feed these animals in a confined space rather than attempt to replicate a natural system. The primary conservation motivation for the park was its exceptional geomorphology and associated plant communities – the mammals were merely additional visitor attractions. No formal burning policy was adopted and the most heavily grazed areas were generally burnt in rotation every September to prevent over-grazing. Particularly important, however, in this park, was the need to provide grazing during the harsh winters.[60]

Of direct importance to an endangered species, the bontebok *Damaliscus pygargus dorcas*, was fire in the Bontebok National Park. As Novellie explained in an important article in *Koedoe* in 1987, to distribute grazing pressure more equally, in 1975 a system of burning blocks of varying sizes had been introduced. Some blocks were managed for grazing and burnt every four years, others to conserve and promote the fynbos. These were burnt every 10–12 years. At first, in the 1960s, red hartebeest and springbok were introduced, but the former never did well and the springbok, not native to the area, were removed in 1975. Bontebok appeared to prefer to graze short grass and the pressure on newly burnt veld was consequently intense. Over a two-year period, Novellie studied experimental plots, measuring the degree of defoliation, height distribution and speed of recovery.[61]

As mentioned, the Pilanesberg National Park in Bophuthatswana was innovative in its conservation science at this time, less hide-bound by regulations and bureaucracy than was the NPB and in which experiment was the order of the day. As well as landscape design, community engagement and restoration ecology, the conservation managers at the Pilanesberg were emboldened to consider fire management differently from the NPB. In the late 1980s, with encouragement from his senior managers and from Michael Mentis at the University of the Witwatersrand and from Arthur Bailey, a rangeland ecologist from the University of Alberta who was taking his sabbatical at Wits, Bruce Brockett (with others) did some trials with random ignition, attempting to replicate lightning strikes. Subsequently, this approach has gained widespread acceptance.[62]

---

[60]P.T. van der Walt and L.J. van Zyl, 'Die invloed van veldbrand op bewegings-patrone van wildsbokke in die Golden Gate Hoogland Nasionale Park', *Koedoe* 25 (1982): 1–11.

[61]P. Novellie, 'Interrelationships between fire, grazing and grass cover at the Bontebok National Park', *Koedoe* 30 (1987): 1–17.

[62]B. Brockett, 'Implementing a patch-mosaic burning system in southern African savanna conservation areas' (MSc diss., University of Cape Town, 2001). See www

Plate 1. Augrabies Falls National Park.
Photograph courtesy of SANParks.

Plate 2. Tankwa-Karoo National Park.
Photograph courtesy of SANParks.

Plate 3. Mapungubwe National Park.
Photograph courtesy of Vincent Carruthers.

Plate 4. Kruger National Park.
Photograph by the author.

Plate 5. West Coast National Park.
Photograph by the author.

Plate 6. Diepwalle, Garden Route National Park.
Photograph courtesy of SANParks

Plate 7. Golden Gate National Park.
Photograph courtesy of SANParks

Plate 8. Richtersveld National Park.
Photograph courtesy of SANParks

Plate 9. Table Mountain National Park, Lion's Head.
Photograph courtesy of Nicola van Wilgen

Plate 10. Agulhas National Park.
Photograph by the author

Plate 11. Courney River, Nyati Section, Addo Elephant National Park.
Photograph courtesy of Dirk Roux

A national park in which fire did not play an important role was KGNP in the arid Northern Cape. In 1983 a symposium was held in Pretoria on the Kalahari ecosystem and the voluminous proceedings were published in a special edition of *Koedoe* in 1984. Commenting on the rarity of veld fires in the arid Kalahari, P.T. van der Walt and E.A.N. le Riche explained in a short, descriptive paper that fire had no use as a management tool in the KGNP. They continued that after a season of good rain, a fire had swept through the Nossob River valley destroying many *Vachellia* (*Acacia*) *erioloba*, a tree important for nutrition and for enhancing the aesthetic tourist experience. The conclusion was that priority should in future be given to protecting *Vachellia erioloba* from conflagration.[63]

Invasive Species

Like fire ecology, invasion biology was a science that emerged as a distinct scholarly field after 1960. For many scientists, Charles Elton's 1958 *The Ecology of Invasions by Animals and Plants* was the seminal text that drew attention to the environmental change introduced plants and animals could cause.[64] Davis, however, has argued that it was the 1964 meeting of the International Union of Biological Sciences at Asilomar, California that alerted many scientists to the urgency of the invasive species problem. This meeting produced the 1965 classic *The Genetics of Colonizing Species*, edited by H.G. Baker and G.L. Stebbins, which foregrounded ecological theory as the tool most needed for studying colonising species.[65] Whatever the relative importance of the two publications and the different vocabularies, both warned scientists of the potential of invasion as a science and to the explicit link between conservation initiatives

.researchgate.net/profile/Bruce_Brockett/publication/35737922_Implementing_a_patch-mosaic_burning_system_in_Southern_African_savanna_conservation_areas_/links/540480010cf2c48563b09850.pdf (accessed 10 December 2015).

[63]P.T. van der Walt and E.A.N. le Riche, 'The influence of veld fire on an *Acacia erioloba* community in the Kalahari Gemsbok National Park', in 'Proceedings of a symposium on the Kalahari ecosystem 1983', eds G. de Graaff and D.J. van Rensburg, supplement, *Koedoe* (1984): 103–106.

[64]C. Elton, *The Ecology of Invasions by Animals and Plants* (London: Methuen, 1958).

[65]M.A. Davis, 'Invasion biology 1958–2005: The pursuit of science and conservation', in *Conceptual Ecology and Invasion Biology*, eds M.W. Cadotte, S.M. McMahon and T. Fukami (Dordrecht: Springer, 2006), 35–64; H.G. Baker and G.L. Stebbins, *The Genetics of Colonizing Species* (New York, NY: Academic Press, 1965); M.A. Davis, *Invasion Biology* (Oxford: Oxford University Press, 2009).

and unwanted, aggressively colonising biota. Understandably, the detrimental effects of invasive species were acutely felt in national parks and other protected landscapes that were being managed as 'pristine', stable and natural. Davis has argued that invasion biology would be a 'dream dissertation topic' for a historian of science. A South African dimension to this topic would certainly be appropriate, because South Africa was an early contributor to the discipline and has consistently maintained a position of leadership.[66]

Although invasion biology accelerated as a field of study after 1990, it had been noted long before that unwanted plants had the potential to transform landscapes. As a result, research into the mechanisms for the success of introduced biota was commenced. In South Africa it focused initially on Cape fynbos, because of the growing international awareness of this ecosystem's particular significance as a varied floral kingdom. Moreover, fynbos was facing competition from similarly adapted introduced plants, particularly from Australia. A bibliography related to invasive species, compiled by V.C. Moran and P.M. Moran in 1982,[67] was followed by several volumes of the Scientific Committee on Problems of the Environment (SCOPE) on this subject as part of the CSP.[68]

Moreover, the NPB had already had to take note of the damage non-native plants had done to landscapes in some of the national parks under its control. It seems that the initial concern was aesthetic rather than scientific (biodiversity had not yet emerged as a term), although this prioritisation is not spelt out in the documents that survive. In March 1960, for example, Pieter Barnard, the biologist then responsible for Cape national parks, began the control of prickly pear *Opuntia* spp. from

---

[66]Davis, 'Invasion biology 1958–2005', 35.

[67]V.C. Moran and P.M. Moran, *Alien Invasive Vascular Plants in South African Natural and Semi-natural Environments: Bibliography from 1830*. South African National Scientific Programmes Report 65 (Pretoria: CSIR, 1982).

[68]A.A. Ferrar and F.J. Kruger, comp., *South African Programme for the SCOPE Project on the Ecology of Biological Invasions*. South African National Scientific Programmes Report 72 (Pretoria: CSIR, 1983); I.A.W. Macdonald, F.J. Kruger and A.A. Ferrar, eds, *The Ecology and Management of Biological Invasions in Southern Africa* (Cape Town: Oxford University Press, 1987); I.A.W. Macdonald and M.L. Jarman, eds, *Invasive Alien Plants in the Terrestrial Ecosystems of Natal, South Africa*. South African National Scientific Programmes Report 118 (Pretoria: CSIR, 1985); I.A.W. Macdonald, D.L. Clark and H.C. Taylor, 'The history and effects of alien plant control in the Cape of Good Hope Nature Reserve, 1941–1987', *South African Journal of Botany* 55 (1989): 56–75.

Mountain Zebra National Park.[69] The previous year (December 1959), he had produced a long report for the NPB on the chemical control of 'ongewenste plante in natuurlike veld' (unwanted plants in natural veld). In it, Barnard noted that the effects of alien plants first came to scientific attention in the 1930s, particularly with respect to agriculture, and he proposed using herbicides developed for weeds in crop-fields in national parks. In March 1960, alien plants – 1350 syringas *Melia azedarach*, 155 prickly pears and 30 guavas *Psidium guajava* – were controlled in parts of the KNP using a selective herbicide.[70] By 1963, chemicals were being used on invading plants in Addo,[71] and in 1972 on prickly pear and other species in Bontebok National Park, as part of the efforts to preserve the renosterbos.[72]

The interest in alien vegetation sparked by the SCOPE initiative and the many CSP publications on the topic spurred the NPB into further action in the 1980s. In 1984 KNP botanist Willem Gertenbach initiated a survey of invasive plants in southern Africa's protected areas. He collaborated with Ian Macdonald, of the Percy Fitzpatrick Institute of African Ornithology at the University of Cape Town and, at that time, one of the leaders in the developing field of invasion biology. Ian Macdonald and S.A. Macdonald did a rapid survey of invasive plants in Kruger in winter 1984. This, together with Gertenbach's survey questionnaire and his herbarium list of 1985, formed the basis of a list of alien plants in the KNP published in *Koedoe* in 1988. At that time, there were 156 alien plant species recorded in the national park, of which 113 were considered 'invasive'. The authors noted a rapid increase since the original list of six species noted by Obermeijer in 1937, 32 by Codd in 1951 and 76 by van der Schijff in 1969. They ascribed this proliferation in part to more careful data collection and new invasions. The article provided the date the species was first recorded in the KNP, the reason for its introduction, its growth form and whether the ecological impact was slight, moderate or high. Twenty-seven species, dispersed primarily by water and by animals,

---

[69]Minutes of a meeting of the NPB, 23 March 1960, Annexure C, SANParks archives, Groenkloof, Pretoria. See also NPB *Annual Report for 1958/1959*.

[70]Minutes of a meeting of the NPB, 23 March 1960, Annexure C and Annexure E, SANParks archives, Groenkloof, Pretoria.

[71]Minutes of a meeting of the NPB, 28 November 1963, SANParks archives, Groenkloof, Pretoria.

[72]Minutes of a meeting of the NPB, 1 September 1972, SANParks archives, Groenkloof, Pretoria.

were regarded as having a moderate to high impact. The authors warned that most of the water-dispersed species originated from upstream infestations and that a coordinated regional campaign to control them would be required.[73]

In an article that appeared in the *Transactions of the Royal Society of South Africa* that same year, Macdonald expanded on the topic as it applied to the KNP. In discussing introduced species of microbes, plants and animals, Macdonald noted that 'there is very little about the Park's ecological functioning that can today be considered strictly "natural"', and that the growing number of visitors and expanded amenities for staff and visitors would accelerate the potential problem of alien organisms – he did not then dub them 'invasive'. Stevenson-Hamilton's aversion to introduced species in 1937 was noted, although there was no mention by him at that time of how, or whether, they might be controlled. Macdonald's article was more sophisticated and better elucidated the topic than the checklist in *Koedoe* because he dealt with invasions of all biota more generally, discussed the pattern of invasion and the control of introduced species.[74]

As the years went by, the proliferation of invasive species in national parks made their elimination an urgent priority. The mechanisms of invasion were not researched in the NPB prior to 1990, but managing for stability and 'nature' resulted in a growing realisation that introduced species were not only out of place in the veld – 'discordant' and 'incongruous', in Stevenson-Hamilton's words[75] – but, in the jargon of a later period, transformed habitats and impoverished biodiversity.

Land-use Planning, Soil and Climate

Other disciplines relevant to national parks were also given attention during this period, and to an extent not repeated in later years. Despite the board's legal mandate to study history and archaeology, as well as disciplines such as geology and climatology, no permanent staff member had expertise on abiotic issues.

---

[73]I.A.W. Macdonald and W.P.D. Gertenbach, 'A list of alien plants in the Kruger National Park', *Koedoe* 31 (1988): 137–150.

[74]I.A.W. Macdonald, 'The history, impacts and control of introduced species in the Kruger National Park, South Africa', *Transactions of the Royal Society of South Africa* 46, no. 4 (1988): 251–276.

[75]Macdonald, 'The history, impacts and control of introduced species in the Kruger National Park', 255.

The *Koedoe* supplement of 1977, the 'Proceedings of a symposium on the state of nature conservation in southern Africa' was path-breaking in including landscape planning as part of the general brief for protected areas. In 1976, Willem van Riet, doyen of South African landscape architects and much influenced by the wilderness movement in the USA, had been invited to compile a detailed report on the planning of Mountain Zebra National Park, including suggestions for its better management and expansion. Quoting Aldo Leopold, Roderick Nash and Leo Marx, in his *Koedoe* article van Riet explained how tourist visitors to national parks needed to be guided into the wilderness experience through landscape planning and appropriate recreational activities. Critically important to the tourist experience was the rest-camp landscape and road planning, with attention being paid to visual fields and vistas, such as plateaus, ridges, valleys and plains. A strong advocate of peripheral development and local community beneficiation which, together with his ideas on landscape, he was to bring to fruition in the Pilanesberg National Park,[76] van Riet urged that the landscape and tourist facilities of the Mountain Zebra be maximised with these philosophies in mind.[77]

Even broader ideas were expressed in the same issue of *Koedoe* by J.J. la Grange, director of environmental issues in the government's new Department of Planning and the Environment. He urged national park authorities to work with all the other government departments – for example, water affairs, forestry, agriculture, defence, Bantu administration, mining – and the provinces so that nature conservation would become part of a coordinated system of land-use planning. Because all government

---

[76]J. Carruthers, 'Designing a wilderness for wildlife: The case of the Pilanesberg National Park, South Africa', in *Designing Wildlife Habitats*, ed. J. Beardsley (Washington, DC: Dumbarton Oaks Research Library and Collection, 2013), 107–130; J. Carruthers, 'Pilanesberg National Park, North West Province, South Africa: Uniting economic development with ecological design – a history, 1960s to 1984', *Koedoe* 53, no. 1 (2011), doi: 10.4102.

[77]B. Farrell and W. van Riet, 'Beplannings-, bestuurs- en uitbreidingsvoorstelle vir die Bergkwagga Nasionale Park.' Unpublished National Parks Board Report, 1976; W. van Riet, 'The importance of wilderness landscape analysis in development planning schemes for national parks, with special reference to the Mountain Zebra National Park', in 'Proceedings of a symposium on the state of nature conservation in southern Africa, Kruger National Park, 1976', eds G. de Graaff and P.T. van der Walt, supplement, *Koedoe* (1977): 55–67. Van Riet had obtained one of the first doctoral degrees in landscape with his thesis 'An ecological planning model for use in landscape architecture' (PhD diss., University of Pretoria, 1978).

activities overlapped with natural resource management, cooperation and synergy were required to make best use of those resources.[78]

Of fundamental research importance to management have been geology and climate, which have featured frequently in *Koedoe* articles. Articles about the former were generally written by government and consulting geologists and soil scientists rather than national park staff. Basic descriptions were the first order of the day. Important examples are the geohydrology of the KGNP by P.J. Smit of the Geological Survey and based in Kuruman, and the soil types of that national park by P.A. Louw, of the Department of Agricultural Technical Services.[79] In the late 1960s and 1970s, these were followed by pieces on the basic geology of Bontebok, Golden Gate, Addo, Mountain Zebra and Tsitsikamma.[80]

In 1979, in response to prolonged and recurrent drought, E. Martinelli and G.L. Hubert published a paper in *Koedoe* on the use of electrical geophysical techniques for the identification of groundwater supplies and the development of boreholes in the KGNP and the Nwanetsi area of the KNP.[81] In 1980, Kruger biologist Gertenbach analysed the patterns of rainfall in the KNP,[82] and in 1985 warden Pienaar contributed an extensive overview of rainfall in the region. Using historical data and modern climate research, he argued that if regular patterns could be discerned – as the work of P.D. Tyson of the University of the Witwatersrand and others suggested – then wildlife management planning and the appropriate provision of water supplies throughout Kruger would be greatly facilitated. Pienaar further argued that desiccation of the larger region was progressive

---

[78]J.J. la Grange, 'Die erkenning van die noodsaaklikheid van natuurbewaring ten opsigte van basiese grondgebruiksbeplanning in die Republiek van Suid-Afrika', in 'Proceedings of a symposium on the state of nature conservation in southern Africa, Kruger National Park, 1976', eds G. de Graaff and P.T. van der Walt, supplement, *Koedoe* (1977): 68–78.

[79]P.J. Smit, 'Die geohidrologie van die Nasionale Kalahari-Gemsbokpark', *Koedoe* 7 (1964): 153–155; P.A. Louw, 'Bodemkundige aspekte van die Kalahari-Gemsbokpark', *Koedoe* 7 (1964): 156–172.

[80]J.M. Theron, 'Die geologie van die Bontebokpark, distrik Swellendam', *Koedoe* 10 (1967): 147–148; J.J. Spies, 'Die geologise en geomorfologiese geskiedenis van Golden Gate Hoogland Nasionale Park', *Koedoe* 12 (1969): 184–198; D.K. Toerien, 'Geologie van die Addo-Olifant Nasionale Park', *Koedoe* 15 (1972): 67–75; D.K. Toerien, 'Geologie van die Tsitsikamakusstrook', *Koedoe* 19 (1976): 31–41; *Koedoe* 29 (1986) contains numerous articles on Kruger Park geology and geomorphology.

[81]E. Martinelli and G.L. Hubert, 'The use of electrical geophysical techniques for the development of groundwater supplies in SA National Parks', *Koedoe* 22 (1979): 199–209.

[82]W.P.D. Gertenbach, 'Rainfall patterns in the Kruger National Park', *Koedoe* 23 (1980): 35–43.

and that the NPB's policy of simulating and manipulating 'natural mechanisms' required such artificial interventions. He warned that KNP simply had to forestall a catastrophic crash of animal populations during severe drought, which could 'spell the end of the park as a viable, self-sustaining wildlife sanctuary and destroy its well-established tourist industry'. He added that 'special measures will have to be taken to safeguard the perennial rivers of the park and their unique aquatic life from the calamitous effects of progressive desiccation or serious pollution', a problem that was to become increasingly important with the passing of the years.[83]

Two special issues of *Koedoe* from the 1980s are particularly significant for their multidisciplinary focus on one national park. The first, the 'Proceedings of a two-day symposium on the Kalahari ecosystem' held in Pretoria in October 1983 and attended by some 200 people, appeared in 1984. This was a tribute to Dr Fritz Eloff, chairman of the NPB since 1979 and soon to retire as professor of zoology at the University of Pretoria. The symposium was also in celebration of the close relationship between the NPB and Pretoria University, for Eloff had helped establish the Mammal Research Institute at that university (with Waldo Meester the first Director) and had encouraged Anton Rupert's endowment of the Eugène Marais Chair of Wildlife Management in 1970. Eloff took a close interest in the lions of the KGNP and became a consultant for the Cat Specialist Group as well as for the Survival Service Commission of the International Union for the Conservation of Nature and Natural Resources (IUCN). The contents of this issue of *Koedoe* were wide-ranging and included articles on geology and soil; water resources and vegetation; fire; mammal, bird and invertebrate studies; as well as a list of relevant publications on the national park.

As Anthony Hall-Martin pointed out in his conclusion, the symposium and the publication provided a welcome synthesis of the state of knowledge about the KGNP, while also identifying important gaps. These, he noted, included poorly defined research goals, the absence of a research strategy and programme and a lack of coordination of the studies by NPB staff or visiting scientists. Importantly, he mentioned that without studies of ecosystem functioning, the level of understanding would remain extremely limited.[84]

[83]U. de V. Pienaar, 'Indications of progressive desiccation of the Transvaal Lowveld over the past 100 years, and implications for the water stabilization programme in the Kruger National Park', *Koedoe* 28 (1985): 93–165.
[84]G. de Graaff and D.J. van Rensburg, eds, 'Proceedings of a symposium on the Kalahari ecosystem, Pretoria 11–12 October 1983', supplement, *Koedoe* (1984).

An issue of *Koedoe* devoted to the KNP followed in 1986, celebrating 60 years since its establishment.[85] Perhaps given the considerable attention KNP had been given in other issues of *Koedoe*, the 1986 journal focused on detailed aspects of Kruger's geology. A useful 'textbook'-type format was adopted for it, with many contributions and an introduction and conclusion by Salomon Joubert, then park warden. In the latter, 'Management and research in relation to ecosystems of the Kruger National Park', Joubert, while ostensibly foregrounding ecosystems, does not deal with ecosystem functioning, but seems to assume that once the components of the system have been collected and studied, their interrelationship will become apparent.[86]

Humanities and Social Sciences

Far more so than is currently the case, research attention was devoted to history and archaeology between 1960 and 1990. This emphasis, while not nearly as strong as research into elements of nature, fitted into the programme of 'nationalising' national parks according to prevailing government ideology and gave rise to a particular view of history in which Afrikaner suffering was prioritised. The very first article in *Koedoe* in 1958 was by W.H.J. Punt, a local antiquarian with a flair for microhistory, particularly the minutiae of explorer routes and how explorers opened up the southern African interior to 'white civilisation'. Naturally, this kind of historical research chimed with the data collection in other disciplines, as it was extremely detailed but lacked an over-arching framework, analysis and a research hypothesis.

Punt's first article, 'Die verkenning van die Krugerwildtuin deur die Hollandse Oos-Indiese Kompanje, 1725' ('The reconnaissance of the Kruger Game Reserve by the Dutch East India Company, 1725') linked the KNP to the founder of 'white South Africa', Jan van Riebeeck, who had established the Dutch East India Company replenishment station at Cape Town in 1652. Later, the NPB also published Punt's book on this topic, *Die Eerste Europeane in die Nasionale Krugerwildtuin 1725/The First Europeans in the Kruger National Park*.[87] The object of Punt's attention

[85]G.H. Groenewald, 'Geology of the Golden Gate Highlands National Park', *Koedoe* 29 (1986): 165–181.

[86]S.C.J. Joubert, 'Management and research in relation to ecosystems of the Kruger National Park', *Koedoe* 29 (1986): 157–163.

[87]W.H.J. Punt, *Die Eerste Europeane in die Nasionale Krugerwildtuin 1725/The First Europeans in the Kruger National Park* (Pretoria: National Parks Board, 1975).

was a group from the Netherlands that briefly penetrated the Lowveld from Lourenço Marques (Maputo) in Mozambique, thereby, in his view, initiating a European presence of long-standing in the vicinity of the KNP.[88] In another article, Punt identified the location of the murder by Africans in 1836 of the Great Trek party led by J.J.J. (Lang Hans) van Rensburg. To identify the exact spot, Punt led an expedition into the KNP.[89] Commemoration of martyrs ('slagoffers') such as those in the KNP or Piet Retief, who was killed by Dingane, the Zulu king, was a key strand in the Afrikaner nationalist historiography of the time. It also ennobled the KNP in Afrikaner mythology as a site of sacrifice.

The van Rensburg saga continued the following year with an article in *Koedoe* by T.J.W. Jorden of the South African Iron and Steel Corporation (ISCOR). He established that an anvil discovered at the site was of English origin and dated to about 1820.[90] The same issue of *Koedoe* contained a copy of the proclamation of 26 March 1898, signed by President Paul Kruger of the Transvaal Republic, establishing the Sabi Game Reserve.[91] In 1962 Punt followed up with an overview of 'historical research' in the Kruger Park, which dealt exclusively with the Voortrekker routes in the Transvaal. In this endeavour, he was pleased to acknowledge the support of various politicians as well as KNP staff.[92] In a similar vein, in 1969, B.V. Lombaard, geologist-cum-historian, identified the origins of the name Pretoriuskop.[93] This form of chronological research and detailed anti-quarianism was to dominate studies of Kruger for many years to come.[94]

Other historical articles were broader in scope, but still reflected a white settler perspective. N.J. van der Merwe wrote about nature conservation in South Africa within a historical framework that valorised

---

[88]W.H.J. Punt, 'Die verkenning van die Krugerwildtuin deur die Hollandse Oos-Indiese Kompanje, 1725', *Koedoe* 1 (1958): 1–18.

[89]W.H.J. Punt, 'Waar die Van Rensburgtrek in 1836 vermoor is', *Koedoe* 3 (1960): 206–237.

[90]T.J.W. Jorden, 'Verslag oor die ondersoek i.v.m. ou aambeeld wat vermoedelik tot die Van Rensburg-trek behoort het', *Koedoe* 4 (1961): 45–53.

[91]Editorial office, 'Proklamasie van die Sabie-Wildtuin, 26 Maart 1898', *Koedoe* 4 (1961): 1–3.

[92]W.H.J. Punt, ''n Beknopte oorsig van die historiese navorsing in die nasionale Krugerwildtuin', *Koedoe* 5 (1962): 123–127.

[93]B.V. Lombaard, 'Herkoms van die naam Pretoriuskop', *Koedoe* 12 (1969): 53–56.

[94]See, for example, U. de V. Pienaar, *Goue Jare: Die Verhaal van die Nasionale Krugerwildtuin 1947–1991* (Stilbaai: The Author, 2010); U. de V. Pienaar, *Neem uit die Verlede* (Pretoria: Protea Boekhuis, 2007); U. de V. Pienaar, *A Cameo from the Past* (Pretoria: Protea Boekhuis, 2012); S.C.J. Joubert, *The Kruger National Park: A History*. 3 vols. (Johannesburg: High Branching, 2012).

white conservation efforts. So did A.P.J. van Rensburg, who was commissioned by the NPB to write a history of Golden Gate National Park in 1968 and of Bontebok National Park seven years later.[95] Not until the current author's article on the Pongola Game Reserve in *Koedoe* in 1985 was there a paradigm shift. For the first time, African involvement, science and politics were incorporated into the history of a protected area.[96] Since then, I have published other work on nature conservation and the KNP in academic journals, often focusing on the political expedients associated with protectionism, in particular African dispossession. This perspective has met with the considerable disapproval of numerous national park managers and Afrikaner nationalist historians.[97] Nonetheless, my article on African participation in shaping Kruger was published in *Koedoe* in 1993.

As far as the recording of animal species is concerned, NPB zoologist Penzhorn contributed an account of the naming of the quagga and of the records of hartebeest in the Transvaal Lowveld.[98] N.J. van der Merwe wrote about 'Die Bontbok' in *Koedoe* in 1968, outlining the history of the species and its protection in the Cape.[99]

Koedoe also published archaeological research. Much of this related to the KNP, where there were numerous precolonial settlement sites. The first of these articles appeared in 1961 and was entitled *Place Names of the*

---

[95]Van der Merwe, 'The position of nature conservation in South Africa'; A.P.J. van Rensburg, 'A Golden Gate: Die geskiedenis van twee plase wat 'n nasionale park geword het', *Koedoe* 11 (1968): 83–138; A.P.J. van Rensburg, 'Die geskiedenis van die Nasionale Bontebokpark, Swellendam', *Koedoe* 18 (1975): 165–190.

[96]J. Carruthers, 'The Pongola Game Reserve: An eco-political study', *Koedoe* 28 (1985): 1–16.

[97]My 1988 PhD thesis was published as *Game Protection in the Transvaal, 1846 to 1926* (Pretoria: Archives Year Book for South African History, 1995). I also wrote *The Kruger National Park: A Social and Political History* (Pietermaritzburg: Natal University Press, 1995); 'Defending Kruger's honour? A reply to Professor Hennie Grobler', *Journal of Southern African Studies* 22, no. 3 (1996): 473–480; 'Dissecting the myth: Paul Kruger and the Kruger National Park', *Journal of Southern African Studies* 20, no. 2 (1994): 263–284; '"Police boys" and poachers: Africans wildlife protection and national parks, the Transvaal 1902–1950', *Koedoe* 36, no. 2 (1993): 11–22; 'Creating a national park, 1910 to 1926', *Journal of Southern African Studies* 15, no. 2 (1989): 188–216; 'Game protectionism in the Transvaal, 1900–1910', *South African Historical Journal* 20 (1988): 33–56.

[98]B.L. Penzhorn, ''n Nota oor die gebruik van die benaming "Kwagga"', *Koedoe* 12 (1969): 104–105; B.L. Penzhorn, 'An old reference to "Hartebeest" in the Transvaal lowveld', *Koedoe* 28 (1985): 69–71.

[99]N.J. van der Merwe, 'Die Bontbok', *Koedoe* 11 (1968): 161–168.

Figure 7.4. A reconstructed village at Masorini, one of the many significant archaeological sites in the Kruger National Park.
Courtesy of SANParks.

Kruger National Park/Plekname van die Kruger Nasionale Park.[100] Written by N.J. van Warmelo, a government ethnologist in the Department of Bantu Administration, it provided a detailed list of known names in various African languages, giving type of locality (hill, river, watercourse, etc.), pronunciation, meaning and compass coordinates. In 1963, district game ranger Don Lowe located the site of 'Makahane' and the NPB requested J.F. (Hannes) Eloff, a well-known archaeologist and anthropologist from the University of Pretoria, to investigate it. His findings, co-authored with J.B. de Vaal, appeared in a formal report and also in an article in *Koedoe* in 1965.[101] Given the close ties with the University of Pretoria, and the fact that Hannes Eloff was the brother of Fritz Eloff, it is not surprising that the NPB assigned its archaeological and ethnological research projects to that university, with Hannes Eloff as leader. His group unearthed

---

[100]N.J. van Warmelo, *Place Names of the Kruger National Park/Plekname van die Kruger Nasionale Park.* Ethnological Publications No. 47 (Pretoria: Department of Bantu Administration, 1961). Other revised editions have followed. See, for example, J.J. Kloppers and H. Bornman, *A Dictionary of Kruger National Park Place Names* (Barberton: S.A. Country Life, 2005).

[101]J.F. Eloff and J.B. de Vaal, 'Makahane', *Koedoe* 8 (1965): 68–74.

and restored the site of Masorini, which indicated an African precolonial presence in the KNP area of at least 1500 years.

Broadly speaking, the type of archaeology that was done by the Pretoria group in national parks more generally in the 1960s and 1970s was 'organised around the idea of race' and resembled colonial archaeology – with its concentration on 'elite residences, royal burials and gold, and its persistent mythologising of the relation between archaeologist and subject'.[102] It certainly did not include the newer revisionist archaeology that was becoming internationally current and was being taught at the universities of the Witwatersrand and Cape Town.

Archaeological research reflecting a different school of thought was conducted in the late 1960s and early 1970s in Tsitsikamma by Hilary and Janette Deacon of the University of Stellenbosch. Hilary Deacon's ecological study, 'Two shell midden occurrences in the Tsitsikama National Park, Cape Province: A contribution to the study of the ecology of the Strandloopers', was commissioned by then Tsitsikamma warden Richard Liversidge, who was concerned by the destruction of many coastal caves in the wake of the recreational development of the Garden Route.[103] Later, warden Robbie Robinson also took an interest in archaeology and discussed the riddle of FitzSimon's 'Tzitzikama cave' in *Koedoe* 1977.[104] Work in Mountain Zebra was done by Stellenbosch student Mary Brooker in November 1973 and published in 1977. It consisted principally of a five-day research visit to 30 archaeological sites, three of which yielded scrapers and other artefacts in the various Smithfield series, as well as a number of rock paintings.[105]

[102]N. Shepherd, 'State of the discipline: Science, culture and identity in South African archaeology, 1870–2003', *Journal of Southern African Studies* 29, no. 4 (2003): 823–844; M. Schutte, 'Die tromme praat oor Masorini', *Custos* 15, no. 6 (1986); J. Verhoef, 'Notes on archaeology and prehistoric mining in the Kruger National Park', *Koedoe* 29 (1986): 149–156. See also I. Plug, 'The faunal remains from Iron Age sites in the Mahlangeni District, Kruger National Park'. Unpublished Report of the Department of Archaeozoology, Transvaal Museum, Pretoria, 1982; I. Plug, 'The faunal remains from TSH 1, an early Iron Age site in the Tshokwane district'. Unpublished Report of the Department of Archaeology, Transvaal Museum, Pretoria, 1985.
[103]H.J. Deacon, 'Two shell midden occurrences in the Tsitsikama National Park, Cape Province: A contribution to the study of the ecology of the Strandlopers', *Koedoe* 13 (1970): 37–50.
[104]G.A. Robinson, 'The riddle of FitzSimons' Tzitzikama cave', *Koedoe* 20 (1977): 95–99.
[105]M. Brooker, 'The archaeology of the Mountain Zebra National Park', *Koedoe* 20 (1977): 77–93.

The research section of the NPB began in 1951 and in 1986, after 25 years of research and on the 60th anniversary of the NPB and the KNP, a retrospective evaluation was published. It was a rather subdued anniversary because 1986 was an extremely difficult year for the NPB. The country was going through a period of violent convulsion, there was a substantial military presence in the KNP,[106] international visitor numbers were at an all-time low and funding for research – indeed for staff and infrastructure – was becoming increasingly constrained. The research team was particularly upset at veld fires lit by Mozambicans that spoilt years of carefully collected data from scheduled and monitored burns. The situation for the NPB was far from rosy, and it was already becoming dependent on private donors, particularly for land purchases for national parks, which the state was increasingly reluctant to fund.

In a special anniversary issue of *Custos* in 1986, Salomon Joubert, the newly appointed KNP warden, and Johan Kloppers, the chief game ranger who had been promoted in 1979 to the head of management, took the opportunity to explain the research trajectory of the KNP and how it had altered over the decades. The authors conceded that, in the absence of a clear initial strategy, the research staff had eventually realised that there were three components to research: articulation of objectives, the collection of appropriate data and determination of a plan of action. While the research team had initially adopted a scatter-gun approach to data collection, it had subsequently been decided that all research had to be directed by management. Thus, the purpose of research was not to learn per se, but – as was also the case in US national parks – to provide answers to questions about wildlife and vegetation management *in situ*. Even after 25 years, therefore, the argument for data collection remained strong. Knowledge, in the first instance, therefore meant baseline studies and counts of fauna and flora. Veld burning, agreed to be a necessity, needed experimentation and documentation. Only after data collection and experimentation could management policies be developed. Initially,

---

[106]In terms of the Defence Amendment Act 49 of 1978, the South African Defence Force created a military buffer along all of the country's international boundaries. The army therefore had a large presence in the KNP, the KGNP and in northern Natal, and it was able to construct roads and other infrastructure in accordance with its needs. Many employees of the KNP joined an active commando, led by P. van Wyk, and young men awaiting their period of conscription were, where possible, provided with employment in the national parks. M.S. Steyn, email to the author, 29 September 2015.

these would be constructed around vegetation community analyses, and subsequently around landscape types. The latter would be employed to guide management interventions once the dynamic properties of eco-systems within those landscape types were understood.[107] It sounded extremely logical.

However, in another publication in the early 1980s, 'A monitoring programme for an extensive national park', Joubert admitted that senti-ment rather than sound scientific evidence was often used for manage-ment intervention. Evidence was hard to find and often lagged behind a problem requiring urgent solution. Joubert also seemed to imply that understanding ecological processes was, in any event, impossible because conservation areas were fenced and only incomplete processes sur-vived within them. Nonetheless, he argued that inventory surveys were required to establish the variety of components in the ecosystem, and that a programme for monitoring fluctuation in these components over time should be brought into play so that, subsequently, basic research projects might begin to establish cause and effect.[108] There is, however, no description of the exact management questions for which answers were sought. In truth, much of the information emanating from the NPB during this period suggests a high and intensive level of effort rather than clearly considered management and research objectives and goals.

The over-arching philosophy had been made clear in 1976 in Pienaar's contribution to a significant NPB initiative, namely, a symposium on the state of nature conservation in southern Africa convened in the KNP. Pienaar's paper was seminal, and it addressed research objectives in South African national parks. The primary purpose of any national park, he averred, was to 'maintain an area's ecosystems in as nearly pristine a con-dition as possible. This means that ecological processes, including plant succession and the natural regulation of animal numbers, should be per-mitted to proceed as far as possible as they did under pristine conditions, and that modern man must be restricted to generally non-consumptive uses of these areas.' The word pristine is not defined, nor is there any indi-cation of how deviations from the pristine would be evaluated through research. Pienaar explained his views thus. Because few of South Africa's

---

[107]Joubert and Kloppers, 'Advancing by the decade'.

[108]S.C.J. Joubert in *Management of Large Mammals in African Conservation Areas: Proceedings of a Symposium held in Pretoria, South Africa*, 29–30 April 1982, ed. N. Owen-Smith (Pretoria: HAUM, 1983): 204–205.

national parks were ecological units, they had to be managed in terms of clear scientific objectives. The aim of ecological management in national parks was to diversify, not simplify the systems (unlike agriculture and forestry). In order to do so, 'firm and factual biological data, obtained through research' was required. And for this purpose, basic surveys, historical data, zoning and manipulation were indispensable activities.[109]

[109]U. de V. Pienaar, 'Research objectives in South African national parks', in 'Proceedings of a symposium on the state of nature conservation in southern Africa, Kruger National Park, 1976', eds G. de Graaff and P.T. van der Walt, supplement, *Koedoe* (1977): 38–48.

8 · *Zoology*

While acquiring knowledge of vegetation, geology, weather and fire in particular was extremely important for the scientific division of the National Parks Board (NPB), the major research emphasis was, and remains, the fauna, especially the large mammals. Protecting them (or most species) had been the original rationale for establishing the Sabi and Singwitsi Game Reserves in the early 1900s and for the enlargement of the protected estate in the 1930s with the establishment of new national parks.

Until the 1960s, protecting, preserving and propagating wildlife was extremely successful in all South Africa's national parks, and indeed in other game reserves as well. With the exception of wild dog, which had been decimated by disease in the 1920s and had never recovered their previous abundance, the numbers of large mammals increased and there seemed to be sufficient lion, leopards, cheetah and other carnivora to provide tourists with a satisfying, not to say exciting, experience. Under strict protection, impala and other antelope species that had so entranced earlier sport-hunters began to be numbered in their hundreds if not thousands and buffalo and hippopotamus were plentiful. Even the elephant population burgeoned in the KNP after migrants moved in from Mozambique and became the nucleus of substantial herds. As far as the Bontebok, Addo Elephant and Mountain Zebra parks were concerned, the targeted protected species grew in number and other species were added from different parts of South Africa in order to replicate what was believed to be the precolonial mix of species in the area.[1] In time, the large parks, namely Kruger (KNP) and Kalahari Gemsbok (KGNP), began to be considered as 'balanced, pristine and stable' environments.

As noted earlier, the small group of scientists employed in the NPB, together with outside experts, generally invited, were diligent in publishing their work in *Koedoe*. It is not surprising that in the first 25 issues

---

[1] See, for example, L.C.C. Liebenberg, 'Die grotere soogdiere wat vroë dae voorgekom het in die omgewing van die Golden Gate-Hoogland Park', *Koedoe* 7 (1964): 99–104.

of the journal (1958–1983), most articles deal with individual species, of which mammal species were the most numerous by far. Other taxa were not, however, totally neglected: invertebrates, birds and fishes were included by way of checklists, surveys and species descriptions. Given the international focus on endangered animals, this listing of species and, where possible, recording their abundance or scarcity, coincided with the initial publication of the International Union for the Conservation of Nature and Natural Resources (IUCN) Red Data Lists. It also coincided with the founding of the Endangered Wildlife Trust in Johannesburg in 1973 by wildlife artist Clive Walker specifically to raise funds for research into endangered and rare species.[2] The environmental movement had highlighted the fragility of particular species and the prospect of their extinction at a time of exponential human population growth loomed large in debates about the future of many biota.

In zoology, as in other disciplines, the preferred mode of research throughout the NPB between 1960 and 1990 was the biological survey. Although useful, this approach meant that new connections and fresh systemic knowledge were neither generated nor encouraged. Nor was careful ecological and environmental planning incorporated into an overall strategy or into national park management. As early as 1978, Brian Huntley had warned that conservation science, to fulfil its function, needed to become more multidisciplinary and give greater attention to long-term issues and to causation. In his view, current policy concentrated on solutions to short-term effects without generating greater understanding of the larger picture. Huntley thus argued that ecosystems, not their individual components, should be prioritised in national park research. Even at that time he also believed that constructive engagement with local African communities was vital to the future of conservation.[3] This issue, hitherto totally neglected, was becoming more urgent as fences proliferated and rural populations around many national parks grew as a

[2]G.R. McLachlan, *South African Red Data Book: Reptiles and Amphibians*. South African National Scientific Programmes Report 23 (Pretoria: CSIR, 1978); W.R. Branch, ed., *South African Red Data Book: Reptiles and Amphibians*. South African National Scientific Programmes Report 151 (Pretoria: CSIR, 1988); R.K. Brooke, *South African Red Data Book: Birds*. South African National Scientific Programmes Report 97 (Pretoria: CSIR, 1984). EWT was to become an energetic and important conservation body in South Africa, entering into many partnerships with specialist bodies, beginning with a large symposium in 1976.

[3]B.J. Huntley, 'Ecosystem conservation in southern Africa', in *Biogeography and Ecology of Southern Africa*, vol. 2, ed. M.J.A. Werger (The Hague: Junk, 1978), 1333–1384.

result of the large-scale population relocations undertaken in the name of apartheid. After 1994, this was to become a critically important issue. Huntley's cautions and advice on both fronts went unheeded. The NPB merely forged ahead – it must be said with energy and dedication – with taking detailed stock of the biodiversity under its control, and with producing long lists of insects, spiders, fish and other fauna.

Lists, Surveys and Observations

From the very first issue of *Koedoe*, the smaller invertebrates and insects were included in the published material. For many years, the NPB did not employ an entomologist and much of the survey work was done by outside specialists. In 1958, the Dutch-born educationist Anthonie Janse, who later became an outstanding South African entomologist (and advocate for a zoological survey of South Africa), recorded three new species of the gall-forming moth *Acutitornus* (including *A. kalahariensis*) in the KGNP.[4] Reptiles of this park also featured in the first issue of *Koedoe*, as did its bird life and small mammals. Also published in this first issue was a survey of the Culicine mosquitoes in the KNP.[5]

In 1964, André Prins of the Plant Protection Institute listed the ants of the KNP, and three years later produced an expanded description of the ants of the national parks in general.[6] At much the same time, Reginald Lawrence, then director of the Natal Museum and later of the Albany Museum, contributed the first systematic survey of myriopods (the subphylum of terrestrial arthropods containing millipedes, centipedes, etc.) in a sub-region of the Transvaal in his article, 'The Myriopoda of the Kruger National Park', which appeared in an early issue of *Zoologica Africana*, the journal of the Zoological Society of South Africa.[7]

---

[4] A.J.T. Janse, 'Three new species of *Acutitornus* from the Kalahari', *Koedoe* 1 (1958): 95–98.

[5] V. FitzSimons and C.K. Brain, 'A short account of the reptiles of the Kalahari Gemsbok National Park', *Koedoe* 1 (1958): 99–104; J.S. de Villiers, 'A report on the bird life of the Kalahari Gemsbok National Park', *Koedoe* 1 (1958): 143–161; D.H.S. Davis, 'Notes on some small mammals in the Kalahari Gemsbok National Park, with special reference to those preyed upon by barn owls', *Koedoe* 1 (1958): 184–188; K.H. Schultz, J.J. Steyn and R. Rose-Innes, 'A Culicine mosquito survey of the Kruger National Park', *Koedoe* 1 (1958): 189–200.

[6] A.J. Prins, 'A revised list of the ants collected in the Kruger National Park', *Koedoe* 7 (1964): 77–93; A.J. Prins, 'The ants of our national parks', *Koedoe* 10 (1967): 63–81.

[7] R.F. Lawrence, 'The Myriopoda of the Kruger National Park', *Zoologica Africana* 2, no. 2 (1966): 225–262; R.F. Lawrence, 'The Solifugae, scorpions and Pedipalpi of the Kruger National Park', *Koedoe* 7 (1964): 30–39. See also A.S. Dippenaar-Schoeman, 'Annotated

This study, which included expert identification by scientists at the universities of Lund and Nancy, was based on the extensive material on many species (some new to science) gathered over several years by KNP warden Pienaar and his staff, and on Lawrence's previous publications and specialised knowledge. Lawrence also contributed articles to *Koedoe* in 1966 on the arachnid fauna of the KNP.[8] William Coaton, the termite specialist in the division of entomology in the Department of Agriculture (and head of the national insect collection), published a 'Survey of the termites of the Kruger National Park' in 1962 and of the Kalahari and bushveld the ensuing year, while L. Vari, who had worked in various national parks on butterflies and moths, published his species list in 1962.[9] A checklist of mites in the South African national parks was contributed by Magdalena Meyer in 1970 and by Meyer and her co-workers in 1988.[10] J.F. Barker provided a list of grasshoppers in the KGNP in 1984.[11]

In 1983, L.E.O. Braack, the son of an NPB employee and brought up in the KNP, was taken on as a laboratory and museum technician at Skukuza. After obtaining his PhD from the University of Natal in 1984 on 'An ecological investigation of insects associated with exposed carcasses in the northern Kruger National Park', he went on to distinguish himself as an entomologist. In 1991 he authored the *Field Guide to Insects of the Kruger National Park*. Later, in 1997, Braack became KNP's head of research and information and in 1998 was promoted to head office in Pretoria.

---

check list of the spiders (Araneae) of the Mountain Zebra National Park', *Koedoe* 31 (1988): 151–160.

[8] R.F. Lawrence, 'Supplementary list of the Solifugae, scorpions and Pedipalpi of the Kruger National Park', *Koedoe* 10 (1967): 82–86; R.F. Lawrence, 'The Pseudoscorpioins (False-scorpions) of the Kruger National Park', *Koedoe* 10 (1967): 87–91.

[9] W.G.H. Coaton, 'Survey of the termites of the Kruger National Park', *Koedoe* 5 (1962): 144–156; W.G.H. Coaton, 'Survey of the termites (Isoptera) of the Kalahari thornveld and shrub bushveld of the RSA', *Koedoe* 6 (1963): 38–50; L.Vari, 'South African Lepidoptera, 2', *Koedoe* 5 (1962): 162–167; L.Vari, 'South African Lepidoptera, 4', *Koedoe* 7 (1964): 43–51.

[10] M. Meyer, 'South African ACARI II checklist of mites in our Parks (Part 1)', *Koedoe* 13 (1970): 29–36; M. Meyer and E.A. Ueckermann, 'South African ACARI III. On the mites of the Mountain Zebra National Park', *Koedoe* 31 (1988): 1–29; E.A. Ueckermann and M. Meyer, 'South African ACARI IV. Some mites of the Addo Elephant National Park', *Koedoe* 31 (1988): 31–51; M. Meyer and E.A. Ueckermann, 'South African ACARI V. Some mites of the Kalahari Gemsbok National Park', *Koedoe* 32, no. 1 (1989): 25–38.

[11] J.F. Barker, 'Preliminary list of the grasshoppers (Acridoidea) found in the Kalahari Gemsbok National Park', *Koedoe* 27 (1984): 1–4.

Figure 8.1. Covers of some Kruger National Park guidebooks published in the 1970s and 1980s.
Photograph by the author.

Warden Pienaar was personally knowledgeable about and interested in all the biota in the KNP, including its birds, frogs, fish and reptiles. He identified many of these fauna himself and strongly encouraged others to assist with and contribute to identification lists and guides. A prolific writer, enthusiastic and meticulous data recorder and collector and an extremely diligent and hard-working man, Pienaar published extensively in *Koedoe* on almost every aspect of life in the KNP.[12] The recording of

[12]He was the most published author in *Koedoe* during the period 1958–2006 with 32 papers, followed by G.J. Bredenkamp (28) and J. du P. Bothma (23), both of the University of Pretoria. See, for example, U. de V. Pienaar, 'The zoogeography and systematic list of Amphibia in the Kruger National Park', *Koedoe* 6 (1963): 76–82; U. de V. Pienaar, 'The freshwater fishes of the Kruger National Park', *Koedoe* 11 (1968): 1–82; U. de V. Pienaar, 'A supplementary checklist of Decapoda, freshwater fish, Amphibia, reptiles and small mammals recorded in the Kruger National Park', *Koedoe* 4 (1961): 167–177;

the amphibian and reptile fauna of other national parks took place more slowly, the preliminary checklist of reptiles and amphibians in Mountain Zebra appearing only in 1981 and of Addo and Tsitsikamma national parks six years later.[13]

While most of this work appeared in *Koedoe*, the board was extremely supportive of all research whether intended for the in-house journal or not. Some authors contributed to other, more academic, journals, although at that time publication did not have the urgency (or the citation indices) associated with today's scientific scholarship. The board even subsidised books on the lesser animals – including butterflies – throughout the 1970s.[14] Those who were invited to work in the national parks were often provided with accommodation and research assistance. Researchers always had to have their projects approved by the NPB and their topics had to conform to what the board or the individual national park wished to have done. For many years, a detailed report of research projects was provided to the board at its meetings. The NPB also hosted a number of international conferences, some quite large. For example, in 1975 there was a well-attended symposium on herpetology and ichthyology at Skukuza, and in 1988, the third international symposium

U. de V. Pienaar, 'An amended check-list of the birds of the Kruger National Park', *Koedoe* 4 (1961): 117–140.

[13]J.H. Grobler and P.J. Bronkhorst, 'A preliminary checklist of reptiles and amphibians in the Mountain Zebra National Park', *Koedoe* 24 (1981): 193–197. Grobler also recorded the leopard tortoise in MZNP; see J.H. Grobler, 'The leopard tortoise in the Mountain Zebra National Park', *Koedoe* 25 (1982): 49–53; W.R. Branch and N. Hanekom, 'The herpetofauna of the Tsitsikamma Coastal and Forest National Parks', *Koedoe* 30 (1987): 49–60; W.R. Branch and H.H. Braack, 'Reptiles and amphibians of the Addo Elephant National Park', *Koedoe* 30 (1987): 61–111.

[14]U. de V. Pienaar, W.D. Haacke and N.H.G. Jacobsen, *The Reptiles of the Kruger National Park* (Pretoria: National Parks Board, 1966); U. de V. Pienaar, *The Reptile Fauna of the Kruger National Park* (Pretoria: National Parks Board, 1978); U. de V. Pienaar, N.I. Passmore and V.C. Carruthers, *The Frogs of the Kruger National Park* (Pretoria: National Parks Board, 1976); U. de V. Pienaar, *The Freshwater Fishes of the Kruger National Park* (Pretoria: National Parks Board, 1978); J. Kloppers and the late G. van Son, *The Butterflies of the Kruger National Park* (Pretoria: National Parks Board, 1978). See also W.R. Branch and H.H. Braack, 'Reptiles and amphibians of the Karoo National Park: A surprising diversity', *The Journal of the Herpetological Association of Africa* 36, no. 1 (1989): 26–35. G. van Son had published 'On some butterflies of the Kalahari Gemsbok National Park, with descriptions of three new forms' in *Koedoe* 2 (1959): 52–59 and 'Records of butterflies of the Kruger National Park 1', *Koedoe* 7 (1964): 52–55, while M.C. Ferreira published 'A contribution to the study of the Coleoptera from the Kalahari Gemsbok National Park (Scarabaeidae, Buprestidae, Cerambycidae)', *Koedoe* 2 (1959): 77–86.

on neuropterology (insects of the order Neuroptera) took place at Berg-en-Dal, attracting 30 delegates (including world authorities), 21 of them from outside South Africa. Thus the record of research supported in various ways by the NPB is a significant one.

Probably the most exciting national park proclaimed in the 1960s was the Tsitsikamma Coastal and Forest National Park (1964). Consisting – as its name implies – of a marine and a forest zone, it was a novelty among national parks in not being dominated by large mammals. Enthusiastically managed by G.A. (Robbie) Robinson, Tsitsikamma soon became a popular destination for both visitors and researchers. Situated along the scenic Garden Route of the Cape province, and close to holiday destinations such as Knysna and the Wilderness Lakes area, Tsitsikamma offered a fascinating shoreline to explore and opportunities to walk along the cliffs overlooking the sea. In the forest section, the remnant of an extensive indigenous forest region, there were rambles among the large yellowwood trees *Podocarpus* spp. and the rare stinkwood *Ocotea bullata*. Robinson soon built a partnership with the ichthyologists at Rhodes University and drew on their considerable knowledge of the fishes of the subcontinent.[15] As a former employee of the South African Department of Sea Fisheries, he also had access to the considerable research the department had done over many years in regulating and managing the lucrative offshore fisheries. For marine researchers, the national park provided an ideal site for studying unexploited stocks.

In the absence of large and dangerous mammals, visitors were able to explore the Tsitsikamma coastline on foot and peer into tidal pools and they were provided with a fish identification guide published in 1966 by J.L.B. Smith and Margaret Smith. Both were leading ichthyologists at Rhodes University, where the former had made world headlines with his identification of the coelacanth *Latimeria chalumnae* in 1938, and had established a renowned Institute of Ichthyology. After 1974, visitors also had access to a guide to the marine invertebrate fauna in a publication, compiled by Rosamund Tietz of Port Elizabeth Museum, together with Robinson.[16]

---

[15]J.L.B. Smith, *The Sea Fishes of Southern Africa* (Johannesburg: South African Fish Book Fund, 1949).

[16]J.L.B. Smith and M.M. Smith, *Fishes of the Tsitsikama Coastal National Park* (Pretoria: National Parks Board, 1966); R.M. Tietz and G.A. Robinson, *The Tsitsikama Shore: A Guide to the Marine Invertebrate Fauna of the Tsitsikama Coastal National Park* (Pretoria: National Parks Board, 1974).

75 **Stingray Pylstert** *Myliobatis cervus** (Myliobatidae)

S.A. SPEARFISHING RECORD: 25 LBS.

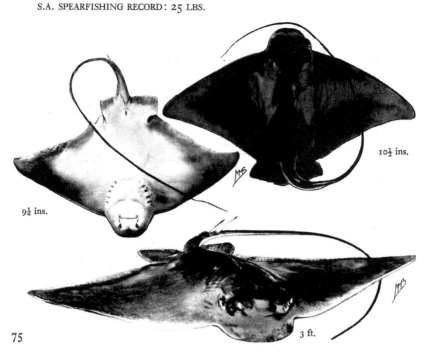

10¼ ins.

9¼ ins.

75   3 ft.

Figure 8.2. Stingrays *Myliobatis cervus,* illustration by M.M. Smith.
From J.L.B. Smith and M.M. Smith, *Fishes of the Tsitsikama Coastal National Park* (1966),
p. 30. Courtesy of SANParks.

With his experience of the national parks in the USA, where he had
obtained a PhD at the University of Washington in Seattle, the top institution worldwide in marine biology, Robinson was keen to attract visitors
to the marine national park.[17] He appreciated that many South Africans
were unfamiliar with the biological world of the sea and believed that in
this national park they would require specialised guidance and innovative
forms of interpretation. In a detailed five-year plan presented to the NPB,
Robinson included ideas for an interpretation centre, self-guided under-
water trails, rocky shore trails, low-tide beach hikes, observation boats and

---

[17]Robinson's PhD dissertation (1972) was entitled 'A study of the Pacific Ocean perch
  fisheries of the north-eastern Pacific Ocean'.

even for an aquarium.[18] The list of research projects Robinson encouraged at Tsitsikamma is a long one, although few articles saw the light of day in *Koedoe* as the ichthyologists generally preferred to publish in their own well-established disciplinary journals. No doubt the overwhelmingly terrestrial focus of *Koedoe* made it an unattractive publication for them, although Robinson, as an NPB employee, did publish in this journal.[19]

By contrast, visitors to the KNP were confined to their vehicles and had no opportunity to identify the majority of smaller creatures in the field apart from those encountered in rest camps. Nonetheless, it is a great pity that the book series on such creatures has not been maintained by the next generation of NPB managers and many of these publications are now sadly out of date.[20] Fortunately, better illustrated guidebooks have been published by commercial publishers in response to the growing demand for field guides in recent decades.

Bird-watching was not always as popular a pastime in South Africa as it has become. Aided by improvements in field guides and their multiplicity, the many courses on bird identification, and affordable binoculars and telescopes, bird-watching has grown into one of the world's most widespread leisure activities. However, there have long been specialist ornithologists in South Africa's museums, at the Percy Fitzpatrick Institute of African Ornithology (founded 1959) at the University of Cape Town, as well as extremely competent enthusiasts and bird artists. Many of these people, both professional and amateur, were involved in the compilation of the authoritative reference work, *Roberts Birds*. First published in 1940, it has now run into numerous editions. *Koedoe* also featured a number of bird lists and brief observations by reputable ornithologists such as J.M. Winterbottom (Percy Fitzpatrick Institute), Gordon Maclean (Natal University), G.J. Broekhuysen (University of Cape Town), C.J. Skead (Amathole Museum),[21] O.P.M. Prozesky (Transvaal Museum) and Richard Liversidge (warden of Tsitsikamma National Park from 1964 and later director of the McGregor Museum, Kimberley). Kenneth Newman, an

[18]Minutes of a meeting of the NPB, 14 September 1973, SANParks archives, Groenkloof, Pretoria.

[19]See G.A. Robinson, 'Sex reversal in the dageraad *Chrysoblephus cristiceps* (Pisces: Sparidae)', *Koedoe* 19 (1976): 43–48. There are many examples of marine research conducted in the TCNP.

[20]One of the later of these books was L.E.O. Braack, *Field Guide to Insects of the Kruger National Park* (Cape Town: Struik and National Parks Board, 1991).

[21]C.J. Skead, 'The need for a zoological survey in South Africa', *South African Museum Association Bulletin* 6, no. 4 (1955): 101–103.

artist turned bird-illustrator and ornithologist, compiled the first bird field guide for the KNP in 1980 as part of the series *Birds of Southern Africa*.[22] Alan Kemp of the Transvaal Museum obtained his PhD from Rhodes University in 1972 on the ecology, behaviour and systematics of hornbills, much of his research being conducted in the KNP.[23] Later, he wrote about the importance of the KNP for bird conservation in South Africa.[24] Many studies in the KGNP focused on the numerous raptor species found there.[25] Over the years, *Koedoe* has included updated surveys and lists and unusual sightings of birds for almost all the national parks.[26]

[22]B.L. Penzhorn and A.K. Morris, 'A supplementary check-list of birds recorded in the Addo Elephant National Park', *Koedoe* 12 (1969): 106–107. Ornithological research was done by Gordon Maclean in the Kalahari and some of the UCT ornithologists at the PFIAO, for example, by J.M. Winterbottom and later by Roy Siegfried in other national parks. See K. Newman, *Birds of Southern Africa. 1: Kruger National Park* (Johannesburg: Macmillan, 1980); J.M. Winterbottom, 'Bird densities in coastal renosterbosveld of the Bontebok National Park', *Koedoe* 11 (1968): 139–144; J.M. Winterbottom, 'A preliminary list of the birds of the Bontebok National Park, Swellendam', *Koedoe* 5 (1962): 183–188; J.M. Winterbottom, 'The birds of the Augrabies Falls National Park', *Koedoe* 13 (1970): 171–180; G.J. Broekhuysen, M.H. Broekhuysen, J.E. Martin, R. Martin and H.K. Morgan, 'Observations on the bird life of the Kalahari Gemsbok National Park', *Koedoe* 11 (1968): 145–160; R. Martin, J. Martin, E. Martin and H.H. Braack, 'A preliminary list of the birds of the Karoo National Park', *Koedoe* 31 (1988): 203–225; C.J. Skead, 'Report on the bird-life in the Mountain Zebra National Park, Cradock, CP, 1962–1964', *Koedoe* 8 (1965): 1–40; C.J. Skead, 'The birds of the Addo National Park', *Koedoe* 8 (1965): 41–67; C.J. Skead and R. Liversidge, 'Birds of the Tsitsikama Forest and Coastal National Park', *Koedoe* 10 (1966): 43–62; O.P.M. Prozesky and C. Haagner, 'A check-list of the birds of the Kalahari Gemsbok Park', *Koedoe* 5 (1962): 171–182. See also M.G.L. Mills, 'A revised check-list of birds in the Kalahari Gemsbok National Park', *Koedoe* 19 (1976): 49–62.
[23]A.C. Kemp, 'The ecology, behaviour and systematics of *Tockus* hornbills' (PhD diss., Rhodes University, 1972).
[24]A.C. Kemp, 'The importance of the Kruger National Park for bird conservation in the Republic of South Africa', *Koedoe* 23 (1980): 99–122.
[25]Some of the work involved long-term raptor monitoring. This began in 1974 and included workers such as Chris and Karin Olwagen, Takagoya Breeding Unit, Pretoria, for the research on birds of prey and falconry; C.W. Sapsford, Department of Biology, University of Natal, on the water and energy requirements of pygmy falcon and other birds of prey in KGNP. Meeting and agenda of NPB, 7 December 1959, SANParks archives, Groenkloof, Pretoria.
[26]Martin *et al.*, 'A preliminary list of the birds of the Karoo National Park'. Harold Braack (brother of L.E.O. Braack) and his wife Toni Braack were well known and very knowledgeable research assistants in the KNP and later became wardens of the Bontebok and Karoo National Parks.

Figure 8.3. Kites, kestrel, falco, buzzard, goshawk and gymnogene.
From National Parks Board, *Voëls van der Krugerwildtuin en Ander Nasionale Parke/
Birds of the Kruger and Other National Parks*, vol. 1 (1974), opp. p. 14.
Courtesy of SANParks.

Considerable attention was devoted to checklists of the smaller mammals in the national parks. Many articles about them and their taxonomy appeared in *Koedoe*, as did a number of observational studies of specific populations. In 1958, D.H.S. Davis wrote a series of notes on the small mammals of the KGNP that were preyed upon by barn owls.[27] An unusual contributor to early issues of *Koedoe* was Niels Bolwig, senior lecturer in zoology at the University of the Witwatersrand from 1946 to 1959. Bolwig, who had emigrated from Denmark after the Second World War, was an acclaimed scientist and one of the first ethologists to study primates in the wild. He also had an interest in small mammals and contributed papers to *Koedoe* on aspects of animal ecology in the Kalahari (1958), on facial mimicry (1959) and on the physiological and behavioural characteristics of small animals in the southern Kalahari (1959).[28] Bolwig was forced to leave South Africa in 1959 on account of his opposition to apartheid and spent the rest of his life working on primates in other parts of Africa and was associated with the universities of Makerere, Ibadan and Lesotho.

The first systematic record of small mammals in the KNP was compiled by Pienaar and published in *Koedoe* in 1964.[29] Little more appeared until the employment of Gerrit de Graaff in 1969 as liaison and research officer. A graduate of the universities of the Witwatersrand and Pretoria, he had been employed in the department of zoology at the latter institution. He was a small-mammal taxonomist whose doctoral work at Pretoria in 1965 had been revision of the Bathyergidae,[30] and in 1981 he published the authoritative *The Rodents of Southern Africa: Notes on their Distribution, Ecology and Taxonomy*.[31] The name of de Graaff, who

[27]Davis, 'Notes on some small mammals in the Kalahari Gemsbok National Park'.

[28]N. Bolwig, 'Aspects of animal ecology in the Kalahari', *Koedoe* 1 (1958): 115–135; N. Bolwig, 'Observations and thoughts on the evolution of facial mimic', *Koedoe* 2 (1959): 60–69; N. Bolwig, 'Further observations on the physiological and behavioural characteristics of small animals in the southern Kalahari', *Koedoe* 2 (1959): 70–76.

[29]U. de V. Pienaar, 'The small mammals of the Kruger National Park: A systematic list and zoogeography', *Koedoe* 7 (1964): 1–25. See also P. Swanepoel, 'Small mammals of the Addo Elephant National Park', *Koedoe* 18 (1975): 103–130.

[30]Published as G. de Graaff, *The Mammals of Africa: An Identification Manual. 16. Rodentia: Bathyergidae* (Washington, DC: Smithsonian Institution, 1968).

[31]G. de Graaff, 'Notes on the small mammals of the Eastern Cape National Parks', *Koedoe* 13 (1970): 147–150; 'On the mole-rat (*Cryptomys hottentotus damarensis*) (Rodentia) in the Kalahari Gemsbok National Park', *Koedoe* 15 (1972): 25–35; 'Notes on the occurrence of rodents in South African National Parks', *Koedoe* 17 (1974): 173–183. See also G. de Graaff, *The Rodents of Southern Africa: Notes on their Distribution, Ecology and*

was to rise through the NPB ranks to become head of scientific liaison in 1974, appears often in *Koedoe* in relation to small mammals, as does that of his colleague I.L. Rautenbach, also a taxonomist (with a special interest in bats) and formerly the curator of the mammal department at the Transvaal Museum.[32] In 1980, Rautenbach and de Graaff, together with Pienaar, produced *The Small Mammals of the Kruger National Park*,[33] while in 1982, Rautenbach authored *Mammals of the Transvaal*.[34]

Like F.C. (Fritz) Eloff, head of the zoology department at Pretoria University, and J. du P. Bothma, holder of the Eugène Marais Chair of Wildlife Management there, John Skinner, the Cambridge-trained director of the Mammal Research Institute (MRI) at the university from 1972 to 1998, had a profound influence on science in South Africa's national parks.[35] His influence arose less from his expertise in animal husbandry and game ranching[36] than through his many personal connections with,

---

Taxonomy (Durban: Butterworths, 1981); G. de Graaff, 'A systematic revision of the Bathyergidae (Rodentia) of southern Africa' (PhD diss., University of Pretoria, 1965); J.A.J. Nel and L. Pretorius, 'A note on the smaller mammals of the Mountain Zebra National Park', *Koedoe* 14 (1971): 99–110.

[32]I.L. Rautenbach and J.A.J. Nel, 'Further records of smaller mammals from the Kalahari Gemsbok National Park', *Koedoe* 18 (1975): 195–198. See also I.L. Rautenbach and I.W. Espie, 'First records of occurrence for two species of bats in the Kruger National Park', *Koedoe* 25 (1982): 111–112; I.L. Rautenbach, D.A. Schlitter and L.E.O. Braack, 'New distribution records of bats for the Republic of South Africa, with special reference to the Kruger National Park', *Koedoe* 27 (1984): 131–135; J.A.J. Nel, I.L. Rautenbach, D.A. Else and G. de Graaff, 'The rodents and other small mammals of the Kalahari Gemsbok National Park', in 'Proceedings of a symposium on the Kalahari ecosystem 1983', eds G. de Graaff and D.J. van Rensburg, supplement, *Koedoe* (1984): 195–220; I.L. Rautenbach, M.B. Fenton and L.E.O. Braack, 'First records of five species of insectivorous bats from the Kruger National Park', *Koedoe* 28 (1985): 73–80.

[33]U. de V. Pienaar, I.L. Rautenbach and G. de Graaff, *The Small Mammals of the Kruger National Park* (Pretoria: National Parks Board, 1980).

[34]I.L. Rautenbach, *Mammals of the Transvaal*. Ecoplan Monograph No.1 (Pretoria: Ecoplan, 1982).

[35]R.H.N. Smithers, *The Mammals of the Southern African Subregion* (Pretoria: University of Pretoria, 1983); J.D. Skinner and R.H.N. Smithers, *The Mammals of the Southern African Subregion*, 2nd edn (Pretoria: University of Pretoria, 1990); J.D. Skinner and C.T. Chimimba, *The Mammals of the Southern African Subregion* (Cambridge: Cambridge University Press, 2005).

[36]See, for example, J.D. Skinner, R.H. Monro and I. Zimmermann, 'Comparative food intake and growth of cattle and impala on mixed tree savanna', *South African Journal of Wildlife Research*, 14, no. 1 (1984): 1–9; J.D. Skinner, 'An appraisal of the eland as a farm animal in Africa', *Animal Breeding Abstracts* 35 (1967): 177–186; J.D. Skinner, 'Game farming in South Africa', *Journal of the African Biological Society* 6 (1975): 8–15;

for example, the zoology department at Oxford University. Many of his students, including Anthony Hall-Martin, Albert van Jaarsveld, Rudi van Aarde, Michael Knight and others were, thanks to these connections, exposed to a well-developed ecological perspective. This generation of young scientists (with whom he frequently co-authored papers) was introduced by Skinner to the NPB, although the relationship between Skinner and the board was never very harmonious. Together with researchers such as Norman Owen-Smith, a postdoctoral fellow at the MRI, they were probably the first to approach research projects in national parks with some kind of hypothesis in advance.[37] Skinner carefully planned the MRI's research agenda and ensured that its work appeared in leading international publications and not only in *Koedoe*.[38] An early example of the resultant international collaboration was the complex and synthetic research project on small mammals begun in 1982 under David Macdonald from the conservation research unit at Oxford and today a world authority on meerkats *Suricata suricatta*. The small-mammal studies were coordinated by Knight, by then an employee of the NPB and stationed in the KGNP as a scientific research officer.

Translocation and Modelling

During the 1960s, there were three major developments in scientific research and its application in southern Africa and in other parts of the world. These were game management, or game ranching as it was often called, the successful technology of tranquillisation and transportation of wild animals, and the implications of computerisation.

Fresh thinking was evident in the USA thanks to the work of Aldo Leopold, who as early as 1933 had devised and explained the term 'game management' in a book of the same name. Leopold defined the concept as 'the art of making land produce sustained annual crops of wildlife' for

---

J.D. Skinner, 'Game ranching in southern Africa', in *Wildlife Production Systems: Economic Utilisation of Wild Ungulates*, eds R.J. Hudson, K.R. Drew and L.M. Baskin (Cambridge: Cambridge University Press, 1989), 286–306.

[37] Anthony Hall-Martin. Interview with the author. Cape Town, 14 February 2012. In 1978 Hall-Martin was transferred from AENP to KNP. Skinner himself published one article in *Koedoe*, see J.D. Skinner, 'Productivity of mountain reedbuck *Redunca fulvorufula* (Afzelius, 1815), at the Mountain Zebra National Park', *Koedoe* 23 (1980): 123–130.

[38] N. Bennett, 'The Mammal Research Institute 1966–2006', *Transactions of the Royal Society of South Africa* 63, no. 1 (2008): 53–60.

recreational use.[39] Leopold believed game should be 'positively produced, rather than negatively protected', and that it was a 'crop which nature will grow'.[40] He therefore advocated moving away from strict preservation to 'wise use' not only of agricultural lands and areas set aside for sportsmen, but even of national parks and game reserves. Leopold's thinking had no impact in southern Africa until the 1960s, when a 'game farming' revolution was inaugurated in what was then Rhodesia by Raymond Dasmann, later the chief ecologist of the IUCN,[41] and Archie Mossman, whose interest in the subject had first been piqued by Transvaal mammalogist Berndt Lundholm in 1952.[42]

The game farming project in Rhodesia (which was politically more agreeable than South Africa at the time) took place under the auspices of the UN Food and Agricultural Organisation (FAO).[43] It was facilitated by Reay Smithers, an outstanding zoologist and the then director of the Rhodesian National Museums. Together with the FAO's Thane Riney, Dasmann and Mossman postulated in their studies between 1958 and 1961

[39]A. Leopold, *Game Management* (Madison, WI and London: University of Wisconsin Press, 1986), 3–4.

[40]C. Meine, *Aldo Leopold: His Life and Work* (Madison, WI: University of Wisconsin Press, 1988), 240.

[41]R. Jarrell, 'A giant among ecologists: Raymond F. Dasmann, 1919–2002', *Wildlife Society Bulletin* 31, no. 1 (2003), 324.

[42]B. Lundholm, 'Game farming: Is it a feasible proposition?' *African Wildlife* 6, no. 2 (1952): 121–128, 137–138; R. Dasmann, *Environmental Conservation* (New York, NY: Wiley, 1959); R.F. Dasmann, *A System for Defining and Classifying Natural Regions for Purposes of Conservation*. IUCN Occasional Paper No. 7 (Morges: IUCN, 1973), iii–47; R.F. Dasmann and A.S. Mossman, 'Commercial use of game animals on a Rhodesian ranch', *Wild Life* 3, no. 3 (1961): 7–14; R.F. Dasmann, *African Game Ranching* (Oxford: Pergamon and Macmillan, 1964); R.S. Dasmann, *A Different Kind of Country* (New York, NY: MacMillan, 1968); R.F. Dasmann, *Wildlife Biology* (New York, NY: John Wiley, 1964); S. Mossman and A. Mossman, *Wildlife Utilization and Game Ranching: Report on a Study of Recent Progress in this Field in Southern Africa* (Morges: IUCN, 1976). See also J. Carruthers, '"Wilding the farm or farming the wild": The evolution of scientific game ranching in South Africa from the 1960s to the present', *Transactions of the Royal Society of South Africa* 63, no. 2 (2008): 160–181 and D. D'A Nell, 'The development of wildlife utilisation in South Africa and Kenya, c.1950–1990' (PhD diss., University of Oxford, 2003).

[43]See L.M. Talbot, 'The concept of biomass in African wildlife research', *Mammalia* 28 (1964): 613–619; L.M. Talbot, W.J.A. Payne, H.P. Ledger, L.D. Verdcourt and M.H. Talbot, *The Meat Production Potential of Wild Animals in Africa: A Review of Biological Knowledge*. Technical Communication No.16, Commonwealth Bureau of Animal Breeding and Genetics, Edinburgh (Farnham Royal: Commonwealth Agricultural Bureau, 1965).

that not only could wildlife survive on cattle ranches alongside domestic stock, but that wildlife ranching could enormously augment Africa's protein supply and add economic value to rural enterprises through the more sustainable and productive use of pasture grasses.[44] It was because of the exponential growth of the human population after the Second World War and the concomitant pressure on food resources – especially protein – that the FAO had first become involved in this emerging agri-business.[45]

The scientific study of wild mammals as suitable candidates for commercial husbandry had an impact on wildlife management in South Africa's national parks in perhaps unexpected ways. Above all, it encouraged wildlife cropping in protected areas and it provided justification for the active and deliberate manipulation of animal numbers as an economic pursuit. On one hand, tourism and the revenues it generated could be safeguarded by reducing the 'unsightly' environmental damage caused by the growing numbers of certain species. On the other, there was also a limited demand for venison and an expanding market for live animals (South Africa being unusual in allowing the legal sale of wild animals). An income could be generated from the sale of such animals and animal products, and there were also savings to be had by using animal flesh as rations for NPB staff and neighbouring communities.[46]

The utilisation of wildlife along the lines proposed by Riney, Dasmann and Mossman was ultimately constrained by the difficulties of killing the animals and of transporting and marketing the meat both at home and abroad. However, their model did expand the scope of wildlife protection generally by encouraging private nature reserves and placing a monetary value on wildlife species.[47] Given the growing interest

[44]J.D. Ovington, ed., *The Better Use of the World's Fauna for Food* (London: Institute of Biology, 1963).

[45]FAO funding supported the Serengeti Research Project (1962–1966, then called the Serengeti Research Institute until 1977) with the intention of bolstering studies on food production through wildlife research. See A.R.E. Sinclair and M. Norton-Griffiths, eds, *Serengeti: Dynamics of an Ecosystem* (Chicago, IL: University of Chicago Press, 1979); A.R.E. Sinclair and P. Arcese, eds, *Serengeti II: Dynamics, Management and Conservation of an Ecosystem* (Chicago, IL: University of Chicago Press, 1995); A.R.E. Sinclair, C. Packer, S.A.R. Mduma and J.M. Fryxell, eds, *Serengeti III: Human Impacts on Ecosystem Dynamics* (Chicago, IL: University of Chicago Press, 2006); A.R.E. Sinclair, *Serengeti Story: Life and Science in the World's Greatest Wildlife Region* (Oxford: Oxford University Press, 2012).

[46]Carruthers, '"Wilding the farm or farming the wild"'.

[47]B.J. Huntley, 'Ecosystem conservation in southern Africa', in *Biogeography and Ecology of Southern Africa*, vol. 2, ed. M.J.A. Werger (The Hague: Junk, 1978): 1333–1384.

in wildlife ranching, in 1963 the second symposium of the Zoological Society of South Africa, held in Salisbury, Rhodesia (presently Harare, Zimbabwe) focused on African mammals. The most illuminating aspect of the meeting was the discussion on the 'scientific management and planned cropping to preserve the larger animals for their own sake and as an ecological asset, yielding as high a return financially as cattle ranching'.[48]

Key to the consideration of wildlife farming as a viable economic enterprise was the growing technical feasibility of more careful study of the biology, energy requirements and grazing habits of wild animals, and of interventions in their lives. Technical developments included aerial census surveys (in the KNP at first using helicopters in 1972 and 1975 and then fixed-wing aircraft);[49] marking and identifying with coloured or radio-controlled tags and collars; non-lethal immobilisation through such means as chemical darting; developing humane means of gathering tranquillised animals in pens ('bomas'); and relocating them safely.

The technology that enabled wildlife managers to move animals around to suit human needs grew quickly after the 1960s and, of course, after 50 years of strict protection, the numbers of edible and valuable wild species in national parks had greatly increased. Much of the knowledge and practice relating to translocation was applied technology rather than creative scientific theory, and the NPB made good use of it. The KNP in particular afforded almost unlimited opportunities for experimentation with a very large variety of animals. Apparently also, pharmaceutical companies were keen to use the KNP as a testing ground for their new products, and they were given an enthusiastic reception.[50] The new techniques made an enormous difference to the management possibilities in almost all South Africa's protected areas and also on private land. As Joubert and Kloppers recorded for the KNP, in 1962 white rhinoceros were imported from Natal's game reserves. Then, red duiker, mountain reedbuck and grey rhebuck and even Lichtenstein's hartebeest were reintroduced in the 1980s. The idea was to re-establish through relocation all the large mammals known to have existed in the KNP

---

[48] *Zoologica Africana* 1 (1965).

[49] U. de V. Pienaar, P.W. van Wyk and N. Fairall, 'An aerial census of elephant and buffalo in the Kruger National Park and the implications thereof on intended management schemes', *Koedoe* 9 (1966): 40–108.

[50] S.C.J. Joubert, *The Kruger National Park: A History*, vol. 2 (Johannesburg: High Branching, 2012): 196–197.

region in the past.[51] Chemical darting also meant that animals could be targeted for inoculations, a practice first used to vaccinate roan antelope against anthrax in 1971.[52] With these techniques, the manipulation of nature reached new heights.

For instance, in June 1965 the KNP management reported to the NPB meeting on the aerial census of elephant done the previous year. The argument was made that definite, not imprecise, numbers of species were required, as was the case in East Africa, and that more aircraft and funding for chemicals and darting equipment were needed. Estimating from various recorded observations showed that elephant numbers had grown from 10 in 1905 to 100 in 1925, 250 by 1936, 450 by 1946, and 1000 by 1957. In 1967 a helicopter census team confirmed a number of 6586.[53] Importantly, aerial censuses had provided details of how many adult males and females and calves inhabited the KNP. These figures had been extremely helpful in determining the age structure of elephant herds and in calculating the future medium-term population. The KNP was also able to compare its elephant numbers with those in Tsavo National Park in Kenya and in Uganda. Similar calculations were being made for the buffalo population.[54]

Because of the sophisticated technology and its experimental nature, marking and translocating large mammals became a collaborative endeavour. The cutting-edge work in the field was being done in East Africa under the leadership of veterinary physiologist A.M. (Toni) Harthoorn, then recognised as one of the great innovators in the field of chemical darting and its associated technology. Based in East Africa, Harthoorn

---

[51]U. de V. Pienaar, 'The recolonisation history of the squarelipped (white) rhinoceros *Ceratotherium simum simum* (Burchell) in the Kruger National Park (October 1961–November 1969)', *Koedoe* 13 (1970): 157–170; G. de Graaff and B.L. Penzhorn, 'The reintroduction of springbok *Antidorcas marsupialis* into South African national parks', *Koedoe* 19 (1976): 75–82; B.L. Penzhorn, 'An old reference to "hartebeest" in the Transvaal lowveld', *Koedoe* 28 (1985): 69–71.

[52]Joubert, *Kruger National Park*, vol. 2, 197.

[53]I.J.Whyte, R. van Aarde and S.L. Pimm,'Kruger's elephant population: Its size and consequences for ecosystem heterogeneity', in *The Kruger Experience: Ecology and Management of Savanna Heterogeneity*, eds J.T. du Toit, K.H. Rogers and H.C. Biggs (Washington, DC: Island Press, 2003), 332–348, table of population estimates, 336.

[54]Minutes of a meeting of the NPB, 22 June 1965, Annexure (68 pages) on aerial census report by Pienaar, van Wyk and Fairall, SANParks archives, Groenkloof, Pretoria; see also U. de V. Pienaar, 'A lasting method for the marking and identification of elephant', *Koedoe* 13 (1970): 123–126.

made his expertise widely available and was extremely helpful to numerous conservation authorities in Africa. In South Africa, Harthoorn's initial cooperation was not with the NPB but with Ian Player of the Natal Parks Board (through Jack Vincent, head of that organisation, who had met Harthoorn at the IUCN meeting in Warsaw in 1960). This collaboration was focused on relocating some of the growing numbers of white rhinoceros to various points around the subcontinent.[55] This dispersal of rhinoceros ensured the survival of the species, at least for a number of decades thereafter, and its wider dissemination. So enthusiastic was the Natal Parks Board to distribute excess white rhinoceros around South Africa that it offered four to the Bontebok National Park, which regretfully refused them on the grounds that the species had never occurred in that locality.[56]

In an article published in *Oryx* in 1967 and later in *The White Rhino Saga* (1972), Player explained how Harthoorn had been invited to Natal to experiment with the latest cocktails of drugs. The first to be used was gallamine triothiodide, which was tested on ten white rhinoceros but quickly discontinued because of their low tolerance for it. In June 1961 a combination of Themalon (diethylthiambutene hydrochloride) and Sernyl (1-1-phenylcyclohexyl) piperidine (monohydrochloride) used on twelve animals was more successful, as all of them recovered. However, a very large dose was required, the animals thus suffering from serious dart wounds and also exhibiting uncontrollable behaviour after the administration of the antidote.[57] Sernyl was therefore discontinued for white rhinoceros. First synthesised in 1960, the new and powerful quick-acting drug named M99 (etorphine) appeared on the commercial market in 1963. Produced by Reckitt (along with its antidote Lethidrone – now replaced by the even faster-acting diprenorphine/Revivon/M5050), it was adopted for use in Natal.[58]

[55]I. Player, *The White Rhino Saga* (Glasgow: Collins, 1972), 53. Harthoorn grew up in England and studied veterinary science in London. After the Second World War he went to East Africa and began to experiment with various drugs for tranquillising wild mammals. Married to Sue Hart, a South African veterinarian, the couple became famous on film and television. In 1963 Harthoorn moved to South Africa where he continued his work principally in Natal and in Southern Rhodesia.

[56]Minutes of a meeting of the NPB, 28 November 1963, SANParks archives, Groenkloof, Pretoria.

[57]See A. Hall-Martin and B.L. Penzhorn, 'Behaviour and recruitment of translocated black rhinoceros, *Diceros bicornis*', *Koedoe* 20 (1977): 147–162.

[58]It was also used in the KNP; see U. de V. Pienaar, J.W. van Niekerk, E. Young, P. van Wyk and N. Fairall, 'The use of oripavine hydrochloride (M-99) in the drug immobilization

Figure 8.4. Operation rhino, a photograph of the first transported white rhino to settle in the Kruger National Park, having been darted and tranquillised by Ian Player, Chief Game Warden of Natal.
From R.J. Labuschagne, *The Kruger Park and Other National Parks* (n.d.), p. 78. Courtesy of SANParks.

Rangers there also developed improved methods of capture. The first experiment in translocation involved drugging an animal with the Themalon drug combination and transporting it to Mkuzi game reserve, but it died of blood poisoning after cutting its foot badly as it was being released. Problems were not restricted to the veterinary procedures. There were immense challenges in understanding territorial behaviour, because males were inclined to kill one another when a new dominant male arrived from elsewhere.[59] With experience, however, knowledge was augmented and shared and soon calves were being born to translocated rhinoceros. Between June 1962 and September 1964, 92 white rhinoceros were transported to the KNP, a distance of about 500 km, and even further afield to Mozambique and Rhodesia. All the relocated animals were marked so they could be identified and studied further.[60]

---

and marking of wild African elephant (*Loxodonta africana* Blumenbach) in the Kruger National Park', *Koedoe* 9 (1966): 108–124.

[59] See, for example, J. Carruthers, 'Designing a wilderness for wildlife: The case of the Pilanesberg National Park, South Africa', in *Designing Wildlife Habitats*, ed. J. Beardsley, (Washington, DC: Dumbarton Oaks Research Library and Collection, 2013), 107–130.

[60] I. Player, 'Translocation of white rhinoceros in South Africa', *Oryx* 9, no. 2 (1967): 137–150; Player, *White Rhino Saga*.

The NPB was extremely keen to participate in the darting and translocating initiatives. Initially, this had less to do with KNP than with the urgent need to move bontebok to the new site of Bontebok National Park, since by the end of 1959 the animals in the old park were not thriving. There was also a plan to populate the Addo with a greater variety of mammals, particularly rhinoceros and hippopotamus. A key player in this programme was P.J. Barnard, biologist for the Cape national parks. His first step was to contact game wardens in Kenya, Tanganyika, Uganda and Northern and Southern Rhodesia to establish the grazing and other habitats of the target species.[61]

Further discussion of methods of capturing wild animals occurred at a conference at NPB headquarters on 15 February 1960. It was attended by key NPB officials, Fritz Eloff and others with an interest in the subject. Barnard's comprehensive report on the various methods available at the time formed the basis of the discussion and his knowledge guided his colleagues in other national parks on the issue. Later in the year, the conference report was presented to the board, which learned that while no progress had been made with the Addo introductions, communication had been established with Harthoorn. More positively, it also learned that Barnard, with the help of the Cape Nature Conservation Department, had successfully removed 61 bontebok to the new park.[62] Barnard's contribution did not end there: he was also knowledgeable about wildlife migrations and he presented a report to the board in November 1960 on migration from and into the KGNP and, drawing on experience in the USA, made suggestions about how best to mark animals in order to track their movements.[63]

In subsequent years, many successful translocations took place involving black rhinoceros,[64] cheetah, red duiker, oribi, Livingstone's suni, giraffe,

[61]Minutes of a meeting of the NPB, 7 December 1959, SANParks archives, Groenkloof, Pretoria; P.J. Barnard and K. van der Walt, 'Translocation of the bontebok (*Damaliscus pygargus*) from Bredasdorp to Swellendam', *Koedoe* 4 (1961): 105–109.

[62]Minutes of meetings of the NPB, 7 December 1959; 23 March 1960, Annexure C; 4 June 1960; 19 September 1960 (Barnard's report to the September meeting is extremely long and detailed), SANParks archives, Groenkloof, Pretoria.

[63]Minutes of a meeting of the NPB, 24 November 1960. See also Minutes of meetings of the NPB, 22 September 1964 and 1 September 1972, SANParks archives, Groenkloof, Pretoria. See also P.J. Barnard, 'The phenomenon of game migration in the Kalahari Gemsbok National Park, with a discussion of various marking methods to facilitate a study of the routes followed', *Koedoe* 4 (1961): 178–194.

[64]V. de Vos, 'The changing face of research in national parks', *Custos* 15, no. 6 (1986): 35–45.

as well as other species.[65] A considerable number of translocations were within the KNP, either to spread animals more widely or to enable them to use suitable habitats in parts of the park to which they would not normally migrate.[66] Because of the drugs and other procedures involved in darting, translocation and marking, associations with the veterinary community were strengthened. There were also a number of wildlife diseases rampant at this time, anthrax being the most important. In 1961 J.W. van Niekerk, a full-time state veterinarian (i.e. not in the employ of the NPB) was stationed at Skukuza to ensure that diseases within the KNP did not spread to domestic stock beyond its boundaries. He collaborated with others in the KNP on the drug issue and published on the topic in *Koedoe*. In 1974, Valerius (Vossie) de Vos, one of the government veterinarians stationed at Skukuza, was appointed NPB veterinary ecologist.

Many were the publications on chemicals and drugs that sedated wild animals and allowed them to be moved, but also, as explained below, to be killed. *Koedoe* was replete with such articles. The first, 'Adaptations of the immobilizing technique to the capture, marking and translocation of game animals in the Kruger National Park', co-authored by van Niekerk and Pienaar, appeared in 1962. In the 1963 issue of *Koedoe*, the two collaborated on a description of the R05-2807/B-5F tranquilliser produced by Roche. This article appeared alongside two others in similar vein, one by the same two authors on the various drugs then available and the other by Neil Fairall on benzodioxane hydrochloride. Between 1960 and 1990, *Koedoe* published nearly 20 articles on marking and darting and the drugs applicable to many species. Indeed, so wide was the number and variety of drugs that multiple experiments were possible.[67]

---

[65]See, for example, A.J. Hall-Martin and G. de Graaff, 'A note on the feasibility of introducing giraffe to the Kalahari Gemsbok National park', *Koedoe* 21 (1978): 191–193.

[66]Minutes of meetings of the NPB, 7 December 1959 and September 1964, SANParks archives, Groenkloof, Pretoria; de Vos, 'The changing face of research in national parks'; Joubert, *Kruger National Park*, vol. 2, 199.

[67]See, among many others, for example, J.W. van Niekerk and U. de V. Pienaar, 'Adaptations of the immobilizing technique to the capture, marking and translocation of game animals in the Kruger National Park', *Koedoe* 5 (1962): 137–143; J.W. van Niekerk and U. de V. Pienaar, 'The capture and translocation of three species of wild ungulates in the Eastern Transvaal with special reference to R05-2807/B 5F (Roche) as a tranquilliser in game animals', *Koedoe* 6 (1963): 83–90; J.W. van Niekerk, U. de V. Pienaar and N. Fairall, 'A preliminary note on the use of Quiloflex (Benzodioxane Hydro-chloride) in the immobilization of game', *Koedoe* 6 (1963): 109–114; J.W. van Niekerk and U. de V. Pienaar, 'A report on some immobilizing drugs used in the capture of wild animals in

One of the many effects of the easy relocation of wild animals was that new game reserves and national parks could be established and older protected areas stocked with any number of new species. Farmland might be reclaimed for wildlife and the economic benefits of protected areas shared in parts of the country in need of them. One of the most successful initiatives of this sort was the establishment in the 1970s of the Pilanesberg National Park. From modest beginnings, it has become an important case study in successful conservation at a number of levels.[68]

Computers entered the lives of wildlife scientists and managers after the 1960s. They brought the potential to revolutionise many aspects of scientific research as well as management techniques. In particular, in

---

the Kruger National Park', *Koedoe* 6 (1963): 126–133; U. de V. Pienaar, J.W. van Niekerk, E. Young, P. van Wyk and N. Fairall, 'The use of oripavine hydrochloride (M-99) in the drug immobilization and marking of wild African elephant (*Loxodonta africana* Blumenbach) in the Kruger National Park', *Koedoe* 9 (1966): 108–124; U. de V. Pienaar, 'The use of drugs in the management and control of large carnivorous animals', *Koedoe* 12 (1969): 177–183; E. Young, 'A useful marking method for free living animals', *Koedoe* 14 (1971): 131–136; G.F. Barkhuizen, 'Notes on the use of Azaperone and Fentanyl in the immobilization of the bontebok (*Damaliscus dorcas dorcas*) in the Bontebok National Park', *Koedoe* 15 (1972): 101–105; E. Young, 'Notes on the chemical immobilisation and restraint of the Addo elephant (*Loxodonta africana*)', *Koedoe* 15 (1972): 97–99; E. Young and B.L. Penzhorn, 'The reactions of the Cape mountain zebra (*Equus zebra zebra*) to certain chemical immobilisation drugs', *Koedoe* 15 (1972): 95–96; G.L. van Rooyen and P.J. de Beer, 'A retractable barb needle for drug darts', *Koedoe* 16 (1973): 155–158; G.L. Smuts, 'Ketamine hydrochloride – A useful drug for the field immobilization of the spotted hyaena *Crocuta crocuta*', *Koedoe* 16 (1973): 175–180; G.L. Smuts, 'Xylazine hydrochloride (Rompun) and the new retractable-barbed dart ("drop-out dart") for the capture of some nervous and aggressive antelope species', *Koedoe* 16 (1973): 159–173; V. de Vos, 'A new potent analgesic for chemical immobilization of gemsbok *Oryx gazella gazella*', *Koedoe* 21 (1978): 173–180; V. de Vos, 'Do it yourself remote chemical immobilization equiment', *Koedoe* 22 (1979): 177–186; H. Hattingh, V. de Vos, M.F. Ganhao and N.I. Pitts, 'Physiological responses of the buffalo *Syncerus caffer* culled with Succinyldicholine and Hexamethonium', *Koedoe* 31 (1988): 91–97; R.R. Henwood, 'Black rhinoceros *Diceros bicornis* capture, transportation and boma management by the Natal Parks Board', *Koedoe* 32, no. 2 (1989): 43–47.

[68]Among the protected areas made possible because of the streamlined and successful process of relocation were the Pilanesberg National Park and Madikwe Game Reserves, Marakele National Park and many other state and private reserves. See, for one example from this period, Carruthers, 'Designing a wilderness for wildlife'. An example that caught the public imagination at this time was 'Operation Noah', the successful translocation of many wild animals from the site of Kariba Dam in Rhodesia. See C. Lagus, *Operation Noah* (London: Fauna Preservation Society with William Kimber, 1959) and E. Robins and R. Legge, *Animal Dunkirk* (London: Herbert Jenkins, 1959).

the KNP they were first used to calculate population simulation models derived from census data collected in the field.[69] Population dynamics and numbers had intrigued naturalists for decades, including Stevenson-Hamilton, and were critically important to sport-hunters. Computing came within the purview of the NPB in the early 1970s when Robinson returned from his studies in Seattle. He was introduced there to the modelling techniques used by scientists to forecast the number of fish shoals along the North American West Coast. In the process he had become well acquainted with computer techniques and aware of the potential of computerisation for research and management.[70] Robinson persuaded the NPB of the value of quantitative modelling and in 1974 he was offered the post of NPB quantitative biologist provided he moved from Tsitsikamma to Skukuza.[71] Naturally, as a marine specialist, he was reluctant to do so.[72] Others therefore took the lead, including G.L. (Butch) Smuts, a KNP scientist who had studied the zebra population and then predator relationships more generally (especially lion), and Peter Retief, a computer expert recruited by Anthony Starfield, who later became head of Southern Parks. Retief was the first to produce computerised maps (the first GIS) of KNP using data collected over many years but never used. By then, there were computer models for a number of animal populations and experiments were being done to encompass ecosystem modelling, a more complex procedure. In these early computer initiatives, KNP benefited considerably from the assistance of Anthony Starfield, a mathematician at the University of the Witwatersrand and one of South Africa's leading experts in computer modelling.[73] Modelling

[69]Huntley, 'Ecosystem conservation in southern Africa'.

[70]Minutes of a meeting of the NPB, 21 and 22 October 1973, SANParks archives, Groenkloof, Pretoria.

[71]Minutes of a meeting of the NPB, 28 February 1974, SANParks archives, Groenkloof, Pretoria. Robinson had submitted a proposal for acquiring a computer and for appointing a scientific data coordinator. In the ensuing discussion, the board noted that they had already recognised the need for a quantitative biologist and appreciated that they already had such an employee in the person of Robinson himself.

[72]Joubert, *Kruger National Park*, vol. 2, 27. G.A. Robinson. Interview with the author. Johannesburg, 7 July 2012.

[73]NPB, *Research Report 1987/1988* (Pretoria: NPB, n.d.); NPB, *35th Annual Report for the year 1978–1979*. See also A.M. Starfield, G.L. Smuts and J.D. Shiell, 'A simple wildebeest population model and its application', *South African Journal of Wildlife Research* 6 (1975), 95–98; A.M. Starfield and A.L. Bleloch, *Building Models for Conservation and Wildlife Management* (Edina, MN: Burgess Press, 1991); A.M. Starfield and A.L. Bleloch, 'Expert systems: An approach to problems in ecological management that are difficult

was at the forefront of the new thinking in NPB and in 1978 a work-shop on modelling the Auob River and its vegetation was held in the KGNP. Participants included Retief, Ian Noble from the Australian National University and Starfield, who provided the statistical expertise (after Starfield left South Africa in 1979, Frederick Lombard, professor of statistics at the University of South Africa, stepped in to assist Retief).[74]

By the 1960s there were many theories about population dynamics, but there was little firm evidence owing to the complexity of the subject and the many species to be dealt with. Aspects such as intraspecific competition (regulation of numbers) and its interspecific counterpart (niche parti-tioning) further complicated the picture, as did the study of mutualism/symbiosis and/or commensalism/facilitation.[75] At the time, these issues were not part of the formal training of South Africa's zoologists, although they were important to managing animals in the wild. Warden Pienaar held that species requiring particular management – because they were vulnerable or had a greater influence on habitats – should be studied first, and that detailed species studies, and even individual studies, should be conducted before community dynamics were explored.[76]

Starfield worked in the KNP for a number of years, making use of the data sets already collected. He shared Robinson's opinion that the isolation of South Africa's scientists, particularly those in the NPB, had deprived them of contact with international peers and hence with familiarity with the developments in technology and scientific philosophy. Modelling was being done by, for example, D.A. Jameson at Fort Collins in the USA and there was some ecosystem modelling in Australia. Starfield firmly believed, and apparently said as much to the KNP management, that modelling should be simple and should be to assist decision-making – indeed it *was*

---

to quantify', *International Journal of Environmental Management* 16 (1983): 261–268; A.M. Starfield, 'A pragmatic approach to modeling for wildlife management', *Journal of Wildlife Management* 61 (1997): 261–270; K. Ralls and A.M. Starfield, 'Choosing a management strategy: Two structured decision-making methods for evaluating the predictions of stochastic simulation models', *Conservation Biology* 9 (1995): 175–181.

[74]See A.M. Starfield, S.M. Shapiro, P.R. Furness, *et al.*, 'A developing computer model of the Auob River ecosystem, Kalahari Gemsbok National Park', in *Ecological Studies. Vol. 42. Ecology of Tropical Savannas*, eds B.J. Huntley and B.H. Walker (Berlin: Springer Verlag, 1982), 610–625.

[75]Sinclair, *Serengeti Story*, 21, 78, 94.

[76]U. de V. Pienaar, 'Research objectives in South African national parks', in 'Proceedings of a symposium on the state of nature conservation in southern Africa, Kruger National Park, 1976', eds G. de Graaff and P.T. van der Walt, supplement, *Koedoe* (1977): 38–48.

structured decision-making because the use of evidence from data allowed for comparison of the effects of different decisions. These suggestions came at a time when general decision-making in the NPB was under scrutiny, and when consideration was being given by the management committee to the introduction of a system of management by objectives with appropriate training that was 'results'-orientated. However, as Joubert explains, although some objectives were adopted, the system itself was not a success.[77]

Meanwhile, Starfield and one of his students, Julian Shiell, worked with Smuts to build a model to unlock the answer to the problem of the dramatic growth and collapse of wildebeest herds.[78] This became the first predator–prey model developed in the KNP.[79] Although KNP managers thought that fencing the western boundary of the park lay behind the problem, the model, developed over a mere fortnight, demonstrated that culling 'excess' wildebeest might have created a predation pit, thus leading to the diminution of the species.[80] Smuts was also able to use modelling to answer many questions about lion cub synchronisation and pack size, while Joubert made use of the technique for his research on roan antelope. Understanding of the relationship between predator and prey that had so intrigued Stevenson-Hamilton had now entered a new era. The modelling techniques developed by Starfield, Owen-Smith, Retief, Smuts and Joubert resulted in a workshop at the University of the Witwatersrand, which included short modelling courses for KNP rangers. Through this initiative, many people in the NPB were inducted into the field of experimental ecology and hence into modern conservation biology.

However, not all NPB zoologists, veterinarians and botanists favoured the use of computers and modelling. Some felt that biology was too complicated to be modelled, others preferred their traditional roles as observers, naturalists and data collectors. They were also influenced by the authoritarian and hierarchical nature of decision-making in the NPB. Starfield has argued that the flexibility allowed wildlife managers working

[77]Joubert, *Kruger National Park*, vol. 2, 8.

[78]Starfield, Smuts and Shiell, 'A simple wildebeest population model'.

[79]G.L. Smuts, *Lion* (Johannesburg: Macmillan, 1982), 59. Smuts joined the NPB in 1969, obtained his PhD from the University of Pretoria, and left in 1978 to become Chief Professional Officer of the Natal Parks Board.

[80]See I.J. Whyte and S.C.J. Joubert, 'Blue wildebeest population trends in the Kruger National Park and the effects of fencing', *South African Journal of Wildlife Research* 18, no. 3 (1988): 78–87.

in conservation agencies outside the NPB, particularly those trained in Natal or outside the University of Pretoria,[81] led to research hypotheses that accelerated and facilitated modelling at this time.[82] As already mentioned, management and decision-making was a thorny topic for the NPB in the late 1970s and early 1980s. When the proceedings of a symposium on the Kalahari ecosystem were published as a supplement to *Koedoe* in 1984, the NPB's lack of clearly defined goals and a programme to achieve them were singled out, as was the lack of coordination between the work of in-house scientists and visiting experts. Moreover, it was noted, modelling was lacking, and even energy flows were not being undertaken.[83]

Controlling Large Mammal Populations

As has been frequently noted above, the NPB's primary focus was the large mammals – the megafauna – in South Africa's national parks. Not only were these most easily visible to tourists from their cars, but large, dangerous and charismatic, especially African mammals, elicit fascination, excitement and dread in many human beings. Tales of humans in danger from predators abound in the world's folklore, as do tales of hunting large animals for subsistence, to safeguard humans and domestic stock and for economic gain, such as hunting elephants for ivory. Species were divided in many cultures into good (game) and evil (vermin) depending on their usefulness to humans. Indubitably, large animals simply thrill the majority of humans more than smaller creatures and garner more public interest and support. It is therefore hardly surprising that most of the work undertaken by the NPB was on large mammals and was conducted in the KNP and KGNP, where such species abounded, although the Addo elephants and the bontebok and mountain zebra in other national parks were also closely studied. Field guides and other information on large mammals appeared regularly between 1960 and 1990, the majority of which harked back to the naturalist writing of the nineteenth and early twentieth centuries.[84]

---

[81] For example, Jeremy Anderson, Peter Goodman and Ricky Tayler.

[82] Tony Starfield. Interview with the author. Johannesburg, 19 April 2012.

[83] G. de Graaff and D.J. van Rensburg, eds, 'Proceedings of a symposium on the Kalahari ecosystem, Pretoria 11–12 October 1983', supplement, *Koedoe* (1984).

[84] For the national parks, see R.J. Labuschagne and N.J. van der Merwe, *Soogdiere van die Krugerwildtuin en ander Nasionale Parke/Mammals of the Kruger and other National Parks*

Predictably, *Koedoe* carried numerous observations, notes and detailed studies of large mammals. Between 1958 and 2006, more than one-third of the articles (225 of 706) published in the journal dealt with individual mammal species. While a community approach is discernible in vegetation studies published in the journal, fauna were studied principally at a species level. Nearly 70% of the faunal articles in *Koedoe* were descriptive and much of this published material was linked to postgraduate study in wildlife management in the University of Pretoria's department of zoology or Mammal Research Institute.[85] The primacy of the University of Pretoria in this regard was not only that it, like the NPB, was a predominantly Afrikaans institution (although DScs could be in English), making for easy staff relationships and shared philosophies between the two bodies, but it was also the only South African university at the time that, according to Penzhorn, took an active interest in the zoology of indigenous fauna and wildlife management in the field.[86] Thus, for example, Professors Fritz Eloff and Bothma spent a great deal of time in the KGNP and published many papers in *Koedoe* as well as in international journals. They were also of great assistance to the numerous game rangers who steadily improved their knowledge and understanding through observation and study of species that interested them to the point where they obtained higher degrees.[87]

It also should be remembered that the field of scientific wildlife management was still new. Consequently, the NPB was simply unable to tap into a well of already-trained experts: essentially, there were no South African wildlife managers with higher academic training in the field in the 1960s. (This was why George Petrides, professor at Michigan State University, led the first postgraduate course in wildlife management at the University of Pretoria.) Most learnt on the job and had an enthusiasm for and love of the veld and the outdoors: a research strategy was unheard of. Apart from Stevenson-Hamilton in an earlier period, the best example of such a man was Pienaar, a histologist by training, a game ranger

(Pretoria: NPB, n.d.); U. de V. Pienaar, S.C.J. Joubert, A. Hall-Martin, G. de Graaff and I.L. Rautenbach, *Field Guide to the Mammals of the Kruger National Park* (Cape Town: Struik, 1987).

[85] S. Webb, 'A bibliometric survey of the *Koedoe* journal publications from 1958–2006', unpublished report, SANParks archives, Groenkloof, Pretoria.

[86] Banie Penzhorn. Interview with the author. Pretoria, 19 June 2015.

[87] See G. de Graaff, 'Prof. Dr. F.C. Eloff: An appreciation', in 'Proceedings of a symposium on the Kalahari ecosystem 1983', eds G. de Graaff and D.J. van Rensburg, supplement, *Koedoe* (1984): 1–9. For a list of Eloff's publications, see 7–9.

and only later an acclaimed wildlife manager. He was also the author of the first comprehensive article on the large mammals of the KNP, which appeared in *Koedoe* in 1963. Similar in vein to Stevenson-Hamilton's *Wild Life in South Africa* (1947), it provides lengthy descriptions of the geography and vegetation of the KNP and uses historical material to evidence where within this area certain species had been observed. He also considered their current status. A systematic list of 35 large mammals followed, each with a short introductory paragraph and listing feeding habits, breeding and latest estimation of numbers.[88] In 1969, he produced another, even more substantial article, this time on predator–prey relationships among the park's large mammals. Based on a wide literature, together with details garnered from Stevenson-Hamilton's careful notes and the observations and records of game rangers over the years, this article – with its 30 tables – provides a fascinating and almost exhaustive set of data about which animals prey on others, and to what extent.[89]

In time, between 1960 and 1990 numerous other specialists contributed detailed information about the animals they studied and thus built up a valuable body of information relating to South Africa's national parks. This can be accessed through *Koedoe*, but also in their postgraduate theses, and – for some, not many – their publications in other, including international journals. Among this latter group, M.G.L. (Gus) Mills is particularly deserving of mention. A predator and hyena specialist, his initial degree was from the University of Cape Town. He first worked in the KGNP on hyena (obtaining a doctorate on their behavioural ecology under Bothma at Pretoria) and his work on the species has subsequently been featured in *Nature*.[90] Unlike many other NPB scientists, Mills has never sought a senior managerial position within the parks organisation.

---

[88]U. de V. Pienaar, 'The large mammals of the Kruger National Park – Their distribution and present-day status', *Koedoe* 6 (1963): 1–37.

[89]U. de V. Pienaar, 'Predator–prey relationships amongst the larger mammals of the Kruger National Park', *Koedoe* 12 (1969): 108–176.

[90]The minutes of a meeting of the NPB on 1 September 1972 record Mills working in KGNP on brown hyenas as Bothma's student. SANParks archives, Groenkloof, Pretoria. Much of Mills' research was funded from outside sources, including the South African Nature Foundation, the Wild Life Society of Southern Africa, Coca-Cola and the Endangered Wildlife Trust. See M.G.L. Mills, P. Wolff, E.A.N. le Riche and I.L. Meyer, 'Some population characteristics of the lion *Panthera leo* in the Kalahari Gemsbok National Park', *Koedoe* 21 (1978): 163–171; M.G.L. Mills and M.E.J. Mills, 'The diet of the brown hyaena *Hyaena brunnea* in the southern Kalahari', *Koedoe* 21 (1978): 125–149; M.G.L. Mills, 'The socio-ecology and social behaviour of the brown hyena

One scientist who did rise through the ranks was Anthony Hall-Martin. He studied at the University of Natal, focusing particularly on giraffe (the topic of his PhD from the University of Pretoria) before settling on elephants.[91] Hall-Martin began his career with the NPB as the replacement researcher for Banie Penzhorn in 1976. He then succeeded Butch Smuts as senior research officer in 1979, and concentrated on studying the fast-growing elephant population. A decade later he was promoted to director of special services, with responsibility for the export of wildlife to other countries in Africa and liaison with external nature conservation authorities.[92] Another was Peter Novellie, whose Pretoria DSc was on kudu *Tragelaphus strepsiceros* (1986). He completed his career as coordinator of conservation services in head office.[93] Then there was Salomon Joubert, who began his career as a game ranger in the KNP on completion of his BSc and subsequently obtained his DSc from Pretoria in 1976 for work on roan antelope *Hippotragus equinus equinus*. When he finally retired in 1994, he had held the position of KNP warden since 1987.[94]

Hyena brunnae Thunberg 1820 in the southern Kalahari' (DSc diss., University of Pretoria 1981); M.G.L. Mills, 'Related spotted hyaenas forage together but no not cooperate in rearing young', *Nature* 316 (1985): 61–62; M.L. Gorman, M.G.L. Mills, J.P. Raath and J.R. Speakman, 'High hunting costs make African wild dogs vulnerable to kleptoparasitism by hyaenas', *Nature* 391, no. 29 (1998): 479–480.

[91] A.J. Hall-Martin, 'Food selection by Transvaal Lowveld giraffe as determined by analysis of stomach contents', *Journal of the Southern African Wildlife Management Association* 4 (1974): 191–202; A.J. Hall-Martin and H. Ruther, 'Application of stereo photogrammetric techniques for measuring African elephants', *Koedoe* 22 (1979): 187–198; A.J. Hall-Martin, 'A note on the feeding habits, ectoparasites and measurements of the Black-backed jackal *Canis mesomelas* from Addo Elephant National Park', *Koedoe* 23 (1980): 157–162; A.J. Hall-Martin and L.A. van der Walt, 'Plasma testosterone levels in relation to musth in the male African Elephant', *Koedoe* 27 (1984): 151–153.

[92] These countries included Swaziland in 1987 (with funding from the SANF) to which a herd of elephants was exported and later (1994) lion; Malawi, which donated Lichtenstein's hartebeest *Sigmoceros lichtensteinii* to the KNP in 1986 and to which black rhinoceros were exported; as well as relationships, including traineeship programmes, in subsequent years between conservation authorities in Tanzania, Namibia, Côte d'Ivoire and Togo.

[93] P.A. Novellie, 'Feeding ecology of the kudu *Tragelaphus strepsiceros* (Pallas) in the Kruger National Park' (DSc diss., University of Pretoria, 1983); P.A. Novellie, 'Interrelationships between fire, grazing and grass cover at the Bontebok National Park', *Koedoe* 30 (1987): 1–17.

[94] S.C.J. Joubert, 'A study of the social behaviour of the roan antelope, *Hippotragus equinus equinus* (Desmarest, 1804), in the Kruger National Park' (MSc diss., University of

Among other NPB researchers who produced a large body of work that added to the knowledge of many species there is Banie Penzhorn himself, who completed innovative research on the Cape Mountain Zebra in the Mountain Zebra National Park,[95] G.L. Smuts on Burchell's Zebra *Equus burchelli antiquorum* and on lion[96] and Bruce Bryden on lion.[97] Outside researchers included Neil Fairall on the sex physiology of impala *Aepyceros melampus*[98] and Michael Cohen on the biology and behaviour of steenbok *Raphicerus campestris* in the KNP.[99] The archives of the KNP are replete with studies written by zoologists working there between 1960 and 1990, and towards the end of the period more adventurous and analytical studies began to appear. One such was Johan du Toit's University of the Witwatersrand PhD (1988) on patterns of resource use

---

Pretoria, 1970); S.C.J. Joubert, 'The population ecology of the roan antelope *Hippotragus equinus* (Damarest) in the Kruger National Park' (DSc diss., University of Pretoria, 1976); S.C.J. Joubert and P.J.L. Bronkhorst, 'Some aspects of the history and population ecology of the tsessebe *Damaliscus lunatus lunatus* in the Kruger National Park', *Koedoe* 20 (1977): 125–146.

[95] B.L. Penzhorn, 'Behaviour and population ecology of the Cape Mountain Zebra *Equus zebra zebra* Linn.1758 in the Mountain Zebra National Park' (DSc diss., University of Pretoria, 1975); B.L. Penzhorn, 'A note on the sex ratio of steenbok *Raphicerus campestris* in the Kalahari Gemsbok National Park', *Koedoe* 14 (1971): 61–64; B.L. Penzhorn, 'Social organisation of the Cape Mountain Zebra, *Equus zebra zebra* in the Mountain Zebra National Park', *Koedoe* 22 (1979): 115–156; B.L. Penzhorn, 'Soil eating by Cape Mountain Zebra, *Equus zebra zebra* in the Mountain Zebra National Park'; 'Age determination of Cape Mountain Zebra, *Equus zebra zebra* in the Mountain Zebra National Park'; and 'Home range sizes of Cape Mountain Zebras *Equus zebra zebra* in the Mountain Zebra National Park', all in *Koedoe* 25 (1981): 83–108.

[96] G.L. Smuts, 'Seasonal movements, migration and age determination of Burchell's Zebra (*Equus burchelli antiquorum*, H. Smith 1841) in the Kruger National Park' (MSc diss., University of Pretoria, 1972); G.L. Smuts, 'Growth, reproduction and population chracteristics of Burchell's Zebra (*Equus burchelli antiquorum*, H. Smith 1841) in the Kruger National Park' (DSc diss., University of Pretoria, 1974); G.L. Smuts, 'Population characteristics and recent history of lions in two parts of the Kruger National Park', *Koedoe* 18 (1975): 139–146; G.L. Smuts, *Lion* (Johannesburg: Macmillan, 1982); G.L. Smuts and I.J. Whyte, 'Relationships between reproduction and environment in the hippopotamus *Hippopotamus amphibius* in the Kruger National Park', *Koedoe* 24 (1981): 169–185.

[97] B. Bryden, 'The biology of the African lion (*Panthera leo*, Linn. 1758) in the Kruger National Park' (MSc diss., University of Pretoria, 1976).

[98] N. Fairall, 'Sex physiology of the impala (*Aepyceros melampus* Licht.)' (DSc diss., University of Pretoria, 1971).

[99] M. Cohen, 'Aspects of the biology and behaviour of the steenbok *Raphicerus campestris* (Thunberg 1811) in the Kruger National Park' (DSc diss., University of Pretoria, 1987).

within the browsing ruminant guild in the central KNP.[100] A scientist with a long-standing involvement with the NPB is Norman Owen-Smith, a widely acclaimed international researcher with an interest in behavioural ecology who studied chemistry at Natal and later, ecology at the University of Wisconsin, Madison before joining the University of the Witwatersrand.[101] Other prominent scientists working in the KNP in particular include the team of P.T. van der Walt, G. de Graaff and L.J. van Zyl,[102] H. Jungius of the University of Kiel[103] and Lynn Irby of Texas A&M.[104]

For obvious reasons, scientists are reluctant to criticise their peers in print or to make comparative evaluations of their work in public. More often, there are whispers in corridors over inadequate scientific rigour, or about the quality of a particular higher degree or publication. But even without the benefit of expert public evaluations, it is clear that the work conducted by the NPB varied tremendously in quality, particularly in terms of conceptual advances and innovative hypotheses.

[100]J.T. du Toit, 'Patterns of resource use within the browsing ruminant guild in the central Kruger National Park' (PhD diss., University of the Witwatersrand, 1988). The thesis was supervised by Norman Owen-Smith. Du Toit later became director of the MRI.

[101]Owen-Smith's MSc was in chemistry and his PhD thesis was 'The behavioural ecology of the white rhinoceros' (University of Wisconsin, Madison, 1973). He is widely published in international journals. See, for just a few examples, R.N. Owen-Smith, 'The social ethology of the white rhinoceros *Ceratotherium simum* (Burchell 1817)', *Zeitschrift Fur Tierpsychologie* 38 (1975): 337–384; N. Owen-Smith, 'On territoriality in ungulates and an evolutionary model', *The Quarterly Review of Biology* 52, no. 1 (1977): 1–38; R.N. Owen-Smith, *Megaherbivores: The Influence of Very Large Body Size on Ecology* (Cambridge: Cambridge University Press, 1988). The University of Wisconsin, Madison, created a Chair in Game Management for Aldo Leopold in 1933 and in 1939 Leopold formed the Department of Wildlife Management, the first academic department in this field in the world. In 1967 the name of the department was changed to the Department of Wildlife Ecology as being more appropriate to the area of study.

[102]P.T. van der Walt, G. de Graaff and L.J. van Zyl, 'Lewensloop van 'n roooihartbeesbevolking *Alcelaphus buselaphus caama* in die Bontebok Nasionale Park', *Koedoe* 19 (1976): 181–183; P.T. van der Walt, L.J. van Zyl and G. de Graaff, 'Lewensloop van 'n Kaapse buffelbevolking *Syncerus caffer* in die Bontebok Nasionale Park', *Koedoe* 19 (1976): 189–191; G. de Graaff, P.T. van der Walt and L.J. van Zyl, 'Lewensloop van 'n elandbevolking *Taurotragus oryx* in die Bontebok Nasionale Park', *Koedoe* 19 (1976): 185–188.

[103]H. Jungius, 'Studies on the food and feeding behavior of the reedbuck (*Redunca arundinum* Boddaert 1785) in the Kruger National Park', *Koedoe* 14 (1971): 65–97.

[104]See L.R. Irby, 'The ecology of mountain reedbuck in southern and eastern Africa' (PhD diss., Texas A&M University, 1976). Irby was on the faculty of the Fish and Wildlife Management Program at Montana State University for many years.

One issue that did, however, provoke very public scientific disagreement among wildlife scientists and managers was the culling, cropping, controlling, limiting of – such was the variety of euphemisms used for killing – so-called 'excess' animals in protected areas. It was also rare for the NPB to be obliged to set out its rationale for scientific action and to defend its research and management before an international and local audience. Between the 1960s and 1990s controlling the 'over-population' of certain wild species in protected areas was a flashpoint and, even at the time of writing (2016), the issue remains controversial and divisive. In recent years, the old guard of scientists and managers has moved on and the issue has assumed other dimensions. For the historian, however, another reason to dwell on culling, which insofar as it involved the NPB was principally confined to the KNP, is because the debate brought the different scientific paradigms into focus.

Technological developments that enabled wild animals to be counted, darted, marked, tranquillised, transported, inoculated, vaccinated, sold and bartered were bound to encourage the attitude that humans had the power to control the lives of wild creatures. The power to do so was in the hands of the scientists and managers of the land on which these animals occurred. The manipulation of even the largest and most dangerous species that was now more feasible than ever, together with the philosophy of 'carrying capacity'[105] and also of commercial game farming meant that national parks and other protected areas could indeed be managed in exactly the same way as very large farms, with offtake regarded as legitimate, indeed economically desirable. The culling of large numbers of wild mammals was the most interventionist management technique used in the KNP, dwarfing others such as fire. Culling led not only to deaths, sales and exchanges, but affected the built environment too. Close to Skukuza rest camp (the KNP's largest) an abattoir was constructed out of sight of visitors. Here a factory processed the by-products of culling, principally hides and meat, the latter being disposed of as dried biltong, fresh, or canned on site. The food items were distributed to staff (mostly black) as rations and to workers at nearby mines. Thus wildlife was transformed into a saleable item at state expense. Or, as the veterinarian in the Kruger Park responsible for the culling put it, 'sold commercially to offset the considerable investment in equipment and manpower needed

[105]The phrase 'grazing unit' came into use. See discussion in J. du P. Bothma, N. van Rooyen and M.W. van Rooyen, 'Using diet and plant resources to set wildlife stocking densities in African savannas', *Wildlife Society Bulletin* 32, no. 3 (2004): 840–851.

for control operations'.[106] Over a 15-year period (1968–1983), 9456 elephant, 25 857 buffalo and 828 hippopotamus were killed: these are substantial numbers.[107]

The whole issue of reducing the number of large mammals in conserved areas had begun to rear its head in the 1950s in response to the very success of the principles and practice of protect, preserve and propagate. This was an issue not only for South Africa, but also for many of the protected areas in East Africa and in some of the national parks in the USA. In Yellowstone, for example, elk numbers had grown so much that the damage they were doing to the vegetation was both visible and of growing concern. Bison, too, had increased over the previous 100 years from around 1000 to 250 000, mostly on private property.[108] In his 1963 report to the National Parks Service (NPS), Starker Leopold argued that scientists and managers needed to get involved in the management of elk. At first, predators had been controlled so that elk numbers could grow. This they did, but then, predictably, the elk consumed more food and around 4500 of them were shot in 1961, an intervention that provoked a public outcry. The official Robbins report to the NPS that followed Leopold's did not clarify the science: scientists simply could not say 'how many' of every species was 'enough'. Despite all the expertise that had been built up on taxonomy, animal and plant communities and behavioural issues, decrypting population dynamics proved elusive. 'Balance', the approach adopted by naturalists of yore and based upon personal observation, remained the best fall-back position. Yet while historical data might be gathered about precolonial populations, current data could be collected on predators and prey; the consumption of trees and seeds by large mammals could be observed; the effects of flood and drought could

---

[106]A.M. Brynard, 'Game control in national parks', *African Wildlife* 21, no. 2 (1967): 93–99. In this article, Brynard stated categorically that there would be 'no canning factory' in the KNP. In the same period there was contention over trophy hunting in other national parks, including the Pilanesberg, situated in the then Bophuthatswana; see J.L. Anderson, 'Sport hunting in national parks: Sacrilege or salvation?', in *Management of Large Mammals in African Conservation Areas. Proceedings of a Symposium held in Pretoria, South Africa, 29–30 April 1982*, ed. R.N. Owen-Smith, (Pretoria: HAUM, 1983), 271–280.

[107]V. de Vos, R.G. Bengis and H.J. Coetzee, 'Population control of large mammals in the Kruger National Park', in Owen-Smith, ed., *Management of Large Mammals in African Conservation Areas*, 213–231.

[108]D.A. Nesheim, 'Profit, preservation, and shifting definitions of bison in America', *Environmental History* 17 (2012): 547–577.

be postulated; later, the terminology of 'biodiversity' might be used; no one could definitely state an optimum number in any biome. The question was, and remains, 'how much is too many?' This is a philosophical and aesthetic issue as much as it is scientific, and the interface between science and management has never been sharper than over this topic.[109]

The need to husband certain species and limit the numbers of others was driven by worries of an overconsumption that would either destroy the aesthetics of a landscape (or compromise its ability to regenerate) or create the likelihood of an irreversible population crash as was projected by computer models. Beyond that, wildlife managers were concerned that should the method of reduction by those tasked with protecting species become commonly known, the visiting public would turn against national parks. The risk of this was greater because the sophisticated debates and differences of opinion about the scientific rationale for culling were not easily reducible to the language of newspapers and popular magazines, making justification more difficult.[110]

The NPB did not embark on its culling programme lightly. Culling predators such as lion, leopard, hyenas and wild dog was, as has been noted, common among sport-hunters or farmers with antelope or domestic stock to protect. Over the centuries the assumption had taken root that prey and predators would eventually come into 'balance' and that humans could assist this process by limiting the predators and treating prey preferentially. NPB policy on 'carnivora control' was often erratic, but in 1959 alone, 14 lion, 22 wild dog and five leopards were killed, the lion and leopard apparently 'for protection of life and property', and the wild dog (and an unspecified number of hyena) because they preyed on the mountain reedbuck *Redunca fulvorufula* in a waterless part of the KNP. It was at the board meeting in December 1959 that these statistics were reported and it was at this meeting that the fateful question of controlling elephant numbers was first formally broached.[111]

---

[109]W.J. Robbins *et al.*, 'National Academy of Sciences Advisory Committee on Research in the National Parks, National Park Service' and A. Starker Leopold *et al.*, 'The goal of park management in the United States', in *Wildlife Management in the National Parks*. National Park Service (www.craterlakeinstitute.com/online-library/leopold-report/complete.htm., accessed 30 September 2015). (Reprinted in L.M. Dilsaver, *America's National Park System: The Critical Documents* (Lanham, MD: Rowman and Littlefield, 1994). www.nps.gov/parkhistory/online_books/anps/accessed 30 September 2015.)

[110]D.R. Mason and P.A. van der Walt, 'Sex and age data from cropping of buffalo *Syncerus caffer* in the Kruger National Park', *Koedoe* 27 (1984): 73–78.

[111]The board meeting of December 1959 listed carnivora control as 14 lion, 22 wild dog and 5 leopards, and all except wild dog were destroyed for protection of life and

Figure 8.5. Culled elephant in the KNP.
A photograph from the 1990s that appeared in *The Star*, 12 January 2006.

The culling of elephants posed a much greater challenge, because this is a species beloved of humans, not vilified by them. Although elephants are dangerous when aroused, their behaviour resonates anthropomorphically – family parties are delightful to watch, maternal care is evident as are family connections and social order, and death seems to be recognised and the dead mourned. Killing this particular species could provoke outrage.[112] Elephants had been brought to the brink of extermination in southern Africa by ivory hunters, but subsequent hunting restrictions and

---

property. Hyena were also 'controlled'. See Minutes and agenda of a meeting of the NPB, 7 December 1959, SANParks archives, Groenkloof, Pretoria.

[112] See J. Carruthers, A. Boshoff, R. Slotow, H. Biggs, G. Avery and W. Matthews, 'The elephant in South Africa: History and distribution', in *Scientific Assessment of Elephant Management in South Africa*, eds R.J. Scholes and K.G. Mennell (Johannesburg: Wits University Press, 2008), 23–83; J. Carruthers, 'Romance, reverence, research, rights: Writing about elephant hunting and management in southern Africa, c.1830s to 2008', *Koedoe* 52, no. 1 (2010): 1–6; J. Carruthers, '"Hunter of elephants, take your bow!" A historical analysis of nonfiction writing about elephant hunting in southern Africa', in *Environment at the Margins: Literary and Environmental Studies in Africa*, eds B. Caminero-Santangelo and G. Myers (Athens, OH: Ohio University Press, 2011), 73–84.

protective measures had resulted in rebounding numbers and expanding ranges. This phenomenon was not unique to southern Africa, for it was also an issue in East Africa. By 1956 – although there was no scientific count – the loss of habitat from elephant depredations was noted in Tsavo Game Reserve[113] and in 1960 culling was being undertaken on the Galana River Scheme. Under such circumstances elephants then gravitated to the 'safe' areas of national parks, and it was very difficult to decide what to do next. No scientist knew what the 'normal number' of elephants should be, or even how this might be calculated.[114]

In November 1959, KNP warden Louis Steyn, an old-style game ranger who distrusted scientists, began discussion of killing elephants at a meeting of the nature conservation department in Skukuza. It was attended by the biologists and game rangers of the KNP and gave rise to the report presented to the board the following month. The concern expressed was that elephants were congregating in what they considered the most desirable parts of the KNP and that they needed to be dispersed more widely. It was noted that tourists were reluctant to visit parts of the park where elephants were scarce.[115] However, so dense were the numbers becoming in certain places, Steyn predicted that rangers would soon have to kill them on a large scale, as was the case with some carnivora. This would create unwelcome publicity. He recommended immediate commencement of small-scale culling, rather than waiting until drastic measures became necessary. In his view, the underlying need for taking action lay in the problems growing numbers of elephant would cause with KNP neighbours, their destruction of trees and consumption of large volumes of water, and the diseases they spread to other species via pathogens lodged on their foot-pads. In response, the board urged extreme caution before action was taken. R.J. (Lappies) Labuschagne, the chair, recommended that the biological division set time aside to thoroughly investigate the issue of elephant over-population.[116]

The division (there is no single author) had its report, 'Elephant control in southern Kruger National Park', ready for the board meeting in March

---

[113]The elephant population in the Tsavo reserves collapsed totally in 1970–1971, an episode which naturally impacted on the decisions taken by the NPB in KNP.

[114]J. Schauer, 'The elephant problem: Science, bureaucracy, and Kenya's national parks, 1955–1975', *African Studies Review* 58, no. 1 (2015): 177–198.

[115]Pienaar, 'The large mammals of the Kruger National Park', 22.

[116]Minutes of a meeting of the NPB, 23 March 1960, Annexure F, SANParks archives, Groenkloof, Pretoria.

the following year. In it, carrying capacity was said to not only refer to food supply, but also to the availability of water and shelter and the need to allow for intraspecies competition and 'lebensraum' for breeding herds. The biologists believed that the damage to vegetation from the large-scale immigration of elephant and natural population expansion would increase, and soon the '*ewewigsvlak*' – the balance level – between elephants and their environment would be reached. Elephant control would soon have to be considered and, given the lack of research, such control would have to be arbitrary. Almost as a form of exculpation, the report went on to note that the national park could take pride in its custodianship of the KNP, to which elephant had felt safe in returning to play their proper part in the natural economy of their home range, or *tuisveld*.[117]

The biologists recommended that, firstly, the exact number and age cohorts of the elephants be determined, as had been done in Uganda and elsewhere. Secondly, that this information, along with a consideration of the water supply, should be used to compute a quota of elephant for the southern KNP. Thereafter, any 'surplus' to this number should be removed annually, this task to be undertaken in boundary areas not frequented by tourists. Moreover, care was to be taken to ensure the survival of breeding bulls and large animals with impressive tusks. Control in other parts of the KNP was also recommended, but with caution and in accordance with specific circumstances. Further recommendations included proper training for game rangers in darting methods and weaponry, and, most importantly, mounting an effective public relations campaign to justify deliberate and scientific control of animal numbers as consistent with nature conservation and for the good of the animals themselves.[118] Indeed, the argument should be made that humans, the 'natural enemy' of elephants, had always controlled their number and that this practice had merely been stayed when the KNP was proclaimed.[119]

By 1963, the question of 'too many' had been ramped up and elephants were not the only animals subject to population control. By November that year, there was unanimous concern that certain species of

[117]Minutes of a meeting of the NPB, 23 March 1960, Annexure F, SANParks archives, Groenkloof, Pretoria.
[118]See A.M. Brynard, 'Game control in national parks', *African Wildlife* 21, no. 2 (1967): 93–99.
[119]Minutes of a meeting of the NPB, 23 March 1960, Annexure F, SANParks archives, Groenkloof, Pretoria.

plants and animals were being 'over-protected' in South Africa's national parks. Examples included hippopotamus and elephant in the KNP and some species of vegetation in Golden Gate.[120] The board then decided to host a symposium, including scientific representatives, during which the whole issue could be aired. Pending such symposium, up to 100 hippopotamus along the Letaba River were to be killed 'for . . . purposes of intensive scientific research', the meat obtained to be used as rations for African staff.[121] Some of this research was published in *Koedoe* in 1966 and 1967.[122] However, definitive research into and answers about the relationship between animal numbers and the total ecosystem were not forthcoming. In 1965, the board, noting that 'how and when to do control measures' remained unanswered by biologists, again called for more data on the biomass and total area of the KNP. Clearly, the board was reluctant to authorise anything more than experimental culling and believed that peaceful interaction between humans and animals in protected areas was a cardinal consideration. In the meantime, biologists reported regularly to the board on drugs used and numbers killed. Zoologists' interest in the skeletons and histological material from culled hippopotamus was also reported, as was veterinarians' interest in blood serum and parasite load. All animals, it was noted, were weighed, their stomach content analysed and their age and reproductive level recorded.[123] Yet still there was no clear answer about how many was 'too many'.

The proposed scientific symposium on culling took place on 30 November 1965. A very crucial meeting, it was chaired by NPB Director Rocco Knobel and attended by more than 60 people. Seven board members were there along with Eloff of the University of Pretoria, museum and zoo personnel, senior members of the Natal and Transvaal nature conservation authorities and senior state veterinarians, as well as many officials from the KNP and other national parks. Presentations were made by Knobel, Brynard, van Wyk, Fairall, van Niekerk, Pienaar,

---

[120]Minutes of a meeting of the NPB, 28 November 1963, SANParks archives, Groenkloof, Pretoria.

[121]Minutes of a meeting of the NPB, 28 November 1963 and 22 September 1964, SANParks archives, Groenkloof, Pretoria.

[122]U. de V. Pienaar, P. van Wyk and N. Fairall, 'An experimental cropping scheme of hippopotami in the Letaba River of the Kruger National Park', *Koedoe* 9 (1966): 1–33; U. de V. Pienaar, 'The field immobilization and capture of hippopotami in their aquatic element', *Koedoe* 10 (1967): 149–164.

[123]Minutes of a meeting of the NPB, 22 June 1965, SANParks archives, Groenkloof, Pretoria.

Labuschagne and van der Merwe. In his opening comments – which included the exhortation that people should speak freely and without fear in either official language – the chairman emphasised the need for cool heads. Mistakes had been made in other areas of science and management, but no mistake could be allowed over culling. Board member D.F. Gilfillan (representing the Wild Life Society) was not alone in singling out the oversupply of water points in the KNP and the previous policy of lion culling as mistaken.[124] Discussion was lively and involved most of the delegates. The issue was not culling itself, which had already been adopted in smaller protected areas, but its applicability to the KNP in particular. Here was a large institution of national importance and pride, and the public – local and international – had been persuaded that in such extensive regions, nature could find a 'balance'. These perceptions would be hard to shift.

The discussions revealed how little was really understood about either the rationale for culling or its outcomes. McGregor Museum director Richard Liversidge emphasised the existence of barely understood elements of constant change and dynamism in the system. Eloff agreed that basic research on population dynamics was missing. Nonetheless, action was, apparently, necessary, because it was 'obvious' that habitat was being transformed by the 'excess' wildlife populations. It was also clear from the emerging discussion that numerous species, including impala, giraffe, hippopotamus, blue wildebeest, buffalo, zebra and elephants, and even giraffe, were now so numerous that managers believed they threatened the grazing and water resources in the KNP. Strong arguments were advanced that irregular and sporadic control should be formalised if future disaster was to be avoided. Large-scale killing required careful handling. For one thing, what should happen to the carcasses? All agreed they could not be left in the veld to spread disease and encourage more predation. Commercial considerations seemed to offer a solution, for there was a market. Accruals might be spent on improving the grazing

---

[124]Never afraid to advance a different point of view, Gilfillan advocated closing the waterholes in order to force the wildlife to disperse more widely. On addressing a board meeting on his retirement in September 1972 after ten years membership of the board, the English-speaking Gilfillan made reference to the frequent differences of opinion between himself and fellow board members, but that he (Gilfillan) had believed it to be his duty to provide an honest opinion and not merely to agree with everything that other board members or officials did, thought or said. NPB Meeting, Minutes, 1 September 1972.

and water supplies in the KNP, vehicles, as well as the refrigeration, canning and disposal of the fresh meat. Although no decision was made, the recommendations were that systematic control of impala, hippo, blue wildebeest, buffalo, giraffe, zebra and elephant commence; that the NPB's nature conservation department work out the appropriate methods; and that the division of veterinary services be approached about how best to dispose of specific animal products.[125]

In the event, culling was approved and soon commenced. Impala were culled: 18 236 of them between 1966 and 1974, along with hippo and buffalo.[126] One of the first initiatives that convinced the board that culling was needed was a full aerial census (and 600 photographs) of elephant and buffalo conducted by Pienaar, Fairall and van Wyk. Featuring a long literature list, many tables, examples from history and from East Africa, and with photographs of family groups and individuals and recognition of the intellectual capacity of the elephant, this extremely detailed study went to the board for discussion in November 1967. Subsequently published in *Koedoe*, the article underlined how difficult accurate computation of anything like 'carrying capacity' was in a vast and variable area like the KNP. Theoretical considerations had therefore to be balanced against practicability.[127]

In 1967, Pienaar authored a further article in *Koedoe*, 'Operation "Khomandlopfu"', the title being derived from the Tsonga expression for 'capture the elephants'. This dealt with the capture of a limited number of elephants sanctioned by the board in September 1966. The background to this initiative, not highlighted in the article, was that it was part of the preliminary trials before elephant culling commenced. The idea was that, although many elephants would be killed, as many as possible should be saved to be sold or given away. As the article noted, before 1966 no adult females or juveniles had been captured, and it was the latter that were attractive to buyers. Using a helicopter, and with the help of B.H. Carter, who had experience in Kenya and Uganda (he was with

---

[125]This was reported on at the meeting of the NPB on 22 March 1966, Annexure A, SANParks archives, Groenkloof, Pretoria.

[126]M. Reardon, *Shaping Kruger: The Dynamics of Managing Wildlife in Africa's Premier Game Park* (Cape Town: Struik Nature, 2012), 41; Pienaar, van Wyk and Fairall, 'An experimental cropping scheme of hippopotami'; Pienaar, 'The field immobilization and capture of hippopotami'; Mason, 'Sex and age data from cropping of buffalo'.

[127]U. de V. Pienaar, P. van Wyk and N. Fairall, 'An aerial census of elephant and buffalo in the Kruger National park and the implication thereof on intended management schemes', *Koedoe* 9 (1966): 40–107.

Kenya's Game Department and was temporarily employed as a KNP ranger), drugs supplied free of charge by Reckitt, and a cross-bow manufactured by Gert van Rooyen, the KNP's instrument-maker from 1968 to 1987, 27 elephants under the age of five were captured. Twenty were sold to an A. Jones and were to be translocated (at his expense) to a proposed elephant reserve in California. The article included photographs of an elephant cow pathetically guarding her calf as it was about to collapse and then trying to raise it off the ground, or trying to attack the helicopter as it buzzed her to drive her away.[128]

By 1969 there was a strong demand for wild animals and the practice of buying, selling or bartering them flourished. Although mortality was high, the KNP was vigorously selling 'surplus' zebra to farmers and private nature reserves, exchanging them for cheetah, giving them to provincial authorities and stocking national parks such as Golden Gate.[129]

The public relations campaign was not neglected either. As early as 1967 Brynard had written an article in *African Wildlife* on 'Game control in national parks'. It included few details but stressed that the over-abundance of certain species had resulted in the over-use of local resources and that, 'for obvious reasons', reducing numbers was the only solution.[130] In the January 1972 issue of *Custos*, the popular national parks magazine published from 1971 to 1998, Pienaar dealt with culling. Beginning with references to its prevalence in Uganda, Kenya and the USA (Yellowstone), he wrote that the increase in some species meant that obviously 'numbers should be checked', but added that 'it is . . . comforting . . . that the animals which have to forfeit their lives, contribute to the protection and survival of their living brothers in our precious natural heritage'. The money accruing from 'various by-products' flowed back into conservation projects.[131] The balance of nature thus continued to be the dominant management paradigm and popular trope. However, although culling was never denied by the NPB, it was certainly sanitised, and no tourist or newspaper recorded the event, or was given free access to the abattoir, nor was any visual image presented in an annual report or similar publication. Obtaining a visual image of this practice is almost

---

[128]U. de V. Pienaar, 'Operation "Khomandlopfu"', *Koedoe* 10 (1967): 158–164.

[129]Minutes of a meeting of the NPB, 8 September 1969, SANParks archives, Groenkloof, Pretoria. There were other publications by Pienaar on capture and transport, see *Acta Zoologica et Pathologica Antverpeinsia* 46 (1968).

[130]A.M. Brynard, *African Wildlife* 21, no. 2 (1967): 93–99.

[131]U. de V. Pienaar, *Custos* (January 1972).

impossible, although there are a few of elephants, dead and/or drugged, being loaded onto trucks by cranes. Rudi van Aarde, a highly respected elephant scientist and professor of zoology at the University of Pretoria, recalled that even scientists involved were not allowed to take pictures.[132]

By the 1970s, culling in the KNP was routine. After an annual census, a quota was set and a certain number 'removed'. Between 1974 and 1978, 335 lions were killed and 297 spotted hyenas, both for experimental reasons. Wildebeest and impala had been killed since the 1960s and their meat used for rations. During the 1970s, however, numbers of wildebeest and zebra plunged, giving rise, as earlier noted, to modelling in the mid- and late 1970s.[133] Warnings about unexpected outcomes were also beginning to surface. Among them was Huntley's contention that wildlife management and conservation science were beginning to undergo a paradigm shift away from a 'balance of nature' perspective towards a detailed understanding of ecosystem dynamics, especially stability and resilience. This emerging understanding had to inform management strategy in, for instance, the KNP. Indeed, factoring long-term ecosystem oscillations (as described by Stevenson-Hamilton) rather than short-term observations into planning might show the habitat–herbivore–predator manipulation programmes there to be superfluous. Huntley recommended a strong information base, employment of good scientists, an integrated approach to understanding complex systems and the necessary institutional support.[134] Similar ideas were expressed by Norman Owen-Smith in a letter to Salomon Joubert in 1979: 'we still understand very little about the wider impact of elephant populations within an ecosystem framework', he wrote, because population stability was not a general feature of natural ecosystems.[135] By this time, the work on resilience by Holling and Walker was being widely accepted by the scientific community, but it would be many years before the NPB would follow suit.[136] Indeed, the NPB *Annual Report* reported that during 1978–1979 the programme

[132]Rudi van Aarde, email to author, 3 August 2016.
[133]Reardon, *Shaping Kruger*, 131–132.
[134]Huntley, 'Ecosystem conservation in southern Africa'.
[135]Owen-Smith to Joubert, 13 October 1979, A4 Besoeke van wetenskaplikes en andere, KNP archives, Skukuza.
[136]B.H. Walker, 'An appraisal of the systems approach to research on and management of African wildlife ecosystems', *Journal of the South African Wildlife Management Association* 4 (1974): 129–136; C.S. Holling, 'Resilience and stability of ecological systems', *Annual Review of Ecology and Systematics* 4 (1973): 1–23; C.S. Holling, ed., *Adaptive Environmental Assessment and Management* (New York, NY: Wiley, 1978).

for providing 'water for game' was in full swing, and that 570 elephant, 1560 buffalo, 40 lions and 31 hyaenas had been culled.[137] Surprisingly, at least to the NPB, the numbers of the targeted species continued to grow. Between 1970 and 1985, 10 264 elephants were destroyed and 465 sold, while 31 374 buffalo and 1105 hippopotamus were destroyed.[138] By 2002 the total number of elephant that had been officially culled since 1966 was 14 629 and 486 family units, 1339 juveniles and 111 adult bulls had been translocated – a total of 16 666 elephant removed.[139] There were also concerns at this time that some of the drugs used for immobilisation and culling (particularly scoline) were inhumane.[140] However, of the many articles that appeared in *Koedoe* about tranquillisation, culling and large mammal studies, none dealt with animal ethics, behavioural change and stress levels.

Apartheid may well have fostered a sense of hubris among many NPB scientists. Deprived of active contacts with international scientists in their field, it was difficult for them to keep abreast of emerging developments, and perhaps difficult to demonstrate humility in confronting them. Indeed, the NPB seemed reluctant to accept advice from experts in South Africa outside the close NPB–University of Pretoria network; men such as Brian Huntley, Brian Walker, Ken Tinley or John Hanks, or the growing numbers of wildlife managers immigrating from troubled Zimbabwe.[141] Continued membership by the NPB in various IUCN committees was no substitute for lively exchanges with peers. Political gulfs led to scientific gulfs, some of them fuelled by competition between East and South African conservation bodies and by different worldviews and national economic circumstances. Yet by the late 1970s, the whole issue of 'locally abundant wild mammals' was gaining international attention. With the emergence of philosophies more sophisticated than numerical balance or 'carrying capacity', and the growing concerns of civil society about culling, the time was ripe for an international dialogue on the matter.

A seminal workshop was held in September–October 1980 in Cape Cod, Massachusetts, the product of which was a significant book entitled *Problems in Management of Locally Abundant Wild Mammals: A Workshop to*

[137]NPB, *35th Annual Report for the Year 1978–1979.*
[138]Joubert, *Kruger National Park*, Vol. 2, 174.
[139]Whyte, van Aarde and Pimm, 'Kruger's elephant population', 339.
[140]Joubert, *Kruger National Park*, Vol. 2, 172–178.
[141]Among them might be mentioned Jeremy Anderson and Roger Collinson.

306 · **Zoology**

Examine the Need for and Alternatives to Culling of Wild Animals, and edited by Peter Jewell and Sidney Holt of Cambridge University.[142] Suggested by Holt,[143] the workshop was sponsored by the International Federation for Animal Welfare (IFAW), an animal rights organisation that questioned whether intervention in growing populations of animals was really necessary. The objective was to have a discussion about culling on neutral territory, and to introduce comparisons (marine, terrestrial as well as geographical) in order to be open to different opinions and experiences about a contentious topic, rather than judgmental. The meeting was to explore the meaning of over-abundance and to critique the methods used to deal with it.

Almost 40 delegates attended from places as diverse as Peru, Canada, Rhodesia, East Africa, Australia, Israel, the UK and the USA (including Alaska). Also in attendance were a number of South Africans from institutions of higher learning and state conservation authorities. The NPB was represented by Salomon Joubert and he was accompanied by colleagues from the Natal and Cape departments of nature conservation. John Hanks attended from the Institute of Natural Resources at the

[142](New York, NY: Academic Press, 1981). Among the attendees (there were a number of others who did not present papers) were: from the UK: Sidney Holt; Peter A. Jewell; Peter Scott; John R. Beddington; S.K. Eltringham, Applied Biology Cambridge; John Harwood, Sea Mammal Research Cambridge; W.J. Jordan, Trust for Endangered Species, UK; Richard M. Laws, British Antarctic Survey. From other parts of Africa: R.H.V. Bell, Malawi; Stephen Cobb, University of Nairobi; David H.M. Cumming, National Parks and Wildlife Management, Rhodesia. From other parts of the world: Graeme Caughley, CSIRO Canberra; Imanuel Noy-Meir, Hebrew University of Jerusalem; David M. Lavigne, Guelph University. From the USA: Daniel Botkin, UC Santa Barbara; Douglas G. Chapman, Seattle; James A. Estes, Santa Cruz; David R. Klein, Alaska; Burney J. le Boeuf, UC Santa Cruz; Robert M. May, Princeton; G. Carleton Ray, Virginia; A.R.E. Sinclair, University of British Columbia. From South Africa: W.D. Densham and G.L. Smuts, Natal Parks Board; John Hanks, INR University of Natal; J.F. Jooste, Cape Department of Nature Conservation; S.C.J. Joubert, NPB, KNP; Norman Owen-Smith and Brian H. Walker, Centre for Resource Ecology, University of the Witwatersrand. From Peru: R.K. Hofmann and K.C. Otte, Vicuna Protection, Peru.

[143]Peter Jewell was an interdisciplinary biologist with strong interests in ecology and sustainability. His Cambridge PhD was in physiology but he became expert in agriculture, pharmacology, zoology and reproductive physiology. He held the post of professor of biology in Nigeria for some years. Sidney J. Holt is an important founder of fisheries science, best known for his classic book *On the Dynamics of Exploited Fish Populations* (1957). He was active in the FAO and other UN agencies as well as with the International Whaling Commission.

University of Natal[144] and Brian Walker and Norman Owen-Smith from the University of the Witwatersrand.

New Zealander Graeme Caughley reported that Africa was out of step with the rest of the world, where the recent trend was towards reduction of human intervention in national parks. Richard Bell, then working in Malawi, declared the entire issue to be one of aesthetics, not science. He believed that for southern Africans culling had become a system from which they could not break free simply because they could not reorient their thinking and consider any alternative. David Cumming from Zimbabwe agreed: there was no science behind the decision to cull. Brian Walker emphasised there was no need for a rigid dichotomy in approaches, there were positions between the two extremes, including heterogeneity and multiple equilibria. Robert May, author of an article on the multiplicity of stable states published in *Nature* in 1977, agreed.[145] Discussion of case studies was wide-ranging, and covered white rhinoceros, vicuña, domestic stock, baleen whales, sea otter, leopard, northern fur seals and even vegetation. Several of the South African representatives presented a joint paper on the 'Management of locally abundant mammals: The South African experience'.[146] This described the modern economy of South Africa, and its rapidly growing human population, which had increased by 27% over ten years. In such a country, protected areas, apart from the KNP, were small (less than 500 km^2) and were based on the principle of island biogeography. They were fast being hemmed in by farmland and by the 'independent' states the government was creating for African communities. South Africa was therefore different in having fenced off and limited protected areas, and had particular challenges in dealing with over-abundance, when compared with countries that had extensive areas of wild country or open sea.[147]

---

[144]Hanks had obtained his PhD in 1971 from Cambridge on the reproductive physiology, growth and population dynamics of the African elephant in the Luangwa Valley, Zambia.

[145]R.M. May, 'Thresholds and breakpoints: Ecosystems with a multiplicity of stable states', *Nature* (London) 269 (1977): 471–477.

[146]The authors were Hanks, Densham, Smuts, Jooste, Joubert, P. le Roux (OFS) and P. Milstein (Transvaal) – the last two were not present at the meeting.

[147]'Management of locally abundant mammals: The South African experience', in *Problems in Management of Locally Abundant Wild Mammals: A Workshop to Examine the Need for and Alternatives to Culling of Wild Animals, 29 September–3 October 1980, Cape Cod, USA*, eds P.A. Jewell and S. Holt (New York, NY: Academic Press, 1981), 21–55.

Caughley was quick to note that ultimately the problem was the absence of a rigorous definition of 'over-population'.[148] Daniel Botkin led the session on diagnostic characteristics. How might one gauge if a population was over-abundant? Soil degradation would be critical, but soil analysis was seldom undertaken. The meeting concluded that many of the factors in controlling 'over-abundant species' were social, political and economic, not ecological. No formula was likely to be universally applicable, and the philosophy of management – Bell's value system – was the important issue. Other points of agreement were that managing protected areas scientifically required defined management objectives; careful identification of problems; and an experimental approach based on probabilities, possible alternative outcomes and actively adaptive management. It was also agreed that researchers and managers should refuse to supply spurious scientific justification for culling being undertaken for political, social or financial ends. On many other matters there was no unanimity, but that – all agreed – had never been the goal of the workshop.

The 1980 meeting at Cape Cod was followed a couple of years later by two gatherings – one in Pretoria and one at Olifants camp in the KNP – focused specifically on culling and over-population in southern Africa and intended to deal with the many issues not finalised at the earlier meeting. This was in accordance with a process introduced by Huntley to have, first, an open or public meeting that exposed the issues and, second, a smaller gathering during which the contentious matters were synthesised and written up in a formal report. At these subsequent encounters, perhaps because of the personalities involved and the divisions among savannah scientists, the debate was more lively and contentious than at Cape Cod. Both meetings produced important publications that appeared in 1983. The first, *Management of Large Mammals in African Conservation Areas: Proceedings of a Symposium held in Pretoria, South Africa, 29–30 April 1982*, was edited by Norman Owen-Smith[149] and the second, the proceedings of the more practically oriented five-day meeting at Olifants Camp in the KNP shortly afterwards, appeared as *Guidelines for the Management of Large Mammals in African Conservation Areas*, and was edited by Tony Ferrar.[150]

---

[148]Caughley, a widely published New Zealander who studied in Sydney under Harry Frith and Charles Birch, worked on the ecology of kangaroos and on tahr to discover whether Thane Riney's eruption and stabilisation patterns that applied to deer also applied to tahr. He died in 1994.

[149](Pretoria: HAUM, 1983). The author attended this meeting.

[150]South African Scientific Programmes Report 69 (Pretoria: CSIR, 1983).

These were intended as twinned publications, with the first serving as conceptual background for the second. Both workshops were convened by the committee for nature conservation research of the South African National Programme for Environmental Sciences, with funding from the CSIR, the SA Nature Foundation, the Endangered Wildlife Trust and Total oil company. The meetings were unusual in terms of the NPB's reluctance to collaborate with the CSIR programmes and also in attempting to facilitate cooperation between the many people involved in the debates on the philosophy, science and practicalities of culling. A glance at the authorship of the CSP programmes makes it clear that the participation of the NPB was extremely thin, and in the main, totally absent.[151]

At the Pretoria meeting in April 1982, strong opinions were expressed.[152] Pienaar, for example, was adamant that managers and scientists had to intervene in population dynamics and control certain species – it was the only 'pragmatic/economic' option. Most visitors to national parks were not interested in plants, 'let alone the concept of ecosystem conservation' and national parks had to cater to the visitors' fixation on large mammals. Non-intervention was a 'luxury' that South Africa and its national parks could not afford. In order to reach the desired African landscape as it was when 'first visited by the White man', nothing other than interference could be countenanced. He compared the starving of elephants to the starving of people, and argued that the use of elephants to feed people was justified. Moreover, the cropping of species in the KNP had between 1969 and 1980 brought in a net income of R2 855 723.[153] The East African scientist Tony Sinclair, based at the University of

---

[151]I am grateful to Brian Huntley for his analysis.

[152]Presentations were made by R.C. Bengis, H.J. Coetzee, V. de Vos, S.C.J. Joubert and U. de V. Pienaar from the NPB; J.L. Anderson, Pilanesberg National Park; P.M. Brooks and O.S. Goodman, Natal Parks Game and Fish Preservation Board; I.A.W. Macdonald, Hluhluwe Game Reserve, Natal; A.J. Königkrämer, KwaZulu-Natal Development Corporation; R.H.V. Bell and A. Kombe, Department of National Parks and Wildlife, Malawi; D.H.M. Cumming, R.B. Martin and R.D. Taylor, Department of National Parks and Wildlife Management, Rhodesia; I.S.C. Parker, Kenya; R.N. Owen-Smith and B.H. Walker, Centre for Resource Ecology, University of the Witwatersrand; A.R.E. Sinclair, Institute for Animal Resource Ecology, University of British Columbia; G. Caughley, CSIRO, Canberra; K.R. Miller, School of Natural Resources, University of Michigan, Ann Arbor; R.A. Pellew, Physiological Laboratory, University of Cambridge.

[153]U. de V. Pienaar, 'Management by intervention: The pragmatic/economic option', in *Management of Large Mammals in African Conservation Areas. Proceedings of a Symposium held in Pretoria, South Africa, 29–30 April 1982*, ed. R.N. Owen-Smith (Pretoria: HAUM, 1983), 23–26.

British Columbia, strongly disagreed that scientists needed to 'play God', particularly when their understanding was so limited. According to Brian Walker and Peter Goodman, in the absence of understanding of ecosystem processes, interventionists were merely 'fiddling'. The KNP's Salomon Joubert conceded that sentiment often drove management intervention but averred that without scientific data – which were still being collected – there was little other option. However, the desired objective in national parks, by whatever means and with whatever knowledge, should always be the 'maintenance of natural equilibria'. Most of the papers focused on culling, but some raised other issues in this context that were emerging in the science of wildlife and conservation biology and that would later become extremely influential. One was the role of society in national park knowledge systems and management, the other was about how to model and how best to use computers for this purpose.[154]

However, perhaps the most innovative ideas to emerge from the meeting were those of Richard Bell. His presentation, 'Decision-making in wildlife management with reference to problems of over-population', like a number of others (although not from within the NPB) pointed towards adaptive management. In his paper, Bell elevated the debate to the level of how decisions were taken, rather than the decisions themselves. Using control theory – cybernetics – Bell suggested that trial, error and negative feedback were integral to identifying, refining and achieving any desired objective. He agreed with Joubert that decisions were based on aesthetic value systems, not technical facts. And even if there were technical facts, he pointed out, values would determine which option for further action would be chosen. Even the compilation of data, he reminded the audience, was determined by the general outlook of the collectors. The word 'natural' had no meaning, except in association with values. He appealed to the audience to recognise the role of 'gut feeling', human influence, subjectivity, emotion and irrationality in wildlife

[154]A.J. Köningkramer, 'Influencing public attitudes: The socio-politics of culling in Natal', in *Management of Large Mammals in African Conservation Areas: Proceedings of a Symposium held in Pretoria, South Africa, 29–30 April 1982*, ed. R.N. Owen-Smith (Pretoria: HAUM, 1983), 233–240; A. Kombe, 'Governmental and public reactions to culling in conservation areas in Malawi', in *Management of Large Mammals in African Conservation Areas: Proceedings of a Symposium held in Pretoria, South Africa, 29–30 April 1982*, ed. R.N. Owen-Smith (Pretoria: HAUM, 1983), 241–248; J.L. Anderson, 'Sport hunting in national parks: Sacrilege or salvation', in *Management of Large Mammals in African Conservation Areas: Proceedings of a Symposium held in Pretoria, South Africa, 29–30 April 1982*, ed. R.N. Owen-Smith (Pretoria: HAUM, 1983), 271–280.

management and conservation biology, especially because these were not definitive fields.[155]

About 40 of the participants in the Pretoria workshop went to the follow-up session at Olifants Camp to thrash out some of the practical issues of managing large mammals in protected areas.[156] The themes of the meeting were establishing clearly stated goals; considering the ecological basis of wildland management; the rising competition between rural people and conservation areas; the decision-making process; and, finally, approaches to research and its monitoring. Some of the discussion drew on Bell's analysis of the factors affecting decision-making, specifically that cause and effect was not only less obvious than it seemed, but that the context of time and space was also important. Considerable discussion was devoted to stability – what it was and even whether this should be a goal, given that stabilisation did not imply steady density. Moreover, what 'looks natural' is an essentially emotional judgement of value and that while freezing a moment might well be desirable, it needed to be acknowledged openly and not confused with science in both the public propaganda and the formal literature.[157] The leitmotif was summed up by Caughley and Walker as: 'The more one tries to prevent change, the more management effort will be needed in the future.'[158]

The issue of controlling and manipulating large mammals in African protected areas and in other parts of the world was well aired in the late 1970s and early 1980s. It was perhaps courageous of the KNP to put its policies under the international microscope, but while new and exciting ideas about conservation and wildlife biology arose from these discussions and were strongly championed by individual scientists and managers, it would take many more years – and important societal changes – before the new attitudes and policies found a firm footing in the NPB.

[155]In *Management of Large Mammals in African Conservation Areas: Proceedings of a Symposium held in Pretoria, South Africa, 29–30 April 1982*, ed. R.N. Owen-Smith (Pretoria: HAUM, 1983), 145–172.

[156]A.A. Ferrar, ed., *Guidelines of the Management of Large Mammals in African Conservation Areas*. South African Scientific Programmes Report 69 (Pretoria: CSIR, 1983).

[157]See the various papers in Ferrar, *Guidelines of the Management of Large Mammals*.

[158]Ferrar, *Guidelines of the Management of Large Mammals*, iv.

Part III · *Integration, Innovation and Internationalisation, 1990 to 2010*

9 · *Overview*

The early 1990s mark an appropriate chronological break in the evolution of South Africa's national parks, including the science undertaken within and about them. From that time onwards, scientific philosophy, research and national park management acquired a new focus, reach and sophistication. In the international context, there have also been fresh initiatives, revised bureaucracies and innovative scientific understandings of national parks. And South Africa was no longer as cut off from such wider trends as before.

One crucial factor in this shift was that South Africa itself finally became a democratic country under a new, elected and fully representative government, a transformation that has had enormous implications not only for national politics, but also for society, the economy, international relations and the environment. South Africa's transformation in the 1990s mirrored – and was intertwined with – far-reaching changes to the underpinnings of the global order that had been in place since the 1950s. A huge tsunami swept over international relations in the 1980s, leaving the USSR much diminished in power and eventually in a state of collapse. It also had implications for our understanding of the environment, for in this new, more integrated global village without competing power blocs, the vocabulary of the 'Anthropocene' and Climate Change came to the fore and gained the world's attention.[1] The 'environment' and sustainable life on earth itself took on new meaning and new urgency.[2] South Africa's national parks and the research conducted in them could not but be affected by this torrent of political, social and intellectual change. Indeed, the post-1990 period witnessed a flurry of new

---

[1] See, for example, P.J. Crutzen and E.F. Stoermer. 'The "Anthropocene"', *Global Change Newsletter* 41 (2000): 17–18.

[2] L. Robin, S. Sörlin and P. Warde, eds, *The Future of Nature: Documents of Global Change* (New Haven, CT: Yale University Press, 2013).

institutions, new priorities, new stakeholders and new *modus operandi* in protected area research and administration.

Part I of this book focused on national parks and the imperative to protect, preserve and propagate (the 3Ps) desirable animals, attractive landscapes and monumental scenery. The success of the 3Ps made possible the 3Ms (Part II) – the measurement, monitoring and manipulation of the creatures and landscapes protected in the previous period. Indeed, coping with 'over-protection' became an issue. By the 1990s, the 3Ms had been successful – at least in South Africa – and an enabling environment emerged for including innovative thinking about integrating and internationalising knowledge systems.

This final section, Part III, sets out to explain how – at almost every level – national park science in South Africa was characterised by the 3Is: integration, innovation and internationalisation. The science of conservation itself became more intellectual, less emotional, finally jettisoning ideas of 'pristine balance' and 'stability', while developments in technology and communication made the rapid and wide sharing of knowledge possible.[3] Much of what had previously been studied in discrete silos was integrated, shedding new light on how the elements of 'nature' worked, but also raising new questions. New and more intellectually sophisticated and innovative thinking was required. This was produced by a different cohort of managers and scientists working under a different political regime and, in South Africa, these professionals were now answerable, for the first time, to the public.

Internationalisation and integration were not only the hallmarks of national park science in South Africa in the 1990s. After 1994, a transformed South Africa was positively fêted by the global community, itself better integrated after the fall of the Iron Curtain in 1989, and provided with opportunities to showcase its achievements to the outside world. In environmental terms, this included hosting the second World Summit on Sustainable Development (WSSD) in Johannesburg in 2002 and the Fifth World Parks Congress in Durban in 2003. International recognition also brought international funding into the country through the growth of eco-tourism and, of particular relevance, financial, logistical and personnel support for the innovative scientific projects that have helped transform thinking in and about protected areas.

---

[3] G. Cooper, 'Must there be a balance of nature?' *Biology and Philosophy* 16 (2001): 481–506; J. Kricher, *The Balance of Nature: Ecology's Enduring Myth* (Princeton, NJ: Princeton University Press, 2009).

South African Context

When on 2 February 1990, President F.W. de Klerk announced in parliament the unbanning of the African National Congress (ANC), Pan Africanist Congress (PAC), the South African Communist Party (SACP) and other liberation movements, together with the imminent release of Nelson Mandela, the country's most famous political prisoner, South Africa was poised for total political integration after centuries of segregation and decades of apartheid. An entirely new constitution was up for discussion. Many factors were responsible for the National Party's change of heart, including a military stalemate on the borders of the country and in the townships, a shortage of government revenue and the efficacy of economic sanctions. In addition, in a referendum among white South Africans in March 1992, nearly 70% of voters indicated a willingness to accept political change.[4] At least as important as these domestic factors in bringing about change was the collapse of communism, independence for South West Africa as Namibia and other related changes in the geopolitical order. South Africa could no longer count on backing from the USA and Western powers, while the exiled liberation movements could no longer count on Soviet support to sustain their attacks on the South African state and for the maintenance of camps in third countries. Compromise was thus in the interests of both sets of protagonists.

After Mandela's release and the unbanning of the liberation movements, South Africa experienced considerable turmoil. Nonetheless, a new constitution was hammered out at the Convention for a Democratic South Africa (CODESA I and CODESA II). It was decided at CODESA to introduce proportional representation, 11 official languages and a mixed legal and land-holding system to accommodate the country's complex history. The population itself, formerly segmented into 'tribes' and ethnic groups in accordance with the dictates of apartheid, was subsumed under a single South African nationality. Political integration also meant ending the geopolitical atomisation of the country and the landscape through the reincorporation of the apartheid-era 'homelands' and 'independent states'. Nine provinces were created to replace the original four established in 1910. The first democratic election was held in April 1994 and

---

[4]The referendum question was 'Do you support continuation of the reform process which the State President began on 2 February 1990 and which is aimed at a new Constitution through negotiation?' The Northern Transvaal (Pietersburg/Polokwane) was the only district that recorded a majority 'no' vote.

Nelson Mandela became the first president. He has been followed by Thabo Mbeki (1999–2008), Kgalema Motlanthe (2008–2009) and Jacob Zuma (from 2009).[5]

Meanwhile, as the process of political change gathered unstoppable momentum, the country was reaccepted as a full member of international organisations such as the World Health Organisation and UNESCO. Moreover, the bureaucracies and responsibilities of the former provinces and African areas had to be integrated and reapportioned – roads, education, health services, housing, taxation systems and land management. Political integration also placed heavy new demands on state finances, because basic services and other infrastructure were now to be provided equitably to the entire population and not just to a small minority. This process of political, administrative and fiscal transformation was long, complicated and fraught and was to directly affect national parks and other organs of state that relied on government assistance.

Also much changed after 1994 were the echelons of senior politicians and officials. At first, there was local and international anxiety that many of the country's resources and assets would be nationalised or incompetently managed by the untried new government. For this reason, senior members of the old guard were retained in cabinet portfolios and in the bureaucracy. Many state bodies and parastatals, including the National Parks Board (NPB), underwent a phased transformation. As senior managers retired, they were replaced by black South Africans, and new board members were drawn from constituencies very different from those of their predecessors. The new, integrated South African nation took a while to take shape, but the integration of black staff and managers was hastened by the many early retirements and 'golden handshakes' offered to white employees in almost all sectors of the economy and civil service. This policy of Black Economic Empowerment remains firmly in place.

Other changes that impacted the NPB as well as the country at large related to environmental justice. This trend was not dissimilar to the Green Politics becoming more evident internationally, except that hitherto the NPB had been largely insulated from such trends. However, by the early 1990s, as democracy in South Africa drew closer, many environmental non-governmental organisations (NGOs) sprang up and robust debates about environmental justice within an anticipated socialist order took place.

---

[5]An interim constitution Act 200 of 1993 was superseded by the Constitution of the Republic of South Africa 1996, approved by the Constitutional Court in December 1996 and it took effect on 4 February 1997.

These discussions prioritised 'brown' issues such as clean water, minimising industrial pollution, advancing worker safety and acquiring land for housing and subsistence farming for the poor and marginalised, while 'green' issues such as wilderness, national parks and protected areas, perceived as being the pet interests of wealthier whites, were criticised or downplayed. Under slogans like 'apartheid divides, ecology unites' and 'the greening of our country is basic to its healing', environmentalism rode a wave of euphoria. The expectation was that all South Africans, regardless of race, class or age, would care for the physical environment because now environmentalism was a form of grassroots mobilisation for 'our future and for our children' within a united democratic nation.[6] In 1991, at the University of the Western Cape, was held the first National Conference on Environment and Development at which liberation movements, trade unions and representatives of many religions sought to 'ecologise politics and politicise ecology' and to find common ground on the issue of the environment.[7] Saliem Fakir, a land activist at that time and subsequently a board member of the South African National Biodiversity Institute (SANBI) and currently employed by the World Wide Fund for Nature in South Africa (WWF-SA),[8] acknowledged that the 'one great window of opportunity . . . was the roaring 1990s'.[9] In these years, civil society was

[6]See, for example, J. Cock and E. Koch, eds, *Going Green: People, Politics and the Environment in South Africa* (Cape Town: Oxford University Press, 1991), 15; E. Koch, D. Cooper and H. Coetzee, *Water, Waste and Wildlife: The Politics of Ecology in South Africa* (London: Penguin, 1990); B. Huntley, R. Siegfried and C. Sunter, *South African Environments into the 21st Century* (Cape Town: Human and Rousseau Tafelberg, 1989); B.J. Huntley, ed., *Biotic Diversity in Southern Africa: Concepts and Conservation* (Cape Town: Oxford University Press, 1989). The incoming African National Congress (ANC), together with its alliance partner the South African Communist Party, had been strongly aligned to the USSR and, as Douglas Weiner has shown, the Soviets were at the 'cutting edge of conservation theory and practice'; see D.R. Weiner, *Models of Nature: Ecology, Conservation and Cultural Revolution in Soviet Russia* (Pittsburgh, PA: University of Pittsburgh Press, 2000), viii.

[7]National Conference on Environment and Development. See http://research.omics group.org/index.php/South_African_National_Conference_on_Environment_and_ Development (accessed 18 October 2015).

[8]SANBI is itself a product of the general movement towards integration of the late twentieth and early twenty-first centuries in South Africa. In 1989 the Botanical Research Institute (founded 1903) amalgamated with the National Botanical Gardens (founded 1913) as the National Botanical Institute, the ambit of which was broadened into biodiversity generally with the passage of the National Environmental Management: Biodiversity Act 10 of 2004.

[9]*Business Day*, 15 November 2004. See also J. Porritt, 'Environmental politics: The old and the new', in *Greening the Millennium: The New Politics of the Environment* ed. M. Jacobs

environmentally engaged. Africans, no longer cowed by apartheid, were vociferous in their demands – particularly the communities bordering on national parks – as were elements of white society, including environmental justice organisations and the animal rights community, whose pleas, policies and agendas had been ignored in the past.

The political expression of this optimism was that, based on the premise that environmental dysfunction was rooted in apartheid and white domination, the incoming ANC government created a cabinet portfolio for the Reconstruction and Development Programme (RDP), a developmental initiative with a strong pro-environmental agenda. However, the RDP proved to be a momentary flash. Just two years later, in June 1996, it was replaced by a conventional macroeconomic initiative dubbed Growth, Employment, and Redistribution (GEAR). This free-market-oriented economic directive was silent on the environment but seemed to assume that environmentalism was incompatible with economic growth. To create employment, secure investment and eradicate poverty by whatever means, environmental health might well have to be sacrificed.[10]

International Context

Over the course of the twentieth century national parks had become a permanent and prominent feature of the globalised land-holding regime, even if rationales, management styles, scientific bureaucracies, public access and facilities, state of the environment and biodiversity vary greatly among them. In 1900, there was no model for a system of national parks, but by the 1960s such systems existed in many countries. By then, the International Union for the Conservation of Nature and

---

(Oxford: Blackwell, 1997), 62; N. Carter, 'Prospects: The parties and the environment in the United Kingdom', in *Greening the Millennium: The New Politics of the Environment*, ed. M. Jacobs (Oxford: Blackwell, 1997), 192; A. Bramwell, *The Fading of the Greens: The Decline of Environmental Politics in the West* (New Haven, CT and London: Yale University Press, 1994); and, in the South African context, see T. le Quesne, 'The divorce of environmental and economic policy under the first ANC government, 1994–1999', *Journal of Environmental Law and Policy* 7 (2000): 1–20; P. Steyn and A. Wessels, 'The emergence of new environmentalism in South Africa, 1972–1992', *South African Historical Journal* 42 (2000): 125–158.

[10]W.M. Adams, R. Aveling, D. Brockington, et al., 'Biodiversity conservation and the eradication of poverty', *Science* 306, no. 5699 (2004): 1146–1149.

Natural Resources (IUCN) had assumed leadership through its various commissions and regular meetings, the WWF had become a major project funder, the first World Parks Conference was in train (Seattle 1962) and the IUCN was actively discussing a hierarchy of protected areas. Moreover, over the next 30 years robust international environmental structures came into being, many of them under the aegis of the UN and UNESCO. Within civil society, particularly in the West, environmentalism was strong. Moreover, with the Brundtland Report of 1987, entitled *Our Common Future*, a watershed in environmental thinking began. It built on the philosophy formally introduced in Bali and set the agenda that continues to dominate the literature and guide international action. With *Our Common Future*, the link between poverty, development and the environment had been made explicit and national parks were expected to form part of this new, multi-pronged international agenda.[11]

By the 1990s, then, national parks were no longer exceptional or rare. In 1992, there were many hundreds of them (along with other kinds of protected areas) in almost every country of the world. The literature and publicity about them was enormous – especially the television coverage; World Parks Congresses were held every decade and an improved global economy led to eco-tourism as a popular and profitable undertaking. Bird-watching had become fashionable and twitching a serious business, while viewing Africa's 'Big 5' was on the wish list of many thousands of people. Once South Africa had regained international respectability, it was able to share in these trends and its national parks were poised to welcome a deluge of international tourists who had earlier been deterred by the high level of violence in the country, the sanctions that had been imposed and the apartheid regime's pariah status. Importantly, in 1993 South Africa was at last able to take its seat at the IUCN as a state party and its national parks received even more publicity than previously. After rejoining UNESCO in 1994, South Africa was affiliated with the World Heritage Convention of 1972 that linked natural and cultural heritage through the IUCN, the International Council on Monuments and Sites (ICOMOS) and the UNESCO Man and the Biosphere Programme (MAB).[12]

---

[11] World Commission on Environment and Development (WCED), *Our Common Future (The Brundtland Report)* (Oxford: Oxford University Press, 1987).

[12] World Heritage Convention Act 49 of 1999; K.L. Coetzer, E.T.F. Witkowski and B.F.N. Erasmus, 'Reviewing Biosphere Reserves globally: Effective conservation action or bureaucratic label?' *Biological Reviews* 89 (2014): 82–104.

As a new and highly regarded member of the world community, post-apartheid South Africa was extremely warmly welcomed. Nelson Mandela was lauded as a wise and heroic statesman, and the image of a 'rainbow nation' based on forgiveness, dignity and peace resonated widely. South Africa successfully nominated a number of World Heritage Sites and Biosphere Reserves,[13] and was named as host of the Fifth World Parks Congress, which took place in Durban in September 2003. A great success, the congress attracted more than 3000 delegates from 157 countries, many of whom went on to visit game reserves and national parks in South Africa and beyond.[14] It did not take long for South Africans to assume positions of international environmental leadership. For example, Mohammed Valli Moosa, who had been the minister of environmental affairs and tourism from 1999 to 2004, became the IUCN president from 2004 to 2008.

The idea that national parks, clearly demarcated areas carefully policed to maintain the 'pristine ecosystems', might also be motors of rural and regional development for the poor communities surrounding them had gained considerably in international importance since 1980. The notion of 'Parks for Development' had arisen in the context of the World Conservation Strategy of 1980, the Convention on Biological Diversity (CBD, finally signed in 1992) and the UN World Charter for Nature of 1982. Indeed, it was adopted as the theme of the Third World Parks Congress held in Bali in 1982.

The 1987 Brundtland Report spawned the United Nations Conference on Environment and Development in Rio de Janeiro in 1992, and this in turn linked with the Fourth World Parks Congress, themed 'Parks for Life' and held in Caracas later that year. Two questions dominated proceedings in Caracas. First, how could protected areas contribute to economic welfare without compromising nature conservation, and second, how could marginalised local communities be made more aware

[13]In 2016, South Africa had nine inscribed World Heritage Sites: the Fossil Hominid Sites of South Africa (Cradle of Humankind), iSimangaliso Wetland Park, Robben Island, Maloti-Drakensberg Park, Mapungubwe Cultural Landscape, Cape Floral Region Protected Areas, Vredefort Dome, and the Richtersveld Cultural and Botanical Landscape. In 2016, the eight Biosphere Reserves were Kogelberg, Cape Winelands, Cape West Coast Reserve, the Waterberg, Vhembe, Kruger to Canyons, the Magaliesberg and the Gouritz Cluster.
[14]See A. Hall-Martin and J. Carruthers, eds, *South African National Parks: A Celebration* (Johannesburg: Horst Klemm, 2003). www.iucn.org/about/work/programmes/gpap_home/gpap_capacity2/gpap_parks2/?2137/2003-Durban-World-Parks-Congress (accessed 20 October 2015).

of the benefits of biodiversity and thus champion its conservation? The World Parks Congress in Durban took this even further with its theme 'Benefits beyond Boundaries' and with the Durban Accord signed at the event.[15] National parks now had the mandate to uplift society as well as protect natural resources and encourage visitors.

The world at the turn of the millennium was thus quite different from that of 50 years before. At the end of the Second World War, there had emerged a strong belief in progress, particularly technological progress, but a few decades later it was clear that overall progress everywhere was a chimera. Instead, there was a widening gulf between the developed and underdeveloped world and even greater poverty. Industrial capitalism had not solved the economic problems of the world and its benefits were demonstrably uneven. Prophets of environmental doom, such as the Club of Rome and Paul Ehrlich, proved popular in these years,[16] and the Gaia hypothesis had evoked an image of a world that, although self-regulating, was subject to abuse by humans.[17]

Thus, it was with excitement, a sense of community and a sense of urgency that many representatives of South African organisations attended the first 'Earth Summit' in Rio de Janeiro in 1992. The summit demonstrated how ordinary citizens could come together with governments to discuss the world's resources and how best to distribute them equitably and use them sustainably.[18] It was a new avenue for alternative voices and an opportunity to speak truth to power. There were two major results, Agenda 21 and the Convention on Biological Diversity of 1992, which was ratified by South Africa in 1995.

South Africa was privileged to host the second of these world summits in Johannesburg from 26 August to 4 September 2002 (Rio+10) and to contribute to the debates about sustainability and development from a specifically African perspective.[19]

[15]www.danadeclaration.org/pdf/durbanaccordeng.pdf (accessed 18 October 2015).

[16]D.L. Meadows, J. Randers and W.W. Bekrens, *The Limits to Growth: A Report of the Club of Rome's Project on the Predicament of Mankind* (New York, NY: Universe Books, 1972); P. Ehrlich, *The Population Bomb* (New York, NY: Ballantine Books, 1971).

[17]J.E. Lovelock, 'Gaia as seen through the atmosphere', *Atmospheric Environment* 6, no. 8 (1972): 579–580; J.E. Lovelock and L. Margulis, 'Atmospheric homeostasis by and for the biosphere: The Gaia hypothesis', *Tellus* (Series A) 26, nos. 1–2 (1974): 2–10.

[18]R.P. Wynberg, 'Exploring the Earth Summit: Findings of the Rio United Nations Conference on Environment and Development: Implications for South Africa' (MPhil diss., University of Cape Town, 1993).

[19]A.Y. So, *Social Change and Development: Modernization, Dependency, and World-system Theories* (London: Sage, 1990); J.A. du Pisani, 'Sustainable development: Historical roots

National Parks

The changed international context affected national parks everywhere, but, combined with profound domestic changes, nowhere more so than in South Africa. Perhaps more than most other national parks, South Africa's had indeed been 'fortresses' and areas of exclusion. Henceforward, the NPB would have to take into account sustainability and environmentalism as well as 'benefits beyond boundaries'. Moreover, after 1994 South Africa's national parks had had to compete with protected areas enjoying even higher international profiles. These included World Heritage Sites and Biosphere Reserves elsewhere and in South Africa itself. While national parks were creatures of the colonial and apartheid eras, World Heritage Sites and Biospheres had the advantage of being associated with the 'new South Africa' and regarded as inclusive for that reason.

As will become apparent below, the new South Africa confronted the NPB with challenges the like of which it had never encountered before. National parks were seen as 'white playgrounds', offering government-supported outdoor recreation, and staffed in their upper echelons entirely by white males, the vast majority of whom were Afrikaans-speaking and government-supporting.[20] Given a desperate shortage of land among black South Africans, who had been hemmed into 'homelands' to live in conditions of social deprivation and environmental degradation, in 1994 the NPB was poised between survival and abolition. There was no guarantee that national parks would continue. In addition, the Restitution of Land Rights Act was passed in 1994, which enabled those whose land had been expropriated for racially based reasons to seek restitution. This, too, had implications for the integrity of the national parks, as people who had been evicted forcibly from the KNP and other national parks were thus entitled to reclaim what they had lost.

A further threat to the national parks came from private game reserves that were catering to an ever-growing niche market. There had been a marked decline in the commercial agricultural sector that had begun before the end of apartheid and owed much to popular boycotts of

---

of the concept', *Journal of Integrative Environmental Sciences* 3, no. 2 (2006): 83–96. See also www.earthsummit2002.org/ (accessed 18 October 2015).

[20] Notable exceptions were Johan du Toit, originally Zimbabwean, who joined the KNP in the early 1980s, and Harry Biggs and Rina Grant, South African veterinarians working in South West Africa/Namibia, who were employed by the KNP in 1990, Biggs as the quantitative biologist (biometrician) to replace Peter Retief who had been promoted to Head: Southern Parks.

South African produce as well as international limitations on subsidised exports. This, together with the unsettled and violent conditions in the South African countryside, led to the emergence of private game ranching as an alternative form of land use. Ranches of this sort began to compete with the long-established national parks as tourist destinations,[21] as did private game reserves and lodges that offered wildlife viewing in luxurious circumstances very different from the rudimentary facilities in the national parks. The NPB also lagged behind other state-run protected areas, including the Pilanesberg National Park and Madikwe Game Reserve in North West Province as well as the game reserves of KwaZulu-Natal, which not only offered superior visitor experiences but were also more than competitive in terms of wildlife management and scientific study. Certainly, cognisance of developments in KwaZulu-Natal, in areas currently referred to as 'parks' rather than 'game reserves', together with more collegial relationships between structures of government on matters ecological, would have been beneficial to the country at large.[22] On the other hand, given their greater institutional flexibility and familiarity with the demands of local African communities, the government agencies running these parks could also be more innovative and even experimental, particularly in terms of the concept of community conservation that was gaining currency in Zimbabwe, as well as in other parts of Africa.[23]

Offsetting these challenges for the NPB were opportunities. Of these, the greatest was the chance, made possible by the ending of military engagements on South Africa's boundaries with neighbouring Zimbabwe, Botswana, Mozambique and Namibia, for the NPB to

---

[21]J. Carruthers, '"Wilding the farm or farming the wild?": The evolution of scientific game ranching in South Africa from the 1960s to the present', *Transactions of the Royal Society of South Africa* 63, no. 2 (2008): 160–181.

[22]J.P.G.M. Cromsigt, S. Archibald and N. Owen-Smith, eds, *Conserving Africa's Mega-Diversity in the Anthropocene: The Hluhluwe-iMfolozi Park Story,* (Cambridge: Cambridge University Press, 2016).

[23]See, for example, H. Suich, B. Child and A. Spenceley, eds, *Evolution and Innovation in Wildlife Conservation: Parks and Game Ranches to Transfrontier Conservation Areas* (London: Earthscan, 2009); J.D. Hackel, 'Community conservation and the future of Africa's wildlife', *Conservation Biology* 13, no. 4 (1999): 726–734; D. Hulme and M. Murphree, 'Communities, wildlife and the "new conservation" in Africa', *Journal for International Development* 11 (1999): 277–285; M. Wells and K. Brandon, *People and Parks: Linking Protected Area Management with Local Communities* (Washington, DC: International Bank for Reconstruction, 1992).

collaborate in the Transfrontier Conservation Areas (TFCAs), later to become known as 'Peace Parks'. These held out the promise of expanding the protected area estate with bi- or tri-lateral government support as well as of forming the basis for friendly relations with neighbouring countries. Moreover, it did not take the incoming government long to appreciate that, as state enterprises, national parks offered many employment opportunities in rural parts of the country lacking other motors of development.

The NPB responded to the new circumstances by embarking on an almost total self-reconfiguration. In 1991, at a crucial transitional moment, after a long, energetic and productive career, Pienaar retired as chief director of the NPB, to be succeeded, perhaps surprisingly to many, by Robbie Robinson, with the new title of executive chief director.[24] As has already been explained, Robinson was not part of the University of Pretoria wildlife fraternity and was both more flexible and more modest than others in the NPB. He was the first non-savannah scientist to achieve a senior position in the organisation and the first to reorient the NPB away from the dominance of the Kruger National Park (KNP) – an initiative he handled with some success. He even suspended elephant culling in 1994, to the dismay of many KNP managers. Moreover, unlike quite a few of his senior colleagues, he was not entrenched in the National Party nor a supporter of its racist policies and he was therefore able to chart a new course for the NPB at a time of great domestic and international change relatively unencumbered by political 'baggage'.[25] He initiated reorganisations that resulted in greater decentralisation and gave greater powers to each region and to each national park, a move not generally favoured in, for example, the KNP.[26]

In 1994, Robinson was the first and currently remains only one of two South Africans (the other is Mavuso Msimang) to have received the important Packard Award from the IUCN. The citation applauded him for leading the NPB 'into new fields and to new endeavours' and for playing a crucial role in the transition to a democratic society 'in developing appropriate policies to ensure that the National Parks of South Africa

[24]S.C.J. Joubert, *The Kruger National Park: A History*, Vol. 2 (Johannesburg: High Branching, 2012), 277.

[25]In February 1994 he presented a document to the board entitled 'Towards an affirmative action policy and strategy for the National Parks Board', SANParks archives, Groenkloof, Pretoria.

[26]Joubert, *Kruger National Park*, Vol. 2, 282–289.

are relevant to the lives of all its people, and specially to those previously excluded and alienated from those areas'.

Under Robinson's influence, the corporate culture was further altered when English became the sole language of formal communication in 1996. That same year, the organisation adopted a new name, South African National Parks (SANParks), a move intended to signify a break with the former culture and ethos. In addition, Robinson took to heart the need for SANParks to take up community conservation and to reach out to African communities on national park boundaries, an unthinkable move in previous years. The culture of South Africa's national parks had indubitably been National Party-leaning and thus alienating to other groups. Denis Beckett, one of South Africa's leading journalists, jokingly described the 1980s national parks experience as 'dirt cheap, rule-bound, paraffin-powered and Boereparadys [paradise for Boers] De Luxe. Even your card-carrying South African English-speaker could feel like an outsider, to say nothing of a Finn or a Japanese or – unthinkable! – a Disenfranchised.'[27] This, too, had to change. So did employment practices. Africans had only been employed in the lowest echelons of the organisation and opportunities for advancement were entirely based on race. In addition, while in 1991 the board comprised 11 white males, since that time the racial and gender composition has changed entirely.[28]

When Robinson took early retirement in 1997 (over the splitting of SANParks into separate conservation and commercial sections) he was replaced by Mavuso Msimang, who had extensive experience with UN organisations in Africa and Canada. Msimang had been an ANC activist in exile, and had obtained a BSc in entomology and biology from the University of Zambia and an MBA from the International University in San Diego, California. In 2004, Msimang was succeeded by David Mabunda, who had been the executive director[29] of the KNP since 1998 and who had graduated with a doctorate from the University of Pretoria, the topic of which was integrated tourism management in the KNP.[30]

---

[27] *The Star*, 13 September 1993.
[28] See www.sanparks.co.za/about/annual/ for SANParks Annual Reports from 2003 to the present. SANParks is governed by a board of 18 members, nine directly nominated by the Minister and nine by the premiers of each province. The Minister has a direct supervisory role.
[29] The title was changed from warden to executive director in 1992.
[30] The topic of David Mabunda's PhD thesis (2003) was 'An integrated tourism management framework for the Kruger National Park, South Africa'. He also holds a Master's

At the time of the 1994 elections, considerable attention was given in the media to the future of national parks under a new political dispensation. There was evidence that Africans believed national parks to be examples of 'apartheid repression', with 'game wardens part of Pretoria's security forces'.[31] 'A new government should let cattle graze in some sections of the reserve' was one example of the prevailing rhetoric.[32] 'Whither Kruger Park after April elections?' was another, which mimicked Julius Nyerere's question about a similar situation in Tanzania at the time of its independence, 'Why should the animals live if my people are dying of hunger?'[33] As the *Baltimore Sun* noted in May 1995:

> To the tens of thousands of people who enter it each year, Kruger National Park offers the chance to mingle with lions, elephants and the other wild beasts of Africa. But for the impoverished millions of black people who live on the park's border, it represents an anachronistic bastion of white privilege. For generations, the people on the outside of the park's electrified fence have been like street urchins with their noses pressed up against the window of a showplace. In South Africa's new democracy, those people are now demanding to be allowed inside, to benefit from the potential riches there.[34]

In view of its history, changing the name of the Kruger National Park was also an option considered at this time. Many cities, towns, streets and large dams were being renamed in South Africa in a process of reconciliation and redress, and for a while it seemed that the KNP would be among their number.[35]

---

degree in environmental management (Victoria Manchester University) and a postgraduate diploma in development studies from the University of the Witwatersrand.

[31] Koch, Cooper and Coetzee, *Water, Waste and Wildlife*.

[32] *Weekly Mail and Guardian*, 4–10 February 1994; J. Carruthers, 'Designing a wilderness for wildlife: The case of the Pilanesberg National Park, South Africa', in *Designing Wildlife Habitats*, ed. J. Beardsley (Washington, DC: Dumbarton Oaks Research Library and Collection, 2013), 107–130; J. Carruthers, 'Pilanesberg National Park, North West Province, South Africa: Uniting economic development with ecological design – a history, 1960s to 1984', *Koedoe* 53, no. 1 (2011), doi. 10.4102/koedoe.V53i1.1028. 2011.

[32] *The Star*, 13 September 1993.

[33] *The Star*, 26 January 1994.

[34] M. Hill, 'Fenced-out villagers await South African park reforms', *Baltimore Sun*, 24 May 1995, http://articles.baltimoresun.com/1995-05-24/news/1995144104_1_kruger-national-park-south-africa-wildlife-parks (accessed 25 July 2015).

[35] African National Congress, daily news briefing, 29/30 November 1994, Pretoria. South African Press Association.

In 1998, after extensive consultations with all staff, SANParks adopted a corporate plan sub-titled 'A Framework for Transformation'. The document read in part: 'The transformation process is driven by the over-riding need to shed organisational principles, policies and practices that have for decades been nurtured by the apartheid philosophy of the *ancien regime*.'[36] Other proposed reforms included consideration of how best to serve SANParks' functions and its enlarged constituency. These encompassed modern concepts of conservation and progressive biodiversity management, organisational structures dedicated to excellent public service, openly ethical tourism practices and, most importantly, financial viability. In the course of just a few years, SANParks was further restructured with the creation of new divisions. These included a Social Ecology Unit, founded in 2002, to extend the conservation mandate to the cultural heritage component of national parks. In fact, this had been part of the NPB's mandate from the earliest legislation of 1926, but had been ignored or given scant attention.

Needless to say, the changes described above did not always unfold smoothly, and an older generation recorded bygone days with nostalgia, and the advent of the new with regret. Much as Stevenson-Hamilton had mourned the passing of the liberty of the wilderness he had found when he first arrived in favour of 'rubberneck waggons and tourists'[37] and feared that 'scientists' (veterinarians) would convert the landscape and its wildlife into a zoo, Pienaar wrote a nostalgic chronicle entitled *Goue Jare: Die Verhaal van die Nasionale Krugerwildtuin 1947–1991* (*Golden Years: The Story of the Kruger National Park 1947–1991*) about the period when he held office.[38] Tellingly, too, Salomon Joubert's *The Kruger National Park: A History* has a similar thread.[39] Some of the pre-1994 NPB personnel,

---

[36]M. Msimang, H. Magome and J. Carruthers, 'Transforming South African National Parks', in *South African National Parks: A Celebration*, eds A. Hall-Martin and J. Carruthers (Johannesburg: Horst Klemm 2003), 153.

[37]J. Carruthers, '"Full of rubberneck waggons and tourists"': The development of tourism in South Africa's national parks and protected areas', in *Tourism and National Parks: International Perspectives on Development, History and Change*, eds W. Frost and C.M. Hall (London: Routledge, 2009), 211–214.

[38]U. de V. Pienaar, *Goue Jare: Die Verhaal van die Nasionale Krugerwildtuin 1947–1991* (Stilbaai: The Author, 2010).

[39]Joubert, *Kruger National Park*, see in particular Vol. 2, 280–290. Joubert engaged in spirited argument with David Mabunda, former chief executive of SANParks, on the role of national parks in South African society. See *Africa Wild*, January 2012, http://sagr.co.za/forum/viewtopic.php?f=19&t=194 (accessed 24 December 2013).

particularly in KNP, found coming to terms with the changing political context and affirmative action just as difficult as did those affected by the triumph of Afrikaner nationalism in 1948.

In the new South Africa, SANParks has had to become more account-able to government. The relevant cabinet ministers took a more active role than their predecessors had done. For instance, Marthinus van Schalkwyk, minister of environmental affairs and tourism between 2004 and 2009 (and a former leader of the National Party), demanded a full assessment of elephant management (2006–2008).[40] This was the min-ister's right, because in 2003, just in time for the World Parks Congress in Durban, the new National Environmental Management: Protected Areas Act 57 was promulgated.[41] This gave wide powers to the minister, including oversight and approval of management plans. There have also been external reviews of the organisation – something that would have been out of the question in previous years.

SANParks has also had to be more receptive to integration with other national and governmental environmental initiatives and to the more reg-ular monitoring of all environmental indicators.[42] By the same token, the organisation was able to benefit from the 'Working for Water' and 'Working on Fire' programmes funded by what is now the Department of Environmental Affairs. Many thousands of poor people have been employed on contracts awarded to emerging entrepreneurs, drawn – in cases involving SANParks – from communities that abut on national parks. The aim of 'Working for Water' is controlling the spread of invasive alien biota that threaten South Africa's biodiversity by out-competing indig-enous species and threatening the country's meagre supply of riparian and sub-artesian water. By 2002, 14 national parks were participating in this programme. The emphasis on fire control came in the wake of wild fires, particularly around Table Mountain. Local entrepreneurs have been encouraged to become SANParkts' partners by participating in road works, game drives and tourist initiatives in several national parks.

---

[40]R.J. Scholes and K.H. Mennell, eds, *Scientific Assessment of Elephant Management in South Africa* (Johannesburg: Wits University Press, 2008).

[41]It was amended in 2004, twice in 2009 and again in 2014.

[42]Department of Environmental Affairs and Tourism, *State of the Environment: South Africa 1999: An Overview* (Pretoria: Department of Environmental Affairs and Tourism, 1999); Department of Environmental Affairs and Tourism, *South Africa Environment Outlook: A Report on the State of the Environment* (Pretoria: Department of Environmental Affairs and Tourism, 2006).

As noted earlier, another political dimension related to the transfrontier conservation initiatives. Apartheid South Africa was a beleaguered place at war with itself and, by extension, its neighbours. Quite obviously, in such circumstances transfrontier conservation had scant chance of success. Subsequently, however, transfrontier conservation in southern Africa has taken root and there is some cooperative management of biodiversity among countries with contiguous protected areas. Although such projects have their critics,[43] they are widely regarded as fostering regional unity and knowledge-sharing. In 2000, the Kgalagadi Transfrontier Park (South Africa and Botswana) was proclaimed, and in 2002 the Great Limpopo Transfrontier Park (straddling South Africa, Mozambique and Zimbabwe). A number of other such parks are imminent or under discussion. These include the Richtersveld (South Africa and Namibia), the Maloti–Drakensberg (South Africa and Lesotho), and Limpopo-Shashe, which would bestride the borders of South Africa, Zimbabwe and Botswana.[44]

A key challenge for SANParks since 1994 has been to transcend attitudes, impressions and thinking about national parks and to demonstrate unequivocally that these 'landscapes' are managed inclusively for the material, cultural and ecological benefit of all: in other words, to integrate national parks as part of the totality of South African society as well as to comply with international conventions and treaties. Just as the 1960s witnessed a spurt in the number of proclaimed national parks, so too did the 1990s. Some of these were unusual arrangements that would not have been countenanced in years gone by. The South African state was in no financial position to purchase land for national parks and so began a period of philanthropic donor interest in national park acquisition, with contractual parks becoming the order of the day.

The first to come on-stream in 1991 was the Richtersveld National Park and Robinson was responsible for negotiating the complicated arrangements that made it possible. Covering an area of 162 445 ha on the border with Namibia, and part of the Succulent Karoo Biome, it was South Africa's first contractual park. Discussions with the local communities that occupied the communal land were protracted but

[43]See, for example, M. Ramutsindela, *Transfrontier Conservation in Africa: At the Confluence of Capital, Politics and Nature* (Wallingford: CABI, 2007).

[44]A. Hall-Martin, L. Braack and H. Magome, 'Peace parks or Transfrontier Conservation Areas', in *South African National Parks: A Celebration*, eds A. Hall-Martin and J. Carruthers (Johannesburg: Horst Klemm, 2003), 233–244.

ultimately productive. The pastoralists retained agreed rights to the land, including continued access for their herds, and they were also involved in the structures of management. In 1994, Marakele Park followed, comprising 65 542 ha in the Waterberg in the central part of the country. The land was donated by Dr N. Troost, with additions by Dutch business magnate Paul Fentener van Vlissingen. That same year, a smaller version of the Dongola Wild Life Sanctuary was resuscitated (7859 ha) in the form of the Vhembe-Dongola National Park. This proclamation had the effect of bringing the Mapungubwe archaeological site within the formal protected estate. Subsequently (2004), the name was changed to the Mapungubwe National Park after it had been inscribed into the UNESCO World Heritage List as a Cultural Landscape.[45]

The most difficult national park to have been brought into existence was the Cape Peninsula National Park (1995), later renamed Table Mountain National Park (TMNP). After extensive and acrimonious public and private consultations, the multitude of landowners on and around Table Mountain eventually agreed that the area required management as a unit and that the NPB was best placed to undertake this task. Given the variety of vested interests and the deep suspicion of the NPB in the Western Cape province, it is doubtful whether anyone but Robinson in the NPB together with powerful local allies would have been able to pull this off. In 1999, with Mavuso Msimang now at the helm, two more national parks were founded. One was Agulhas National Park (8528 ha) at the southernmost tip of Africa and the official meeting point of the Atlantic and Indian Oceans. This was largely funded by the National Parks Trust,[46] the Park Development Fund and Fauna and Flora International of the United Kingdom. The other was the Namaqua National Park (41 561 ha), near Kamieskroon in Namaqualand. This had begun as a small wildflower reserve in 1992 and was expanded into a national park in 1999 with generous funding from WWF-South Africa and from a private donor, Leslie Hill. This, too, involved local

---

[45]J. Carruthers, 'Mapungubwe: An historical and contemporary analysis of a World Heritage Cultural Landscape', *Koedoe* 41 (2006): 1–14.

[46]Anton Rupert, long-standing supporter and founder of the South African Nature Foundation (SANF) and founder and chairman of the Peace Parks Foundation, established the National Parks Trust in 1986. Funding of US$2 million was obtained from two Saudi Arabian individuals and this sum was matched by the South African government. Members of the Board of Trustees included A.M. Brynard and F.C. Eloff of the NPB and Rupert himself and Frans Stroebel of the SANF.

communities: Soebatsfontein and Kamieskroon. Money for land purchases to enlarge Addo and Mountain Zebra national parks was provided by the Global Environmental Fund of the World Bank, WWF–South Africa, private donors and corporations such as South African Breweries and Sasol.[47]

Scientific Paradigm and Management Regime

SANParks also had to reconsider its position in the field of science and wildlife management. As we have seen, there had already been critical rumblings from beyond the NPB of the organisation's measure, monitor and manipulate paradigm as well as its territorial attitude, but the NPB, and especially KNP, had brushed aside the criticisms or ignored them. After 1994, this attitude was no longer viable. To access the new scientific world and to survive in it, SANParks' response was the adoption of integration, innovation and internationalisation as its key thrusts. The 1998 'Framework for Transformation' included the duty to implement modern concepts of conservation and a progressive biodiversity management. Inclusion of the descriptors 'modern' and 'progressive' in this document is perhaps a recognition that what was being done in South Africa's national parks before 1994 lagged behind practice in these fields in the rest of the world and behind scientific thinking among South African academics.

Conservation biology was indeed changing and a 'new paradigm' was emerging, even if it harked back in some ways to the conservation philosophy of less control and greater understanding that had first emerged before the Second World War. Scientific knowledge, far from being timeless, emanates from its historical context and after a generation of monitoring, measuring and manipulation, new pressures on scientific endeavour became apparent. It was no longer enough to identify and list biota, valuable though that might be. Where possible – and especially in places like the KNP, with its enormous potential for savannah study – this knowledge was to be integrated to provide an understanding of the workings of the ecological system itself. It was already clear that the collection of data in silos would not allow the jigsaw to be pieced together. For that to happen, some other approach to study was required.

[47]A. Hall-Martin and J. van der Merwe, 'Developing a national park system', in *South African National Parks: A Celebration*, eds A. Hall-Martin and J. Carruthers (Johannesburg: Horst Klemm, 2003), 43–62.

Senior managers were probably better able to adjust to the new circumstances in South Africa, including the new scientific mandate, than staff on the ground: game rangers, biologists and white tourism staff in the national parks, particularly the KNP, which constituted a settled community with common purpose and shared values. Notwithstanding this predicament, SANParks was fortunate to have some genuinely forward-thinking people already in its employ. It also had the prospect of being able to recruit more widely from the ranks of black and women scientists and managers. In place of a hierarchical and mechanistic scientific approach, a culture of innovativeness, greater questioning and greater humility eventually emerged. Consequently, SANParks proved more willing to call upon outside scientific assistance. Importantly, too, without the government support it had previously enjoyed, SANParks tapped into international research funding and partnerships, thereby enabling it to make real strides in the acquisition of knowledge.

As regards the KNP specifically, the support of the Andrew W. Mellon Foundation has been crucial. The foundation had previously been involved in strengthening humanities research at South Africa's liberal universities during the dying years of apartheid. After 1994, the Conservation and the Environment Programme under William Robertson arranged scientific project partnerships – 'research bridges' – between US and South African universities and SANParks, particularly in the KNP. Robertson shared the view of the renowned ecologist G. Evelyn Hutchinson that research is 'the point of view of the mind that delights in understanding nature rather than in attempting to reform her'.[48] And 'reforming nature' by controlling wildlife numbers and other rigid management mechanisms had, as we have seen, been precisely the objective of the NPB from the 1960s onwards. The era of research and discovery that was about to begin thus represented a significant tectonic shift in South Africa's environmental sciences, particularly as regards the KNP.

The ecology and conservation biology that emerged at this time encouraged a view of nature as complex, diverse and unpredictable. Within 'ecology' there were now many specialisations and experts within SANParks were expected to publish their work in the best international journals, not in obscure internal research reports. Over time, the number of publications in reputable peer-reviewed international journals by

---

[48]W. Robertson, 'Conservation and the Environment: A brief retrospective', in *Annual Report of the Andrew W. Mellon Foundation, 2013*. https://mellon.org/news-publications/articles/conservation-and-environment-brief-retrospective/ (accessed 19 October 2015).

SANParks staff and partners proved remarkable.[49] *Koedoe* also underwent a transformation under the editorship of Llewellyn Foxcroft, an invasion biologist: an editorial advisory board made up of experts was appointed, peer review was instituted, high-quality articles were solicited and citation indices were compiled.[50]

There was thus a change in scientific actors and networks as well as in paradigm – with control giving way to strategic adaptive management – and in methodology, as hypothesis–driven research took root in SANParks. 'People' had also to be considered, not only as the beneficiaries of biodiversity or of employment and development opportunities, but also as participants in the science and management paradigm. As will be shown below, it was, for instance, the public that played a key role in stopping the practice of elephant culling. As significant as this change was, some of the ground had, as we have seen, been laid by the likes of Brian Huntley, Brian Walker and others,[51] as well as in the Cooperative Scientific Programmes of the CSIR. Consequently, there was thus a tradition to exploit and expertise on which SANParks might call as it moved towards greater flexibility, team work and partnerships; began prioritising new conservation sciences such as invasion biology and savannah heterogeneity; and adopted new technologies such as LiDAR, a laser-based means of achieving finer geographical accuracy.[52]

By adopting the philosophies of integration, innovation and internationalisation, SANParks began to carve out new roles for South Africa's national parks for the twenty-first century. Principally, 1994 offered the opportunity for parks to be reinvented politically, socially and

---

[49]See, for example, D. Roux, M. McGeoch and L. Foxcroft, 'Assessment of selected in-house research achievements for the period 2008–2011', *Scientific Report 01/2012* (Pretoria: SANParks, 2012).

[50]See the *Koedoe* website, www.koedoe.co.za/index.php/koedoe/index.

[51]Huntley, *Biotic Diversity in Southern Africa*; Huntley, Siegfried and Sunter, *South African Environments into the 21st Century*; B. Walker and M. Westoby, 'States and transitions: The trajectory of an idea, 1970–2010', *Israel Journal of Ecology and Evolution* 57 (2011): 17–22; B.H. Walker, 'An appraisal of the systems approach to research on and management of African wildlife ecosystems', *Journal of the South African Wildlife Management Association* 4 (1974): 129–136; B.H. Walker and I. Noy-Meir, 'Aspects of the stability and resilience of savanna systems', in *Ecology of Tropical Savanna Systems*, eds B.J. Huntley and B.H. Walker (Berlin: Springer-Verlag, 1982):556–590; B.H. Walker and D. Salt, *Resilience Thinking: Sustaining Ecosystems and People in a Changing World* (Washington, DC: Island Press, 2006).

[52]LiDAR is a remote sensing technology that measures distances by using the reflected light from a target illuminated by a laser.

intellectually. It is to the reinventions in conservation science (or, at least, the most important of them) that we turn in the next three chapters.

The following is a list of dates relevant to conservation research in South Africa's national parks, *c.*1990 to *c.*2010.

1987   A.M. Brynard retired as NPB chief director and was succeeded by U. de V. Pienaar (until 1991).

1987   S.C.J. Joubert appointed KNP warden (until 1994).

1990   2 February. ANC, PAC and SACP unbanned. Nelson Mandela released on 11 February.

1990   IUCN 18th General Assembly, Perth, Australia.

1990   National Parks Amendment Act 23 of 1990.

1991   Report on the NPB by the National Productivity Institute.

1991   G.A. Robinson, formerly head of all national parks except KNP, appointed NPB chief director on retirement of U. de V. Pienaar.

1991   Population Registration Act Repeal Act 114.

1991   Richtersveld National Park.

1992   Fourth World Parks Congress, Caracas, Venezuela: 'Parks for Life'.

1992   National Parks Amendment Act 91.

1992   External review of IUCN.

1992   Publication of journal *Biodiversity and Conservation*.

1992   Rio de Janeiro 'Earth Summit': UN Conference on Environment and Development.

1993   South Africa signed Convention on Biological Diversity, ratified it in 1995, and became party to the convention in January 1996.

1994   Publication of A. Phillips, *The IUCN Management Categories: Speaking a Common Language About Protected Areas*.

1994   April. First democratic election in South Africa, Nelson Mandela became president (until 1999).

1994   Commencement of Phase 2 of the Rivers Research Programme.

1994   Robinson suspends elephant culling in the KNP.

1994   Harold Braack appointed KNP warden (to 1997).

1994   IUCN 19th General Assembly, Buenos Aires, 1994. Major revision of IUCN statutes.

1994   Marakele National Park.

1994   Meeting of IUCN Commission on National Parks and Protected Areas (CNPPA) African Regional Working Session in Skukuza, KNP, October.

1995   Cape Peninsula National Park.

1995 NPB Social Ecology Unit instituted.
1995 Richard Bell, Report on KNP Scientific Services.
1995 National Parks Amendment Act 38.
1995 Vhembe-Dongola National Park (later named Mapungubwe National Park).
1996 NPB renamed SANParks to reflect new image and mandate.
1996 IUCN 1st World Conservation Congress (General Assembly), Montreal.
1996 8 May. Formal adoption of new South African Constitution. Nine provinces, 11 official languages.
1996 National Register for Protected Areas in South Africa listed 422 properties.
1996 Public debate on elephant culling, November.
1996 Report on South Africa's National Park system by Harold Eidsvik, former chairman of IUCN Commission on Protected Areas and of Parks Canada.
1996 Special issue of *Biodiversity and Conservation* on South Africa.
1997 First Mellon-funded projects considered in South Africa.
1997 David Mabunda appointed KNP warden.
1997 KNP Research Symposium held at Skukuza, 5 and 6 November.
1997 Mavuso Msimang replaces Robinson as CEO of SANParks.
1997 National Parks Amendment Act 70 of 1997.
1997 Peace Parks Foundation established.
1997 White Paper on Conservation and Sustainable Use of South Africa's Biological Diversity.
1997 South Africa ratified the World Heritage Convention.
1997 Global Invasive Species Programme began.
1998 KNP research symposium held at Skukuza.
1998 Kumleben Commission into the Institutional Arrangements for Nature Conservation in South Africa appointed.
1998 Southern African Institute of Ecologists and Environmental Scientists founded.
1999 Agulhas National Park.
1999 Namaqua National Park.
1999 Review of NPB tourism operations and decision to outsource them. Refocus on biodiversity management as core function.
1999 South Africa's World Heritage Convention Act No. 49.
1999 Thabo Mbeki became president of South Africa (to 2008).
2000 IUCN 2nd World Conservation Congress, Amman.
2000 Kgalagadi Transfrontier Conservation Area.

2001 World Wilderness Congress in Port Elizabeth, November.

2001 Initiation of the Millennium Ecosystem Assessment by Kofi Annan, UN Secretary-General.

2002 University of KwaZulu-Natal launched MSc in Protected Area Management in collaboration with University of Montana.

2002 First Savannah Science Network Meeting held at Skukuza with funding from the Mellon Foundation.

2002 Great Limpopo Transfrontier Park formalised.

2002 Johannesburg World Summit on Sustainable Development, September.

2002 McKinsey Report on SANParks.

2002 Reorganisation of South African higher education.

2003 Fifth World Parks Congress, Durban: 'Benefits beyond Boundaries'.

2003 Mapungubwe inscribed as a World Heritage Site (Cultural Landscape).

2003 National Environmental Management: Protected Areas Act No. 57.

2003 Publication of J. du Toit, K. Rogers and H. Biggs, eds, *The Kruger Experience: Ecology and Management of Savanna Heterogeneity* (Washington, DC: Island Press).

2003 Social Ecology Unit becomes Directorate: People and Conservation.

2004 3rd World Conservation Congress, Bangkok, Thailand. Mohammed Valli Moosa, former South African minister for environmental affairs and tourism elected IUCN president (until 2008). Attendance reached 4800, including ministers, scientists, business representatives and many hundreds of non-governmental organisations.

2004 NGO 'Elephants Alive' initiative to challenge anticipated resumption of culling.

2005 National Party disbanded.

2005 Camdeboo National Park.

2007 Mokala National Park.

2007 Society for Conservation Biology Congress held in Port Elizabeth.

2008 Publication of R. Scholes and K. Mennell, eds, *Scientific Assessment of Elephant Management in South Africa* (Johannesburg: Wits University Press).

2008 IUCN 4th World Conservation Congress, Barcelona.

2008   Publication of N. Dudley, ed., *Guidelines for Applying Protected Area Management Categories* (Gland, Switzerland: IUCN, 2008); S. Stolton, P. Shadie and N. Dudley, *IUCN WCPA Best Practice Guidance on Recognising Protected Areas and Assigning Management Categories and Governance Types*, Best Practice Protected Area Guidelines Series No. 21 (Gland, Switzerland: IUCN, 2013); N. Dudley and S. Stolton, eds, *Defining Protected Areas: An International Conference in Almeria, Spain* (Gland, Switzerland: IUCN, 2008).

2008   Kgalema Motlanthe, president of South Africa (until 2009).

2009   Garden Route National Park created by amalgamating the Tsitsikamma and Wilderness National Parks with the Knysna Lake Area and by the addition of other state properties.

2009   Jacob Zuma became president of South Africa.

2009   May. Department of Environmental Affairs and Tourism split in two: Water and Environmental Affairs, and Tourism.

2010   June. Republic of South Africa, Department of Environmental Affairs, review of institutional arrangements for management of protected areas.

10 · *New Thinking in Conservation Science*

In addition to – and sometimes in association with – the dramatic political changes in the country, three elements conspired to thrust science in SANParks into a new era. First was a series of reports that interrogated the past of the National Parks Board (NPB) and identified new directions. Second were fresh ideas in conservation biology and changes and challenges in the suite of sciences engaged with wildlife; and third was the new management framework that emerged, which acknowledged the uncertain and changing state of scientific knowledge. From an era of maximal interference, SANParks set out to minimise manipulation and engage in theoretical innovation.

Reviews and Inquiries

In the early 1990s, there was great ferment in international environmentalism. In 1992 the World Summit on Sustainable Development took place in Rio and Agenda 21 was adopted. The latter directive acknowledged that national parks and protected areas had a role to play in sustainable economic and social development. These new and wider responsibilities were further endorsed that year at the Caracas World Parks Congress. Moreover, after more than a decade of diplomatic and bureaucratic wrangling, the Convention on Biological Diversity was finally concluded in Nairobi in May 1992, just a week before the Rio summit, and came into force on 29 December 1993.[1] This important convention provided guidelines to be followed by signatory nations to conserve national biodiversity, not least through the management and creation of protected areas. Biodiversity conservation has become the lodestar of national parks – South Africa's included – ever since.

---

[1] B.J. Lausche, *Weaving a Web of Environmental Law* (Berlin: IUCN Environmental Law, 2008), 310–313.

The transformation of national parks from discrete areas in which certain landscapes and biota were protected into institutions legally required to contribute to socio-economic upliftment and to manage national biodiversity created unease within the International Union for the Conservation of Nature (IUCN), particularly its Commission for National Parks and Protected Areas (CNPPA), now named the World Commission of Protected Areas (WCPA). Global environmentalism had brought into sharper relief some of the dissension within the organisation, which had a distinct Western bias, particularly with regard to the growing role of, and emphasis on, developing countries. After some 50 years of existence, the IUCN faced a near-revolution among its members and the secretariat was obliged to institute a review of the whole organisation. Various internal appraisals of IUCN programmes were conducted and one, in 1992, covered the entire organisation. This led in 1994 to a full external report. In these early reviews, there was praise for the Species Survival Commission (SSC) and the CNPPA as being well run, while the other four IUCN commissions were severely criticised. Such assessments have subsequently become almost routine and have resulted in major revisions to IUCN statutes, ongoing decentralisation, as well as more integrated and results-oriented programmes.[2]

With the unfolding of the new post-apartheid era and the election of Mandela as president in April 1994, South Africa's national parks were better placed to tap into the new attitudes and approaches of the IUCN, and to gain the support of the World Wide Fund for Nature (formerly the World Wildlife Fund, WWF) and the United Nations Environment Programme (UNEP), and of many South African environmental organisations and commercial sponsors. Robinson, the then chief executive director of the NPB, prevailed upon the CNPPA's African regional working session to meet at Skukuza in October 1994. Given the new politics of South Africa, and the need for national parks to prove themselves amenable to supporting socio-economic development, much of the meeting was taken up with presentations and discussions on community conservation, eco-tourism, environmental education and funding models, with examples being drawn from Zimbabwe and other parts of Africa. The resulting Skukuza Declaration highlighted the benefits of national parks and protected areas to African economic development, peace-making and partnerships, and called on African governments to

[2]Lausche, *Weaving a Web of Environmental Law*, 288–302.

prepare realistic and properly funded plans for the protected areas under their jurisdiction.[3] Given the preoccupation with developmental priorities, very little attention was paid to the scientific role of national parks at this meeting. However, the topic 'Research and monitoring' was raised and one of the formal action items was undertaking 'research to reveal monitoring needs and to develop protocols for statistically robust and cost-effective monitoring'.[4] The session on 'Research and monitoring challenges' made no mention of basic research, but prioritised that research which underpinned 'informed management of protected areas'.[5]

At much the same time as the IUCN was undergoing reorganisation and the first of the international environmental initiatives mentioned above was unfolding, South Africa's national parks were coming under closer and more hostile scrutiny from within the country. As noted earlier, in light of African land-hunger and the association of these parks with white 'fortress conservation', apartheid and an Afrikaner '*volk*' identity, they faced the threat of abolition. It can be argued, however, that they were spared by the trend towards using them as instruments of poverty alleviation and sustainable economic and community development. There was also the expectation that international eco-tourism would accelerate and national parks would become financially self-sufficient. These considerations, together with the international conventions to which South Africa adhered after 1994 – the Convention on Biological Diversity (CBD) and the World Heritage Convention in particular – plus the prospect of the Johannesburg World Summit in 2002 and the Durban World Parks Congress in 2003, turned the tide of popular opinion in favour of national parks.

Given this new political context and the new expectations, and with the advantage of a different cohort of managers at the helm, the time was therefore propitious for the NPB to review its overall mission and to plan a different way forward. To this end the NPB submitted itself to a number of external reviews. The first, in 1990, was undertaken by the National Productivity Institute (NPI), a parastatal, which was commissioned to investigate various aspects of the NPB, particularly its lack

[3]R. Robinson, ed., *African Heritage 2000: The Future of Protected Areas in Africa. Proceedings of the IUCN Commission on National Parks and Protected Areas African Regional Working Session, Skukuza, Kruger National Park, South Africa, 11–17 October 1994* (Pretoria: NPB, 1995), 132.

[4]See R. Siegfried, 'Conference report', in Robinson, *African Heritage 2000*, 134.

[5]See Section 10, 'Research and monitoring challenges', in Robinson, *African Heritage 2000*.

of productivity. Three important issues were flagged for urgent attention: taking economic, social and political change into account; reversing racial discrimination; and improving staff management capabilities. A new organogram was approved in 1991 that decentralised some operations but also integrated all parks other than the Kruger National Park (KNP) into 'Southern Parks', as had been the case before 1983. As far as science in the KNP was concerned, a new Wildlife Management and Research Division was created with Willem Gertenbach as manager.[6] Decentralisation was, however, resisted by many people, particularly in the KNP. Further reviews took place in 1992, 1993 and 1994. By then, Robinson was firmly in the driving seat, and his 1994 restructuring plans were far-reaching. Again, many staff disagreed with Robinson's proposals, including Salomon Joubert, who took early retirement as KNP warden in 1994. Perhaps not surprisingly, during this period there was little emphasis on scientific research because of the overwhelming focus on internal politics and management.

One of Robinson's boldest innovations was the establishment of the NPB's Social Ecology Unit in 1995, at the suggestion of the sociologist board members newly appointed that year.[7] The unit's responsibilities included the long-neglected study of the historical and other cultural aspects of South Africa's national parks. Other responsibilities included liaising and cultivating good relations with the communities neighbouring the national parks. However, it soon emerged that the Social Ecology Unit had a more activist agenda for changing society. Perhaps because of its unfamiliarity with processes of engineering social change through protected area management or its adhesion to the stridently egalitarian and partisan version of the Murray Bookchin school of social ecology, the unit was not a success. Ill-fitted to the ethos and history of the NPB, it ran its course first as a unit, then as a full directorate before being downgraded in 2003 to the Division of People and Parks. Currently this division focuses on improving the relationship between national parks and adjacent communities. It also eschews the arcane

[6]Originally founded in 1969, the NPI was rebranded as 'Productivity SA' in 2007. See S.C.J. Joubert, *The Kruger National Park: A History*, Vol. 2 (Johannesburg: High Branching, 2012), 280–291.

[7]L. Meskell, *The Nature of Heritage: The New South Africa* (Oxford: Wiley-Blackwell, 2012), 136–146. See also A. Ekblom, L. Gillson and M. Notelid, 'A historical archaeology of the Limpopo and Kruger National Parks and Lower Limpopo Valley', *Journal of Archaeology and Ancient History* 1 (2011): 1–29.

jargon earlier favoured by the unit.[8] Overall, the project of reversing the long-term neglect of social sciences and humanities in South Africa's national parks may have been badly damaged by this bruising brush with radical social ecology.

In 1996, Harold Eidsvik, who had attended the 1994 CNPPA meeting at Skukuza, was invited by Robinson to visit all South Africa's national parks and to prepare a report on them in relation to the national parks of the USA and Canada. Eidsvik was also tasked with evaluating how the parks measured up to the IUCN definitions drafted in 1993, but was not asked to comment on science in South Africa's national parks in particular. Robinson was again being innovative in launching this initiative, as a formal international comparison of South Africa's parks had never before been undertaken. With his past experience in Parks Canada, the IUCN and UNESCO, Eidsvik was well qualified for the task, which he undertook between March and late May 1996. In many respects, Eidsvik was critical, and his report came at a time of flux within the national parks structure and in government thinking about protected areas generally. The creation of nine provinces in place of the previous four plus the Bantustans necessitated many reconfigurations in the South African civil service. Eidsvik noted the lack of consistency in management, in area and in financial support among South Africa's national parks. Pointing to the fact that national parks in the USA and Canada were part of the public service, he concluded that the NPB's parastatal status was, on balance, disadvantageous to the protected area estate. He further noted the need for coherent and systematic planning. In recommending a major review of national parks, he advised South Africa to work more closely with the international community and with the South African public and even to be unafraid of abolishing national parks that did not meet accepted international criteria.

Eidsvik felt that the KNP received far too much attention in comparison with the other parks in terms of staffing and financial support. Following interviews with KNP scientific staff, he concluded that KNP was a conservative, top-heavy institution and that scientific expertise should be more equitably shared among national parks. Admiring of the number of partnered scientific projects, he was nonetheless sharply critical of the neglect of research dedicated to the social sector, predicting

[8]Fax Catherine Senatle, Manager: Social Ecology to Jane Carruthers, 13 July 1998, in connection with a symposium to be held at Berg-en-Dal, 25–27 August 1998, entitled 'Voices, Values and Identities'.

that increasing attention would need to be directed to cultural and historical resources. In his view, far too much attention had been devoted to natural resources and the 'Big 5'.[9]

Two years after Eidsvik's report, Pallo Jordan, the assertive minister of environmental affairs and tourism since 1996, instituted just such a thorough investigation of the institutional arrangements of the national nature conservation sector under the chairmanship of Justice M.E. Kumleben. Never before had the South African government instituted a full overview of the entire conservation sector. The terms of reference were published on 13 March 1998, the responses and interviews followed shortly afterwards, and the final report was submitted in October. Like Eidsvik's report, Kumleben's confined itself to institutional arrangements. He noted the range of sizes of protected areas, the different nomenclature used to describe them and the variety of financial models applying to them. They were, in short, uncoordinated and fragmented. He recommended a 'scientific appraisal' of all protected areas in the country, including funding, ministerial support by way of a specialist technical committee ('an experienced and impartial body of biodiversity specialists') and a separate ministerial portfolio for environmental affairs alone. Like Eidsvik, Kumleben gave science and research very little attention, devoting only one page to the matter (Part XII, 'The employment of specialised staff'). Essentially, Kumleben noted that although centralisation might at first seem desirable for specialised scientific staff, given that they were likely to be specialists in just a few ecosystems at most, the present situation of informal skills-sharing should continue.[10]

From this time on, SANParks, as it was now called, began to submit itself to regular internal and external reviews. A key decision in this regard was the hiring of McKinsey to become involved in national park affairs, a new field for this international business consultancy. The McKinsey investigation of 2002 was fairly ruthless and noted the need for further advice, planning and external assessment.

With all these reviews and reports, it was clear that SANParks was re-evaluating its role and function in South Africa – never before

[9]H.K. Eidsvik, 'A technical assessment of South Africa's national parks in relation to the national parks of the United States and Canada' (Ottawa: Parcs International, June 1996). Unpublished report, SANParks archives, Groenkloof, Pretoria.
[10]M.E. Kumleben, S.S. Sangweni and J.A. Ledger, *Board of Investigation into the Institutional Arrangements for Nature Conservation in South Africa: Report October 1998* (Pretoria: Government of South Africa, 1998), 55.

questioned – and was also being made aware that it needed to operate on sound business principles. During the reviews it also emerged that there was a mismatch between regional structures and the objectives of the science programme, that the leadership style was suboptimal, and that conservation services and scientific services were often misaligned.[11] In light of the recommendations and associated debates, staff positions and functions have been reorganised and financial resources redeployed. Yet, given the preponderance in size and importance of the KNP, and also the government's apparent unwillingness to place all protected areas under one bureaucratic umbrella, comprehensive institutional integration has not been achieved.

Nonetheless, the institutional arrangements for protected areas in the new South Africa were and still are a priority. Just in time for the World Parks Congress in 2003, new legislation was hurriedly passed – the National Environmental Management: Protected Areas Act 57 (amended in 2004, 2009 and 2014). This tidied up some of the loose ends, but not many. In 2010 yet another thorough investigation, titled a 'Review of institutional arrangements for management of protected areas', was launched. Authored by the Department of Environmental Affairs, the document noted that delays in responding to Kumleben's 1998 report meant that the social, economic and conservation landscape had meanwhile changed so much, and fragmentation was even more marked, that a fresh investigation was needed. This document provides an excellent overview of the institutional arrangements at that time, a great deal of data and many comparisons with countries elsewhere. As far as SANParks was concerned, the landmark decision in 1997 to out-source tourist operations meant that the organisation could refocus on its core function of managing biodiversity. To this end, the biodiversity management structures in the country, as well as in national parks, have been reorganised.[12]

The government also devoted real attention to the broader issues of environmentalism and environmental and social justice. As regards SANParks, while it could congratulate itself on its protectionist successes,

---

[11]McKinsey & Co., 'SANParks and McKinsey: Building a strong constituency for conservation: Final meeting report' (2002). 183 pp. Unpublished report, SANParks archives, Groenkloof, Pretoria.

[12]Republic of South Africa, Department: Environmental Affairs, *Review of Institutional Arrangements for Management of Protected Areas* ('Kumleben II'). June 2010. Information on SANParks is located on p. 130.

it had neglected basic environmental conservation and initially was not even subject to environmental regulations, such as impact assessments for new developments. This was to change after 1994, and a development in protected areas has to comply with the same environmental regulations as any other. Moreover, more general ideas on environmentalism – such as water and electricity conservation, control of invasive vegetation – were adopted after 1994. Work conducted in the late 1980s and early 1990s by Guy Preston, an environmental academic and activist from the University of Cape Town, highlighted the national parks' neglect of basic conservation thinking. Preston undertook his research in Mopani Camp in the KNP, and was able to demonstrate how resource conservation increases once visitors using camp facilities are charged the price of water and other resources. The environmental value of this finding is not, of course, limited to national parks.[13]

After 1994, SANParks also became more accountable to the South African public, and this was frequently an uncomfortable new relationship. Previously, the word of a park warden was law, the NPB was politically conservative, and the public had no say in how national parks were run and what they offered.[14] It took the NPB some time to recognise that it needed to justify itself to the public. Certainly, the cries to abolish national parks were one wake-up call, as was the fact that the voting public was no longer just South Africa's whites. In May 1995, Valerius de Vos, then manager of scientific services in the KNP, wrote to Joubert, then warden of the park, about 'going public' on major management issues, something that had never happened in de Vos' 30 years of NPB service. Noting that national parks were supposed to reflect the will of the people and encourage partnerships, de Vos described how the South African public had never been asked for its opinion on roads, fencing, zoning, rest camps and other issues that directly affected their national park experience. He argued that a more democratic approach was now needed in order to encourage co-ownership.[15]

[13]Guy Preston. Interview with the author. Pretoria, 5 March 2013. See G. Preston, 'The effects of a user-pays approach, and resource-saving measures on water and electricity use by visitors to the Kruger National Park', *South African Journal of Science* 90 (1994): 558–561.

[14]Johan du Toit. Interview with the author. Johannesburg, 25 February 2013. Du Toit was only one of many informants who expressed this opinion.

[15]De Vos to Warden, 29 May 1995, A21 Wetenskaplike Skakelings [Scientific links], KNP archives, Skukuza.

Perhaps the most uncomfortable encounter that lay ahead for the NPB and the public was with regard to land restitution. This put the NPB in the position of having to give up ownership, if not control, of areas within national parks that had been taken from local people for nature conservation purposes. One of the most important claims was the return of the Pafuri triangle, in the northernmost part of the KNP, to the Makuleke community in 1998. This was a taxing experiment for all parties. Since then, land restitution has become more confrontational, more contentious and more bureaucratic. While some claims have been settled (e.g. the Kalahari Gemsbok National Park, KGNP), almost all national parks are subject to unresolved claims. There are fears that claimants – so far content to engage in contractual arrangements to continue land management under SANParks authority – might compromise scientific endeavours, but so far, no cases of this have been recorded.[16]

Among the many organisational reviews there was one that was science-specific: in 1994 Robinson, strongly supported by Anthony Hall-Martin, invited Richard Bell to evaluate the Scientific Services Section in the KNP. Bell, a graduate of Oxford and Manchester and an outspoken critic of culling in the 1980s, had worked for more than 30 years in Central, East and southern Africa in wildlife research and conservation, both government and private, and was highly regarded as an innovative but practical scientific thinker and manager. His sometimes radical views were well – if bluntly – argued, supported by evidence and sought to encourage fresh thinking.[17] Appointing him to undertake this analysis

---

[16]See, for example, M. Ramutsindela, 'Land reform in South Africa's national parks: A catalyst for the human–nature nexus', *Land Use Policy* 20 (2003): 41–49; M. Ramutsindela, *Transfrontier Conservation in Africa: At the Confluence of Capital, Politics and Nature* (Wallingford: CABI, 2007); J. Carruthers, '"South Africa: A world in one country": Land restitution in national parks and protected areas', *Conservation and Society* 5, no. 3 (2007): 292–306; D. Brockington and J. Igoe, 'Eviction for conservation: A global overview', *Conservation and Society* 4, no. 3 (2006): 424–470; Centre for Development and Enterprise, *Land Reform in South Africa: A 21st Century Perspective*. CDE Research Policy in the Making No. 14 (Johannesburg: CDE, 2005); B. de Villiers, *Land Claims and National Parks: The Makuleke Experience* (Pretoria: Human Sciences Research Council, 1999); M. Rangarajan and G. Shahabuddin, 'Displacement and relocation from protected areas: Towards a biological and historical synthesis', *Conservation and Society* 4, no. 3 (2006): 359–378; S. Robins, 'NGOs, "Bushmen" and double vision: The ≠khomani San land claim and the cultural politics of "community" and "development" in the Kalahari', *Journal of Southern African Studies* 27, no. 4 (2001): 833–853.

[17]J.S. Adams and T.O. McShane, *The Myth of Wild Africa: Conservation Without Illusion* (Berkeley, CA: University of California Press, 1996), 98–103.

was a bold move on Robinson's part. Indeed, it was likely that Bell's conclusions would be painful to an organisation that prided itself on a long history of 'science', but which had never been subjected to peer review.[18]

Bell's main task was to examine the masterplan as a template and guide for Scientific Services. The masterplan had first come into being in 1985, and despite Joubert's best efforts to update and refine it, Bell found it deeply flawed: woolly in language, full of irrelevancies, conceptually vague and containing nothing about how scientific research should be conducted or what its goals should be. Of the KNP's Scientific Services more generally, Bell acknowledged its long-term monitoring and robust infrastructure, but found many more weaknesses. Admonishing the KNP scientists for their insularity and lack of collaborative effort, he also noted the absence of any awareness of political and public interest in their work. He advocated employing Africans as a priority, particularly in junior positions, so that skills and techniques could be imparted. Bell criticised the NPB's data collection for being unnecessarily exhaustive and for lacking strategic direction or any sense of how the data sets might usefully be analysed. He recommended that external scientists and properly coordinated and integrated projects were required, and that a review panel might be useful. Noting the importance of peer review and publication to respectable scientific research, Bell suggested that publication in such journals be mandatory for all scientific staff. He also condemned NPB's bias towards the natural sciences (contrary to the law) and recommended employment of a senior scientist in 'human studies'. Some of these problems, he noted, could be addressed by standardising job descriptions and through closer integration with other departments within the KNP. Bell also highlighted the dichotomy between management-related and academic research and recommended that both were equally needed. And finally, he reminded his readers that the argument that the KNP is 'natural' or 'pristine', or even that it could be, was a fundamental fallacy.[19] The report was discussed by de Vos to his staff at a workshop at the end of the following month.[20]

---

[18]Johan du Toit. Interview with the author. Johannesburg, 25 February 2013. Another person who was a catalyst for change was Mike Mentis, a former faculty member of the University of the Witwatersrand.

[19]R. Bell, 'A review of the programme of the Scientific Services Section, Kruger National Park. December 1994'. SANParks unpublished report.

[20]De Vos to Warden, 29 May 1995, A21 Wetenskapleke Skakelings [Scientific links], KNP archives, Skukuza.

A decade after Bell's review, in December 2006, an internal workshop for the Conservation Services Division was conducted by research staff at a small game lodge retreat.[21] The aim was to develop ideas about science as a basis for decision-making and to explore 'research' for the division of conservation services generally, rather than at park level. Some of the key ideas to emerge were to make research in SANParks an indispensable part of national and international conservation agendas. They also led to improved linkages between scientific knowledge and conservation decisions, particularly through partnerships with academic and other recognised research institutions. Attention was also given to beneficiation of natural resources under SANParks control through resilience thinking and strategic adaptive management. Some of these were issues that had been raised by Bell in his ground-breaking review.

The twists and turns, achievements and ongoing challenges discussed above and below should not obscure the fact that since 1994 the scientific profile of SANParks has increased in terms of volume of peer-reviewed articles and books, scholarly respectability, conceptual sophistication and international reach. It is much to the credit of the current cohort of natural scientists in the organisation that, within an enabling framework and with vital financial and academic partnerships, there have been significant knowledge-generating projects. From lagging behind other conservation agencies in the country, SANParks has caught up relatively quickly.[22] The organisation took most of Bell's and other critiques to heart. However, the World Parks Congress in 2003, with its emphasis on 'Benefits beyond Boundaries', the Durban Accord and the relationship between national parks and national politics, has so far had little or no impact on the SANParks' formal scientific research agenda.[23] This is despite the observations by a group consulted by the George Wright Forum that the social dimension of national parks – 'the interface between sciences, resources management and politics' – had dominated proceedings in Durban.[24]

---

[21]Finfoot Report, 'A corporate strategy for Conservation Services Division'. Unpublished report, December 2006 in KNP archives, Skukuza.

[22]See J.P.G.M. Cromsigt, S. Archibald and N. Owen-Smith, eds, *Conserving Africa's Mega-Diversity in the Anthropocene: the Hluhluwe-iMfolozi Park Story* (Cambridge: Cambridge University Press, 2016).

[23]See Meskell, *The Nature of Heritage*, 136–146. See also Ekblom, Gillson and Notelid, A historical archeology.

[24]George Wright Forum, 'Voices from Durban: Reflections on the 2003 World Parks Congress', *The George Wright Forum* 20, no. 4 (2003): 8–27.

Figure 10.1. Cover of delegate's package for Vth World Parks Congress, Durban 2003.
Photograph by the author.

SANParks' openness to partners and outside experts has resulted in many more publications about South Africa's national parks that have no SANParks staff authors, further enhancing the quality and quantity of knowledge about the country's protected area estate. Very little of this literature is of the 'inventory' and 'observational' variety, and while the KNP still dominates, credible knowledge is being generated about other national parks as well.[25] In addition, instead of resting on its laurels,

[25]SANParks, Peer-reviewed journal and chapter publications related to South African National Parks by SANParks research staff and by non-SANParks research staff,

SANParks has become a more humble and introspective organisation, and unafraid of critiquing its performance and setting future goals. Although more could be done, regular research reporting has recommenced, staff are encouraged to join disciplinary societies, apply where possible through academic partners for National Research Foundation accreditation, improve qualifications and, where finance permits, to attend conferences, symposia and workshops. Regular internal criticism is solicited as well as views on improving research quality and impact, staff retention and satisfaction and the identification of future research leaders.[26] Most importantly, the Savannah Science Network Meeting, held annually in the KNP since 2002 with support from the Andrew W. Mellon Foundation, has become a major networking and information-sharing event and provides a model for the other research nodes to follow.

Innovative and Integrative Sciences

David Ehrenfeld's editorial in the first issue of *Conservation Biology*, published in 1987, defined conservation biology as a 'recognisable and coherent body of facts, theories and technologies . . . at the heart of all phases of conservation'.[27] Earlier, he had also referred to it as the 'turbulent and vital area where biology meets the social sciences and the humanities'.[28] In 1990, Reed Noss, a major thinker on biodiversity,[29] asked whether conservation biology was qualitatively different from wildlife biology and concluded that, for several reasons, it was. First, it was a science with ethical norms and a mission. Second, there was no

2003–2014. www.sanparks.org/conservation/scientific_new/publications/peer_reviewed_articles.php/ (accessed 24 December 2015).

[26]D. Roux, M. McGeoch and L. Foxcroft, 'Assessment of selected in-house research achievements for the period 2008–2011', *SANParks Scientific Report, 01/2012*.

[27]D. Ehrenfeld, 'Editorial', *Conservation Biology* 1, no. 1 (1987): 6–7. See also M.E. Soulé, 'What is conservation biology?', *Bioscience* 35, no. 11 (1985): 727–734; M.E. Soulé, 'History of the Society for Conservation Biology: How and why we got here', *Conservation Biology* 1 (1987): 4–5; M.E. Soulé and B.A. Wilcox, eds, *Conservation Biology: An Evolutionary-Ecological Perspective* (Sunderland, MA: Sinauer Associates, 1980); M.E. Soulé, ed., *Conservation Biology: The Science of Scarcity and Diversity* (Sunderland, MA: Sinauer Associates, 1986).

[28]D.W. Ehrenfeld, *Biological Conservation* (New York, NY: Holt, Rinehart and Winston, 1970), vii.

[29]R. Noss, 'Indicators for measuring biodiversity: A hierarchical approach', *Conservation Biology* 4 (1990): 355–364.

specific training for conservation biologists, all specialised in fields such as botany, zoology or ecology. Nonetheless, conservation biology might be distinguished from these by being integrated and cooperative, innovatively responsive to local ecosystems but also encompassed within an international scope.[30]

In 1994, Graeme Caughley explained conservation biology very differently in an article listed as among the 100 most influential papers over the century of the existence of the British Ecological Society.[31] His 'Directions in conservation biology' in the *Journal of Animal Ecology* dealt entirely with population ecology, introducing fresh arguments to the small- versus declining-population paradigm and using Australia as the model.[32] More recently (2012), Kareiva and Marvier asked 'What is conservation science?' and described it as an umbrella science of which biology is only part. In this era of the Anthropocene, 'biology' has too strong, too narrow, a reference to the non-human world, whereas 'today, one of the most important intellectual developments is the recognition that ecological dynamics cannot be separated from human dynamics'. Biology must include ethics, climate science, sustainable development and philanthropy.[33]

In July 2007, the Society of Conservation Biology held its highly successful 21st annual meeting in Port Elizabeth. The conference theme was: 'One World, One Conservation, One Partnership', with the emphasis on unity towards a common international goal and the promotion of multi- and inter-disciplinary work. It was attended by hundreds of people, only six of whom were SANParks staff.[34] Indeed, SANParks scientists are not formally referred to, and never have been, as 'conservation biologists'. Rather surprisingly, apart from one excellent article in *Ecosystems* (2008), there has never been an exhaustive conversation about nomenclature, philosophy or disciplinary structure in official documents

---

[30]R. Noss, 'Is there a Special Conservation Biology', *Ecography* 22, no. 2 (1999): 113–122.

[31]P. Grubb and J. Whittaker, *British Ecological Society 1913–2013: 100 Influential Papers, Published in 100 years of the British Ecological Society Journals* (British Ecological Society, 2013).

[32]G. Caughley, 'Directions in conservation biology', *Journal of Animal Ecology* 63, no. 2 (1994): 215–244.

[33]P. Kareiva and M. Marvier, 'What is conservation science?' *Bioscience* 62, no. 11 (2012): 962–969.

[34]Society for Conservation Biology, 21st Annual Meeting South Africa 2007, Programme: One World, One Conservation, One Partnership. Arranged discussion: Co-management of Protected Areas – Idealists', Sceptics' and Pragmatists' Views.

Figure 10.2. Society for Conservation Biology Conference 2007, Port Elizabeth. Courtesy Nelson Mandela Metropolitan University.

or in *Koedoe*.[35] The people working for 'Scientific Services' render a service to the parks through any kind of science or knowledge field, although they are sometimes called 'conservation scientists'. However, although SANParks pays obeisance to the literature that links natural and human systems, not one of the approximately 120 journal papers cited in an assessment of SANParks research deals with a human factor – all are natural science-related.[36]

As mentioned previously, the NPB was given to almost relentless reorganisation. One such occurred in 1991, and involved assessment of the board's scientific research function. The mission, in accordance with the National Parks Act 57 of 1976 as amended, was 'to develop and promote a thorough understanding of the ecosystems in National Parks and to provide high-quality scientific knowledge, skills and resources, in order

[35]F. Venter, R. Naiman, H. Biggs and D. Pienaar, 'The evolution of conservation management philosophy: Science, environmental change and social adjustments in Kruger National Park', *Ecosystems* 11 (2008): 173–192.

[36]Roux, McGeoch and Foxcroft, 'Assessment of selected in-house research achievements'.

to facilitate and verify management of national parks'. In the assessment, it was noted that in the past the board's scientists had conducted original research on the systems and species of the parks in which they were stationed, focusing on taxonomy, animal behaviour and other biological studies only marginally relevant to effective environmental management. It was now time to move beyond traditional ecology and biology and to provide scientific information upon which sound management decisions could be taken. This, in turn, would mean that scientists should play leading roles in planning and environmental management in national parks, and would have to determine priorities carefully. 'Research' was considered to be an inappropriate indicator of what scientists do, and so the name of the department became Scientific Services. The scientists were to apply their knowledge to the entire organisation and bring coastal and inland parks closer together. Branches of this department would exist in the KNP, in Kimberley in the Northern Cape and in Rondevlei near Cape Town. The organogram was approved in June 1991.[37]

'Scientific Services' currently exists with three sub-sections arranged geographically: the Savannah and Arid Research Unit, the Cape Research Centre and the Garden Route. After a long hiatus from the 1990s to 2012, regular research reports recommenced and these usefully chart research developments, with the strong caveat that SANParks is not primarily a research organisation, but mainly focused on managing a system of national parks that represent the indigenous fauna, flora, landscape and associated cultural heritage of the country. Its mandate in this regard mainly flows from national legislation and international agreements rather than the impulse to know and understand.[38]

Perhaps the NPB/SANParks has been wary of the term 'conservation biology' because it is 'mission-driven'. As Meine, Soulé and Reed have noted, this represents a fundamental contradiction: conservation biology is value-laden and ethical while seeking to promote conservation through 'rigorous scientific analysis'.[39] These two impulses are sometimes difficult to align – conservation can be thought of as management, biology as hypothesis-driven scientific research. In South Africa before the

[37]Current assessment and planning of scientific research in the National Parks Board. (n. d.) [1991]. KNP archives, Skukuza.

[38]SANParks Research Report 2012. See www.sanparks.org/conservation/reports/research_report.php (accessed 20 December 2015).

[39]C. Meine, M. Soulé and R.F. Noss, '"A mission-driven discipline": The growth of conservation biology', *Conservation Biology* 20, no. 3 (2006): 631–651.

1950s, science was in the service of protection, preservation and propagation and subsequently of monitoring, measuring and manipulating
separated biota.[40] Since the late twentieth century, the watchword has
been conserving the entire biotic and abiotic components of a landscape
through biodiversity conservation. This requires flexibility, many skills
and disciplines and straddling the porous interface between management
and science.[41]

Other national parks organisations have also struggled to define
what their scientists do and how best to describe their 'science'. The
US National Park Service (NPS), like the NPB, underwent internal and
external review in the early 1990s. As in the NPB, the NPS assumed that
national park management and research provided national environmental
leadership, and was concerned that something professional was lacking.
A major conference in Vail, Colorado, in October 1991 addressed this
subject, and the National Academy of Science weighed in during 1992
with a report entitled *Science and the National Parks*. However, the NPS
took little notice of the comments, concerns and critiques at the Vail
meeting or of the Academy's analysis. Sellars has asserted that the official
response has been empty promises of change, while the successes in terms
of scientific research and training remained 'minor'.[42] While often agreeing with Sellars' assessment, Wright has argued that the reason research
has so limited a role in US national parks can only partly be attributed
to organisational structures. He suggests rather that it is the treatment of
each management or scientific 'problem' as separate and requiring immediate and focused attention that has been detrimental to any long-term
integrated studies. Wright blames the NPS for not placing scientists in
senior managerial positions, and the scientists themselves for not publishing their findings in peer-reviewed professional journals, although
they might retort that the applied nature of their work makes their contributions less readily publishable.[43] The scientific role of NPS was again
raised in 2004 in a special issue of *Ecological Applications*, which contained

---

[40]See C.S. Holling and G.K. Meffe, 'Command and control and the pathology of natural
resource management', *Conservation Biology* 10 (1996): 328–337.

[41]See also C. Meine, 'It's about time: Conservation biology and history', *Conservation
Biology* 13 (1999): 1–3.

[42]R.W. Sellars, *Preserving Nature in the National Parks: A History* (New Haven, CT: Yale
University Press, 1997), 267–290.

[43]R.G. Wright, *Wildlife Research and Management in the National Parks* (Urbana and
Chicago, IL: University of Illinois Press, 1992), 177–191.

the proceedings of an Ecological Society of America (ESA) symposium in Madison, Wisconsin, in 2001. In the journal, David Parsons castigated the NPS for a 'well-documented history of indifference, if not hostility, to the support of basic research', although he also welcomed recent NPS efforts to support science because, eventually, the need to 'understand natural ecosystems' would prevail.[44]

The ESA's special issue on research in national parks also provided an international opportunity for outsiders from South Africa and Costa Rica to compare the NPS approach with that in their own countries. Harry Biggs, then the programme manager of systems ecology research in the KNP, described the South African approach as 'a very forward-thinking set of research goals tied directly to management activities'.[45] Park scientists in SANParks were engaged in 'research facilitation' with carefully selected self-funding partners and he itemised some of the particular activities in which SANParks and its scientific partners were involved. He acknowledged challenges: since the 1990s a cohort of natural scientists had worked in every park which, owing to inherent park differences and staffing inadequacies, had resulted in uneven research, overlap and some antagonism. He referred to this as the 'one organisation, twenty parks' problem, a challenge familiar to the more diverse NPS.[46]

Resilience Theory

The study of the ecosystem has been drawn to systems theory for some decades. This theory recognises that identifying fundamental building blocks is not as meaningful as discovering the totality of a community and its environment. The view of an ecosystem as a web, rather than a hierarchy, is a form of process thinking that looks for interactions and has altered the scientific mind-set of South Africa's national parks completely and impacted the type of scientific work conducted in them since the mid-1990s.[47]

---

[44]J.S. Baron, 'Forum: Research in national parks', *Ecological Applications* 14, no. 1 (2004): 3–4; D.J. Parsons, 'Supporting basic ecological research in US national parks: Challenges and opportunities', *Ecological Applications* 14, no. 1 (2004): 5–13.

[45]Baron, 'Forum: Research in national parks'.

[46]H.C. Biggs, 'Promoting ecological research in national parks: A South African perspective', *Ecological Applications* 14, no. 1 (2004): 21–24.

[47]P. Marshall, *Nature's Web: An Exploration of Ecological Thinking* (London: Simon and Schuster, 1992), 342–345.

Conservation science and ecology are extremely wide fields and in recent years newly named sciences and defined areas of study have emerged within them. Sometimes these innovations are distinguished by the philosophies that underpin them and infuse the scientific thinking associated with them. One of the most important examples is the integrative idea of resilience, a revolutionary concept that has totally upended the notion of ecosystem stability that dominated ecosystem science in previous eras.[48] The leading resilience theorist was C.S. (Buzz) Holling of the University of British Columbia, whose work impressed Brian Walker, the most prominent early resilience theorist in South Africa.[49] Like Holling, Walker was 'grappling with fitting biological world views into the modelling paradigm of the International Biological Programme (IBP)'. They, and others, questioned whether Clementsian climax theory had any validity or relevance. 'Holling was keen to see if there were mathematically simple rules that did not need to assume the stability of an ecosystem'. He was seeking a model that would allow ecosystems to adapt and would shed light on environmental change. Because stability did not create the preconditions for adaptation, he excluded it from the model. He concluded: 'High variability not low variability [is] necessary to maintain existence and learning.'[50] Resilience, and with it the requirement for heterogeneity and variance, have become fundamental to the type of ecology conducted in South Africa's national parks.

Resilience directly contradicts the notion of nature as 'primeval, fragile, and at risk of collapse from too much human use and abuse', the prevailing assumption from the 1950s to the 1990s. National parks were themselves creatures of this way of thinking, namely, a means of saving

---

[48]Although it has to be said that those with a bent for natural history, such as Stevenson-Hamilton, believed that nature had the capacity to right itself if 'left alone'.

[49]L. Robin, 'Resilience in the Anthropocene', in *Rethinking Invasion Ecologies from the Environmental Humanities*, eds J. Frawley and I. McCalman (London: Routledge, 2014), 45–64; C.S. Holling, 'Resilience and stability of ecological systems', *Annual Review of Ecology and Systematics* 4 (1973): 1–23; see also L.H. Gunderson and C.S. Holling, eds, *Panarchy: Understanding Transformations in Human and Natural Systems* (Washington, DC: Island Press, 2002) and J. Tempelhoff, 'Exploring panarchy and social–ecological resilience: Towards understanding water history in precolonial southern Africa', *Historia* 61, no. 1 (2016): 92–112, http://dx.doi.org/1o.17159/2309-8392/2016/v61n1a8.

[50]Robin, 'Resilience in the Anthropocene'; Buzz Holling, 'A Journey of Discovery' (2006), www.resalliance.org/files/Buzz_Holling_Memoir_2006_a_journey_of_discovery_buzz_holling.pdf (accessed 24 December 2015). See also Gunderson and Holling, *Panarchy*, chapters 2, 3 and 11.

part of that primeval and fragile nature in its 'original' form. However, according to Lalasz *et al.*, 'the data simply do not support the idea of a fragile nature at risk . . . nature is so resilient that it can recover rapidly from even the most powerful human disturbances'.[51] Mathematical modelling by Buzz Holling and Brian Walker, along with Ross Westoby and Imanuel Noy-Meir, indicated that these transitions might occur relatively quickly but that the system did not revert to a previous stable state, but 'flipped' into a new state.[52] Nonetheless, until the 1990s the NPB was resistant to abandoning the idea of stability, crucial to the project of maintaining a 'pristine' environment.

The early modelling and systems work in the KNP conducted by Starfield, Retief and Owen-Smith referred to in a previous chapter, and later augmented by Harry Biggs and Kevin Rogers, demonstrated this flipping conclusively with regard to certain wildlife species in the savannah. This finding resonated with systems theory that had arisen from the 1940s onwards. These new avenues of research encouraged some (not all) scientists in the NPB/SANParks to change 'the paradigm' and to incorporate resilience and heterogeneity into ecological thinking. Maintaining and encouraging variability at all levels of the ecosystem became the guiding principle of science and, as will be explained, of management. Because resilience is complex and mathematical and requires many case studies and the involvement of many disciplines, it has itself been a further catalyst for scientific internationalisation and integration. Much of the literature has been generated by collaborating teams of authors, as recent publications statistics for SANParks attest.[53]

---

[51]R. Lalasz, P. Kareiva and M. Marvier, 'Conservation in the Anthropocene: Beyond solitude and fragility', *Breakthrough Journal* 2 (2011). http://thebreakthrough.org/index.php/journal/past-issues/issue-2/conservation-in-the-anthropocene/(accessed 25 July 2015).

[52]B.H. Walker and D. Salt, *Resilience Thinking: Sustaining Ecosystems and People in a Changing World* (Washington, DC: Island Press, 2006), 54–55, 81–83, 91. See also M. Westoby, B. Walker and I. Noy-Meir, 'Opportunistic management for rangelands not at equilibrium', *Journal of Range Management* 42, no. 2 (1982): 266–274; M.T. Mentis, D. Grossman, M.B. Hardy, T. O'Connor and P.J. O'Reagain, 'Paradigm shifts in South African range science, management and administration', *South African Journal of Science* 85 (1989): 684–687.

[53]See R. Sooryamoorthy, 'Scientific research in the natural sciences in South Africa: A scientometric study', *South African Journal of Science* 109, nos. 7/8 (2013): 57–67. This article explains that publications with South African scientific co-authorship between 1975 and 2005 rose from 66% to 89%, 67% of which were domestic collaborations, although there was a notable increase in international cooperation over the period.

Another scientific perspective that became evident in this period has been that of 'ecosystem services'. The best-known exposition of this notion was Gretchen Daily's *Nature's Services: Societal Dependence on Natural Ecosystems* (1997). The fact that national parks may be optimal governance regimes for studying and providing ecosystem services (the rivers of the KNP are a prime example[54]) has had a considerable impact on the science and management of such parks in South Africa. Ecosystem services, whether provided by soil, water, pollinators, forests, etc., can be of value to life on earth in various ways. Certainly providing economic benefit is one much-vaunted value and tangibly and directly supports arguments for conserving functioning ecosystems.[55] Unlike earlier conservation philosophies that invoked 'the spiritual and transcendental value of untrammelled nature', ecosystem services speaks to a generation, particularly in the developing world, that demands concrete human benefits.[56] South African scientists have played an important role in the implementation of this concept.[57]

The ecosystem services approach has direct links with restoration ecology, a branch of science particularly relevant to many of South Africa's newer national parks, which have been established in areas previously farmed or where the indigenous vegetation and fauna have been compromised through over-utilisation. These include Marakele, Mokala and Tankwa-Karoo. Apart from the reintroduction of wild animal species into national parks such as Addo and Golden Gate, restoration ecology was first put to the test with the proclamation of the Pilanesberg National Park in the Bophuthatswana 'homeland' on rather degraded farmland in order to attract tourists to the nearby Sun City resort.[58]

---

[54]See next chapter.

[55]G. Daily, ed., *Nature's Services: Societal Dependence on Natural Ecosystems* (Washington, DC: Island Press, 1997). See also R.B. Norgaard, 'Commentary on Gretchen Daily, *Nature's Services* (1997)', in *The Future of Nature: Documents of Global Change*, eds L. Robin, S. Sörlin and P. Warde (New Haven, CT: Yale University Press), 462–464.

[56]Lalasz, Kareiva and Marvier, 'Conservation in the Anthropocene'; B.N. Egoh, 'Integrating ecosystem services into conservation planning in South Africa' (PhD diss., Stellenbosch University, 2009).

[57]R.M. Cowling, B. Egoh, A.T. Knight, P. O'Farrel, *et al.*, 'An operational model for mainstreaming ecosystem services for implementation', *Proceedings of the National Academy of Sciences* 105, no. 28 (2008): 9483–9488.

[58]J. Carruthers, 'Designing a wilderness for wildlife: The case of the Pilanesberg National Park, South Africa', in *Designing Wildlife Habitats*, ed. J. Beardsley (Washington, DC:

Invasion ecology (or invasion biology) is another science that has become a priority within SANParks – as well as elsewhere in South Africa, particularly in the fynbos vegetation of the Western Cape province. It is directly related to ecosystem services because invading vegetation can quickly compromise services from soil, water and other resources. Despite managing for a 'pristine' ecosystem, alien flora quickly invaded the KNP and other national parks. As noted earlier, the rampant spread of alien flora spawned 'Working for Water', an enormous poverty relief programme initiated in 1995 by Guy Preston.[59] The first Working for Water team conducted the initial alien plant control project in the KNP in 1997.[60]

The literature on invasion biology has grown exponentially since Charles Elton's 1958 *The Ecology of Invasions by Animals and Plants* and Alfred Crosby's 1986 *Ecological Imperialism: The Biological Expansion of Europe, 900–1900*.[61] So important has this science become, and so detrimental have invasive species become to national parks, that Springer has launched a book series dedicated to the field. One of the most important titles in the series is *Plant Invasions in Protected Areas: Patterns, Problems and Challenges*, edited by, among others, Llewellyn Foxcroft, a SANParks employee.[62] The concerns about invading alien vegetation and its

Dumbarton Oaks Research Library and Collection, 2013), 107–130; J. Carruthers, 'Pilanesberg National Park, North West Province, South Africa: Uniting economic development with ecological design – a history, 1960s to 1984', *Koedoe* 53, no. 1 (2011), Art #1028, 10 pages, doi: 10.4102/koedoe.V53i1.1028. 2011.

[59]See www.environment.gov.za/projectsprogrammes/wfw (accessed 26 December 2015).

[60]L.C. Foxcroft and S. Freitag-Ronaldson, 'Seven decades of institutional learning: Managing alien plant invasions in the Kruger National Park, South Africa', *Oryx* 41, no. 2 (2007): 160–167.

[61]C. Elton, *The Ecology of Invasions by Animals and Plants* (London: Methuen, 1958); A.W. Crosby, *Ecological Imperialism: The Biological Expansion of Europe, 900–1900* (New York, NY: Cambridge University Press, 1986); D.R. Richardson, ed., *Fifty Years of Invasion Ecology: The Legacy of Charles Elton* (Oxford: Wiley-Blackwell, 2011).

[62]L.C. Foxcroft, P. Pyšek, D.M. Richardson and P. Genovesi, eds, *Plant Invasions in Protected Areas: Patterns, Problems and Challenges* (Dordrecht: Springer, 2013). See also I.A.W. Macdonald and D.M. Richardson, 'Alien species in terrestrial ecosystems of the fynbos biome', in *The Ecology and Management of Biological Invasions in Southern Africa*, eds I.A.W. Macdonald, F.J. Kruger and A.A. Ferrar (Cape Town: Oxford University Press, 1986), 77–91; I.A.W. Macdonald and M.L. Jarman, eds, *Invasive Alien Plants in the Terrestrial Ecosystems of Natal, South Africa*, SA National Scientific Programmes Report 118 (Pretoria: CSIR, 1985); I.A.W. Macdonald, D.L. Clark and H.C. Taylor, 'The history and effects of alien plant control in the Cape of Good Hope Nature Reserve,

Figure 10.3. Working for Water.
Photograph by Brian van Wilgen.

accelerating impact have become more acute over the years, and this issue is now a significant scientific thrust within SANParks.[63] The history of invasion ecology – an intellectually dynamic and emotionally charged topic – has yet to be fully explored. However, as Davis briefly notes, it has always been connected with conservation, specifically of the 'original' flora or fauna 'invaded' by the newcomers. Global change science, encapsulating many different kinds of change, including climate change, and the emphasis on biodiversity, both characteristics of the 1990s, facilitated the evolution of invasion biology and its institutionalisation within research and conservation structures, including SANParks.[64]

1941–1987', *SA Journal of Botany* 55 (1989): 56–75; I.A.W. Macdonald, 'The history, impacts and control of introduced species in the Kruger National Park, South Africa', *Transactions of the Royal Society of South Africa* 46, no. 4 (1988): 251–276.

[63]Foxcroft, Pyšek, Richardson and Genovesi, *Plant Invasions in Protected Areas*; *Diversity and Distributions* is a highly cited journal devoted to invasion biology, edited by David Richardson of the Centre for Invasion Biology, University of Stellenbosch.

[64]M.A. Davis, 'Invasion biology 1958–2005: The pursuit of science and conservation', in *Conceptual Ecology and Invasion Biology*, eds M.W. Cadotte, S.M. McMahon and T. Fukami (Dordrecht: Springer, 2006), 35–64. See also M.A. Davis, *Invasion Biology* (Oxford: Oxford University Press, 2009).

Strategic Adaptive Management

Within the complex and changed context outlined above, the time had
arrived for a totally new approach to science and management in South
Africa's national parks. Fortunately, as the old guard left, there was a
new generation of scientists and managers who were not wedded to the
past, nor over-awed by the previous hierarchy and its philosophies and
achievements. They proved ready to strike out in a new direction and
the reactionary elements were not allowed to derail the larger project of
change. That change was made especially visible in a more productive
partnership between science and management through the adoption of
adaptive management, or in SANParks parlance, strategic adaptive management (SAM), in place of the old command-and-control model.

Adams and McShane credit Richard Bell with this 'most far-reaching
effort to ground science firmly in the day-to-day realities of wildlife management'. They reiterate his point that a specific kind of research was
needed, research 'to improve the understanding of complex ecological,
economic and social systems in order to allow conservation agencies to
achieve their objectives more effectively'. This is, as Robin points out,
exactly what resilience thinking implied: it was 'a key concept in shifting
ecosystem thinking from science into management'.[65] Furthermore, Bell
believed that 'managing science is akin to gambling', with his form of
gambling being called 'adaptive management', which aimed to formalise
trial and error. Essentially, SAM meant adapting to uncertainties, learning from feedback loops, carefully recording procedures and monitoring
results. Such management requires 'a complete rethinking of the professions of wildlife management and of science'. As Adams and McShane
explain, Bell's arguments – as early as the 1980s – are, despite his being
no romantic, predicated on conservation as values-based.[66] Moreover, by
acknowledging imperfect knowledge and recognising that overconfidence
and control can be damaging, the air of arrogance that had enshrouded
wildlife science in South African national parks began to dissipate. A further distinction between the policy of the 3Ms and SAM was that a wide
group of managers and stakeholders were invited to participate in developing joint vision and objectives hierarchies. This expanded participative

[65]L. Robin, 'Commentary on C.S. Holling, *Resilience and Stability of Ecological Systems* (1973)', in *The Future of Nature: Documents of Global Change*, eds Robin, Sörlin and Warde, 257.
[66]J.S. Adams and T.O. McShane, *The Myth of Wild Africa: Conservation Without Illusion* (Berkeley, CA: University of California Press, 1996), 98–100.

element has become recognised in the international literature as essential to the adaptive governance of complex social ecological systems.[67]

Bell did not invent adaptive management, but he may have been the first to appreciate its relevance to African wildlife and to advocate its adoption as a research and management tool. These new ideas began to permeate particular scientific echelons, especially the rangeland scientists outside the NPB. Adaptive management links directly to the work of Holling and his colleagues in Canada and the USA in the 1970s on resilience theory, and also to his work in the early 1990s when he was director of the International Institute for Applied Systems Analysis in Vienna. As these ideas spread through the work of Walker and other rangeland scientists in southern Africa beyond the orbit of the University of Pretoria, older ideas began to give way more widely to adaptive management.[68] It was first introduced into the NPB in 1995.

One of the attractions of SAM was precisely its potential to bring management and scientific research closer in a productive, mutually supportive relationship.[69] In 2011 an extended special issue of *Koedoe* was published on the theme of strategic adaptive management, with articles by many of the people involved in its initiation and perpetuation.[70] In their *Koedoe* editorial, Roux and Foxcroft describe it as 'an

[67]I am grateful to Peter Novellie for alerting me to this point. D.J. Roux and L.C. Foxcroft, 'The development and application of strategic adaptive management within South African National Parks', *Koedoe* 53, no. 2 (2011), 5 pages, doi: 10.4102/koedoe. v53i2.1049; P. Cilliers, H.C. Biggs, S. Blignaut, A.G. Choles, J.S. Hofmeyr, G.P.W. Jewitt and D.J. Roux, 'Complexity, modeling, and natural resource management', *Ecology and Society* 18, no. 3 (2013): 1, http://dx.doi.org/10.5751/ES-05382-180301; S. Freitag, H. Biggs and C. Breen, 'The spread and maturation of strategic adaptive management within and beyond South African national parks', *Ecology and Society* 19, no. 3 (2014): 25, http://dx.doi.org/10.5751/ES-06338-190325. See also D.J. Snowden and M.E. Boone, 'A leader's framework for decision making', *Harvard Business Review*, November (2007): 1–8.

[68]Mentis, Grossman, Hardy, O'Connor and O'Reagain, 'Paradigm shifts in South African range science'; K.H. Rogers and H.C. Biggs, 'Integrating indicators, endpoints and value systems in strategic management of the Kruger National Park', *Freshwater Biology* 41 (1999): 439–451.

[69]K.H. Rogers, 'Managing science/management partnerships: A challenge of adaptive management', *Conservation Ecology* [online] 2, no. 2 (1998), www.consecol.org/vol2/iss2/resp1/ (accessed 20 December 2015); D.J. Roux, K.H. Rogers, H.C. Biggs, P.J. Ashton and A. Sergeant, 'Bridging the science–management divide: Moving from unidirectional knowledge transfer to knowledge interfacing and sharing', *Ecology and Society* 11, no. 1 (2006): 4, www.ecologyandsociety.org/vol11/iss1/art4/(accessed 26 December 2015).

[70]*Koedoe* 53, no. 2 (2011).

appealing approach to deal with inherent uncertainty in complex and interactive social–ecological systems', 'learning-by-doing in a scientific way, adapting behaviour and overall direction as new information becomes available'. In addition, the importance of setting 'thresholds of potential concern' (TPCs) – a vocabulary and process that emerged from a workshop held in February 1997 – rather than establishing firm outcomes is explored in this number. Kevin Rogers and Harry Biggs played a key role in developing TPCs, which are crucial to SAM. The tools needed to establish the probability of potential TPCs are complex,[71] and according to many, even in international terms, TPCs are extremely innovative and have forced people to think clearly and hard about all aspects of SAM.[72]

As will be seen in the following chapter, the open debate around culling as a tool of elephant management was characteristic of the changed attitude of SANParks in the early years of the twenty-first century. Once almost completely closed off from other scientists – whether South African or from abroad – SANParks seemed keen to engage with any knowledgeable expert as well as with the public. It was indeed a new face of South Africa's national park, in the forefront of which were Harry Biggs of the KNP, mentioned above, and Hector Magome, who replaced Anthony Hall-Martin at SANParks head office in 1996. Magome was the first black ecologist employed in the conservation sector. He joined Bophuthatswana National Parks in 1986, thereafter obtaining his MSc from the University of the Witwatersrand and his prize-winning PhD in conservation biology from the University of Kent. Magome became SANParks' energetic – and charismatic and, indeed, courageous – executive director of Conservation Services. His motto was: 'the biggest impediment to new thinking is old thinking . . . the largest obstruction to learning and change is what you already know',[73] sentiments that accorded well with the new era.

---

[71]Roux and Foxcroft, 'The development and application of strategic adaptive management'. See also H. Biggs and P. Novellie, 'Science for biodiversity management', in *South African National Parks: A Celebration*, eds A. Hall-Martin and J. Carruthers (Johannesburg: Horst Klemm, 2003), 67–84.

[72]William Bond. Interview with the author. Cape Town, 3 September 2012.

[73]Hector Magome, paper presented at the Royal Society of South Africa Spring Science Showcase, Johannesburg, September 2012. Both Mabunda and Magome left SANParks abruptly in 2014. Fundisile Mketeni was appointed CEO in place of Mabunda and Magome's current replacement (acting) is Michael Knight.

Although SAM is presented in *Koedoe* as a scientific approach, it strongly resonates with changes in other fields of knowledge, the humanities and social sciences in particular. They, too, have been influenced by post-modern ideas about the reliability of evidence and the recognition that human experience and knowledge are not objective, certain or subject to reason. It is now held that knowledge is shaped by cultural biases and modes of expression, is not progressive and has to be constantly recreated. SAM is not without critics, some on account of the ideas mentioned above, others because SAM begins from the premise that because the world is complicated and complex and always behaves differently, the past is a poor indicator of the future. This then raises the awkward question of whether any knowledge gained will ever be useful for the future.[74] However, SANParks scientist/managers would probably respond that it is the best available tool at the moment and that one should simply remain open to new thinking as it develops.

With hindsight, it is remarkable how quickly a totally different and innovative approach to science and management pervaded the NPB/SANParks in the 1990s. However, one may argue that the very tumultuousness of the times locally and globally was conducive to innovation. In addition, many of the 'old guard' in the NPB retired, thus creating leadership space for newcomers with fresh thinking. SAM is most readily applicable to ecosystem research and management, and therefore first took root in the KNP rather than the smaller national parks. With the strong or dogmatic scientific leaders of the past gone from the park by 1997, and with the support thereafter of the charismatic David Mabunda, not a scientist but an expert in tourism, middle-ranking scientists in the KNP were able to demonstrate how advantageous their ideas could be. In addition, they had the support at headquarters of Robinson, and subsequently of his successor Mavuso Msimang, a manager by profession and

---

[74]See H. Biggs, S. Ferreira, S. Freitag-Ronaldson and R. Grant-Biggs, 'Taking stock after a decade: Does the "thresholds of potential concern" concept need a socio-ecological revamp?', *Koedoe* 53 (2011): 9; J.E. Mcfadden, T.L. Hiller and A.J. Tyre, 'Evaluating the efficacy of adaptive management approaches: Is there a formula for success?', *Journal of Environmental Management* 92 (2011): 1354–1359; L. Rist, B.M. Campbell and P. Frost, 'Adaptive management: Where are we now?', *Environmental Conservation* 1 (2012): 1–14; B.W. van Wilgen and H.C. Biggs, 'A critical assessment of adaptive ecosystem management in a large savanna protected area in South Africa', *Biological Conservation* 144 (2011): 1179–1187.

a man who encouraged innovation.[75] Thus, scientific research was able to break free and the new guard were able to bring together scientific research and management as part of the SAM strategy.[76]

These changes in leadership allowed scientific research to flourish and take new directions, but they also heralded change in the balance of power within SANParks towards professional management and commercially viable tourism and away from research and management. With this change came the need for research funding and research partners, both of which – at least for the KNP – were forthcoming during the first two decades of the 'new' South Africa, as will be explained in the next chapter. By contrast, the emphases on biodiversity and community cooperation led to the establishment of a new group of national parks with different scientific priorities. These will be examined in Chapter 12.

[75]These changes in top management were also, of course, politically driven. See B. Maguranyanga, '"Our battles also changed": Transformation and black empowerment in South Africa's national parks, 1991–2008' (PhD diss., University of Michigan, 2009). https://books.google.co.za/books?id=b3hp0AVJyxsC&printsec=copyright#v=onep-age&q&f=false (accessed 7 November 2015).

[76]See M. Knight and G. Castley, 'Conservation management', in Hall-Martin and Carruthers, eds, *South African National Parks: A Celebration*, 98–110.

11 · *The Kruger National Park*

As we have seen in previous chapters, international and local socio-political transformations totally altered scientific research in South Africa's national parks, as well as its management. The Kruger National Park (KNP) continued to attract the lion's share of attention. In this period, it was to prove an almost incomparably rich source for knowledge and its scientific and management structures were immeasurably more sophisticated than those elsewhere on the subcontinent and beyond. By 1990, the KNP was a mine of scientific information waiting to be tapped, and in this period it was also considered a potential global asset on account of its fame for the long-term protection of its landscape. Indeed, once the threat of its abolition passed after 1994, it was regarded as of major international significance, despite the failure of the application for world heritage status in 1994.[1]

The data sets mentioned as being part of the 3Ms were long and potentially useful, but required analysis. Nor were these data sets and other collections perfect, because no research hypothesis framed their collection, and many of the inventories (which required tedious maintenance) were wasted effort because of the gaps and deficiencies in them. Because the data had not been structured in a logical or scientific manner, they could not be retrofitted into innovative research projects.[2]

Certainly, the knowledge domain that was SANParks had been energised in the 1990s, but so too had the need to attract tourists and generate revenue increased at a time when the national exchequer faced demands as never before. After 1994, the new state was obliged to provide support

---

[1] Van der Walt to Robinson and Joubert, 7 January 1994. A concept document in preparation for applying for world heritage status for the KNP was submitted for evaluation. A21 Wetenskaplike skakelinge. KNP archives, Skukuza. It is not entirely clear from the record how far this application proceeded.

[2] Morné du Plessis. Interview with the author. Cape Town, 20 January 2014. Johan du Toit. Interview with the author. Johannesburg, 25 February 2013.

to nine provinces and to meet enormous pent-up expectations of black South Africans on whom very little had been spent under apartheid. Expenditure on national parks was a very low priority. It did not take the country long to realise that local and, particularly, international, tourism could become a source of significant revenue, providing that accommodation and services were tailored to a modern and sophisticated tourist market. More directly for SANParks, obtaining such revenue was the means of its salvation.

Manoeuvring a large and inflexible organisation like SANParks in new directions; curtailing expenditures on unproductive staff, administration and existing tourism services; introducing a new philosophy such as management by objective while at the same time maintaining a high standard of conservation management and scientific research was never going to be easy. Inevitably, there was considerable fall-out and within and outside SANParks there was a loud chorus of criticism from those who had supported the philosophies of the 1970s and 1980s and had benefited from the lavish spending of that era. Certainly, it was strenuously argued that sufficient 'luxury' tourism existed in South Africa's private game reserves and that national parks should offer a different experience, focused on looking at biodiversity, not pandering to tourist demands. There was an equally strong argument that it was not the task of the state to run a hospitality industry, nor was it a core state competency. Dissension over the commercial direction the SANParks board of directors insisted on at this time resulted in Robinson's early retirement, and the replacement of him and others by businessmen actively interested in commercialising tourism in national parks (in the same way as the US and other national parks had done). The board also realised that professional management was needed and strove to make appointments that reflected these modern business concerns.[3] For a while there was considerable unhappiness among staff and white visitors to national parks, which still surfaces from time to time.[4]

The overall management of SANParks bifurcated in the mid-1990s into sustainable tourism and sustainable science. With the introduction of Strategic Adaptive Management (SAM), conservation management and

[3]Particularly David Mabunda, Director of the KNP and subsequently Chief Executive Officer of SANParks, an acknowledged authority on sustainable tourism.
[4]See, for example, the summary of the situation in P. Fearnhead and D. Mabunda, 'Towards sustainability', in *South African National Parks: A Celebration*, eds A. Hall-Martin and J. Carruthers (Johannesburg: Horst Klemm, 2003), 184–204.

conservation science came together. As Folke *et al.* noted: 'When adaptive management is practiced, policies become hypotheses and management actions become the experiments to test those hypotheses.'[5] However, the relationship is not always harmonious, particularly in smaller national parks where the implementation of adaptive management is more difficult. Moreover, there are certain areas in which management trumps science, for example, rhino poaching and problem animal control.[6] The matter of rhino poaching has reached endemic and very worrying proportions and it has become evident that this trade is of international reach and is linked to other aspects of illegal and corrupt trade, including money laundering and drugs. So serious is the matter that considerable resources have had to be reallocated from other business, including scientific research, and the older principles of protect, preserve and propagate reinstated together with stringent procedures of monitoring and manipulation.

During the turbulent transitional years of 1994–1996 several issues became clear. First, global conservation science was changing focus and paradigm and second, that the South African public would demand more of its protected areas, not only politically and economically, but also in terms of scientific output. Third, that the new group of protected area scientists in South Africa were open to new ideas, new partnerships and innovative administrative arrangements. Fourth, that these scientists would no longer be sheltered by a hierarchical and outmoded institution. They would have to be well qualified, active in the academic and scholarly community and would also have to share their knowledge by publishing in reputable, high-impact journals. Fifth, that the Internet and rapid computerisation was revolutionising communication and opening up opportunities for integrated, collaborative science. And finally, that financing protected area science in South Africa and finding good partners after years of isolation was going to be extremely difficult.

[5]D.J. Roux and L. Foxcroft, 'The development and application of strategic adaptive management within South African National Parks', *Koedoe* 53, no. 2 (2011): 5 pages, doi: 10.4102/koedoe.v53i2.1049.
[6]See, for example, the tension between the work of M. Knight and G. Castley, 'Conservation management', and that of H. Biggs and P. Novellie, 'Science for biodiversity management', both chapters published in *South African National Parks: A Celebration*, eds A. Hall-Martin and J. Carruthers (Johannesburg: Horst Klemm, 2003), 97–120, 67–98.

Mellon Foundation: Conservation and the Environment Programme

It was SANParks' good fortune to attract the attention of the Mellon Foundation, an institution with a long history of funding and supporting worthwhile endeavours. Rather than engage in advocacy like other foundations, Mellon sought to strengthen institutions and individuals by encouraging objective research and public education. Among the initiatives was 'Conservation and the Environment' managed by programme officer William (Bill) Robertson from 1979 until his retirement in 2013. This programme, which had originated in 1974 in response to environmental issues relevant in the USA, began in South Africa in 1997 when the Mellon trustees accepted a proposal to establish a collaborative ecosystems research project in the KNP. The contribution of the foundation was to revolutionise scientific research in the KNP and elsewhere in South Africa and demonstrate the extraordinary potential of the area to contribute to ecological knowledge.

It was fortunate that Robertson was at the helm of this programme at the time. A biologist who had served on the staff of the National Academy of Sciences and the National Research Council, he had been involved in ocean and freshwater pollution and global monitoring and other projects, and was attracted to the possibilities of ecosystem studies in South Africa, the KNP in particular. An active member of many scientific societies and a recipient of several distinguished awards, he was, and is, an extremely clear-thinking and helpful person and many have paid tribute to his ability to encourage and empower creative scientists and to his continuing interest in projects.[7]

According to Robertson, in 2003 a transition in the then existing 'Conservation and the Environment' programme began, with more support being afforded basic investigation into how natural ecosystems work. Until it closed in 2013, there was a formally named subprogramme, 'Research Bridges to South Africa'. Importantly, and in marked contrast to pre-1994 science in South Africa's national parks, the foundation sought through this programme to support what George Evelyn Hutchinson had described in 1943 as 'the point of view of the mind that delights in understanding nature rather than in attempting

---

[7]Since 2003, Robertson has greatly assisted a consortium of more than 240 herbaria in 70 countries to develop a coordinated digital database of type specimens.

to reform her'.[8] Curiosity, not box-ticking, was to be the order of the day, as indeed it had been in the KNP before the Second World War. Robertson spelt this approach out clearly to a potential grantee in 2006: proposed research had to be field research and not merely analysis, modelling, work on correlations or proving whether a model was appropriate to a different set of circumstances. Grants, which had stringent reporting requirements, did not routinely provide assistance for administration or overhead costs.[9] The ultimate purpose of the foundation's intervention was not to support discrete projects alone, but to create intellectual capital at a number of levels and across networks and groups within South Africa and beyond. In addition, the foundation has supported Island Press, journal digitisation projects such as JSTOR and the Global Plants Initiative for botanical specimens.

Pivotal to the partnership between the Mellon Foundation and SANParks was a brief but productive meeting between Robertson and Mabunda, the then head of SANParks. Mabunda understood Robertson's point that, to be effective, scientists should not be instructed about what kind of research to undertake but be free to follow their own ideas. Moreover, he recognised that to benefit KNP, fundamental research needed to be lifted out of the ordinary and energised by drawing on ideas and theories beyond the closed circuit of SANParks scientists and their historical partner, the University of Pretoria.[10]

The advent of the Mellon Foundation in South Africa's ecological science created a flurry of activity and raised the quality and quantity of research enormously. The outputs showed the potential of protected areas to increase scientific knowledge in South Africa, just as had been demonstrated in East Africa by the Serengeti Research Institute.[11]

[8]W.R. Robertson, 'Conservation and the Environment: A brief retrospective', 30 June 2014. 'A history of the Foundation's program in Conservation and the Environment', published in *Annual Report, 2013*. https://mellon.org/about/annual-reports/2013-conservation-and-environment-brief-retrospect/ (accessed 17 November 2015). See also J. Carruthers, 'G. Evelyn Hutchinson in South Africa, 1926 to 1928: "An immense part in my intellectual development"', *Transactions of the Royal Society of South Africa* 66, no. 2 (2011): 87–104.

[9]Grant: 30600713 Utah State University, email from Robertson to Andrew Kulmatiski. Archives of the Mellon Foundation, New York, 2006 to 2009.

[10]Bill Robertson. Interview with the author, New York, 20 March 2014 and personal meetings and discussion, New York, 2–4 April 2012.

[11]See A.R.E. Sinclair and M. Norton-Griffiths, eds, *Serengeti: Dynamics of an Ecosystem* (Chicago, IL: University of Chicago Press, 1979); A.R.E. Sinclair and P. Arcese, eds,

Certainly, generous Mellon funding was extremely welcome to a financially strapped research sector, but money was not merely thrown at projects, there were strategic and well-considered benefits in addition. Most importantly, there were genuine partnerships and collaborations, with no hint of US scientific imperialism, foreign agendas or top-down directives. At first the group of collaborators was relatively small: SANParks, the University of the Witwatersrand, the University of Washington and the Institute of Ecosystem Studies (Milbrook, New York). However, by 2012, the range of institutions that were supported by the foundation also included Princeton, Oxford, Stanford and the universities of California (Santa Barbara and Davis), Minnesota, Alaska, San Francisco, Cape Town, Utah State and Fort Hare, as well as the Organization of Tropical Studies (OTS) (Durham, NC) and the Carnegie Institution (Washington, DC).[12] Many of South Africa's top scientists who had not been able to work easily in the KNP before 1994 now found themselves welcomed. Even South African universities that had never before collaborated found productive opportunities to work with others at the cutting edge of ecosystems research. The roles of education and research were combined and it was hoped that through these initiatives the next generation of South African scientists would be more diverse. Student support was robust. For example, Grant 40000769 recruited two students from different departments at the University of the Witwatersrand (Wits) and one each from Cape Town and Kansas State universities to work together.[13] Bearing in mind that every funded project was in partnership with SANParks and usually also a South African university, and that the total amount of grant funding eventually exceeded $20 million, this was an unprecedented investment in South African ecosystem science.[14]

Serengeti II: Dynamics, Management and Conservation of an Ecosystem (Chicago, IL: University of Chicago Press, 1995); A.R.E. Sinclair, C. Packer, S.A.R. Mduma and J.M. Fryxell, eds, *Serengeti III: Human Impacts on Ecosystem Dynamics* (Chicago, IL: University of Chicago Press, 2006); A.R.E. Sinclair, *Serengeti Story: Life and Science in the World's Greatest Wildlife Region* (Oxford: Oxford University Press, 2012).

[12]The range of topics included soils ecology, primary production and nutrient cycling, isotope and savannah plant–tree interactions; riparian nutrients; field laboratory and training; research and education and LiDAR. The range of support varied from $25 000 to $900 000.

[13]Grant 40000769 $200 000, 72 months. Archives of the Mellon Foundation, New York, 2000–2009.

[14]'Summary of Research Bridges Program'. Archives of the Mellon Foundation, New York, 2006–2009.

There was much synergy and cross-fertilisation of ideas after 1994. American researchers were able to do fieldwork in South Africa while South African graduate and postdoctoral students were able to attend workshops and courses with partner institutions abroad. SANParks' personnel were exposed to and worked with international scientists as never before.[15] There are very many examples of the internationalisation of South African environmental science after 1994. For instance, in 1996, stimulated by the International Long Term Ecological Research (LTER) project,[16] South Africa's Foundation for Research Development (now the National Research Foundation, NRF) together with other stakeholders, and with Mellon financing, began the long process of establishing a South African LTER. By the early 2000s, this had developed into the South African Environmental Observation Network (SAEON), comprising several nodes around the country.[17] In 2003, a large and long (10–15-year) grant was instituted specifically for capacity-building. Its aim was attracting, training and retaining scientific staff from disadvantaged backgrounds in the KNP. For its part, SANParks would provide fieldwork and mentorship. The experiment had mixed success, but was a worthwhile endeavour at an opportune time.[18]

It did not take long for the scientific polarisation that existed before 1994 to dissipate, prejudices to be challenged and many imagined and practical barriers simply to disappear.[19] Without the leverage of the Mellon Foundation it is extremely doubtful that any of this would have happened, for such transformations are beyond the power of individuals or even universities. Over little more than a decade, some 87 projects were funded, many of them pioneering and path-breaking. Several of them have been sustained and all of them have ensured that SANParks and the KNP are counted today among the world leaders in ecosystem science. In addition, tribute should be paid to the welcome and assistance these researchers received from scientists in the KNP,[20] particularly – as

[15]Grant 10300699. Proposal 21 March 2003. Archives of the Mellon Foundation, New York, 2003–2009.

[16]International Long Term Ecological Research. See www.ilternet.edu (accessed 8 August 2016).

[17]Grant 20300654. Archives of the Mellon Foundation, New York, 2003–2006. See www .saeon.ac.za/ (accessed 6 August 2016).

[18]Grant 30300644. Archives of the Mellon Foundation, New York, 2003–2008.

[19]Morné du Plessis. Interview with the author. Cape Town, 20 January 2014. Johan du Toit. Interview with the author. Johannesburg, 25 February 2013.

[20]In 2001 there were 24 posts within KNP Scientific Services. At the head was D. Pienaar, and other senior positions were H. Biggs, Principal Scientist: Systems Ecology;

many informants have noted – Harry Biggs, the extremely congenial master of acquiring and maintaining networks.[21]

One Mellon Foundation intervention was helping the OTS establish a semester-abroad programme in the KNP.[22] Named 'African Ecology and Conservation in South Africa', the programme was designed to bring US and South African students together. This proved more difficult than anticipated because of the differences in the syllabuses in the two countries. Eventually, however, the project had a firm footing and became a key tool for enticing students into ecosystem studies. It is now a respected educational programme in the KNP and among Ivy League universities in the USA and has links with many South African universities and academics.[23]

Even more successful have been other science support partnerships financed by Mellon. One important grant (2002–2004) dealt with the management of the process by which KNP approves and supports outside research projects and ensures that they remain focused and meet objectives. Raising funds to sustain projects was also a priority. In the event, David Mabunda – by then chief executive of SANParks – took the lead in this, investigated other schemes of this nature and established the post of scientific liaison officer.[24] In addition, the flood of scientific research, welcome though it was, created a bottleneck in KNP's Scientific Services Section as staff found it difficult to accommodate the flood of researchers and their information. To ameliorate this, Biggs proposed unifying the various support elements so that SANParks could take over once Mellon funding ceased. A further small grant (2003–2006) was made available for improving the KNP's library and archival systems and for transforming the library into an effective knowledge resource centre.[25]

S. Freitag-Ronaldson, Specialist Scientist: Environmental Management; H. Eckhardt, Specialist Scientist: Spatial Ecology; F. Venter, Specialist Scientist: Spatial Ecology: Rivers; L. Foxcroft, Technician: Alien Biota; M.G.L. Mills, Specialist Scientist: Predators; I. Whyte, Specialist Scientist: Large Herbivores; A. Deacon, Specialist Scientist: Small Vertebrates, and M. Hofmeyr, Specialist Veterinary Researcher.

[21] Johan du Toit. Interview with the author. Johannesburg, 25 February 2013. Greg Kiker. Interview with the author. Skukuza, March 2013. Biggs retired from SANParks at the end of 2014.

[22] See the website www.ots.ac.cr/index.php?option=com_frontpage&Itemid=1 (accessed 20 December 2015).

[23] Grant 10100613, 2001–2004; Grant 30100649, 2001–2004; Grant 30100650, 2002–2005; Grant 40200680. Archives of the Mellon Foundation, New York, 2001–2009.

[24] Grant 20200754. Archives of the Mellon Foundation, New York, 2002–2004.

[25] Grant 30300685. Archives of the Mellon Foundation, New York, 2003–2006. It has to be said that this is one of the less successful projects in terms of sustainability. The library and the historical archives in Skukuza leave a great deal to be desired.

Without doubt, however, the most important Mellon legacy for SANParks science is the regular Savannah Science Network Meetings that have been held at Skukuza since 2002. Extremely informal, they involve no paid keynote speakers and no long presentations. Research findings are briefly presented by the widely varied participants, and there is ample time for networking and for developing new projects. Currently they last about five days, are attended by around 150 people and involve more than 100 presentations. These meetings originated in the mid-1990s when rivers and boundaries researchers organised information workshops for their colleagues from SANParks and the universities of the Witwatersrand and Cape Town. At the invitation of L.E.O. (Leo) Braack, then the KNP's manager of Scientific Services, the two-day event in September 1997 was restricted to presentations by KNP researchers. However, responding to the open philosophy that was developing, Braack made it clear that this was to be an annual event in which researchers from other institutions could actively participate.[26] The second symposium took place in August the following year at the formal invitation of M.G.L. (Gus) Mills, at which many outside researchers reported on their KNP projects.[27] The symposium has become an established tradition and it has grown in significance and attendance since receiving Mellon Foundation support in 2002. The tenth Savannah Science Network Meeting in March 2012 was a celebration and it is worth noting that the wide range of work presented at the meetings in 2012 and 2013 appeared in 35 scholarly journals, all of them peer-reviewed and some of the highest rank.[28]

In addition, support from the Mellon Conservation and Environment programme enabled the publication of an important book by Island

[26]Braack (manager Scientific Services) to 'Visiting researcher/Fellow-conservationist', 22 August 1997, invitation to Research Symposium to be held on 5 and 6 November 1997, A/21 Wetenskaplike skakelings. KNP archives, Skukuza.

[27]Program for KNP Research Symposium Goldfields Centre, Skukuza, 13–14 August 1998, A/21 Wetenskaplike skakelings. KNP archives, Skukuza.

[28]They were *Ecology Letters, Land Degradation and Development, Global Change Biology, IEEE Transactions on Geoscience and Remote Sensing, Remote Sensing of Environment, Biogeosciences, Ecological Applications, Remote Sensing, PloS ONE, Comparative Immunology, Microbiology and Infectious Diseases, Environmental Conservation, Conservation Biology, Wildlife Research, Ecological Applications, Energy Policy, ISPRS Journal of Photogrammetry and Remote Sensing, Animal Behaviour, International Journal of Applied Earth Observation and Geoinformation, Austral Ecology, Koedoe, Journal of Arid Environments, The American Naturalist, Behavioral Ecology and Sociobiology, Ecology, Landscape Ecology, Ecography, Environmental Research Letters* and *Forest Ecology and Management*.

Figure 11.1. Group exchanging research at one of the annual Savannah Science
Network Meetings.
Photograph by Andrew Deacon.

Press in 2003,[29] *The Kruger Experience: Ecology and Management of Savanna
Heterogeneity*, which synthesises and integrates much of the current ecological knowledge about the KNP. Edited by Johan du Toit (formerly of
the Mammal Research Institute, University of Pretoria), Kevin Rogers
(Centre for Water in the Environment, Wits) and Harry Biggs (KNP) and
partly modelled on the three volumes that dealt with the Serengeti ecosystem,[30] *The Kruger Experience* is not a long, disjointed list of projects and
topics going back over decades.[31] Rather, it is a focused, modern, peer-
reviewed science text with specialist authors addressing aspects of savannah heterogeneity, the ultimate source of biodiversity. Of the 51 authors,
10 were SANParks staff, and many were, and still are, world-renowned
figures in their fields. The editors paid tribute to Salomon Joubert, whose
annual ecological surveys greatly assisted in establishing the research

[29]J.T. du Toit, K.H. Rogers and H.C. Biggs, eds, *The Kruger Experience: Ecology and
Management of Savanna Heterogeneity* (Washington, DC: Island Press, 2003).
[30]See Sinclair and Norton-Griffiths, *Serengeti*; Sinclair and Arcese, *Serengeti II*; Sinclair,
Packer, Mduma and Fryxell, *Serengeti III*; Sinclair, *Serengeti Story*. See also K.H.
Rogers, 'Operationalizing ecology under a new paradigm: An African perspective', in
*The Ecological Basis for Conservation: Heterogeneity, Ecosystems, and Biodiversity. 6th Cary
Conference, 1995: Institute of Ecosystem Studies*, eds S.T.A. Pickett, R.S. Ostfeld, M. Shachak
and G.E. Likens (New York, NY: Chapman and Hall, 1997), 60–77.
[31]See, for example, S.C.J. Joubert, *The Kruger National Park: A History* (Johannesburg: High
Branching, 2012).

378 · **The Kruger National Park**

agenda of the twenty-first century. They also acknowledged the relevance to the book of the 'Malawi Principles' of 1998, which recognised the inter-relationship between society (stakeholders) and conservation.[32]

The work falls into several sections: historical and conceptual framework; template for savannah heterogeneity; and interactions between biotic components, humans and savannahs. This project was brought to life at a workshop at Berg-en-Dal camp in April 2002, attended by many of the contributors as well as those who would later critique the chapter drafts (115 people in total). One chapter that best summarises the changes in science and management in SANParks after 1994 is by Kevin Rogers. In it, he traces how, within the KNP, the dominant studies of charismatic species ignored scale and were instead heavily influenced by habitat stability, an approach developed for commercial agriculture. Rogers explained that conservation managers are often risk-averse (and sometimes intent on protecting their turf), so that monitoring tends to become an end in itself. The result is paralysed decision-making, because information is unstructured. He reiterated that policy must be translated into achievable and scientifically defensible operational goals, the attainment of which can be audited and adjusted – and also tested against societal values.[33] In sum, *The Kruger Experience* exemplifies the integration, innovation and internationalisation of SANParks science from the 1990s onwards and reflects a moment in which, to quote Thomas Mellon once more, beneath the eddies and ripples of events, an under-current of the changing stream of scientific endeavour can be discerned.[34]

Although the intervention of the Mellon Foundation was very successful, one innovative project did not get off the ground: the initiative to create a permanent (although changing) science advisory board to monitor and assist SANParks in its scientific endeavours. People of the highest calibre were suggested as members, including Jane Lubchenco, Peter Crane, Brian Huntley and William Bond. Such a board – mingling internationals and South Africans – would have created an international

[32]A.R.E. Sinclair and B.H. Walker, 'Foreword', in *The Kruger Experience: Ecology and Management of Savanna Heterogeneity*, eds J.T. du Toit, K.H. Rogers and H.C. Biggs (Washington, DC: Island Press, 2003), xiii–xv.

[33]K.H. Rogers, 'Adopting a heterogeneity paradigm: Implications for management of protected savannas', in *The Kruger Experience: Ecology and Management of Savanna Heterogeneity*, eds J.T. du Toit, K.H. Rogers and H.C. Biggs (Washington, DC: Island Press, 2003), 41–58.

[34]*Thomas Mellon and his Times*, 338. Quoted in D. Cannadine, *Mellon: An American Life* (London: Allen Lane/Penguin, 2006), 583.

science presence for SANParks (and South Africa) and ensured its lead-ership in the field. A proposal was written in 2004, and a grant provided. This board was initially intended as an advice panel for the KNP, but its remit was widened to apply to all of South Africa's national parks because Robertson had begun to take an interest in the kind of science that might be conducted in the Cape national parks. Some of the proposal's wording harked back to Richard Bell's 1995 recommendation that such a body be established, but the plea was also made for a social science and humanities presence to help the board chart a productive way forward. Delay followed delay. Eventually, perhaps out of fear that such a board would impact management decisions about restructuring the organo-gram, perhaps because top management believed that the three scientists then on the SANParks board were sufficient, the project ended and the money was returned in full in 2009.[35]

Comparing the progress reports on research projects in 1993 and 1994 with the details of the projects later supported by the Mellon Foundation provides an indication of the enormous changes in the quality of the scientific research conducted in the KNP. The primary objective in 1993 was to 'establish inventories'. In that year, there were 154 registered projects, the large majority of which were being conducted by outside researchers in isolation from one another and from SANParks staff. Only one was multidisciplinary, while veterinary studies accounted for 30% of the total, mammalian studies 22.6% and vegetation studies 15.6%. Given that the veterinary studies were probably largely mammalian, these latter comprised more than half the total. Not one project related to the eco-system per se. The following year (1994) was in a similar vein, but included Preston's innovative 'user pays' work on sustainability and Starfield's frame-based, management-oriented spatial models.[36] A decade later, the picture had changed entirely. A new group of scientists had been brought into the KNP and collaborations had linked them with the top eche-lons of international research. Moreover, SANParks and KNP research had become interlocked with the international community of ecosys-tem scholarship. Many KNP researchers moved away from publishing in *Koedoe* alone (even though it was now subject to rigorous peer review)

---

[35] Grant 40400672. Archives of the Mellon Foundation, New York, 2004–2009.

[36] KNP, Scientific Services, Progress report of research projects undertaken in the Kruger National Park during 1993. Scientific Report 10/94; Scientific Services, Kruger National Park, Progress Report of research projects undertaken in the Kruger National park during 1994. Unpublished report 12/95.

and shared their expertise more widely through international journals. The annual SANParks research reports from 2012 to 2014 shed further light on this remarkable increase in accredited research output.[37]

Mellon-funded teamwork and partnerships helped provide greater knowledge of the Kruger ecosystem and resulted in real advances in understanding. For many years, South Africa had lagged behind the kind of research that had been done by the Serengeti Research Institute because the focus had been on particular species and not on any fundamental drivers of the system or even on synthesising the knowledge that had been obtained.[38] Beginning in the 1990s, several projects began to shed some light on the drivers of the KNP ecosystems. For instance, Oliver Chadwick (UC Santa Barbara), Rogers and Frederik (Freek) Venter (SANParks) along with others began research to understand plant communities by modelling soil–plant interactions along catenas.[39] Another project, led by Steward Pickett and Mary Cadenasso among others, and involving SANParks, the University of San Francisco and the Institute of Ecosystem Studies, focused on the Shingwedzi drainage system, specifically the heterogeneity of riparian zones and their role in modulating flows.[40] Through Edward February, the University of Cape Town became a partner in a large project to investigate the ecological relationship between grassland and trees and to augment investigations published by Steven Higgins, William Bond and Winston Trollope in the *Journal of Ecology* in 2000.[41] These are just a few of the cumulatively important landmarks in ecosystem studies undertaken in the KNP in these years.

Before 1994, as we have seen, the National Parks Board (NPB) and especially the KNP had been able to act unilaterally as a protected area fortress without interacting with the broader academic community or with the South African public at large. Legally, this was justifiable because the board had no mandate beyond park boundaries and therefore,

[37]SANParks, *Research Reports 2012–2014*. See www.sanparks.org/conservation/reports/research_report.php (accessed 20 December 2015).

[38]Sinclair and Norton-Griffiths, *Serengeti*; Sinclair and Arcese, *Serengeti II*; Sinclair, Packer, Mduma and Fryxell, *Serengeti III*.

[39]Grant 10300699. Archives of the Mellon Foundation, New York, 2003–2005.

[40]Grant 20300655. This was the first intensive study undertaken in the northern KNP. Archives of the Mellon Foundation, New York, 2003–2008.

[41]S.J. Higgins, W.J. Bond and W.S.W. Trollope, 'Fire, resprouting and variability: A recipe for grass-tree coexistence in savanna', *Journal of Ecology* 88 (2000): 213–229. Grant 30100651. Archives of the Mellon Foundation, New York, 2001–2008.

management believed, no responsibility for matters 'on the other side of the fence'. Since Stevenson-Hamilton's departure in 1946, the landscape on the 'other side' had undergone profound transformation. Increasingly heavily populated by impoverished Africans obliged, under apartheid, to live in 'self-governing' tribal reserves, these areas were home to widespread and unsustainable subsistence agriculture, and were enmeshed within burgeoning industries such as plantation forestry and intensive white commercial agriculture.[42] In addition, with a priority to manage the landscape and its biota within the fence, there was no need, the NPB believed, to involve people outside the KNP in any management or research activity. It was this attitude that not only begat arrogance, but also prevented the NPB from contributing to the savannah Cooperative Scientific Programmes (CSP) of the 1980s.

River Research

There was, however, one unavoidable exception to this isolationist philosophy, namely rivers, a 'fugitive resource' that 'knows no boundaries'. It was rivers that, together with the wider socio-political changes in the country, eventually opened up the KNP to cooperative research agendas.[43]

A relatively narrow and long strip along the South African border with Mozambique, the KNP is traversed by six complex and geologically and geomorphologically diverse rivers. They rise in high ground far west of the KNP, flow eastwards through the park and eventually discharge into the Indian Ocean off Mozambique. They also have different spatial zonations and each river (and its catchment) has a different vegetation and landscape structure.[44] All have highly variable flow

---

[42]S. Pollard, C. Shackleton and J. Carruthers, 'Beyond the fence: People and the lowveld landscape', in *The Kruger Experience: Ecology and Management of Savanna Heterogeneity*, eds J.T. du Toit, K.H. Rogers and H.C. Biggs (Washington, DC: Island Press, 2003), 422–446.

[43]S. Pollard, D. du Toit and H. Biggs, 'River management under transformation: The emergence of strategic adaptive management of river systems in the Kruger National Park', *Koedoe* 53, no. 2 (2011): 14 pages, doi: 10.4102/koedoe.v53i2.1011.

[44]The literature is now extensive and includes A.L. van Coller and K.H. Rogers, *Riparian Vegetation of the Sabie River: Relating to Spatial Distribution Patterns to Characteristics of the Physical Environment*, Report 1/95 (Johannesburg: Centre for Water in the Environment, University of the Witwatersrand, 1995); F.J. Venter and A.R. Deacon, 'Managing rivers for conservation and ecotourism in the Kruger National Park', *Water Science and Technology*

regimes, in part because of seasonal rainfall (summer) and of irregular, but massive, floods and droughts. It has also been impossible for the KNP water supply to escape the impact of human activities upstream.[45] Water quality has deteriorated, impoundments have attempted to regulate the flow and biotic life in the rivers has changed. Considerable management attention was given to smoothing out these variables by constructing dams (inside and outside the KNP) and by providing alternative surface water to which wildlife could have continual access. It was not until the 1980s that, owing to research by the CSP Rivers Research Programme, it began to be appreciated that big events could not be smoothed out without disrupting the Lowveld savannah system, which is characterised by inherent heterogeneity and flux.[46] The understanding that these rivers

---

32, nos. 5/6 (1995): 227–233; A.L. van Coller, K.H. Rogers and G.L. Heritage, 'Linking riparian vegetation types and fluvial geomorphology along the Sabie River within the Kruger National Park, South Africa', *African Journal of Ecology* 35 (1997): 194–212; K.H. Rogers and J. O'Keeffe, 'River heterogeneity: Ecosystem structure, function, and management', in *The Kruger Experience: Ecology and Management of Savanna Heterogeneity*, eds J.T. du Toit, K.H. Rogers and H.C. Biggs (Washington, DC: Island Press, 2003), 189–218; G.P.W. Jewitt, G.L. Heritage, D.C. Weeks, *et al.*, *Modelling Abiotic–Biotic Links in the Sabie River: Kruger National Park Rivers Research Programme.* Water Research Commission Report, 777/1/98 (Pretoria: Water Research Commission, 1998).

[45] S. Freitag-Ronaldson and L. Foxcroft, 'Anthropogenic influences at the ecosystem level', in *The Kruger Experience: Ecology and Management of Savanna Heterogeneity*, eds J.T. du Toit, K.H. Rogers and H.C. Biggs (Washington, DC: Island Press, 2003), 391–421.

[46] Rogers and O'Keeffe, 'River heterogeneity'; Pollard, du Toit and Biggs, 'River management under transformation', S.R. Pollard and D.R. du Toit, *Recognizing Heterogeneity and Variability as Key Characteristics of Savannah Systems: The Use of Strategic Adaptive Management as an Approach to River Management Within the Kruger National Park, South Africa.* Report of UNEP/GEF Project No. GF/2713-03-4679. Ecosystems, Protected Areas and People Project, 2005; R.T. Kingsford, H.C. Biggs and S.R. Pollard, 'Strategic adaptive management in freshwater protected areas and their rivers', *Biological Conservation* 144 (2010): 1194–1203; D.J. Roux, J. Nel, A. Deacon, *et al.*, 'Designing protected areas to conserve riverine biodiversity: Lessons from a hypothetical redesign of the Kruger National Park', *Biological Conservation* 141 (2008): 100–117; F. de Moor, J. Cambray and H. Barber-James, 'Use of landscape-level river signatures in conservation planning: A South African case study', *Conservation Ecology* 6, no. 2 (2002). Online: www.consecol .org/vol6/iss2/art6 (accessed 26 December 2015); K. Rogers, D. Roux and H. Biggs, 'Challenges for catchment management agencies: Lessons from bureaucracies, business and resource management', *Water SA* 26, no. 4 (2000): 505–511; K.H. Rogers and H.C. Biggs, 'Integrating indicators, endpoints and value systems in strategic management of the Kruger National Park', *Freshwater Biology* 41 (1999): 439–451; K.H. Rogers and R. Bestbier, *Development of a Protocol for the Definition of the Desired State of Riverine Systems in South Africa* (Pretoria: Department of Environmental Affairs and Tourism, 1997).

were not mere water flows across the park but an ecosystem linking the inland with the ocean and all that occurs in between by way of ground elevation and riparian areas drew on international thinking that was influenced by work done in Chesapeake Bay and on the rivers in the northern USA that flow into the Pacific.[47]

As mentioned in Chapter 6, river research came into prominence in the KNP in the late 1980s. As a public good, water has always been inherently political. Throughout the twentieth century, South Africa has had a strong cabinet ministry responsible for water affairs, which has not been shy about intervening in the interests of agriculture, industry and urban services. In 1986, during a protracted dry phase when the KNP suffered greatly from shortages of river water, a four-day workshop involving the park and the department was convened.[48] This led, in 1988, to the KNP adding a river research component to the existing general ecosystem project begun under the direction of Salomon Joubert.[49] However, more important than this in-house project was the CSP water research programme, which was wider and far more interdisciplinary. The latter programme was, moreover, important not only for the scientific research it undertook but because, of necessity, the KNP was brought in as an accessory.[50]

In order to discharge their mandates, the Rivers Research Programme (RRP) and specifically its Kruger National Park Rivers Research Programme (KNPRRP) had to be interdisciplinary and could not act in isolation from the KNP (and vice versa).[51] In addition, the research group working to the west of the KNP was itself collaborative, and included the University of the Witwatersrand's Rural Facility at Bushbuckridge

Online: www.ccwe.ac.za/knprrp/index.html (accessed 26 December 2015); Rogers and O'Keeffe, 'River heterogeneity'; Rogers, 'Adopting a heterogeneity paradigm'; Rogers, 'Operationalizing ecology under a new paradigm'.

[47]Johan du Toit. Interview with the author. Johannesburg, 25 February 2013. This was the work of Bob Naiman and Steward Pickett. See S.T.A. Pickett, J. Kolasa and C. Jones, *Understanding in Ecology: The Theory of Nature and the Nature of Theory* (San Diego, CA: Academic Press, 1994).

[48]NPB, *Jaarverslag Nasionale Kruger Wildtuin 1986–1987*.

[49]Director's Archive File Index. Nature Conservation and Research updated in 2006. Files NK1 (Fauna and Flora), NK53 (Alien Plants), A/7/1/ (General Research), Algemeen Ekosisteemprojek. KNP archives, Skukuza.

[50]B.J. Huntley, 'Ten years of cooperative ecological research in South Africa', *South African Journal of Science* 83, no. 2 (1987): 72–79.

[51]Norman Owen-Smith. Interview with the author. Johannesburg, 22 May 2012.

384 · **The Kruger National Park**

and the Association for Water and Rural Development in Acornhoek (AWARD). The programme also came to include Kevin Rogers, who is passionate about linking science and society, a topic on which he frequently expounds.[52] Highly praised as a clear, original and multi-disciplinary thinker, he specifically nests aquatic science (by definition, interdisciplinary) within ecosystem studies.[53] Leading the programmes for the Council for Scientific and Industrial Research (CSIR), with considerable assistance from the Department of Water Affairs and the CSIR's National Institute for Water Research (NIWR), were Charles Breen (University of Natal), assisted by Graham Noble (an aquatic scientist and leader of the CSP projects).[54] There were those who considered that water needed only to be 'managed' as it traversed the park and that cooperation was only necessary insofar as it achieved this end, and persuading them that it also needed to be theoretically and systematically researched was one of the major challenges facing the programme.[55]

The KNPRRP went through three phases between 1988 and 2000. It began its start-up phase as a fully cooperative venture between the Department of Water Affairs, the Water Research Commission and the Foundation for Research and Development (later the National Research Foundation). From 1994 to 1999, Breen managed this initiative with the assistance of Rogers, Biggs, Venter and others. In the first phase, the work consisted of separate projects, but second- and third-phase projects were better aligned with one another under Breen's direction. The TPC decision-making system within SAM was generated within this broader programme as a project with the specific mandate to link river science and management. Led by Rogers with collaboration from Biggs, a report entitled 'A protocol for defining the desired state of river systems' had the innovative SAM as its outcome.[56] By way of political context, almost immediately after coming to power in 1994, the new government gave

[52]K.H. Rogers, 'Limnology and the post-normal imperative: An African perspective', *Verhandlungen des Internationalen Verein Limnologie* 30, no. 2 (2008): 171–185.
[53]See, for example, Rogers, 'Operationalizing ecology under a new paradigm'.
[54]Kevin Rogers. Interview with the author. Skukuza, March 2013.
[55]Robust scientific data were required, along the lines of C.A. Moore, 'A survey of the conservation status and benthic biota of the six major rivers of the Kruger National Park' (MSc diss., University of Pretoria, 1991); A.L. van Coller, 'Riparian vegetation of the Sabie River: Relating spatial distribution patterns to the physical environment' (MSc diss., University of the Witwatersrand, 1992).
[56]I thank Kevin Rogers for his comments here. D.J. Roux, C.M. Breen and J. Carruthers, 'Reflections on the history of aquatic science in South Africa with particular reference

Figure 11.2. Damage to Sabie River high water bridge after the floods of February 2000.
Photograph by Joep Stevens.

its attention to water equity. The Water Services Act 108 of 1997 and the National Water Act 36 of 1998 were passed. While dealing principally with the quality of piped water supplies, this legislation impacted on South Africa's rivers because the water law was changed to ensure sustainability and to redress past imbalances in water provision. It also changed the institutional arrangements for water management by establishing catchment-based water management agencies, of which the KNP straddles three.[57] The KNPRRP formally ended in 1999, but river research in the region continued with funding from Mellon to the riparian boundaries and after 2007 as the Shared Rivers Initiative (SRI).[58]

---

to the period after 1994', *Water SA* 40, no. 2 (2014): 255–262; Rogers and O'Keeffe, 'River heterogeneity'.

[57]Pollard, du Toit and Biggs, 'River management under transformation'; E. van Wyk, J. Jaganyi, B. van Wilgen, *et al.*, 'Developing a protocol for managing the biophysical condition of a water management area: The Sabie catchment case study', *African Journal of Aquatic Science* 25 (2000): 162–168.

[58]J.H. O'Keeffe, *Ecological Research on South African Rivers: A Preliminary Synthesis.* South African National Scientific Programmes Report 121 (Pretoria: CSIR, 1986); A.A. Ferrar, J.H. O'Keeffe and B.R. Davies, *The River Research Programme.* South African

These developments in the water sector created further opportunities for international engagement, the first of which was in 1995 when KNPRRP hosted an international conference on integrated catchment management in Skukuza.[59] Additionally, the rivers programme spawned an important suite of Mellon Foundation projects in response to the tremendous flooding that occurred along the Sabie River in 1999–2000. Much damage resulted, but the floods enabled ecosystem scientists to investigate the system of flux at work. Mellon provided two grants to enable Wits and SANParks to investigate, under the direction of Rogers, the ecosystem response to the catastrophic floods.[60] Thereafter, a longer-term grant was awarded to investigate how a riparian ecosystem remains productive and recovers after a series of large floods. Led by Robert Naiman of the University of Washington, this project yielded many significant publications.[61] Even before the floods, however, there was fresh thinking about riparian systems, specifically their linkage not only to streams but also to the surrounding landscape. This River Savannah Boundaries Programme had many international and local collaborators, including students. At least four Mellon grants supported this research from 2000 to 2005.[62]

Invasion Biology

Invasion biology, less often referred to as invasion ecology, was another science new to the KNP.[63] Its prehistory there dates to the slowly growing awareness of the undesirability of non-indigenous flora in the KNP, the spread of some species[64] and their arrest or control in terrestrial and aquatic habitats by physical work and the use of chemicals. Its growth as

---

National Scientific Programmes Report 146 (Pretoria: CSIR, 1988); C.M. Breen, M. Dent, J. Jaganyi, *et al.*, *The Kruger National Park Rivers Research Programme: Final Report*. Water Research Commission Report TT130/2000 (Pretoria: Water Research Commission, 2000).

[59]Pollard, du Toit and Biggs, 'River management under transformation'.

[60]Grant 10000658 and Grant 10000659. Extension of Flood grant to Plant Ecosystem Response to Catastrophic floods. Archives of the Mellon Foundation, New York, 2000–2001.

[61]Grant 30300642. Archives of the Mellon Foundation, New York, 2003–2009.

[62]Grant 49700613; Grant 19900623; Grant 29900704; Grant 29900705; Grant 30300643; Grant 30400668. Archives of the Mellon Foundation, New York, 1998–2009.

[63]M.A. Davis, 'Invasion biology 1958–2005: The pursuit of science and conservation', in *Conceptual Ecology and Invasion Biology*, eds M.W. Cadotte, S.M. McMahon and T. Fukami (Berlin: Springer Verlag, 2006), 35–64.

[64]In 2004, 372 alien species were recorded in the KNP. See note 75.

a science in the KNP, however, was linked to developments elsewhere (see Chapter 10) and the emergence of invasion biology as an important cluster of sciences with implications for faunal and floral conservation. Invasion biology has a strong link to restoration ecology, although this has not yet become as important in the KNP as it has in protected areas established on former farmland or in other SANParks.[65]

The hub of invasion biology in South Africa is the Centre for Invasion Biology (CIB), a centre of excellence at Stellenbosch University. It was founded in 2004. Llewellyn Foxcroft, one of only two scientists in SANParks to have achieved NRF rating,[66] is attached to the CIB as a research associate. He is based at Skukuza and under his direction the partnership with the CIB and its many institutional affiliates has blossomed, resulting in many important invasion biology studies. (One might speculate that other scientists in SANParks are also worthy of NRF status, but as they have no affiliation with an institution of higher learning, they do not quality for evaluation.)

Invasion biology gained its first academic journal in 1996, when *Biodiversity Letters* (1993) changed its name to *Diversity and Distributions*. Another disciplinary journal, *Biological Invasions*, began publication in 1999. Since the 1990s, the discipline has burgeoned. It came into its own as a science in the KNP with the introduction of decision-oriented and scientifically based management, SAM in particular.[67] It then became part of threshold theory, because invading and alien species had to be taken into consideration in relation to other potential concerns. Such biota also required monitoring to ensure the maintenance of biodiversity.[68]

---

[65]See, for example, J.L. Anderson, 'Restoring a wilderness: The reintroduction of wildlife to an African national park', *International Zoological Yearbook* 24/25 (1986): 192–199; B. Child, 'Recent innovations in conservation', in *Parks in Transition: Evolution and Innovation in Wildlife Conservation: Parks and Game Ranches in Transfrontier Conservation Areas*, eds H. Suich and B. Child (Washington, DC: Island Press, 2008), 277–287; R.F.H. Collinson and P.S. Goodman, 'An assessment of range condition and large herbivore carrying capacity of the Pilanesberg Game Reserve, with guidelines and recommendations for management', *Inkwe* 1 (1982): 1–55.

[66]The other is Dirk Roux, freshwater ecologist and aquatic scientist based at Garden Route National Park.

[67]L.C. Foxcroft and M. McGeoch, 'Implementing invasive species management in an adaptive management framework', *Koedoe* 53, no. 2 (2011): 11 pages, doi: 10.4102/koedoe.53i2.1006.

[68]L. Foxcroft, 'Developing thresholds of potential concern for invasive alien species: Hypotheses and concepts', *Koedoe* 51, no. 1 (2009): 11–16.

Figure 11.3. Invasion of *Opuntia* sp. in the Kruger National Park.
Photograph by Llewellyn Foxcroft.

The adoption of invasion biology also coincided with the Working for Water programme, which allowed the KNP to interact with the national government on issues of unemployment and to take advantage of the Poverty Relief Fund, as well as donor finance. Thus, physical control is now occurring on a scale unimaginable in a previous era, when the only labour resources were those of SANParks alone. Funded very generously by the South African government, it is, however, sometimes criticised because its effectiveness is not being measured.[69]

Moreover, partnerships with the CIB have enabled KNP to benefit from the latest thinking on biological control, first adopted in the park in 2002.[70] Nonetheless, the group of ecologists working on savannah-related

[69]B. van Wilgen, G.G. Forsyth, D.C. le Maitre, *et al.*, 'An assessment of the effectiveness of a large, national-scale invasive alien plant control strategy in South Africa', *Biological Conservation* 148 (2012): 28–38; B. van Wilgen and A. Wannenburgh, 'Co-facilitating invasive species control, water conservation and poverty relief: Achievements and challenges in South Africa's Working for Water programme', *Current Opinion in Environmental Sustainability* 19 (2016): 7–17.

[70]L.C. Foxcroft and S. Freitag-Ronaldson, 'Seven decades of institutional learning: Managing alien plant invasions in the Kruger National Park, South Africa', *Oryx* 41, no. 2 (2007): 160–167; L.C. Foxcroft, M. Rouget and D.M. Richardson, 'Risk assessment

biological invasion science in South Africa is small, because the Cape floristic region has garnered most of the attention. Therefore, understanding and predicting invasions and using them as a way to study core concepts and theories of evolution and ecology is not yet as advanced as is the conservation imperative to be rid of invasive plants.[71] However, the extension of invasion biology to include fauna[72] suggests the elaboration of the science in the KNP and perhaps its potential to contribute to invasion biology internationally.

Among his other achievements, Foxcroft was one of the editors of a significant book about plant invasions in protected areas worldwide.[73] Through his work, and that of others, it has become clear that protected areas can provide excellent research sites for the study of the mechanisms of biotic invasion. Not only is the level of research higher in protected sites than elsewhere, but their boundaries are under intense scrutiny and may serve as a 'natural filter' for introductions from elsewhere.[74] It is also possible that invasion biology will become increasingly important in the multidisciplinary mix needed to manage an area for maximum heterogeneity and flux.[75]

Fire Science

As explained in Chapter 7, veld burning has been a bone of contention in the KNP from the start. The first time that the two words 'fire ecology'

---

of riparian alien plant invasion into protected areas: A landscape approach', *Conservation Biology* 21 (2007): 412–421; L. Foxcroft, L. Henderson, G.R. Nichols and B.W. Martin, 'A revised list of alien plants for the Kruger National Park', *Koedoe* 46, no. 2 (2003): 21–44; L.C. Foxcroft, D.M. Richardson and J.R.U. Wilson, 'Ornamental plants as invasive aliens: Problems and solutions in Kruger National Park, South Africa', *Environmental Management* 41 (2008): 32–51.

[71]M.A. Davis, 'Invasion biology 1958–2005: The pursuit of science and conservation', in *Conceptual Ecology and Invasion Biology*, eds M.W. Cadotte, S.M. McMahon and T. Fukami (Berlin: Springer Verlag, 2006), 53–54.

[72]K.N. de Kock and C.T. Wolmarans, 'Invasive alien freshwater snail species in the Kruger National Park, South Africa', *Koedoe* 50, no. 1 (2008): 49–53.

[73]L.C. Foxcroft, P. Pyšek, D.M. Richardson and P. Genovesi, *Plant Invasions in Protected Areas: Patterns, Problems and Challenges* (Dordrecht: Springer Verlag, 2013).

[74]L.C. Foxcroft, V. Jarošík, P. Pyšek, D.M. Richardson and M. Rouget, 'Protected-area boundaries as filters of plant invasions', *Conservation Biology* 25, no. 2 (2011): 400–405.

[75]L.C. Foxcroft, D.M. Richardson, M. Rouget and S. MacFadyen, 'Patterns of alien plant distribution at multiple spatial scales in a large national park: Implications for ecology, management and monitoring', *Diversity and Distributions* 15 (2009): 367–378.

were combined was in 1962 when Ed Komarek, the influential executive secretary of Tall Timbers Research Station and Land Conservancy
in Tallahassee, Florida, and an advocate of controlled fire, organised the
first fire ecology conference to draw attention to this 'most neglected
ecological subject'.[76] In Stevenson-Hamilton's time, unless fires threatened staff houses and infrastructure, there was no question of curtailing
them, let alone studying them scientifically. The staff complement was
limited and the philosophy behind allowing their spread was that grazing would improve the next season, provided there was sufficient rain.
However, within South Africa at large, and particularly in the Cape, a
fierce debate raged based on the view that fires not only damaged fynbos,
but destroyed it.[77] This philosophy had an impact on savannah management in the KNP. For a period after 1946, fires were suppressed as far as
possible, but it was soon clear that this biome responded differently to
fire than Cape flora. The CSP programmes of the 1980s, together with
the innovative thinking of Winston Trollope[78] and later of William Bond
of the University of Cape Town – in addition to the considerable basic
literature on fire in the KNP by Brynard and van Wyk[79] – ensured that
fire ecology was a well-established branch of conservation management
and an emerging science in the KNP by the 1990s. However, it was a
matter of worry to many fire ecologists by then that perhaps the regular
burnings aimed at stabilising the 'pristine ecosystem' were not having the
desired effect, and, once heterogeneity had been established as an aspect

[76]With thanks to Brian van Wilgen for alerting me to this fact.

[77]C.L. Wicht, *Report of the Committee on the Preservation of the Vegetation of the South Western Cape* (Cape Town: Royal Society of South Africa, 1945).

[78]W.S.W. Trollope, 'Fire regime of the Kruger National Park for the period 1980–1992', *Koedoe* 36, no. 2 (1993): 45–52.

[79]G.U. Schirge and A.H. Penderis, *Fire in South African Ecosystems: An Annotated Bibliography.* South African National Scientific Programmes Report 33, October 1978 (Pretoria: CSIR, 1978). See also M.V. Gandar, *Description of a Fire and its Effects in the Nylsvley Nature Reserve: A Synthesis Report.* South African National Scientific Programmes Report 63 (Pretoria: CSIR, 1982); A.M. Brynard, 'The influence of veld burning on the vegetation and game of the Kruger National Park', in *Ecological Studies in Southern Africa*, ed. D.H.S. Davis (The Hague: Junk, 1964), 371–393; P. van Wyk, 'Veld burnings in the Kruger National Park: An interim report of some aspects of research', in *Proceedings of the Annual Tall Timbers Fire Ecology Conference 11, 1971*, 9–31; W.P.D. Gertenbach and A.L.F. Potgieter, 'Veldbrandnavorsing in die struikmopanieveld van die Nasionale Krugerwildtuin', *Koedoe* 22 (1979): 1–28.

of resilience and sustainability, that regular fires were actually detrimental by decreasing variability.[80]

The carefully monitored consequences of previous fires gave fire ecology in the 1990s a head start in terms of being incorporated into SAM. The amount of data collected and the records kept facilitated the integration of fire management into ecosystem studies as well, including the new studies the Mellon-funded partnerships were suggesting. Indeed, concerns about the management of fire were not limited to South African savannahs or protected areas, because grassland ecologists such as Michael Mentis, as well as Trollope the fire ecologist, were giving creative thought to how and to what extent fire might be an ecosystem driver.[81] There is no doubt the work on fire at Nylsvley, which showed that a regular fire regime simplified an ecosystem and thus weakened it, had an eventual influence on the KNP. Once the emphasis shifted from large mammals and embraced a wider perspective, Trollope's work on fire gained in pertinence. In 1992, as had been the case for years in the Pilanesberg National Park, discussion centred on a lightning-driven fire regime. However, Mentis, with Trollope and Bond, recognised that the KNP landscape was one where the impact of humans had been felt for many centuries, and included the kind of patchy burning that pastoralists would have undertaken. This, too, was built into the matrix.[82]

In 2007, Brian van Wilgen of the CIB and CSIR, together with Navashni Govender and Harry Biggs of SANParks, contributed a retrospective critical review to the *International Journal of Wildlife Fire* of the long-term fire experiment that had taken place in the KNP. This experiment had not been designed as such, and although the data were potentially rich, little had been extracted from them or analysed with a hypothesis in mind. The authors summarised the history of fire policy in the KNP, noting that the philosophies behind its application mirrored

---

[80]H.C. Eckhardt, B.W. van Wilgen and H.C. Biggs, 'Trends in woody vegetation cover in the Kruger National Park, South Africa, between 1940 and 1998', *African Journal of Ecology* 38 (2000): 108–115.

[81]B.W. van Wilgen, W.S.W. Trollope, H.C. Biggs, A.L.F. Potgieter and B.H. Brockett, 'Fire as a driver of ecosystem variability in the Kruger National Park', in *The Kruger Experience: Ecology and Management of Savanna Heterogeneity*, eds J.T. du Toit, K.H. Rogers and H.C. Biggs (Washington, DC: Island Press, 2003): 149–170; R. Buitenwerf, W.J. Bond, N. Stevens and W.S.W. Trollope, 'Increased tree densities in South African savannas: 50 years of data suggests CO_2 as a driver', *Global Change Biology* 18, no. 2 (2012): 675–684.

[82]M.T.B. Mentis and A.W. Bailey, 'Changing perceptions of fire management in savanna parks', *Journal of the Grassland Society of Southern Africa* 7 (1990): 81–85.

the times, and listed the journal articles, theses and reports that had been published on the subject. They showed that in the 1990s, with the introduction of non-equilibrium theory, flexibility and new thinking, publications had soared. However, their main conclusion was that the experiment itself, although begun in order to influence policy, had not, in fact, done so, principally because it did not cater for variability. The authors described how, between 1992 and 1996, the KNP had become a vital component in a large, international field experiment in atmospheric chemistry, known as SAFARI-92. Responding to criticism, KNP scientists had begun to analyse the data sets to provide – with the aid of models of heterogeneity and disequilibrium – information about how the KNP's fire regime should be understood. During the course of the 1990s a 'natural' fire policy was introduced, a hybrid system of mosaic burning within SAM and also within mathematically formulated TPCs.[83]

As with other specialisations that are becoming integrated into ecosystem studies, fire has brought new players into SANParks science, as well as creating synergy between more senior and younger scientists such as Navashni Govender and Sally Archibald.[84] Mellon funding for multidisciplinary projects was crucial to research in this field. So too has been the Carnegie Airborne Observatory (CAO) developed by Greg Asner

[83]B.W. van Wilgen, N. Govender and H.C. Biggs, 'The contribution of fire research to fire management: A critical review of a long-term experiment in the Kruger National Park, South Africa', *International Journal of Wildland Fire* 16 (2007): 519–530. (This article has an excellent and very full list of references.) The group had previously published B.W. van Wilgen, N. Govender, H.C. Biggs, *et al.*, 'Response of savanna fire regimes to changing fire management policies in a large African national park', *Conservation Biology* 18 (2004): 1533–1540. See also B.W. van Wilgen, H.C. Biggs, S. O'Regan, *et al.*, 'A fire history of the savanna ecosystems in the Kruger National Park, South Africa between 1941 and 1996', *South African Journal of Science* 96 (2000): 167–178; S.I. Higgins, W.J. Bond, E.C. February, *et al.*, 'Effects of four decades of fire manipulation on woody vegetation structure in savanna', *Ecology* 88, no. 5 (2007): 1119–1125. As far as TPCs are concerned, see B.W. van Wilgen, H.C. Biggs and A.L.F. Potgieter, 'Fire management and research in the Kruger National Park, with suggestions on the detection of thresholds of potential concern', *Koedoe* 41 (1998): 69–87.

[84]Sally Archibald, based at the University of the Witwatersrand, is involved in many collaborative research projects that, among other aspects, integrate fire–grazer interactions and a global theory of fire. Her priority is to integrate field and modelling data in the context of global change. Her work has been supported by the Mellon Foundation. See S. Archibald, A. Nickless, R.J. Scholes and R. Schulze, 'Methods to determine the impact of rainfall on fuels and burned area in southern African savannas', *International Journal of Wildland Fire* 19 (2010): 774–782.

in 2007 and located at the Department of Global Ecology at Stanford University. CAO is a plane with very sensitive remote-sensing equipment that images vegetation in 3D by sweeping across it with laser light. The images are later analysed with sophisticated software (LiDAR).

The data obtained are extremely detailed and can include the location and size of individual trees at a resolution of 1.1 m. With this technology, understanding the effect of fires and wildlife impact is taken to a higher

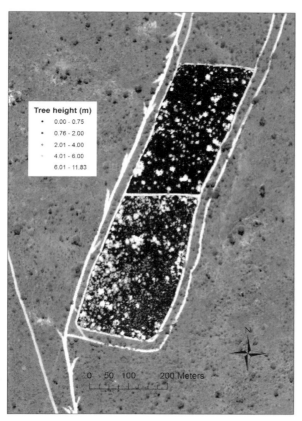

Figure 11.4. Diagram redrawn from photograph 3 in Smit *et al.* in the *Ecological Society of America Bulletin*, July 2010 (http://onlinelibrary.wiley.com/ doi/10.1890/0012-9623-91.3.343/full) based on work conducted in I.P.J. Smit, G.P. Asner, N. Govender, *et al.*, 'Effects of fire on woody vegetation structure in African savanna', *Ecological Applications* 20 (2010): 1865–1875. http://esajournals .onlinelibrary.wiley.com/hub/journal/10.1002/(ISSN)2327-6096/about/ permissions-Bulletin.html.
Courtesy of Izak Smit.

level and knowledge of the relationship between trees, grass and fire has been significantly augmented.[85] Izak Smit is the LiDAR expert within the scientific team in the KNP and he summarises the benefits of the technology in terms of fine-scale mapping of landscape patterns and woody vegetation, vegetation dynamics and the ability to compare land-scapes within the KNP but also with private protected areas and densely populated neighbouring communities.[86]

Surface Water Management[87]

As well as an overall reconsideration of fire policy in this period was another: surface water policy. In this regard, a total transformation has occurred, as has also elephant management as will be explained below. During Stevenson-Hamilton's time as KNP warden it was frequently noted that during times of drought, some of which were extreme, 'away from the main rivers and a few permanent pools, the country was water-less'. Grazing was thus concentrated in these places, to the detriment of the vegetation and to the physical condition of the growing numbers of wild animals. Moreover, wildlife was drawn to water resources more readily available on the private farms outside of the unfenced park where they were often poached. Intent on keeping wildlife within the park's boundaries and on extremely limited resources, Stevenson-Hamilton's team constructed a few earth dams. These too dried up in difficult times, and the warden began to consider sinking boreholes, but the cost was prohibitive. An idea was mooted to plant tsamma melons *Citrullus lanatus*, a source of water for desert mammals, and some 50 lbs of seed were planted, unsuccessfully, in 1930. As explained in Stevenson-Hamilton's memoirs as well as in the archives of the KNP, Bertram Jearey, a regular visitor from Cape Town, keen photographer and author of *Pride of Lions*

---

[85]S.R. Levick, G.P. Asner and I.P.J. Smit, 'Spatial patterns in the effects of fire on savanna vegetation three-dimensional structure', *Ecological Applications* 22, no. 8 (2012): 2110–2121; I.P.J. Smit, G.P. Asner, N. Govender, *et al.*, 'Effects of fire on woody vegetation structure in African savanna', *Ecological Applications* 20 (2010): 1865–1875; I.P.J. Smit, G.P. Asner, N. Govender, *et al.*, 'Fire on the African savanna: Using LiDAR', *Bulletin of the Ecological Society of America* 91 (2010): 343–346.

[86]Izak Smit, email to author, 10 August 2016.

[87]I would like to thank Norman Owen-Smith for alerting me to the importance of surface water management in the dismantling of the 'command-and-control' model of research in the KNP.

(London: Longmans, Green, 1936), a book about the KNP, offered a solution: a publicity fund-raising campaign in the popular press. Perhaps unexpectedly, this was a great success and between 1933 and 1935, at the insistence of the Department of Water Affairs, a number of concrete dams and drinking troughs were built, later to be replaced by more natural-looking waterholes in which wildlife might wallow. Not unexpectedly, these water points were extremely popular with many mammal (and other) species, but they also altered the population density of creatures by encouraging concentration around these artificial water points.[88]

After the Second World War and the advent, particularly in the 1960s, of an explicit policy of manipulation according to agriculturally based carrying capacity principles, the provision of surface water to mitigate drought conditions became ever-more generous. In addition to an active fire policy came an active water policy, 'water for game' also based on stabilisation. Begun initially by warden Sandenbergh, with backing from a survey by the Soil and Water Conservation Board of 1947, 'water for game' became a major pillar of landscape control. By the 1980s, boreholes dotted the KNP, eventually some perennial rivers were impounded and some very large dams had been constructed. In 1985, Pienaar, then KNP warden, summarised the various water policy history in an extensive article in *Koedoe*, and ended with a quotation from the chief director: 'Nobody should be allowed to look down with scorn upon the achievements of the past. Every borehole drilled, every windmill erected, every wheelbarrow of concrete, and every bucketful of soil were accompanied by hard labour, more often than not, under difficult circumstances, many hours of planning and often meagre funds that were needed in many places at the same time. The Kruger National Park and its animals can look back gratefully to what had been done for them.'[89]

However, even during Pienaar's wardenship there was concern that perhaps while individual animals benefited from this policy, the ecosystem itself was disturbed by it. It is well known (although not formally recorded) that Gus Mills, for example, was a critic of any expansion to the

---

[88]See J. Stevenson-Hamilton, *South African Eden* (Johannesburg: Penguin, 2008), 285–289; Box K38 file KNP38, Pollution of Sabi River; Box K39 file KNP 5.1, Water for game. KNP archives, Skukuza.

[89]U. de V. Pienaar, 'Indications of progressive desiccation of the Transvaal lowveld over the past 100 years, and implications for the water stabilization programme in the Kruger National Park', *Koedoe* 28 (1985): 93–165, quotation p. 160.

programme.[90] Given that a number of artificial dams and waterholes had been donated by the public with some fanfare, criticism remained below the surface and was certainly not heeded by the NPB or by the KNP warden and senior management at that time. However, in the 1990s, with the total re-evaluation of research, the rise of heterogeneity and studies of scales, together the impetus provided by the Mellon Foundation for serious study, water provision – together with fire and culling – was put under the spotlight.

In their chapter in *The Kruger Experience* on this topic, Gaylard, Owen-Smith and Redfern summarised the history of surface water provision, noting that as an experiment in maintaining certain populations of rare animals in times of drought, it had failed dismally. Soil erosion and over-grazing around surface water had occurred (known as 'piospheres' that affect woody vegetation as well as grass species) and nutrient distributions had been thereby disturbed. Moreover, many of the expensive water points and dams dried up. From 1997, therefore, the policy has been reversed and many water points have been closed and weirs across rivers dismantled.[91]

Elephant Management

The controversial issue of culling has been the subject of scientific debate since the late 1970s (see Chapter 8). Although it was recognised at the

---

[90]Norman Owen-Smith. Interview with the author. Johannesburg, 22 May 2012.

[91]A. Gaylard, N. Owen-Smith and J. Redfern, 'Surface water availability: Implications for heterogeneity and ecosystem processes', in *The Kruger Experience: Ecology and Management of Savanna Heterogeneity*, eds J.T. du Toit, K.H. Rogers and H.C. Biggs (Washington, DC: Island Press, 2003), 171–188; N. Owen-Smith, 'Ecological guidelines for water-points in extensive protected areas', *South African Journal of Wildlife Research* 26, no. 4 (1996): 107–112; R. Harrington, N. Owen-Smith, P.C. Viljoen, *et al.*, 'Establishing the causes of the roan antelope decline in the Kruger National Park, South Africa', *Biological Conservation* 90, no. 1 (1999): 69–78; C.C. Grant, T. Davison, P.J. Funstan and D.J. Pienaar, 'Challenges faced in the conservation of rare antelope: A case study on the northern basalt plains of the Kruger National Park', *Koedoe* 45, no. 2 (2002): 45–66, doi: 10.4102/koedoe.v45i2.26; I.P.J. Smit, 'Systems approach towards surface water distribution in Kruger National Park, South Africa', *Pachyderm* 53 (2013): 91–98; I.P.J. Smit and C.C. Grant, 'Managing surface-water in a large semi-arid savanna park: Effects on grazer distribution patterns', *Journal for Nature Conservation* 17, no. 2 (2009): 61–71; I.P.J. Smit, C.C. Grant and B.J. Devereau, 'Do artificial waterholes influence the way herbivores use the landscape? Herbivore distribution patterns around rivers and artificial surface water sources in a large African savanna park', *Biological Conservation* 136, no. 1 (2007): 85–99.

time that scientific understanding about large mammal populations was extremely meagre, and that culling was a decision based on values rather than science, throughout the 1980s the NPB continued to insist that culling was necessary. After the meetings in the USA (1979) and in South Africa (1982) discussed in an earlier chapter,[92] the issue of culling was not seriously reconsidered by the NPB. Instead, it had become routine to hold the population of elephants, hippopotamus and buffalo to a certain level in the KNP. The procedure was that following the annual aerial census, management took action aimed at sustaining stability.

However, a warning had been sounded by Graeme Caughley and Brian Walker during meetings in the 1980s that:

> The world is not simple and things are not always as they seem. In many instances the obvious response to a problem is not appropriate, it might even produce an effect directly opposite to that intended. This reflects the inherent difficulty in establishing cause and effect relationships in complex, poorly understood systems. Change in itself is not a bad thing, but is in fact a requirement for the maintenance of high resilience. In many cases culling is by no means either the conservative or the safe option.[93]

The general validity of this warning was already becoming apparent in the unexpected consequences of providing artificial water supplies and of regular veld burning in the KNP.[94] However, together with the dawning of SAM that responded to changes in scientific belief and conservation practice, there was another impetus that led to change in elephant management, namely, and as Richard Bell had predicted, human values.[95] This was, in fact, an aspect of ecosystem management for which the NPB, even with SAM, had no working tools. Nor was SANParks prepared for the scientific and emotional onslaught against culling that persisted for more

---

[92]P. Jewell and S. Holt, eds, *Problems in Management of Locally Abundant Wild Mammals: A Workshop to Examine the Need for and Alternatives to Culling of Wild Animals, 29 September–3 October 1980, Cape Cod, USA* (New York, NY: Academic Press, 1981); N. Owen-Smith, ed., *Management of Large Mammals in African Conservation Areas: Proceedings of a Symposium Held in Pretoria, South Africa, 29–30 April 1982* (Pretoria: HAUM, 1983); A.A. Ferrar, ed., *Guidelines of the Management of Large Mammals in African Conservation Areas.* South African Scientific Programmes Report 69 (Pretoria: CSIR, 1983).

[93]Ferrar, *Guidelines of the Management of Large Mammals*, iv.

[94]Joubert, *The Kruger National Park*, Vol. 2, 437, 453.

[95]In Owen-Smith, *Management of Large Mammals in African Conservation Areas*, 145–172.

Figure 11.5. Formal regular culling of elephant ended in the Kruger National Park in 1994, enabling elephant numbers to grow.
Photograph by Chantal Knoetze.

than a decade. For the first time in the history of the park, science was being driven by local and international public opinion and values.

Between 1966 and 1994, 16 330 elephants were killed or otherwise removed from the KNP. This stabilised the population at between 7000 and 8500 animals at any one time. After 1985, the park was divided into four management zones, each with a different culling regime.[96] By the 1990s the mass slaughter of animals such as elephants had become controversial internationally. The first conference on over-population, held at Cape Cod in 1979, had been sponsored by the International Fund for Animal Welfare (IFAW), an animal rights activist group whose influence had grown in the 1980s and 1990s. Over the years, animal rights and

[96]I.J. Whyte, R.J. van Aarde and S.L. Pimm, 'Kruger's elephant population: Its size and consequences for ecosystem heterogeneity', in *The Kruger Experience: Ecology and Management of Savanna Heterogeneity*, eds J.T. du Toit, K.H. Rogers and H.C. Biggs (Washington, DC: Island Press, 2003): 332–348, information from 338–339. See also M. Grainger, R.J. van Aarde and I. Whyte, 'Landscape heterogeneity and the use of space by elephants in the Kruger National Park, South Africa', *African Journal of Ecology* 43 (2005): 369–375.

biosphere rights had been championed by a growing cohort of lobbyists and philosophers and the literature on environmental ethics had burgeoned. Along with the scientific approach of managing ecosystems with minimal interference went the work in a quite different vein of the likes of Arne Naess, Roderick Nash, Peter Singer and others, who championed the rights and the freedom of individual species. Culling, therefore, ran counter to the rights of natural phenomena to exist without human interference, and to the belief that their value is intrinsic and not contingent upon human use.[97] Given the closeness of the historical relationship between humans and elephants worldwide, it is not surprising that elephant culling evoked such powerful emotions and debate. Adding to the mix was the growing understanding of just how 'human' elephants were in terms of social organisation and behaviour, based on what seemed to be emotions.[98] In short, philosophers and animal behaviourists and others – particularly in the West – were redefining animal ethics.[99]

In addition, South Africa was no longer able to dismiss world opinion as it had under apartheid, nor were national parks immune to public opinion within the country. The mantra that 'government knows best' had been undermined not only by the transition to democracy but also by the growth of easily available electronic communications. While South Africa's elephant population may have been sustainable, or even growing

[97]H. Rolston III, *Conserving Natural Value* (New York, NY: Columbia University Press, 1994); H. Rolston III, *Genes, Genesis and God: Values and their Origins in Natural and Human History* (Cambridge: Cambridge University Press, 1999); A. Naess, *Ecology, Community and Lifestyle: Outline of an Ecosophy*, trans. David Rothenberg (New York, NY: Cambridge University Press, 1989); P.W. Taylor, *Respect for Nature: A Theory of Environmental Ethics* (Princeton, NJ: Princeton University Press, 1986); P. Singer, *Animal Liberation* (Wellingborough: Thorsons, 1983); R.F. Nash, *The Rights of Nature: A History of Environmental Ethics* (Madison, WI: University of Wisconsin Press, 1989).

[98]See, for example, J. Poole, *Coming of Age with Elephants: A Memoir* (New York, NY: Hyperion, 1996); M. Garstang, *Elephant Sense and Sensibility* (Waltham, MA: Academic Press, 2015).

[99]A summary of this altered thinking is to be found in C. Wemmer and C.A. Christen, eds, *Elephants and Ethics: Toward a Morality of Coexistence* (Baltimore, MD: Johns Hopkins University Press, 2008); B. Page, R. Slotow and R. van Aarde, 'A scientific perspective on the management of elephants in the Kruger National Park and elsewhere', *South African Journal of Science* 102 (2006): 389–394; A. Paterson, 'Elephants (!Xó) of the Cederberg Wilderness Area: A re-evaluation of the San paintings previously referred to as "Elephants in boxes"', *The Digging Stick* 24, no. 3 (2007); R. Sukumar, *The Living Elephants: Evolutionary Ecology, Behaviour, and Conservation* (New York, NY: Oxford University Press, 2003).

in protected areas, this was not the case elsewhere in Africa,[100] and South Africa's responsibility to protect this iconic species had a global dimension as well. There were many conventions and international responsibilities applying to certain species and after 1994 the international spotlight fell on South Africa's discharge of these duties. Earlier, in 1989, CITES had listed the African elephant on Appendix 1, thus effectively banning trade in elephants and elephant products.[101]

As South Africa became more receptive to democratic 'people and parks' ideas and community conservation, the KNP culling programme came under attack from another quarter, the local African communities around the national park. This was because the financial benefits and other by-products of culling (meat, hides, etc.) accrued to the NPB and were not shared with neighbours, some of whose fields were sometimes trampled by elephants that had broken through the fence. If culling were to continue, the argument ran, the wider community should benefit. Thus, even politicians began to sit up and take note of the issue.

Moreover, as we have seen, there was a change in leadership in the NPB. Unlike his predecessors in the NPB's top position, Robinson was not heavily invested in the KNP's routines or particularly anxious to perpetuate them. Moreover, Joubert, who had become KNP warden in 1987, was a relatively flexible and ecosystem-oriented scientist and had attended the over-population meetings held in previous years. He was thus well aware of the arguments against arithmetical culling and of the absence of reliable evidence and experimentation concerning the regulation of elephant populations. There was, moreover, one scientist in the NPB who did become an elephant specialist, Ian Whyte. He had joined the KNP in 1974 as an assistant to de Vos, the veterinarian. By 1990 he had risen to become the senior research officer responsible for compiling census results and culling quotas.[102] Whyte went on to make scholarly study of elephant management in the form of a University of Pretoria

[100]See I. Parker, *What I Tell You Three Times is True: Conservation, Ivory, History and Politics* (Moray: Librario, 2004); R.E. Leakey, *Wildlife Wars: My Fight to Save Africa's Natural Resources* (New York, NY: St Martin's Press, 2001).

[101]See H.T. Dublin and L.S. Niskanen, eds, *Guidelines for the* in situ *Translocation of the African Elephant for Conservation Purposes. The African Elephant Specialist Group in Collaboration with the Re-introduction and Veterinary Specialist Groups, 2003* (Gland: IUCN, 2003); D. Cumming and B. Jones, *Elephants in Southern Africa: Management Issues and Options.* WWF-SARPO Occasional Paper Number 11 (Harare: WWF-SARPO, May 2005). Southern Africa elephant returned to CITES Appendix II in 1997.

[102]Joubert, *The Kruger National Park*, vol. 2, 437, 453.

DSc entitled 'Conservation management of the Kruger National Park Elephant population' (2001) and was to play an important role in the ongoing culling debate.

Elephants in Africa, as well as elsewhere, began to attract considerable attention after the late 1980s. South Africa's management of its elephants stood in stark contrast to East Africa's. There, elephants were poached relentlessly for their ivory and numbers were plummeting, whereas in southern Africa where protection was more effective, numbers were growing and culling was the order of the day. The latter issue even gave rise to a 'Symposium on the African elephant as a game ranch animal', held in the KNP in April 1991, which concentrated on culling, capture, confinement, disease, economic returns and other practical matters, to the exclusion of what became the most important issue in later debates – ethics and ecosystem management.[103]

The whole question of elephant management, whether in terms of game farming or conservation science, was being opened up for public discussion, a discussion that has continued unabated. In 1993, the debate ratcheted up when IFAW undertook to pay to translocate KNP elephants earmarked for culling to other areas of the country.[104] This, together with his personal aversion to automatic culling and appreciation of the need to cultivate non-governmental sources of funding, persuaded Robinson to impose a moratorium on culling in 1994.[105] The revised KNP management plan for 1995–1996 reflected the uncertain path ahead. The total ceiling for elephants in the KNP was uplifted in accordance with the theories of heterogeneity and change, and overall culling was to be evaluated against a non-equilibrium paradigm. There was recognition in the plan that decision-makers acted in terms of value systems – of which culling was one – and not scientific necessities. This realisation was strengthened by the appreciation that conservation science and ecology in its SAM incarnation were not predictive but uncertain. Thus, the argument that elephants were destroying vegetation and required culling was

[103]L. Colly, 'Diseases of elephants', in *Proceedings of a Symposium on the African Elephant as a Game Ranch Animal, Berg-en-Dal, Kruger National Park, 29–30 April 1991* (Pretoria: Wildlife Group of the South African Veterinary Association), 106–114. See also A.J. Hall-Martin, 'Distribution and status of the African elephant *Loxodonta africana* in South Africa, 1652–1992', *Koedoe* 35 (1992): 65–88.

[104]Joubert, *The Kruger National Park*, vol. 2, 436.

[105]The last cull took place in 1994.

a value judgement. Consequently, when values changed or were questioned, they could be – indeed had to be – reconsidered.

Because of opposition to the moratorium and the view that it was 'obvious' there were 'too many' elephants as evidenced by the uprooted trees littering the veld, Robinson arranged a public debate on culling in Midrand, near Johannesburg, on 4 May 1995. This was the first occasion the NPB had asked the public to contribute to the running of national parks. At that meeting, the NPB undertook to suspend elephant culling and to review its elephant management policy. The next step was a workshop in Skukuza on 8 February the following year involving the African Elephant Specialist Group, which would assist in developing the policy review. This resulted in an internal report, which was subject to further debate. Finally, in October 1996, the decision was taken in principle not to impose a predetermined ceiling but to allow elephant numbers to fluctuate according to certain criteria relating to heterogeneity.[106] These decisions were presented to the public in Midrand the following month. Comments were solicited, but few were received.[107] By now, many scientists, and not only within the NPB, were interested in elephant management and the pool of expertise was growing.

A major concern about the presence of large herds of huge mammals was how to maintain biodiversity, the guiding principle behind all conservation practice in the country and also an international commitment by South Africa.[108] In February 1997, a workshop attended by international and local scientists tackled this very issue, namely, the extent to which elephant transformations of habitat threaten biodiversity. The idea of a 'grand plan' was abandoned in favour of small, carefully monitored steps aligned with the concept of TPCs. The KNP would be managed not as a unit but in terms of discrete elephant management zones (within which culling might be done as needed).[109] The proposed new policy was compiled in 1997 by the KNP team of Ian Whyte, Harry

---

[106]D. Mabunda, *Report to the Minister of Environmental Affairs and Tourism on Developing Elephant Management Plans for National Parks with Recommendations on the Process to be Followed* (Pretoria: SANParks, 2005), Appendix 4. The Skukuza workshop was held on 30 October 1996.

[107]Mabunda, *Report to the Minister of Environmental Affairs and Tourism*. The public debate in Midrand was held on 12 November 1996.

[108]See A. Gaylard, 'Exploring management of biodiversity in the Kruger National Park: Elephants as agents of change', *Rhino and Elephant Journal* 12 (1998): 16–19.

[109]Mabunda, *Report to the Minister of Environmental Affairs and Tourism*. This workshop was held from 11 to 13 February 1997.

Biggs, Angela Gaylard and Leo Braack and published on the Internet.[110] Before long, the views of outsider scientists appeared in print.[111] The public reacted positively to renewed culling in accordance with the plan when this option was presented at an open meeting in Nelspruit on 31 October 1998. However, various animal rights groups counselled awaiting analysis of the results of the experiments that had been taking place with elephant contraception. These experiments had involved Whyte as well as Rudi van Aarde of the University of Pretoria and Stuart Pimm of Duke University, and required thorough investigation of elephant population dynamics.[112] Nothing like this had been done during the many years of culling and, given the lifespan of the elephant and its particular physiology and biology, this would obviously be a long-term project.[113] Reacting to the opinion of their peers and the public, the KNP team of Whyte, Biggs, Gaylard and Braack published their policy document in *Koedoe* in 1999, after approval by the SANParks board on 12 March 1999.[114] In terms of this document, the moratorium on culling was to be extended.

Another idea that gained currency at the time – and one particularly attractive to many scientists (including van Aarde) – was the notion of elephant as a metapopulation in southern Africa, not a series of isolated populations in KNP and elsewhere.[115] Here the influence can be

[110]I.J. Whyte, H.C. Biggs, A. Gaylard and L.E.O. Braack, 'A proposed new policy for the management of the elephant population of the Kruger National Park', in *Policy Proposals Regarding Issues Relating to Biodiversity Maintenance, Maintenance of Wilderness Qualities, and Provision of Human Benefits* (Skukuza: SANParks, 1997), 117–139.

[111]For example, S.L. Pimm and R.J. van Aarde, 'Managing the elephants of Kruger National Park', *Animal Conservation* 1 (1998): 77–83.

[112]R.J. van Aarde, I. Whyte and S.L. Pimm, 'The consequences of culling for the dynamics of the African elephant population of Kruger National Park', *Animal Conservation* 2 (1999): 287–294.

[113]H. Bertschinger, 'Reproductive control of elephants', in *Scientific Assessment of Elephant Management in South Africa*, eds R.J. Scholes and K.G. Mennell (Johannesburg: Wits University Press, 2008), 257–328; R.A. Fayrer-Hosken, D. Grobler, J.J. van Altena, H.J. Bertschinger and J.F. Kirkpatrick, 'Immunocontraception of African elephants', *Nature* 407 (2000): 149–150; S.L. Pimm and R.J. van Aarde, 'African elephants and contraception', *Nature* 411 (2001): 766.

[114]I.J. Whyte, H.C. Biggs, A. Gaylard and L.E.O. Braack, 'A new policy for the management of the Kruger National Park's elephant population', *Koedoe* 42 (1999): 111–132.

[115]R.J. van Aarde and T.O. Jackson, 'Megaparks for metapopulations: Addressing the causes of locally high elephant numbers in southern Africa', *Biological Conservation* 134 (2007): 289–298.

discerned of Ilkka Hanski of the University of Helsinki, whose book *Metapopulation Ecology* had appeared in 1999.[116] Viewing elephants as a subcontinental metapopulation has been useful in considering their range beyond formally protected areas, but the notion has also drawn criticism from neighbouring countries, especially Mozambique, which have concerns about increased elephant–human conflict.[117]

During the moratorium, elephant numbers increased in the KNP, resulting in visible damage to the vegetation and renewed pressure to begin culling again.[118] Three important meetings were convened and public debate was again joined. The first was a 'Great Elephant Debate', organised on 6 August 2004 in Nelspruit by the Wildlife and Environment Society of Southern Africa (WESSA). Thereafter, from 19 to 21 October, SANParks arranged a 'Great Elephant Indaba: Finding an African solution to an African problem' at Berg-en-Dal in the KNP. More than 200 stakeholders attended. In his opening address, David Mabunda alluded to the immense changes in South Africa's legislation on protected areas and biodiversity, which had coincided with the elephant's rise to international importance as a socio-political issue. South Africa was the custodian of elephants, not their owner. The discussion was fairly heated – indeed, was sometimes referred to as a battleground[119] – and it was soon apparent that no solution would satisfy both the pro- and anti-culling lobbies. The scientists themselves could not, apparently, agree on the 'facts'. Beyond that, Justice for Animals representatives castigated apartheid for creating a culture of violence (which included culling) and transforming conservation from a praiseworthy moral commitment into a merely profitable exercise. Delegates from neighbouring African communities retorted that animal rights was a Western imposition, not an African position, and they both demanded and would welcome a share in any profits. The group favouring a return to culling was outspoken in its insistence that the view of 'too many' fallen trees equalled 'too many' elephants, an equation no

[116] I. Hanski, 'Metapopulation dynamics', *Nature* 396 (1998): 41–49; I. Hanski, *Metapopulation Ecology* (Oxford: Oxford University Press, 1999).

[117] www.sanparks.co.za/parks/kruger/conservation/scientific/key_issues/plans/elephant/pdfs/chapter_03.pdf. Chapter 3 (accessed 23 November 2015).

[118] I.J. Whyte, 'The ecological basis of the Kruger National Park's new elephant management policy and expected outcomes after its implementation', *Pachyderm* 36 (2004): 99–108.

[119] Author's notes from the Indaba, 19–21 October 2004. The word was used in the address by David Mabunda. The keynote speaker was David Cumming.

amount of science could alter.[120] The debate continued into 2005, with community workshops in March and April at which the neighbours of protected areas once again supported culling and expressed the wish to benefit from it.[121]

Moreover, by this time, elephant management as an issue had reached far beyond the KNP. In Zimbabwe, the African Wildlife Consultative Forum, under the auspices of the Southern African Development Council, hosted a meeting of all the region's elephant range states in May 2005 to reach agreement on a regional elephant conservation and management strategy.[122] In addition, a non-governmental consortium named Elephants Alive began an initiative to challenge the anticipated resumption of culling and convened a workshop of its own at Wits from 18 to 20 July 2005. One of the concerns expressed by this consortium was the existence of a 'cabal' of scientists in SANParks whose ideas needed to be tested by 'independent' scientists.[123] IFAW, for its part, voiced concern about the conflation of 'science' with 'values' in SANParks reports.[124]

The high emotions that were triggered among interested parties by the publicity accorded to the culling of elephant through the many meetings and the attendant media attention also spilled over into often exaggerated reports of the disparity of views expressed by different scientists thus leading to public distrust of their ability to take valid ecological decisions. Particularly concerned by this element in the debate, senior SANParks managers Hector Magome and Harry Biggs asked Kevin Rogers to facilitate a workshop of 50 scientists with a mandate to develop consensus among the group on the current state of elephant science and management. This was held at Luiperdskloof in March 2005 and, in record time, a 30-page summary and executive outline appeared. Obviating the need for a plethora of published scholarly papers, this document synthesised existing information and presented it clearly to a wide variety of readers.[125]

---

[120]SANParks, *The Great Elephant Indaba: Finding an African Solution to an African Problem* (Pretoria: SANParks, 2004).

[121]Mabunda, *Report to the Minister of Environmental Affairs and Tourism*, 11–13.

[122]Mabunda, *Report to the Minister of Environmental Affairs and Tourism*, 13–14, Appendix 5.

[123]*Mail and Guardian*, 15 December 2005, 'Minister to discuss elephant culling with scientists'. Report by Elvira Van Noort.

[124]IFAW, *The Debate on Elephant Culling in South Africa: An Overview* (Cape Town: IFAW, 2005).

[125]I am grateful to Kevin Rogers for a copy of the summary document, 'Elephant and biodiversity: An executive synthesis of current understanding of the role and management

More importantly, the gaps in scientific knowledge and the controversy and confusion also concerned Marthinus van Schalkwyk, the former leader of the New National Party who had been rewarded with the environmental affairs and tourism ministerial portfolio after joining the African National Congress in 2005. He was thus in a position not only to receive reports about all these meetings, especially as they were now online, but also to act on them. Van Schalkwyk was not pleased to see the divisive issue of elephant culling dominate the conversation, and recognised the urgency of doing more to regulate the policy framework.[126] During late 2005 and early 2006, he mounted an 'international roadshow' with members of SANParks management to the UK, the Netherlands, Switzerland, Italy, Germany and the USA, aimed at testing opinion and explaining South Africa's dilemma.[127]

After the Luiperdskloof meeting, he had also convened his own panel of ten scientists involved in elephant management to answer specific questions and enable him to compile an objective document on the norms and standards of elephant management.[128] This compilation had recently been recommended by Mabunda.[129] However, whereas Mabunda had anticipated a March 2006 completion date, van Schalkwyk convened yet another roundtable in early 2006, followed by one more in August 2006.[130] The scientists disputed the degree of uncertainty, and stressed that there was consensus on the absence of compelling evidence for culling, yet they also felt it might be required in certain areas at certain

---

of elephant in savanna ecosystems. Outcomes of the Science Workshop Luiperdskloof, March 2005', by K.H. Rogers, Animal Plant and Environmental Sciences, University of the Witwatersrand, Johannesburg.

[126]*Mail and Guardian*, 15 December 2005, 'Minister to discuss elephant culling with scientists'. Report by Elvira Van Noort.

[127]*Mail and Guardian*, 16 November 2005. 'Roll up for the culling circus'. Report by Fiona MacLeod. See also: www.sanparks.co.za/parks/kruger/conservation/scientific/key_issues/plans/elephant/pdfs/chapter_03.pdf. Chapter 3 (accessed 23 November 2015).

[128]N. Owen-Smith, G.I.H. Kerley, B. Page, R. Slotow and R.J. van Aarde, 'A scientific perspective on the management of elephants in the Kruger National Park and elsewhere', *South African Journal of Science* 102 (2006): 389–394, quotation p. 389. The Minister had accepted responsibility for compiling a formal document on norms and standards of elephant management and a draft document was ready in March 2007.

[129]Mabunda, *Report to the Minister of Environmental Affairs and Tourism*, 7.

[130]*Mail and Guardian*, 15 December 2005, 'Minister to discuss elephant culling with scientists'. Report by Elvira Van Noort.

times.[131] Apparently, the minister was struck anew by the diversity of scientific opinion and the paucity of knowledge on key questions related to elephant management, the highest profile branch of South African protected area science. According to J.P. Louw, head of communications in the department of environmental affairs and tourism, 'it was disturbing that scientists appear intolerant of each other's views'. Clearly, piecemeal responses to elephant management were proving extremely unsatisfactory and gaining South Africa unwelcome international publicity. Many scientists were beginning to argue that impact did not depend only on numbers and that issues such as regional ecosystem management required careful study.[132]

Scientific findings and opinions on how best to manage elephants in the future were found in scattered publications and full synthesis of the state of knowledge was needed. The government thus stepped in as arbitrator. Consequently, at the final meeting between van Schalkwyk and the scientific advisors it was agreed that a full assessment be conducted along the lines of the CSIR's millennium ecosystem assessment undertaken in 2004.[133] Chosen as leader was Robert (Bob) Scholes, an award-winning systems ecologist at the CSIR and a well-respected science administrator and coordinator who had been involved in the millennium ecosystem assessment. Given the need of a solution to this protracted problem, no time was to be lost in compiling the assessment. Scholes invited a large team to compile the synthesis, emphasising that the objective was to 'document what is known, unknown and disputed on the topic of elephant–ecosystem–human interactions in South Africa' and to 'synthesise and communicate the information in such a way that decision-making and the reaching of social consensus is facilitated'.[134] In the event, the

---

[131]Owen-Smith, Kerley, Page, Slotow and van Aarde, 'A scientific perspective on the management of elephants', 389–394, quotation p. 389.

[132]Owen-Smith, Kerley, Page, Slotow and van Aarde, 'A scientific perspective on the management of elephants'. See also R.J. van Aarde, T.P. Jackson and S.M. Ferreira, 'Conservation science and elephant management in southern Africa', *South African Journal of Science* 102 (2006): 385–388.

[133]R.J. Scholes and R. Biggs, eds, *Ecosystem Services in Southern Africa: A Regional Assessment. A Contribution to the Millennium Ecosystem Assessment, Prepared by the Regional-Scale Team of the Southern African Millennium Ecosystem Assessment* (Pretoria: Council for Scientific and Industrial Research, 2004).

[134]R.J. Scholes and K.G. Mennell, 'Preface', in *Elephant Management: A Scientific Assessment of Elephant Management in South Africa*, eds R.J. Scholes and K.G. Mennell (Johannesburg: Wits University Press, 2008), xxx–xxxiv.

assessment was published as a book by Wits University Press in 2008, and, like *The Kruger Experience* that appeared five years earlier, has become a classic in environmental science in South Africa.[135]

Work on it began in earnest in mid-2007, and involved 62 experts as authors and as members of the review panel. There were two rounds of review: one by experts qualified to comment on technical accuracy and the second by stakeholders to ensure that all issues were canvassed adequately and in a balanced fashion. The topics covered included elephant history, ecosystems and biodiversity, human–elephant interactions, translocation, control of elephant reproduction, distribution, lethal management, ethics, legislation and decision-making. The final 'Norms and Standards for the Management of Elephants in South Africa', which included many graphs, tables and figures, was published in the *Government Gazette* on 29 February 2008. Provision was made for revision of the norms and standards every four years. For the first time, an important conservation management tool, based on scientific evidence, had been taken out of the hands of protected area administrators and brought into the domain of national politics. No longer was SANParks able to cull elephants at will, but now required the authority of the Minister to do so.[136] However, it is important to observe that it was because SANParks had begun to operate democratically that, thanks to a cohort of senior managers, it had nurtured a societally acceptable process to elephant management in the country.[137] Among the 'eddies and ripples' described above, and that form part of the quotation with which the Introduction to this book begins, the elephant management process is one of the 'undercurrents changing the main channel of the stream'.

The elephant management debate had shown the power of local and international civil society to influence science, and indeed provide positive incentives for research and experimentation. It had also shown that conservation science was indeed a science with a mission – a mission underpinned by value systems, not scientific evidence alone. Thus for the first time, the South African public – and politicians – had become involved in a science that was innovative, integrative and international and, despite the divergences of opinion, had thereby improved the

---

[135]Scholes and Mennell, *Elephant Management*.

[136]'Norms and Standards for the Management of Elephants in South Africa', Notice 251, *Government Gazette*, 29 February 2008.

[137]Kevin Rogers has been extremely helpful in assisting me with the analysis of the elephant management debate.

science and helped persuade conservation scientists in national protected areas to become more accountable to the human constituency they served. Moreover, the great elephant culling issue had brought together South and southern Africa with the rest of Africa, and indeed the wider international world of elephant science.

Cultural, Historical and Archaeological Heritage Conservation Science

Unlike in the natural sciences, there was no champion, intellectual or financial, for the other fields of study in the KNP, or indeed, the other national parks. No senior manager emerged to negotiate top-level partnerships with rock art specialists, creative archaeologists or professional archivists and museologists. Some good work was done and published by the likes of Lynn Meskell of Stanford, Marie Küsel, then at the University of South Africa, and T.I. Nemaheni.[138] However, the absence of a suitably trained senior manager within SANParks has often meant that archaeological finds, such as Thula Mela, are over-sensationalised, treated as 'prehistoric', and not nested within a wider context of careful scholarship. Moreover, without ongoing financial support or publicity and marketing by SANParks, the valuable sites that have been worked on have not been well preserved or promoted as tourist highlights. After almost a century of conservation in the KNP, there is still little to show in the way of humanities and social science research.

Since 1994, the KNP has gained world renown for the ecosystem research and conservation management conducted within its boundaries by a wide array of experts from South Africa and abroad. In previous decades, the national park was renowned for its megafauna and the almost unrivalled opportunities it offered for sightings. Since the 1990s, however, it has embellished that reputation by becoming a reputable site for serious, hypothesis-driven research that has added significantly to our understanding of the workings of ecosystems generally and savannah ecosystems in particular.

[138]L. Meskell, 'Falling walls and mending fences: Archaeological ethnography in the Limpopo', *Journal of Southern African Studies* 33, no. 2 (2007): 383–400; M.M. Küsel, 'A preliminary report on settlement layout and gold melting at Thula Mela, a Late Iron Age site in the Kruger National Park', *Koedoe* 35, no. 1 (1992): 55–64; T.I. Nemaheni, 'A cultural heritage resource management plan for Thulamela heritage site' (MA diss., University of Pretoria, 2003).

12 · *Other National Parks*

While the Kruger National Park (KNP) continued to be the main focus of scientific attention within South African National Parks (SANParks) – indeed, its preponderance may have grown thanks to the activities and enthusiasm unleashed by Mellon Foundation support – from the 1990s onwards more attention was paid to South Africa's other national parks. After 1990 many new national parks were proclaimed and there was also a concerted attempt to convert smaller parks into viable entities by expanding them where possible. This entailed significant organisational and administrative rearrangements, and it was these, rather than scientific output, that were the main focus of attention. A recent phase of the reorganisation of the agency has involved grouping all national parks into broad ecological units rather than by location. In this regard, the influence of the international conventions to which South Africa became party is apparent: both the Biodiversity Convention and the resultant South African Biodiversity Act 10 of 2004 required that representative national biomes be identified and conserved. SANParks was tasked with this responsibility for some of the previously neglected biomes, as the new nine provinces were struggling just to provide basic human services. Interestingly, there is no record of the consideration of formal partnerships between SANParks and the provincial conservation authorities or even of scientific partnerships or capacity-building arrangements with them. The silo-type organisation of government has continued to hold sway.

In addition, as has been explained, national parks were now expected to be creators of employment and to ensure a continued and expanded flow of international eco-tourists in the face of competition from game ranches and protected areas in private hands. Those national parks that were large, contained representative charismatic megafauna, were easy to access and situated in areas of the country regarded as crime-free were better suited to these tasks than others. Moreover, SANParks was coming under pressure to reach out in various ways to neighbouring states with which apartheid-era South Africa had had hostile relations. The identification and declaration of appropriate Transfrontier Conservation Areas (TFCAs), or 'Peace Parks', was a key plank in this strategy.[1] The Peace Parks Foundation was founded by Anton Rupert in 1997[2] and since then three transfrontier parks have been declared. The first, in 2000, was the Kgalagadi protected area, covering some 38 000 km², which was an amalgamation of the Kalahari Gemsbok National Park and Botswana's Gemsbok National Park. By a formal treaty signed in December 2002, the Great Limpopo Transfrontier Park came into being. It combines the KNP, the Limpopo National Park in Mozambique (created out of 16 hunting areas in 2001), and a substantial area of south-eastern Zimbabwe, including Gonarezhou National Park. The resulting protected area is also some 38 000 km². Despite the intent to promote regional peace and appeals by the Peace Parks Foundation (and indeed SANParks) for African cooperation and conflict resolution, this park has been criticised as being part of the neoliberal economic agenda on account of the World Bank's involvement in its creation. Moreover, the promise of scientific research in a larger ecosystem straddling international borders has yet to bear fruit.[3] Finally, in August 2003 agreement was reached between South Africa and Namibia to create the |Ai-|Ais/Richtersveld

[1]S.H. Ali, *Peace Parks: Conservation and Conflict Resolution* (Cambridge, MA: MIT Press, 2007); J.A. Andersson, M. de Garine-Wichatitsky, D.H.M. Cumming, V. Dzingirai and K.E. Giller, eds, *Transfrontier Conservation Areas: People Living on the Edge* (Abington: Routledge, 2013).

[2]See Peace Parks, www.peaceparks.org/.

[3]W. Whande and H. Suich, 'Transfrontier conservation initiatives in southern Africa: Observations from the Great Limpopo Transfrontier Conservation Area', in *Evolution and Innovation in Wildlife Conservation: Parks and Game Ranches to Transfrontier Conservation Areas*, eds H. Suich, B. Child and A. Spenceley (London: Earthscan, 2009), 373–391; W. Dressler and B. Büscher, 'Market triumphalism and the CBNRM "crises" at the South African section of the Great Limpopo Transfrontier Park', *Geoforum* 39 (2008): 452–465; D.M. Hughes, 'Third nature: Making space and time in the Great Limpopo Conservation Area', *Cultural Anthropology* 20 (2005): 157–184; W. Wolmer, 'Transboundary conservation: The politics of ecological integrity in the Great Limpopo Transfrontier Park', *Journal of Southern African Studies* 29 (2003): 261–278; A. Spenceley, 'Tourism in the Great Limpopo Transfrontier Park', *Development Southern Africa* 23 (2006): 649–667; C. Mavhunga and M. Spierenburg, 'Transfrontier talk, cordon politics: The early history of the Great Limpopo Transfrontier Park in southern Africa, 1925–1940', *Journal of Southern African Studies*, 35 no. 3 (2009): 715–735; M. Spierenburg, C. Steenkamp and H. Wels, 'Enclosing the local for the global commons: Community land rights in the Great Limpopo Transfrontier Area', *Conservation and Society* 6, no. 1 (2008): 87–97; K. Berglund, 'Framing transfrontier nature conservation: The Great Limpopo Transfrontier Park and the vision of "peace parks" in southern Africa' (MA diss., Uppsala University, 2015).

TFCA (604 500 ha) that straddles their Orange River border. Others are in the planning stages: the Gariep Transfrontier Park around Augrabies Falls National Park, involving Namibia and South Africa; the Limpopo–Shashe River boundary between Botswana, South Africa and Zimbabwe (around Mapungubwe National Park); and the Maloti-Drakensberg Transfrontier Conservation and Development Area, involving South Africa and Lesotho.[4]

Some of this flurry of activity in the 1990s was driven by the international attention focused on South Africa in the lead up to the World Summit on Sustainable Development to be held in Johannesburg in 2002 and especially, the fifth World Parks Congress in Durban in 2003. It was important that South Africa demonstrate commitment, enterprise and energy in the protected area sector. With a fresh cohort of senior managers in Pretoria, and with the eagerness to showcase the 'new country', there was an excitement about new beginnings and the initiation of new strategies.

As explained previously, national parks other than the KNP had always been lower in the pecking order. Some did not – and do not – meet IUCN criteria for national parks and none has the variety and interest of the Kruger ecosystem. However, some of the other national parks had been in existence since the 1930s and without appealing to parliament to abolish them – a step not lightly taken – SANParks was obliged to continue to manage them.

With the appointment of Robinson as head of the National Parks Board (NPB) in 1991, more attention was devoted to parks other than Kruger by the top management. Part of the impetus for this shift, especially towards the Western Cape, stemmed from the complex and politically fraught negotiations to establish a national park around Cape Town that would include Table Mountain and the Cape Peninsula. Attention to this area was also drawn not only by the beautiful scenery and winelands, but also by the enormous stature of Nelson Mandela and the inscription of Robben Island, where he and others had been held prisoner for so many years, as a World Heritage Site in 1999. An even greater influx of foreign tourists to the region was thus anticipated. There is also no doubt that Robinson had a different vision for national parks than the previous coterie of Pretoria-trained savannah scientists.

[4]Ali, *Peace Parks*; A. Hall-Martin, L. Braack and H. Magome, 'Peace Parks or Transfrontier Conservation Areas', in *South African National Parks: A Celebration*, eds A. Hall-Martin and J. Carruthers (Johannesburg: Horst Klemm, 2003), 224–244.

In anticipation of the advent of democracy, the NPB's 1992 annual report noted many changes to the administration of the NPB and also to board membership. This was a watershed year with the retirement of many of the old guard, the appointment of Enos Mabuza as the first black board member and the appointment of B.N. Mokoatle as the first black human resources director. It also marked the enlistment of the National Productivity Institute to improve the management and administration of the board and its parks by way of updated systems and higher productivity. As importantly, the 'inland' and 'southern' parks were combined into a single management unit, headquartered in Cape Town and led by Anthony Hall-Martin. Property in Kimberley and near Sedgefield was purchased as research headquarters for these parks.

There were signs that research interest in these other parks was already increasing. In Addo Elephant, the valley bushveld vegetation was beginning to be viewed as more significant than the elephant population. A database of plant species in Augrabies Falls National Park (including invasive species) had been generated, while in Bontebok, identifying genetic markers for the bontebok, literature searches and grazing and fire research were proceeding well. A number of other catalysts drew increasing scientific attention to South Africa's suite of national parks. Vegetation assumed cardinal importance in a scientific milieu that demanded the conservation of areas of high irreplaceability and vulnerability but also large enough to allow for viable management,[5] hence, for example, the efforts to place the fragmented and small 'biodiversity hotspots' around Cape Town under closer management and conservation. Also of particular interest was arid area vegetation, especially in the provinces of the Northern and Eastern Cape. Expanding existing protected areas or creating new national parks in these regions also chimed well with the government's strategy to utilise national parks as nodes of economic development in areas that were extremely poor and lacking in job opportunities.

Thus, a variety of considerations ranging from biological conservation, biogeography and an ecosystem approach, together with economic instrumentalism, environmental justice and transfers of power, brought

[5] A. Hall-Martin, 'Developing a national park system', in *South African National Parks: A Celebration*, eds A. Hall-Martin and J. Carruthers (Johannesburg: Horst Klemm, 2003), 44–62, quote p. 52.

great changes to South African national parks.[6] For the first time in decades the national government began to purchase land for conservation or to enter into innovative land tenure and ownership arrangements with partners or with concessionaires with whom they could share costs.[7] These initiatives facilitated growth in the number of national parks and the expansion of existing parks. For instance, agreement with the Richtersveld community on a contractual national park had been concluded, while Tsitsikamma National Park was expanded by some 30 000 ha, even though NPB did not acquire ownership of the land.[8] Interestingly, no national parks were created in KwaZulu-Natal. That province, however, is well served by Ezemvelo KZN Wildlife, the provincial conservation authority that manages a number of game reserves, and there is also the World Heritage Site at St Lucia, the iSimangaliso Wetland Park, managed as a separate authority.

North West is the other province where there is no SANParks presence, but there, too, the provincial conservation authorities own and manage a number of well-run and respected national parks and game reserves, including Pilanesberg and Madikwe. In addition, careful forward planning became the order of the day, including long-term strategies exemplified by the integrative plan put forward in 2002 by the Department of Environmental Affairs and Tourism, *A Bioregional Approach to South Africa's Protected Areas*.[9]

Yet in many ways, NPB science was ill-equipped to meet these challenges in the 1990s. In this period some 20 scientists were employed by NPB along with technicians and other assistants. It was difficult to coordinate the group or even to generate synergy among them. Because of the great variability in geography, size, ecology and facilities – and also in scientific interest – in parks other than the KNP, learning was not shared among them. There was no science forum, or formal structure that brought them together in terms of research priorities and

---

[6]B. Child, 'Conservation in transition', in *Evolution and Innovation in Wildlife Conservation: Parks and Game Ranches to Transfrontier Conservation Areas*, eds H. Suich, B. Child and A. Spenceley (London: Earthscan, 2009), 3–15.

[7]G. Castley, C. Patton and H. Magome, 'Making "conventional" parks relevant to all of society', in *Evolution and Innovation in Wildlife Conservation: Parks and Game Ranches to Transfrontier Conservation Areas*, eds H. Suich, B. Child and A. Spenceley (London: Earthscan, 2009), 393–407.

[8]NPB, Jaarverslag van die Nasional Parkeraad, 1992, pp. 3–25.

[9]See also, Anon., *The National Protected Area Expansion Strategy 2008–2012: A Framework for Implementation* (Pretoria: SANBI, 2008).

methodology. Generally, work in these parks reflected the preferences of individual managers, some of them old-style game rangers more interested in routine administration than scientific findings. Some may perhaps have even felt threatened by the jargon emanating from the KNP about strategic adaptive management (SAM) and thresholds of potential concern (TPCs). Also unsettling to certain people in the NPB was the increasing emphasis on engagement with society. Indeed, the culture of South Africa was changing dramatically in the 1990s and with it the type of studies deemed relevant to protected areas.

Science and Other Parks

Currently, SANParks has responsibility for 19 national parks. Six were established before 1960, one of which, Dongola Wild Life Sanctuary, was abolished in the late 1940s. Four were proclaimed in the 1930s, three of them – Bontebok, Addo Elephant and Mountain Zebra – were extremely small and they, along with the larger Kalahari Gemsbok National Park (KGNP), were intended as shelters for mammal species regarded as rare. These four have survived. Between 1960 and 1990 a further seven national parks were proclaimed, in each case to conserve a specific environment rather than a single mammal species. They included the country's first coastal, marine, highland and arid karoo national parks – Golden Gate Highlands, Tsitsikamma Coastal and Forest (the Forest section was deproclaimed in 1989 and the name of the remaining area changed to the Tsitsikamma National Park), Karoo, West Coast, Knysna National Lake Area, Wilderness and Vaalbos. A successful land claim by previous inhabitants led to the abolition in 2007 of Vaalbos, a karoo area requiring extensive restoration, after the wildlife had been removed to the recently established Mokala National Park. Eight new national parks have been proclaimed in many locations since 1990. They encompass a wide, but not yet nationally comprehensive, range of habitats. They are Mapungubwe (first named Vhembe-Dongola), Table Mountain (formerly Cape Peninsula National Park), Marakele, Namaqua, Richtersveld, Agulhas, Camdeboo (originally the Karoo Nature Reserve), Mokala and Garden Route (GRNP). In addition, there have been expansions and consolidations of boundaries in national parks such as the Garden Route (around the Knysna estuary, and encompassing southern coastal lake and forest areas), Addo Elephant, West Coast, Agulhas, Namaqua and Augrabies. As already mentioned, there have also been a number of extensions across international boundaries as TFCAs.

Acquiring land in South Africa is costly, because about 85% of it is privately owned.[10] Government has provided some of the funding for SANParks' enormous expansion of protected estate, but most of it has been directed through the Park Development Fund, WWF-South Africa, land transfers between government departments (particularly Forestry) and generous donor funding from individuals and corporations. Also successful have been the contractual and partnership parks, whereby SANParks is not invariably the owner of the land under its jurisdiction. Innovative strategies were used to acquire land and enlarge national parks in the cases of Garden Route, Namaqua (originally the Skilpad Wild Flower Reserve owned and managed by what is now the South African Worldwide Fund for Nature, WWF-SA), Mountain Zebra, Augrabies, Mapungubwe, Marakele, Table Mountain and Camdeboo.[11]

However, it is noteworthy that there have been no scientific liaison partnerships with other government departments (such as Science and Technology), nor with provincial nature conservation agencies. It is also clear that this rapid expansion has been at the expense of SANParks' ability to fund professional staffing and even its capacity to administer and manage such enormously varied landholdings.

The sheer diversity of these national parks makes their management and administration, and particularly scientific research in them, inherently difficult to accomplish. They form no organic unit, and their histories and standards differ, as does the level of record-keeping and the type of scientific research required. While some need monitoring and study, others require ecological restoration and attention to invasive vegetation. Some need intensive management and research, others do not. Recreational considerations loom large in some parks, and their historical and heritage value varies greatly. Being remote, some are not attractive long-term locations for researchers who require access to research facilities and colleagues. Moreover, marine scientists, foresters and arid area scientists do not share a knowledge or information base and therefore including them within a single scientific structure does not always work well. In comparison with developments in the KNP, the scant scientific achievements in the other parks to date appear rather old-fashioned, being based on

---

[10]http://mg.co.za/article/2013-09-05-up-to-21-of-land-is-state-owned-says-surveyor-general (accessed 9 December 2015). The amount in communal ownership is not reflected in the statistics. Much remains in the hands of the apartheid 'trust' system and has not yet been transferred to individual ownership.

[11]Castley, Patton and Magome, 'Making "conventional" parks relevant', 397.

recording and listing (although listing is now justifiable in terms of the biodiversity convention to which South Africa adheres). An understanding of the systems that link the various biota appears to be less highly regarded in these parks. From time to time, some national parks have had talented science champions, but as these professionals move on, the gap they leave is not always filled. The assortment of priorities, geography and administrative needs that has haunted the NPB since the 1930s regarding parks other than the KNP continues to bedevil the organisation and it is not clear how the latest administrative regime – ecological clusters – will stand the test of time.

Prior to 2006, parks other than the KNP were grouped together for a while, but in that year SANParks Scientific Services was rearranged into three research clusters – the Savannah and Arid Research Unit, the Cape Research Centre and the Garden Route Research Centre. This approach was undertaken in order to link parks with commonalities and to spread and maximise expertise at a time when recruitment proved both difficult and expensive. Despite challenges, this arrangement appears more scientifically defensible than previous iterations. It creates the opportunity for senior and junior scientists to support and assist one another and can thus serve as a nursery for future professional capacity. Nonetheless, there is still no senior humanities or social scientist with a competent supporting department, a surprising omission given the socioeconomic importance of sustainable conservation heritage and other disciplines. However, Wendy Annecke, a social scientist, has recently been appointed general manager of the Cape Research Centre in Cape Town, and it is to be hoped that she will be able to grow this portfolio, at least in the Cape unit.

The absence of trained people outside the natural sciences within SANParks (with the exception of tourism) means that some of the literature on history, archaeology, etc. encouraged by SANParks is undertaken by untrained people: it is thus often academically naïve and politically and economically polemical.[12] Nonetheless, the recent groupings and partnerships among national parks have been innovative and new arrangements have encouraged greater integration. However, in perusing SANParks websites and other information it is evident that priority has been accorded attracting tourists and establishing stable systems of

---

[12]Examples would include much of the literature on TFCAs and on heritage sites such as Thula Mela in the KNP.

Figure 12.1. Headquarters of the SANParks Cape Research Centre, Tokai, Cape Town.
Photograph by Nicola van Wilgen.

management and administration, as is required by the legislation. In terms of science, monitoring biodiversity, removing alien vegetation and breeding wildlife species is the main concern and far less effort is devoted to scientific projects that aid understanding or produce new and significant breakthroughs.

The KNP has been able to augment its knowledge and gain understanding of ecosystem functioning and drivers because of the Mellon Foundation grants, but nothing similar has transpired for other national parks. There is nothing akin to the annual Savannah Science Network Meetings among these other parks. However, there is a regular Fynbos Forum meeting that includes presentations, workshops, field trips and posters and that has a wide brief to include not only research, but also conservation and communication about the fynbos biome. The Cape fynbos national parks are key participants in these meetings.[13]

[13]See www.fynboshub.co.za/ (accessed 28 July 2016).

While clustering has its merits, it does mean that personnel have responsibilities for huge and diverse areas, and keeping abreast of relevant scientific developments – even in this age of electronic communication – is not easy.

Savannah and Arid Research Unit

In the current cluster groupings, geography and location (inland, marine, southern, etc.) have given way to an ecological rationale. Within the overall ambit of scientific services, the Savannah and Arid Research Unit covers more than half of South Africa's national parks. The 11 widely scattered parks, other than Kruger, are grouped into regions. The frontier region comprises Addo, Karoo, Mountain Zebra and Camdeboo national parks; the northern region consists of Golden Gate Highlands, Mapungubwe and Marakele; and the arid region, Kalahari Gemsbok (Kgalagadi), Richtersveld (|Ai-|Ais/Richtersveld), Augrabies Falls, Mokala and Namaqua, although the latter is the responsibility of the Cape Research Centre.

The programmes undertaken by the Savannah and Arid Research Unit are divided into systems ecology, knowledge support, park interface and restoration ecology. As the unit is new, it has still to prove its worth. Apart from the management team, the staff is large: 14 qualified scientists with a variety of fields of expertise in different national parks and a large but thinly spread support staff. Employees are based at various research centres and at smaller park-based satellite facilities. These centres are in Kimberley in central South Africa, and in Knysna in the south (servicing Addo, Mountain Zebra, Camdeboo and Karoo national parks). There are small offices in Marakele, KGNP and Addo.[14]

Two members of this unit – a biotechnician and a research assistant – are based in Addo, one of the oldest national parks and the site of considerable monitoring and recording work over the years. Expanded from its 1931 area of 7735 ha to 122 553 ha, it has become 'the most biologically diverse protected area in Africa',[15] including sandy beaches, the offshore Bird Island and St Croix, the dune-fields of Alexandria, the estuary of the Sundays River, coastal and Afro-Montane forest and fynbos. Most importantly, it includes Succulent and Nama Karoo and Xeric

[14]www.sanparks.co.za/conservation/scientific_new/savannah_arid/default.php (accessed 13 December 2015).
[15]Hall-Martin, 'Developing a national park system', 53.

Succulent Thicket, biomes that have recently attracted considerable botanical attention. The expansion of Addo, known as the 'greater Addo Elephant National Park' (gAENP), has been assisted by private funding and a grant from the World Bank Global Environmental Fund, established in 1991 shortly before the Rio summit. The team tasked with assisting the national park to expand was driven by the need to maximise regional economic growth as well as to conserve fauna and flora.[16] There has been some criticism that this expansion has been detrimental to the farmworkers of the area, rather than benefiting them.[17] The park, once extolled for protecting the remnants of a small local elephant herd, now hosts an elephant population so overwhelming that it is threatening the thicket vegetation and the area's status as a hub of endemism.

Addo is fortunate in being close to the Nelson Mandela Metropolitan University (NMMU, formerly the University of Port Elizabeth), where there is a group of botanists and zoologists working in, or with, the Centre for African Conservation Ecology, one of whose foci is the ecology and conservation of the Eastern Cape and adjacent regions. The work of the director Graham Kerley, Richard Cowling, an A-rated scholar of the National Research Foundation, and Guy Castley, now at Griffith University in Australia, together with other academics has been prolific, important and of high quality. It is also extremely helpful to SANParks.[18]

---

[16]See G. Castley, M. Knight and J. Gordon, 'Making conservation work: Innovative approaches to meeting biodiversity conservation and socio-economic objectives (an example from the Addo Elephant National Park, South Africa)', in *Evolution and Innovation in Wildlife Conservation: Parks and Game Ranches to Transfrontier Conservation Areas*, eds H. Suich, B. Child and A. Spenceley (London: Earthscan, 2009), 308–323; Hall-Martin, 'Developing a national park system', 59; A.F. Boshoff, G.I.H. Kerley, R.M. Cowling and S.L. Wilson, 'The potential distributions, and estimated spatial requirements and population sizes, of the medium to large-sized mammals in the planning domain of the Greater Addo Elephant National Park project', *Koedoe* 45, no. 2 (2002): 85–116; F. Retief, 'The quality and effectiveness of Strategic Environmental Assessment (SEA) as a decision-aiding tool for national park expansion: The greater Addo Elephant National Park case study', *Koedoe* 49, no. 2 (2006): 103–122.

[17]T. Connor, *Conserved Spaces, Ancestral Places: Conservation, History and Identity among Farm Labourers in the Sundays River Valley, South Africa* (Pietermaritzburg: KwaZulu-Natal University Press, 2014); M.C. Rose, 'A critical analysis of the socioeconomic impact assessments of the Addo Elephant National Park' (MComm diss., Rhodes University, 2010).

[18]Some examples are: A.T. Knight, A. Driver, R.M. Cowling, *et al.*, 'Designing systematic conservation assessments that promote effective implementation: Best practice from South Africa', *Conservation Biology* 20, no. 3 (2006): 739–750; J.G. Castley,

Figure 12.2. Portulacaria afra, one of the dominant succulent species in the Greater Addo Elephant National Park.
Photograph by the author.

M.H. Knight, M.G.L. Mills and C. Thouless, 'Estimation of the lion, *Panthera leo*, population in the south-western Kgalagadi Transfrontier Park using a capture–recapture survey', *African Zoology* 37, no. 1 (2002): 27–34; J.G. Castley, A.F. Boshoff and G.I.H. Kerley, 'Compromising South Africa's natural biodiversity: Inappropriate herbivore introductions', *South African Journal of Science* 97 (2001): 344–348; J.G. Castley, J.-S., Bruton, G.I.H. Kerley and A. McLachlan, 'The importance of seed dispersal in the Alexandria Coastal Dunefield, South Africa', *Journal of Coastal Conservation* 7 (2001): 57–70; J.G. Castley and G.I.H. Kerley, 'The paradox of forest conservation in South Africa', *Forest Ecology and Management* 85 (1996): 35–46; A.J. Mills, R.M. Cowling, D. Steyn, *et al.*, '*Portulacaria afra* is constrained under extreme soil conditions in the Fish River Reserve, Eastern Cape, South Africa', *South African Journal of Botany* 77 (2011): 782–786; A.J. Mills and R.M. Cowling, 'Below-ground carbon stocks in intact and transformed subtropical thicket landscapes in semi-arid South Africa', *Journal of Arid Environments* 74 (2009): 93–100; A.M. Sigwela, G.I.H. Kerley, A.J. Mills and R.M. Cowling, 'The impact of browsing-induced degradation on the reproduction of subtropical thicket canopy shrubs and trees', *South African Journal of Botany* 75 (2009): 262–267; A.J. Mills and R.M. Cowling, 'Rate of carbon sequestration at two thicket restoration sites in the Eastern Cape, South Africa', *Restoration Ecology* 14 (2006): 38–49; R.G. Lechmere-Oertel, G.I.H. Kerley and R.M. Cowling, 'Patterns and implications of transformation in semi-arid succulent thicket', *South African Journal of Arid Environments* 62 (2005): 459–474.

If there is modern scientific research to be uncovered in Golden Gate Highlands National Park, established in 1963 to cater to tourists and hikers, it may be in connection with the spread and eradication of invasive vegetation. Initially, the autumnal colours of the introduced poplar trees were regarded as attractive embellishments, but subsequently they have come to be regarded as ecologically damaging. Situated in an economically marginal region – but with a rich human and palaeontological heritage – Golden Gate may provide research opportunities that could assist with employment and community participation as well as in understanding settlement patterns in this area.[19] Most of the work conducted in this park comprises basic listing and fairly rudimentary geology and geomorphology (which shows future promise) and it is uncertain whether without a resident scientist this is likely to change.[20]

First established in 1995 as the Vhembe-Dongola National Park and renamed the Mapungubwe National Park in 2004, this area of 7859 ha is much smaller than the short-lived Dongola Wild Life Sanctuary proclaimed in 1947 and abolished in 1949. Between that date and 1995, mining and agriculture prospered in the area, driving up land values and making land acquisitions for a park expensive. The treasure of this national park is the extraordinary archaeological ruins, a World Heritage Site since 2003 and one of the very few in the category of Cultural Landscapes, rather than its vegetation or wildlife.[21] Not enough has

---

[19]P. Taru, W. Chingombe and G. Mukwada, 'South Africa's Golden Gate Highlands National Park management plan: Critical reflections', *South African Journal of Science* 109, nos. 11/12 (2013): 17–19; M.E. Marker, 'Golden Gate Highlands National Park', in *Field Guide to Geocryological Features in the Drakensberg UNESCO/IGCP Project* 297, ed. P.M. Hanvey (Grahamstown: Rhodes University, 1990), 70–79; B.K. Reillly, G.K. Theron and J. du P. Bothma, 'Food preferences of oribi *Ourebia ourebi* in the Golden Gate Highlands National Park', *Koedoe* 33, no. 1 (1990): 55–61; M.F. Bates, 'A provisional check list of the reptiles and amphibians of the Golden Gate Highlands National Park', *Koedoe* 34, no. 2 (1991): 153–155; M.E. Marker, 'Dating of valley fills at Golden Gate Highlands National Park', *South African Journal of Science* 90 (1994): 361–363.

[20]S.W. Grab, A.S. Goudie, H.A. Viles and N. Webb, 'Sandstone geomorphology of the golden Gate Highlands National Park, South Africa, in a global context', *Koedoe* 53, no. 1 (2011), Art. #985, 14 pages, doi: 10.4102/koedoe. v53i1.985.

[21]P. Kotzé, 'Riparian vegetation: Shedding light on Mapungubwe's disappearing riverine forest', *The Water Wheel*, July/August (2015): 28–31; A.R. Götze, S.S. Cilliers, H. Bezuidenhout and K. Kellner, 'Analysis of the riparian vegetation (Ia land type) of the proposed Vhembe-Dongola National Park, Limpopo Province, South Africa', *Koedoe* 46, no. 2 (2003): 45–64; A.R. Götze, S.S. Cilliers, H. Bezuidenhout and K. Kellner, 'Analysis of the vegetation of the sandstone ridge (Ib land type) of the north-eastern

been done by SANParks on the site and its relationships with other similar sites in the region (including Great Zimbabwe), although there is considerable expertise on the topic both in South Africa and internationally.[22] Indeed, there is criticism that the growing elephant numbers in the national park threaten the archaeological values and that SANParks does not have the skills required to manage national parks with heritage research potential, although it makes some attempts to do so.[23] As with Golden Gate, there is no scientist or professional heritage expert resident in the national park.

Marakele, by contrast, does boast at least a resident biotechnician. Founded as the Kransberg National Park in 1994 with the purchase of 15 021 ha, it was renamed shortly afterwards. By 1999, it had expanded to almost its current extent of 67 339 ha. Situated at the edge of the Waterberg massif, Marakele comprises mostly woodland, and many species of animals have been reintroduced. The original land was donated by Dr N. Troost and was augmented by the late Dutch industrialist Paul Fentener van Vlissingen, who owned hunting farms in the area and elsewhere in the world.[24] This national park was attractive to the NPB not only because the property was donated, but also because it is the only park in the western part of the old Transvaal province. There is very little literature on Marakele and its importance in terms of ecosystem

---

parts of the Mapungubwe National Park, Limpopo Province, South Africa', *Koedoe* 50, no. 1 (2008): 72–81; J.F. Durand, 'Die ontdekking van 'n voorwerp naby Mapungubwe wat moontlik as 'n abakus gebruik was', *Suid-Afrikaanse Tydskrif vir Natuurwetenskap en Tegnologie* 23, no. 3 (2004): 46–51.

[22]J. Carruthers, 'The Dongola Wild Life Sanctuary: "Psychological blunder, economic folly and political monstrosity" or "more valuable than rubies and gold"?' *Kleio* 24 (1992): 82–100; J. Carruthers, 'Mapungubwe: An historical and contemporary analysis of a World Heritage Cultural Landscape', *Koedoe* 41 (2006): 1–14; T.N. Huffman and J. du Piesanie, 'Khami and the Venda in the Mapungubwe Landscape', *Journal of African Archaeology* 9, no. 2 (2011): 189–206; L. Meskell, 'Falling walls and mending fences: Archaeological ethnography in the Limpopo', *Journal of Southern African Studies* 33, no. 2 (2007): 383–400; L. Meskell, *The Nature of Heritage: The New South Africa* (Oxford: Wiley-Blackwell, 2012). Like others, Meskell is highly critical of the lack of attention to heritage conservation in South Africa's national parks.

[23]See the Mapungubwe interpretation centre at www.sanparks.co.za/parks/mapungubwe/tourism/interpretation_centre.php (accessed 13 December 2015).

[24]A. Hall-Martin, 'Donors and donations to national parks', in *South African National Parks: A Celebration*, eds A. Hall-Martin and J. Carruthers (Johannesburg: Horst Klemm, 2003), 63–64. Troost appears to have had a connection with ESKOM and may have been the owner of a game farm in the area.

study would appear to be slight, although its value in terms of restoration ecology would appear to be significant. Between 1994 and 2010, only two articles about Marakele appeared in *Koedoe*, and these were floristic analyses.[25]

Between 1960 and 1990, the KGNP, covering 960 029 ha, received considerable research attention. As is so often the case, this was owing to a personal interest among specific scientists, particularly large mammal researchers, notably Gus Mills, Fritz Eloff and Johan Bothma. Eloff was interested in lions and Bothma in a variety of animal species, and also in vegetation and habitat mapping. As a student of Bothma at the University of Pretoria, Mills first worked on the behavioural ecology of brown and spotted hyenas and studied the two species in the KGNP. He later relocated to the KNP and became a highly acclaimed expert on large and predatory cats. As outlined in previous chapters, there were symposia on the Kalahari ecosystem (but not ecosystem studies) and this national park featured prominently in articles in *Koedoe*. In recent years, however, despite the fact that the KGNP has been included in a formal TFCA with Botswana, a project close to the heart of SANParks CEO Mavuso Msimang,[26] interest has abated, although quality articles by Mills, Michael Knight and Anette Knight-Eloff regularly appear.[27] Knight's PhD on the gemsbok was completed in 1991 and since then he has been a SANParks regional ecologist, head of research for 'inland' parks (as they were once called) and manager of park planning and development.

Vegetation studies of the park have largely supplanted mammalian studies since the 1990s,[28] but despite the extensive area covered

[25]P.J. van Staden and G.J. Bredenkamp, 'Major plant communities of the Marakele National Park', *Koedoe* 48, no. 2 (2005): 59–70; P.J. van Staden and G.L. Bredenkamp, 'A floristic analysis of forest and thicket vegetation of the Marakele National Park', *Koedoe* 49, no. 1 (2006): 15–31.

[26]*SANParks Annual Report 1999–2000*.

[27]M.H. Knight, 'Ecology of the gemsbok *Oryx gazella gazella* (Linnaeus) and blue wildebeest *Connochaetes taurinus* (Burchell) in the southern Kalahari' (PhD diss., University of Pretoria, 1991); M.H. Knight, 'Drought-related mortality of wildlife in the southern Kalahari and the role of man', *African Journal of Ecology* 33 (1995): 377–394; M. Herbst and M.G.L. Mills, 'Techniques used in the study of African wildcat, *Felis sylvestris cafra*, in the Kgalagadi Transfrontier Park (South Africa/Botswana)', *Koedoe* 52, no. 1 (2010), Art. #939, 6 pages, doi: 10.4102/koedoe.v52i1.939.

[28]N. van Rooyen, D. Bezuidenhout, G.K. Theron and J. du P. Bothma, 'Monitoring of the vegetation around artificial watering points (windmills) in the Kalahari Gemsbok National Park', *Koedoe* 33, no. 1 (1990): 63–88; F.W. Gess and S.K. Gess, 'A preliminary survey of the aculeate wasps and the bees of the lower reaches of the Nossob River

by the TFCA no scientist from the unit is permanently located there. The KGNP was the subject of a large and high-profile land claim, by the ≠Khomani San community on the basis of their eviction from the national park by E.A. le Riche and other managers between 1930 and the 1960s. An extremely large financial and land package settlement was made, involving the purchase of farmlands outside the park and certain use rights within it. Unfortunately, this success has been followed by considerable dissension within the community and other ongoing problems.[29] A sizeable literature on this social and economic dilemma has arisen, but SANParks has not made the most of this learning experience in terms of formal research and scholarly publications.[30] Probably the most important recent corpus of scientific papers on the Kalahari ecosystem – and mainly focused on the KGNP – arose from a Royal Society of South Africa colloquium convened in 1998. Comprising 18 articles by a multidisciplinary team that included eminent international scientists, this publication deserves to be better known and used.[31]

Located in probably the most arid part of South Africa, with less than 50 mm of rainfall per annum, is the Richtersveld National Park, established in 1991 on 162 455 ha. Robinson struggled to negotiate the creation of this national park, given the complexity of the co-ownership and co-management arrangements with the local Nama community. Conflicts over land and access to land have as long a history as human settlement itself in southern Africa. Eventually, the deal included recognition of Nama grazing rights and an annual lease fee payable to the

---

Valley, Kalahari Gemsbok National Park, South Africa', *Koedoe* 34, no. 2 (1991): 77–88; N. van Rooyen and H. Bezuidenhout, 'New records of flowering plants and ferns from the Kalahari Gemsbok National Park', *Koedoe* 40, no. 2 (1997): 105–116.

[29] J. Carruthers, '"South Africa: A world in one country": Land restitution in national parks and protected areas', *Conservation and Society* 5, no. 3 (2007): 292–306; E. Bregin, *Kalahari Rainsong* (Scottsville: UKZN Press, 2004); www.culturalsurvival.org/ourpublications/csq/article/the-khomani-san-land-claim (accessed 13 December 2015).

[30] Carruthers, '"South Africa: A world in one country"'; J. Carruthers, 'Past and future landscape ideology: The Kalahari Gemsbok National Park and Uluru-Kata Tjuta compared', in *Social History and African Environments Past and Present*, eds W. Beinart and J.M. McGregor (Oxford: James Currey and Cape Town: David Philip, 2003), 255–266; W. Ellis, 'The ≠Khomani San land claim against the Kalahari Gemsbok National Park: Requiring and acquiring authenticity', in *Land, Memory, Reconstruction, and Justice: Perspectives on Land Claims in South Africa*, eds C. Walker, A. Bohlin, R. Hall and T. Kepe (Athens, OH: Ohio University Press, 2010), 81–197.

[31] 'The Kalahari Colloquium', special issue *Transactions of the Royal Society of South Africa* 53, no. 2 (1998).

community. It seems that the conservation imperatives of a national park have not been negated by the presence of livestock. This is a remote and harsh part of South Africa, the terrain is difficult and the accommodation in the park is only for the adventurous. It is, however, fascinating in terms of plant life, the study of which may come into its own as climate change studies increase.[32] The Richtersveld contains almost one-third of South Africa's succulent species and is a centre of endemism because its mountainous desert is shaped by coastal fog.

An older park situated in the Northern Cape, and also along the Orange River (due south of the KGNP), is Augrabies Falls, established in 1966 to protect the spectacular waterfall from commercial exploitation. This park, totalling 52 083 ha, is relatively well represented in the literature. It comprises Nama Karoo habitat of a specific type, and contains characteristic arid area trees. Using *Koedoe* as an indicator, there is no doubt that since 1990 it has received much less professional attention than previously. Hugo Bezuidenhout, an extremely productive and knowledgeable ecologist based in Kimberley, is working on the major vegetation communities and issues of ecological restoration, but other activities seem extremely limited.[33] It may well be that this national park is of limited scientific value.

Proclaimed in June 2007, the newest national park covered by the Savannah and Arid Research Unit is the relatively small Mokala National Park (19 611 ha) near Plooysberg, 37 km south-west of Kimberley. It lies in the transition zone between Nama Karoo and Savannah. The ultimate intention is to enlarge it and rationalise its complex boundaries. Apparently, it is an appropriate locality for regenerating species such as rhinoceros and roan antelope, but whether for the purpose of sale or conservation is not clear. This national park lies closest to the Kimberley research office, where there is a relatively large scientific staff headed by a regional ecologist with expertise in arid landscapes.

---

[32]G. Williamson, *Richtersveld National Park* (Pretoria: Umdaus Press, 1995); L. Webley, F. Archer and J. Brink, 'Die Toon: A Late Holocene site in the Richtersveld National Park, Northern Cape', *Koedoe* 36, no. 2 (1993): 1-9; C.M. Shackleton, G. Guthrie, J. Keirungi and J. Stewart, 'Fuelwood availability and use in the Richtersveld National Park, South Africa', *Koedoe* 46, no. 2 (2003): 1-8.

[33]H. Bezuidenhout, 'The major vegetation communities of the Augrabies Falls National Park, Northern Cape. 1. The southern section', *Koedoe* 39, no. 2 (1996): 7-24; C. Plug and L. Plug, 'Popups on Moon Rock, Augrabies Falls National Park', *Koedoe* 40, no. 2 (1997): 75-84.

To some extent, Mokala is the replacement for the Vaalbos National Park, an area of 22 697 ha proclaimed in 1986. The scant literature on Vaalbos indicates that it was founded for political reasons in order to evict the local community. Its landscape bears the scars of alluvial diamond mining and would have required considerable money to rehabilitate, without any real assurance a valuable conservation area would emerge.[34] However, in the early 2000s a successful land claim by the evicted community put paid to this national park and it was abolished without ado by the House of Assembly in 2007.

It is worth noting that in this same general area of the Northern Cape there is an extremely large property that has been well researched by scientists. This is Tswalu, a property of 100 000 ha owned by the Oppenheimer family, who welcome and support scientific research in this part of South Africa. Like the national parks, it too is open to tourists, but researchers are a priority. For example, innovative work on the physiology of several arid wild animal species has been conducted by the likes of Duncan Mitchell, a renowned international wildlife physiologist based at the University of the Witwatersrand.[35]

In 1979, the town of Beaufort West in the Western Cape donated 7000 ha of commonage for the Karoo National Park in a venture partnered with Anton Rupert's South African Nature Foundation. Comprising three vegetation types of the Nama Karoo Biome, it was considered at the time to be an important adjunct to the rest of the suite of national parks.[36] The endangered Riverine Rabbit *Bunolagus monticularis* occurs

[34]P.C. Zietsman, P.J. du Preez and H. Bezuidenhout, 'A preliminary check list of flowering plants of the Vaalbos National Park', *Koedoe* 35, no. 1 (1992): 89–98; H. Bezuidenhout, 'An ecological study of the major vegetation communities of the Vaalbos National Park, Northern Cape. 1. The Than-Droogeveld section', *Koedoe* 37, no. 2 (1994): 19–42; I.A. Russell, 'Spatial variation in the structure of fish assemblages in the Vaalbos National Park, South Africa', *Koedoe* 40, no. 1 (1997): 113–123; C.M. Bancroft, H. Bezuidenhout and J.G. Nel, 'Use of veld condition assessment to set objectives and targets for an ISO 14001 environmental management system for Vaalbos National Park', *Koedoe* 41, no. 2 (1998): 1–12.

[35]One example is B. Rey, M-A. Costello, A. Fuller, *et al.*, 'Chemical immobilization and anesthesia of free-living aardvarks (*Orycteropus afer*) with ketamine–medetomidine–midazolam and isoflurane', *Journal of Wildlife Diseases* 50, no. 4 (2014): 864–872, others are to follow.

[36]F. Rubin and A.R. Palmer, 'The physical environment and major plant communities of the Karoo National Park, South Africa', *Koedoe* 39, no. 2 (1996): 25–52; A.S. Dippenaar-Schoeman, A. Leroy, M. de Jager and A. van den Berg, 'A check list of the spider fauna of the Karoo National park, South Africa (Arachnida: Araneae)', *Koedoe* 42,

there and over time the restoration of the over-grazed karoo landscape and the removal of vestiges of human habitation has continued. The experiment to recreate the quagga *Equus quagga quagga* began in 1987 and for a time SANParks participated in the project by locating a proto-quagga in this park.[37]

Near Cradock in the Eastern Cape lies the Mountain Zebra National Park, established in 1937 and comprising 24 848 ha. As described in an earlier chapter, it was founded in response to international pressure on South Africa to preserve its remaining mountain zebra herd. It has been fortunate in consistently attracting excellent scientists to study its biota. In earlier decades, Banie Penzhorn studied the structure of the mountain zebra herd and he was followed by Peter Novellie, whose interest continued into the 1990s, even after he had been transferred to Pretoria headquarters.[38] Norman Owen-Smith of the University of the Witwatersrand, one of South Africa's most acclaimed wildlife scientists, has also worked with his students in this park.[39] Nor has the vegetation been neglected in the current period. Bezuidenhout has shown consistent interest, as, among others, has Leslie Brown, the head of the applied behavioural ecology and ecosystem research unit at the University of South Africa.[40]

---

no. 1 (1999): 31–42; M. Saayman, A. Saayman and M. Ferreira, 'The socio-economic impact of the Karoo National Park', *Koedoe* 51, no. 1 (2009), Art. #158, 10 pages, doi: 10.4102/ koedoe.v51i1.158.

[37]E.H. Harley, M.H. Knight, C. Larder, B. Wooding and M. Gregor, 'The Quagga project: Progress over 20 years of selective breeding', *South African Journal of Wildlife Research* 39 (2009): 155–163.

[38]P.A. Novellie, 'Monitoring the condition of mountain zebra habitat in the Mountain Zebra National Park', *Koedoe* 37, no. 1 (1994): 35–40.

[39]A. Winkler, 'The feeding ecology of the Cape mountain zebra (*Equus zebra zebra* Linn., 1758) in the Mountain Zebra National Park, South Africa' (MSc diss., University of the Witwatersrand, 1993); A. Winkler and N. Owen-Smith, 'Habitat utilisation by Cape mountain zebras in the Mountain Zebra National Park, South Africa', *Koedoe* 38, no. 1 (1995): 83–93.

[40]D. Wessels and L. Kappen, 'Photosynthetic performance of rock-colonising lichens in the Mountain Zebra National Park, South Africa', *Koedoe* 36, no. 1 (1993): 27–48; L.R. Brown and H. Bezuidenhout, 'The phytosociology of the De Rust section of the Mountain Zebra National Park, Eastern Cape', *Koedoe* 43, no. 1 (2000): 1–18; J. de Klerk, L.R. Brown, H. Bezuidenhout and G. Castley, 'The estimation of herbage yields under fire and grazing treatments in the Mountain Zebra National Park', *Koedoe* 44, no. 1 (2001): 9–15; U. Pond, B.B. Beesley, L.R. Brown and H. Bezuidenhout, 'Floristic analysis of the Mountain Zebra National Park, Eastern Cape', *Koedoe* 45, no. 1 (2002): 35–58; J. de Klerk, L.R. Brown and H. Bezuidenhout, 'Plant communities of the Ebenhaezer section of the Mountain Zebra National Park', *Koedoe* 46, no. 2 (2003): 35–58; L.R. Brown

The core of Camdeboo National Park (19 405 ha) was the Karoo Nature Reserve, which almost totally surrounds the historical and beautiful small town of Graaff-Reinet, a favourite among tourists.[41] The topography varies from lowland to the Sneeuberg mountain range and there are some fascinating geological formations in the Valley of Desolation. It was, apparently, Marthinus van Schalkwyk, minister of environmental affairs, who advocated the proclamation of this national park and WWF-SA, which owned the Karoo Nature Reserve, duly donated the land to the state. The area is rich in archaeology and history, none of which has been professionally explored by SANParks. There is a plan to link Camdeboo with Mountain Zebra to form an enormous conservation area of about half a million hectares. Innovative partnerships are envisaged for a Mountain Zebra–Camdeboo Corridor Project, a project that would link SANParks and the Wilderness Foundation through the Critical Ecosystems Partnership Fund, which focuses on grasslands. Whether significant scientific research interest will follow remains to be seen.

Garden Route Research Centre

The spectacular Garden Route stretches along South Africa's southern coast from Mossel Bay to Storms River. With the sea on one side and forested mountains on the other, it is a popular tourist itinerary and abounds in beautiful sites and visitor and vacation amenities. The now extensive Garden Route National Park has been years in the making and originally comprised three separate conservation areas. Initially, there was the Tsitsikamma Coastal and Forest National Park, founded in 1964. It owed its origins to the need expressed during the 1962 World Parks Congress for increased marine conservation areas worldwide. The marine component was initially 34 300 ha extending 5.56 km offshore. There are many habitats along this coast and the high cliffs facing the

---

and H. Bezuidenhout, 'The vegetation of the farms Ingleside and Welgedacht of the Mountain Zebra National Park, Eastern Cape', *Koedoe* 48, no. 2 (2005): 23–42; A.J.F.K. Craig, P.E. Hilley and D. Parker, 'A re-assessment of the avifauna of the Mountain Zebra National Park', *Koedoe* 48, no. 1 (2005): 95–113; H. Bezuidenhout and L.R. Brown, 'Vegetation description of the Doornhoek section of the Mountain Zebra National Park (MZNP), South Africa', *Koedoe* 50, no. 1 (2008): 82–92.

[41]M.L. Masubelele, L.C. Foxcroft and S.J. Milton, 'Alien plant species list and distribution for Camdeboo National Park, Eastern Cape Province, South Africa', *Koedoe* 51, no. 1 (2009), Art. #515, doi: 10.4102/Koedoe.v51i1.515.

sea are covered in coastal fynbos or extensive Afromontane forests. Over many decades, the forests were depleted, but they have recovered to some extent. Second came the Wilderness National Park, proclaimed almost 20 years later. Covering only 7688 ha, the park is important to conservation because of its unusual coastal lake and wetlands. It is a Ramsar site. Surrounded by urban developments, it required conservation from too intensive use and against development pressures. So too did the third component, the Knysna National Lake Area, 15 000 ha in extent and proclaimed in 1985. Not established as a national park, it was instead protected under the Lake Areas Development Act 39 of 1975 and placed under NPB management. The purpose of the designation was to protect the lower reaches of the Knysna River and the estuary, which is unusual in South Africa by being permanently open and in forming an estuarine bay.

In recent years there have been great changes to the management of this coastal area, including the creation of the new Garden Route National Park in 2009. The Tsitsikamma and Wilderness National Parks were formally included in it, while the De Vasselot section was a nature reserve under the forestry department, later incorporated into Tsitsikamma before the GRNP was created. In total, the new combined national park is about 1210 km² in extent, of which about half formed part of the original national parks. Reflecting an increased focus on the southern forests, it includes about 605 km² of indigenous forest. Since 2011, the park has included 120 566 ha of state forests and mountain catchments, previously the responsibility of the Department of Forestry.[42] The priority so far has been restoring the physical environment and controlling the enormous infestation of invasive vegetation.

It was obvious that a new administrative, management and scientific regime was required for this now-unified cohort of parks situated along a highly developed coastline and in a much-visited recreational area. A Garden Route Research Centre was established, comprising a substantial team to develop internal scientific capacity and bring together previously disparate research and management agendas. Three offices serve the scientific needs of this complex national park. One is in the town of Knysna, the second at Rondevlei near Sedgefield, and the third at Saasveld, near George, the region's largest town. Originally a forestry

---

[42]G.P. Durrheim, 'Monitoring for sustainable indigenous forest management in the Garden Route National Park', unpublished report, South African National Parks, Scientific Services, Knysna, 2010.

college, Saasveld was taken over by the Port Elizabeth Technikon in 1985 and 20 years later became a satellite campus of the NMMU.

Between the 1960s and 1980s, work in the lakes and coastal national parks involved detailing aquatic landscapes and biota. Robinson, then warden of Tsitsikamma, worked closely with other aquatic and marine scientists in the region and beyond. Administration from Tsitsikamma, which is remote, proved difficult and by 1991 had moved to Rondevlei, where the marine biologist, aquatic scientist and terrestrial ecologist were based. Together with biotechnicians and an earth scientist, they were also responsible for other southern parks. When the state forests and Outeniqua and Tsitsikamma mountain catchments became part of the new national park in 2005, the Department of Water Affairs and Forestry's scientific team, which included specialists in forestry, fynbos and GIS, became integrated into SANParks. It was clear that continuing to take responsibility for other southern parks in addition to the expanded Garden Route park would overtax the team, so a separate Cape Research Centre (see below) was established, thus enabling the Garden Route scientific services, comprising 20 permanent staff positions (not all of them filled), to concentrate on the national park. Half the staff is located at Rondevlei, eight at Knysna and one, a freshwater conservation specialist, at Saasveld. At the time of writing (2016), senior KNP science manager Stefanie Freitag-Ronaldson has been appointed to head the science team in this region. The team also includes a regional ecologist, while half a dozen other scientists work on fauna, forest and marine studies and GIS. There are also four biotechnicians. Only a few of these scientists have doctorates, but Dirk Roux at Saasveld is one of only two National Research Foundation-rated scientists in SANParks.

Melding this group into a team has not been easy. As can be appreciated, the complexities of forming a coherent research agenda from disparate elements forced together by the state, and with different training and corporate cultures, will take time. While the public communications stress 'integration and collaboration, to conduct and facilitate monitoring and research of fynbos, forest, fresh water, estuarine and marine systems in the region, with a view to provide scientific information in support of park planning and management', this, it appears, has yet to be fully achieved.[43] However, South Africa has a strong community of marine

[43]www.sanparks.co.za/conservation/scientific_new/garden_route/default.php (accessed 13 December 2015).

biologists, dating back to the colonial period and predicated on the importance of fisheries to the national economy.[44] Marine and aquatic research has been important at the University of Cape Town and at Rhodes University, and there is thus a solid base upon which SANParks can draw for knowledge of the Western and Eastern Cape marine environment. During her career at SANParks before leaving for the NMMU, energetic researcher Tineke Kraaij, a PhD student of Brian van Wilgen, published a large number of papers relating to the GRNP.[45]

[44]C.L. Attwood, C.L. Moloney, J. Stenton-Dozey, *et al.*, 'Conservation of marine biodiversity in South Africa', in *Summary of Marine Biodiversity Status Report*, eds B.C. Durham and J.C. Pauw (Pretoria: NRF, 2000), 68–83; G.A. Robinson, 'Benguela upwelling: How does it affect South Africa's conservation philosophy?' *South African Journal of Marine Science* 12 (1992): 1063–1067; R.L. Tilney, G. Nelson, S.E. Radloff and C.D. Buxton, 'Ichthyoplankton distribution and dispersal in the Tsitsikamma National Park marine reserve, South Africa', *South African Journal of Marine Science* 17 (2000): 1–14; A.D. Wood, S.L. Brouwer, P.D. Cowley and T.D. Harrison, 'An updated checklist of the ichthyofaunal species assemblage of the Tsitsikamma National Park, South Africa', *Koedoe* 43, no. 1 (2000): 83–95; N. Hanekom, J.B. Mann-Lang, B.Q. Mann and T.V.Z. Carinus, 'Shore-angling catches in the Tsitsikamma National Park, 1989–1995', *Koedoe* 40, no. 2 (1997): 37–56; A. Götz, P.D. Cowley and H. Winker, 'Selected fishery and population parameters of eight important shore-angling species in the Tsitsikamma National Park no-take marine reserve', *African Journal of Marine Science* 30 (2008): 519–532; J. Turpie, B. Clark and K. Hutchings, *The Economic Value of Marine Protected Areas Along the Garden Route Coast, South Africa, and Implications of Changes in Size and Management.* Report prepared for WWWF-SA (Cape Town: Anchor Environmental Consultants and FitzPatrick Institute, University Cape Town, 2006); S.L. Brouwer, 'Dispersal of red steenbras (*Petrus rupestris*) from the Tsitsikamma National Park, a marine protected area in the Eastern Cape, South Africa', *South African Journal of Marine Science* 24 (2002): 375–378; S.L. Brouwer, M.H. Griffiths and M.J. Roberts, 'Adult movement and larval dispersal of *Argyrozona argyrozona* (Pisces: Sparidae) from a temperate marine protected area', *African Journal of Marine Science* 25 (2003): 395–402; P.D. Cowley, S.L. Brouwer and R.L. Tinley, 'The role of the Tsitsikamma National Park in the management of four important shore angling fishes along the south-east Cape Coast', *South African Journal of Marine Science* 24 (2002): 27–35; C.G. Attwood, J.M. Harris and A.J. Williams, 'International experience of marine protected areas and their relevance to South Africa', *South African Journal of Marine Science* 18 (1997): 311–332.

[45]See, for example, T. Kraaij, R.M. Cowling and B.W. van Wilgen, 'Past approaches and future challenges to the management of fire and invasive alien plants in the new Garden Route National Park', *South African Journal of Science* 107, nos. 9/10 (2011), Art. #633, 11 pages, doi: 10.4102/sajs.v107i9/10.633; T. Kraaij, R.M. Cowling and B.W. van Wilgen, 'Fire regimes in eastern coastal fynbos: Imperatives and thresholds in managing for diversity', *Koedoe* 55, no. 1 (2013), Art. #1104, 9 pages, http://dx.doi.org/10.4102/koedoe.v55i1.1104; T. Kraaij, R.M. Cowling, B.W. van Wilgen and A. Schutte-Vlok, 'Proteaceae juvenile periods and post-fire recruitment as indicators of minimum fire

Initial synthetic work was focused on the compilation of a Garden Route National Park State of Knowledge (SoK) report, a document that can be regularly updated. It has grown out of the SoK reports of the three aquatic sections (Tsitsikamma, Wilderness and Knysna), but with their amalgamation and the addition of the forests, a single SoK was deemed desirable. First compiled in 2014 and intended for SANParks staff and other interested parties, the most recent version (April 2015) involved 13 contributors in various fields. A useful document (about 140 pages) with an extensive bibliography, it can be employed as a reference tool to identify areas requiring research. Primarily intended as an ecological and biophysical SoK, it is nonetheless disappointing that only two pages are dedicated to archaeology and history, and that the scholarly information on these topics is anecdotal, incorrect and based on outdated sources. No doubt, in future, attempts will be made to augment the information in the SoK. For the historical aspects this will not be difficult as this region is rich in both history and reputable historiography. A further disappointment is the absence of sections on a future research agenda, what gaps have been uncovered, which are more urgent and where synergies and collaborations would be most effective.[46] Nonetheless, a beginning has been made and one hopes that within a few years a vibrant research culture will have been nurtured.

Cape Research Centre

The third scientific node is the Cape Research Centre (CRC) that was opened at Tokai near Cape Town in 2008. It was established by Melodie McGeoch, who headed it until she emigrated to Australia in 2012 to take up a position at Monash University. McGeoch's research interests are wide-ranging and include what she has referred to as 'Conservation

---

return interval in eastern coastal fynbos', *Applied Vegetation Science* 16 (2013): 84–94; T. Kraaij, R.M. Cowling and B.W. van Wilgen, 'Lightning and fire weather in eastern coastal fynbos shrublands: Seasonality and long-term trends', *International Journal of Wildland Fire* 22 (2012): 288–295, http://dx.doi.org/10.1071/WF11167; T. Kraaij, J.A. Baard, R.M. Cowling, B.W. van Wilgen and S. Das, 'Historical fire regimes in a poorly understood, fire-prone ecosystem: Eastern coastal fynbos', *International Journal of Wildland Fire* 22 (2013): 277–287, http://hdl.handle.net/123456789/1553.

[46]South African National Parks, 'Garden Route National Park: State of Knowledge', unpublished report, South African National Parks, 2014, www.sanparks.co.za/assets/docs/conservation/scientific/coastal/state-of-knowledge.pdf (accessed 13 December 2015).

Scaling'. She was, at the time of establishing the CRC, also an honorary professor at Stellenbosch University. With the most skeleton of initial staffs, the CRC took over responsibility for five national parks, some of them distant. Despite these and other challenges, under McGeoch's direction the CRC appeared to be heading for a great future, but procrastination over choosing her successor has not been helpful, and nor have the many staff changes that have taken place.

When the CRC began, it suffered from a lack of archival material and previous research on which to build. Entirely new baseline data had to be compiled. Although personnel were appointed, all were new, and they needed time to settle in, learn the ropes and work together as a team. Owing to the lack of a cohesive scientific records system for national parks, the CRC struggled to discover 'what it knew'. Some material for Table Mountain National Park (TMNP) was in the hands of CapeNature[47] and the Cape Town city council, but some was on individuals' computers, in unmarked boxes, on shelves and under desks. Moreover, much of what information was unearthed was written for annual reports, not scholarly journals. Despite these difficulties, currently the CRC is conducting several projects, including one related to global environmental change (necessary for national reporting on issues such as alien vegetation, climate change, etc.) and another addressing land-use changes through history.[48]

[47]This was the renamed (and re-energised) provincial nature conservation authority, a parastal established in 1999 in the Western Cape to replace the nature conservation authority that previously existed for the old Cape province.

[48]Author's record of meeting at SANParks Cape Research Centre, Tokai, 6 September 2013. There are a number of talented younger researchers in the CRC who are worth watching in the future. One example is Nicola van Wilgen, a few of whose publications are N.J. van Wilgen, V. Goodall, S. Holness, S.L.C. Chown and M.A. McGeoch, 'Rising temperatures and changing rainfall patterns in South Africa's national parks', *International Journal of Climatology* (2015), doi: 10.1002/joc.4377; N.J. van Wilgen and M.A. McGeoch, 'Balancing effective conservation with sustainable resource use in protected areas: Precluded by knowledge gaps', *Environmental Conservation* (2014), doi: 10.1017/S0376892914000320; N.J. van Wilgen, M. Dopolo, A. Symonds, *et al.*, 'An inventory of natural resources harvested from national parks in South Africa', *Koedoe* 55, no. 1 (2013), Art. #1096, 5 pages, http://dx.doi.org/10.4102/koedoe.v55i1.1096; N.J. van Wilgen and D.M. Richardson, 'The roles of climate, phylogenetic relatedness, introduction effort, and reproductive traits in the establishment of non-native reptiles and amphibians', *Conservation Biology* 26 (2012): 267–277; N.J. van Wilgen, D.M. Richardson

The CRC is responsible for a wide variety of national parks: Agulhas, West Coast, Bontebok, Tankwa Karoo, Namaqua and Table Mountain. SoK reports have already been compiled for the first three.[49] In addition, there are separate bibliographies for TMNP and Tankwa Karoo.[50] These are very diverse national parks. Consequently, the CRC has responsibility for Succulent Karoo and the Cape Floral Kingdom as well as marine and coastal areas.

The oldest national park in this cluster, Bontebok, was founded in 1931, but, as noted in an earlier chapter, the animals were moved in about 1960 to 3435 ha of land on the coastal plateau a few kilometres outside Swellendam. There, the new national park was proclaimed in 1961. Despite being only five years younger than the KNP, Bontebok has never been extensively researched. Even the research on bontebok that might have interested wildlife veterinarians or on the quality of the veld was not sufficiently comprehensive to attract international attention. In any event, any interest in bontebok, whose numbers have recovered, has since been superseded by the importance of the biome in which they live. It is the rich variety of lowland fynbos – renosterveld – in this small national park that today merits scientific attention.

The SoK for Bontebok, one of the CRC's two inland parks, lists many of the park's biotic and abiotic attributes. The management of the park is summarised, many references and a number of maps have been provided and there are appendices listing plants, invertebrates, fish and amphibians. Once again, disappointingly, the human sciences are given short shrift, with the rich and extremely well-recorded history of the Swellendam area being relegated to two paragraphs derived from a single seven-page

and E.H.W. Baard, 'Alien reptiles and amphibians in South Africa: Towards a pragmatic management strategy', *South African Journal of Science* 104 (2008): 13–20.

[49]N. Hanekom, R.M. Randall, P. Nel and N. Kruger, 'West Coast National Park: State of Knowledge', unpublished report, SANParks, 2009, www.sanparks.org/docs/conservation/scientific/coastal/West%20Coast/WCNP_SOK_Mar2009.pdf (accessed 20 December 2015); T. Kraaij, N. Hanekom, I.A. Russell and R.M. Randall, 'Agulhas National Park: State of Knowledge', unpublished report, SANParks, 2009; T. Kraaij, R.M. Randall, P. Novellie, I.A. Russell and N. Kruger, 'Bontebok National Park: State of Knowledge', unpublished report, SANParks, 2009 (updated September 2011).

[50]www.google.co.za/webhp?sourceid=chrome-instant&ion=1&espv=2&ie=UTF-8#q=tankwa%20karoo%20blbiography and https://www.google.co.za/webhp?sourceid=chrome-instant&ion=1&espv=2&ie=UTF-8#q=table+mountain+national+park+blbiography (accessed 13 December 2015).

Figure 12.3. Evidence of past farming practices in Tankwa Karoo National Park showing the need for ecological restoration and cultural heritage conservation. Photograph by Dirk Roux.

source published in *Koedoe* in 1975.[51] Equally regrettable is that this national park has, after 50 years, yielded little ecological knowledge.[52] However, it is to be hoped the SoK will alert researchers, including well-managed citizen scientists from the Swellendam community and educational institutions, as to the scientific potential of this national park. Moreover, with the increased interest in fire ecology throughout the Western Cape, it may be that Bontebok will yield information on the role of fire in this particular ecosystem.[53]

Tankwa Karoo, another inland park and a semi-desert landscape, was proclaimed in 1986. It is very distant from the CRC, situated west of Sutherland and not far from the Cederberg, the mountainous area which – although desired by the NPB in decades past – remains a protected area

[51]N.J. van der Merwe, 'Die Bontbok', *Koedoe* 11 (1968): 161–168.
[52]Kraaij, Randall, Novellie, Russell and Kruger, 'Bontebok National Park: State of Knowledge'.
[53]T. Kraaij, 'Changing the fire management regime in the renosterveld and lowland fynbos of the Bontebok National Park', *South African Journal of Botany* 76 (2010): 550–557; T. Kraaij, 'The flora of the Bontebok National Park in regional perspective', *South African Journal of Botany* 77, no. 2 (2011): 455–473.

under the aegis of CapeNature. Like many national parks, Tankwa Karoo (named after the Tankwa River that runs through it) started as a relatively small park (27 000 ha), but has since grown to 143 600 ha. The eventual aim is a protected area of some 200 000 ha.[54] As this is a remote and not densely populated area, this may well prove feasible. Tankwa Karoo incorporates three distinct ecosystems – pure desert, open grassland and the mountainous Roggeveld, the edge of the interior escarpment. It also includes some of the succulent karoo. In time, this arid biodiversity, not to mention the highly degraded state of the land, might attract research interest, but up to 1998 (12 years after proclamation) not a single article about the park appeared even in *Koedoe*. The (short) bibliography for the Tankwa Karoo available from SANParks includes only four articles on restoration ecology, two of which are international and none specific to the national park.[55]

The northernmost coastal national park for which CRC is responsible, Namaqua National Park was established in 1999 and covers 41 561 ha. It began life as the small Skilpad (Tortoise) Flower Reserve, established in 1992 by WWF-SA (with public access only during the spectacular spring flowering season). This particular part of Namaqualand has many endemic species and, apparently, the richest bulb flora of any arid region in the world. There have been various additions to the park, which now includes part of the coastline. Assistance for this enlargement came from WWF-SA and the Leslie Hill Foundation, which funded the purchase of 38 000 ha from the De Beers mining company. Other less formal and quantifiable assistance came from the local community, which partners this venture and hopes to benefit from it.[56] No doubt both the government and SANParks hope that this park will become a catalyst for regional development in an impoverished part of South Africa.

Further south, not far from Cape Town, lies the West Coast National Park, founded in 1983 as Langebaan National Park. A Ramsar site, it consists of a lagoon and the offshore islands near Saldanha Bay, as well as a narrow but substantial inland area consisting of fynbos thicket. This area is rich in South African maritime history and holds promising fossil

[54]Hall-Martin, 'Developing a national park system', 59.

[55]F. Rubin, 'The physical environment and major plant communities of the Tankwa-Karoo National Park', *Koedoe* 41, no. 2 (1998): 61–94; www.google.co.za/webhp? sourceid=chrome-instant&ion=1&espv=2&ie=UTF-8#q=tankwa%20karoo%20 blbiography (accessed 13 December 2015).

[56]Hall-Martin, 'Developing a national park system', 59.

material that will, it is hoped, shed light on palaeontology and possibly even geological events. The SoK for this national park indicates that considerable work has been done on the marine and avian fauna in particular.[57] Moreover, the park is contractually bound to the Postberg Syndicate, which controls the Postberg Nature Reserve (renowned for its spring flowers) and also to the marine and coastal management authorities that manage the Langebaan Lagoon Marine Protected Area.[58]

Although the Cape Nature Conservation authority had managed De Hoop nature reserve in the south-western Cape (34 000 ha) from 1957, SANParks had no foothold on this part of the southern coast prior to procuring a small parcel of land in 1999 that has subsequently been expanded to some 22 000 ha. The acquisition of the iconic Cape Agulhas, the southernmost tip of Africa and billed as the meeting place of the Atlantic and Indian Oceans, was a coup for SANParks. With its Khoekhoen middens and fish-traps, its lighthouse and shipwrecks, the heritage value of this park is almost incomparable. It is therefore disappointing to find in the otherwise welcome SoK produced a decade after the park was acquired so little mention of the abundant scholarly work in these fields. Nevertheless, the SoK does acknowledge the potential of this park for palaeo-environmental studies.[59] Like Namaqua, this is a park of the late 1990s, and it is a complex one. Agulhas point itself lies within the national park, but part of the Agulhas plain is not included. This is of high conservation significance and the SoK relates to both park and plain, which is 72 km long and extends up to 25 km inland. Money to purchase the park was donated by Fauna and Flora International in the UK, the National Parks Trust and Park Development Fund, and the estate of nature and bird-lover Elizabeth Harding through WWF-SA.[60]

---

[57]Hanekom, Randall, Nel and Kruger, 'West Coast National Park'.

[58]T.B. Robinson, C.L. Griffiths and N. Kruger, 'Distribution and status of marine invasive species in and bordering the West Coast National Park', *Koedoe* 47 (2004): 79–87; G. Avery, D. Halkett, J. Orton, *et al.*, 'The Ysterfontein 1 Middle Stone Age rock shelter and the evolution of coastal foraging', *South African Archaeological Society Goodwin Series* 10 (2008): 66–89; R.G. Klein, G. Avery, K. Cruz-Uribe, *et al.*, 'The Ysterfontein 1 Middle Stone Age site, South Africa, and early human exploitation of coastal resources', *Proceedings of the National Academy of Sciences* 101, no. 16 (2004): 5708–5715.

[59]Kraaij, Hanekom, Russell and Randall, 'Agulhas National Park: State of Knowledge'.

[60]Harding's bequest has enabled WWF to purchase almost 20 000 ha of conservation land in the Agulhas, Cederberg, Riverlands, Table Mountain, West Coast and Overberg regions. *Panda Bulletin* (August 2011): 7.

Referred to in the SoK as a 'developing park', much needs to be done to restore the marshlands that had been drained for white agriculture hundreds of years earlier. In addition, the management structure of this park is complex and includes Transnet (the management authority for South Africa's lighthouses), WWF-SA and SANParks, sometimes on a contractual basis. Moreover, this is a populated area and there are many fishing towns of up to 10 000 people along, the coast, as well as many smaller villages.

Without doubt, however, the most complex of the recreational national parks in the Western Cape is Table Mountain National Park. In its current form, the park that comprises much of the mountain chain that defines the Cape Peninsula is not contiguous. It consists of three sections: Table Mountain, Silvermine-Tokai and Cape Point, and includes some 1000 ha of marine reserves. The history of the park's creation is long and extremely complicated and does not need to be addressed in detail here. A good summary of the park's protracted birth pangs has, in any event, been written by David Daitz and Brett Myrdal, and an interpretive guide to the park written by environmental journalist John Yeld has been published by SANParks.[61] Essentially, the urban development and sprawl in the Cape Peninsula and the growing awareness of the Cape Floral Kingdom as a draw for tourists and for its conservation and scientific interest led to recognition of the need for a single administrative and conservation authority capable of managing professionally and systematically all parts of this floristic wonder, situated on and around one of the world's best known landscapes, Table Mountain. In addition, Table Mountain has been a powerful political and aesthetic symbol in the subcontinent and archives and museums abound with visual depictions dating back to 1634, before white settlement began, not to mention manuscript and literary references. The Cape of Good Hope was described by many early travellers as the most beautiful in the world and over the centuries the rich history of the town at the foot of the mountain came to hold a particularly important place in the hearts and minds

[61]D. Daitz and B. Myrdal, 'Table Mountain National Park', in *Evolution and Innovation in Wildlife Conservation: Parks and Game Ranches to Transfrontier Conservation Areas*, eds H. Suich, B. Child and A. Spenceley (London: Earthscan, 2009): 325–339; SANParks, *Mountains in the Sea: Table Mountain to Cape Point* (Cape Town: SANParks, 2004). This book also includes brief descriptions of other Cape national parks, Agulhas, West Coast, Bontebok and Karoo.

Figure 12.4. The overseer's hut that is available to visitors to Table Mountain National Park.
Photograph by the author.

of white middle-class Capetonians.[62] Given the mountain's importance in the colonial and imperial eras and to the Khoekhoen people, the original inhabitants of the area who were displaced by white settlement, the historiography of this area is extremely rich.

In 1978, in response to the Environmental Planning Act, Douglas Hey, then director of nature conservation in the Cape province, produced a report on how best to conserve Table Mountain and its surroundings through the legislative opportunities then available. Entitled the *Report on the Future Control and Management of Table Mountain and the Southern Peninsula Mountain Chain*, the report seems to have begun consideration of a process that eventually culminated in more effective conservation of Table Mountain, which until then had largely been managed by the Cape Town city council.[63] However, only many years later, in

[62]L. van Sittert, 'The bourgeois eye aloft: Table Mountain in the Anglo urban middle class imagination, *c*.1891–1952', *Kronos* 29 (2003): 161–190.

[63]S. Pooley, *Burning Table Mountain: An Environmental History of Fire on the Cape Peninsula* (Houndmills: Palgrave Macmillan, 2014), 157; D. Hey, *Report on the Future Control and*

1989, did the Cape Peninsula Protected Natural Environment come into being and with it an institutional mechanism for joint administration and management.

However, by the 1990s yet stronger legal protections were needed, particularly as the Peninsula was fairly regularly ravaged by fires that were inadequately handled by the myriad management authorities. At about this time, Brian van Wilgen, a forester and fire ecologist at the Council for Scientific and Industrial Research (CSIR), published a very useful paper in *Biodiversity and Conservation* that outlined the challenges and the potential of a unified conservation authority.[64] Indeed, it may not have been fortuitous that the entire issue of the journal was devoted to the Cape Peninsula.[65] However, action was needed not only for conservation reasons but also because the ecology was a fairly powerful restorative philosophy (or unifying factor) as South Africa began its reincarnation as a full democracy. Another trigger for the TMNP was the announcement in 1995, the year after the advent of democracy, that the Western Cape provincial government (the National Party) intended to create a national park that would include as much of the Cape Peninsula Protected Natural Environment as possible. This was in response to reports produced in 1994 by a team from the University of Cape Town's Environmental Evaluation Unit and the attorney-general of the Cape on environmental policy development in respect of the Cape Peninsula.[66]

As the forces aligned behind the idea of unifying the conservation management of a landscape administered by 14 public authorities at all three levels of government, and involving almost 200 private owners, it was the future national park's good fortune that the calm voice in the fracas was that of Brian Huntley, then head of the National Botanical Institute and based at Kirstenbosch. He chaired the Table Mountain Advisory

---

Management of Table Mountain and the Southern Peninsula Mountain Chain (Pretoria: Government Printer, 1978); J. Carruthers, 'From "land" to "place": Communities and conservation in the Magaliesberg area', *Kleio* 34 (2002): 72–103.

[64]B. W. van Wilgen, 'Management of the natural ecosystems of the Cape Peninsula: Current status and future prospects', *Biodiversity and Conservation* 5, no. 5 (1996): 671–684.

[65]The introduction to the 1996 special issue of *Biodiversity and Conservation* on South Africa recognises that, after long period of isolation, the time had come to give a wider world 'some idea of local developments in this field'. However, also recognising that there was too much material for a single journal issue, rather surprisingly in view of the large reputation of the KNP, it had been decided to concentrate on Table Mountain and the Cape Peninsula.

[66]Pooley, *Burning Table Mountain*, 158–161.

Committee set up by Environmental Affairs and Tourism Minister Dawie de Villiers that negotiated the process between 1995 and 1998.[67] His wisdom and long experience in handling environmental politics as well as in cooperative and collaborative projects was invaluable, and his recommendation that future management of the protected area that comprised Table Mountain and the Peninsula be transferred to the National Parks Board was fundamental to success. It was also fortunate that Robinson, a politically neutral English-speaker from the Western Cape, was involved in the negotiations on behalf of the NPB. In January 1996 Robinson recruited a project coordinator with a broad mandate to take the matter further and he kept a close eye on the process. It is doubtful whether Robinson's understanding and diplomacy could have been matched by his predecessors in the NPB, an organisation not regarded with much affection by the citizens of Cape Town. They feared that land accessible to the public would be out of bounds if a national park was declared, that fences would be erected, charges levied and big and dangerous game introduced.[68]

Transparency, public participation and effective public relations were critically important to the deliberations that began in 1996, as were frank discussions about what the financial arrangements would be once the consolidated conservation authority was in place. With some reluctance on all sides, in April 1998 agreement was eventually reached and SANParks became the controlling authority when the national park was gazetted the following month. In 2004, after a public poll, the name was changed from the Cape Peninsula National Park to Table Mountain National Park.

To enable work to commence on this massive project, money was secured from the World Bank's Global Environmental Fund (GEF) and from the French Fonds Francais Pour L'Environnement (FFEM). Soon the government's poverty relief fund, Working for Water, was also involved through the clearing initiatives to rid the area of unwanted exotic and invasive vegetation. Some management strategies, such as clearing the pine trees from Table Mountain, the sometimes unattractive and slow restoration of fynbos, and the eradication of the introduced Himalayan tahr *Hemitragus jemlahicus* from the slopes of Table Mountain, offended many in Cape Town, who considered them and the introduced flora with affection. SANParks had also to contend with crime in parts of the national park as well as veld fires, some of them started by arsonists.

---

[67]Pooley, *Burning Table Mountain*, 59.
[68]I thank both Brian Huntley and Robbie Robinson for the detailed information they so kindly shared with me.

Never before had SANParks had to manage a national park in a highly populated urban area with all the difficulties that entailed, including providing recreational facilities for about 4 million visitors annually.[69] Over the past few years, park forums have been created to channel public feedback. World Heritage Status (obtained in 2004) for the Cape Floral Region (553 000 ha) has been helpful in terms of positive publicity, and the present division of the national park into three management areas with separate staff has brought some of the operational challenges under control. As is evident from this summary, management took precedence over research, although it was assumed this would follow.

However, the new national park is the only one in South Africa that can lay claim to centuries of Western research.[70] As the oldest city in South Africa and with strong links to international ideas, Cape Town could boast many firsts relevant to science and conservation: the first museum, the first scientific societies, the first national botanical garden, the first university, the first observatory, and the first authoritative journals and other publications. Not only were these firsts, but they were long-lasting and involved exchanges with and peer review by colleagues elsewhere in the British Empire.[71] From the end of the nineteenth and into the first half of the twentieth centuries, expertise on the Cape flora had grown even more, as had appreciation of it among the middle-class public.[72]

---

[69]B. W. van Wilgen, G.G. Forsyth and P. Prins, 'The management of fire-adapted ecosystems in an urban setting: The case of Table Mountain National Park, South Africa', *Ecology and Society* 17, no. 1 (2012), 8 pages, http://dx.doi.org/10.5751/ES-04526-170108; B.W. van Wilgen, 'Management of the natural ecosystems of the Cape Peninsula: Current status and future prospects', *Biodiversity and Conservation* 5, no. 5 (1996): 671–684; Daitz and Myrdal, 'Table Mountain National Park'.

[70]The literature is replete with botanical, astronomical, geological, zoological and other studies of the Cape Peninsula. A reputable source for some of the early research emanating from the Cape can be found in various chapters of A.C. Brown, ed., *A History of Scientific Endeavour in South Africa* (Cape Town: Royal Society, 1977). Because the Cape was of importance to Europe, particularly environmentally, European sources are also prolific.

[71]J. Carruthers, 'Scientists in society: A history of the Royal Society of South Africa', *Transactions of the Royal Society of South Africa* 63, no. 1 (2008): 1–30; S. Dubow, 'A commonwealth of science: The British Association in South Africa, 1905 and 1929', in *Science and Society in Southern Africa*, ed. S. Dubow (Manchester: Manchester University Press, 2000): 66–99; S. Dubow, *A Commonwealth of Knowledge: Science, Sensibility, and White South Africa, 1820–2000* (Oxford: Oxford University Press, 2006).

[72]L. van Sittert, 'From mere weeds and bosjes to Cape floral kingdom: The re-imagining of the indigenous flora at the Cape *c.*1890–1939', *Kronos* 28 (2002): 102–126; B.M.

As mentioned in a previous chapter, robust research had been conducted into the fynbos biome by the CSIR in the 1970s and 1980s.[73] Because fynbos is a fire-driven system, the contentious issue of fire has received a good deal of attention in the Cape Peninsula from botanists, foresters, ecologists and, more recently, professional historians.[74] Indeed, fire management and control were key drivers in the genesis of the new national park.

TMNP is thus well served by the scientific literature on many aspects of conservation, but little – if any – so far authored by SANParks scientists. However, with a rich base, as evidenced by a still incomplete bibliography exceeding 500 entries, research is well poised to develop quickly.[75] A special issue of *Ecology and Society* has been devoted to social and urban ecological research pertinent to Cape Town,[76] fire management has been carefully reconsidered,[77] and monitoring appears to be well under way.[78] What is probable is that with this wealth of literature, three universities nearby, a large educated population and an iconic site,

Bennett and F.J. Kruger, *Forestry and Water Conservation in South Africa: History, Science, Policy* (Canberra: ANU Press, 2015); B. Bennett, 'Model invasions and the development of national concerns over invasive introduced trees: Insights from South African history', *Biological Invasions* 16, no. 3 (2014): 499–512; F. Kruger and B. Bennett, 'Wood and water: An historical assessment of South Africa's past and present forestry policies as they relate to water conservation', *Transactions of the Royal Society of South Africa* 68, no. 3 (2013): 163–174; B.M. Bennett, 'The rise and demise of South Africa's first school of forestry', *Environment and History* 19, no. 1 (2013): 63–85.

[73]See, for example, *A Description of the Fynbos Biome Project*. South African National Scientific Programmes Report 28 (Pretoria: CSIR, 1978); D. Day, W.R. Siegfried, G.N. Louw and M.L. Jarman, *Fynbos Ecology: A Preliminary Synthesis, South African Programme for the SCOPE Mid-Term Project on the Ecological Effects of Fire*. South African National Scientific Programmes Report 40 (Pretoria: CSIR, 1979); M.L. Jarman, R.M. Cowling, R. Haynes, *et al.*, *A Bibliography of Fynbos Ecology*. South African National Scientific Programmes Report 53 (Pretoria: CSIR, 1981).

[74]Pooley, *Burning Table Mountain*.

[75]www.google.co.za/webhp?sourceid=chrome-instant&ion=1&espv=2&ie=UTF-8 #q=sanparks%20bibliography%20of%20table%20mountain (accessed 13 December 2015).

[76]P. Anderson and T. Eimqvist, 'Urban ecological and social ecological research in the City of Cape Town', *Ecology and Society* 17, no. 4 (2012): 23, http://dx.doi.org/10.5751/ ES-05076-170423.

[77]G.G. Forsyth and B.W. van Wilgen, 'The recent fire history of the Table Mountain National Park, and implications for fire management', *Koedoe* 50, no. 1 (2004): 3–9.

[78]T.G. Rebelo, S. Freitag, C. Cheney and M.A. McGeoch, 'Prioritising species of special concern for monitoring in Table Mountain National Park', *Koedoe* 53, no. 2 (2011), Art. #1019, 14 pages, doi: 10.4102/koedoe.v53i2.1019.

TMNP will not want for either researchers or research topics relevant to its future.

Conclusion

Owing to the enormous diversity of these national parks, no strand of systematic scientific research into ecosystems stands out. Instead, the two decades since 1990 have witnessed considerable upheaval in SANParks: the number of protected areas under its control has grown; management priorities have expanded to include human development; there has been a significant staff turnover; and there have been frequent organisational reconfigurations. In short, the institutional environment has not been conducive to scientific research: rather the contrary is true. A perusal of the published material suggests that the new research units are still orienting themselves through SoKs, building teams and honing skills prior to launching research projects. However, the SoK reports, and even the copious bibliographies, disappoint in not identifying gaps in understanding or future priorities.

Moreover, research in parks other than the KNP still has no lodestar. It also requires a rationale that will enable all the component parks to mesh in the production of hypothesis-based research that adds value to the South African ecological enterprise. Certainly, there are talented individuals within SANParks undertaking quality research, but it is also true that there are more scientists outside SANParks who do so. This is not necessarily a criticism, but researchers tend to be individualists and one cannot gauge to what extent research in SANParks reflects corporate priorities rather than individual preferences. The lessons and examples of the old CSP programmes could usefully be reconsidered and adopted, and collaborative work encouraged, even formalised. Yet strong internal scientific leadership by the conservation body involved is not indispensable to collaborative research, as a recent book extracting the 'lessons' from the Hluhluwe-iMfolozi Park[79] in KwaZulu-Natal reveals. This park, the descendant of two nineteenth-century game reserves, now linked by a corridor, covers some 96 000 ha of savannah. None of the editors or lead authors of the book are Ezemvelo KZN Wildlife staff members, but this has not been an obstacle to their research. Modelled on work done in

---

[79]Note the change of terminology, but not formal designation, from 'game reserve' to 'park'.

the KNP and in the Serengeti,[80] the book explains how research in this provincial game reserve has increased scientific understanding of ecological disturbance, the role of the smaller fauna in ecological processes, what constitutes 'degraded grass patches' versus 'grazing lawns' in terms of nutrients, 'demographic bottlenecks', the role of bush encroachment in creating savannah and grassland, fire ecology and, most importantly, the role of megafauna in a savannah system.[81] That these important conceptual breakthroughs have occurred in a relatively small area suggests that South Africa's other smaller national parks, particularly those in less-studied non-savannah areas, have considerable potential to enhance the country's ecological knowledge.

Post-1994, SANParks has befriended many of the research constituencies previously antagonistic towards it. From an outsider's perspective it seems regrettable that the proposed Scientific Advisory Council, made up of eminent international and local scientists, came to nought in 2004. Such an institution, with members from several disciplines, possibly including human and social sciences, might not only have assisted conservation science within SANParks, but provided networks to maximise synergies and collaborations among research institutions.[82] It is also noteworthy that nothing akin to *The Kruger Experience* has been mooted for the 'other' national parks, or even an edited volume collecting the high-quality papers that have appeared in various journals about these parks.

In recent years, SANParks has been careful to record its scientific output and there has been an annual SANParks Research Report

---

[80]J.T. du Toit, K.H. Rogers and H.C. Biggs, eds, *The Kruger Experience: Ecology and Management of Savanna Heterogeneity* (Washington, DC: Island Press, 2003); A.R.E. Sinclair and M. Norton-Griffiths, eds, *Serengeti: Dynamics of an Ecosystem* (Chicago, IL: University of Chicago Press, 1979); A.R.E. Sinclair and P. Arcese, eds, *Serengeti II: Dynamics, Management and Conservation of an Ecosystem* (Chicago, IL: Chicago University of Press, 1995); A.R.E. Sinclair, C. Packer, S.A.R. Mduma and J.M. Fryxell, eds, *Serengeti III: Human Impacts on Ecosystem Dynamics* (Chicago, IL: University of Chicago Press. 2006); A.R.E. Sinclair, K.L. Metzger, S.A.R. Mduma and J.M. Fryxell, eds, *Serengeti IV: Sustaining Biodiversity in a Coupled Human–Natural System* (Chicago, IL: University of Chicago Press, 2015).

[81]J.P.G.M. Cromsigt, S. Archibald and N. Owen-Smith, eds, *Conserving Africa's Mega-Diversity in the Anthropocene: The Hluhluwe-iMfolozi Park Story* (Cambridge: Cambridge University Press, 2016).

[82]Grant 40400672. Archives of the Mellon Foundation, New York, 2004–2009. See Chapter 11.

since 2012. In this literature, however, the lacunae in SANParks research outside Kruger are laid bare. The cumulative index for articles in *Koedoe* between 1992/3 and 2001 lists 56 articles relating to the KNP. The next highest figure is six (Addo Elephant and Kalahari Gemsbok), five on Vaalbos, four on Tsitsikamma, three each on Wilderness and Karoo, and one each on Richtersveld, West Coast and Golden Gate. At the time there were 20 national parks,[83] meaning that half the national parks got no mention even in the organisation's own research journal.[84] The lists from 2003 to 2010 of peer-reviewed journal publications by SANParks research staff show some improvement and many more co-authored publications began to appear in reputable journals. Just two examples will suffice to demonstrate the continuing dearth of publishable research on parks other than the KNP. In 2004, SANParks scientists published work on only three national parks (13 articles on the KNP and one each on the KGNP and the Richtersveld), while outside scientists published on nine (but including 31 articles on KNP, more than half the total). In 2006, SANParks scientists published work on five national parks: 16 articles on the KNP, two on the Garden Route and one each on Agulhas and Augrabies. That year, external researchers published articles on 12 national parks. Again, by far the majority concerned the KNP (41), the next highest being Addo with nine and KGNP with six.[85]

The SANParks Research Report of 2012 indicates that 37 SANParks research staff authored 15 peer-reviewed journal articles and co-authored 32 – a good tally by any measure. Six of these articles appeared in *Koedoe*, four in the *Journal of Zoo and Wildlife Medicine*, three each in *PLoS ONE* and *Pachyderm*, two in *Ecological Applications* and one each in journals such as *Ecology and Society, Proceedings of the Royal Society, Biological Sciences*, the *South African Journal of Wildlife Research, South African Journal of Botany* and *Journal of Ecology*. The impact factors of these journals ranged from 0.286 (*Pachyderm*) to 6.419 (*Annual Review of Environment and Resources*). Once more, the disparity between KNP and the others parks is stark. Of articles relating to specific South African national parks there were 146,

---

[83]Hall-Martin and Carruthers, *South African National Parks*, 53–62. The number decreased when the GRNP was proclaimed.

[84]J.C. Rautenbach, comp., 'Third cumulative index for *Koedoe*: Volumes 35/2–44/1', *Koedoe* 44, no. 2 (2001): 85–113.

[85]The peer-reviewed publications of SANParks staff from 2003 can be found at www .sanparks.org/assets/docs/conservation/publications/2014-publications.pdf. Insert the required year in the place of 2014 in the URL above (accessed 16 December 2015).

27 of which had SANParks authors. The KNP garnered 69, GRNP was next with 20, Table Mountain with 14, Addo with 11 and the others ranging from one to three. There were no research articles on Bontebok, Camdeboo and Mokala.[86]

A recent (2016) more analytical, and informative, bibliometric study on the role of embedded research in South Africa's national parks identified similar trends and statistics, taking into account all researchers, not only SANParks staff. Of the 1026 identified papers published between 2003 and 2013, the authors of the paper at hand noted that some 2003 authors from 578 organisations had contributed to the 1026 under evaluation. With a mean of 3.8 authors per paper, a single-authored contribution was a rarity. Some 87% of the papers had at least one South African author and embedded researchers contributed to 30% of the papers, many of them from universities in South Africa. Also, perhaps not surprisingly, a small cohort of researchers produced a disproportionate number of contributions: 2% contributed to 31% of papers and some 85% of these concerned research in only five of the 19 parks: KNP, GRNP, TMNP, Addo and Kalahari Gemsbok. Interesting though these data are, there is no evaluation so far as to how other protected area authorities perform on similar measures.[87]

The question arises of the value of many of South Africa's national parks to the generation of knowledge. If this is slight, then this should be acknowledged and the parks subjected to the protection and propagation, monitoring and measuring regime of an earlier era. On the other hand, the opportunities for collaboration and partnerships and for the integration of knowledge among conservation agencies, universities and the South African National Biodiversity Institute (SANBI) are enormous and would benefit not only SANParks but conservation science in South Africa more generally.

[86]The reports can be accessed from www.sanparks.co.za/conservation/reports/research_report.php (accessed 28 July 2016).

[87]B.W. van Wilgen, N. Boshoff, I.P.J. Smit, S. Solano-Fernandez and L. van der Walt, 'A bibliometric analysis to illustrate the role of an embedded research capability in South African National Parks', *Scientometrics* (2016), doi: 10.1007/s11192-016-1879-4.

Conclusion

This account of conservation science over a century in, or relating to, South Africa's national parks has unearthed a number of issues with which it is appropriate to conclude. Among the final comments are cautious responses to the research questions outlined in the Introduction and that have guided the direction of this book.

The first observation, however, is to underscore the process of scientific, or formal, research related to understanding South Africa's environment as being a very long one. The evolution of this understanding – that will not, of course, ever be complete or comprehensive – has occurred because of a concatenation of multiple factors. These have involved local and international dynamics, among which are legal governance, bureaucratic organisation and procedure, the state of higher education, the emergence of new fields of study, individual personalities and, perhaps most significantly, the ever-changing socio-political and economic milieux. As Thomas Mellon noted, these all alter with the passing of time and what might have been regarded as extremely important in one decade or period is determined as being less so in another, and these eddies and ripples may indeed obscure the main factors that bring momentous change to the main channel of the stream.[1]

A further aim of this book has been to avoid a unilinear, simplistic trajectory and rather to provide a multilinear and complex understanding of the contexts in which the different scales of change have occurred.

---

[1]'In the short voyage of a lifetime, we can see the eddies and ripples upon the surface, but not the under-currents changing the main channel of the stream. History alone can determine the deep seated causes which have been at work to bring them about.' *Thomas Mellon and His Times*, 338, as quoted by David Cannadine in *Mellon: An American Life* (London: Allen Lane/Penguin, 2006), 583. For a dissection of the meaning and use of ignorance, see F. Uekötter and U. Lübken, 'Introduction: The social functions of ignorance', in *Managing the Unknown: Essays on Environmental Ignorance* (New York, NY and Oxford: Berghahn, 2014), 1–12.

Another has been to offer scientists, non-government organisations and policy-makers in the conservation sector in South Africa a critical perspective on their work and not to extract direct 'lessons' or 'chart the way forward', although such observations may be made. I have also eschewed any assessment of 'progress', a word that is both loaded and emotive, and instead concentrate on the legal, societal, technological and intellectual possibilities within their own time.

The purpose of a work of history is to reflect on events and people within their contexts, cognisant of the real possibilities and limits within which they operate. In the Anthropocene – a concept only recently given expression and one germane to conserving our planet – history remains an intellectual journey, not a recitation of facts, dates and a timeline, let alone the exposition of general laws. It is an explanation, or an interpretation, of how we have come to be where we are. Essentially, too, it is as well to recall that 'The ideas of conservation biology have a history of constructing different understandings of biodiversity, and of the sustainability science that strives to preserve it.'[2] It has been my intention to uncover this history as it relates to South Africa in the twentieth century and a little beyond.

Each of the three periods into which this work is divided has, as has been shown, to have had a general leitmotif, particularly, but not solely, pertaining to South Africa. Early ideas of wildlife decimation and ensuing scarcity gave rise to the need to protect, preserve and propagate particular species within clearly demarcated areas that were called 'game reserves' or 'game preserves'. The species to be protected in this manner were those valued by sport and subsistence hunters, 'vermin' animals were routinely culled, even destroyed. As these phrases had a rather old-fashioned ring to them while 'national park' had a cachet of the modern, emanating from the USA (the new world) and democratic in terms of public access, it was this term that became current even though elements – such as hiking, camping, swimming in or rafting on the rivers and similar outdoor pursuits – could not be conducted in a sanctuary full of dangerous wildlife. By the 1960s, the protectionist goals had largely been accomplished in certain areas and, together with technological developments of many kinds, a regime of measuring, monitoring and manipulating animal populations and their habitats became the fact-gathering

[2] L. Robin, 'New science for sustainability in an ancient land', in *Nature's End: History and the Environment*, eds S. Sörlin and P. Warde (Houndmills: Palgrave Macmillan, 2009), 188–211, quotation 205–206.

routine and it was a long while before this logical compilation was transformed into scientific knowledge or understanding, let alone wisdom. This information-collecting period coincided with a time of economic prosperity and strong government support for national parks in South Africa and its consequence was to extend the reach and influence of the then National Parks Board. Later, because the world and South Africa had altered by the 1990s, more innovation, integration and an internationalisation of nature conservation had become the order of the day. However, I hope that I have indicated that this categorisation is far from water-tight. For example, the current scourge of international rhinoceros poaching in many of South Africa's protected areas (not only in national parks operated by SANParks) has recreated a need to revert to methods of protection, preservation and propagation of this individual species, while the tick-box approach to biodiversity and the IUCN 'Red-listing' of only a chosen few recalls an era of monitor and measure.

The first research question posed in the Introduction concerned the extent to which scientific research in South African national parks has been externally or internally driven. Certainly, both environments have been influential. The internal drivers produced the enabling (or disabling) circumstances in which this research has taken place and the localities selected for national parks. These factors also determined the calibre and qualifications of researchers and other staff as well as their race and gender. Constraints and opportunities included the nature, scope and quality of education in institutions of higher learning and other academic institutions and, perhaps most critically important, has been local funding and official and public support. Internal (South African) drivers have come from organisations like the Council for Scientific and Industrial Research (CSIR) and its Cooperative Scientific Programmes (CSP), the research done in game reserves in what is now the province of KwaZulu-Natal and even the experimental agenda of the Pilanesberg National Park in North West province.

As far as external drivers are concerned, the international community and global ideas have also played a large role, a role that amplified over the globalising twentieth century. An injection of expertise and funding from the Mellon Foundation to the Kruger National Park (KNP) in the 1990s and early 2000s was unparalleled and extremely productive. Without doubt, too, global environmentalism and the large number of international conventions and agreements to which South Africa now adheres have also shaped the type of conservation science that is validated at national level. And, as has also been alluded to throughout this work, the formal bureaucracy – by way of organisation and administration – together with competition around international, national, regional and even local governance has determined what has been possible in the genre of national parks. All these elements have also, of course, created competition among the various state as well as private conservation actors. At times this competition has been healthy and created an atmosphere in which a variety of different thinking has flourished productively, but when it has been unhealthy, inwardness, a sense of hubris and autocracy has resulted, with consequences that I have explained.

Like many, probably the majority of conservation agencies with long histories (it certainly applies to the USA), there has not been a long-term or lasting strategy for environmental research within SANParks or within South Africa. In terms of an internal driver of conservation science, a glimpse into overall strategic thinking came with the CSIR's CSP agenda of the 1980s and the publication at the time of *Biotic Diversity in Southern Africa: Concepts and Conservation* and *South African Environments into the 21st Century*, but nothing similarly broad-ranging and thoughtful emanated from SANParks or its predecessor the National Parks Board (NPB).[3] In its absence, it has been national legislation debated in parliamentary forums and informed by international obligations that has provided the framework and reflects the aspirations of the state and its citizens in connection with national parks, and indeed, other protected areas in South Africa.[4] The purpose of state-owned protected areas in the category of 'national parks' in South Africa has had three major legal iterations: initially in 1926, in consolidating legislation of 1976 and in fresh legislation in 2003.

The National Parks Act 56 of 1926 applied only to the newly established KNP. Although the law provided for the proclamation of future national parks, it did not specify objectives for them. At the time, paragraph 1, 'Constitution of Kruger National Park', read that it had been established as an area 'for the propagation, protection and preservation therein of wild animal life, wild vegetation and objects of geological, ethological, historical or other scientific interest for the benefit, advantage

---

[3] B.J. Huntley, ed., *Biotic Diversity in Southern Africa: Concepts and Conservation* (Cape Town: Oxford University Press, 1989); B.J. Huntley, W.R. Siegfried and C. Sunter, *South African Environments into the 21st Century* (Cape Town: Human & Rousseau Tafelberg, 1989).

[4] See P. Novellie, H. Biggs and D. Roux, 'National laws and policies can enable or confound adaptive governance: Examples from South African national parks', *Environmental Science and Policy* 66 (2016): 40–46, http://dx.doi.org/10.1016/j.envsci.2016.08.0051462-9011/ã 2016.

and enjoyment of the inhabitants of the Union'. There was no specific mandate to study the fauna, flora, geology, history or other aspects of interest, although it might be argued that doing so would benefit and advantage the Union's citizens.

In 1962, the word 'study' was inserted into this sentence in the law at the suggestion of Douglas Mitchell, an Opposition MP from the province of Natal and a prominent member of the competitive, and at times leading, South African conservation authority, the Natal Parks Game and Fish Preservation Board.[5] This was further incorporated into a major revision and consolidation of the law at a time when the number of national parks had greatly increased. The National Parks Act 57 of 1976, paragraph 4, then applicable to all national parks, read:

> The object of the constitution of a park is the establishment, preservation and study therein of wild animal, marine and plant life and objects of geological, archaeological, historical, ethnological, oceanographic, educational and other scientific interest and objects relating to the said life of the first-mentioned objects or to events in or the history of the park, in such a manner that the area which constitutes the park shall, as far as may be and for the benefit and enjoyment of visitors, be retained in its natural state.

From 1962, therefore (and enshrined in subsequent 1976 legislation), 'study' (the gaining of academic knowledge, detailed investigation, research, scholarship, etc.) applied legally and equally to all the aspects listed, although many disciplines, e.g. history and ethnography, were simply ignored within the organisation as has been described in the foregoing pages. Unlike the National Parks Service of the USA, historical monuments and other heritage places have not been part of national park bureaucracy but subject to the National Monuments Council, or currently the South African Heritage Resources Agency (SAHRA). There can be no doubt that the NPB and its successor, SANParks, were in breach of their legal obligation in this regard, simply preferring (it would seem) to concentrate on acquiring knowledge relating to the natural environment alone.[6] In the most recent major revision, hastily drafted to coincide

---

[5]Union of South Africa *House of Assembly Debates*, 26 May 1961, cols. 7292–7316.
[6]One of these reports, strongly worded, was by R. Bell, 'A review of the programme of the Scientific Services Section, Kruger National Park. December 1994'. SANParks unpublished report.

with the World Parks Congress in Durban in 2003 (and subsequently amended), the law was substantially changed to encompass all protected areas, not only those at national level and not only those named national parks – a development that resonates better with the categorisation of the International Union for the Conservation of Nature/World Conservation Union (IUCN) of which the 'protected area' is the core unit.[7] Entitled the National Environmental Management: Protected Areas Act 57 of 2003 (as amended), it is one of a number of Acts underpinning national environmental management as a whole, rather than its fragments as was previously the case. A complex and wide-ranging piece of legislation, it makes no overt reference to 'study' or 'research'. Its objective is 'the protection and conservation of ecologically viable areas' which form part of a varied system of protected areas that includes 'special nature reserves, national parks, nature reserves (including wilderness areas) and protected environments', World Heritage Sites, marine protected areas, specially protected forest areas and mountain catchment areas. Thus, in respect of coordinated legislation to encompass disparate elements of the conservation estate, this law marks a welcome change from fragmentation, without providing a straitjacket.

National parks in South Africa, therefore, are currently merely one of many conservation areas that have been banded together under a single legislative framework, a development unimaginable in the earlier years of the twentieth century when any kind of protected area, whether game reserve or national park, was a rarity, and when categories such as World Heritage Sites and Biosphere Reserves had not been invented. Also differing from past practice are the considerable powers vested in the responsible cabinet minister, particularly in prescribing norms and standards for many of the Act's objectives. Government intervention and oversight has increased. Management plans and management and supervision indicators are obligatory for all protected areas and require regular ministerial review and approval. Section 17 of the Act sets out a long list of what protected areas are intended to accomplish. In reading this part of the law, there are strong indications that the mandate of conservation science has reverted in some respects to 'protect' and 'preserve' (6 of the 12 purposes), reference to disciplines other than conservation biology have been removed, and modern objectives have been added, such as using natural and biological resources sustainably, rehabilitating and restoring degraded

---

[7]National Environmental Management: Protected Areas Act 57 of 2003, including National Environmental Management: Protected Areas Amendment Act 21 of 2014.

ecosystems and promoting the recovery of endangered and vulnerable species. Moreover, there are key economic and social desiderata: creating and augmenting nature-based tourist destinations and managing the inter-relationship between biodiversity, human settlement and economic development so as to promote human well-being.[8] Cultural heritage sites appear in Section 20(a)(i) only insofar as national parks may be declared to protect them. Thus the legal obligation for scientific research in South Africa's national parks is vague and seemingly can only be justified in connection with fulfilling one or more of the purposes set out in Section 17. Of these, protecting, preserving and conserving environmental elements, tourism and ecological restoration have been highlighted as important.[9] The Act is silent on whether these are in-house obligations of the various conservation agencies, or can be collaborative or even outsourced. The paradigm articulated in the South African legislation, including nesting national parks within a wider framework of environmental management, accords well with the current worldwide framing suggested by Georgina Mace as 'people and nature'.[10] This is a development totally different from earlier periods of 'nature without people'.

[8]Paragraph 17 reads: Purpose of protected areas
The purposes of the declaration of areas as protected areas are:
(a) to protect ecologically viable areas representative of South Africa's biological diversity and its natural landscapes and seascapes in a system of protected areas;
(b) to preserve the ecological integrity of those areas;
(c) to conserve biodiversity in those areas;
(d) to protect areas representative of all ecosystems, habitats and species naturally occurring in South Africa;
(e) to protect South Africa's threatened or rare species;
(f) to protect an area which is vulnerable or ecologically sensitive;
(g) to assist in ensuring the sustained supply of environmental goods and services;
(h) to provide for the sustainable use of natural and biological resources;
(i) to create or augment destinations for nature-based tourism;
(j) to manage the interrelationship between natural environmental biodiversity, human settlement and economic development;
(k) generally, to contribute to human, social, cultural, spiritual and economic development; or
(l) to rehabilitate and restore degraded ecosystems and promote the recovery of endangered and vulnerable species.
[9]A. de Vos, G.S. Cumming, C.A. Moore, K. Maciejewski and G. Duckworth, 'The relevance of spatial variation in ecotourism attributes for the economic sustainability of protected areas', *Ecosphere* 7 (2016), e01207.10.1002/ecs2.1207.
[10]G. Mace, 'Whose conservation? Changes in the perception and goals of nature conservation require a solid scientific basis', *Science* 345, no. 6204 (2014): 1558–1560.

It is important to note that neither current nor past South African legislation has provided a definition of a national park. However, as we have seen, the IUCN has done so. Its definitions and schedules are regularly revised according to environmental priorities, international politics and the socio-economic milieu, like South Africa's own legislation. However, even there, the exact role of national parks in promoting scientific research has never been clarified.[11] The first internationally agreed IUCN definition of a national park was in 1969: they had to be 'large', contain one or more 'materially unchanged' ecosystems, involve the highest official authorities in the country and be open to the public under certain conditions.[12] Many protected areas in the world referred to as national parks did not meet this definition – including in South Africa – and it has been revised to become more inclusive and also to better distinguish national parks from other kinds of protected areas.

According to the 2008 guidelines updated and launched at the World Conservation Congress in Barcelona, the IUCN defines a protected area,[13] of which there are six categories.[14] National parks fall into

---

[11]See R.F. Dasmann, 'Towards a system for classifying natural regions of the world and their representation by national parks and reserves', *Biological Conservation* 2 (1972): 247–255; R.F. Dasmann, *A System for Defining and Classifying Natural Regions for Purposes of Conservation.* IUCN Occasional Paper No. 7 (Morges: IUCN, 1973), iii–47; IUCN, *United Nations List of National Parks and Equivalent Reserves.* IUCN Publications No. 33 (Morges: IUCN, 1975); IUCN Commission on National Parks and Protected Areas, *United Nations List of National Parks and Equivalent Reserves* (Gland: IUCN, 1980); IUCN Committee on Criteria and Nomenclature Commission on National Parks and Protected Areas, *Categories, Objectives and Criteria for Protected Areas: A Final Report* (Morges: IUCN, 1978); International Union for the Conservation of Nature, *Guidelines for Protected Area Management Categories* (Gland and Cambridge: IUCN, 1994).

[12]The IUCN uses the definition from the Agreement on Biological Diversity in which an ecosystem is understood as a dynamic complex of vegetable, animal and microorganism communities and their non-living environment that interact as a functional unit. Ecosystems may be small and simple, like an isolated pond, or large and complex, like a specific tropical rainforest or a coral reef in tropical seas. The various 'ecosystems' in South Africa's national parks are not itemised, nor is their scale inherent in the proclamation of the national park.

[13]A protected area is a clearly defined geographical space, recognised, dedicated and managed, through legal or other effective means, to achieve the long-term conservation of nature with associated ecosystem services and cultural values (IUCN Definition 2008).

[14]www.iucn.org/theme/protected-areas/about/categories (accessed 18 August 2016).
The IUCN Protected Area Management Categories are Category Ia, Strict Nature Reserve; Category Ib, Wilderness Area; Category II, National Park; Category III, Natural Monument or Feature; Category IV, Habitat/Species Management Area; Category V,

Category II, and these are 'large natural or near natural areas set aside to protect large-scale ecological processes, along with the complement of species and ecosystems characteristic of the area, which also provide a foundation for environmentally and culturally compatible, spiritual, scientific, educational, recreational, and visitor opportunities'. Thus, by this definition, opportunities for science are to be provided in national parks. Attached to IUCN Category II national parks are objectives, distinguishing features, and an explanation of their role. National parks are distinctive principally in welcoming visitors and in having the maintenance of a whole ecosystem as their management objective. There has been no clear exposition of which South African national parks are indeed 'large' enough 'to protect large-scale ecological processes'. What is clear is that very many of them are not, and do not. Interestingly, not one category of protected area as defined by the IUCN has scientific research as a core mandate, although Strict Nature Reserves (Category Ia) may serve as reference areas for scientific research and monitoring. However, it has been argued that scientific research is fundamental to many protected areas, among them strict reserves but also many, although not all, national parks. Evaluation of protected areas to meet the specific criteria of IUCN categories is not enough: some are ideal sites for both fundamental and applied research, but a research agenda is seldom a consideration in their proclamation.[15] As noted by Götmark, Kirby and Usher, perhaps the most science-friendly category is that of IUCN Type 1(a).[16]

South Africa's legislation makes no reference to these definitions (or indeed even to the IUCN), nor does it explain how protected areas in the country might comply with them. Essentially, these are ignored and, as has often been observed, 'national park' is just a brand open to almost infinite interpretation, in South Africa as everywhere else. Unlike World Heritage Sites, national parks are not regulated by international

---

Protected Landscape/Seascape; Category VI, Protected Area with sustainable use of natural resources. Full descriptions of their characteristics and how they differ from one another can be found on this website.

[15] F. Götmark, K. Kirby and M.B. Usher, 'Strict reserves, IUCN classification, and the use of reserves for scientific research: A comment on Schultze et al. (2014)', Biodiversity Conservation 24 (2015): 3621–3625. doi: 10.1007/s10531-015-1011-8; G.S. Cumming, 'The relevance and resilience of protected areas in the Anthropocene', Anthropocene 108 (2016), http://dx.doi.org/10.1016/j.ancene.2016.03.003.

[16] Götmark, Kirby and Usher, 'Strict reserves, IUCN classification'.

law or convention, standards are not scrutinised and the label cannot be denied.[17]

Although South Africa has a multitude of types of protected areas, SANParks is responsible for just one single category: national parks. It has no strict nature reserves under its control, no wilderness areas, no natural monument or feature, no habitat or species management area, no protected landscape or seascape and no protected area within which natural resources are sustainably used. The IUCN's definitions of these other categories indicate that many of South Africa's national parks under SANParks administration should not be Category II at all, but belong better to other categories. The Augrabies Falls, for example, is a 'natural monument or feature', while Bontebok and Mountain Zebra national parks are surely 'habitat/species management areas'.[18]

Another initial research question concerned the 'scientists' in SANParks over the course of its history and an investigation of their range of expertise and their scientific contribution and their partnerships and collaborations. This too has been shaped by internal and external contexts, but also by the dominance of certain individuals and certain institutions over the years. In this regard, until about 20 years ago, the 'warden' of the KNP was a particularly powerful position, as was, and indeed still is, the Chief Executive Officer of SANParks itself, as this person has considerable authority delegated by the board. Nonetheless, although a strong personality can be beneficial in providing charismatic leadership, organisational direction and personal loyalty, it can also promote sycophantism and a reluctance to accept opinion that might contradict the leader. And in the case of South African national parks, it is evident that new thinking has, until recently with the initiation of strategic adaptive management and its ramifications, been generated from outside the organisation, not from within it. The entry of the US Mellon Foundation was critically important in vitalising conservation science in the KNP from the mid-1990s onwards.

Reference to the KNP in particular is important because this single national park has occupied a dominant position since the 1920s.

---

[17]C.M. Hall and W. Frost, 'Introduction: The making of the national parks concept', in *Tourism and National Parks: International Perspectives on Development, History and Change*, eds W. Frost and C.M. Hall (London: Routledge, 2009), 3–15, quotation p. 3.

[18]www.iucn.org/theme/protected-areas/about/categories (accessed 18 August 2016).

Its history, not always accurately communicated,[19] has eclipsed and even obliterated more creative and adventurous protected areas and national parks, such as the earlier Natal National Park and the scientific Dongola Wild Life Sanctuary, let alone the studies that have taken place within the game reserves of KwaZulu-Natal. Often titles of books and articles that refer grandly to 'South Africa's protected areas' turn out to be about the KNP or, at best, the 'other parks' become footnotes to the main story of the KNP. Thus, the context of 'which space?' or 'which place?' is itself important too. As well as careful reconsideration of the IUCN categorisation, differentiating between the sciences and the scales required to benefit each of the various national parks in South Africa might strengthen the portfolio generally.

As has been explained, the ever-changing and unstable organisational structure of the NPB and its successor SANParks has been detrimental to coherent or cohesive management and science in what are clearly regarded as the 'lesser' parks, although arguably this instability has affected them all. Certainly, as has been shown, very little research has thus far emanated from these parks, although a start will be made once the state of knowledge reports are more complete. Perhaps, too, there is too little coordinated research within SANParks for a variety of reasons including the wide span of ecological regions under its control. However, one might argue that this is not a critical gap, because biologists in the Cape Floral Region and in the Karoo, regardless of the status of the properties that they study or the organisations to which they are affiliated, have made considerable strides in understanding and studying non-savannah ecosystems. It may be that, as was the CSP agenda of the 1980s, it is the quality of the research that matters, not the legal status of the locality in which the research is done, or the employment affiliation of the researchers. Nonetheless, in terms of answering the research question about the partnerships and collaborations that have been generated over the years, it is clear that many of the properties in the stable of SANParks do not yet contribute to the national scientific agenda in a meaningful way. There is, however, currently no indication that these parks will be moved into other portfolios (e.g. provincial), or be recategorised any time soon. It remains to be seen whether their contribution to the national well-being, through employment creation and tourist attraction, makes good

---

[19]There are countless references to the KNP having been founded in 1898. This is totally incorrect: a small game reserve south of the Sabi River was proclaimed in 1898, as were numerous other game reserves at that time.

this deficiency in scientific research. Nor are there organisational links between SANParks' protected areas (all named national parks) and the wide diversity of the rest of the protected area estate in the country. The time may arrive when South Africa's newer internationally relevant protected areas – Biosphere Reserves and World Heritage Sites, wilderness areas, protected natural environments – come into their own as sites of formal study, as well as being more efficacious in leading sustainable development, a vitally urgent national necessity. So far, the network of Biosphere Reserves has begun to cooperate as a unit within South Africa and within the region, and this cooperative and multi-level model might proliferate with beneficial consequences.[20]

Changes in Conservation Science

Conservation science more broadly has operated in this confusing and bewildering institutional context, and has itself been in almost constant flux in South Africa, as elsewhere.[21] Indeed, one may ask of current conservation science itself, what *is* it? In a special issue of *Conservation Biology* in 2013, Michael Soulé, the 'originator' of the term conservation biology, came out strongly against the notion that conservation science should have linkages to economic development and poverty alleviation – issues integral to South Africa's conservation science agenda.[22] Many of his peers disagreed with him and, appreciating that conservation is a science of values, have argued that all human values should be embraced in its furtherance and that no scientist should assume the role of an 'arbiter of moral purity'.[23]

[20]R. Pool-Stanvliet, 'A history of the UNESCO Man and the Biosphere Programme in South Africa', *South African Journal of Science* 109 (2013): Art. #a0035, 6 pages. http://dx.doi.org/10.1590/sajs.2013/a0035; R. Pool-Stanvliet and M. Clüsener-Godt, eds, *Afrimab: Biosphere Reserves in Sub-Saharan Africa: Showcasing Sustainable Development* (Pretoria and Paris: Department of Environmental Affairs and UNESCO, 2013).

[21]K. Cuddington and B.E. Beisner, eds, *Ecological Paradigms Lost: Routes of Theory Change* (Burlington, MA: Elsevier, 2005); C. Meine, 'It's about time: Conservation biology and history', *Conservation Biology* 13 (1999): 1–3; F. Venter, N. Naiman, H. Biggs and D. Pienaar, 'The evolution of conservation management philosophy: Science, environmental change and social adjustments in Kruger National Park', *Ecosystems* 11 (2008): 173–192.

[22]M. Soulé, 'The "New Conservation"', *Conservation Biology* 27 (2013): 895–897.

[23]M. Marvier, 'A call for ecumenical conservation', *Animal Conservation* 17, no. 6 (2014): 518–519, quotation p. 518; B. Miller, M.E. Soulé and J. Terborgh, '"New conservation" or surrender to development?' *Animal Conservation* 17, no. 6 (2014): 509–515.

Kareiva and Marvier have pointed out that much has changed since 1985 when conservation biology first entered the lexicon and overshadowed any ideas of an older natural history. They observe, nonetheless, that the distinction between conservation biology and conservation science has become increasingly evident. The former, they argue, was 'the application of biological science to address the problems of species, communities, and ecosystems perturbed by humans'. Conservation science, by contrast, is an integrated and multidisciplinary field of study which recognises that ecological dynamics are inseparable from human dynamics and that 'a key goal of conservation science is the improvement of human wellbeing through the management of the environment'. Because conservation is an expression of human values, conservation science 'focussed primarily on biology is likely to misdiagnose problems and arrive at ill-conceived solutions'.[24] Many, but not all, South African conservation scientists would agree.[25]

Biologists and other natural scientists generally work with spatial scales, but, as Curt Meine avers, 'it is the temporal scales that define our research questions, our interpretation of results, and our conservation recommendations'.[26] Many scholars have noted the difficulties in integrating history and conservation science because the disciplines are so far apart: '[N]atural scientists and environmental historians may gaze upon the same landscape, but they see different things and draw different conclusions'.[27] The training differs between the disciplines as do intellectual

---

[24]P. Kareiva and M. Marvier, 'What is conservation science?' *Bioscience* 62, no. 11 (2012): 962–969.

[25]K.H. Rogers, 'Operationalizing ecology under a new paradigm: An African perspective', in *The Ecological Basis for Conservation: Heterogeneity, Ecosystems, and Biodiversity*, eds S. Pickett, R.S. Ostfeld, M. Shachak and G. Likens (New York, NY: Chapman and Hall, 1997), 60–77; G. Castley, M. Knight and J. Gordon, 'Making conservation work: Innovative approaches to meeting biodiversity conservation and socio-economic objectives (an example from the Addo Elephant National Park, South Africa)', in *Evolution and Innovation in Wildlife Conservation: Parks and Game Ranches to Transfrontier Conservation Areas*, eds H. Suich, B. Child and A. Spenceley (London: Earthscan, 2009), 308–323.

[26]Meine, 'It's about time'.

[27]Meine, 'It's about time'. See also M. Welch-Devine and L.M. Campbell, 'Sorting out roles and defining divides: Social sciences at the World Conservation Congress', *Conservation and Society* 8, no. 4 (2010): 339–348; H. Els and P. Bothma, 'Developing partnerships in a paradigm shift to achieve conservation reality in South Africa', *Koedoe* 43, no. 1 (2000):19–26; D. Brockington, R. Duffy and J. Igoe, *Nature Unbound: Conservation, Capitalism and the Future of Protected Areas* (London: Earthscan, 2008). There are many examples.

traditions and discourses, and seldom do members of one group read the literature of the other.[28] Szabó and Hédl agree, but note that differing worldviews are productive for generating knowledge, but that the 'social sciences' are often lumped together as an undifferentiated whole, as they should not be, any more than should be the 'natural sciences'.[29] It must also be acknowledged that some scientists consider themselves writers of 'history', but neglect even the basic skills historians must acquire in terms of critical approach, reliance on primary sources and broad contextual knowledge.[30] This is not to dismiss their attempts at recording the past, but it does highlight the fact that no historian would take such liberties with the sciences.

However, conservation science has not been neglected, not at least by SANParks, although aspects of that science have received little attention, the study and management of the Fungal kingdom being a case in point despite its critical role in any ecosystem. As Roux and his colleagues have argued, to be successful, conservation requires effective research. Taking three case studies, the team explains the difficulties confronting research within a conservation agency, but insist that such research should satisfy two key criteria: reliability through the normal channels of peer-reviewed publications and, as legally mandated and publicly funded, political and policy relevance through stakeholder engagement. The first criterion is easier to measure and does not require a researcher to have a foothold in a conservation agency. The second does, they suggest, because while productive academics may be contracted by conservation agencies and publish in quality journals, it is only an agency like SANParks that has access to managers, policy-makers and the public and shares the values of the polity at large.[31] Thus, they conclude, it is the partnership between

---

[28]Meine, 'It's about time'.

[29]P. Szabó and R. Hédl, 'Advancing the integration of history and ecology for conservation', *Conservation Biology* 25, no. 4 (2011): 680–687; but see also S. Pooley, 'Historians are from Venus, ecologists are from Mars', *Conservation Biology* 27, no. 6 (2013): 1481–1483, doi: 10.1111/cobi.12106; L. Robin and W. Steffen, 'History for the Anthropocene', *History Compass* 5 (2007): 1694–1719.

[30]See, for example, D. Mabunda, D.J. Pienaar and J.Verhoef, 'The Kruger National Park: A century of management and research', in *The Kruger Experience: Ecology and Management of Savanna Heterogeneity*, eds J.T. du Toit, K.H. Rogers and H.C. Biggs (Washington, DC: Island Press 2003), 3–21; S.C.J. Joubert, *The Kruger National Park: A History*. 3 vols (Johannesburg: High Branching, 2012).

[31]D.J. Roux, R.T. Kingsford, S.F. McCool, M.A. McGeoch and L.C. Foxcroft, 'The role and value of conservation agency research', *Environmental Management*, doi: 10.1007/

sound academic research and a commitment to the polity at large that should define the conservation science conducted by SANParks. Perhaps this is not an unexpected conclusion for scientists within such organisations to come to, but if this is true, then stronger links with other state or semi-state conservation and environmental agencies would clearly be even more beneficial. As for the future, Roux, McGeoch and Foxcroft propose a coordinated strategy to deal with priority research themes and urgent research questions, and at a lower level, recommend improved communications between managers and researchers through, for example, an annual science forum, and the encouragement of early-career scientists.[32] Why this should be restricted to SANParks alone is not clear, as many of these characteristics apply to provincial and other nationally protected areas too.

Another research question posed at the outset was about how the scientific outputs of national park research have been communicated. As explained in previous chapters, employees in the science sector of the NPB and SANParks have contributed to many publications, some of them highly prestigious.[33] For this they should be congratulated as one of the major features of academic life in the twenty-first century is a rate of publication and the citation level of authors. There is less emphasis on environmental education, however, and little in the published literature about how scientific knowledge generated in the national parks spills over into school learners, environmental educational curricula, or even disseminated among the general public. It is the tourist arm of

s00267-015-0473-5. Published online 4 April 2015. See also B.W. van Wilgen, N. Boshoff, I.P.J. Smit, S. Solano-Fernandez and L. van der Walt, 'A bibliometric analysis to illustrate the role of an embedded research capability in South African National Parks', *Scientometrics* (2016), doi: 10.1007/s11192-016-1879-4 and B.G. Lovegrove and S.D. Johnson, 'Assessment of research performance in biology: How well do peer review and bibliometry correlate?' *BioScience* 58, no. 2 (2008): 160–164.

[32] D. Roux, M. McGeoch and L. Foxcroft, 'Assessment of selected in-house research achievements for the period 2008–2011'. *Scientific Report 01/2012* (Skukuza: SANParks, 2012).

[33] SANParks, 'Peer-reviewed journal and chapter publications related to South African National Parks by SANParks research staff and by non-SANParks research staff, 2003–2014', www.sanparks.org/conservation/scientific_new/publications/peer_reviewed_articles.php/ (accessed 24 December 2015); Roux, McGeoch and Foxcroft, 'Assessment of selected in-house research achievements for the period 2008–2011'.

SANParks that generally guides visitors and perhaps not always is the level of knowledge as professionally accurate as it might be.

A relatively small country like South Africa does not have a large group of conservation scientists and partnerships with universities and other conservation agencies – private and public – might perhaps be extended and even formalised, and should certainly include relevant academic social sciences and humanities. This aspect of environmental study has been almost entirely absent – history, archaeology, aesthetics, psychology, political science have not been championed as they should have. Conservation science workshops and conferences are convened by organisations such as SANParks, the Endangered Wildlife Trust, the Diamond Route, and some provincial authorities, but these are often poorly attended by external scientists.[34] A comprehensive central database of publications could be maintained by a professional organisation such as the Southern African Institute of Ecologists and Environmental Scientists (founded in 1998) and could include disciplines beyond the natural sciences.[35] Fewer silos and more synergy and collaboration would lead to further integration, innovation and internationalisation to the benefit of conservation science in South Africa, and particularly to good and meaningful research in the smaller national parks and protected areas.

On this topic of partnerships and collaborations, the preceding overview of conservation science in South Africa's national parks has brought to light a number of 'moments' at which a high-powered, integrated and flexible protected area and environmental research agenda and structure might have come into being – the 'what ifs' in the account that has been given. Although not possible here, it might be salutary to compare them and to consider in detail why all ended in failure. The first firm attempt at some form of national coordination occurred in 1945 when a provincial consultative committee was appointed to coordinate the activities of all bodies controlling national parks, game reserves and botanical gardens. It never got off the ground.[36] Just a few years later, in January 1949, the Scientific Advisory Council for National Parks and Nature Reserves

---

[34]For example, www.diamondroute.com/research-downloads/5th%20Annual%20Diamond %20Route%20Research%20Conference%202014%2 (accessed 18 December 2015); www.ewt.org.za/BUSINESSDEVELOPMENT/events.html (accessed 18 December 2015).

[35]www.saiees.org/ (accessed 18 December 2015).

[36]Central Archives Depot, National Archives of South Africa. SAB BNS 1/1/477, 6/5/85.

was created.[37] In 1955 a steering committee for scientific research in the national parks in cooperation with the Scientific Advisory Board for National Parks and Nature Reserves was established.[38] It too, fizzled out, just three years later. So did the potentially more promising Council for the Environment and a National Committee for Nature Conservation (NACOR) of the 1980s. In the mid-1990s, the Mellon Foundation provided financial support for creating a permanent (although changing) science advisory board of local and international luminaries to monitor and assist SANParks and this would have secured the organisation international leadership and prominence. However, it, too, came to naught.[39] One of the most outspoken critics of the KNP and the national parks organisation was Richard Bell, whose 1995 report has already been described. He too recommended a panel of advisory external scientists and also condemned the NPB's bias towards the natural sciences (contrary to the law), recommending the employment of a senior scientist in 'human studies'.[40]

The resistance to any overall advisory body, it would appear, remains strong within SANParks. However, given the existence of a growing network of biosphere reserves and the increasing strength of the Western Cape's Fynbos Forum organisation, let alone the increasing importance of arid ecology – and the weakness of the South African National Biodiversity Institute (SANBI) as a strong partner and national agenda-setter (at least to date, it is certainly gaining traction and influence) – many would argue that an overall mechanism for the formal exchange of conservation science would be beneficial. Moreover, there is at the apex of SANParks a board (including the CEO of SANParks), the latest of which was appointed by government in 2015. Certainly the role of government in national parks and other protected areas has strengthened over the century, but it has not yet had a direct effect on integrating conservation science and research more widely in the country at large.

---

[37]Bigalke archives (per kind favour of Dr R. Bigalke), Bigalke to Smith, 5 January 1949.

[38]C.S.L. Schutte, 'Oor die hoofdoel van nasionale parke en die stigting van 'n ekologiese instituut', n.d., 5. Box K8, KNP archives, Skukuza. See also Minutes of a meeting of the NPB, 22/23 September 1954, Item 13, File KNP 1/13, KNP archives, Skukuza; Minutes of the first meeting of the Steering Committee, 10 May 1955, file KNP K1/16, K1/19/1, KNP archives, Skukuza; Minutes of a meeting of the NPB, 23 March 1956, item 25F, annexure L, file KNP K1/16, K1/19/1, K1/20, KNP archives, Skukuza.

[39]Grant 40400672. Archives of the Mellon Foundation, New York, 2004–2009.

[40]R. Bell, 'A review of the programme of the Scientific Services Section, Kruger National Park. December 1994'. SANParks unpublished report.

One should not view conservation science as separate from the history of a country or from the international context, which have been the predominant shapers of ideas, and which have enabled opportunities and possibilities as well as set limitations. No formal research happens in a vacuum, it is not self-generating, and it is not solely influenced by powerful individuals. It is the interplay of many factors that has shaped conservation science. As this book has shown, conservation science is a malleable discipline that changes over time. It is not yet possible to discern the contours of future major change, although this is inevitable, but it is hoped that this book has illuminated and analysed some of what Thomas Mellon referred to as the 'under-current changing the main channel of the stream' and some of the 'deep seated causes', as well as explained many of the 'eddies and ripples upon the surface'.[41] It is also to be hoped that this book overturns some of the over-simplified versions of the past, and encouraged innovative thinking about what conservation science in South Africa can contribute to the country's future environmental well-being and sustainability.

[41] *Thomas Mellon and His Times*, 338, as quoted by David Cannadine in *Mellon: An American Life* (London: Allen Lane/Penguin, 2006), 583.

Selected Source List

Acocks, J.P.H. 'Veld types of South Africa'. *Memoirs of the Botanical Survey of South Africa* 28 (1953): 1–192.

Adams, C.C. *Guide to the Study of Animal Ecology* (New York, NY: Macmillan, 1913).
'Ecological conditions in national forests and in national parks'. *The Scientific Monthly* 20 (1925): 561–593.

Adams, W.M. *Against Extinction: The Story of Conservation* (London: Earthscan, 2004).

Adams, W.M., R. Aveling, D. Brockington, B. Dickson, J. Elliott, J. Hutton, D. Roe, B. Vira and W. Wolmer. 'Biodiversity conservation and the eradication of poverty'. *Science* 306, no. 5699 (2004): 1146–1149.

African Regional Scientific Conference, Johannesburg, 17–28 October 1949. *Vol. I, Proceedings and Resolutions*. G-PS 10461–1949; vol II. *Statements and Communications*. G-PS 10462–1949 (Pretoria: Government Printer, 1949).

Albright, H.M. 'Research in the national parks'. *The Scientific Monthly* 36 (1933): 483–501.

Ali, S.H. *Peace Parks: Conservation and Conflict Resolution* (Cambridge, MA: MIT Press, 2007).

Allen, R. 'Marine parks: The Cinderella of conservation'. *New Scientist* 67 (1975): 366–369.

American Committee for International Wild Life Protection. *The London Convention for the Protection of African Fauna and Flora*. Special Publication of the American Committee for International Wild Life Protection, No. 6 (Cambridge, MA: American Committee for International Wild Life Protection, 1935).

Anderson, D. and R. Grove, eds. *Conservation in Africa: People, Policies and Practice* (Cambridge: Cambridge University Press, 1987).

Andersson, J.A., M. de Garine-Wichatitsky, D.H.M. Cumming, V. Dzingirai and K.E. Giller, eds. *Transfrontier Conservation Areas: People Living on the Edge* (Abingdon: Routledge, 2013).

Anon. *Environmental Research Perspectives in South Africa*. South African National Scientific Programmes Report 66 (Pretoria: CSIR, 1982).
Environmental Research Perspectives in South Africa. South African National Scientific Programmes Report 84 (Pretoria: CSIR, 1984).
'American authority's impressions of Union's game reserves'. *Farmer's Weekly* 80, no. 7 (1951): 58.

Asibey, E.O.A. 'Wildlife as a source of protein in Africa south of the Sahara'. *Biological Conservation* 6 (1974): 32–39.

Asner, G.P., S.R. Levick, T. Kennedy-Bowdoin, *et al.* 'Large-scale impacts of herbivores on the structural diversity of African savannas'. *Proceedings of the National Academy of Sciences* 106 (2009): 4947–4952.

Attwood, C.G., J.M. Harris and A. Williams. 'International experience of marine protected areas and their relevance to South Africa'. *South African Journal of Marine Science* 18 (1997): 311–332.

Barber, L. *The Heyday of Natural History, 1820–1870* (London: Jonathan Cape, 1980).

Barnard, P.J. and K. van der Walt. 'Translocation of the Bontebok (*Damaliscus pygargus*) from Bredasdorp to Swellendam'. *Koedoe* 4 (1961): 105.

Barrett-Hamilton, G.E.H. *A History of British Mammals* (London: Gurney and Jackson, 1910).

Basalla, G. 'The spread of western science'. *Science* 156 (1967): 611–622.

Beatty, J. 'Ecology and evolutionary biology in the war and postwar years: Questions and comments'. *Journal of the History of Biology* 21 (1988): 245–263.

Behnke, R.H, I. Scoones and C. Kerven. *Range Ecology at Disequilibrium* (London: Overseas Development Institute, 1993).

Bell, R.H.V. 'The ecologist in Africa: His role for the next two decades'. *Bulletin of the Ecological Society of America* 66 (1985): 11–14.

    'Conservation with a human face: Conflict and reconciliation in African land use planning'. In *Conservation in Africa: People, Policies and Practice*, edited by D. Anderson and R. Grove, 79–101 (Cambridge: Cambridge University Press, 1987).

Bengis, R.G., R. Grant and V. de Vos. 'Wildlife diseases and veterinary controls: A savanna ecosystem perspective'. In *The Kruger Experience: Ecology and Management of Savanna Heterogeneity*, edited by J.T. du Toit, K.H. Rogers and H.C. Biggs, 349–369 (Washington, DC: Island Press, 2003).

Bennett, N. 'The Mammal Research Institute 1966–2006'. *Transactions of the Royal Society of South Africa* 63 (2008): 53–60.

Bews, J.W. 'The vegetation of Natal'. *Annals of the Natal Museum* 2 (1912): 253–331.

    'An oecological survey of the Midlands of Natal with special reference to the Pietermaritzburg district'. *Annals of the Natal Museum* 2 (1913): 485–545.

    'The plant ecology of the Drakensberg Range'. *Annals of the Natal Museum* 3 (1917): 511–566.

    'An account of the chief types of vegetation in South Africa, with notes on the plant succession'. *Journal of Ecology* 4 (1916): 129–159.

Bigalke, R. 'A biological survey of the Union'. *South African Journal of Science* 31 (1934): 396–404.

    A Guide to Some Common Animals of the Kruger National Park (Pretoria: Van Schaik, 1939).

    National Parks and their Functions, with Special Reference to South Africa. South African Biological Society pamphlet No. 10 (Pretoria: South African Biological Society, 1939).

    'Science and the conservation of wild life in South Africa'. *Journal of the South African Veterinary Medical Association* 21 (1950): 166–172.

'Wild life conservation in the Union of South Africa'. *Fauna and Flora* 1 (1950): 5–42.

'Science and nature conservation in Transvaal: A short historical account'. *Fauna and Flora* 27 (1976): 13–15.

Bigalke, R. and G. de Kock. 'The conservation and control of wild life in South Africa'. In *African Regional Scientific Conference, Johannesburg, 17–28 October, 1949. Vol. 2, Statements and Communications*, 211–219 (Pretoria: Government Printer, 1949).

Bigalke, R. and J. Skinner. 'The Zoological Survey: An historical perspective'. *Transactions of the Royal Society of South Africa* 57 (2002): 38.

Biggs, H. and P. Novellie. 'Science for biodiversity management'. In *South African National Parks: A Celebration*, edited by A. Hall-Martin and J. Carruthers, 67–84 (Johannesburg: Horst Klemm, 2003).

Biggs, H.C. 'Integration of science: Successes, challenges, and the future'. In *The Kruger Experience: Ecology and Management of Savanna Heterogeneity*, edited by J.T. du Toit, K.H. Rogers and H.C. Biggs, 469–487 (Washington, DC: Island Press, 2003).

'Promoting ecological research in national parks: A South African perspective'. *Ecological Applications* 14 (2004): 21–24.

Biggs, H.C., G.I.H. Kerley and T. Tshiguvho. 'A South African long-term ecological research network: A first for Africa?' *South African Journal of Science* 95 (1999): 6–7.

Biggs, H.C. and A.L.F. Potgieter. 'Overview of the fire management policy of the Kruger National Park'. *Koedoe* 42 (1999): 101–110.

Biggs, H.C. and K.H. Rogers. 'An adaptive system to link science, monitoring and management in practice'. In *The Kruger Experience: Ecology and Management of Savanna Heterogeneity*, edited by J.T. du Toit, K.H. Rogers and H.C. Biggs, 59–80 (Washington, DC: Island Press, 2003).

Bishop, K., N. Dudley, A. Phillips and S. Stolton. *Speaking a Common Language: The Uses and Performance of the IUCN System of Management Categories for Protected Areas* (Cardiff: Cardiff University, IUCN and UNEP, 2004).

Boardman, R. *International Organization and the Conservation of Nature* (London: Macmillan, 1981).

Bocking, S. *Ecologists and Environmental Politics: A History of Contemporary Ecology* (New Haven, CT: Yale University Press, 1997).

'Nature on the home front: British ecologists' advocacy for science and conservation'. *Environment and History* 18 (2012): 261–281.

Bond, W.J. and B.W. van Wilgen. *Fire and Plants* (New York, NY: Springer, 1996).

Braack, L.E.O. *Field Guide to Insects of the Kruger National Park* (Cape Town: Struik & National Parks Board, 1991).

Bramwell, A. *Ecology in the 20th Century: A History* (New Haven, CT: Yale University Press, 1989).

Braun-Blanquet J. *Plant Sociology; The Study of Plant Communities* (New York, NY: McGraw-Hill, 1932).

Breen, C.M., M. Dent, J. Jaganyi, *et al. The Kruger National Park Rivers Research Programme: Final Report.* Water Research Commission Report TT130/00 (Pretoria: Water Research Commission, 2000).

Brink, C. v.d. M. 'Trends and challenges for science in South Africa'. *Transactions of the Royal Society of South Africa* 43 (1978): 223–229.

Brockett, B.H., H.C. Biggs and B.W. van Wilgen. 'A patch mosaic burning system for conservation areas in southern African savannas'. *International Journal of Wildland Fire* 10 (2001): 69–183.

Brockington, D. *Fortress Conservation: The Preservation of the Mkomazi Game Reserve. Tanzania* (Oxford: James Currey, 2002).

Broekhuysen, G.J., M.H. Broekhuysen, J.E. Martin, R. Martin and H.K. Morgan. 'Observations on the bird life of the Kalahari Gemsbok National Park'. *Koedoe* 11 (1968): 145–160.

Brooks, S. 'National parks for Natal? Zululand's game reserves and the shaping of conservation management policy in Natal 1920s to 1940s'. *Journal of Natal and Zulu History* 22 (2004): 73–108.

Brown, A.C., ed. *A History of Scientific Endeavour in South Africa* (Cape Town: Royal Society of South Africa, 1977).

Bruton, M.N. and S.V. Merron. *Alien and Translocated Aquatic Animals in Southern Africa: A General Introduction, Checklist and Bibliography.* South African National Scientific Programmes Report 113 (Pretoria: CSIR, 1985).

Bryden, H.B. and V. de Vos. 'A scientific bibliography on the national parks of South Africa'. In supplement, *Koedoe* (1994): 1–3. doi: 10.4102/koedoe.v1i1.343.

Brynard, A.M. 'The influence of veld burning on the vegetation and game of the Kruger National Park'. In *Ecological Studies in Southern Africa*, edited by D.H.S. Davis, 371–393 (The Hague: Junk, 1964).

'Game control in national parks'. *African Wildlife* 21, no. 2 (1967): 93–99.

'Controlled burning in the Kruger National Park: History and development of a veld burning policy'. In *Proceedings of the Annual Tall Timbers Fire Ecology Conference, April 22–23, 1971, Tallahassee, Florida*, 219–231 (Tallahassee, FL: Tall Timbers Research Station, 1972).

'Die nasionale parke van die Republiek van Suid-Afrika: Die verlede en die hede'. In 'Proceedings of a symposium on the state of nature conservation in southern Africa, Kruger National Park, 1976', edited by G. de Graaff and P.T. van der Walt, supplement, *Koedoe* (1977): 24–37.

Cadotte, M.W., S.M. McMahon and T. Fukami, eds. *Conceptual Ecology and Invasion Biology* (Berlin: Springer Verlag, 2006).

Cahalane, V.H., ed. *National Parks: A World Need* (New York, NY: American Committee for International Wildlife Protection, 1962).

Caldwell, K. 'Game preservation: Its aims and objects'. *Journal for the Society of the Preservation of the Fauna of the Empire* 4 (1924): 45–56.

Callicott, J.B. 'Whither conservation ethics?' *Conservation Biology* 4 (1990): 15–20.

Campbell, C.E., ed. *A Century of Parks Canada, 1911–2011* (Calgary: University of Calgary Press, 2011).

Cannadine, D. *Mellon: An American Life* (London: Allen Lane/Penguin, 2006).

Carr, E. *Mission 66: Modernism and the National Park Dilemma* (Amherst, MA: University of Massachusetts Press, 2007).

Carruthers, E.J. 'The Pongola Game Reserve: An eco-political study'. *Koedoe* 28 (1985): 1–16.

Carruthers, J. 'The Dongola Wild Life Sanctuary: "Psychological blunder, economic folly and political monstrosity" or "More valuable than rubies and gold?"'. *Kleio* 24 (1992): 82–100.

'"Police boys and poachers": Africans, wildlife protection and national parks, the Transvaal 1902 to 1950'. *Koedoe* 36 (1993): 11–22.

Game Protection in the Transvaal 1846 to 1926 (Pretoria: Archives Yearbook for South African History, 1995).

The Kruger National Park: A Social and Political History (Pietermaritzburg: University of Natal Press, 1995).

'Lessons from South Africa: War and wildlife protection in the southern Sudan, 1917–1921'. *Environment and History* 3 (1997): 299–322.

Wildlife and Warfare: The Life of James Stevenson-Hamilton (Pietermaritzburg: University of Natal Press, 2001).

'Past and future landscape ideology: The Kalahari Gemsbok National Park'. In *Social History and African Environments*, edited by W. Beinart and J. McGregor, 255–266 (Oxford: James Currey, 2003).

'Mapungubwe: An historical and contemporary analysis of a World Heritage Cultural Landscape'. *Koedoe* 41 (2006): 1–14.

'Influences on wildlife management and conservation biology in South Africa c.1900–c.1940'. *South African Historical Journal* 58 (2007): 65–90.

'"South Africa: A world in one country": Land restitution in national parks and protected areas'. *Conservation and Society* 5 (2007): 292–306.

'Conservation and wildlife management in South African national parks 1930s–1960s'. *Journal of the History of Biology* 41 (2008): 203–236.

'Scientists in society: A history of the Royal Society of South Africa'. *Transactions of the Royal Society of South Africa* 63 (2008): 1–30.

'"Wilding the farm or farming the wild": The evolution of scientific game ranching in South Africa from the 1960s to the present'. *Transactions of the Royal Society of South Africa* 63, no. 2 (2008): 60–81.

'"Full of rubberneck waggons and tourists": The development of tourism in South Africa's national parks and protected areas'. In *Tourism and National Parks: International Perspectives on Development, History and Change*, edited by W. Frost and C.M. Hall, 211–224 (London: Routledge, 2009).

'Romance, reverence, research, rights: Writing about elephant hunting and management in southern Africa, c.1830s to 2008'. *Koedoe* 52 (2010): 1–6.

'G. Evelyn Hutchinson in South Africa, 1926 to 1928: "An immense part in my intellectual development"'. *Transactions of the Royal Society of South Africa* 66, no. 2 (2011): 87–104.

'Pilanesberg National Park, North West Province, South Africa: Uniting economic development with ecological design – a history, 1960s to 1984'. *Koedoe* 53 (2011): 10 pages. doi: 10.4102/koedoe.v53i1.1028.

'The Royal Natal National Park, Kwazulu-Natal: Mountaineering, tourism and nature conservation in South Africa's first national park c.1896 to c.1947'. *Environment and History* 19 (2013): 459–485.

Carruthers, J., A. Boshoff, R. Slotow, H. Biggs, G. Avery and W. Matthews. 'The elephant in South Africa: History and distribution'. In *Scientific Assessment of*

Elephant Management in South Africa, edited by R.J. Scholes and K.G. Mennell, 23–83 (Johannesburg: Wits University Press, 2008).

Carson, R. *Silent Spring* (New York, NY: Houghton Mifflin, 1962).

Castley, G., M. Knight and J. Gordon. 'Making conservation work: Innovative approaches to meeting biodiversity conservation and socio-economic objectives (an example from the Addo Elephant National Park, South Africa)'. In *Evolution and Innovation in Wildlife Conservation: Parks and Game Ranches to Transfrontier Conservation Areas*, edited by H. Suich, B. Child and A. Spenceley, 308–323 (London: Earthscan, 2009).

Castley, G., C. Patton and H. Magome. 'Making "conventional" parks relevant to all of society'. In *Evolution and Innovation in Wildlife Conservation: Parks and Game Ranches to Transfrontier Conservation Areas*, edited by H. Suich, B. Child and A. Spenceley, 393–407 (London: Earthscan, 2009).

Caughley, G. 'Directions in conservation biology'. *Journal of Animal Ecology* 63 (1994): 215–244.

Caughley, G. and A.R.E. Sinclair. *Wildlife Ecology and Management* (Oxford: Blackwell, 1994).

Chalmers Mitchell, P. *The Childhood of Animals* (London: Heinemann, 1912).

Centenary History of the Zoological Society of London (London: Zoological Society of London, 1929).

Chase, A. *Playing God in Yellowstone: The Destruction of America's First National Park* (San Diego, CA: Harcourt Brace, 1987).

Child, B. 'Innovations in park management'. In *Parks in Transition: Biodiversity, Development and the Bottom Line*, edited by B. Child, 165–188 (London: Earthscan, 2005).

Child, G. 'Growth of modern nature conservation in southern Africa'. In *Parks in Transition: Biodiversity, Development and the Bottom Line*, edited by B. Child, 7–28 (London: Earthscan, 2005).

Cioc, M. *The Game of Conservation: International Treaties to Protect the World's Migratory Animals* (Athens, OH: Ohio University Press, 2009).

Clements, F.E. *Plant Succession: An Analysis of the Development of Vegetation* (Washington, DC: Carnegie Institution of Washington, 1916).

Clements, F.E. and V.C. Shelford. *Bio-ecology* (New York, NY: John Wiley, 1939).

Cock, J. and E. Koch, eds. *Going Green: People, Politics and the Environment in South Africa* (Cape Town: Oxford University Press, 1991).

Codd, L.E.W. *Trees and Shrubs of the Kruger National Park*. Department of Agriculture Division of Botany and Plant Pathology. Botanical Survey Memoir No. 26 (Pretoria: Government Printer, 1951).

Coleman, D.C. *Big Ecology* (Berkeley, CA: University of California Press, 2010).

Courtenay-Latimer, M. and G.G. Smith. *The Flowering Plants of the Tsitsikama Forest and Coastal National Park* (Pretoria: National Parks Board, 1967).

Cowling, R.M., D.M. Richardson and S.M. Pierce, eds. *Vegetation of Southern Africa* (Cambridge: Cambridge University Press, 1997).

Cowling, R.M. and P.W. Roux, eds. *The Karoo Biome: A Preliminary Synthesis. Part 2: Vegetation and History*. South African National Scientific Programmes Report 142 (Pretoria: CSIR, 1987).

Cromsigt, J.P.G.M., S. Archibald and N. Owen-Smith, eds. *Conserving Africa's Mega-Diversity in the Anthropocene: the Hluhluwe-iMfolozi Park Story* (Cambridge: Cambridge University Press, 2016).

Cumming, G.S. 'The relevance and resilience of protected areas in the Anthropocene'. *Anthropocene* 108 (2016). http://dx.doi.org/10.1016/j.ancene.2016.03.003.

Curson, H.H. and J.M. Hugo. 'Preservation of game in South Africa'. *South African Journal of Science* 21 (1924): 400–424.

Daily, G.C., ed. *Nature's Services* (Washington, DC: Island Press, 1997).

Daitz, D. and B. Myrdal. 'Table Mountain National Park'. In *Evolution and Innovation in Wildlife Conservation: Parks and Game Ranches to Transfrontier Conservation Areas*, edited by H. Suich, B. Child and A. Spenceley, 325–339 (London: Earthscan, 2009).

Darling, F. Fraser. *Wildlife in an African Territory* (Oxford: Oxford University Press, 1960).

Dasmann, R. *Environmental Conservation* (New York, NY: Wiley, 1959).

Dasmann, R.F. *African Game Ranching* (Oxford and New York: Pergamon and Macmillan, 1964).

    Wildlife Biology (New York, NY: John Wiley, 1964).

    'Towards a system for classifying natural regions of the world and their representation by national parks and reserves'. *Biological Conservation* 2 (1972): 247–255.

    A System for Defining and Classifying Natural Regions for Purposes of Conservation. IUCN Occasional Paper No. 7 (Morges: IUCN, 1973).

Davis, D.H.S., ed. *Ecological Studies in Southern Africa* (The Hague: Junk, 1964).

Davis, M.A. 'Invasion biology 1958–2005: The pursuit of science and conservation'. In *Conceptual Ecology and Invasion Biology*, edited by M.W. Cadotte, S.M. McMahon and T. Fukami, 35–64 (Berlin: Springer Verlag, 2006).

    Invasion Biology (Oxford: Oxford University Press, 2009).

Dawes, B. *A Hundred Years of Biology* (London: Duckworth, 1952).

De Graaff, G. *Animals of the Kruger National Park* (Cape Town: Struik, 1987).

De Graaff, G., G.A. Robinson, P.T. van der Walt, B.R. Bryden and E.A. van der Hoven. *The Karoo National Park, Beaufort West* (Pretoria: National Parks Board, 1979).

De Graaff, G. and P.T. van der Walt, eds. 'Proceedings of a symposium on the state of nature conservation in southern Africa, Kruger National Park, 1976', supplement, *Koedoe* (1977).

De Graaff, G. and D.J. van Rensburg, eds. 'Proceedings of a symposium on the Kalahari ecosystem, Pretoria 11–12 October 1983', supplement, *Koedoe* (1984).

De Villiers, B. *Land Claims and National Parks: The Makuleke Experience* (Pretoria: Human Sciences Research Council, 1999).

De Villiers, J.S. 'A report on the bird life of the Kalahari Gemsbok National Park'. *Koedoe* 1 (1958): 143–161.

De Vos V., R.C. Bengis and H.J. Coetzee. 'Population control of large mammals in the Kruger National Park'. In *Management of Large Mammals in African Conservation Areas. Proceedings of a Symposium Held in Pretoria, South Africa, 29–30 April 1982*, edited by R.N. Owen-Smith, 213–231 (Pretoria: HAUM, 1983).

Dennis, J.G. 'Building a science program for the national park system'. *The George Wright Forum* 4, no. 3 (1985): 11–20.

Diamond, J.M. 'The island dilemma: Lessons of modern biogeographic studies for the design of natural reserves'. *Biological Conservation* 7 (1975): 129–146.

Dilsaver, L.M. *America's National Park System: The Critical Documents* (Lanham, MD: Rowman and Littlefield, 1994).

Dommisse, E. *Anton Rupert: A Biography* (Cape Town: Tafelberg, 2009).

Du Toit, J.T., K.H. Rogers and H.C. Biggs, eds. *The Kruger Experience: Ecology and Management of Savanna Heterogeneity* (Washington, DC: Island Press, 2003).

Dubow, S. 'A commonwealth of science: The British Association in South Africa, 1905 and 1929'. In *Science and Society in Southern Africa*, edited by S. Dubow, 66–99 (Manchester: Manchester University Press, 2000).

    A Commonwealth of Knowledge: Science, Sensibility, and White South Africa, 1820–2000 (Oxford: Oxford University Press, 2006).

Dudley, N., ed. *Guidelines for Applying Protected Area Management Categories* (Gland: IUCN, 2008).

Dudley, N. and S. Stolton. *Defining Protected Areas: An International Conference in Almeria, Spain* (Gland: IUCN, 2008).

Duncan, D. 'George Melendez Wright and the national park idea'. *The George Wright Forum* 26, no. 1 (2009): 4–13.

Dunlap, T.R. 'Values for varmints: Predator control and environmental ideas, 1920–1939'. *Pacific Historical Review* 53, no. 2 (1984): 141–161.

    Saving America's Wildlife: Ecology and the American Mind, 1850–1990 (Princeton, NJ: Princeton University Press, 1991).

Eckhardt, H.C., B.W. van Wilgen and H.C. Biggs. 'Trends in woody vegetation cover in the Kruger National Park, South Africa, between 1940 and 1998'. *African Journal of Ecology* 38 (2000): 108–115.

Edwards, D. 'Survey to determine the adequacy of existing conserved areas in relation to vegetation types'. *Koedoe* 17 (1974): 2–37.

Egerton, F.N. 'Changing concepts of the balance of nature'. *The Quarterly Review of Biology* 48, no. 2 (1973): 322–350.

    'Essay review: A worldwide inventory of the history of ecology'. *Journal of the History of Biology* 16, no. 1 (1983): 171–175.

    'The history of ecology: Achievements and opportunities, part 1'. *Journal of the History of Biology* 16, no. 2 (1983): 259–311.

    'The history of ecology: Achievements and opportunities, part 2'. *Journal of the History of Biology* 18, no. 1 (1985): 103–143.

Egerton, F.N. and R.P. McIntosh, eds. *History of American Ecology* (New York, NY: Arno Press, 1977).

Ehrenfeld, D.W. *Biological Conservation* (New York, NY: Holt, Rinehart and Winston, 1970).

    'Conservation biology: Its origin and definition'. *Science* 255 (1992): 1625–1626.

Elliott, H. *Second World Conference on National Parks* (Morges: IUCN, 1974).

Eloff, F.C. 'Theoretiese aspekte van ekologie en die toepassing daarvan in Suidelike Afrika'. *Tydskrif vir Wetenskap en Kuns* 17 (1957): 105–139.

    'The Kalahari ecosystem'. In *Proceedings of a Symposium on the Kalahari Ecosystem, Pretoria 11–12 October 1983*, edited by G. de Graaff and D.J. van Rensburg, supplement, *Koedoe* (1984): 11–20.

Eloff, J.F. and J.B. de Vaal. 'Makahane'. *Koedoe* 8 (1965): 68–74.

Elton, C. *Animal Ecology* (London: Sidgwick & Jackson, 1927).

    The Ecology of Invasions by Animals and Plants (London: Methuen, 1958).

Everhart, W.C. *The National Park Service* (Boulder, CO: Westview Press, 1983).

Farber, P.L. *Finding Order in Nature: The Naturalist Tradition from Linnaeus to E.O. Wilson* (Baltimore, MD: Johns Hopkins University Press, 2000).

Farnham, T. *Saving Nature's Legacy: The Origins of the Idea of Biological Diversity* (New Haven, CT: Yale University Press, 2007).

Ferrar, A.A., ed. *Guidelines for the Management of Large Mammals in African Conservation Areas*. South African Scientific Programmes Report 69 (Pretoria: CSIR, 1983).

Ferrar, A.A. and F.J. Kruger, comp. *South African Programme for the SCOPE Project on the Ecology of Biological Invasions*. South African National Scientific Programmes Report 72 (Pretoria: CSIR, 1983).

Ferrar, A.A., J.H. O'Keeffe and B.R. Davies. *The Rivers Research Programme*. South African National Scientific Programmes Report 146 (Pretoria: CSIR, 1988).

Festa-Bianchet, M. and Apollonio, M., eds. *Animal Behavior and Wildlife Conservation* (Washington, DC: Island Press, 2003).

Fitter, R. and P. Scott. *The Penitent Butchers: The Fauna Preservation Society, 1903–1978* (London: Fauna Preservation Society, 1978).

Flint, W. and J.D.F. Gilchrist, eds. *Science in South Africa: A Handbook and Review* (Cape Town: Maskew Miller, 1905).

Forsyth, G.G. and B.W. van Wilgen. 'The recent fire history of the Table Mountain National Park, and implications for fire management'. *Koedoe* 50 (2008): 3–9.

Fourie, J. 'Comments on national parks and future relations with neighbouring communities'. *Koedoe* 37 (1996): 123–136.

Foxcroft, L. 'Developing thresholds of potential concern for invasive alien species: Hypotheses and concepts'. *Koedoe* 51 (2009): 11–16.

Foxcroft, L.C., P. Pyšek, D.M. Richardson and P. Genovesi, eds. *Plant Invasions in Protected Areas: Patterns, Problems and Challenges* (Dordrecht: Springer, 2013).

Frankel, O.H. and M.E. Soulé. *Conservation and Evolution* (Cambridge: Cambridge University Press, 1981).

Freitag, S., 'The Kruger National Park and the analysis of historic data sets: Where are we going?' *South African Journal of Science* 94 (1998): 146.

Freitag, S., H. Biggs and C. Breen. 'The spread and maturation of strategic adaptive management within and beyond South African national parks'. *Ecology and Society* 19, no. 3 (2014). http://dx.doi.org/19.5751/ES-06338-190325.

Freitag-Ronaldson, S., M.A. McGeoch and M. Joubert, eds. *Biodiversity, Science and SANParks: Conservation in Times of Change* (Pretoria: SANParks Scientific Services, 2010).

Frost, W. and C.M. Hall, eds. *Tourism and National Parks: International Perspectives on Development, Histories and Change* (Abingdon: Routledge, 2009).

Fuggle, R.F. and M.A. Rabie. *Environmental Concerns in South Africa: Technical and Legal Perspectives* (Cape Town: Juta, 1983).

Gaylard, A. 'Exploring management of biodiversity in the Kruger National Park: Elephants as agents of change'. *Rhino and Elephant Journal* 12 (1998): 16–19.

Gaylard, A., N. Owen-Smith and J.V. Redfern. 'Surface water availability: Implications for heterogeneity and ecosystem processes'. In *The Kruger Experience: Ecology and Management of Savanna Heterogeneity*, edited by J.T. du Toit, R.H. Rogers and H.C. Biggs, 171–199 (Washington, DC: Island Press, 2003).

Gertenbach, W.P.D. 'Landscapes of the Kruger National Park'. *Koedoe* 26 (1983): 9–121.

Gillson, L. and K.I. Duffin. 'Thresholds of potential concern as benchmarks in the management of African savannahs'. *Philosophical Transactions of the Royal Society of London Series B – Biological Sciences* 362 (2007): 309–319.

Gissibl, B., S. Höhler and P. Kupper, eds. *Civilizing Nature: National Parks in Global and Historical Perspective* (New York, NY: Berghahn Books, 2012).

Glazewski, J. *Environmental Law in South Africa* (Durban: Butterworths, 2000).

Golley, F.B. *A History of the Ecosystem Concept in Ecology: More than a Sum of the Parts* (New Haven, CT: Yale University Press, 1993).

Götmark, F., K. Kirby and M.B. Usher. 'Strict reserves, IUCN classification, and the use of reserves for scientific research: A comment on Schultze *et al.* (2014)'. *Biodiversity and Conservation* 24 (2015): 3621–3625.

Govender, N., W.S.W. Trollope and B.W. van Wilgen. 'The effect of fire season, fire frequency, rainfall and management on fire intensity in savanna vegetation in South Africa'. *Journal of Applied Ecology* 43 (2006): 748–758.

Greyling, T. and B.J. Huntley, eds. *Directory of Southern African Conservation Areas*. South African National Scientific Programmes Report 98 (Pretoria: CSIR, 1984).

Grumbine, R.E. 'What is ecosystem management?' *Conservation Biology* 8 (1994): 27–38.

Gunderson, L.H. and C.S. Holling, eds. *Panarchy: Understanding Transformations in Human and Natural Systems* (Washington, DC: Island Press, 2002).

Haagner, A.K. 'Game and bird protection in South Africa: A short comparison with some other countries'. *South African Journal of Science* 12, no. 11 (1916): 519–529.

Hagen, J.B. 'Ecologists and taxonomists: Divergent traditions in twentieth-century plant geography'. *Journal of the History of Biology* 19, no. 2 (1986): 197–214.

'Research perspectives and the anomalous status of modern ecology'. *Biology and Philosophy* 4 (1989): 433–455.

An Entangled Bank: The Origins of Ecosystem Ecology (New Brunswick, NJ: Rutgers University Press, 1992).

'Environmentalism and the science of conservation biology'. *Conservation Biology* 9 (1995): 975–976.

'Teaching ecology during the environmental age, 1965–1980'. *Environmental History* 13 (2008): 704–723.

Hailey, Lord. *An African Survey: A Study of the Problems Arising in Africa South of the Sahara* (London: Oxford University Press, 1938).

Hall, A.V., ed. *Conservation of Threatened Natural Habitats*. South African National Scientific Programmes Report 92 (Pretoria: CSIR, 1984).

Hall-Martin, A. and J. Carruthers, eds. *South African National Parks: A Celebration* (Johannesburg: Horst Klemm, 2003).

Hall-Martin, A.J. 'Distribution and status of the African elephant *Loxodonta africana* in South Africa, 1652–1992'. *Koedoe* 35 (1992): 65–88.

Halvorson, W.L. and G.E. Davis, eds. *Science and Ecosystem Management in the National Parks* (Tucson, AZ: University of Arizona Press, 1996).

Hanski, I. *Metapopulation Ecology* (Oxford: Oxford University Press, 1999).

Harrison, A.-L. 'Who's who in conservation biology: An authorship analysis'. *Conservation Biology* 20 (2006): 652–657.

Hey, D. 'The history and status of nature conservation in South Africa'. In *A History of Scientific Endeavour in South Africa*, edited by A.C. Brown, 132–163 (Cape Town: Royal Society of South Africa, 1977).

A Nature Conservationist Looks Back (Jonkershoek: Cape Nature Conservation, 1995).

Higgins, J. and L. Green. 'The necessary conjunction: Science and the humanities'. *Scrutiny2* 12, no. 1 (2007): 5–18.

Higgins S.I., W.J. Bond, E.C. February, *et al.* 'Effects of four decades of fire manipulation on woody vegetation structure in savanna'. *Ecology* 88, no. 5 (2007): 1119–1125.

Hingston, R.W.G. 'Proposed national parks for Africa'. *The Geographical Journal* 97, no. 5 (1931): 401–428.

The Meaning of Animal Colour and Adornment (London: Edward Arnold, 1933).

Hockings, M., J. Ervin and G. Vincent. 'Assessing the management of protected areas: The work of the World Parks Congress before and after Durban'. *Journal of International Wildlife Law and Policy* 7 (2004): 32–42.

Hockings, M., S. Stolton, N. Dudley, F. Leverington and J. Courrau. *Evaluating Effectiveness: A Framework for Assessing the Management of Protected Areas* (Gland: IUCN, 2006).

Hoffman, M.T. 'Major P.J. Pretorius and the decimation of the Addo elephant herd in 1919–1920: Important reassessments'. *Koedoe* 36, no. 2 (1993): 23–44.

Holdgate, M.W. *The Green Web: A Union for World Conservation* (London: Earthscan, 1999).

Holling, C.S. 'Resilience and stability of ecological systems'. *Annual Review of Ecology and Systematics* 4 (1973): 1–23.

ed. *Adaptive Environmental Assessment and Management* (New York, NY: Wiley, 1978).

Holling, C.S. and G.K. Meffe. 'Command and control and the pathology of natural resource management'. *Conservation Biology* 10 (1996): 328–337.

Hornaday, W.T. *Wild Life Conservation in Theory and Practice* (New Haven, CT: Yale University Press, 1914).

Hornaday, W.T. and A.K. Haagner. *The Vanishing Game of South Africa: A Warning and an Appeal* (New York, NY: Permanent Wild Life Protection Fund, 1922).

Houston, D.B. 'Ecosystems in national parks'. *Science* 172 (1971): 648–651.

Howkins, A., J. Orsi and M. Fiege, eds. *National Parks Beyond the Nation* (Norman, OK: University of Oklahoma Press, 2016).

Huntley, B.J. 'Terrestrial ecology in South Africa'. *South African Journal of Science* 73 (1977): 366–370.

'Ecosystem conservation in southern Africa'. In *Biogeography and Ecology of Southern Africa*, Vol. 2, edited by M.J.A. Werger, 1333–1384 (The Hague: Junk, 1978).

'Ten years of cooperative ecological research in South Africa'. *South African Journal of Science* 83 (1987): 72–79.

ed. *Biotic Diversity in Southern Africa: Concepts and Conservation* (Cape Town: Oxford University Press, 1989).

'Developing the capacity to manage protected areas: South African experience'. In *Strategic Innovations in Biodiversity Conservation: The South African Experience*, edited by G.I. Cowan, J. Yawitch and M. Swift, 31–38 (Pretoria: Department of Environmental Affairs & Tourism, 2003).

Huntley, B.J. and S. Ellis. 'Conservation status of ecosystems in southern Africa'. In *Proceedings of the 21st Working Session of the Commission for National Parks and Protected Areas*, 13–22 (Gland: IUCN, 1984).

Huntley, B.J., W.R. Siegfried and C. Sunter. *South African Environments into the 21st Century* (Cape Town: Human & Rousseau Tafelberg, 1989).

Huntley, B.J. and B.H. Walker, eds. *Ecology of Tropical Savannas* (Berlin: Springer, 1982).

Hutchinson, G.E. 'What is science for?' *American Scientist* 71 (1983): 639–644.

Huxley, J. *Wild Lives of Africa* (London: Collins, 1963).

International Union for the Conservation of Nature. *United Nations List of National Parks and Equivalent Reserves*. IUCN Publications No. 33 (Morges: IUCN, 1975).

    United Nations List of National Parks and Equivalent Reserves (Gland: IUCN Commission on National Parks and Protected Areas, 1980).

    World Conservation Strategy: Living Resource Conservation for Sustainable Development (Gland: IUCN-UNEP-WWF, 1980).

    Guidelines for Protected Area Management Categories (Gland and Cambridge: IUCN, 1994).

    Guide to the WPC Recommendations Procedures Vth World Parks Congress (Gland: IUCN, 2003).

    An Introduction to the African Convention on the Conservation of Nature and Natural Resources. IUCN Environmental Policy and Law Paper No. 56 (Gland: IUCN, 2004).

International Union for the Conservation of Nature (1948–2012). www.iucnworldconservationcongress.org/about/congress_history/congress-archives/ (accessed 10 December 2015).

International Union for the Conservation of Nature, Committee on Criteria and Nomenclature Commission on National Parks and Protected Areas. *Categories, Objectives and Criteria for Protected Areas: A Final Report* (Morges: IUCN, 1978).

International Union for the Protection of Nature. *The Position of Nature Protection throughout the World in 1950* (Brussels: IUPN, 1951).

    Proceedings of the Third International Conference: Protection of the Fauna and Flora of Africa, 1953 (Bukavu, Belgian Congo: IUCN, 1953).

Janse, A.J.T. 'A short history of the South African Biological Society'. *South African Biological Society Pamphlet* 10 (Pretoria: South African Biological Society, 1939).

Jardine, N., J.A. Secord and E. Spary, eds. *Cultures of Natural History* (Cambridge: Cambridge University Press, 1996).

Jewell, P.A. and S. Holt, eds. *Problems in Management of Locally Abundant Wild Mammals: A Workshop to Examine the Need for and Alternatives to Culling of Wild Animals, 29 September–3 October 1980, Cape Cod, USA* (New York, NY: Academic Press, 1981).

Jones, K.R. and J. Wills. *The Invention of the Park: Recreational Landscapes from the Garden of Eden to Disney's Magic Kingdom* (Cambridge: Polity, 2005).

Joubert, S.C.J. 'Management and research in relation to ecosystems of the Kruger National Park'. *Koedoe* 29 (1986): 157–163.

    'The Kruger National Park: An introduction'. *Koedoe* 29 (1986): 1–11.

    The Kruger National Park: A History. 3 vols (Johannesburg: High Branching, 2012).

Kareiva, P. and M. Marvier. 'What is conservation science?' *Bioscience* 62 (2012): 962–969.

Keller, D.R. and F.B. Golley. *The Philosophy of Ecology from Science to Synthesis* (Athens, GA: University of Georgia Press, 2000).

Kerley, G.I.H., S. Wilson and A. Massey. *Elephant Conservation and Management in the Eastern Cape*. Terrestrial Ecology Research Unit Report No. 35 (Port Elizabeth: Terrestrial Ecology Research Unit, University of Port Elizabeth, 2006).

Kingsford, R.T. and H.C. Biggs. *Strategic Adaptive Management Guidelines for Effective Conservation of Freshwater Ecosystems in and Around Protected Areas of the World* (Sydney: IUCN Freshwater Taskforce, Australian Wetlands and Rivers Centre, 2012).

Kingsland, S.E. *Modeling Nature: Episodes in the History of Population Ecology* (Chicago, IL: University of Chicago Press, 1985).

The Evolution of American Ecology 1890–2000 (Baltimore, MD: Johns Hopkins University Press, 2005).

Kingwill, D.G. *The CSIR: The First 40 Years* (Pretoria: CSIR, 1990).

Klopfer, P.H. and J.P. Hailman. *An Introduction to Animal Behavior: Ethology's First Century* (Englewood Cliffs, NJ: Prentice-Hall, 1967).

Kloppers, J.J. and H. Bornman. *A Dictionary of Kruger National Park Place Names* (Barberton: S.A. Country Life, 2005).

Kloppers, J. and the late G. van Son. *The Butterflies of the Kruger National Park* (Pretoria: National Parks Board, 1978).

Knight, M. and G. Castley. 'Conservation management'. In *South African National Parks: A Celebration*, edited by A. Hall-Martin and J. Carruthers, 98–100 (Johannesburg: Horst Klemm, 2003).

Knobel, R. 'The I.U.C.N'. *South African Biological Society Pamphlet* 18 (Pretoria: South African Biological Society, 1956).

'The economic and cultural values of South African National Parks'. In *Voices of the Wilderness*, edited by I. Player, 230–234 (Johannesburg: Jonathan Ball, 1979).

Kohler, R.E. *Landscapes and Labscapes: Exploring the Lab–Field Border in Biology* (Chicago, IL: University of Chicago Press, 2002).

Kraaij, T. 'Changing the fire management regime in the renosterveld and lowland fynbos of the Bontebok National Park'. *South African Journal of Botany* 76 (2010): 550–557.

Kuhn, T.S. *The Structure of Scientific Revolutions* (Chicago, IL: University of Chicago Press, 1970).

Kumleben, M.E., S.S. Sangweni and J.A. Ledger. *Board of Investigation into the Institutional Arrangements for Nature Conservation in South Africa: Report October 1998* (Pretoria: Government of South Africa, 1998).

Kupper, P. *Creating Wilderness: A Transnational History of the Swiss National Park* (Oxford: Berghahn Books, 2014).

Küsel, M.M. 'A preliminary report on settlement layout and gold melting at Thula Mela, a Late Iron Age site in the Kruger National Park'. *Koedoe* 35 (1992): 55–64.

Labuschagne, R.J. *The Kruger Park and Other National Parks* (Johannesburg: Da Gama, n.d.).

Labuschagne, R.J., comp. *60 Years Kruger Park* (Pretoria: National Parks Board, 1958).

Labuschagne, R.J. and N.J. van der Merwe. *Soogdiere van die Krugerwildtuin en ander Nasionale Parke/Mammals of the Kruger and Other National Parks* (Pretoria: National Parks Board, n.d.).

Landman, M.G., G.I.H. Kerley and D.S. Schoeman. 'Relevance of elephant herbivory as a threat to important plants in the Addo Elephant National Park, South Africa'. *Journal of Zoology* 274 (2008): 51–58.

Lang, H. 'Game reserves and wild life protection'. In *South Africa and Science: A Handbook Prepared under the Auspices of the South African Association for the Advancement of Science for the Meeting of the British Association in Capetown and Johannesburg, South Africa, 1929*, edited by H.J. Crocker and J. McCrae, 241–250 (Johannesburg: South African Association for the Advancement of Science, 1929).

Larson, B. *Metaphors for Environmental Sustainability: Redefining Our Relationship with Nature* (New Haven, CT: Yale University Press, 2011).

Latour, B. *Science in Action: How to Follow Scientists and Engineers through Society* (Cambridge, MA: Harvard University Press, 1987).

Lausche, B.J. *Weaving a Web of Environmental Law* (Berlin: IUCN Environmental Law Programme, 2008).

Leopold, A. *Game Management* (Madison, WI: University of Wisconsin Press, 1986).

Levick, S.R., G.P. Asner, T. Kennedy-Bowdoin and D.E. Knapp. 'The relative influence of fire and herbivory on savanna three-dimensional vegetation structure'. *Biological Conservation* 142 (2009): 1693–1700.

Lindeman, E.C. 'Ecology: An instrument for the integration of science and philosophy'. *Ecological Monographs* 10, no. 3 (1940): 367–372.

Lindenmayer, D. and M. Burgman. *Practical Conservation Biology* (Melbourne: CSIRO Publishing, 2005).

Louw, G.N. 'The biological sciences in South Africa: Present state and future trends'. *Transactions of the Royal Society of South Africa* 43 (1978): 261–265.

Lubchenco, J. 'Entering the century of the environment: A new social contract for science'. *Science* 279 (1998): 491–497.

Maberly, C.T. Astley. *What Buck is That? A Guide to the Antelope and Other More Notable Animals of the Kruger National Park* (Bloemfontein: A.C. White, 1951).

Mabunda, D., D.J. Pienaar and J. Verhoef. 'The Kruger National Park: A century of management and research'. In *The Kruger Experience: Ecology and Management of Savanna Heterogeneity*, edited by J.T. du Toit, K.H. Rogers and H.C. Biggs, 3–21 (Washington, DC: Island Press, 2003).

MacArthur, R.H. and E.O. Wilson. *The Theory of Island Biogeography* (Princeton, NJ: Princeton University Press, 1967).

Macdonald, I.A.W. 'The history, impacts and control of introduced species in the Kruger National Park, South Africa'. *Transactions of the Royal Society of South Africa* 46, no. 4 (1988): 251–276.

Macdonald, I.A.W., D.L. Clark and H.C. Taylor. 'The history and effects of alien plant control in the Cape of Good Hope Nature Reserve, 1941–1987'. *South African Journal of Botany* 55 (1989): 56–75.

Macdonald, I.A.W., F.J. Kruger and A.A. Ferrar, eds. *The Ecology and Management of Biological Invasions in Southern Africa* (Cape Town: Oxford University Press, 1986).

Marshall, P. *Nature's Web: An Exploration of Ecological Thinking* (London: Simon & Schuster, 1992).

Masubelele, M.L., L. Foxcroft and S.J. Milton. 'Alien plant species list and distribution for Camdeboo National Park, Eastern Cape Province, South Africa'. *Koedoe* 51 (2009): 80–89.

Mavhunga, C. and M. Spierenburg. 'Transfrontier talk, cordon politics: The early history of the Great Limpopo Transfrontier Park in southern Africa, 1925–1940'. *Journal of Southern African Studies* 35, no. 3 (2009): 715–735.

McIntosh, R.P. *The Background of Ecology: Concept and Theory* (Cambridge: Cambridge University Press, 1985).

Meadows, D.H., D.L. Meadows, J. Randers and W.W. Behrens. *The Limits to Growth: A Report of the Club of Rome's Project on the Predicament of Mankind* (New York, NY: Universe Books, 1972).

Meine, C. *Aldo Leopold: His Life and Work* (Madison, WI: University of Wisconsin Press, 1988).

  'It's about time: Conservation biology and history'. *Conservation Biology* 13 (1999): 1–3.

Meine, C., M. Soulé and R.F. Noss. '"A mission-driven discipline": The growth of conservation biology'. *Conservation Biology* 20 (2006): 631–651.

Mentis, M.T. and A.W. Bailey. 'Changing perceptions of fire management in savanna parks'. *Journal of the Grassland Society of Southern Africa* 7 (1990): 81–85.

Mentis, M.T., D. Grossman, M.B. Hardy, T. O'Connor and P.J. O'Reagain. 'Paradigm shifts in South African range science, management and administration'. *South African Journal of Science* 85 (1989): 684–687.

Meskell, L. 'Falling walls and mending fences: Archaeological ethnography in the Limpopo'. *Journal of Southern African Studies* 33, no. 2 (2007): 383–400.

  The Nature of Heritage: The New South Africa (Oxford: Wiley-Blackwell, 2012).

Mills, M.G.L. 'Related spotted hyaenas forage together but do not cooperate in rearing young'. *Nature* 316 (1985): 61–62.

Moran, V.C. and P.M. Moran. *Alien Invasive Vascular Plants in South African Natural and Semi-natural Environments: Bibliography from 1830*. South African National Scientific Programmes Report 65 (Pretoria: CSIR, 1982).

Mossman, A.S. 'International game ranching programs'. *Journal of Animal Science* 40, no. 5 (1975): 993–999.

Myer, E. *The Growth of Biological Thought* (Cambridge, MA: Harvard University Press, 1982).

Myers, N. 'National parks in Africa'. *Science* 178 (1972): 1255–1263.

Nash, R.F. *Wilderness and the American Mind* (New Haven, CT: Yale University Press, 1983).

  The Rights of Nature: A History of Environmental Ethics (Madison, WI: University of Wisconsin Press, 1989).

Newman, K. *Birds of Southern Africa. 1: Kruger National Park* (Johannesburg: Macmillan, 1980).

Nicholson E.M. *Handbook to the Conservation Section of the International Biological Programme*. IBP Handbook No. 5 (Oxford: Blackwell, 1968).

Noble, G. 'An evaluation of the conservation of aquatic biotopes'. *Koedoe* 17 (1974): 71–83.

Noss, R.F. 'Indicators for monitoring biodiversity: A hierarchical approach'. *Conservation Biology* 4 (1990): 355–364.

'The naturalists are dying off'. *Conservation Biology* 10 (1996): 1–3.

'Is there is a special conservation biology?' *Ecograph* 22 (1999): 113–122.

O'Keeffe, J.H. *Ecological Research on South African Rivers: A Preliminary Synthesis.* South African National Scientific Programmes Report 121 (Pretoria: CSIR, 1986).

Odendal, A.W. and I.M. Krige. 'Social science research projects in South African National Parks: Introductory notes'. *Koedoe* 31 (1988): 105–113.

Odum, E.P. and H.T. Odum. *Fundamentals of Ecology* (Philadelphia, PA: Saunders, 1953).

Odum, H.T. *Systems Ecology: An Introduction* (New York, NY: Wiley, 1983).

Ecological and General Systems: An Intoduction to Systems Ecology (Niwot, CO: University Press of Colorado, 1994).

Owen-Smith, R.N., ed. *Management of Large Mammals in African Conservation Areas: Proceedings of a Symposium Held in Pretoria, South Africa, 29–30 April 1982* (Pretoria: HAUM, 1983).

Megaherbivores: The Influence of Very Large Body Size on Ecology (Cambridge: Cambridge University Press, 1988).

'Ecological guidelines for waterpoints in extensive protected areas'. *South African Journal of Wildlife Research* 26 (1996): 107–112.

Owen-Smith R.N., G.I.H. Kerley, B. Page, R. Slotow and R.J. van Aarde. 'A scientific perspective on the management of elephants in the Kruger National Park and elsewhere'. *South African Journal of Science* 102 (2006): 389–394.

Pabst, M. *Transfrontier Peace Parks in Southern Africa* (Stuttgart: SAFRI, 2002).

Passmore, J. *Man's Responsibility for Nature: Ecological Problems and Western Traditions* (London: Duckworth, 1974).

Perry, A.H.T. *National and Other Parks* (n.p.: n.p.), (1929).

Peterson, D.L. 'Research in parks and protected areas. Forging the link between science and management'. In *National Parks and Protected Areas: Their Role in Environmental Protection*, edited by R.G. Wright, 417–433 (Oxford: Blackwell Science, 1996).

Phillips, A. 'Turning ideas on their head: A new paradigm for protected areas'. *The George Wright Forum* 20, no. 2 (2003): 8–32.

'The history of the international system of protected area management categories'. *Protected Area Categories* 14, no. 3 (2004): 4–14.

Phillips, J.F.V. 'The biotic community'. *Journal of Ecology* 19 (1931): 1–24.

'Succession, development, the climax, and the complex organism: An analysis of concepts. Part 1'. *Journal of Ecology* 22 (1934): 554–571.

'Fire in Africa: A brief re-survey'. In *Proceedings: Annual Tall Timbers Fire Ecology Conference, April 22–23, 1971, Tallahassee, Florida*, 1–7 (Tallahassee, FL: Tall Timbers Research Station, 1972).

Pienaar, U. de V. 'Research objectives in South African national parks'. In '*Proceedings of a Symposium on the State of Nature Conservation in Southern Africa, Kruger National Park, 1976*', edited by G. de Graaff and P.T. van der Walt, supplement, *Koedoe* (1977): 38–48.

The Freshwater Fishes of the Kruger National Park (Pretoria: National Parks Board, 1978).

The Reptile Fauna of the Kruger National Park (Pretoria: National Parks Board, 1978).

'Management by intervention: The pragmatic/economic option'. In *Management of Large Mammals in African Conservation Areas: Proceedings of a Symposium Held in Pretoria, South Africa, 29–30 April 1982*, edited by R.N. Owen-Smith, 23–26 (Pretoria: HAUM, 1983).

'Indications of progressive desiccation of the Transvaal lowveld over the past 100 years, and implications for the water stabilization programme in the Kruger National Park'. *Koedoe* 28 (1985): 93–165.

'An overview of conservation in South Africa and future perspectives'. *Koedoe* 34, no. 1 (1991): 73–80.

Neem uit die Verlede (Pretoria: Protea Boekhuis, 2007).

Goue Jare: Die Verhaal van die Nasionale Krugerwildtuin 1947–1991 (Stilbaai: The Author, 2010).

A Cameo from the Past (Pretoria: Protea Boekhuis, 2012).

Pienaar, U. de V., W.D. Haacke and N.H.G. Jacobsen. *The Reptiles of the Kruger National Park* (Pretoria: National Parks Board, 1966).

Pienaar, U. de V., N.I. Passmore and V.C. Carruthers. *The Frogs of the Kruger National Park* (Pretoria: National Parks Board, 1976).

Pienaar, U. de V., I.L. Rautenbach and G. de Graaff. *The Small Mammals of the Kruger National Park* (Pretoria: National Parks Board, 1980).

Player, I. *The White Rhino Saga* (Glasgow: Collins, 1972).

ed. *Voices of the Wilderness* (Johannesburg: Jonathan Ball, 1979).

Pocock, R.I. 'The Quagga'. *Journal of the Society for the Preservation of the Fauna of the Empire* 2 (1922): 26–37.

Pollard, S.R. and D.R. du Toit. *Recognizing Heterogeneity and Variability as Key Characteristics of Savannah Systems: The Use of Strategic Adaptive Management as an Approach to River Management Within The Kruger National Park, South Africa*. Report of UNEP/GEF Project No. GF/2713-03-4679, Ecosystems, Protected Areas and People Project, 2005.

Guidelines for Strategic Adaptive Management: Experiences from Managing the Rivers of the Kruger National Park. Guidelines of UNEP/GEF Project No. GF/27-13-03-4679. Ecosystems, Protected Areas and People Project, 2007.

Pollard, S., D. du Toit and H. Biggs. 'River management under transformation: The emergence of strategic adaptive management of river systems in the Kruger National Park'. *Koedoe* 53, no. 2 (2011): 14 pages. doi: 10.4102/koedoe.v53i2.1011.

Pooley, S. *Burning Table Mountain: An Environmental History of Fire on the Cape Peninsula* (Houndmills: Palgrave Macmillan, 2014).

Pritchard, J. *Preserving Yellowstone's Natural Conditions: Science and the Perception of Nature* (Lincoln, NB: University of Nebraska Press, 1999).

Punt, W.H.J. ''n Beknopte oorsig van die historiese navorsing in die nasionale Krugerwildtuin'. *Koedoe* 5 (1962): 123–127.

Die Eerste Europeane in die Nasionale Krugerwildtuin 1725/The First Europeans in the Kruger National Park (Pretoria: National Parks Board, 1975).

Radkau, J. *The Age of Ecology* (Cambridge: Polity, 2014).

Ramutsindela, M. 'Land reform in South Africa's national parks: A catalyst for the human–nature nexus'. *Land Use Policy* 20 (2003): 41–49.

Rautenbach, J.C., comp. 'Second cumulative index to Koedoe: Volumes 26–35/1 (1983–June 1992)'. *Koedoe* 35, no. 1 (1992): 131–151.

comp. 'Third cumulative index for Koedoe: Volumes 35/2–44/1'. *Koedoe* 44, no. 2 (2001): 85–113.

Reardon, M. *Shaping Kruger: The Dynamics of Managing Wildlife in Africa's Premier Game Park* (Cape Town: Struik Nature, 2012).

Rebelo, T.G., S. Freitag, C. Cheney and M.A. McGeoch. 'Prioritising species of special concern for monitoring in Table Mountain National Park: The challenge of a species rich, threatened ecosystem'. *Koedoe* 53, no. 2 (2011): Art. #1019, 14 pages. doi: 10.4102/koedoe.v53i2.1019.

Reid, W.V. 'Science: who needs it?' *Conservation Biology* 19 (2005): 1341–1343.

Reiger, J.F. *American Sportsmen and the Origins of Conservation* (Corvallis, OR: Oregon State University Press, 2001).

Republic of South Africa. *The National Protected Area Expansion Strategy 2008* (Pretoria: Government of South Africa, 2010). www.environment.gov.za/sites/default/files/docs/nationalprotected_areasexpansion_strategy.pdf (accessed 28 December 2015).

Reyers, B., A.E. Ginsburg, J.L. Nel, P.J. O'Farrell, D.J. Roux and R.M. Cowling. 'From conservation biology to conservation science: Moving beyond disciplinary divides'. In *Exploring Sustainability Science: A Southern African Perspective*, edited by M. Burns and A. Weaver, 135–178 (Stellenbosch: Sun Press, 2008).

Reyers, B., D.J. Roux and P.J. O'Farrell. 'Can ecosystem services lead ecology on a transdisciplinary pathway?' *Environmental Conservation* 37, no. 4 (2010): 501–511.

Roberge, J.-M., G. Mikusinski and H. Possingham. 'Has the term "conservation biology" has its day?' *Frontiers in Ecology and the Environment* 8 (2010). http://dx.doi.org/10.1890/10.WB.010.

Robin, L. 'Ecology: A science of empire?' In *Ecology and Empire: Comparative History of Settler Societies*, edited by T. Griffiths and L. Robin, 63–75 (Edinburgh: Keele University Press, 1997).

How a Continent Created a Nation (Sydney: UNSW Press, 2007).

'Resilience in the Anthropocene: A biography'. In *Rethinking Invasion Ecologies from the Environmental Humanities*, edited by J. Frawley and I. McCalman, 45–63 (London: Routledge, 2014).

Robin, L., S. Sörlin and P. Warde, eds. *The Future of Nature: Documents of Global Change* (New Haven, CT: Yale University Press, 2013).

Robinson, G.A. 'Marine conservation in the Republic of South Africa with special reference to marine parks and reserves'. In 'Proceedings of a symposium on the state of nature conservation in southern Africa, Kruger National Park, 1976', edited by G. de Graaff and P.T. van der Walt, supplement, *Koedoe* (1977): 230–242.

ed. *African Heritage 2000: The Future of Protected Areas in Africa. Proceedings of the IUCN Commission on National Parks and Protected Areas African Regional Working Session, Skukuza, Kruger National Park, South Africa, 11–17 October 1994* (Pretoria: National Parks Board, 1995).

Rogers, K.H. 'Operationalizing ecology under a new paradigm: An African perspective'. In *The Ecological Basis for Conservation: Heterogeneity, Ecosystems, and Biodiversity*, edited by S. Pickett, R.S. Ostfeld, M. Shachak and G. Likens, 60–77 (New York, NY: Chapman and Hall, 1997).

'Adopting a heterogeneity paradigm: Implications for management of protected savannas'. In *The Kruger Experience: Ecology and Management of Savanna Heterogeneity*, edited by J.T. du Toit, K.H. Rogers and H.C. Biggs, 41–58 (Washington, DC: Island Press, 2003).

'The real river management challenge: Integrating scientists, stakeholders and service agencies'. *River Research and Applications* 22 (2006): 269–280.

'Kilham Memorial Lecture, Limnology and the post-normal imperative: An African perspective'. *Verhandlungen des Internationalen Verein Limnologie* 30, no. 2 (2008): 171–185.

Rogers, K.H. and J. O'Keeffe. 'River heterogeneity: Ecosystem structure, function, and management'. In *The Kruger Experience: Ecology and Management of Savanna Heterogeneity*, edited by J.T. du Toit, K.H. Rogers and H.C. Biggs, 189–218 (Washington, DC: Island Press, 2003).

Roux, D. J. and L. Foxcroft. 'The development and application of strategic adaptive management within South African National Parks'. *Koedoe* 53 (2011), 5 pages. doi: 10.4102/koedoe.v53i2.1049.

Roux, D.J., R.T. Kingsford, S.F. McCool, M.A. McGeoch and L.C. Foxcroft. 'The role and value of conservation agency research'. *Environmental Management* 55 (2015): 1232–1245. doi: 10.1007/s00267-015-0473-5.

Roux, D., M. McGeoch and L. Foxcroft. 'Assessment of selected in-house research achievements for the period 2008–2011'. *Scientific Report 01/2012* (Skukuza: South African National Parks, 2012).

Roux, D.J., K.H. Rogers, H.C. Biggs, P.J. Ashton and A. Sergeant. 'Bridging the science-management divide: Moving from unidirectional knowledge transfer to knowledge interfacing and sharing'. *Ecology and Society* 11, no. 1 (2006). www.ecologyandsociety.org/vol11/iss1/art4/ (accessed 28 July 2016).

Runte, A. *National Parks: The American Experience* (Lincoln, NB: University of Nebraska Press, 1979).

Yosemite: The Embattled Wilderness (Lincoln, NB: University of Nebraska Press, 1990).

Saayman, M., A. Saayman and M. Ferreira. 'The socio-economic impact of the Karoo National Park'. *Koedoe* 51 (2009): 26–35.

Sagarin, R. and A. Pauchard. *Observation and Ecology: Broadening the Scope of Science to Understand a Complex World* (Washington, DC: Island Press, 2012).

Scholes, R.J. and R. Biggs. 'A biodiversity intactness index'. *Nature* 434, no. 3 (2005): 45–49.

Scholes, R.J. and K.G. Mennell, eds. *Elephant Management: A Scientific Assessment of Elephant Management in South Africa* (Johannesburg: Wits University Press, 2008).

Scholes, R.J. and B.H. Walker. *An African Savanna: Synthesis of the Nylsvley Study* (Cambridge: Cambridge University Press, 1993).

Schwarzenbach, A. *Saving the World's Wildlife: WWF – The First 50 Years* (London: Profile Books, 2011).

Seagrief, S.C. *The Seaweeds of the Tsitsikama Coastal National Park/Die Seewiere van die Tsitsikama-Seekus Nasionale Park* (Pretoria: National Parks Board, 1967).

Sellars, R.W. *Preserving Nature in the National Parks: A History* (New Haven, CT: Yale University Press, 1997).

Sheail, J. *Seventy-five Years in Ecology: The British Ecological Society* (Oxford: Blackwell, 1987).

    Nature Conservation in Britain: The Formative Years (London: The Stationery Office, 1998).

Siegfried, W.R. and B.R. Davies. *Conservation of Ecosystems: Theory and Practice.* South African National Scientific Programmes Report 61 (Pretoria: CSIR, 1982).

Simberloff, D. 'Flagships, umbrellas, and keystones: Is single-species management passé in the landscape era?' *Biological Conservation* 83 (1998): 247–257.

Sinclair, A.R.E. *Serengeti Story: Life and Science in the World's Greatest Wildlife Region* (Oxford: Oxford University Press, 2012).

Sinclair, A.R.E. and P. Arcese, eds. *Serengeti II: Dynamics, Management and Conservation of an Ecosystem* (Chicago, IL: University of Chicago Press, 1995).

Sinclair, A.R.E., K.L. Metzger, S.A.R. Mduma and J.M. Fryxell, eds. *Serengeti IV: Sustaining Biodiversity in a Coupled Human–Natural System* (Chicago, IL: University of Chicago Press, 2015).

Sinclair, A.R.E. and M. Norton-Griffiths, eds. *Serengeti: Dynamics of an Ecosystem* (Chicago, IL: University of Chicago Press, 1979).

Sinclair, A.R.E., C. Packer, S.A.R. Mduma and J.M. Fryxell, eds. *Serengeti III: Human Impacts on Ecosystem Dynamics* (Chicago, IL: University of Chicago Press, 2006).

Skinner, J.D. and C.T. Chimimba. *The Mammals of the Southern African Subregion* (Cambridge: Cambridge University Press, 2005).

Smit, I.P.J., G.P. Asner, N. Govender, T. Kennedy-Bowdoin, D.E. Knapp and J. Jacobson. 'Effects of fire on woody vegetation structure in African savanna'. *Ecological Applications* 20, no. 7 (2010): 1865–1875.

Smit, I.P.J. and S.M. Ferreira. 'Management intervention affects river-bound spatial dynamics of elephants'. *Biological Conservation* 143 (2010): 2172–2181.

Smith, J.L.B. and M.M. Smith. *Fishes of the Tsitsikama Coastal National Park* (Pretoria: National Parks Board, 1966).

Smithers, R.H.N. *The Mammals of the Southern African Subregion* (Pretoria: University of Pretoria, 1983).

Smuts, G.L. *Lion* (Johannesburg: Macmillan, 1982).

Snow, C.P. *The Two Cultures and the Scientific Revolution* (Cambridge: Cambridge University Press, 1993).

Sooryamoorthy, R. 'Scientific research in the natural sciences in South Africa: A scientometric study'. *South African Journal of Science* 109, nos. 7/8 (2013): 57–67.

Soulé, M. 'The "new conservation"'. *Conservation Biology* 27, no. 5 (2013): 895–897.

Soulé, M.E. 'What is conservation biology?' *Bioscience* 35, no. 11 (1985): 727–734.

    ed. *Conservation Biology: The Science of Scarcity and Diversity* (Sunderland, MA: Sinauer Associates, 1986).

    'History of the Society for Conservation Biology: How and why we got here'. *Conservation Biology* 1 (1987): 4–5.

Soulé, M.E. and J. Terborgh. *Continental Conservation: Scientific Foundations of Regional Reserve Networks* (Washington, DC: Island Press, 1999).

Soulé, M.E. and B.A. Wilcox, eds. *Conservation Biology: An Evolutionary–Ecological Perspective* (Sunderland, MA: Sinauer Associates, 1980).

South African National Parks. *The Great Elephant Indaba: Finding an African Solution to an African Problem* (Pretoria: SANParks, 2005).

Spierenburg, M., C. Steenkamp and H. Wels. 'Enclosing the local for the global commons: Community land rights in the Great Limpopo Transfrontier Area'. *Conservation and Society* 6, no. 1 (2008): 87–97.

Stevenson-Hamilton, J. 'Opposition to game reserves'. *Journal of the Society for the Preservation of the Wild Fauna of the Empire* 3 (1907): 53–59.

'The relation between game and tsetse-flies'. *Bulletin of Entomological Research* 2 (1911): 113–118.

Animal Life in Africa (London: Heinemann, 1912).

'The coloration of the African hunting dog (*Lycaon pictus*)'. *Proceedings of the Zoological Society of London* 27 (1914): 403–405.

The Lowveld: Its Wildlife and its People (London: Cassell, 1929).

'The management of a national park in Africa'. *Journal of the Society for the Preservation of the Fauna of the Empire* 10 (1930): 13–20.

South African Eden (London: Cassell & Co., 1937).

'A game warden reflects'. *Journal of the Society for the Preservation of the Fauna of the Empire* 54 (1946): 17–21.

Wild Life in South Africa (London: Cassell, 1947).

'Tsetse fly and the rinderpest epidemic of 1896'. *South African Journal of Science* 53 (1957): 216–218.

Stirzaker, R.J., D.J. Roux and H. Biggs. 'Learning to bridge the gap between adaptive management and organisational culture'. *Koedoe* 53 (2011), 6 pages. doi: 10.4102/koedoe.v53i2.1007.

Suich, H., B. Child and A. Spenceley, eds. *Evolution and Innovation in Wildlife Conservation: Parks and Game Ranches to Transfrontier Conservation Areas* (London: Earthscan, 2009).

Szabó, P. and R. Hédl. 'Advancing the integration of history and ecology for conservation'. *Conservation Biology* 25, no. 4 (2011): 680–687.

Takacs, D. *The Idea of Biodiversity: Philosophies of Paradise* (Baltimore, MD: Johns Hopkins University Press, 1996).

Tall Timbers Research Station. *Proceedings: Annual Tall Timbers Fire Ecology Conference, April 22–23, 1971, Tallahassee, Florida* (Tallahassee, FL: Tall Timbers Research Station, 1972).

Tansley, A.G. 'The use and abuse of vegetational concepts and terms'. *Ecology* 16 (1935): 284–307.

Our Heritage of Wild Nature: A Plea for Organized Nature Conservation (Cambridge: Cambridge University Press, 1945).

Thorpe, W.H. *The Origins and Rise of Ethology: The Science of the Natural Behaviour of Animals* (London: Heinemann, 1979).

Tietz, R.M. and G.A. Robinson. *The Tsitsikama Shore: A Guide to the Marine Invertebrate Fauna of the Tsitsikama Coastal National Park* (Pretoria: National Parks Board, 1974).

Timko, J.A. and J.L. Innes. 'Evaluating ecological integrity in national parks: Case studies from Canada and South Africa'. *Biological Conservation* 142 (2009): 676–688.

Trollope, W.S.W. 'Veld management with specific reference to game ranching in the grassland and savanna areas of South Africa'. *Koedoe* 33, no. 2 (1990): 77–86.

'Fire regime of the Kruger National Park for the period 1980 to 1992'. *Koedoe* 36, no. 2 (1993): 45–52.

Tweed, W.C. 'An idea in trouble: Thoughts about the future of traditional national parks in the United States'. *The George Wright Forum* 27, no. 1 (2010): 6–13.

Uncertain Path: A Search for the Future of National Parks (Berkeley, CA: University of California Press, 2010).

Tyrrell, I. 'America's national parks: The transnational creation of national space in the Progressive Era'. *Journal of American Studies* 46 (2012): 1–21.

Van Aarde, R.J. and T.O. Jackson. 'Megaparks for metapopulations: Addressing the causes of locally high elephant numbers in southern Africa'. *Biological Conservation* 134 (2007): 289–298.

Van Aarde, R.J., T.P. Jackson and S.M. Ferreira. 'Conservation science and elephant management in southern Africa'. *South African Journal of Science* 102 (2006): 385–388.

Van Aarde, R.J., I. Whyte and S.L. Pimm. 'The consequences of culling for the dynamics of the African elephant population of Kruger National Park'. *Animal Conservation* 2 (1999): 287–294.

Van der Merwe, N.J. 'The position of nature conservation in South Africa'. *Koedoe* 5 (1962): 1–127.

Van der Schijff, H.P. 'Inleidende verslag oor veldbrandnavorsing in die Nasionale Krugerwildtuin'. *Koedoe* 1 (1958): 60–93.

Van Rensburg, A.P.J. 'Golden Gate: Die geskiedenis van twee plase wat 'n nasionale park beword het'. *Koedoe* 11 (1968): 83–138.

'Die geskiedenis van die Nasionale Bontebokpark, Swellendam'. *Koedoe* 18 (1975): 165–190.

Van Warmelo, N.J. *Place Names of the Kruger National Park*. Ethnological Publications No. 47 (Pretoria: Department of Bantu Administration, 1961).

Van Wilgen, B.W. 'Management of the natural ecosystems of the Cape Peninsula: Current status and future prospects'. *Biodiversity and Conservation* 5, no. 5 (1996): 671–684.

'The evolution of fire and invasive alien plant management practices in fynbos'. *South African Journal of Science* 105 (2009): 1–8.

Van Wilgen, B.W. and H.C. Biggs. 'A critical assessment of adaptive ecosystem management in a large savanna protected area in South Africa'. *Biological Conservation* 144 (2011): 1179–1187.

Van Wilgen, B.W., H.C. Biggs and A.L.F. Potgieter. 'Fire management and research in the Kruger National Park, with suggestions on the detection of thresholds of potential concern'. *Koedoe* 41 (1998): 69–87.

Van Wilgen, B.W, N. Boshoff, I.P.J. Smit, S. Solano-Fernandez and L. van der Walt. 'A bibliometric analysis to illustrate the role of an embedded research capability in South African National Parks'. *Scientometrics* 107 (2016): 185–212. doi: 10.1007/s11192-016-1879-4.

Van Wilgen, B.W., N. Govender and H.C. Biggs. 'The contribution of fire research to fire management: A critical review of a long-term experiment in the Kruger National Park, South Africa'. *International Journal of Wildland Fire* 16 (2007): 519–530.

Van Wyk, P. 'Veld burning in the Kruger National Park'. In *Proceedings of the Annual Tall Timbers Fire Ecology Conference, April 22–23, 1971, Tallahassee, Florida*, 9–31 (Tallahassee, FL: Tall Timbers Research Station, 1972).

   Trees of the Kruger National Park. 2 vols (Cape Town: Purnell, 1972, 1974).

   Field Guide to the Trees of the Kruger National Park (Cape Town: Struik, 1984).

Van Wyk, P. and N. Fairall. 'The influence of the African elephant on the vegetation of the Kruger National Park'. *Koedoe* 12 (1969): 57–89.

Van Wyk, P. and E.A.N. le Riche. 'The Kalahari Gemsbok National Park, 1931–1981'. In 'Proceedings of a symposium on the Kalahari ecosystem, Pretoria 11–12 October 1983', edited by G. de Graaff and D.J. van Rensburg, supplement, *Koedoe* (1984): 21–32.

Venter, F., R. Naiman, H. Biggs and D. Pienaar. 'The evolution of conservation management philosophy: Science, environmental change and social adjustments in Kruger National Park'. *Ecosystems* 11 (2008): 173–192.

Venter, F.J. and W.P.D. Gertenbach. 'A cursory view of the climate and vegetation of the Kruger National Park'. *Koedoe* 29 (1986): 139–148.

Verhoef, J. 'Notes on archaeology and prehistoric mining in the Kruger National Park'. *Koedoe* 29 (1986): 149–156.

Vollmar, F. 'Conserving one earth: A look at world conservation'. In 'Proceedings of a symposium on the state of nature conservation in southern Africa, Kruger National Park, 1976', edited by G. de Graaff and P.T. van der Walt, supplement, *Koedoe* (1977): 10–23.

Vorster, W.S., ed. *Are we Killing God's Earth? Ecology and Theology* (Pretoria: University of South Africa, 1987).

Wagner, F. *Yellowstone's Destabilised Ecosystem* (Oxford: Oxford University Press, 2006).

Walker, B. and M. Westoby. 'States and transitions: The trajectory of an idea, 1970–2010'. *Israel Journal of Ecology and Evolution* 57 (2011): 17–22.

Walker, B.H. 'An appraisal of the systems approach to research on and management of African wildlife ecosystems'. *Journal of the South African Wildlife Management Association* 4 (1974): 129–136.

Walker, B.H., D. Ludwig, C.S. Holling and R.M. Peterman. 'Stability of semi-arid grazing systems'. *Journal of Ecology* 69 (1981): 473–498.

Walker, B.H., G.A. Norton, G.R. Conway, H.M. Commins and M. Birley. 'A procedure for multidisciplinary ecosystem research with reference to the South African Savanna Ecosystem Project'. *Journal of Applied Ecology* 15 (1978): 481–502.

Walker, B.H. and I. Noy-Meir. 'Aspects of the stability and resilience of savanna systems'. In *Ecology of Tropical Savanna Systems*, edited by B.J. Huntley and B.H. Walker, 556–609 (Berlin: Springer-Verlag, 1982).

Walker, B.H. and D. Salt. *Resilience Thinking: Sustaining Ecosystems and People in a Changing World* (Washington, DC: Island Press, 2006).

Welch-Devine, M. and L.M. Campbell. 'Sorting out roles and defining divides: Social sciences at the World Conservation Congress'. *Conservation and Society* 8, no. 4 (2010): 339–348.

Wemmer, C. and C.A. Christen, eds. *Elephants and Ethics: Toward a Morality of Coexistence* (Baltimore, MD: Johns Hopkins University Press, 2008).

Werger, M.J.A. 'On concepts and techniques applied in the Zurich–Montpellier method of vegetation survey'. *Bothalia* 11 (1974): 309–323.

  ed. *Biogeography and Ecology of Southern Africa* (The Hague: Junk, 1978).

Westoby, M. 'What does ecology mean?' *TREE* 12, no. 4 (1997): 166.

Westoby, M., B. Walker and I. Noy-Meir. 'Opportunistic management for rangelands not at equilibrium'. *Journal of Range Management* 42, no. 2 (1989): 266–274.

Whande, W. and H. Suich. 'Transfrontier conservation initiatives in southern Africa: Observations from the Great Limpopo Transfrontier Conservation Area'. In *Evolution and Innovation in Wildlife Conservation: Parks and Game Ranches to Transfrontier Conservation Areas*, edited by H. Suich, B. Child and A. Spenceley, 373–391 (London: Earthscan, 2009).

White, L. 'The historical roots of our ecologic crisis'. *Science* 155, no. 3767 (1967): 1203–1207.

Whitehouse, A.M. and A.J. Hall-Martin. 'Elephants in the Addo National Elephant Park, South Africa: Reconstruction of the population's history'. *Oryx* 34 (2000): 46–55.

Whyte, I.J., H.C. Biggs, A. Gaylard and L.E.O. Braack. 'A new policy for the management of the Kruger National Park's elephant population'. *Koedoe* 42 (1999): 111–132.

Whyte, I.J., R.J. van Aarde and S.L. Pimm. 'Kruger's elephant population: Its size and consequences for ecosystem heterogeneity'. In *The Kruger Experience: Ecology and Management of Savanna Heterogeneity*, edited by J.T. du Toit, K.H. Rogers and H.C. Biggs, 332–348 (Washington, DC: Island Press, 2003).

Winterbottom, J.M. *An Introduction to Animal Ecology in Southern Africa* (Cape Town: Maskew Miller, 1971).

Wolmer, W. 'Transboundary conservation: The politics of ecological integrity in the Great Limpopo Transfrontier Park'. *Journal of Southern African Studies* 29 (2003): 261–278.

World Commission on Environment and Development (WCED). *Our Common Future (The Brundtland Report)* (Oxford: Oxford University Press, 1987).

Worster, D. *The Wealth of Nature: Environmental History and the Ecological Imagination* (New York, NY: Oxford University Press, 1993).

  Nature's Economy: A History of Ecological Ideas (Cambridge: Cambridge University Press, 1994).

Worthington, E.B. *Science in Africa: A Review of Scientific Research Relating to Tropical and Southern Africa* (London: Oxford University Press, 1938).

  'The scientific problems of game control and preservation'. In *African Regional Scientific Conference, Johannesburg, 17–28 October, 1949. Vol. II, Statements and Communications*. G-PS 10462-1949, 230 (Pretoria: Government Printer, 1949).

  Science in the Development of Africa: A Review of the Contribution of Physical and Biological Knowledge South of the Sahara (n.p.: n.p., 1958).

  ed. *The Evolution of IBP*. International Biological Programme 1 (Cambridge: Cambridge University Press, 1975).

The Ecological Century: A Personal Appraisal (Oxford: Clarendon Press, 1983).

Wright, G., J. Dixon and B. Thompson. *Fauna of the National Parks of the United States* (Washington, DC: US Government Printing Office, 1933).

Wright, G. and B. Thompson. *Fauna of the National Parks of the United States: Wildlife Management in the National Parks* (Washington, DC: US Government Printing Office, 1935).

Wright, R.G. *Wildlife Research and Management in the National Parks* (Urbana, IL: University of Illinois Press, 1992).

ed. *National Parks and Protected Areas: Their Role in Environmental Protection* (London: Wiley-Blackwell, 1996).

Wynberg, R. and T. Kepe. *Land Reform and Conservation Areas in South Africa: Towards a Mutually Beneficial Approach* (Johannesburg: IUCN, 1999).

Index